Land Battles in
5th Century B.C. Greece

Land Battles in 5th Century B.C. Greece

A History and Analysis of 173 Engagements

Fred Eugene Ray, Jr.

McFarland & Company, Inc., Publishers
Jefferson, North Carolina, and London

The present work is a reprint of the illustrated case bound edition of Land battles in 5th Century B.C. Greece: A History and Analysis of 173 Engagements, *first published in 2009 by McFarland.*

LIBRARY OF CONGRESS CATALOGUING-IN-PUBLICATION DATA

Ray, Fred Eugene, 1949–
Land battles in 5th century B.C. Greece : a history and analysis of 173 engagements / Fred Eugene Ray.
        p.   cm.
Includes bibliographical references and index.

ISBN 978-0-7864-6773-0
softcover : 50# alkaline paper ∞

1. Military art and science — Greece — History — To 500.
2. Armies — Greece.   3. Greece — History, Military — Sources.
I. Title.   II. Title: Land battles in fifth century B.C. Greece.
U33.R395   2011   355.00938 — dc22   2008036085

BRITISH LIBRARY CATALOGUING DATA ARE AVAILABLE

© 2009 Fred Eugene Ray, Jr. All rights reserved

No part of this book may be reproduced or transmitted in any form or by any means, electronic or mechanical, including photocopying or recording, or by any information storage and retrieval system, without permission in writing from the publisher.

On the cover: Detail of a fallen warrior from the Temple of Aphaia in Aegina, Greece, 500-480 B.C. (Erich Lessing/Art Resource)

Manufactured in the United States of America

*McFarland & Company, Inc., Publishers
Box 611, Jefferson, North Carolina 28640
www.mcfarlandpub.com*

To Marleen and my little muses

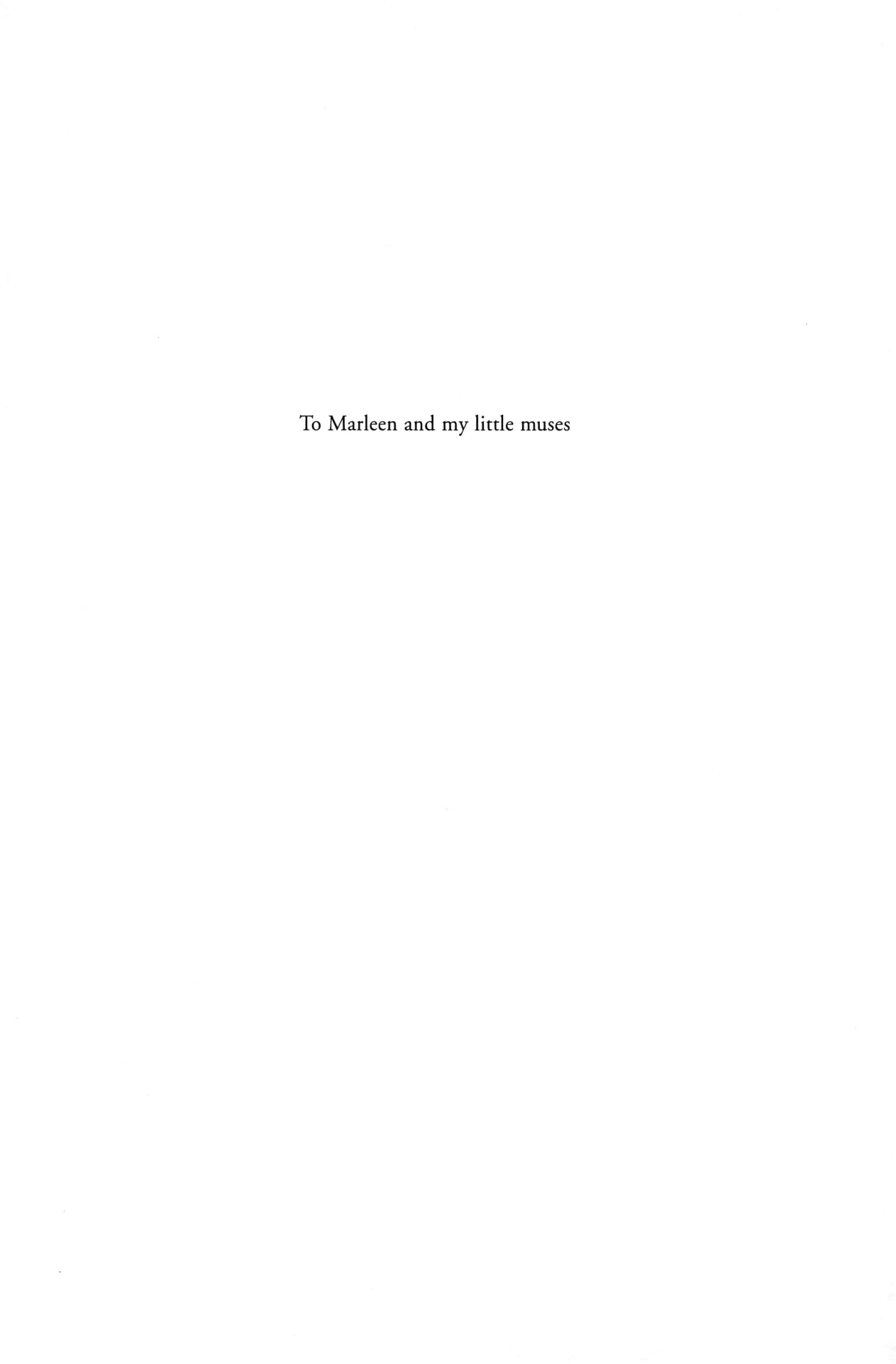

Table of Contents

Preface	1
Introduction	5
I. The Spearmen: Greek Hoplite Warfare (500–401 B.C.)	7
II. Arguing with Socrates: Territorial Disputes, the Ionian Revolt, and the Rise of Sparta and Gela (500–481 B.C.)	21
III. The Strength of Lions: Marathon, Himera, and the Invasion of Greece	59
IV. Prelude to Collision: The Pentacontaetia (478–432 B.C.)	109
V. Danger and Glory: The Archidamian War (431–422 B.C.)	150
VI. Daring and Destruction: The Peace of Nicias and the Sicilian Invasion (421–413 B.C.)	199
VII. A World at Spear's Length: The Decelean/Ionian War to the End of the 5th Century (413–401 B.C.)	237
Conclusion	287
Table 1: Combat Factors in Greek Pitched Battles (500–401 B.C.)	289
Table 2: Decisive Factors in Greek Pitched Battles (500–401 B.C.)	293
Table 3: Pitched Battle Record of Major Combatants (500–401 B.C.)	298
Table 4: Hoplite Losses and Point/Cause of Formation Failure for Greek Pitched Battles (500–401 B.C.)	301
Bibliography	307
Index	313

Preface

My fascination with combat among the ancient Greeks began as a boy, when I found Homer's *Iliad* in the local branch of the Omaha Public Library. Ever since, I've devoted a great deal of effort to collecting and studying works on Greek warfare and taking advantage of a career as an international geologist to visit many of the actual sites where some of classical Greece's most famous battles took place. It was on one of these latter forays that I ran across Victor David Hanson's *The Western Way of War* on the shelf of a small shop in Athens. As I devoured this influential book, I came to much better appreciate the significant impact that Greek military practices have had on the way we view war today. Yet, as a professional scientist accustomed to dealing in hard data, I also realized that this effect might be as much due to myths about ancient battle as to its reality. And if the past is truly a key to the future, then it seemed vitally important to root one's concept of so serious a matter as war firmly in the real world. That was when I first conceived of sorting out fact from fiction on tactical events in this seminal era for western military history through use of the same approaches that work so well in the realm of natural history.

Once I began research in earnest, it soon became obvious that the 5th century B.C. was the ideal starting point for this project. Not only was it a subject for our earliest reliable historians, but it had also hosted enough documented combats to illustrate general trends. Understandably, however, the existing literature on the period provided battlefield details only on its best known combats — those that also received extensive coverage from classical writers. It was, in fact, this very shortcoming that came to set my agenda. The goal was to create a first-ever tactical-level survey on the 5th century's entire catalog of Greek land engagements. I would seek to place each within its proper historical context and document any significant overall patterns of action. The nature of the surviving ancient record made this quite a challenge. These documents seldom preserve specific tactics on any battle, let alone the more obscure ones. Moreover, it is common to find conflicting information regarding even the most celebrated actions whenever there are multiple sources. It was therefore a must to extend the historical database through a series of logical reconstructions. Unlike most scientific methods, which try to "predict" future events, this was a forensic process that in the words of history of science scholar David Kitts (1973, personal communication) strives to "retrodict" the past.

The technique applied here makes heavy use of analogs and correlates various peripheral indicators toward resolving issues that are lacking in direct evidence. A good example of this is the section herein on the battle of Cleonai (c. 500 B.C.). The only specific data for this event consist of dedications on helmets, greaves, and shields from a shrine at Olympia. Location of the action therefore came from knowing that nearly all combats at the time grew out of land disputes, and that Cleonai was by far the most likely bone of contention between the states engaged. Next, since Greek military organization almost always paralleled social institutions, it was possible to deduce that the units present at Cleonai reflected each side's tribal structure. A fair estimate on the number of men present could then be projected not only from other actions where manpower is recorded for the same combatants, but also by analog from common strengths for the kinds of units that were probably on hand. Lastly, both the likely course of events on the field and casualties were derived from statistical norms. This same basic approach has served me well in many a past geologic investigation and appears to be every bit as valid for stretching slim battlefield data to their logical limits.

Applying this process on each battle required a constant search to find mutual support for every deduction from multiple lines of inquiry. The more answers tended to dovetail from different sets of evidence, the more certain it was that I was approaching the truth. At the same time, it was incumbent to never ignore information, no matter how it might appear to disagree with other sources. Every scrap of reference material was therefore treated with equal respect. It had to either be reconciled with an all-inclusive interpretation or have its validity fairly and adequately disputed. As it turned out, it proved surprising just how often a little hard thought and creativity succeeded in tying even the most seemingly disparate data into a consistent and universal narrative. In the end, this approach generated reasonable estimates for many of the factors that must have been present in each engagement, as summarized in the tables at the back of the book. When taken in combination, these various elements can tell quite a vivid story about a combat otherwise long lost in time. Of course, such conclusions must by nature remain somewhat speculative, but they nonetheless represent the very best guess that can be made from the existing evidence. In all cases, I have tried to fully document origins for the raw information or analogs used so that the reader can readily see the path of each reconstruction.

It should be apparent from all of this that one of the most vital aspects of such a forensic survey is an attention to minute details in sifting through all available sources for a small clue or stray fact that will lead the way to a major revelation. And this, more than anything else, highlights the reality that anyone studying ancient Greek warfare owes an immense debt to the efforts of many previous generations of historians. Herodotus, Thucydides, Xenophon, Diodorus, and Plutarch are the ancient authors that provide the core of our knowledge about 5th century events. Among the modern writings that have most influenced this book are Hans Delbruck's highly practical and analog-rich studies; W.K. Pritchett's many wonderful articles that so seamlessly mix the highest quality scholarship with revealing field work; Nick Sekunda's reviews of Persian warfare, which set the standard for me on evaluating the capabilities of barbarian armies — undoubtedly the most overlooked component in previous analyses; Donald Kagan's rich and insightful series on the Great Peloponnesian War that dominated late 5th century Greece; and the aforementioned Victor Davis Hansen's growing canon, which effectively and passionately relates the ancient Greeks to our own time, toward restoring respect for the ongoing value of classical studies. These marvelous authors, both past and present, join a host of others to form the substantial base of literature on which the present work is so dependant, all of which is represented in my own library and detailed in the bibliography. The text makes note of this material either as referrals to ancient sources in the form of author citations or as referrals to modern sources that include lead author, date of publication, and (if needed) page number. These show as inserts within the main body of the text, and the same method is used for additional supporting notes, which appear within parenthetical enclosures.

As to other matters of style, the discussion that follows generally proceeds in chronological order. However, a limited number of events fall into natural geographic groups and are so covered, which creates some minor overlaps in time among a few subsets of subjects. Also regarding sequence, it was often necessary to talk about battles in passages that are at a distance from their principal description (as in either a prior or later chapter). To make it easier to locate the prime discussions of these actions, their date is always listed at first mention. Another stylistic consideration is that transliteration of the Greek alphabet has always posed problems. A common solution has been to balance literal transliterations of Greek words with Romanized or Anglicized forms more familiar to modern readers. I have taken this same approach and made liberal use of Latin and English equivalents. Furthermore, where Greek or other foreign terms make their initial appearance, they are always in italics with an English translation. With respect to units of measure, values (linear, area, and weight) are uniformly expressed in the metric system. Alternatives supplement these only where they provide a strong aide to visualization. Also provided as visual support are maps and battlefield diagrams throughout. Joan Huckaby has ably drafted all of these to the considerable improvement of my own crudely drawn originals.

I would like to make it clear that I do not see this work as any sort of ultimate authority. My main intent is rather to distinguish likelihoods wherever possible and separate them from mythology in order to encourage a more accurate discussion about warfare in 5th century Greece. Additionally, though this is not a comparative study per se, I hope that readers will find some useful lessons in the ancient Greek battle experience that will inform their perspective on combat in other eras up to the present.

Introduction

> "When a man stands firm and remains unmoved in the front rank and forgets all thoughts of disgraceful flight, steeling his spirit and heart to endure, and with words encourages the man standing next to him. This is the man good in war."
> *Tyrtaeus (Spartan poet, 7th Century* B.C.*)*

What really mattered to the ancient Greeks on the field of battle? This is by no means an easy question to resolve in full. That's because making war is among the most human of activities and, like all of humankind's more fundamental undertakings, it is a mixture of things physical, intellectual, and emotional. Indeed, the foregoing quote from Tyrtaeus lays out this intrinsic multiplicity in eloquent terms that are more than two and a half millennia old. To truly understand classical combat we therefore must deal with its material, cerebral, and moral aspects — its body, mind, and spirit, if you will. The following work attempts to do this by separating myth from reality on the original Grecian battlefields of the 5th century B.C.

Knowing the physical factors present in any past battle is critical to grasping what actually took place, with fighting techniques, types and numbers of troops, and casualties among the most basic of such concrete elements. Sadly, our available ancient writings rarely say much about these; thus, this study strives to restore them using a variety of projected and analog information. This has resulted in the generation of estimates on this kind of data for all of the 5th century's 173 significant land engagements. Of course, this is an unavoidably imprecise process that calls for a great deal of guesswork, and it's a must to use its results with great care and no small amount of skepticism. Yet the rewards that can be derived are substantial. Through substituting probability for mere legend, we can deduce some valuable answers about just what it was that made the ancient Greeks so capable in combat.

Nor are our results confined to physical considerations, since this approach also allows a new appreciation for the use of deliberate stratagems. These represent the intellectual side of making war. A key distinction here is that such ploys require a conscious choice on the part of a commander, not just acceptance of things that, at least on the day of battle, are beyond his control. It is this that separates real tactical evolution from inherited physical factors like manpower and acculturated fighting styles, or the emotional influences that dominated the hearts of men going into battle. Despite a common perception that 5th century Greek warfare was simplistic in this area, there were actually a number of designed maneuvers that found employment at that time. The ancient Greeks sometimes invoked these as a prelude to contact with the enemy, while at other times they utilized them in the very midst of combat. Of course, generals of the age differed greatly in both knowledge and skill with regard to such techniques. Some merely followed common past practices, with the most talented or lucky carving out a fair portion of success with these conventional approaches. Others were more inventive or at least more creatively adoptive. These bold leaders sought to bend odds in their favor by doing the unexpected, sometimes taking great risks, but often delivering spectacular results.

Finally, beyond the impact of matters physical and intellectual, this study is equally instructive about the more emotional aspects of ancient warfare. Among these are the effects that fighting on home soil and combat experience or training could have on morale. Dubious products of stirring speeches aside, generals could do little to control these kinds of inputs on the battlefield, and each of them carried a strong psychological impact. They had potential for inspiring warriors to great effort, whether through love (of home or country) or confidence (in skill or winning tradition). Steeped in the romantic mythology of war, it's easy to assume that such elements always had positive effects. Their true nature seems to have been much more complex; in fact, these perceptual aspects of making war could sometimes produce results quite contrary to common expectation.

All of the foregoing physical, intellectual, and emotional factors came together in differing combinations on the battlegrounds of Greece to produce the result of each and every engagement. By working carefully through the surviving records and extending them with logical probabilities as described above, it has then been possible to produce the following series of tactical-level narratives for all of those actions, giving them historical perspective and collecting the derived data in tabular form. An overview of the results of this process has enabled identification of a number of distinct tactical patterns, both within sets of contemporary combats and for the 5th century as a whole.

The picture that emerges from this survey is one of everyday men dealing with practical problems in the perilous and intimidating environment of mortal combat. In doing so, they were prone as much to fear and blundering as to genius and daring. This might seem far less grand than the prevailing image of classical-age warriors, yet it's also much more recognizably human and inspiring. These weren't demigods to be chiseled from marble or cast in bronze, but fallible creatures of flesh and blood just like us. And in light of this fundamental truth, we may well learn more of lasting value from telling their stories in a detailed and realistic fashion than we ever could by repeating broad and heroic, but ultimately misleading fictions.

I

The Spearmen: Greek Hoplite Warfare (500–401 B.C.)

"Come, call up whatever courage you can muster.
Life or death — now prove yourself a spearman."

Achilles (Homer: *The Iliad*)

The Greek world in the 5th century B.C. was a patchwork of over a thousand small and fiercely independent states. An adventurous people, the Greeks had radiated from their homeland at the southeastern edge of Europe during the early first millennium B.C., questing for land and livelihood wherever their ships could reach and their strength of arms wrest possession. Their outposts soon lay scattered from Asia Minor to what is now southern Spain and from the North African coast to the fertile plains above the Black Sea. Each settlement within this loose cultural network acted as a miniature country, with most having a capital city to provide both a political nexus and a sort of national identity. Residents of such city-states or *poleis* in Greek (singular *polis*) were, beyond all else, members of the local community. Indeed, their very survival was bound to its fate.

Life in the classical era was harsh and required grim determination and self-reliance in order to endure. Forming city-states enhanced chances for survival by providing a means of making combined efforts for both commerce and defense. Thus, the health of the polis linked directly to the welfare of its citizens. If their city thrived they would prosper, but its failure would at best leave them as wretched outcasts and more likely bring either slavery or death. So close a tie between the state's security and the well-being of its populace led the Greeks to take great care in their relations with outsiders. Since involvement in the affairs of others might threaten their own existence, it was rare for poleis to form alliances of any great size or duration. Thus, beyond a myth-shrouded expedition to Troy (sacked c. 1270–1190 B.C.), the Greeks never created anything like a national union prior to the early 5th century B.C. (and then, only briefly).

Despite such isolationism, the Greek people had strong ties to common cultural elements. Language was foremost of these. In fact, Greeks identified those speaking foreign tongues as barbarians (*barbaroi*) — aliens whose utterances sounded like "bar-bar" (equivalent to "blah-blah" in modern English). Ability to communicate freely joined with religion and a wide variety of other shared social practices to forge a powerful bond of kinship. All thus felt a unity of culture despite any minor variations in physical make-up and dialect. Prominent among these shared cultural conventions was a unique style of warfare.

War was central to the life of city-state residents, a key element of their political and social organization, as to be a citizen was to be a soldier. Likewise, intellectual and emotional accommodation of combat was a basis of much of their literature and art. Poets, sculptors, philosophers, and architects — all were warriors first. The ability to fight was crucial to a man's self-image and sense of place in the community. It was therefore totally unremarkable in its day that the epitaph for Aeschylus, the great tragic dramatist of classical Athens, made note solely of his participation in the battle of Marathon (490 B.C.). He and his family considered this battlefield service to have been the most memorable achievement in his life. If this shows that warfare lay at the heart of classical Greek society, then it would be fair to say that the armored spearman or hoplite was its soul.

Hoplites

Hoplites (*hoplitai*) had their roots in Mesopotamia, where military advances through the 9th century B.C. had seen use of linear formations of spearmen with helmets, shields, and metal-reinforced corselets. These concepts spread out from Assyria and elsewhere in the Tigris and Euphrates region to the Carians of southern Asia Minor, who developed an improved style of bronze-clad fighter. Such warriors then served not only within Caria, but also found work as hired fighters throughout the eastern Mediterranean.

The ancient Greeks said that Caria was home to the hoplite shield; and though its final form was probably a European Greek development, this tradition remains instructive. Tales of Carian invention chart the direction some aspects of the shield and basic hoplite technology took in migrating across the Greek world — from Caria north into Ionia and thence across the Aegean to Greece proper. The first poleis there to develop hoplites were on the large island of Euboa, which lies just off the eastern coast. The Euboans refined the arming of such soldiers during the 8th century B.C. into something much like its classical form. The men of Euboa were known as Greece's best fighters in those days and the highly skilled metal workers of their leading city of Chalcis reputedly designed the heavy bronze cuirass worn by early hoplites and developed effective short-swords of iron.

The hoplite concept spread rapidly from this island toehold to the warlike Dorian peoples in the Peloponnesian peninsula of southwestern Greece. Here, the artisans of Corinth gained fame for improving hoplite gear in the early 7th century with the development of superior bronze helmets, with their distinctive "Corinthian" helm coming into widespread use throughout Greece. Likewise, craftsmen in nearby Argos improved the shield. Earlier shields had a central grip for the hand and included both round and "Boeotian" designs. The Boeotian shield — named for an illustration found on a gold ring from Boeotia in central Greece — had an oval outline with notches cut out on each side to yield a figure-eight shape. Though hybrid forms persisted for some time, the round and concave "Argive" shield eventually replaced all previous designs. These new shields were carried more efficiently on the forearm, a method of suspension that might have been the original concept contributed by the Carians. As the various elements of hoplite equipment developed, all Greece moved to embrace this more effective style of fighter.

At first, the Greeks deployed hoplites in linear formations that had shallow depth of file. They fought in these arrays using two light spears, throwing one and retaining the other for hand-to-hand action in the front ranks. However, much deeper formations emerged in the first half of the 7th century B.C. that relied on a single, longer spear used only for thrusting. Like aforementioned improvements in the shield, this innovation was created and/or perfected in the Peloponnese, most likely at the city-state of Argos. Undoubtedly, the so-called

Argive shield evolved as an adaptation to the new, deeper-massed formations. Whether the Argives were inventors or merely early adopters of hoplite warfare, they clearly honed its use to a deadly art. Argos fielded the most proficient army of heavy spearmen (*doruphoroi*, singular *doruphoros*) in Greece by the mid 7th century and would hold this advantage until eclipsed by neighbor and chief rival Sparta (Lacedaemon) in the later half of the 6th century.

The hoplite population was largely made up of militiamen from the middle income class. These were mostly farmers (*georgoi*), though urban dwellers formed a minority element and were more significant in the armies of trading centers like Corinth, Athens, and Syracuse. Such amateur spearmen seem to have been available in fairly large numbers, with 27 percent of their battles in the 5th century involving more than 5,000, 22 percent more than 10,000, and the typical Greek army of the period having a mean of around 2,500 hoplites. For most of these men, their introduction to the martial arts must have come in their early teens from male relatives who took time to instruct them on the basics of wearing and handling arms. Some joint training with others of their age group would have followed toward instilling rudimentary formation skills. Community drills might then have further readied young men for combat, allowing them to gather and work in an ordered array alongside veteran countrymen. Ultimately, of course, it was experience gained on actual battlefields that finally turned untried boys into soldiers.

Hoplites supplied their own arms and armor during the 5th century and only men of at least middling means could afford these items. Gear typically included armor of helmet, knee-high bronze greaves (*knemides*) that snapped on, and a cuirass (*thorax*) for the chest. The latter was originally of bronze with a weight of over 11kg, but became much lighter stiffened linen, leather, and metal composite during the subject era, often with protective shoulder pieces (*epomides*) and leather strips (*pteruges*) that formed a shielding kilt below the waist. Helmets of highly shined bronze came in a variety of types. The aforementioned Corinthian model with a nose-guard and an open-faced design now called "Illyrian" were common in the early 5th century. A lighter Corinthian variant known today as "Chalcidian" and a conical, pot-like helm called a *pilos* (after the peaked felt cap on which it was styled) were often worn in later years, the latter being popular with the Spartans and their allies. Other than the pilos, it was commonplace for Greek headgear to sport an attached crest of bristling horsehair. These generally ran front-to-back like a cock's comb (hence the Asian slang term "roosters" for hoplites), but a side-to-side design is known from Sparta where it might have denoted rank. Colorfully dyed and ornamental, crests had some practical value for making a hoplite seem taller and more menacing.

In contrast to shifting fashions in helmet design, the most fundamental piece of the hoplite's defensive gear remained unchanged. This was the rounded Argive shield or *aspis* (plural *aspides*). The term *hoplon* sometimes denoted this piece of equipment, but that word found use most often in the plural (*hopla*) to describe all the tools of war (i.e., arms, with *hoplites* signifying a man at arms). A typical aspis had a base of highly flexible wood such as poplar or willow overlain with a very thin layer (less than 0.5mm thick) of bronze, which could attain a mirror-like finish when polished. The hoplite carried his shield on the left, with his forearm through a metal band at center (*porpax*) and using a leather handgrip (*antilabe*) near the rim. Aspides were heavy (about 8kg), but at 0.8–1.0m wide, they gave protection from knee to chin. The Greeks painted emblems on the front of their shields. These began as images distinct to each warrior or family/clan; a practice that Athens maintained throughout the 5th century. However, other states came to the use of uniform shield devices. These could be a letter (such as *lambda* for Lacedaemon and *sigma* for Sicyon) or a national symbol (per a trident for Mantinea and the club of Hercules for Thebes).

The thrusting spear (*doru* or *enchos*) of some 2.0–2.5m in length was the chief offensive weapon of the hoplite. Held in the right hand, it had a forward-tapering shaft of ash or other light and strong wood, a head of steel, and a base/butt spike (*styrax* or *sauroter*, i.e. "lizard killer") of bronze (steel in later models). A short leather sleeve sewn around the shaft at the point of balance provided a grip for the hand. The hoplite rested this long weapon on the shoulder while marching and carried it upright prior to contact with the enemy, which let the skyward projecting tip provide some protection from missiles. When finally lowered into action (for *doratismos* or spear fighting), men in the first few rows of a close formation all used the length of their spears to strike at the leading line of their rival. They could aim crippling and even lethal underhand thrusts at the legs and lower body of an opponent, while an overhand strike directed over the top of a shield was capable of dealing a mortal blow to the face or throat of even a heavily armored foe.

In addition to his spear, the hoplite carried a sword hanging at his left side and a knife for daily tasks and use as a weapon of last resort. The sidearm of choice was a two-edged sword (*xiphos*) that widened slightly from the hilt before tapering to a final point. A single-edged saber, the *machaira* or *kopis*, was also very popular. "Kopis" was a slang term equally applicable to meat cleavers that might best be translated as "chopper," leaving us a rather unpleasantly vivid idea of the weapon's effect on the human body. The substantial length (up to 60cm) and downward-curving configuration of this saber allowed the wielder to slash down over the top of an opponent's shield from arm's reach, while the single edge protected those in the following rank from a careless backstroke. The xiphos was often long as well (as much as 70cm) and thus also more of a slashing than thrusting weapon. Yet contrary to the general preference for slashing swords, classical Greece's most feared warriors, the Spartans, favored a short version of the straight sword that was better designed for thrusting and their close-in style of fighting.

The term panoply (*panoplia*) denotes Greek heavy infantry equipment in its entirety, with men so outfitted often called *panoploi*. Total weight of this gear early in the 5th century ran to some 32kg or 70 pounds, a heavy load for the average hoplite, who was of rather small stature. It thus made sense to cut down on his burden as much as was practical toward increasing comfort, endurance, and ease of maneuver. The panoply therefore evolved during the 5th century, losing both specific elements and overall metal content. Never, however, did hoplites abandon their characteristic Argive shields or thrusting spears.

The Doric Phalanx

The *phalanx* (literally a "roller") was the standard battle formation of city-state armies. The 7th century development of this array in the Peloponnese by Greeks of the Dorian ethnic group transformed the hoplite from just one more type of armored fighter into the premier soldier of the time. Note that this sort of phalanx predated and was quite distinct from the Macedonian formation of that same name. "Doric phalanx" is a more specific term that best identifies the older arrangement that is the subject here.

The Doric phalanx was a linear body of warriors arrayed by rank and file, with ranks commonly ranging from hundreds to over 1,000 men in width. Conversely, files had a normal count of only eight men, but could increase to provide greater offensive momentum or accommodate terrain restrictions, or could lessen to stretch manpower into matching length of an opposing line. Limits on keeping order while marching were also a consideration. Deeper formations maneuvered with greater ease (Goldsworthy 1996, 196–197) and only the very best troops could long maintain an orderly advance below a depth of six men. Likewise, deep formations gave defensive advantage and imparted moral strength, while at the same time crowding the route of retreat to make it difficult for those at the front to run from a fight. Troops deployed into three groups along the width of the phalanx, forming a center, left wing, and right wing. They kept a more open order when distant from the enemy, but drew together for final approach. Such closing of files meant that the shields of each rank effectively overlapped to create a frontage of about 1m per man (the width of a typical aspis). In this way, the shield of each hoplite protected his left side as well as the right side of the man standing next to him. Intervals between men in file ranged from 1.5–2m per man in open order to about 1m per man during close-order advance and maybe not much more than 0.5m per man when compressed against an enemy.

Keeping order intact at a brisk walk, a phalanx could move forward at around 6km/hr. This allowed it to crash into an opposing front with considerable force, even if the foe remained stationary. The resulting impact often shattered spears and inflicted a number of initial casualties on both sides. Adding a final run over the last few meters or engaging an opponent approaching at similar speed only heightened the effect of this initial collision.

Once engaged, those foremost in each file stabbed and shoved at the enemy in what must have been a noisy, frenzied, and often desperate melee. The majority of ancient depictions show hoplites at this stage striking with spears held in an overhand grip, strongly indicating this to have been the most common practice. However, a few surviving illustrations and evidence for wounds in the leg and groin suggest that some held their weapons couched underhand. This made sense for men in the leading rank, letting them direct a powerful thrust at the lower body of an opponent with all the momentum of the charge. Switching to an overhand grip might then have followed, as it could deal a much more forceful blow (Gabriel and Boose 1994, p. 19). Still, a continued underhand pose along the front would have made it easier for men in the ranks behind to reach out past the shoulders of those ahead for overhand strikes. Yet regardless of details of technique, it's certain that, once a formation made contact with the enemy, only hoplites in the first two or three ranks had sufficient reach to actually engage in hand-to-hand or "shock" combat. Such limited participation was inherent to any deep battle array in this era, but the phalanx was unique in finding a solution to the short range of ancient shock weaponry.

Linear formations traditionally moved ahead behind a line of front-fighters (*promachoi*). This forced those in the rearward ranks to take a passive role, waiting to move up into striking distance as replacements for fallen comrades. In contrast, the after ranks of a Doric phalanx actively affected the front. Each hoplite stood with left foot and shoulder thrust forward to allow the man behind to push a shield into his back. In this way, all ranks pressed ahead to help drive into the enemy. Even grounded spears aided the effort, with those behind thrusting sauroters into the soil to pull and shove against their anchored shafts for additional leverage. This system of concerted pushing, known as *othismos*, was probably the key innovation that gave the phalanx of Argos its original dominance. It's likely that adoption of othismos tactics had inspired 7th century modifications that gave the shield a lip around the rim, since this let a hoplite rest the aspis on his shoulder and put full weight into pushing ahead.

Othismos drove the phalanx forward like a huge threshing machine of bronze and steel. The advancing formation trampled those that went down before it, leaving men deeper in the files to dispatch anyone still alive among the fallen. The muscular demands of othismos made for a particularly exhausting fight. This tended to make actions short in duration, though spontaneous lulls in an evenly matched effort gave periodic respite and could produce a longer contest. Othismos appears to have been the decisive factor in some 30 percent of the victories gained by Greek armies during the 5th century, including an estimated two-thirds of those scored over barbarian foes.

The Doric phalanx, forward-thrusting and powerfully driven from behind, was extremely formidable in frontal attack or defense. A pitched battle (*parataxis*) between two phalanxes thus yielded the proverbial meeting along the front of immovable object and irresistible force. However, the phalanx was at hazard at back and sides. Rear attacks, though potentially devastating, were uncommon, but the edges of the formation were frequent targets of flanking efforts. In fact, it looks like about a quarter of hoplite victories in the 5th century came as a result of some sort of successful flank envelopment. The right wing thus served as the post of honor for an army's best fighters, since men exposed their unshielded and most vulnerable side along that flank. The left wing followed next in prestige, because, though having a shielded flank, it usually faced the enemy's best men on his right. In addition to troop assignments, the Greeks sometimes used natural and artificial barriers to secure their wings. They also deployed both light infantry and cavalry on the flanks for this same purpose.

Front to back in formation, the most dangerous and esteemed station was along the leading line, where contact with the enemy was unavoidable. Yet due to the crowding of men on all sides, only those at the rear of the phalanx actually had the option to run away, and it was vital to assign highly reliable soldiers there as well. The interior of the phalanx was thus the least valued posting. Generals traditionally placed men of lesser experience and/or questionable valor (potential *tresantes*, "tremblers" or "runaways") in the very center, where they could be kept from ignoble flight by the press of more trustworthy troops all around.

A phalanx's security and effectiveness depended in the end on the integrity of its ranks and files. If hoplites lost order, they became isolated as small groups or individuals. Slowed by heavy gear and unshielded from attack on three sides, a lone man had no chance to stand his ground and nearly always gave way to panic and flight. Critical cohesion was not only at risk due to enemy attacks to rear and flank, but also often fell apart during rapid advance or while moving over rough terrain. The need to preserve formation order therefore effectively restricted phalanx actions to ground that was more or less open and level. Furthermore, it was important that hoplites not break ranks to exploit victory by chasing a defeated enemy. Light infantry and/or cavalry therefore became the primary tool for this kind of post-battle pursuit.

Potency of the Doric phalanx rested upon much more than simple equipment technology and formation design. The true strength of this method lay in the courage of the bronze-clad men standing in the ranks, the *stratiotai*. Napoleon once claimed that the value of the moral to the physical was three to one as a factor in military success in his age; and this seems equally valid for the 5th century B.C., as courage born of conviction and confidence was a paramount element in classical Greek warfare. Only determined men with faith in their own ability and tactical doctrine would exert to the limits of endurance in pushing a phalanx toward victory. Likewise, only those with this same solid belief in their system would hold position without wavering that they might fend off so fearsome an assault.

Valor vital to success in phalanx battle seems to have had a firm basis in the native endurance of Greek farmers (Hanson 1995, 127–78), who formed the bulk of the hoplite population. This natural strength of character gained a boost in measure with the level of a hoplite's confidence in his leaders, his belief in his own and his unit's combat superiority, and his devotion to comrades ordered around him. Men lacking in these moral factors usually broke and ran before those who had them in abundance, and this often happened in defiance of the balance of physical strength present on the field of battle. Martial tradition and hard won experience of past success were critical to a hoplite's belief in both his leaders and his own prowess, while a place in the ranks among friends and relatives was a great stimulus to his sense of duty.

Besides inspiring individual and unit confidence, fighting in close order was a prime factor allowing soldiers to overcome a natural aversion to taking the life of another human being. Grossman (1995) has made a strong case for an innate aversion among men for killing their own kind. Such reluctance occurs even when failing to slay puts one's own life or those of friends and family at risk. However, he also proposes that personal bonds inside a team or the group sharing of duty among a weapon's crew can overcome this instinct, noting that the moral dynamics at work within the phalanx effectively turned it into a crew-served weapon. Yet this didn't entirely eliminate mental duress. Shay (1994) has shown close parallels between modern combat-related afflictions such as post-traumatic stress disorder (PTSD) and symptoms described among ancient Greeks. Tritle (2000) draws similar conclusions in comparing veterans of Vietnam and Greece's Great Peloponnesian War of the late 5th century B.C. Nevertheless, supportive aspects of the phalanx did serve to significantly reduce psychic trauma, thus helping to make Greek hoplites into the most effective soldiers of their time.

Beyond the foregoing socio-psychological factors, it's worthwhile to explore the role played by situational tactics in phalanx warfare. The most remarked upon "maneuver" of the Doric phalanx was its tendency to move toward the right during advance. Thucydides said that this was inadvertent, claiming that each hoplite tended to crowd the shield of his comrade on the right for protection as he marched into danger, which caused the man to his left to do the same and so on. The end result of such cheating toward safety by everyone was that the entire phalanx would drift toward the right prior to contact with the enemy. This was often so pronounced that clashing phalanxes could mutually overlap each other at opposite ends of the battlefront. Simultaneous outflanking often led to success for both sides on separate parts of the field and, when enough daylight remained, sometimes brought about a second engagement between the two victorious wings. Still, though the Greeks sometimes exploited this natural tendency of the phalanx to drift, it can't honestly be said that they devised it as a deliberate tactic.

On the other hand, we do have a few reports of maneuvers taking place on command during advance and even in the heat of battle. This proves that not all phalanx movements were natural or accidental. Furthermore, given the dearth of detailed tactical documentation, such actions might have been more common than it at first appears. Who devised these maneuvers and set them into motion? Generals (*strategoi*, singular *strategos*) led a phalanx from within its ranks. These officers performed a number of pre-combat tasks, such as assigning contingents according to prestige and ability; they also arrayed the formation to best use its available manpower and match enemy alignments. And it was these same generals who dictated tactical maneuvers during battle through their supreme commander.

Generals fought in the line like anyone else and therefore had only very limited potential to affect the course of an action already underway. Unable to see what was taking place more than a few feet away from his own position, the commanding officer had to arrange all tactical maneuvers in advance. Based on perception of what was going on in his immediate vicinity, he would then signal a given move via a horn known as a *salpinx*, trusting that the action was following to plan. Since phalanx combat produced only a few tactical patterns, an experienced general had a good chance of programming at least one movement likely to prove appropriate.

Of course, a general's potential to maneuver was limited by the quality of his troops. Most militias could handle little more than signals to move forward and halt. However, highly trained hoplites had greater abilities. Spartans and some picked soldiers (*epilektoi*) of other city-states could shift during advance, strike with one wing prior to the other, wrap around the flank of an enemy line, and feign retreat to tempt a foe into breaking ranks in pursuit. Often a single wing carried out these actions, requiring only a small portion of an army to have such skills. This potential for adapting in the midst of combat added greatly to the effectiveness of the Doric phalanx and helped to produce a military system that would dominate most of the Mediterranean region for over 300 years.

Light Infantry

While hoplites formed by far the greatest part of a typical Greek army in the 5th century B.C., they were not the only foot soldiers (*pezoi*). Modest numbers of light infantrymen (*psiloi*) took the field as well to provide support to the phalanx. Psiloi came from the lower classes and could afford neither expensive weapons nor armor protection. They carried out a wide array of auxiliary duties, such as scouting, foraging, raiding, and constructing siege works, while in combat they hurled missiles of various types at the enemy—javelins, arrows, and sling-bullets.

Unarmored men were rarely decisive in pitched battle. This reflects not only the modest strength of most light infantry deployments, but also the defensive nature of that arm's combat duties. The task of light troops was to neutralize their opposite numbers and prevent them from interfering with the phalanx. If the psiloi on both sides were mutually successful in countering their opponents, which was usually the case, then their actions went virtually unnoticed as the hoplites took center stage to decide the issue unimpeded. Yet one has only to look at the dire results of those few battles where the light-armed on one side failed completely (as at Spartolos in 429 B.C. or Aegitium in 426 B.C.) to see that their contribution could indeed be vital.

Psiloi generally skirmished against other light-armed men in the area between phalanxes during a battle's opening phase. They fought using a dispersed order that gave room for each soldier to discharge his missiles, while keeping enough open space for individuals or small groups to charge and retreat with the ebb and flow of the fight. Psiloi withdrew from the opening skirmish around or through the still widely spread ranks of their phalanx to take up stations in support of the formation flanks. They stood ready there at battle's end to either cover retreat or chase a beaten enemy as appropriate. In all of this, the Greek light infantryman suffered the universal fate of all those assigned to seemingly small roles that are in actuality quite critical—undeserved anonymity in victory and over-stated notoriety in defeat.

Javelinmen

Though both archers and slingers found employment in the subject era, the most common light infantrymen were those that used javelins (*palta* or *akontia*), light, bronze-headed, throwing spears of 1.1–1.6m in length. The javelinman usually wrapped the shaft of his weapon with a leather thong some 50cm in long that ended in a loop for the fingers (an *amentum* in Latin). Unfurling this cord during the throw imparted spin that increased both precision and range much like rifling in a gun barrel. A man on foot could accurately hurl a javelin about 90m when utilizing a throwing thong, versus a range of probably less than half that without this device. Javelin heads could be either tanged (fitted into a notch in the shaft) or socketed (pulled over the end of the shaft). In contrast to contemporary war-arrows, these were not barbed. It was much easier to withdraw an unbarbed point from the body of a fallen foe, an important feature in a weapon carried in very limited quantities (often no more than two at time) and sometimes used hand-to-hand.

Javelin throwers (*akontistai*) were most often the only missile troops in a Greek army of the early 5th century. Though the javelin had shorter range than sling or bow, it required far less training, which accounts for its popularity among part-time militiamen who lacked the free time to drill with more demanding weapons. The earliest Greek javelinmen were a minority among combatants (*makhimoi*) drawn for light support from among the large group of lower-class retainers that normally accompanied a hoplite army. This crowd of attendants (*okhlos*, including baggage carriers —*skeuophoroi*— and shield-bearers —*upaspistae*) usually numbered at least one for each spearman. When they took up arms, most of these men wielded makeshift weapons like rocks or farm tools; thus, they had little effect on pitched battle. However, those armed with javelins were more effective than other psiloi and could be a significant factor in combat.

Javelin fighters normally only engaged other missilemen on the periphery of a battle and thus avoided shock action. They could, however, employ their weapons as short thrusting spears when necessary. This modest shock capability combined with speed of foot to make them well suited for striking down fleeing foes during post-battle pursuit. It was very rare for javelin-armed light infantry to do more than skirmish or pursue; yet when facing opponents short on light forces of their own, they were sometimes able to take advantage of their mobility and range to confront and defeat hoplites.

Peltasts (*peltastai*) emerged in the later 5th century B.C. as a more effective form of javelin-armed auxiliary. This was a type of warrior adopted from Thrace in the northeast, which also supplied Greek armies with peltast mercenaries. These men usually wore helmets and carried a leather-covered, crescent-shaped shield or *pelta* from which they derived their name. This gave them an edge on shieldless psiloi, who could only wrap their cloaks around the non-throwing arm for protection. As effectiveness of javelinmen improved, they gained wider appreciation and their ratio to hoplites in Greek armies increased.

Archers

The bow (*toxon*) had a much stronger tradition in Asia than among the Greeks; therefore, archers (*toxotai*, singular *toxotes*) were never a large component of Greek armies in the classical period. However, the Athenians of southeastern Greece put bowmen to significant use at this time, both in the field and aboard their ships. A good many of these archers were local citizens, but others were mercenary fighters.

The war bow had gone through three distinct stages of development to produce the types used in 5th century warfare: the simple bow (also known as a self or stave bow), the compound bow, and the composite bow. The simple bow was a single piece of wood with an animal-gut string that could project an arrow up to 300m as part of a directional barrage, but only some 90–135m with accuracy against a specific target. Archers on the Greek mainland still commonly used this device, as more advanced bows were both hard to produce and costly. Stave bows were also best suited to their style of grip, which pinched the bowstring between thumb and forefinger. This method was too weak for use with more complex bows, which called for the first three fingers of the hand to pull back the string in a technique known today as the "Mediterranean loose." The latter was mandatory for the somewhat farther-ranging compound bow, comprising two pieces of wood sandwiching an inner layer of hide. It was also required by the composite bow. This was a construct of laminated wood, horn, and animal tendons that could send a barrage out as far as 500m. Despite being fairly accurate anywhere below 220m, this mighty weapon, like all bows, was still most precise at distances less than 90m. The advantage it held over simpler bows at such close range was in delivering an arrow with greater force and ability to penetrate.

Archers tipped their reed shafts with tanged, bronze arrowheads that had thick central spines to improve penetration. There was considerable variation in size and shape of these points. The bowmen of Crete used exceptionally large and heavy heads on their arrows, while others employed tips that were notably more delicate. As archers fought from a distance and could carry a large supply of missiles, it was neither practical nor necessary that they recover their arrows from a victim's body for immediate reuse. Bowmen took advantage of this to fit their war-arrows with barbed heads. These insured that even greater damage would be done to a stricken enemy upon any attempt to remove the arrowhead from his wound.

Yet though they had potential to inflict fearsome injuries, arrows were only a modest threat to hoplites, as they rarely pierced shields or body armor. Arrows most often caused harm by finding gaps between parts of the panoply, and it took a sustained volley for any great number to do so. Only a long and intense pelting could disrupt and defeat a phalanx, something that was a very rare event. This was because a targeted formation would generally move forward into contact with its foe, causing the rear profile of the archers' own men to partially block the line of sight. With bow fire thus restricted, shock fighting settled most actions before the fall of arrows could become decisive. This was the case at Marathon, when hoplites defeated a bow-rich Persian army, and this same scenario played out many other times in the later history of Greco–Persian conflict. Thus, while sometimes of value in defeating hoplites under certain circumstances, the bow was usually little more than a nuisance to such well-protected men.

The amount of drill that it took to become proficient with the bow accounts in part for its lack of popularity among militiamen. It was simply not possible for part-time soldiers to devote so much time and effort. This was especially true for the poorer men that normally filled the role of unarmored warriors. Furthermore, use of the bow did not require the sort of stoic courage prized by Greek society of the day and exemplified by the mandates of shock combat. Simply put, the Greeks viewed striking from a distance with an arrow as less than honorable. Citizens of greater means, who had the free time to seriously pursue archery skills, chose instead to serve as hoplites or ride with the cavalry. Bowmen therefore remained a rarity in Greek warfare until the later part of the 5th century; only then did their value gain greater recognition and inspire more common hiring of mercenary specialists.

Athens was outstanding among mainland Greek states in using the bow to bolster its phalanx. This was a tradition that dated back to 547 B.C., when the tyrant Peisistratos came back from exile in Thrace with a force of bowmen. These were Scythian horse-archers and when we later hear of Athenians using mercenary bowmen as policemen it's likely that these likewise came from Scythia. Employment of archers survived ouster of the last tyrant in 510 B.C. to become part of newly democratic Athens's style of warfare.

Athenian bowmen and hoplites actually worked in tandem. While the archers kept light-armed opponents away from the phalanx, the spearmen reciprocated by shielding them. The Persians had long recognized the weakness of bowmen in hand-to-hand combat and responded by deploying their archers behind a wall of shield-bearers. The Athenians likely learned of this approach from their Scythian mercenaries and were inspired to form a specialized squad of hoplites to front their own bow-troops. First described at Plataea (479 B.C.), this tactic dates from the late 6th century, since we have depictions from that period (as per Sekunda and Hook 2000, 46) showing Scythian archers firing from behind kneeling spearmen. At first, these fronting hoplites used two short "throwing" spears (Wees 2004, 177), but then appear to have rather quickly converted to the longer, thrusting spear used in the regular phalanx.

The Athenians didn't field archers at Marathon, but they used them often from 483 B.C. onward. Their bowmen were about 1,200–1,300 strong in 480–479 B.C., with 800 supporting the army (How and Wells 1928 [Vol. II], 295) and 400–500 with the fleet. They likely formed squads of four (the number on each ship) and deployed for battle in files of eight (just as per the norm for phalanx depth). When the full land force arrayed on the battlefield, it probably stood 12–16m deep, allowing 1.5–2m per man for use of the bow. This created a front of 100m (1m per man), which 300 hoplites could shield at three-deep (the maximum able to engage in active shock combat). By 431 B.C., the number of bowmen reached 1,600. This made it possible to have 800 archers for duty ashore at the same time that another 800 manned 200 ships at sea.

Athens's archery corps began with poorer citizens using wooden-stave bows. Seeking better missile support, the city began in the middle of the 5th century to boost firepower by again bringing in Scythians. These utilized distinct, doubly convex, composite bows. And they might have further increased their effectiveness with poison derived from decomposed vipers — Scythian "medicine" (*pharmakon*). They are said to have applied this venom to their arrowheads from small gold cups on their belts (Mayor 2003, 77–86) and, significantly, the Greek term for poison (*toxikon*) derives from the word for bow. The Athenians also hired archers from Crete later in the century. These used composite weapons with a single-convex design that were superior to native Greek stave bows, but less powerful than those of the Scythians. The large and distinctive arrowheads of the Cretans are a common find in Greek archeological sites, which suggests that archers from Crete were used in a great many city-state armies and/or that others copied their weapons.

Slingers

Slingers never played a role as large as javelinmen or even archers in 5th century Greek armies. Nonetheless, they were present in a number of major actions, most notably in northwestern Greece and on Sicily. Slingers were highly mobile and fought without armor, using the "shepherd's sling," a leather device composed of two long cords attached on either side of a center patch that acted as a pouch for the shot. The cords were knotted at the end to allow the slinger to hold them in one hand and whirl the load above his head at full length before releasing one line to open the pouch and loose the missile at his target.

A good slinger could lob small (usually 25–30g) lead bullets with reasonable precision as far as 185m or even more accurately fire them on a flatter trajectory out to around 70m. This equaled or exceeded the range of many bowmen. During the Greek retreat from Cunaxa in 401 B.C., it was noted that Persian slingers using stone shot outreached both javelinmen and Cretan archers alike, and slingers with metal shot had even greater range. Even more than was the case for arrows, it was very difficult to see and avoid sling bullets, which seemed to come out of nowhere to deal serious damage. Striking shot not only imparted significant concussion, but could also become deeply buried inside a victim's wound.

Mercenaries able to devote many years of training to achieving mastery of the sling came increasingly into demand during the classical era. Great skill with this device was common among herdsmen that used it from early youth to fend off roaming predators and the Greeks recruited slingers from a large number of pastoral areas across the region. These included Aitolia and Acarnia in the northwest, Thessaly and Thrace in the northeast, Elis and Achaea in the southwest, and even Crete. Yet it was the island of Rhodes in the eastern Mediterranean that provided the most famous slingers, with Rhodians allegedly being able to hit designated targets at distances of over 300m.

Horsemen

Mounted troops were rarely present in large numbers in classical Greek armies. Still, the Athenians, Boeotians, Thessalonians, Chalcidians, and Sicilians put cavalry to good use at times, and even the proud hoplites of Sparta fielded a few horsemen by the end of the 5th century B.C. War chariots, on the other hand, were almost extinct in the Grecian world by the beginning of the subject era, though both Phoenicians and Greeks on the island of Cyprus continued to put them to effective use.

Cavalry

Aristocratic cavalry was central to pre-hoplite armies, but horsemen were no more than auxiliaries among 5th century Greeks. Nevertheless, mounted men were major factors in a number of battles during the period of interest and carried out a wide variety of functions away from the battlefield as well. Despite their reduced role, Greek horsemen (*hippeis*, singular *hippeus*) maintained high social status, since only men of very significant means could afford to supply a horse and tack. They rode small, unshod mounts (horseshoes wouldn't appear before the 1st century B.C.) with only a primitive type of saddle and no stirrups (an invention of the 5th century A.D.). So precariously seated, riders weren't well suited for close combat; as a result, they fought for the most part with missiles and used neither shields nor armor beyond a helmet.

Greek cavalrymen usually carried two javelins, hurling one in the main offensive sortie and keeping the other for shock combat or throwing it as a parting shot in retreat. Most also carried a sword for close-in work, favoring the machaira saber, whose curved blade was well suited for striking down at the necks and upper arms of opponents on foot. We have no evidence that Greeks specially trained their mounts to also function as weapons (a practice known from contemporary Persia). In truth, the small and notoriously unruly horses of Greece were often more dangerous to their masters than to the enemy, having a propensity for throwing riders to cause injury or even death. They also bit, with the resulting wounds sometimes turning fatally septic.

Cavalry had a combat role much like that of light infantry, though more restricted in its need for unbroken and reasonably level ground. Useful in countering skirmishers, it could also mount flank/rear attacks against hoplites and was well suited for both pursuit and screening retreat. Greek horsemen took on a wide range of operations off the battlefield as well. These included securing an army on the march, reconnaissance, raiding, and defense of crops.

Mounted forces maneuvered in mass. This injected mob courage into their charges, made it easier to hold formation, and yielded denser and more effective volleys of missiles. Most city-states in southern and central Greece deployed horsemen in a rectangle (Spence 1993, 103), as per Persian practice and the custom in horse-rich Sicily. But in the far north, the preferred formation had the shape of a wedge that tapered to a point—a standard array of the horse-wise Scythians that had found its way to Macedonia via Thrace. The wedge's chief advantage was that it placed a leader at its apex, where he was highly visible for transmitting commands. The Thessalians, Greece's finest horsemen, took this one step further by employing a diamond-shaped array. Essentially a double wedge, this put officers at each corner to increase control and boost potential for complex maneuver.

Spacing between riders varied with both local practice and circumstances. A reasonable arrangement under most conditions would have been 2m width per rider in rank (1m per mount and 1m between horsemen) and 3m deep per rider in file. Existence of a 96-horse Athenian cavalry squadron (known as a tribe or *phyle*) in the late 6th century combines with Polybios's comments on Hellenistic practice to suggest that the standard mounted file was eight deep, just as for hoplites and foot archers. An Athenian phyle thus formed a square of 24m on each side, twelve horses wide and eight per file, while a regiment of five squadrons (*phylai*) in line created a rectangle with a frontage of 120m. Of course, such parade-ground order would have quickly fallen into a jumble once riders began to move at speed. It's therefore likely that most maneuvers took place at a slow pace unless done quite close to the enemy. Facing similar concerns, later British cavalry doctrine forbade moving above a trot until within 40m of an opponent (France 1999, 160).

Lacking stirrups, a man on horseback couldn't use his legs while throwing the javelin, which cut his range to no more than 60m. Opposing light foot troops could best this reach and posed a grave danger to horsemen. Cavalry-rich armies in Sicily, Boeotia, and Thessaly addressed the problem with javelin-armed footmen that were trained to work with mounted troops. These were *hamippoi* (singular *hamippos*), unarmored fighters that took the field in numbers equal to that of the cavalry, running into action while holding onto the tail or mane of a horse as an aid in keeping up to speed. Though able to function broadly as typical psiloi, the first duty of these men was to protect their cavalry from other skirmishers.

Archers were a special danger for ancient horsemen, since even the least powerful bows could have twice the range of a cavalry dart and easily outreached the javelins of hamippoi. Armies in Asia, where bowmen were the rule rather than the exception, had long ago developed a counter measure to this threat in the form of the mounted archer. The Athenians took similar steps in the 5th century by putting together a corps of 200 horse-archers (*hippotoxotai*, singular *hippotoxotes*). These mounted bowmen were of use in general skirmishing, but did their most critical work in support of the regular cavalry, being of great value for fending off all forms of opposing light infantry, including foot archers. In practice, the range advantage for a bowman on foot against a mounted archer might not have been great for the light bows of this period. Such weapons relied mostly on upper-body strength, making the horse archer, who held an edge in elevation, competitive against a man on the ground with similar gear. Yet though an archer on horseback might have matched or exceeded the range of one on foot, his unstable perch made him less accurate. Taking a precise shot at either walk or gallop presented a fair challenge, while trying to do so while bouncing along at a trot must have been near impossible. This indicates that horse archers relied more on mass volleys than on targeting individuals and suggests that, when present in sufficient numbers, they facilitated a concerted barrage by maneuvering apart from the other horsemen.

Chariots

The two-horse two-man war chariot was once state of the art in military technology. However, this weapon had by the early 5th century disappeared from mainland Greece, where unsuitability to the rough terrain must have severely limited use even at the peak of its popularity. The chariot served as a mobile missile platform and cavalry had gradually usurped this role. Horseback riders could operate over rougher ground than a chariot and give twice the firepower (two bows or javelins) for the same cost in horses and men without the added expense of the vehicle itself.

An exception to this pro-cavalry trend existed on Cyprus, where chariots retained a strong combat role into the classical period. Survival of these archaic fighting machines was actually more a tribute to local retention of monarchy than one of military strategy, as a position within the chariot force was an honored status to which no one but royalty and their close retainers could aspire. And social system aside, only the wealthiest of aristocrats could afford to equip himself and his followers with such an expensive implement of war.

The light chariot used by the Cypriots was drawn by a pair of horses and held a driver and passenger/warrior. Based on what we know of chariot fighting in the Middle East (Dawson 2001, 150), each vehicle also had a small team of peltasts, who ran alongside and provided support much like that given by hamippoi to cavalry. The chariot-mounted fighters of Cyprus were archers that drew composite bows, their personal wealth allowing them sufficient leisure time to master this complex weapon. Modern simulations (Gabriel and Metz 1991, 78) suggest that these archers could be highly accurate while being conveyed at speeds commonly around 12–18km/hr and having an all-out top pace of over 37km/hr. This wasn't much slower than a man on horseback. And not only did the chariot approach the speed of a lone horse, but it was also more stable than a saddle without stirrups as a platform for firing a bow. The chariot archer therefore was at least equal in range and very likely superior in accuracy to any other contemporary warrior of similar mobility, which meant that he could outfight anything that he couldn't outrun. The war chariot thus remained highly effective when available in adequate numbers and where it could deploy on suitably flat and open terrain.

* * *

Hoplites reigned supreme on the battlefields of Greece at the beginning of the 5th century B.C. These men were secure in having a highly respected position within the community as well as supreme confidence in their fighting abilities. After all, their phalanx tactics had been a widely accepted standard in the Grecian realms for over a century and a half, during which time little need had been felt to incorporate other warrior types. The Greeks therefore rarely fielded either cavalry or light foot in significant strength, preferring to confine them to no more than a supporting role on the fringes of city-state conflict. However, a new challenge soon arose to expose the parochial nature of this way of war.

The Persian Empire would threaten Greece with a huge national army that was rich in light infantry and supported by large mounted contingents. The Persians employed what today would be called "combined arms" warfare. This was a system that used an array of troop types that expertly blended their different weapons into a single, orchestrated attack. The Persians mixed high mounted mobility on the flanks with dense missile firepower ahead of a shield-protected battlefront to achieve this deadly combination. Such an approach stood in stark contrast to the Greek method of deploying homogeneous phalanxes of spearmen that were single-mindedly focused on shock combat along the leading edge of their formation.

The hoplite would rise magnificently to this new challenge. He fought to victory time and again in selected settings, where his discipline and armored strength could prevail at close quarters over the enemy's greater ranging weapons and speed of maneuver. Moreover, the more innovative of the Greeks would learn from their trials against Persia. Thus, though the armored spearman was to remain dominant in Grecian warfare, other arms would gradually be given a larger role toward making city-state armies more versatile and deadly.

II

Arguing with Socrates: Territorial Disputes, the Ionian Revolt, and the Rise of Sparta and Gela (500–481 B.C.)

"Challenging Socrates to an argument is like challenging cavalry on the plain."
Plato *(Theaitetos)*

The Achaemenid Empire of Persia was the classical world's greatest power, with vassal lands stretching from India to Egypt and across all Asia Minor. The Persian Great Kings seized this vast domain using a mix of foot archers and cavalry that was nearly invincible where its signature firepower and mobility could properly come to bear. But when this mighty war machine reached for Greece in the early fifth century, it met defeat against an incomplete and fractious union of small city-states. Many have taken this as proof of the fundamental superiority of hoplite warfare. However, the first major clash between Persian and Greek ways of war disputes so simple a verdict. Indeed, armies of the Great King won one battle after another against hoplites during the Ionian Revolt of 499–493 B.C.

The Greek phalanx was a slow, methodical grouping of heavy spearmen that had evolved in a land of narrow valleys to match brute strength along the battlefront against foes of equally limited agility. It was short on the sort of light troops needed to protect flanks in open country. This proved a tremendous liability against the highly mobile Persians on the broad plains of Ionia. Another shortcoming was that phalanx warfare didn't simply focus on killing the enemy in large numbers for strategic advantage. Though undeniably brutal and dangerous (some 100,000 hoplites died in action during the fifth century), it had come to serve an important social function as well.

Classical Greek battle emphasized the role of citizen soldiers in promoting the welfare of their communities. These men endured the terrible ordeal of close-order combat so that conflicts might be resolved at minimal cost in blood and treasure. In this way, they were able to settle disputes within a few days, requiring no more than an hour or two of fighting and avoiding extensive damage to their property. It was war waged by pragmatic men of the soil — men who saw folly in rewarding those last standing in a deadly contest of high attrition, since everyone would lose come harvest time.

The restrictive and highly practical tenets of phalanx warfare were internalized among the Greeks. They became part of their innate sense of morality. As we shall see at Sepeia (494 B.C.), ends didn't always justify means in Greek culture; thus, a victory gained without honor could carry a lasting stigma regardless of its strategic value. Given the arbitrary restraints that this imposed on hoplite warfare, it's no surprise that Grecian armies fighting in Asia Minor often met disaster. After all, they were pitted against vastly more mobile opponents that pursued victory by any and all available means. Yet the Greeks put these painful lessons to good use in the years that followed. They would find ways of compensating for their weaknesses and upset Persia at its height to alter the course of history.

Boundaries Marked in Blood

Most wars fought by the early Greek city-states involved rights to farmland in border regions. Incorporation of marginal land (*eschatia*) in areas of rugged terrain or near the fringe of a city's domain was vital to the needs of the private farmers that made up nearly 80 percent of the average polis's citizenry and provided nearly all of its hoplites. These men generally worked small plots that covered less than eight hectares (twenty acres) and couldn't provide an inheritance for more than one son. Thus, growth within this segment of the population created a burning desire to acquire more territory. Some seafaring cities met this need by sending colonists to distant barbarian lands. However, settling on such alien soil was quite an adventure, and it has been wryly said that a good definition of "adventure" is "danger in retrospect." The Greeks therefore tended to view colonies as an extreme measure best suited to resolving highly volatile social situations, such as pacifying a displaced people or getting rid of a troublesome minority. They thus normally sought solutions to the more mundane issue of middle-class expansion much closer to home; and once having absorbed all the wild tracts within their polis, the only remaining option was to seize nearby land from another city by force of arms. Most poleis pursued this with great vigor, not just to bring relief from immediate pressures for expansion, but also in order to burnish a politically valuable military reputation.

A polis asserted possession of borderlands by occupying them and seizing or setting up religious sanctuaries. Each city had these kinds of shrines in the heart of its urban center, most often within its citadel (the *acropolis* or "high city"). Sanctums were also erected at the edge of a city's farmland, where they served to mark the limits of its territory (Polignac 1995, 33–41). Some of these more distant sites could still be seen from town, thus allowing a man to actually look from the political center of his polis to its outer boundary; others were visible only from a vantage point on the acropolis or lay out of sight altogether. Frontier shrines declared a people's right to work and defend the attached ground and therefore became prime foci for arguments over ownership of eschatia. Capturing such a site and/or despoiling associated fields sounded a challenge to war. This usually led to a contest of phalanxes, with combat results yielding a mutually accepted resolution of the land dispute.

The Peloponnese and Lemnos (c. 500–495 B.C.)

Greek speakers first arrived on the Peloponnesian peninsula of southwestern Greece around 1600 B.C. in a flood that overwhelmed the indigenous population. The invaders brought a culture that flourished for some 400 years before a series of social and economic disasters rocked the eastern Mediterranean late in the thirteenth century. At that time, most Greeks either took refuge in the hills or migrated to safer realms toward the east. The original inhabitants thus regained the lowlands, but their restoration proved brief, as a fresh wave of Greek-speaking people soon poured in from the direction of Thessaly. Traditional beliefs held that these newcomers arrived by way of the small city of Doris on the Malian Gulf, and though their origin must have been more complex, they became known as Dorians.

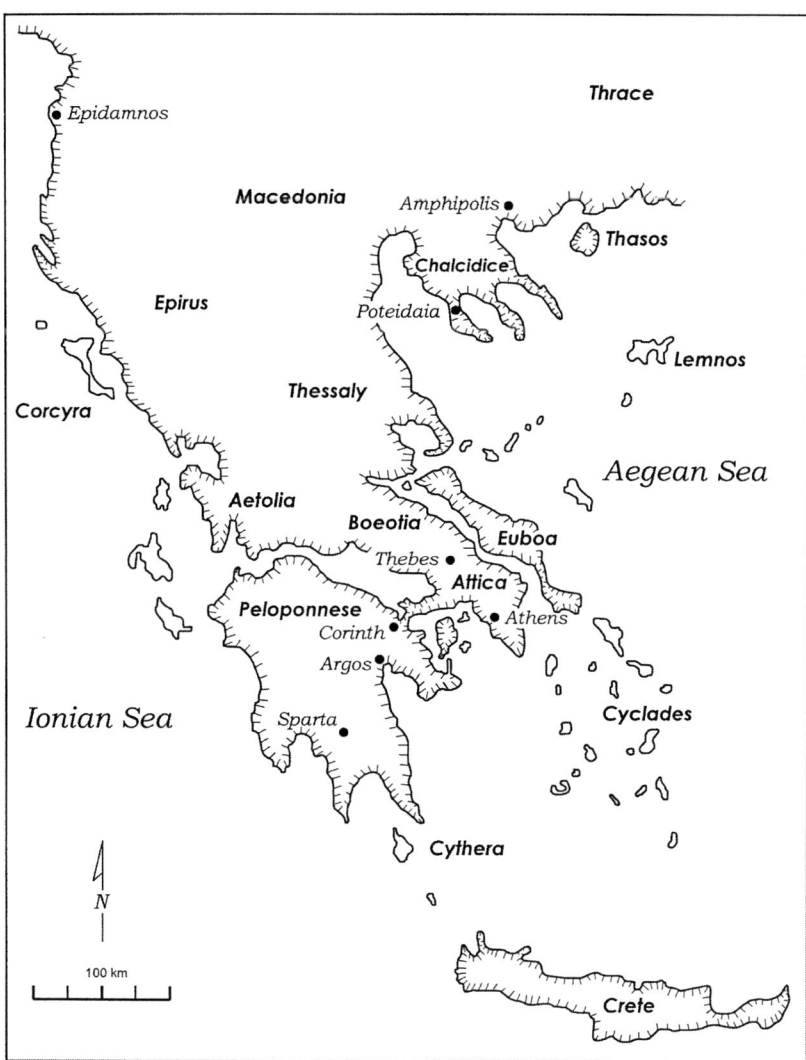

CLASSICAL GREECE

Dorians came to control much of southern Greece, including the Argive plain in the eastern Peloponnese. This is a triangular lowland with mountains on three sides, which opens southward onto the coast and narrows northward into the highlands. In the second millennium B.C., the Argive region contained cities like Mycenae, Tiryns, and Argos itself. So powerful were these communities that Homer referred to the entire Greek race as "Argives." The Argive cities underwent profound decline after 1200 B.C., such that Homer's late eighth century poetry reflected little more than fantasies of past glory. The Dorians changed all that. They reduced the district's natives to subordinate status and had by the early seventh century transformed Argos into the most important city-state in the region.

Argos built its rebirth upon successful exploitation of phalanx tactics. Putting this fearsome methodology to deadly use, the Argives quickly took control of the surrounding plain and went on to exert hegemony to the east as far as Epidauros on the Saronic Gulf. At the same time, they established friendly relations with Mantinea in Arcadia to the west and reached south to contest Sparta for the rich agricultural district of Thyreatis. Corinth was Argos's chief competitor to the north, and it was rivalry with this state that would send the Argives into what appears to be the first significant hoplite action of the fifth century.

Finds at Olympia (Pritchett 1971–1991, Vol. 3, 240–276) indicate that Argos bested Corinth in a major battle c. 500 B.C. Borderland no doubt lay at the heart of this clash, with the district of Cleonai being by far the most likely site. Containing a small plain (10km north to south and 1–4km east to west) along the Longos River, Cleonai sat on the north side of the watershed of Mount Tretus. It thus lay between the Argive plain and the drainage area into the Corinthian Gulf above, which would seem to favor Corinthian control. But Argos had long-standing ties to this tract, as its monarchy had based there during a period of exile in the sixth century. The local sanctuary must therefore have acted as a boundary marker for Argive territory, while a similar shrine just to the east, near Tenea, marked Corinth's southern limit. This set up a natural competition for the fertile land that lay between.

What sort of army marched from Corinth to fight for Cleonai? It was probably similar to the one at Plataea in 479 B.C., which had around 5,000 hoplites. The Dorians of Corinth had reduced the local natives to serfs (known as "wearers of dog skin caps"— Grant 1987, 80) and united eight villages to form their city. This eight-part origin echoed throughout the city's institutions; thus, the army probably had eight regiments or *lochoi* (singular *lochos*) formed from 50-man sub-units (*pentekostyes*— see Connolly 1981, 37–38 on this "archaic lochos"). Lochoi varied in size across Greece, elite contingents often being 300 strong and regular units ranging from 400 to 600 men. The Greeks called up manpower by age groups as needed to insure that lochoi mustered at full strength. Allotment at Corinth of a dozen pentekostyes to each would have yielded 600-man lochoi and an army of 4,800 spearmen.

A full deployment to Cleonai meant calling up all fit men of prime age. It also required Corinth to restrain activity of its fleet. This was because shipboard marines (*epibatai*, singular *epibates*) came from among the younger hoplites and a major sailing would have deprived the army of those men. An all-out effort of this sort (*pandemei*) left city defenses in the hands of reserves. These represented those either too young (teenagers) or beyond the normal years for service in the field (over fifty) plus a few others with disabilities like old wounds. A fair population model for Greek city-states (Hodkinson 1993, 166) suggests that older men made up half of a reserve that comprised around 20 percent of all hoplites (equal in size to a quarter of the regular army). This indicates that Corinth's reserve spearmen numbered around 1,200. Men from the poorer classes (at least 60 percent of the male population) were available as well. Some 5,000 of these would have gone to Cleonai as retainers, including around 500 javelin-armed psiloi at a ratio of one for every ten hoplites. As for the wealthy, there were few or no upper-class horsemen with the army, since Corinth didn't form a regular cavalry force until after 425 B.C. (Spence 1993, 5). Well-to-do Corinthians therefore served as hoplites.

It can be assumed that Argos had also mustered its tribal manpower (the Hylleis, Dymanes, Pamphyloi, and Hyrnathioi) by pentekostyes. This probably took the form of a ten-regiment system, as per contemporary practice at Athens and Sparta that may have been common wherever there was sufficient population. The Argives put at least 6,000 hoplites on the field at Sepeia in 494 B.C., which suggests that their force at Cleonai might have been of like size, with 600 spearmen within each of 10 lochoi. As at Corinth, this field force left behind youth and old-age reservists (some 1,500) to defend the homeland. Non-Dorians provided light-armed support in the form of unarmored javelinmen (*gymnesioi* or "naked" troops). Some 600 of these would have been present at one tenth the army's strength in spearmen. There was no significant mounted force with this mobilization, as Argos paralleled Corinth in its typical Dorian disdain for cavalry and lacked a regular contingent of horsemen at this time.

There are no written records to assist tactical reconstruction of the engagement at Cleonai, but it's possible to frame the action within protocols of the day for a typical clash between two militia phalanxes. We can begin by assuming that the army of Corinth set out during early summer, when crops were vulnerable and streambeds, often used as marching routes, were dry. Moving through the hills along the ancient track from Tenea, the Corinthians descended onto the southern plain of Cleonai and set their attendants to ravaging the area. This served as an insult and challenge for their foe to come out and fight in defense of honor and food supply.

Word of the incursion is sure to have arrived quickly at Argos, where deployment of the army to the north waited only long enough for men to gather from their homes and farms. The Argives mustered at a fixed site (*syllogon*) in or near the city, each bringing his own panoply and supplies for a few days in the field. They then marched up-country to the Cleonai town site to join hoplites from that allied polis. Based on manpower contributed at Mantinea I (418 B.C.), Cleonai probably provided a lochos of around 500 spearman.

The Argives staged near the city as the Corinthians did the same on the plain to the east. Appraising enemy strength, generals on each side would have made an effort to appear confident as they prepared their men for action with a careful arrangement of the ranks, encouraging speeches, and sacrifices to the gods. The Argives had an edge in manpower and must have taken advantage to form up in phalanx at a full eight men deep (or eight "shields" deep to use the terminology of the time). The hoplites from Cleonai likely stood far left in this array, with the commanding Argive and his best troops taking the right wing. On signal, the Argive formation slowly advanced until within 600–800m of the Corinthians, pausing then as its gymnesioi charged out to skirmish with their opposite numbers.

Corinth's generals would have watched their foe's deliberate approach and used the opportunity to shorten their files. They likely arranged their 4,800 hoplites into a phalanx six shields deep, feeding manpower into longer ranks toward matching the width of the enemy front. This was prudent, since the broader Argive array threatened to extend passed them on at least one wing. If not countered, such an overlap would allow the Argives to wrap around the shorter formation to wheel and attack at side or back to devastating effect.

Of course, thinning the files in favor of longer ranks was actually a trade-off of one handicap for another. The Argives now had a better chance of pushing through their opponents' thinner array, something guaranteed to send the foe running in defeat. Even short of such a break-through, stronger shoving/othismos was likely to move the enemy backwards and inspire them with sufficient fear to achieve the same result. Still, a general might hold out reasonable hope that superior physical or moral strength on the part of his men could somehow overcome the disadvantages of facing a deeper array, as had happened numerous times on the battlefields of Greece. But it was something else entirely for him to assume that his soldiers could fight to victory when outflanking allowed the foe to assault unshielded sides or backs. Therefore, though an army might submit on occasion to being overlapped (as implied by Thucydides' comments on the engagement at Olpae in 425 B.C.), this was rare. The preferred response to greater enemy manpower was thus to field a shallower formation rather than a shorter one.

With heavy infantry properly arranged, the generals next signaled for their skirmishers to retire and take post in support of the flanks. Each side then closed ranks to form an 800-meter front of overlapping shields. Though standing still on the defensive was better for maintaining formation integrity, once one army began to move forward (a phase of combat called the *ephodos*), the other usually followed suit in a display of aggression meant to boost its own confidence and lower that of the enemy. Advancing with care to preserve an orderly array, the first line on each side may have lowered its spears underhand toward the foe, those immediately behind shifting to overhand grip, while men in the rear kept their spears upright until needed. The air filled with war songs, as soldiers gave voice to a traditional battle hymn (*paian*). This singing released tension, steeled resolve, and inspired courage; submerging fears, not only of pain and death, but above all else of failing to meet society's lofty standards of manhood before neighbors, friends, and family ranked all about.

Moving steadily ahead and likely drifting slightly toward their right, the phalanxes slowly advanced until fairly close. Both sides then broke into a controlled trot as men gave vent to a bloodcurdling chorus of shrill battle cries. Charging at the enemy like this certainly must have caused some disruption along the ranks, but that seems to have been generally accepted in return for the advantage that forward momentum gave to an initial effort to shove the enemy rearward. Marathon (490 B.C.) is the first recorded instance of such a final run into battle, where it appears to have been something new for the Athenians. However, it's likely that more experienced Peloponnesian armies engaged in the practice at an earlier date, as implied by a foot race in armor that was added to the Olympic games in 520 B.C. (Sekunda and Hook 2000, 6).

The opening collision of bronze and steel must have been bone-jarring and quite a few men at the front of both formations would have gone down, taken by a spear in the legs or groin. Men would have stepped forward over their fallen comrades as those in the first three ranks reached out to strike at the enemy, reversing any weapons shattered in the fearsome initial impact to employ their sauroters. Front fighters clashed hand-to-hand (*en chersi*) amid a hellish din and a rising cloud of choking white dust from the dry, lime-rich soil. A few more hoplites would have fallen in this melee with wounds to face, throat, and/or arms. Meanwhile, men among the rear ranks put their shields into the backs of those ahead and strained forward with all their might. Each grounded the butt of his spear to help push ahead in a desperate attempt to shove through the opposition. Sweating in the summer heat and straining in a powerful mixture of excitement and dread, the combatants struggled to retain footing on ground now growing damp and slick from excretions of frightened men in the ranks and an ever-growing flow of blood at the front.

Given no major overlaps to aid early flanking, this deadly scrum kept up until a differential in manpower, physical strength, endurance, or willpower began to tell. Eventually, the Argive phalanx must have started to move the Corinthians back. Pressing and stabbing their way ahead, the leading Argives would have inched over the bodies of fallen foes, leaving any still alive to downward thrusts from the sauroters of men deeper in the ranks. It's hard to judge just how long it took to reach this turning point, as spontaneous mutual resting could extend an action. In most cases, however, combat reached a decision in less than an hour.

Men within the suffocating press of Corinth's phalanx had to gauge the course of events by feel alone. Swathed in hot, stifling armor and hearing nothing but the cacophony of battle, they could see no more than the backs of those before them. At first, they must have shoved away to the very limits of their strength in hope of victory. They then must have become steadily more frustrated and apprehensive as it grew obvious that their best efforts were not resulting in forward progress. Finally, rising fear blossomed into full-on panic as enemy pressure gradually forced them awkwardly toward the rear. Once such panic surfaced, it quickly rose to a terrified frenzy as unreasoning claustrophobia and the fear of crippling injury or death took over.

With everyone else being confined within the formation's tight press, only those rearmost among the Corinthians had any choice to give up the fight. Stumbling backward and increasingly infected by desperate fear emanating from the front, it was these rear ranks that first broke and ran. Fleeing men would have thrown away their shields (an act known as *rhipsaspia*) to speed their escape, some shedding their helmets and spears as well. Departure of the back rows freed those farther forward, and successive ranks peeled away to utterly dissolve the Corinthian phalanx. As for the Argives, they would have kept on shoving and bowled over those few men remaining in opposition, breaking through in a last stage of battle known as *pararrexis* to complete the total collapse (*trope*) and rout of their foes. Most of those killed among the defeated fell at this stage, going down as their front gave way or caught trying to flee in heavy armor over slippery, blood-soaked ground and amongst a terrible clutter of fallen men, broken spears, and discarded gear. Argos now held both the battlefield and a formal victory in the land dispute.

Their heavy armor encumbered the victorious Argive hoplites and prevented them from giving effective chase to any Corinthians who had discarded their shields. But this was not the case for Argos' fleet gymnesioi, who must have brought down a number of the running men with stabs to the back. This deadly pursuit continued to the eastern edge of the plain, where it broke off as escapees reached the traditional safety zone of the nearby hills.

Ancient reports and modern analogs suggest that the Corinthians probably left 5–15 percent of their hoplites dead on the battleground (a median of around 480 men). About 60 percent of these would have been killed more or less outright, with the rest dying within a few hours from shock and loss of blood. Another 2,400 (a 5 to 1 ratio to those fallen in action) probably got away carrying wounds of various sorts. It's likely that about one in eight among these men eventually died as well, succumbing within a week or so to gangrene, tetanus, peritonitis, and other infections. This suggests a final Corinthian death toll of nearly 800 hoplites — about 16 percent. Argive losses on the field were undoubtedly much lower, at perhaps 2–3 percent (around 150 men). The overwhelming majority of these fatalities came in the horrific initial clash of the charging phalanxes, with later stages claiming only a few more. Adding post-combat deaths would then have yielded a final cost to Argos of only about 250 hoplites, or less than 5 percent.

The Argives would have collected their own dead and wounded at battle's end, then gathered the spoils of victory by retrieving discarded gear and stripping fallen foes. They also would have erected a customary trophy (*tropaion*) of captured armor on a pole or cairn at the spot where the engagement turned in their favor (the trope). The Corinthians undoubtedly arranged a truce very shortly thereafter that they might recover the bodies of their dead and carry them home. This was an important protocol, since it was extremely shameful among the classical Greeks to leave a comrade's body behind in a foreign place. In the end, over a thousand men are likely to have given their lives to confirm the border between Argos and Corinth; a frightful price to be sure, but one well below the cost in death and devastation that would have accompanied total war.

We know of several other battles c. 500 B.C. from dedications of arms and armor at various shrines. The hoplites of Cleonai won another engagement at that time, this one against Orneai, also an ally of Argos in the northern Argolid. These poleis must have come to blows over land along their border in the hills around the shrine at Nemea. This had to have been quite a modestly sized clash, with each state having only around 500 prime-aged spearmen plus some 50–100 psiloi. Elsewhere in the central Peloponnese, Cleitor bested Heraia. These were minor cities in western Arcadia about 35km apart that likely contested arable land in the intervening valley of the Ladon River. Being even smaller than Cleonai or Orneai, these poleis would have fielded no more than a couple of hundred hoplites apiece.

Contests for borderlands could range much farther out for a select few maritime states.

We know from dedications at Athens and Olympus of an Athenian victory sometime 500–495 B.C. over the island of Lemnos. Athens was seeking at this time to claim Lemnos that it might add an outpost along its northern Aegean trade routes. In fact, a holding of this sort was just as important to a trading city as farmland was to an agricultural state; thus, it drew efforts for conquest and defense similar to that for any other eschatia.

The highlight of the campaign on Lemnos came with what was most likely a decisive battlefield win by Miltiades, Athens's governor in the Thraceward region. Miltiades would have gained this triumph with some 1,500–2,000 hoplites, which he led into action from a fleet of 50–60 ships that each carried 30–40 spearmen. Having staged from the nearby mainland, Miltiades seems sure to have timed his landing on Lemnos for very late in the day to get ashore unopposed and set up camp in front of his beached ships. Next morning, he set light-armed men to pillaging the countryside while his spearmen stood ready to meet any response to this traditional challenge.

Herodotus's history tells of a successful siege; still, it's likely that the Lemnians came out to fight first. This better fits the dedications and reflects not only prevailing martial conventions, but also that it was usually worth risking even the worst defeat in the field if it had any chance to prevent a crippling investment. The defenders must therefore have accepted battle somewhere near the Athenian landing site. Based on the force sent by Lemnos to Amphipolis in 422 B.C., the island had potential to muster around 1,000 hoplites. These included some 800 spearmen in their prime, plus 200 or so old-age and youth reservists. Nonetheless, the Athenians held a significant edge in manpower and this let them either roll up a shorter line or, more likely, punch through thinner files to claim the victory, killing perhaps 100–150 Lemnian hoplites at the cost of only a very few Athenian lives.

The handful of engagements known from dedications no doubt represent but a sampling of many such combats, as all Greek states, large and small, fought that they might gain glory and farmland. However, while early fifth century Greece remained focused on such fraternal bloodletting, momentous events were building to the east. Asian affairs would soon bring the Greeks reluctantly into international conflict.

The Ionian Revolt

Greeks settled the islands of the eastern Aegean and the west coast of Anatolia (modern Turkey) sometime before 1,000 B.C. Though the many dialects spoken across this region indicate multiple origins for these immigrants, Ionian settlers from the vicinity of Athens were a dominant element and the term "Ionia" came to identify all of Grecian Asia Minor. Ionian affairs were destined to heavily affect not only Athens, but all of Greece, leading to war with Persia, the latest and greatest empire to rise in the Near East.

A vibrant mountain people, the Persians had come forward under Cyrus the Great to take over the kingdom of the closely related Medes in 550 B.C. From Media they gained land formerly ruled by Assyria and frontier taken from the Lydians in eastern Anatolia up to the boundary of the Halys River. Cyrus conquered Lydia in 546 B.C. and took over the remainder of Anatolia. In doing so, he acquired all of the Greek colonies that had previously fallen under Lydian control.

The Persians formed their conquered lands into provinces, each under a royally appointed "satrap" (a *khshathrapavan* or "protector of the kingdom") backed by key political and military assistants (called *hyparchoi* by the Greeks). The province or "satrapy" headquartered in the city of Sardis was responsible for the former territory of Lydia that included Ionia. This

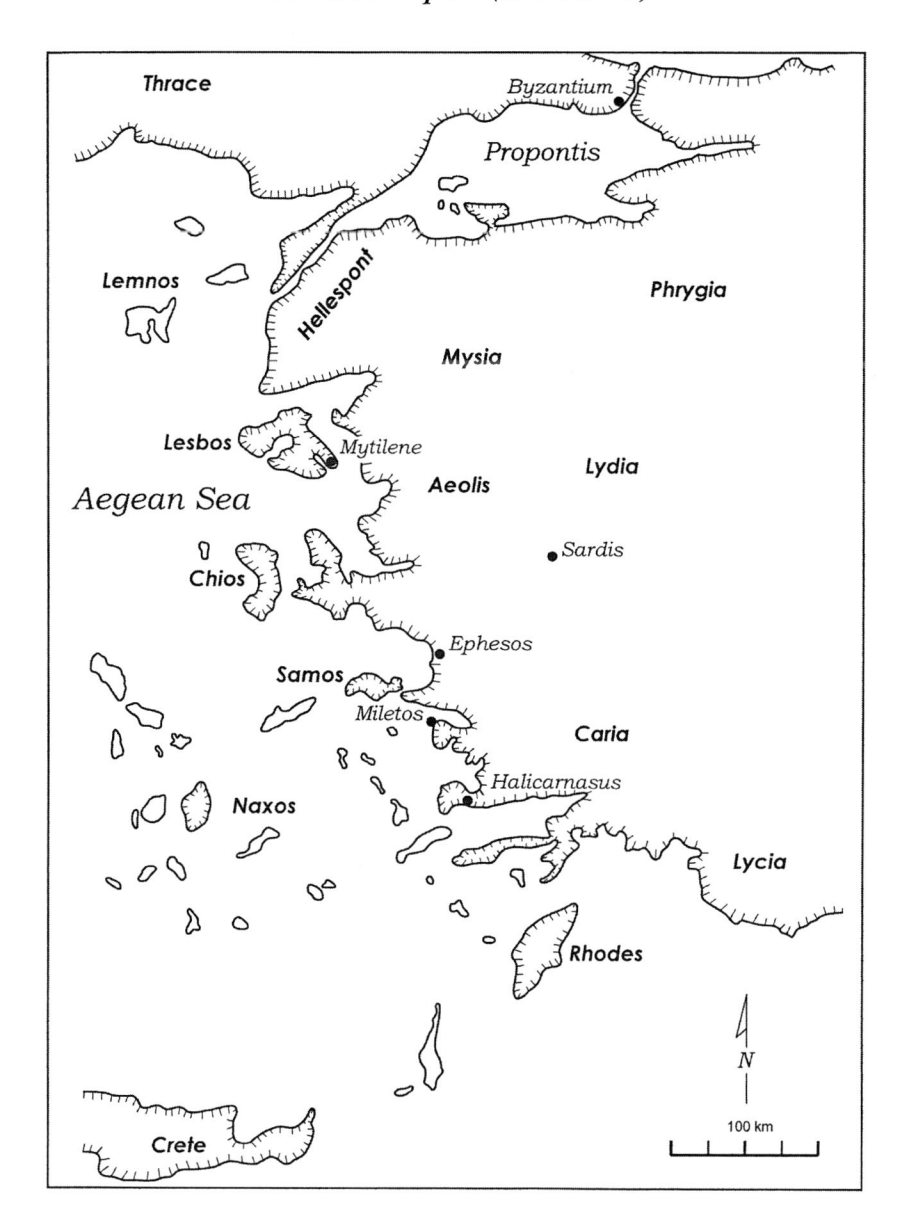

THE GREEK EAST—IONIA/ASIA MINOR

satrapal scheme was quite enlightened for its time. It left much to native leaders or "tyrants" (*tyrannoi* in Greek, singular *tyrannos*), who could run things as per local customs. "Tyrant," likely a Lydian term, didn't always have a negative connotation in this era; in fact, many of these leaders were quite popular. The Asian Greeks got by for nearly half a century under this system without major incident, but they never lost their desire to be truly free.

The Revolt Takes Form

The seeds of Greco–Persian conflict took sprout when Darius I Hystaspes of Persia attempted c. 513 B.C. to attack Scythian tribesmen along the northwestern shores of the Euxine (Black) Sea. This had followed upon a campaign of conquest in Thrace that served the tradition of imperial expansion established by Cyrus the Great and his successor, Cambyses. Darius was the victor in a scramble to seize the throne after the latter's death and must have been under great duress to prove his worthiness to be the next Great King. The new sovereign thus promptly annexed land in northern India and on Persia's eastern frontier, but remained unfulfilled and next turned toward Europe.

After conquering various Thracian tribes, Darius and his army swung northward, bridging the Danube (Hister) River to cross into Scythia. Unfortunately for Darius, the targeted tribesmen proved formidable. They refused pitched battle and used a scorched earth campaign to nearly draw him into disaster. He followed the retreating Scythians deep into the steppes (just how far is unknown, but Cawkwell [2005, 47] has argued that their advance reached the Dniester, the next major river north of the Danube). Failing to bring his foe to grips, the king finally came to realize that his column was in growing peril from badly stretched lines of supply. He swiftly retreated, leaving (per Herodotus) both baggage and wounded men behind in his haste. Potential ruin was averted only when the Ionians under Histiaeus (tyrant of Miletos) preserved an escape route by twice refusing Scythian proposals to destroy the Danube bridge. The Greeks are said to have preserved the span despite advice to the contrary from Miltiades, governor of Athens's colony on the Hellespont. However, Miltiades remained in favor with the Great King, suggesting that this might be a latter-day tale meant to hide his Persian ties.

Asian Greeks had felt a sense of union while supporting Darius's failed northern venture and had also taken due note of the seeming impotence of the Great King's arms against the Scythians. These combined to foster a spirit of independence that would prove costly to their Persian overlords. Histiaeus of Miletus, Darius's savior at the Danube, now came into custody at the imperial court in Susa under suspicion of harboring traitorous ambitions. This distrust would soon prove well-founded. Aristogoras, son-in-law and proxy of Histiaeus, set off a rebellion in 499 B.C. by declaring a democracy in Miletos. Aristogoras next seized the Ionian fleet from those loyal to the crown and set about deposing Persia's friends throughout the region to form a league opposed to the Empire. The Ionians straight away sought aid from their kinsmen in Europe, especially from powerful Sparta and Athens. The Spartans refused, upon learning of the great distances involved, but the Athenians were more sympathetic.

Athens not only claimed a founder's relationship with the Ionians, but also had other incentives to support them. Hippias, an Athenian tyrant exiled in 510 B.C., had sought support for a return from Artaphernes, satrap at Sardis. This encouraged the Athenians to back Ionia in hope that trouble in Artaphernes' back yard would divert him from aiding Hippias. They therefore pledged twenty war galleys or triremes (*trierai*, singular *trieres*, so named for their three banks of oars) and a modest infantry force to the rebellion. This was a significant diversion of strength from their fleet, as they had no more than sixty warships at the time and were already engaged in a contest with the nearby isle of Aigina for naval supremacy in the Saronic Gulf. The Euboan polis of Eretria also came to the assistance of the Ionians, adding five ships to the Athenian flotilla and sending a larger naval force to keep the fleet of Cyprus from sailing to Asia. This timely help from Eretria was said to be in repayment of past aid given by Miletos against Euboan rival Chalcis.

The Army of the Persian Empire

Sparabara ("shield bearers") were the backbone of Persia's infantry in the early fifth century. This warrior type had evolved from an older Assyrian model (a divergent development from that which produced the hoplite) and was common throughout Mesopotamia. Thus, sparabara of several "Iranian" nationalities (Persian, Median, Cissian/Elamite, and Hyrkanian) manned the main front-line units of the Great King's armies.

Sparabara carried lighter equipment than Greek hoplites, with no more than an elite minority having metal body armor. And, in fact, just a few of them normally used the characteristic rectangular wicker shield or *spara* (known as a *gerrhon* to the Greeks) from which their name derived. Fighting as a combined arms force, most fired bows from behind no more than a thin front of shield-bearing spearmen, though the ratio of men with shields to archers could vary to suit circumstances. When there was little risk of shock combat, only men in the front rank carried spara. At other times, when hand-to-hand action was more likely, at least the first two ranks bore shields that they might replace casualties at the front. Like hoplites, sparabara used swords solely as secondary weapons, with the *akinakes*, a straight, double-edged blade of modest length (20–25cm) being the preferred model.

It's likely that more sparabara carried spears than shields. This was surely the case when a shock engagement was expected, and finds support in Persian artwork portraying sparabara with both spear and bow. This allowed greater potential for forward ranks to participate in overhand thrusts at the enemy and/or in replacing fallen comrades. Since his spear lacked a butt-spike (having a rounded counterweight instead), a back-ranker had to ground it by the head in order to free both hands for use of the bow. Bows remained the primary offensive weapon, since, at just under two meters in length, the Persian spear was shorter than that of the Greeks and not as well suited for attack. This relegated the spear to a role of defending the front-line shield wall. In contrast to hoplites, the duty of Persian spearmen was not to project power forward, but rather to hold the enemy in place long enough for other arms to be decisive.

Sparabara often fought in the company of light footmen. The latter were subject national levies of spearmen, peltasts, and archers that took post in the rear or on the flanks of the main battle array. Their job was to ward sparabara from flank attack; however, some archers, most notably the Sakae (of Scythian descent), also added to frontal firepower with longer-ranging composite bows. Cavalry was a key support element as well, and Persians usually deployed large numbers of horsemen on their flanks. The ethnic Iranian horsemen that cored the front line cavalry were for the most part unarmored, though some officers wore a metal cuirass. Herodotus described Persia's heavy horse as mounted sparabara, yet it's unlikely that they ever used the unwieldy spara and no more than 10–20 percent may have had spears, with the rest relying either on the bow or javelins. As for specialist horse archers, the Persians fielded these to enhance missile fire and screen their heavier cavalry, drawing them from allied peoples. The Sakae are again notable here for their use of composite bows. Overall, Persian horsemen functioned much like their Greek counterparts, but differed in one key aspect: mounted flank and rear attacks — so rare in Greece — were their dominant tactic.

Persian boys spent their first five years under their mothers' care at home. They then took formal instruction in the manly arts of riding and archery through age twenty, at which time all were obligated for military service and advanced instruction over a further four years. It was these young men in compulsory service that made up standing units in the regular army. Their assignments included forming elite contingents in the capital at Suza and a number of royal infantry divisions within the various satrapies. The most capable and suited conscripts remained after their regular tour as additions to the army's officer corps. All other veterans 25–50 years of age formed a large pool of experienced soldiers that were entitled to grants of land ("bow land") in return for a familial obligation for further duty in times of need. These men filled the ranks of additional contingents as required to undertake special efforts, like those mounted to seize new territory or in response to crises like the revolt in Ionia.

Persia could call upon its trained reservists to fill a large and highly capable militia — the *kara* or "host." This was the empire's primary tool for major campaigns. A reserve system parallel to that described above for private soldiers supplied line officers to the kara, while the Great King assigned relatives and favorites as generals. Still, even the loftiest royal appointee was a product of the full training regimen and should have been fit for command. All the nations providing sparabara must have used a similar system of conscription and reserve.

The *hazarabam* (plural *hazaraba*) was the primary field unit of the Persian army (Sekunda, 1989, 83–84). This regiment had ten companies or *sataba* (singular *satabam*) with ten squads or *dathaba* (singular *dathabam*) of ten men each. It thus should have held 1,000 men. In fact, strength was usually much lower. Manpower often shrank in the field due to spotty recruiting, detachments (as to garrisons), desertion, combat loss, and illness. Such straying from nominal "paper" or "authorized" strength is common even today within standing units. The Persians coped with this by keeping their dathaba at ten men, but reducing the count of dathaba per satabam.

Data from Egypt and Judaea (Sekunda and Chew 1992, 5–6) indicate that a satabam on long-term duty was commonly at only 30–60 percent of nominal strength. This suggests that satrapal hazaraba had no more than 300–600 men. However, certain picked units (like the guards at Suza) and those called up for short-term duty as part of the kara had greater manpower. Based on an analog from Babylon (Head 1982, 27), these might have set out at up to 80 percent of full strength. Major field forces mustered in ten hazaraba contingents. The Greeks called these "myriads," while the Persians themselves might have used the term *baivaraba* (singular *baivarabam*). Per the staffing norms outlined above, a garrison baivaraba likely had 3–6,000 men, with elite and kara variants being on the order of 8,000 strong.

Persia used linear battle formations with files of ten men (one dathaba). Rank width was similar to that for hoplites at one meter per man, but file depth at a likely 1.5–2m per man would have been greater than among the Greeks to ease use of the bow (save at the head of each file where a unit's best men stood on shield duty). Troops with lighter arms arrayed in a more open order that was better suited for skirmishing. Cavalry must also have used files of ten, spaced at three meters horse-to-horse, for a total formation depth of thirty meters. This combined with a front of two meters for each rider (at one meter per horse and one meter between horses) that extended along ranks wide enough to hold the entire force on hand. An 800-rider hazarabam would therefore have formed a rectangle 160m (80 riders) wide and 30m (10 riders) deep. Any spear-armed troops among the Iranian horsemen took station at the front and (possibly) back of the files, these being the most likely areas where such shock weapons might come into play.

As with the phalanx, Persian infantry should have been vulnerable to the rear and sides. Yet their great strength in cavalry and light foot gave such high security in these areas that the focus of honor actually fell on men in the formation center who had to prevent frontal penetration. Lacking the pushing potential that the Greek aspis made possible from rear ranks, Persia's linear battle array was largely defensive. Its main roles were to fix the foe in place and weaken him with missiles in order for cavalry to carry the day on the flanks. Still, no less than for the Greeks, morale was vital to this fighting style. Courage and confidence thus went equally far among the Persians to determine ultimate success or failure on the field of battle.

Ephesos I (498 B.C.)

The European force sent to support the Ionian uprising eventually arrived at Miletos. Here it joined a fleet from that city and its allies and then sailed north to the port of Ephesos, which lay just west of the city above the hill of Coressos. Uniting with the Ephesians, the Greeks sat down to plan their campaign against royal forces already in the field. The Persians had responded to the revolt by collecting troops for a counterstrike from all the garrisons posted west of the Halys River in former Lydian territory. The Great King had placed this host under three generals — Daurises, Hymaees, and Otanes, each of whom was married to one of his daughters. This trio of commanders arrived on the scene to commit most of their strength in concert against Miletos, flash point for the revolt and strongest of the rebel cities.

Royal troops probably included two baivaraba of sparabara from the satrapies of Sardis and Tyaiy Drayahya ("Those of the Sea," south of the Euxine or Black Sea between Sardis and the Halys). Two hazaraba of cavalry came from reservists in these same provinces and more infantry from locals still loyal to the crown. This assumes (as per Burn 1984, 120–126) that military and political organization of the satrapies differed such that the troops at Sardis also served for Skudra (Thrace and Macedonia) and Caria (see Olmstead 1948, 239–245 for an alternate opinion). There was one more garrison west of the Halys, in Cilicia (east of Caria), but a simultaneous uprising on Cyprus prevented its use in Ionia.

The Greeks at Ephesos surveyed the situation and decided to strike at Sardis, which lay about 75km northeast of their position. It seems to have been their hope that this would not only dispute control of the region and sully the empire's image, but also serve to divert royal forces from the spoiling of Milesian territory. Moreover, this target looked to be only weakly defended, as the local satrap, Artaphernes, could call on no more than a modest force spared from the major effort around Miletos. The Greeks marched on Sardis and, seeing their numbers, Artaphernes wisely refused battle and retired into the city's strongly fortified citadel.

Rebel occupation of Sardis proved short. The city had a large number of reed huts and buildings with thatched roofs; therefore, when the invaders set a few of these ablaze, a general conflagration broke out that consumed much of the urban area. The fire forced the Greeks to abandon Sardis and escape southward along the Pactolos River until reaching the nearby slopes of Mount Tmolos. That night, a powerful force under Darius's triumvirate of sons-in-law approached the city after having detached from the effort around Miletus. This triggered a full-blown Greek retreat. The rebels withdrew across Tmolos and down the Cayster River, with the Lydians in hot pursuit that they might avenge the destruction at Sardis. Thus, while they had succeeded in highlighting Persian vulnerability and relieving pressure against Miletos, the Greeks were now in great peril as they fled across the Cayster all the way to the plain northeast of Ephesos. Having finally reached friendly ground, they turned to confront the enemy. The Persian force from Miletos had by this point linked up with the Lydians to set the stage for a major battle.

Rebel strength included large Ephesian and Milesian levies led by Hermophantos and Charopinos (brother of Aristogoras) of Miletos. Ephesos might have had some 2,000 hoplites ready for action. This represented four of five available lochoi (one for each of the city's tribes) at 500 hoplites each, making for an extensive mobilization (80 percent) consistent with engaging on home soil. For its part, Miletos could muster up to six field-grade lochoi of 500 spearmen apiece. This was one for each of four Ionian and two Carian tribes and in line with manpower for an 80-ship fleet. Miletos wouldn't have sent this entire force with an enemy army already at its gates, but given that Milesians held overall command, they must have at least equaled Ephesian numbers. Such a two-thirds levy was also par for allied contributions to a foreign campaign. Other Ionian cities had likely sent around 1,000 hoplites in a hodgepodge of small contingents. For their part, the Europeans landed 40 spearmen per trireme; thus, Melanthios led 800 Athenians, while Eretria added 200 under the renowned athlete Eualcidas. This brought the entire Greek army up to 6,000 hoplites. A crowd of attendants was also present, with around 1,000 set to serve as psiloi. As for horsemen, the rebels had none. Persia had taken over all mounted duties in the region and the Ionians must have long ago grown accustomed to putting only foot soldiers into the field.

The Greeks likely faced an army based upon 6,000 sparabara from the Sardis garrison (60 percent of its nominal manpower, with all other sparabara in the region remaining at Miletos). There were also some Lydians (armored like hoplites, but having shorter spears) and peltasts from Mysia (north of Ionia). The Lydians and Mysians probably were at 80 percent of paper strength for 8,000 each as per 480 B.C., when they made up a brigade of two baivaraba. If they had split their strength evenly between Miletos and Sardis, then some 4,000 Lydians and the same number of Mysians must have been at Ephesos. This would have brought the Persian infantry up to 14,000 in all. With regard to cavalry, both hazaraba on hand had likely rushed to Artaphernes's rescue, fielding something like 1,600 riders at 80 percent of parade strength (one for each ten foot soldiers).

The Persians approached Ephesos from the east after crossing and following the Greeks down the Cayster. They would have drawn into formation upon nearing their quarry, arraying the sparabara ten deep along a 600-meter front and extending the Lydians at similar depth across another 200 meters on each wing. This created a battle line 1 kilometer wide. Mysian peltasts stood ready to skirmish and guard the flanks, while the cavalry held back, awaiting an opportunity to exploit a weakness in the enemy's formation. As preliminary skirmishing unfolded, the Greek hoplites undoubtedly deployed in a phalanx that matched Persian line length at six shields deep. The Ephesians, fighting before their own city, would have taken the post of honor on the right wing (towards town on the southeast), while the Milesians formed the center division to their left. The other Ionians, Eretrians, and Athenians then filled out the left wing in that order, with the latter holding the northwest flank along the Cayster. By anchoring on the riverbank, Athens's hoplites were secure from cavalry attack and freed all of the army's light-armed men to cover the still exposed right flank. The rebels must have held fast in this array as the enemy closed, thus making it easier for the less experienced Ionians to keep in formation. Standing pat also kept everyone close to escape routes into Ephesos as a hedge against defeat.

As the skirmishers had retired, the sparabara would have moved forward behind their usual front of shields. The Lydians kept pace with this advance along each side, while cavalry moved in rectangular array next to the open left flank. Halting within effective bow range (under 175m), the Persians then unleashed a barrage of arrows from their after ranks. The Greeks had no real choice but to rush forward and put their enemies to the spear. Very quickly, however, they found both shield wall and heavily equipped Lydians up to the challenge of containing this charge and fixing the fight along a static line. The royalist rear ranks would have continued their bombardment, even though its effectiveness was now much reduced as they had to avoid comrades engaged up front. It also must have been very difficult to acquire the narrow target offered by an enemy filed at less than 6 meters deep; thus, this archery assault could be telling only if of great duration. Unfortunately for the Greeks, the opposing bowmen seem to have had just such an extended opportunity.

Asian Greeks either lacked othismos (pushing) tactics or were less practiced at them. In fact, the latter seems more likely, a product of the peaceful conditions that had long prevailed within Persian-administered Ionia. They thus could neither penetrate the enemy front nor get past the cavalry screen to envelop its left flank. As for the cadre of Europeans, this was too small to remedy the situation, especially against Lydian opposition that was equally well-anchored. The Greeks therefore ended up hopelessly mired in place as casu-

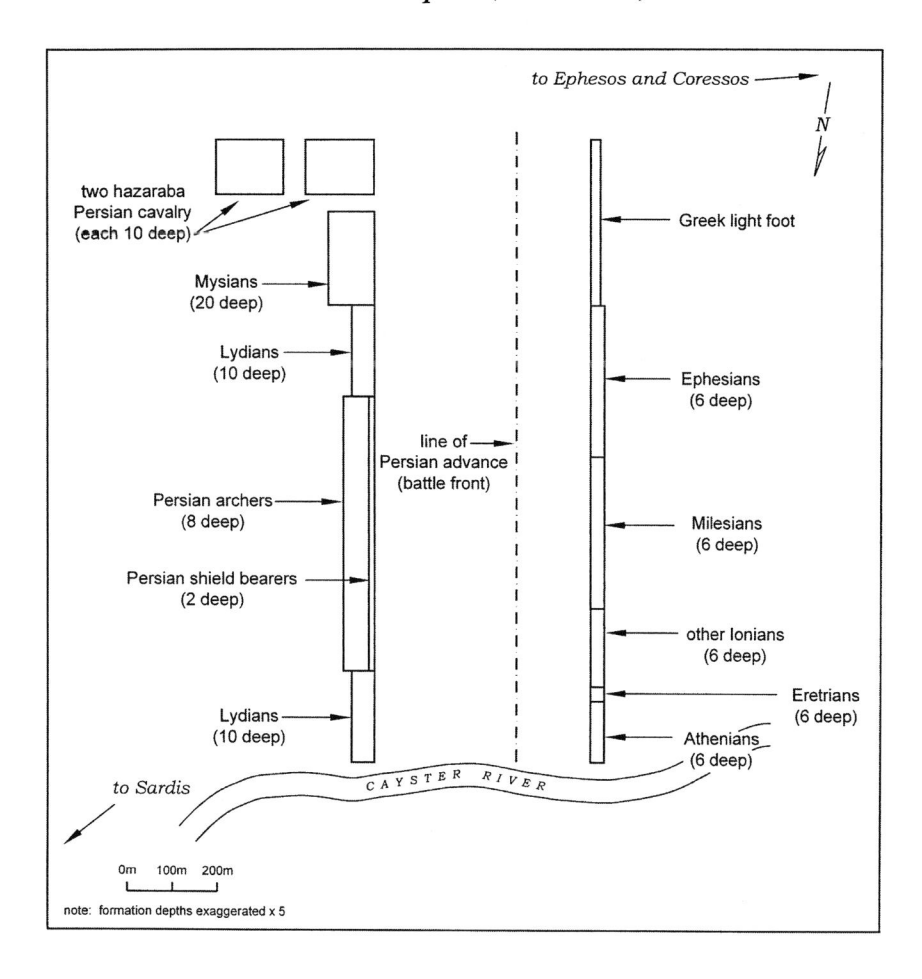

BATTLE OF EPHESOS I (498 B.C.)

alties mounted under a light, but unrelenting shower of projectiles. Arrows punctured thighs, upper arms, and throats with cruelly barbed heads that tore the flesh all the more horribly upon any attempt to pull them free. Unable to escape this deadly rain, hoplites could only make a series of forlorn attempts on the wall of shields holding them in check. All the while, the Persian cavalry added more missile fire and maneuvered to turn the unsecured inland flank.

Low morale seems to have compounded Greek tactical difficulties. Deciding to strike at the soft target of Sardis, rather than seek a direct confrontation at Miletos, suggests fear of Persian might from the very start. Rapid retreat before the threat of a counterattack serves to underscore this point. Then, when the Greeks finally turned to do battle, they did so only with great reluctance, taking a stand where they could more easily escape a defeat. This was a practical move, but also one that smacks of weakness. Such timidity stood in stark contrast to the enemy's poise. The Persians would have had no doubts about their superiority, having defeated mercenary hoplites many times during decades of conquest. They now sent a steady shower of arrows into the Greek ranks to strike without warning and wound with no respect for a man's courage or prowess. This took a toll not only on the rebels' bodies, but also on their already shaky confidence. Bloodied and unsteady, the Greeks must have come to crisis when Persia's cavalry at last managed an envelopment.

The Iranian-style cavalry would have charged repeatedly to pelt the opposing skirmishers with javelins even as the leading rank of lancers threatened violent contact. The shock impact of such mounted rushes was clearly more fearsomely psychological than physical, but proved devastating nevertheless. Having expended most of their darts during this extended action, psiloi on the Greek right could no longer keep the opposing horsemen at bay and, nearly defenseless, they must have finally taken collective fight at a cavalry charge and scattered. This exposed the Ionians' unshielded right, and spread panic (terrible tool of the god Pan) among the hoplites. It was spears and missiles that slew rebel soldiers, but it was actually fear that killed their army. Each man's dread of wounded agony and death now drove him to flee for the nearest safe haven.

Ephesians on the far right broke first, tossing shields and sprinting toward the closest city gate. This ignited a powder train of terror that flashed down the line to send the other Ionians running for either town or their nearby ships. Their collapse exposed the right side of the allied European brigade and vengeful Lydians swarmed to the attack. The Eretrian general Eualcidas likely stood at the right front of his contingent, near the point of this assault. He and a number of his men went down before the remaining Euboans managed to join the more distal Athenians in a fighting retreat to the safety of their triremes.

Due to lengthy combat along the front, casualties were no doubt high among both victor and vanquished. The rebels were hurt not only by extended missile fire, but even more by an after-battle pursuit that inflicted the sort of mounted slaughter that was rare on Greek battlefields. Based on recorded losses to cavalry at Plataea, a force suffering mounted pursuit could expect to lose around 15 percent of its men. We can add these to 5 percent killed in the main action and another 10 percent succumbing later to wounds for an estimated loss of 30 percent of the hoplites engaged at Ephesos. This is about twice the damage that even a very badly beaten army might expect from a clash between two phalanxes. For their part, the Persians likely suffered 4–5 percent killed in the main engagement as well, but their ultimate success limited further loss. Subsequent deaths due to wounds probably amounted to another 2–3 percent for a total of about 700 line troops and 1,000 in total slain on the day — a heavy toll, but well below the Greek body count.

The surviving Athenians and Eretrians set sail for home, never to return. As for the Asian Greeks, they quickly dispersed and left Ephesos in perilous straits. Having taken heavy losses in battle, cut off from supply by sea, the Ephesians were in poor shape to resist a siege, and quickly capitulated. The city's loss was a cruel blow to the Ionian cause; but all the same, the rebellion was now widely set alight and continued to burn fiercely elsewhere.

Cyprian Salamis I (498 B.C.)

Cyprus sits in the southeastern Aegean at a position transitional between Europe and Asia. It comes as no surprise then that in classical times the islanders fell into two camps — one European/Greek and the other Asian/Phoenician. Both these cultures had long been subject to foreign domination. Assyria held Cyprus in the late 8th and early 7th centuries, followed by Egypt in the early 6th century, and then Persia in 545 B.C. Buffered by such outside rule from events on the mainland, Cypriot states never developed the kind of middle-class government that had become common throughout Greece, instead retaining both local royalty and its signal chariot forces.

The eastern coastal city of Salamis was a Grecian center and the largest, most powerful polis on Cyprus. Gorgus ruled there as tyrant at the time of the Ionian revolt and remained loyal to Persia. His brother Onesilus, however, was keen to make a break. This ambitious fellow saw initial Greek success in Lydia and the defeat of a royalist Cypriot fleet by the Eretrians (dispatched in parallel to the Sardis campaign) as an opportunity to seize power. Onesilus waited for his sibling to leave town, then shut him out and assumed the throne. Arousing the other Greek poleis of Paphos, Soloi, Curium, Enkomi, and Idalium, he led the Grecian population in a bid to throw off Persian control. The island's three major Phoenician cities of Amathus, Citium, and Lapethus remained true to the empire (Amathus is named as a Persian ally by Herodotus, and Citium later assisted the siege of Idalium). The Punic Cypriots thus preserved not only their ties to Persia, but also to their motherland, which provided the core of the Great King's fleet. The city of Amathus was the leader among these royalist centers and was the first to come under rebel attack, with its residents then losing no time in calling to their Persian masters for help.

Onesilus learned that the Persian general Artybius was in Cilicia, only 75km to the north, preparing to embark an army for Cyprus aboard Phoenician ships. The rebel leader promptly sent for aid, and the Ionians responded by dispatching their fleet to Salamis. Warships of that time were crowded with rowers and had no space for food or sleeping, thus they needed to put in for meals and rest each evening. This made it impossible to keep station and prevent a Persian landing. It would therefore take two actions to repel the invasion — one at sea and the other ashore. The Ionians had to stay aboard ship to engage the Phoenicians, which left the Cypriots to best the Persian army on their own. As it turned out, the Greeks did prevail at sea, but it was the battle on shore that decided the fate of Cyprus.

The Greek Cypriots mustered at Salamis under Onesilus and his fellow monarchs, gathering near the city at the eastern end of Mesaoria, the island's long central plain. The royals of each city led their levies aboard contingents of war chariots that comprised a total force perhaps 200 vehicles strong. These weapons probably took the field in squadrons of 50, as was the custom in nearby Egypt. If so, it's likely that Salamis, Curium, and Soli each sent a squadron, while Paphos, Enkomi, and Idalium combined to provide one more. Each chariot held two men (a driver with sword and small shield plus a bowman passenger) and had a squad of peltasts running alongside to screen opposing light infantry.

The mounted Greek aristocrats and their attendants likely headed a large infantry force of nearly 10,000 hoplites plus 2,500 psiloi. This is based on Herodotus's note that the hoplites ("picked men") from Salamis and Soli matched fronts with the Persian sparabara (estimated 6,000 strong — see below). They thus must have lined along 600 meters, which required at least 4,800 hoplites at a traditional eight shields deep. Another assumption is that levies from the leading cities of Salamis and Soli were the rebel army's strongest in quantity as well as quality and might then have provided about half of the heavy infantry on hand. As for the number of psiloi, this follows from that for the hoplites in line with the Asian custom of light support at a higher level (one per four spearmen) than on the Greek mainland.

Artybius had one baivarabam of sparabara — the Cilician satrapal garrison — along with some Cabelee peltasts from the area to the west of Cilicia and horsemen drawn from bow land reservists. These were embarked aboard the Phoenician fleet, which was the largest division of the imperial navy, with some 300 triremes. Each of these ships could carry about 30 men above its marines and crew. The sparabara, at 6,000 strong (60 percent nominal), would have filled 200 vessels. Another 40 ships likely transported a cavalry contingent of 200 horsemen and their mounts — two sataba (one for each flank) brought to full complement by drafts out of the satrapy's hazarabam. This assumes (per Bartlett 1983, 5) that a horse and its tack took up about the same space as five men, with five horses and their riders taking the normal passenger space for 30 men. The remaining 60 ships could carry 1,800 peltasts. These picked men must have been from the five Cabelee hazaraba available (as per their reported strength

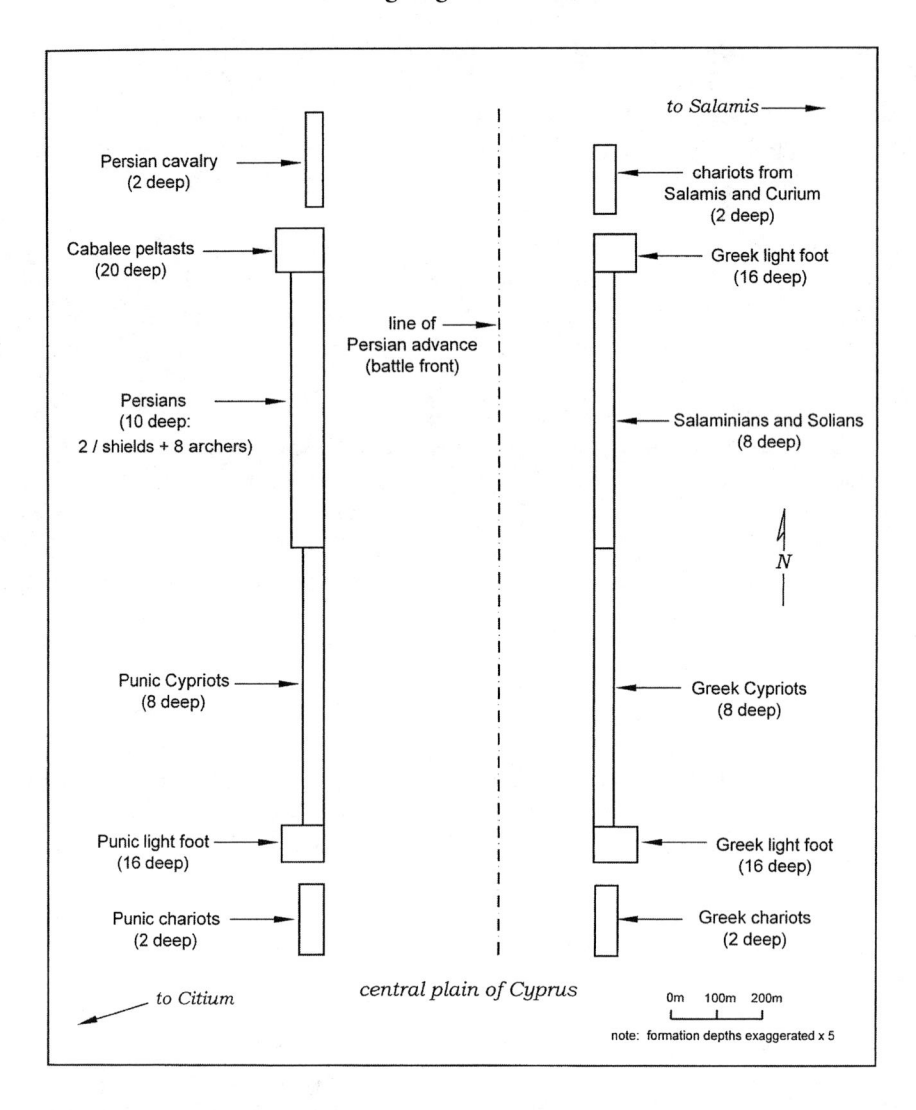

[Diagram: Battle formation showing Persian forces on left (Persian cavalry 2 deep, Cabalee peltasts 20 deep, Persians 10 deep: 2 / shields + 8 archers, Punic Cypriots 8 deep, Punic light foot 16 deep, Punic chariots 2 deep) and Greek forces on right (chariots from Salamis and Curium 2 deep, Greek light foot 16 deep, Salaminians and Solians 8 deep, Greek Cypriots 8 deep, Greek light foot 16 deep, Greek chariots 2 deep), with line of Persian advance (battle front) in the middle, central plain of Cyprus, to Citium arrow, to Salamis arrow, scale 0m 100m 200m, note: formation depths exaggerated x 5]

BATTLE OF CYPRIAN SALAMIS I (498 B.C.)

in 480 B.C.). In all, the embarked force numbered 8,000 men, who, once ashore, were joined by levies from island allies.

Punic Cypriots would have supplied men with armor plus some light foot and chariots. Some of the armored troops were Greek-style hoplites, while others were a sort of heavy peltast (as per descriptions of Phoenician marines) with small round shield, helmet, linen cuirass, and two throwing spears. Numbers are speculative, but at one major loyalist city for every two on the other side, Punic strength might have been half that of the Greeks. This suggests 100 chariots (two squadrons from Amathus, Citium, and Lapethus combined), around 4,800 heavies (perhaps evenly divided between hoplites and armored javelinmen), and 1,200 peltasts. Artybius's army would therefore have had nearly 14,000 footmen (including 6,000 shield-bearing line troops) plus 300 mounted fighters (100 in chariots and 200 on horses).

The Persian general likely mustered near Citium and then marched on Salamis. There, the ethnic Persians must have moved up to form the left side of a battle formation that put them opposite the best Greek troops (the same posting that they would take under similar circumstances at Plataea in 479 B.C., assigning local allies to what they deemed the lesser threat on their right). These sparabara presented a 600-meter front at one dathabam (ten men) deep, while their Cabelee peltasts stood alongside Artybius and his cavalry on the adjacent left flank. Meanwhile, the Punic units lined up their armored men to the right over another 600m at eight shields deep, positioning their light infantry and chariots to protect that flank.

Soldiers from Salamis are sure to have held the place of honor on the Greek right side, which put the Solians next in line as the other rebels filled out toward the men of Paphos on the far left. The phalanx then had to stand eight shields deep in order to match the enemy front. Psiloi and chariots split between the wings, relegating half the javelinmen with the chariots of Soli, Paphos, Enkomi, and Idalium to the left and vehicles from Salamis and Curium plus the remaining light foot to the right. The right-wing position of Onesilus and his chariots was not only culturally fitting for a Greek commander, but it also set the stage for a face-to face confrontation with Artybius.

Action opened with a light infantry skirmish and then the heavy formations closed to fight it out. The Persians must have stopped at a short distance to shower arrows from behind their wall of spara, with the Phoenicians adding throwing spears as the Greeks moved into contact. A fierce melee ensued. Front fighters on the Persian left were able to stall the hoplites in the opening phase, while their Punic allies did the same on the right. Despite the Greek Cypriots' many ties to mainland culture, their hoplites appear to have been more like those of Ionia in lacking advanced tactical skills such as othismos. Whether due to a long history of subordination to aristocratic horsemen or to an equally archaic need to seek personal glory, these men fought more as individuals than as part of a concerted effort, which severely limited shock potential of their phalanx and precluded rapid penetration of the enemy. Hope for Greek victory therefore came to hinge on horsemen battling along the flanks.

The Greeks initially fared well in the mounted dual on their right. This must have been due to the chariot's innate superiority over the saddle as a platform for bowmen. Chariots were rarely available in adequate quantity to counter large numbers of cavalry, but in this instance there were enough to match up well against a force cut to meet the transport limits of its fleet. Opposing riders would have rushed at each other to release flights of missiles and then pulled apart only to wheel and charge again, flowing back and forth in lethal sequence. Amidst this chaotic fight, Onesilus demonstrated the full potential of his chariot by closing at speed to kill Artybius. The Persian had led his men into battle on a horse specially trained to smash at the enemy with its front legs. Onesilus's driver caught this animal's hooves on his shield and crippled it with a sword, sending mount and rider crashing to the earth. Once unhorsed, the bow of Onesilus or javelins of his runners dealt the Persian general a swift death.

The imperial left was put in peril by the loss of Artybius and victory was briefly within the rebels' grasp. At this critical juncture, Stasenor of Curium turned the battle around by deserting with his chariots to the Persians. Onesilus's hold on the aristocrats of Salamis appears to have been very tenuous, as the chariots of that city also defected. It was a move no doubt plotted in advance by Stasenor and conspirators from Salamis still loyal to the deposed Gorgus, who was present on the Persian side. The turncoats surrounded Onesilus and killed him. They then joined the Persian horses in falling upon the rebel right flank and rear. The Greek hoplites, apparently shaken by the death of their leader, broke under this assault and bolted from the field, leaving Aristokypros, king of Soloi, behind on the left wing to be overwhelmed and slain.

The revolt on Cyprus came to a halt for all practical purposes with this single battle. Gorgus reclaimed Salamis, and both Idalium and Paphos fell before year's end (remnants of the siege walls, emergency counter walls, and hundreds of bronze arrowheads have been unearthed at the latter site). Soloi, despite losing its ruler, resisted fiercely. Yet it too was overcome, falling at last to a tunneled mine and ending Cypriot resistance for good in 497 B.C.

Marsyas (497 B.C.)

The population of southwestern Anatolia (Caria) included both Carian and Greek speakers. Greeks had settled near the Aegean and had their strongest concentrations in the port cities of Cnidus and Halicarnassus (both founded around 900 B.C.). Ethnic Carians, though also present in the coastal areas, had their real strength well inland, where they followed a pastoral lifestyle and lived in mountaintop villages associated with a series of national shrines. It ended up being these hinterland barbarians, rather than their Greek countrymen, who led Caria into rebellion.

Carians fought much like pre-phalanx hoplites, wearing armor and carrying distinctive shields sheathed in white leather. They had a long history of fighting abroad for hire, providing "brazen men" to nearby Babylon and Lydia. Both Carian and Ionian soldiers of fortune had also served in Egypt as elite shock troops called *alloglossoi* or "foreign speakers." Many of these men came home to form a pool of seasoned warriors waiting for the next job to come along. However, Persia's conquests dried up all their markets — Lydia in 547 B.C., Babylon in 539 B.C., and Egypt in 525 B.C. Caria itself came under the Great King's sway with the fall of Egypt, and for more than a generation now its fighters had lacked mercenary opportunities. Impoverished and bitter, these hard men no doubt needed very little prodding to join their old Ionian comrades. Taking the sack of Sardis as a clear sign of Persian weakness, much of the Carian interior rose up in revolt, including the major cities of Caunus, Kyndya, and Mylasa.

The Persian host in Ionia had split during the summer of 497 B.C. into three columns. This allowed each Persian general to pursue a separate objective and personal glory. Hymaees moved north and east against Cius in Mysia, perhaps leading a portion of the Sardis sparabara, some Mysian peltasts, and five sataba of cavalry representing half of a satrapal conscription. Meanwhile, Otanes teamed with Artaphernes to subdue Ionia and Aeolis to the immediate north. They most likely advanced with the remainder of the sparabara from Sardis, some Lydians and Mysians, and Sardis's other five sataba of horsemen.

As Hymaees and Otanes set about their tasks, the third column turned north and west. Here, Daurises sought to put down insurgency in the area of the Hellespont. Daurises's strength is highly speculative, but subsequent events suggest that he had the largest of the three divisions. The Phrygian baivarabam of sparabara likely cored this force and had support from their satrapy's full hazarabam of conscript cavalry and the same Lydian and Mysian auxiliaries that had also been at Miletos. Daurises sacked several towns in the north before being told at the end of summer that the Carians had also gone into revolt. He then turned about and marched south to meet this new threat, leaving mopping-up operations in the Hellespont to Hymaees, who had been quickly victorious in his own campaign to the east.

Learning of Daurises's approach, Carian leaders debated the best defense strategy. Pixodarus of Kyndya advised taking post along the northern border with the Meander River at their backs. In proposing this, he argued that the men would make a better effort in the absence of a path to safety. But this was more than exceedingly poor tactics; it was insulting as well, since it implied that a people with a long and glorious warrior tradition must be forced to put up a good fight. Many of the older Carians had substantial mercenary experience and they surely felt no need of such a crutch for their valor. The leadership therefore rejected Pixodarus's plan and elected instead to make their stand south of the river. The Carians set up eastward from the Marsyas, a north-flowing tributary of the Meander, near a sanctuary and traditional place of national assembly known as the White Pillars.

In judging rebel manpower, it seems clear that Herodotus's report of 10,000 Carians killed at Marsyas is much too high. His number most likely reflects the total force engaged. Based on a heavy to light ratio of 4 to 1, this suggests that Caria's army amounted to some 8,000 hoplites and 2,000 peltasts, the latter of a type similar to their Cabelee neighbors. There is no record of horsemen in any Carian action in this era and it seems safe to assume that the highlanders had ceded all mounted functions to imperial forces for the last quarter century. Indeed, this shortcoming must have been a prime factor in their choice of a position beside the Marsyas, where they could counter their foe's superior cavalry by anchoring against the stream bank. So standing, the rebel hoplites would have fronted along a full kilometer at eight shields deep and having peltasts covering their exposed right side.

The Persian army seems to have forded the Meander without difficulty, facing at best only token resistance. Daurises's manpower likely came to just short of 15,000 men, which included 6,000 sparabara (a division at 60 percent nominal strength), 4,000 Lydian heavies, 4,000 Mysian peltasts, and 800 horsemen (a regiment at 80 percent nominal strength). The sparabara must have formed up ten men deep in the center of Daurises's array, with the Lydians split at the same depth on either side. This made for a combined front that equaled that of the enemy. It seems certain that Mysians and cavalry set up along the east flank in optimum position to support the battle line's open end.

Daurises's men would have closed into range and begun bombarding the Carians with arrows. The rebels quickly moved to reduce their exposure, advancing into contact with the enemy's shield wall to open a fearsome shock assault. Despite a spirited effort by the confident and bellicose highlanders, this attack met with little success. Even those Carians who had combat experience were really only familiar with the older style of linear front-fighting favored by their former imperial employers and are thus unlikely to have mastered more effective phalanx tactics. In fact, their shields might not have even had the lipped design best suited for othismos. As a result, the engagement quickly bogged down into a long and stubborn duel along the front ranks that failed to produce a breakthrough.

Herodotus's claim that the rebels gave in solely due to the weight of Persian numbers indicates that they didn't fail on the flank. This reflects the effectiveness of both their riverbank anchoring and peltast screen. There could have been no shortage of Carian courage; still, as the struggle wore on, lengthy missile fire and pressure from the fronting enemy spearmen were finally able to prevail. Even the best of armies needed strong discipline and strength of will to avoid turning into an uncontrollable mob bent only on escaping the hell of combat. In the end, the Carians must not have been able to suppress this instinct, and men began to flee in terror from the rear, allowing the Persians to spear past rapidly thinning files to victory. Many went down where they stood at the front, as their formation literally disintegrated behind them; and even more died trying to run away, cut down by pursuing peltasts and horsemen.

Intense combat and pursuit rendered this action more costly to those defeated than either Ephesos or Salamis. It's likely that some 35–40 percent of the rebels either lost their lives or took a fatal wound, with such severe losses inspiring Herodotus's inflated casualty figure. And the winners paid a hefty butcher's bill as well. Herodotus put the Persian dead at a believable 2,000—nearly 15 percent of those on the field. A fierce and bloody affair, Marsyas was the hardest fought battle of the entire revolt.

Labraunda (496 B.C.)

Survivors from Marsyas regrouped in the spring, coming together at Labraunda, site of a sacred grove dedicated to an axe-wielding god of war (Zeus of Hosts, to the Greeks). The problem they now faced was to find a way of dealing with Daurises, who was poised to penetrate even deeper into Caria. Shaken by the magnitude of their earlier defeat, the nation's leaders were actually debating whether to surrender or simply flee the region. Just then, crucial reinforcements arrived from Miletos and other allies. About a third of the population of Miletos was of Carian origin and the appearance of these kinsmen and their Greek comrades gave the hill men heart to again chance an open battle.

Odds are that the Milesians, having replaced casualties by drawing from the two lochoi not engaged at Ephesos, fielded a contingent of about the same size as the one sent to that earlier battle, with something like 2,000 hoplites and 500 psiloi. The other Ionians probably brought half this number of men. At the same time, the Carians, in spite of their fearful losses, could still call up about 5,000 hoplites and over 1,000 peltasts — 60 percent of their original manpower. Combined rebel strength at Labraunda was therefore comparable to that of the Carian force at Marsyas, with 8,000 spearmen and a large number of psiloi.

Daurises marched to confront the insurgent gathering with a force that must have included around 5,000 sparabara (20 percent or 1,000 bearing shields), 3,500 Lydian heavy infantry, and 3,500 Mysian peltasts, along with some 750 Iranian horsemen. As this host approached, the rebels scrambled to array a phalanx over what should have been a 1-kilometer front at eight shields deep. The Carians likely claimed the right wing on home ground, leaving the Milesians to take the left and the other Ionian allies to hold the center. The Persians would have marched into bow range in a formation that featured the Persian sparabara massed at the center in their usual ten-man files and the Lydians split between the wings at a probable depth of eight men. This allowed them to approximate the width of the Greek line. Skirmishers from both sides drew back as the formations closed for battle, with the Persian cavalry setting up either off one flank or in the rear to await an opportunity to impact the action.

The rebels charged once under missile fire, crashing into the shield wall in an all-out effort to get at their bowmen antagonists. However, our scant description of what followed suggests that the phalanx did no better here in piercing the Persian front than it had at Ephesos, Salamis, or Marsyas. Once more, the Greeks failed to knock back firmly braced sparabara shield-holders with othismos. Once again, Persian archers wrought havoc.

The longer the battle went on as a struggle between a few static ranks of front-fighters, the more the Persian bowmen methodically bombarded rebel ranks to bleed them both physically and psychologically. Even more importantly, Persian horsemen gained critical time to maneuver. Casualties reported by Herodotus for the battle indicate that the critical rebel collapse came on their left wing, as it was here where the Milesians took the worst losses of all those engaged that day. Persian cavalry and peltasts must have dispersed the opposing light foot to finally allow a mounted sweep around that end of the rebel line, causing the men of Miletos to reel away from their left flank and rear in panic. This let the Lydians push through and put the entire wing to rout. The remaining Ionians in the center and the Carians on the far wing then gave way to break up the phalanx from left to right.

Persian light-armed pursuit was mercilessly effective and actually inflicted slaughter even worse than that dealt out at Marsyas. The Carians' dead and fatally wounded probably totaled nearly 40 percent of the force engaged, while adding those with crippling wounds meant that half their army was out of action. Ionians in the formation center must have taken casualties comparable to those of the Carians, yet the Milesians on the broken left wing undoubtedly suffered even worse. The contingent from Miletos very likely left the bodies of over 1,000 of its finest warriors heaped around their collapsed position in the battle line and strewn pitifully along their escape route. It's telling that the Milesians didn't again take the field during the revolt, which underscores the severity of their losses. On the other hand, casualties for Persia were largely confined to the pre-collapse phase of fighting along the front. Though significant, these losses would have been relatively modest in contrast to those of the insurgents, with maybe 5–10 percent dying or taking wounds too serious to continue campaigning.

Pedasos (496 B.C.)

Daurises prepared in late summer 496 B.C. to take the war to Caria by moving against towns in the central hill country. Unable to match the invaders in the field, the Carians heeded advice to consider an alternative. This came from Heracleidas — a veteran possessed of great tactical genius and destined to gain fame for naval stratagems against the Persians at Artemisium in 480 B.C. He proposed that they draw Daurises into an ambush. Bait for this ploy would be a leaked report that they were regrouping near Pedasos in the south.

Daurises eagerly jumped at this lure, his confidence no doubt soaring after an unbroken string of victories. He thus set out on a rapid night march through the hilly terrain along the road to Pedasos, obviously expecting to catch his enemy unprepared and wipe out the last remaining opposition in Caria in one fell swoop. Having suffered only modest loses to date, he had a strong force for this foray. His baivarabam of sparabara would still have numbered nearly 5,000, while the Lydians and Mysians were each about 3,000 strong. Cavalry support came from 700 or so troopers of the same satrapal hazarabam that had been in action at Ephesos.

The Carians at this point could probably field no more than 2,500 hoplites and 500 peltasts of prime age — all that remained from the previous year's host of 10,000 men. Youth and old-age reserves might have added another 2,000 heavies and 500 skirmishers at best. Since Daurises had almost 1,000 sparabara with shields (two ranks or 20 percent) and 3,000 Lydians, the Carians for the first time faced a larger force of shock fighters. Moreover, with half their men reservists, they were looking at a discrepancy in quality as well. Daurises must have been aware of much of this and sensed that his opponents had no chance in a pitched battle.

Daurises and his troops could only move with difficulty along the track to Pedasos, using moonlight and torches to dimly illuminate their way. They would have been strung out over 3–4km at no more than four or five men abreast, with the cavalry leading the way followed by the sparabara, the baggage train, the Lydians, and the Mysians bringing up the rear. Experienced mercenaries among the rebels were without doubt familiar with this standard order and hid in accord on reverse slopes above the road. Placing their hoplites to oppose the sparabara and Lydians in the middle of the column, they could then split their peltasts between the wings to screen out the enemy's van and rear guards.

Under daylight conditions, the Carian army could never have escaped detection, but night provided perfect cover. As the Persians moved opposite, the rebels launched a wild charge over the crest that caught their foes flat-footed with a massive flank attack. Out of combat formation against an unknown number of fanatical assailants screaming down out of the gloom, Daurises and his men could only try to turn into line to meet this threat, but it was hopeless. Panic and flight must have ensued within minutes.

Carian losses would have been light due to their foe's state of disorganization and inability to effectively direct missile fire in the dark. Royalist casualties were very heavy in contrast, with perhaps 4–5,000 dying either on the spot or while trying to flee over poorly lit and unfamiliar terrain. Daurises and his subordinates Amorges and Sisimaces were among the slain as was the Lydian nobleman Myrsos, who had led the corps of heavy auxiliaries. The Mysians would have suffered less than the other footmen. Not only swift of foot, their rearguard post had also placed them away from the main action and closer to an avenue of escape. Likewise, much of the cavalry surely got clear due to its forward position, greater mobility, and the enemy's lack of mounted assets for pursuit.

The Hollows of Chios and Malene (494–493 B.C.)

Persian success from the Hellespont to Caria had by 495 B.C. squelched enthusiasm among the Ionians for another pitched battle. Only six cities on the mainland (Teos, Erythrai, Phocaia, Myous, Priene, and Miletos) and a few island poleis continued to resist. The war now devolved into a series of separate Persian attacks against the remaining rebel strongholds. Among these, Miletos was the most important and had the highest priority.

As other sites fell, Miletos continued to hold out on its well-fortified peninsula, where seaborne supply allowed for resistance as long as the Ionian fleet was intact. Still, the city's leader, Aristogoras, had no stomach for a long investment. Departing on pretext of finding a safe haven in the event of defeat, he fled to Thrace only to die there in pursuit of local conquests. Meanwhile, the Persians had granted release to Miletos's former tyrant, Histiaeus. Ostensibly, he was going to help put down the uprising, but, in reality, he planned to join it. However, the people of Miletos had enjoyed their respite from tyranny and refused to take him back.

Despite this show of strong morale by the Milesians, their freedom wouldn't survive much longer. The Persians crushed a badly disunited Ionian fleet in summer 494 B.C. near the small island of Lade, which lay just offshore from Miletos. This let them slow supply from the sea and take the city by storm that winter. With most of the population either dead or captured, a handful of survivors fled to Italy in remnants of their fleet. The victors relocated their male captives to the modern Persian Gulf area and sold the women and children into slavery. The plains around Miletos now became Persian bow land, while the mountainous interior went to the Carians of Pedasos, who had already come to favorable terms with Persia. With Miletos captured, the Great King's men were soon able to subdue the rest of Ionia.

Histiaeus, meanwhile, had drifted about for a time before finally settling on the island of Lesbos. Accepting eight triremes from the locals, he began raiding to make ends meet and descended upon Chios. His Lesbian allies eagerly joined in this attack, not only seeking economic spoils, but also no doubt out of a spirit of rivalry as Aeolic Greeks going up against the Chians, who were of Attic/Ionic stock. Sadly, it seems that inter-polis fighting for territory and personal gain had not ceased amid the wider struggle with Persia. The party of fighting men with Histiaeus would have been limited to around 320 hoplites (at 40 per ship) plus some lightly armed rowers. As Chian strength was sure to outnumber this modest force, the raiders' only reasonable chance for victory lay in exploiting the element of surprise. Histiaeus thus came ashore secretly and set up a trap in the heavily wooded countryside at a place known as The Hollows, which probably sat along the route between town and fields. Having arranged their ambush, his men then made their presence known by openly attacking nearby cropland.

In fact, the Chian garrison must have been quite small. The island's original force of 4,000 hoplites (complement for a 100-ship fleet) had taken devastating losses at Lade, with half going down in the battle and many others falling near Ephesos in an attempt to escape. Probably no more than 500–600 reserve hoplites (a single lochos) were available to respond against this sudden threat to their crops. The Chians raced toward their fields and right into the waiting ambush. Catching their foe in open order, the raiders butchered most of them on the spot and captured the rest. This left little more than a few hundred reservists to put up a last-ditch defense, and Chios capitulated without further resistance.

Refugees from the war continued to gather around Histiaeus and by spring 493 B.C. had become so numerous as to outstrip the ability of Lesbos to sustain them. Histiaeus recognized that he must get food from the mainland. He therefore sailed to the Aeolic coast of Mysia to plunder stores in the vicinity of Atarneus and the Kaikos plain northwest of Sardis. The size of his expedition is very uncertain, though it must have been substantial considering the magnitude of supplies being targeted. Maximum availability of Lesbian ships for this operation was 70 triremes — the number that had fled from Lade the preceding year. If we add in a few refugee vessels, there may have been up to 3,000 hoplites aboard 75 ships, with all light-armed support coming from the ships' crews.

The raiders began stealing crops near the town of Malene, but were interrupted by the arrival of a strong force of defenders under Harpagos of Persia. This was in all likelihood the same column that had been in action to the immediate north under Hymaees, who had died of disease near Troy and been replaced by Harpagos. It's probable then that the Persians fielded five hazaraba of sparabara (some 2,500 men at a well-worn 50 percent of authorized strength) plus some 1,500 Mysian peltasts. They also had perhaps 300–350 horsemen left from among five cavalry sataba, though these were late to arrive. Greek crewmen caught plundering the fields took to their heels straight away at the approach of these troops, even as Histiaeus rushed to their aid with his hoplites.

The Persians would have closed into bow range, ranking their sparabara ten-deep along a 250-meter front and splitting the peltasts between the flanks at similar depth to extend their formation another 75m on each wing. As for the Greeks, they must have been at a significant psychological disadvantage, having come to steal, not fight. Nonetheless, they moved to accept combat. Possibly they saw an opportunity in the Persians' modest numbers and lack of cavalry; more likely, the enemy blocked escape to the sea and forced them into battle. The hoplites would have formed eight deep, which let them nearly match the length of the approaching enemy line. Then, as the sparabara set up their shield wall and loosed a barrage of arrows, this phalanx charged to initiate shock combat.

The Greeks seem to have held their own in the center as they strove to use their heavier gear in pushing through the lighter peltasts on the wings. But before they could turn a Persian flank, Harpagos's cavalry arrived to set the situation on its ear. The unanticipated mounted assault undoubtedly had a devastating effect on already delicate Greek morale as the horsemen apparently enveloped at least one end of the line. This sent the hoplites on that wing running for their lives and rippled a wave of panic along the rest of their formation to utterly destroy it. Flinging away shields, the raiders desperately raced toward the rear and escape, all the while under pursuit from both cavalry and peltasts. Cut off from retreat to their ships, very few of the Greeks got away, with a great many losing their lives and most of the rest ending up prisoners. Histiaeus was among the captives and Artaphernes swiftly executed him. As it turned out, this act was decried by Darius, who seems to have still harbored some affection for the man whose loyalty had saved his life and reputation at the bridge on the Danube.

Malene was the last major land action in the Ionian Revolt. The major centers of rebellion had fallen with most of the insurrection's leaders dead or having fled, and though a few mop-up operations loomed, the uprising was essentially at its end. Darius moved to reorganize his satrapies toward tighter control in the future. At the same time, he contemplated an appropriate punishment for those who had opposed him. The Persian king appears to have emerged from this early trial of arms against the Greeks with two ideas uppermost. First, he must have felt that heavy hoplite infantry was no match in the field for his lighter equipped, but considerably more versatile Asians. Second, he saw opportunity in mounting a campaign to punish the city-states of Athens and Eretria for their interference. The poor showing of his Ionian opponents no doubt did much to encourage Darius's dreams of conquest against a similar military system in Europe. As sound as such thinking must have appeared at the time, events were to prove the phalanx tactics of the European Greeks to be considerably advanced over those of their kin in Asia Minor.

Peloponnesian Juggernaut

Sparta had the most powerful army among the prospective opponents of Persia on the Greek mainland. This Dorian foundation in the southern Peloponnese was an early 9th-century union of four villages (Pitana, Mesoa, Limnai, and Konosura) on the Eurotas River that might have been the first true polis in Greece (Grant 1987, 91–92). A fifth town (Amyclae) came into the fold during the early 8th century. Sparta had thereupon moved to expand, first taking over all of Laconia and then spreading west into Messenia. Though the Spartans had two kings, these were suborned to officials elected by and from a narrow ruling class of hoplites called spartiates (*spartiatoi*) or peers (*homoioi*). Sparta took in the Doric peoples of annexed lands as subject freemen called perioeci (*perioikoi*, those who "live around"). These latter were vital to the state's security, since they joined the spartiates in providing spearmen for the army. Some of the non–Dorians in Messenia also gained perioecian status, but most became serfs known as helots (*helotoi*).

Little better than slaves, the helots provided an economic base for the ruling class. The spartiates had from some time in the 7th century onward dedicated themselves solely to military training, each using a plot of land farmed by helots to support his lifestyle. Helot enmity for their masters was such that the threat of open revolt always hung heavy over the land. In truth, Sparta's refusal to participate in the Ionian uprising was not derived solely from an aversion to fighting far from home, but stemmed to a large extent from the menace of revolt inherent within its own social system. This was so divisive that the Spartans declared war on the Messenians each year to justify a host of aggressions employed in keeping them subdued.

Another reason that the Spartans refused aid to Ionia was the need to keep a strong army at home. This was critical to maintaining their hegemony. Sparta led an alliance that the ancients called "the Lacedaemonians and their allies," but is known today as the Peloponnesian League. It was actually a network of bilateral compacts that provided a large pool of allied manpower. This gave immense clout for dealing with poleis both within and outside the coalition and also allowed the Spartans to specialize in infantry, with others providing any necessary cavalry and naval support. Yet old rivalries complicated this system; thus, Sparta sometimes needed force to maintain those unions that were more imposed than voluntary.

The Spartan army had evolved from a militia levy representing the three Dorian tribes into a larger muster of both spartiates and perioeci from fixed districts. The spartiate troops came from five such precincts. Known as *obai* (singular *oba*), these districts corresponded to the four founding villages plus a fifth section (Dyme) for all later additions. Each oba provided a unit of hoplites (the Aidolios, Sines, Sarinas, Ploas, and Mesoates contingents) and there was a matching five-part system among the perioeci. This created a field army of ten units. The spartiates and perioeci thus formed separate lochoi in the early 5th century; however, many spartiates lost rights during the century and Sparta seems to have coped by pooling the classes together. (Cawkwell has suggested [2002, 240] that such common units were always the case, with perioeci forming the rear ranks in battle.)

The basic platoon-sized unit or *enomotia* (plural *enomotai*) of the Spartan army in the 5th century usually contained 32 men. A multiple of four and eight, this count was consistent with forming files at either of those depths of shield and the Spartans grouped their enomotai in fours to form pentekostyes (companies) of 128 men. In fact, pentekostyes means "fifties," which suggests an origin in the same "archaic lochos" cited at Corinth and Argos. Furthering the pattern of fours, a quartet of pentekostyes made up a lochos (battalion) of 512 men, which was the levy provided by each oba. A lochos of spartiates and one of perioeci then joined to create a regiment or *mora* (plural *morai*) of 1,024 men. (Note that "mora" and "lochos" might often have been interchangeable terms. This roughly parallels the late-Victorian British army, which featured regiments of both one and two battalions.) Linking lochoi in this way yielded composite units of a size well suited for detached operations.

Besides regular line units, Sparta also fielded a select team of the best young spartiates. These were 300 picked spearmen, 20–30 years of age, that were known as "Hippeis" (Horsemen). Since they were all hoplites, the Hippeis' title suggests roots in a past muster of mounted retainers. Much like Macedonian kings and their "companions," Spartan royals went into battle with an elite bodyguard of 100–300 spearmen drawn for the most part from among past and present Hippeis (Stylianou 1998, 290–294). Other teams of 300 picked men in classical Greece suggest that the Hippeis either set a fashion or reflected a wider, long-standing tradition.

With ten 500-man lochoi forming five mora, the Spartan field army in the 5th century contained around 5,000 hoplites. A sixth mora of reserves (older men and those below 20 years of age) was also available. This additional unit came into the regular army some time after the Great Peloponnesian War, when incorporation of selected helots had expanded prime-aged manpower. The concept of a sixth, reserve mora was at that time replaced with a scheme that divided the reserves among twelve regular lochoi. At 20 percent of total strength, these reserves could boost each lochos from 512 to 640 men. While far below Aristotle's estimate that Laconia could support up to 30,000 hoplites and 1,500 horsemen, such numbers match well with late 5th and early 4th century figures from Thucydides and Xenophon.

A major problem with the foregoing strengths is that they yield a Spartan field army only about half that said by Herodotus to have been at Plataea in 479 B.C. One explanation might be that Plataea was a unique case of full deployment to meet an extraordinary threat from Persia. This would make all other musters on record into partial mobilizations per the two-thirds levies often culled from Spartan allies. It also might explain the report of a huge number of helots at Plataea, since sending these potential troublemakers out of the country would have made up for absence of a large home guard. However, it seems that Plataea wasn't the largest Spartan mobilization of the 5th century, since Thucydides gave that distinction to the levy of 6,200 hoplites that gathered at the start of the Mantinea I campaign in 418 B.C. In fact, we can reconcile this later force with Herodotus only by evoking a catastrophic reduction in Sparta's population. This is not at all likely. The only major disaster that we know of during this period was an earthquake in the mid 5th century, which wouldn't have caused so severe a loss of life in such a rural setting (as noted by Chrimes [1949, 352] and per modern geophysical studies).

A more viable solution to the puzzle of Spartan numbers is that Herodotus might have confused his figures. Swayed by a boastful (and perhaps deliberately misleading) manpower claim by the ex-Spartan king Demaratus, he easily could have mistaken a full army of 5,000 for only the spartiate levy. He might then have doubled the figure to add a matching draft of perioeci. This seems like the best explanation on balance, as a smaller force is more consistent with the details of Spartan organization, better agrees with numbers from later years, and compares well with resources in other city-states of the same era. Any decline in manpower was therefore to spartiate content, rather than overall head count. And it's important to note that such a strength in no way detracted from Sparta's ability to maintain its hegemony. Even at only 5,000–6,500 hoplites (the latter including reserves), its army would still have been among the largest in Greece. Moreover, Spartan power didn't rest on size of the army, but rather on its skill. Spartan hoplites were the world's finest heavy infantry.

The spartiates were ancient Greece's only full-time military force of any size and could drill and perfect tactics to a degree impossible for their amateur militia opponents. Furthermore, they had a superior command structure and seeded spartiate leaders among the perioeci to raise the performance level of their entire army. Spartan mastery of hoplite tactics not only gave a material advantage, but also inspired confidence and spawned a fearsome and intimidating reputation. This widespread conviction of Sparta's invincibility was just as important as physical prowess in explaining its record of military success. Over a period of nearly two centuries, no other hoplite army bested the Spartans in a critical battle. Indeed, many foes ran away at or before first contact in the field. Nevertheless, other armies in Greece had strong warrior traditions of their own that gave them the courage to stand and sternly test the Spartans in combat, and the Doric fighters of Argos were foremost among these worthy foes.

Sepeia (494 B.C.)

The rich farming district of Thyreatis to the south of the Argive plain was an area of contention between Argos and Sparta for centuries. At least three battles took place prior to the classical period in attempts to settle territorial claims in this district: c. 718 B.C. (Thyreatis), c. 669 B.C. (Hysiae), and c. 550 B.C. (Battle of the Champions). The last of these had left Sparta with effective title to the region; however, Argos had grown strong enough in the early 5th century to again challenge for control. Spartan king Cleomenes thus seems to have decided at the end of the current truce with Argos to make a preemptive strike. He first marched his army north to the Erasinos River at the frontier with Argos, but this was merely a feint designed to draw the Argive army into that area. He doubled back and, having gained ships from Sicyon and the island polis of Aigina, ferried his forces across the Gulf of Argos. The Spartans came ashore to the southeast of Tiryns at Asine.

The Argives learned of Cleomenes' landing and turned about to intercept him at Sepeia, a town along the road to Tiryns. Here, the path from the sea opened up between the hills onto the main Argive plain, offering a good defensive position from which to block any advance on the croplands farther north. Once the armies made contact, the Spartan king hesitated to accept battle, bringing about a lengthy standoff. There could even have been a temporary truce negotiated (for seven days according to Plutarch) to allow for a sort of "cooling off" period.

There were clearly a couple of reasons for Cleomenes' reluctance to attack. He had no doubt brought all of his polis's prime-aged hoplites, totaling just over 5,000. Argos could counter with 6,000 spearmen (per a later casualty figure that Herodotus presented as the entire hoplite population of the city), which represented ten lochoi of 600 men each. Crowds of attendants supported these heavy troops, including perhaps one skirmisher for each ten hoplites on either side. As a result, the Argives must have held not only the better field position, but an advantage in numbers as well. Adding these physical factors to the Argives' martial prowess and strong motivation against a much hated rival, it's easy to see good sense in Cleomenes' caution. Practical and clever, the Spartan king began stalling for time as he sought a way to improve his chances for success.

Cleomenes camped close to the Argives, but refused to take the field for several days, either on the pretext of unfavorable omens or under a temporary truce. His men kept to their camp and carried out a regular routine that included sounding a horn to signal the taking of meals. The Argives relaxed their guard after a few days, falling out for their own food at the same time as the Spartans. Herodotus claimed that Cleomenes observed this and arranged for his men to charge out of their camp when the horn for the midday meal was next sounded. Plutarch, in line with the report of a seven-day cease-fire being in effect at the time, suggested that the attack actually took place at night during the third day of truce — Cleomenes rationalizing his breach of the peace agreement by claiming that it specified days and not nights! The two stories can easily be reconciled by placing the assault before the evening meal rather than at midday, but regardless of such details of timing, the Argives were taken by surprise and routed with great loss of life.

While the Spartans were known for being highly focused and emotionally stable in combat, the Argives often suffered from broad swings in mood. This made them capable of either great ferocity or disabling despair depending on the circumstances at hand. That Cleomenes would take advantage of this emotional instability is not unusual, but that he would do so by means of a dishonorable ploy suggests much. It shows that there must have been little difference in skill between the warriors of Sparta and Argos at this time, and that the overall situation might have favored the Argives.

Pursuit and slaughter of a beaten foe was not in keeping with Spartan custom, yet just such a thing took place at Sepeia. While this might have reflected the Spartans' exceptional hatred of Argos, it seems to be more in keeping with the ruthless personal style of Cleomenes. The final Argive casualties were inflicted when the Spartan king had his helots set fire to the sacred grove of Argos, where many of the rout's survivors had sought sanctuary (perhaps overnight if we follow the idea of an evening assault in the main engagement). Cleomenes apparently didn't want to take the men sheltered in the grove by force, since doing so would risk precious spartiate lives against a desperate foe on uncertain ground amongst the trees. He therefore resorted to another trick and called out 50 of the Argives one at a time, using names gained from local allies. Each emerged upon hearing that he was to be ransomed (there was, in fact, a customary fee for this) only to be treacherously killed. Dense vegetation hid this act from the other Argives, who learned of the deadly scam only after one of them scaled a tree to see what was going on. Cleomenes then ordered his helots to set fire to brush around the sanctuary. The resulting blaze rapidly spread to consume the entire sacred grove and, forced out into the open by this blasphemous arson, the last of the fugitives quickly fell victim to waiting Lacedaemonian spearmen.

Herodotus reported that Argive losses at Sepeia left the city's slaves in charge. Elsewhere, we hear that only women were available to defend the walls. While these stories are clearly overstated, they do illustrate the seriousness of the situation. Argos had to arm its underclass (the Orneates) to aid the battle's survivors and citizen reserves in manning the defenses. And the fairer sex did indeed contribute to this effort, with the famed poetess Telesilla gaining praise for organizing the Argive women to help defend their homes, freedom, and lives. This was not actually all that unusual, since stores of votive arms in the temples of Greek cities commonly acted as emergency armories to equip both women and the lower classes in times of extreme crisis.

Sepeia removed the Argives as a threat to Sparta for a full generation and they wouldn't again challenge for hegemony until 470 B.C. (backing an uprising at Tegea). Argive losses were sufficient to not only require a long recovery, but also to trigger major changes in the social order. When next seen fully mobilized in 418 B.C., the phalanx of Argos was smaller and mirrored Spartan organization in its use of perioeci and elite troops supported by the state. The Argives' hatred of Sparta rose to new heights after Sepeia and no doubt had a strong influence 14 years later on their failure to support the Spartan-led alliance against Persia. Argos may even have gone so far as to make a deal with the Persians for leadership of the Peloponnese in return for its neutrality.

Sepeia presents one of Greek history's most underappreciated "what ifs." What if Sparta had been defeated by Argos in 494 B.C.? Such a reversal of the historical result certainly seems to have been possible, maybe even likely if Cleomenes hadn't devised his sneak attack. Sparta's last defeat at the hands of the Argives had derailed its drive for domination in the Peloponnese for over a century. And while a loss at Sepeia may not have set the Spartans back so long again, it certainly could have sidelined them for a generation and profoundly affected the conflict with Persia.

Could Athens have triumphed at Marathon or eleven years later at Mycale if their foes had not been pushed into inopportune offensives by the threat of Spartan reinforcement? Would the Greeks have persevered in 480 B.C. without inspiration from the shining legend of Leonidas and his 300 at Thermopylae? Most of all, could the Persians have been turned back for good at Plataea without the storied steadfastness of the Spartans, who carved out a Greek victory against the enemy's best men on the all-critical right wing? Perhaps the Argives could have done as well or Greece could have gone without, but these alternatives seem doubtful. Greek liberty and all that it engendered might well have fallen to foreign domination in the early 5th century without Sparta.

Though it's hard to admire the often brutal ways of the Spartans, it's equally difficult to ignore the benefits to all Greece of their martial contributions. A century and a half after the struggle against Persia the Greeks again had to face foreign invaders (from Macedonia this time). Sparta, having gone into decline after suffering defeat against Thebes, didn't fight and Greece's independence was finally snuffed out.

Tyrants in the West

The Greeks spread westward in the 8th century, crossing the narrow seaway separating their homeland from southern Italy. This migration began with a trading post (*emporion*) off the west Italian shore on the small isle of Pithecusae in 775–770 B.C., followed by another on the nearby mainland. The second site, at Cumae (Cyme), evolved into a true polis sometime before 725 B.C. and spawned an armed expedition to Sicily in the period 730–720 B.C. that set up camp at Zancle. Arrival of other settlers from Euboa would turn this outpost into a full-fledged colony. Zancle lay across from the toe of Italy on the narrow Sicilian Strait, giving it control of a key choke point along the western trade route from Greece.

Having set up Zancle, Cumae made other settlements along the coast of western Italy to become one of the region's most powerful states. The city reached a peak under the tyrant Aristodemus, who parlayed victories against local barbarians into a dictatorship that endured into the early 5th century. Nor was Cumae alone in the rush to exploit the potential of this

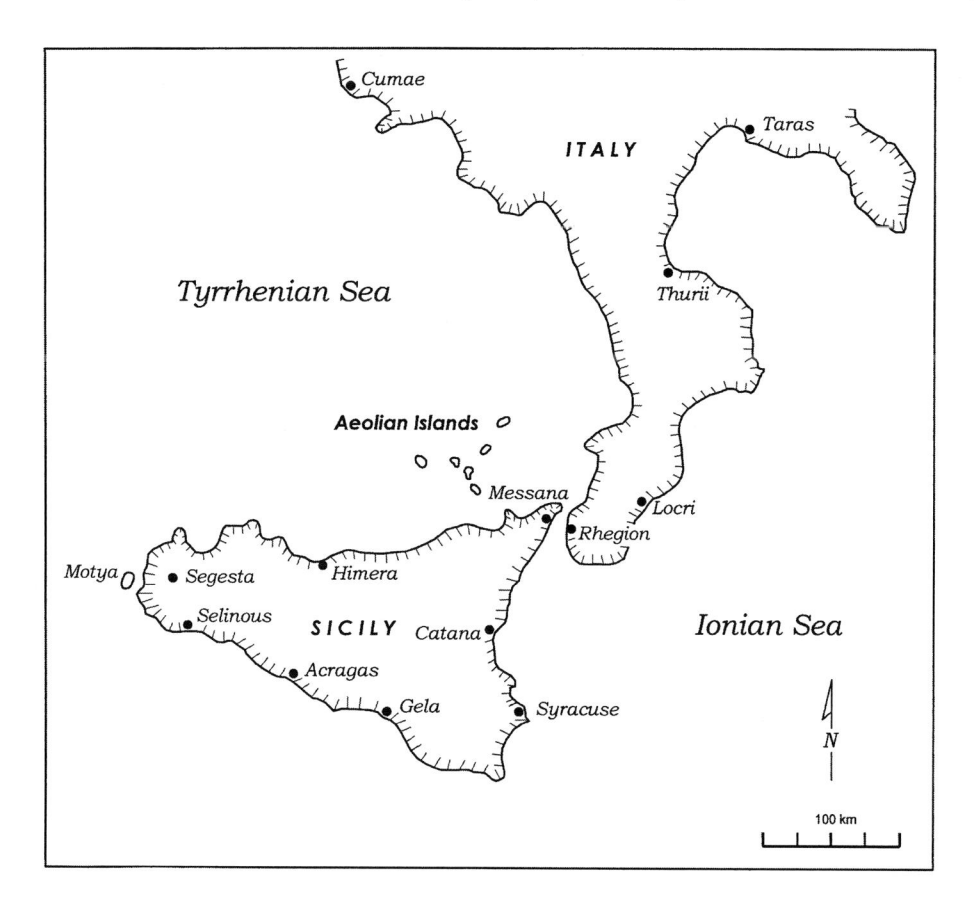

THE GREEK WEST—SOUTHERN ITALY / SICILY

region, as more Greeks settled a host of sites across southernmost Italy (Breltioi). Rhegion was among the most important of these new colonies, having begun at the same time as Zancle at a competing site directly across the strait. Other major foundings around the boot-shaped tip of Italy were at Sybaris (front instep, c. 720 B.C.), Croton (south of Sybaris in 710 B.C.), Taras (back instep, late 8th century), and Locri (south side of the toe in 679–673 B.C.). These had all developed into significant city-states by the early 5th century.

Though Zancle opened up Sicily's northeast sector, it wasn't the first Greek settlement on the island. Immigrants from the islands of eastern Greece had already landed on Sicily in 734 B.C., founding Naxos on the east coast. The following year, a group from Corinth had settled farther south along the same shoreline at Syracuse. These new arrivals quickly came to dominate eastern Sicily and then extended their sway along most of the coastal plain. Native peoples—Elymians in the northwest, Sicans in the southwest, and Siculi in the east—either fled into the interior highlands or became subordinate within the Greek colonies.

There was little resistance to these developments by the island's other non-native inhabitants, the Phoenicians. These seafaring traders occupied commercial outposts on Sicily, but were neither populous nor interested in farming and therefore ceded most of the fertile land to the Greeks. By the beginning of the 5th century, Phoenicians held no more than a few trading centers at the extreme western end of the island. These lay closest to their regional stronghold at Carthage, which sat about 250km southwest on the African coast.

Reflecting their homeland culture, western Greeks were independent and combative. It comes as no surprise then that economic and martial aggression was integral to their way of life. This led to a good many wars, both among the poleis and with native peoples.

Eastern Sicily (500–481 B.C.)

Rhegion was involved in a fierce struggle for control of the Sicilian Strait in the early 5th century. Anaxilas led this polis as a dictator bent on extending his reach not only on the Italian mainland, but into Sicily as well. Finds at Olympia record a victory by this despot c. 500 B.C. over the equally ambitious Sicilian tyrant Cleander of Gela, with the battle most likely being for control of the west side of the strait near Zancle. Concentrated along the coast near that city, it would have matched several thousand hoplites and small groups of psiloi for each side. A few hundred cavalrymen were probably on hand as well, though they would have been of little use in a shoreline setting. We have no description of this engagement, but it could have resembled the contemporary action at Cleonai. Yet Anaxilas failed to take Zancle after the battle and had to fight that polis again sometime 498–492 B.C., when the Zancleans came out on top with help from Hippocrates, the new dictator of Gela. In fact, it wasn't until 490/489 B.C. that Anaxilas finally gained control of Zancle. He then moved colonists from his old home region of Messenia into the town and renamed it Messana. Sometime 487–481 B.C., the tyrant put these new allies to use in an attack on the surviving Zanclean outpost at Mylae, which lay to the west along the north coast of Sicily.

We can deduce the participants at Mylae I from dedications for victories at this time by Rhegion over Locri and by Messana over Mylae and Locri. Though these could have been separate actions, it's more probable that a single battle is referenced. This suggests that the Rhegians and their Messanian vassals assaulted a Mylae that had support from Locri, Rhegion's bitterest rival. Refugees from the recent takeover at Zancle might also have been present to defend their former outpost. Locris would have transported its men by sea, bringing about 600 hoplites—equal to the passenger capacity of a 15-ship fleet (as per later deployments against Athens). Adding these troops to some 800–1,200 local spearmen from Mylae/Zancle (two lochoi—the garrison later recorded for this post) would have given the defenders roughly 1,600 hoplites. Light support came from both the local population and Locrian ship crews.

Rhegion probably had over 5,000 hoplites with strong light foot and mounted support. Yet Anaxilas wouldn't have had so full a mobilization at Mylae, and dedications indicate that he fought only the Locrian portion of the opposing front. This indicates that he had no more than 1,000 spearmen, though this was still sufficient to file at eight shields against a depth of but four or five. The Messanians could easily have fielded more than 2,000 hoplites, completing a phalanx 3,000 strong that held an overall advantage of roughly 2 to 1. With Rhegians on the right and Messanians at center and left, this array must have closed on a facing formation that had the men from Mylae standing right through most of the center and their Locrian allies holding the rest of the line. Once engaged, Anaxilas's men likely exploited their huge edge in manpower to penetrate the thinner opposition, taking both the victory and Mylae.

Sicily was also a hotbed of tyranny at this time. The first Greek settlement on the south coast was at Gela, founded from Rhodes and Crete around 690 B.C. Losing no time, this fledgling colony extended its control into the interior through a series of campaigns against the local tribesmen. Cleander seized Gela in 505 B.C., but suffered assassination in 498, leaving his brother Hippocrates in charge. A ruthless man, Hippocrates fortified the city and beefed up his army with hired men and more cavalry. He used this force to lead Gela to the fore among Sicilian powers, gaining most of the communities along the east coast and avenging his brother's defeat at Zancle. Only Syracuse under its aristocratic *gamoroi* class remained as a last bulwark against Gelan domination of all Greek Sicily.

Hippocrates led an attack on Syracuse in 492 B.C. He crossed into Syracusan territory via a bridge over the deep valley of the Helorus River and set about ravaging the surrounding farmland. The Syracusans reacted swiftly by calling up their gamoroi horsemen, yeoman hoplites, and peasant psiloi, who all rushed to intercept. The Gelan dictator was waiting for them near the Helorus on open ground favorable to his cavalry.

Figures for Gela and Syracuse after their union in 485 B.C. offer clues to the manpower involved here. The combined poleis could field 5–6,000 hoplites within 600-man lochoi (per a picked Syracusan unit of later years). Assuming that mercenaries were not a factor and that Syracuse was the weaker partner suggests a Gelan mobilization of about 3,000 spearmen (five lochoi) plus an unusually strong cadre of 600 horsemen. Gelon, a former member of the tyrant's bodyguard, led the cavalry contingent and a matching team of hamippoi. Syracuse must have stood in opposition with some 2,400 spearmen (four lochoi) and 300 horsemen (at 10–15 percent of hoplite strength) plus hamippoi. The Syracusans, having less heavy infantry, would have matched the Gelan front by filing only six shields deep.

In the ensuring battle, the thinly deployed Syracusans could exert little othismos and must have come under immense pressure from the enemy's deeper files. This might have led to a quick penetration by Gela. Yet subsequent criticism of the mounted aristocracy at Syracuse suggests that the battle turned on a cavalry action. If so, the hoplites of Syracuse must have put up a good fight despite their lesser numbers, probably giving ground only very gradually until Gelon's superior horsemen dispersed the opposing gamoroi riders. Taken then in flank and rear, the Syracusan spearmen would finally have given up their dogged resistance and fled. Without a cavalry screen, the beaten hoplites suffered under a fierce pursuit that might have run their losses up to as high as 20–25 percent. Devastated, the city avoided a siege only by surrendering some of its borderland. The people of Syracuse were enraged by this turn of events and ousted their failed gamoroi leaders in favor of a hoplite democracy.

The area gained by Gela from Syracuse covered Camarina (on the south coast) and the attached interior. This included lands held by the Siculi. These were an Italian people that had (per Diodorus) crossed to the island and displaced previous immigrants from the north (the Sicans). Continuing presence of Siculi on the mainland and typing of their language within the Latin group (Bury 1900, 95–96) tend to support this story. The Siculi were now a collection of rural tribes that had just a few towns surrounding hilltop citadels. Each tribal group was fiercely independent, but common threats could on occasion inspire them to make a united effort for the combined good.

Siculi warfare likely followed that of the Oscan tribesmen on the Italian mainland, but would have included some elements similar to pre-hoplite Latin culture as well. Military organization was therefore probably decimal-based, with tribal levies comprising a main body of spearmen that subdivided into war bands. Some of these men carried two short spears (suitable for both throwing and thrusting) and others a single, longer type (for thrusting only), using either a straight short-sword or one-handed fighting axe as a secondary weapon. They wore bronze armor according to personal wealth. Panoply elements included helmet, a broad belt to protect the mid-section, *pectorale* (a round, square, or rectangular plate fixed over the breast), and strapped shin-guards. Shin protection often consisted of a single guard on the left leg, which was normally placed forward in combat stance. Fighters in the main battle array also bore a large, aspis-sized shield of the oblong Latin type known as a *scutum* (called a *thureos* by the Greeks), which was cored with wood and had an outer covering of hide. A vertical grip in the center of the scutum allowed its user to hold it in his left hand. Many Siculi added elements of hoplite equipment obtained from their Greek neighbors to their native gear and it seems that the cuirass, snap-on greaves, and machaira/kopis sword were the most popular of these adoptions.

Horsemen were certainly significant among the Siculi. Their cavalry would have consisted of mounted nobles that used javelins and wore armor like the best-equipped among their footmen (though they could not have used the bulky scutum). Since each Siculi warrior fitted out in accordance with his personal wealth, many lightly armed soldiers drawn from among the poor must also have been present. These formed a mix of helmeted javelinmen and axemen with small shields that found their primary use in after-battle pursuit.

The Siculi usually relied on ambushes and surprise attacks in open order, but could also fight in linear formation if need be. When working in close order, they seem to have placed those armored warriors that had shorter, multi-purpose spears in front and backed them with the others holding thrusting spears. A basic organization of small war bands would have been well suited to irregular warfare within their rugged homeland and, combined into larger arrays, these combat teams could make them highly flexible and adaptive.

Some of the Siculi tribes openly battled Gela in 491 B.C. Hippocrates led an army against this uprising, perhaps taking around 3,000 hoplites and 600 cavalrymen accompanied by hamippoi, and the Siculi confronted him near Heraian Hybla, which lay inland from Camarina (near modern Ragusa). Deployments during the Athenian invasion of 415–413 B.C. give some idea of tribal strength, as it's probable that the Siculi threw most of their support to Athens at that time, possibly by a ratio of roughly 5 to 1. This means that the 1,000 tribesmen serving Syracuse as infantry might have come from a total force of around 6,000. These men represented all economic levels, from the fully armored down to the lightly equipped poor. With Siculi foot soldiers normally at ten for each horseman (as among the related Oscans and Latins), there should have been some 600 mounted nobles throughout the tribes. Yet this wasn't a nationwide rebellion (something that wouldn't occur until the middle of the 5th century) and but a fraction of total manpower would have been on hand. It's unlikely then that more than half the tribes were at Hybla; thus, the Siculi were seriously short on cavalry and at least somewhat outnumbered in infantry.

We know little about the engagement at Hybla, even whether it was an open battle, guerilla action, ambush, or siege — nor are we told who won. Still, the Greeks appear to have been victorious, given that we hear no more of the rebellion and know Gela held Hybla later in the century. A Greek victory combines with the death of Hippocrates to imply a phalanx action that put the tyrant at hazard while leading from the front. Hippocrates might easily have forced this kind of pitched clash by simply marching into enemy territory just before harvest time The Siculi could then protect their food supply only by winning a stand-up fight, since either pursuing guerrilla tactics or submitting to siege would have cost them both fields and outlying stores. Once battle got underway, superior Gelan cavalry must have driven off the flanking Siculi horsemen and skirmishers, which would have allowed the hoplites to put their heavier gear and othismos to deadly use in breaking through by main force. The Siculi would have taken to their heels as soon as this happened, running toward high ground and Hybla under hot pursuit.

Though their lighter gear was a boon in flight, the Siculi still seem to have taken terrible losses. Casualties among the victorious Greeks must have been contrastingly light; their commander, however, was among the fallen few. Fighting from the traditional general's station at the fore on the right wing, Hippocrates likely went down only in the battle's final phase, when it had minimal effect on his army's morale. Cavalry commander Gelon subsequently deposed the slain dictator's surviving sons, for whom he had become legal guardian, and seized power for himself. His rule got off to a rough start with the loss of Zancle to Rhegion; still, he recovered soon enough and would eventually become one of Grecian Sicily's most successful leaders.

Taras I (c. 490 B.C.)

Conflict with resurgent indigenous tribes in the early 5th century was not confined to Sicily and a dedication at Delphi indicates that the polis of Taras in southern Italy engaged local Messapian tribesmen in the same period. Control of land on the Sallentine Peninsula (heel of the Italian boot) was at issue here, with the colony at Taras occupying a key position along the southern shore at the top of that long headland. This incident was only the latest outbreak of violence in a long-running altercation that had been going on since arrival of the Greeks in the region during the late 8th century. The battle at Taras may well have pitted the full strengths of both sides in a decisive engagement. Without doubt, a great deal of territory was at stake and the results of this action settled the land dispute for most of a generation.

The Messapians were one of three major Iapyian tribes (the Daunians and Peucetians being the other two). These people had crossed into Italy from northern Illyria (modern Albania) in the distant past and had since taken on many Oscan ways, though this trend was stronger at the north end of their range than with the Messapians in the south. Clues to Messapian manpower derive from an all-inclusive gathering of the Iapyians and a few of their allies in 473 B.C. This host numbered 20,000 fighters, of whom the allies are unlikely to have supplied more than 10 percent (2,000 men), while the Messapians brought the most. Thus, an early 3rd century B.C. report that put the Daunians (the weakest tribe) at 4–5,000 warriors, suggests that there were 5–6,000 among the Peucetians and around 8,000 in Messapia. The Messapians were strong in cavalry, with a quarter of their muster being mounted in the late 3rd century B.C. A similar ratio at Taras would have fielded some 2,000 riders to support a 6,000-man force of foot.

Like the Siculi in Sicily, Messapian armored men probably all used large shields (*scuta*) and helmets (mostly of the open-faced, "Illyrian" style), but the rest of their panoply reflected personal wealth. They likely wielded either two multipurpose spears of modest length or a single thrusting spear having greater reach, with the two equipment types perhaps present in near equal numbers. Curved short swords similar to the Greek kopis and one-handed axes were the most popular side arms. Though skirmishers were not common among the Oscans, they were a fixture of the Messapians' Illyrian kin and they thus would have had some light javelinmen, axemen with small shields, and a few slingers. The cavalry would have followed more in the Oscan pattern than that of the horse-poor Illyrians, featuring mounted nobles and their retainers deployed in rectangular formation. These horsemen lacked the scutum shield, but were otherwise armored like the wealthiest infantrymen and carried javelins plus either sword or axe.

The Tarantines hailed from Sparta, with legend making them the banished offspring of Spartan women and helots born during the First Messenian War (743–742 B.C.). And though later known for a dissolute lifestyle, they seem at this time to have retained at least some of the traditions of their fierce homeland. Most notable among these was a Doric-style monarchy that was subordinate to hoplite land owners. The spearmen that cored Taras's army drew light-armed support from men of the poorer classes and, in a setting so favorable for horses, there were without doubt a good many wealthy cavalrymen as well. Taras would become the leading state in Grecian Italy before century's end and had an urban area much like that of

Athens (Cornell 1995, 204), perhaps being able to field somewhere around 4,000 hoplites, 1,000 psiloi (one for each four spearmen), and 400–600 horsemen (10–15 percent of the hoplite count). Another 1,000 spearmen, 250 psiloi, and 100–150 riders would have been available in an old-age/youth reserve.

We have no surviving description of the battle at Taras, but relative strengths suggest a hard-fought and closely decided affair. What is known of later encounters between Romans and Oscans provides at least a broad outline of how this might have played out. The Tarantines must have formed a phalanx near the city, using rough ground and/or dense vegetation to ward the ends of their line from the enemy's horsemen (as per the approach taken by fellow Greeks at the contemporaneous battle of Marathon). Their own riders and psiloi would then have taken post either to safeguard retreat into the city or further protect the flanks. The Greeks most likely invited their foes to approach and engage in open combat. In fact, these tribal warriors were prone to headlong charges into shock confrontation when denied an opportunity to fight from cover.

The Messapians would have put their armored men into a deep linear array that was limited by terrain to the same width as that for the Greeks. Meanwhile, their skirmishers and cavalry must have been forced to stand either in the rear or off the most open flank. Since the axemen lacked missiles to engage at a distance, these probably stayed in the rear to finish off foes overrun by their spearmen and/or pursue in the case of victory. Like their Siculi cousins, the Oscans usually placed men with two shorter spears in the forward ranks, where they could lead the attack by hurling one weapon and then close to engage hand-to-hand with the other. This opening burst of missiles and momentum-driven shock attack were the most effective aspects of Italian tribal tactics and, once the Tarantines weathered it, they must have gotten the better of the close combat that followed. With the Greek cavalry and psiloi holding firm on the flanks, the battle would have come to hinge entirely on fighting in the center, where the men of Taras held a huge advantage against their lighter armed opponents.

Warriors equipped with thrusting spears no doubt manned the Messapian rear ranks. When combat had dragged on long enough to exhaust and/or deplete forward manpower, these spearmen would have moved up into the fight as replacements. Yet once at the front, these fresh fighters seem to have fared no better than those who went before them. Despite any advantage that the tribesmen's more flexible organization might have imparted in broken terrain, the phalanx remained superior on level ground. Denied a quick victory and put under increasing pressure from advance of the closely ordered Tarantines, the Messapians finally broke from the fight.

Casualties among the Greeks were surely minimal, perhaps running no more than 2–3 percent fatalities. Their tribal foes, meanwhile, probably took losses two or three times as high. Even though the presence of significant numbers of Messapian horsemen limited pursuit, the damage inflicted was at least morally significant. It would be 17 years before the Messapians would make another attempt on Taras; and when next in action against a phalanx, they would take care to heavily bolster their ranks with allied manpower.

Tactical Patterns of the Early 5th Century

What were the keys to battlefield success in the early 5th century? The most obvious was cavalry. Horsemen played crucial roles in surprise attacks at Cyprian Salamis and Malene, and pressed to victory in more straightforward fashion at Ephesos, Labraunda, and Helorus River (and possibly at Hybla, as well). The excellent cavalry of Persia was a major factor in that nation's ability to crush its Asian Greek foes without ever tasting defeat in a conventional battle. Likewise, Hippocrates first set Gela on its course to greatness by upgrading his mounted contingent.

Nevertheless, armies with a significant advantage in horsemen weren't always successful. Frederick the Great said that outnumbering the enemy by more than one-third gave a prohibitive edge in combat (Phillips 1985, 314). Still, armies with just such superiority in mounted troops either met failure or had to rely on other arms on at least three occasions (Marsyas, Pedasos, and Taras). This shows that there were effective counter-measures against horsemen even at this early date. Specifically, defeat of the Persian mounted van at Pedasos was due to use of a nighttime ambush, while Marsyas and Taras saw flank barriers frustrate strong cavalry forces.

The strength of cavalry was its great mobility across flat, clear ground. Indeed, mounted troops were nearly unbeatable against infantry caught in the open by day. This was axiomatic among the Greeks and inspired Plato's humorous comment that challenging his old tutor Socrates to an argument was just as hopeless as fighting cavalry on the plain. Yet the far-reaching missiles, light gear, and fast-but-fragile steed that gave a horseman such overwhelming advantage in open country with good visibility turned to weaknesses when darkness or rough terrain forced shock combat with men on foot. By pursuing night actions or prudently anchoring their flanks, hoplites could therefore metaphorically pass on debate with Socrates in favor of a fistfight.

Surprise was another key. Though harder to apply than cavalry superiority, since it called for a certain amount of enemy cooperation, armies carrying out unexpected attacks in the early 5th century won every time. Examples include Curium switching sides at Salamis, the ambushes at Pedasos and Chios, the late-arriving cavalry at Malene, and the sneak attack at Sepeia. Furthermore, it's clear that surprise trumped all other factors in a battle.

At the same time, two other elements that might have been decisive actually failed to have a significant impact in the early 5th century. These were the presence of hoplites and defense of home soil. Armies with a major advantage in shield-bearing spearmen (+33 percent or more) actually lost more often than they won. Hoplite losses came against cavalry on open ground, either as a result of surprise attack or (at Marsyas) under extended missile assault against a foe well supplied with shield-bearers. Therefore, the aura of combat superiority that would ultimately surround the hoplite was definitely not a product of his heavy equipment alone. It would take skillful use of terrain in the service of advanced phalanx tactics to gain that fame.

Likewise, fighting near home wasn't enough on its own to overcome other factors in combat. Armies on home soil lost twice as often as they won in the first decade of the 5th century. Homeland fighting gave a clear edge in knowledge of terrain and might sometimes have fueled a more desperate effort on the battlefield as well. Yet these don't seem to have mattered as much as cavalry superiority, surprise, or simply having more hoplites.

*　*　*

Persia had a nearly unbroken record of victory against the Greeks in Ionia; nonetheless, other early 5th-century actions show that Europe's hoplites were more capable than those of Asia Minor. Moreover, they were at their deadliest when fighting within the sort of mountain valleys where their phalanx had been born and for which it was ideally suited. Darius was either unaware of these facts or remained unimpressed by them. He seems to have seen his recent success as proof that slow-moving Greek militias couldn't match the empire's larger, swifter, and more professional host. Also, contact with exiles from a deeply divided Greece suggested that he could always find a traitor when needed. Thus, by exploiting fraternal hatreds like that of Argos for Sparta, he might greatly reduce enemy resources. Though time and further experience were to prove any such assumptions about Greek politics and martial capability to be faulty, they must have seemed sound at the time. To a great warrior race drunk on fresh triumphs, the lure of pursuing even greater glory on battlefields in Europe proved irresistible.

III

The Strength of Lions: Marathon, Himera, and the Invasion of Greece (490–479 B.C.)

"[N]ot the strength of lions or of bulls shall hold [Xerxes], strength against strength; for he has the power of Zeus …"
                                                 Delphic Oracle *(Herodotus: The Histories)*

The Greek city-states fought desperately in the second decade of the 5th century to avoid being overrun by Persia and Carthage. Facing superior numbers, the Greeks prevailed by employing their more limited assets when and where they could be most effective. While naval forces and the tactics of surprise played key roles in turning the tide, it was the Doric phalanx that literally spearheaded this amazing victory against long odds. From initial resistance at Marathon and Thermopylae to final triumphs at Plataea and Mycale, hoplites emerged as lords of battle and saviors of Greek freedom.

Clashes between the Greeks and Persians at this time show a keen awareness of opposition strengths and weaknesses. The Greeks had learned all too painfully during the fighting in Ionia that Asian cavalry held an overwhelming edge in open country; thus, they avoided battle sites that exposed the vulnerable flanks of their formations to horsemen. For their part, the generals of the Great King were quick to accept that the Doric phalanx was nearly unbeatable in settings that dictated shock combat. This led to an intricate contest of move and countermove as armies sought to engage on ground favorable to their own tactical doctrine. For a variety of largely logistical reasons, the city-states were more successful at this deadly game. With most of the action taking place on Greek soil, they used secure lines of supply to maintain strong positions and lead the Persians into a number of inopportune offensives. Persian skill and valor resulted in several hard-fought battles, yet the Greeks ultimately gained a string of victories that stood in stark contrast to their earlier failures in Asia.

The War Comes to Greece

Having crushed the uprising in Ionia, Darius put his very capable nephew and son-in-law Mardonios in charge of the region. This young general set out with an army and fleet in 492 B.C. that he might secure his northeast frontier and then punish Eretria and Athens for their interference in the revolt. But this venture failed due to fleet damage from a heavy storm and losses on land due to an ambush in Thrace, forcing Mardonios to return to Asia in order to regroup. Still hoping to pave the way for wider conquests, Darius prepared another western expedition.

Marathon (490 B.C.)

Datus the Mede and Artaphernes (son of the satrap of that name during the revolt) replaced Mardonios in command of the European campaign and set out in the early summer of 490 B.C. to strike at Greece. They planned to avoid the hazards of a long overland march by attacking directly from the sea. Phoenicia provided most of the 300 ships needed for this effort, but the fleet included a small Ionian element as well. The latter made up Mardonios's storm losses and provided Greek speakers for communicating with the locals. This also had a political aspect, as bringing Ionian Greeks along forced them to demonstrate loyalty by warring against their European kin.

The Persians sailed first to the isle of Naxos. They quickly subdued this stronghold and then sent out squadrons to take control of the remaining islands of the Cyclades chain off the southeastern shores of Greece. The fleet next proceeded to Eretria, where it landed in late July and, after six days of assaults, captured the city when it was betrayed from within. Setting up base on Euboa at Carystus, the invaders were finally ready to move against Athens.

The deposed Athenian dictator Hippias came with the expedition as a Persian client, and it was upon his suggestion that they touched land on August 12 at the Bay of Marathon. In selecting this particular beachhead, located only 36 km (about 24 miles) east of Athens, Hippias sought to repeat the exploits of his youth. He had landed here in 546 B.C. along with his father Pisistratus, who had also come from Euboa to reclaim leadership of Athens. This region of Attica was aligned with the Pisistratid clan in those days and added men to a force of Argive mercenaries and others that restored his father's tyranny. The aging exile must have remembered this time fondly and chose Marathon that he might garner local support for another such return of his family to power. There was also a good tactical reason for this choice, since flat terrain above the bay was well suited for his allies' cavalry should Athens oppose the landing.

Sparabara cored Persia's army at Marathon, backed by marines from the fleet (Punic heavy peltasts and Ionian hoplites) and a few light archers. There was also cavalry that arrived aboard modified triremes. The Phoenicians had ferried horses to Cyprus in the Ionian Revolt and not needed to alter their ships for so short a voyage; but this longer trip to Europe appears to have required at least some minor conversion. A good guess at the Persians' strength comes from the size of their fleet. Each trireme could carry some 226 men — 186 in the crew (170 rowers or *nautae* and 16 sailors or *hyperesia*) plus 10 marines and 30 passengers. This allowed for 500–600 horsemen and their mounts on 100 ships (replacing the marines and passengers) plus 6,000 infantry and 3,000 marines on the other 200 vessels. Footmen seem to have included four hazaraba of Medean sparabara, one of Persian sparabara, and another of Sakae bowmen. Drafting from units left behind in Asia could have put all of these at nominal strength. The landing force was thus quite large, though nowhere near the size that Athenian legend would later make of it.

A famous painting on the colonnade at Athens (created about 30 years after the battle and described by Pausanius in the 2nd century A.D.) attested that the Phoenician fleet was at Marathon. And its reported strength at this time of 300 ships equals Plato's claim for the number of triremes in the expedition (though he added anachronistic troop transports as well). Alternatively, Herodotus reported 600 ships, but this seems less likely to reflect the actual deployment than a generic size used for Persian fleets in the absence of precise numbers. Perhaps it represented total Persian potential. Regardless, 300 ships is a much more realistic figure for the sort of punitive expedition being attempted here. Indeed, assembling a fleet of even this lesser strength was very demanding and required all that could be gathered from the

Empire's largest naval contingent (that of Phoenicia) plus an Ionian levy. (Ionia reportedly had 100 triremes in 480 B.C., but this was part of an account that [per Burn, 1984, 330–332] likely doubled the real size of the imperial fleet. Given this overstatement plus heavy losses a few years earlier at Lade, the Ionians probably sent less than 50 ships to Marathon.)

Beyond size of their fleet, Herodotus seems to have inflated other data on the Persians, as well. Yet there are clues to true Persian strength within his details. His claim that 6,400 Persians died in the engagement might actually preserve an accurate tradition on total size of the defeated army. In fact, we need only make the very reasonable assumption that the invaders had 40 ships from Ionia to calculate a landing force of precisely this size: 4,000 Medes, 1,000 Persians, 1,000 Sakae, and 400 Ionians (at ten per ship). As per classical descriptions of the battle, this excludes both horsemen and Punic marines, who didn't take part in the main action and became involved only during the retreat and subsequent fighting among the ships.

How do we account for later inflated estimates of the Persians at Marathon? Two sources of misinformation are possible. First, the Athenians very likely embroidered the story in creating a patriotic myth that covered the city and its hoplite defenders in glory. Second, due to the amphibious nature of the campaign, Persian manpower was close to 68,000 sailors, rowers, and soldiers. An impressive figure, this could well have led ancient reports to grossly multiply the force that actually fought in the battle.

Still, even at 300 ships and less than 10,000 combatants, the Persians posed a serious threat. This led the Athenians to marshal their resources while the enemy was busy on Euboa and, shortly after the fall of Eritrea, to send for help from Sparta. Philippides, a professional dispatch carrier, ran over 200km to Sparta in less than two days, arriving on August 9 with the plea for assistance. But it was past the first quarter of the lunar cycle, during the sacred Carnelian Feast, and the highly pious Spartans chose to delay marching until after this major religious event. Nonetheless, they promised to send troops to Athens in just six days, when the festival would end at the full moon on August 15.

With Sparta's pledge in hand, Athenian hoplites departed for Marathon Bay upon learning of the Persian landing. Their decision to engage well away from the city probably stemmed from the poor condition of Athens's walls at this time, Pisistratus having torn down the old barriers. The Athenians marched east through the highlands towards the hamlet of Marathon (near modern Vrana). Here, they took up a strong position in what is now the Vrana Valley in the hills to the west of the coastal lowland. Shortly thereafter, an allied contingent from the Boeotian polis of Plataea arrived to boost their numbers.

Callimachus led the Greeks as an appointed supreme commander (*polemarchos* or polemarch). His subordinates included generals from each Athenian tribe and another from Plataea (Arimnestas), these combining to form a team of advisors and line of succession should the polemarch die in battle. Miltiades was general of the Oeneis tribe and was especially influential, since service in Thrace gave him valuable knowledge of the enemy.

The Athenians seem to have organized their militia on a decimal basis, much as at Argos (where there were ten lochoi) and Sparta (five lochoi each of spartiates and perioeci). Athens thus had one regiment (later called a *taxis*, plural *taxeis*), for each of its ten tribes (the Acamantis, Aiantis, Aegeis, Antiochis, Cecropis, Erechtheis, Hippothoontis, Leontis, Oeneis, and Pandionis). The reformer Cleisthenes had created these in 507 B.C. by dividing the four Ionic clans into smaller groups more equal in size. Each tribe covered three geographic areas: the *parlia* (coast), *mesogeia* (inland), and *astu* (city). These areas subdivided into districts (*demes*) that varied in number from one to nine that they might evenly allot the population. Tribes drafted troops into their taxeis from rolls that included all middle-class males ranging from the late teens up to 60 years of age.

Sekunda and Hook (2000, 14) have proposed that the city's famed lawgiver Solon had introduced a system in 594 B.C. that gave each clan 30 war bands of 30 men each. At 900 men per clan, this created an army of 3,600. Population growth had by the turn of the century allowed for a tribal muster 500 strong — roughly equal to manpower for a contemporary Spartan lochos. Levies doubled in size later in the century to provide each tribe with two such units, much like the two-lochoi mora of Sparta. This growth of the hoplite class reflected an economic boom that had also boosted the size of the fleet and gained further steam with tax cuts in 477 B.C. Garnsey (1988, 90) has estimated that the 13,000 citizen spearmen in the field army (10,000) and aboard ships (3,000) in 431 B.C. came from a pool that was about twice that of 480–479. This indicates an average growth of 135 men per year that expanded the hoplite citizenry from 5,000 in 490 B.C. to 6,500 in 480 and a peak 13,000 in 431. As for contingent size, one lead is Miltiades' recent recruitment of a 500-strong regiment in Thrace. Other clues come from known dimensions of various institutions at Athens. Cleisthenes had formed a 500-man council to rule the city, and this is likely to have run parallel to military organization, having one representative per ten hoplites. Similarly, most juries at Athens had 500 men. We can thus reasonably project that the Athenian army at Marathon probably had 5,000 spearmen (up nearly 40 percent since Solon's day) within ten tribal units, and that Plataea added a further 600 spearmen (per its strength in 479 B.C.).

The Greeks at Marathon would also have included a crowd of attendants, with perhaps 500–600 serving as javelinmen; however, there seem to have been no horsemen or archers. Athens had at least 96 riders at the time (Spence 1993, 11–12), but these must have remained behind — a reasonable move given that the marching route required a climb unsuitable for horses. As for the city's archers, these apparently stayed home as well, maybe with the fleet. The Greek army was thus about the same size as that arrayed for its opponent, there being 6,000–6,500 fighting men on each side. Later estimates of greater Athenian manpower seem likely to have confused unit strength of the four clans from Solon's time with the lesser complements that now resided within the ten new tribal taxeis.

The confrontation at Marathon opened as something of a standoff. The Greeks clearly had no intention of risking a cavalry attack by advancing onto the coastal plain, while their foe was equally unwilling to charge into the hills. The Persians' reluctance derived from the Vrana Valley being only about 1,000m wide where the Greek lines lay at some 150m inside its mouth (Delbruck 1990, 81), which would require them to advance into the valley if they were to engage with their bows. There, the flanks of the phalanx could rest against mountainous terrain that had scattered trees, precluding the sort of mounted envelopment that had worked so well in Asia. The Greeks had also enhanced their natural protection with an *abatis*, a crude wooden impediment or "line of trees" (*arborum tractu*) per Cornelius Nepos. This jerry-built barricade stretched across almost 200m on the north (left) end of their line, shortening the front and allowing their hoplites to cover the remaining gap at greater depth.

Building of artificial barriers to impede cavalry was a tactic borrowed from the crafty Spartan monarch Cleomenes. Frontinus recorded that Cleomenes cut down trees and used their clutter to help defeat the mounted allies of Hippias in 510 B.C., when the dictator was driven from Athens. This ploy reversed the tactical situation, as these same horsemen had repulsed the king's earlier advance on the city. The democratic Athenian allies of Cleomenes, many of whom were among those camped at Marathon, must have put that memory to good use in shoring up their defenses. It's ironic that this tactic would play a role in Hippias's last defeat, much as it had in his first some 20 years earlier.

From their commanding position in the valley, the Greeks could threaten the flank of any march on Athens. Likewise, they could strike from the rear should their foes attempt to reboard. Hampered thus from leaving by either land or sea, the invaders faced a stalemate favoring their opponents. The Persians had weak logistics, subsisting on what they could bring by ship or forage from the countryside. The Greeks, on the other hand, had an unimpeded line of supply through the hills back to Athens. Moreover, the longer the Asians remained in place, the worse things got as they depleted the surrounding area of food and time grew short before the Spartan troops would arrive (warning of this threat had no doubt come from Hippias's friends in Athens). On August 16, a day after the Spartans had promised to depart, the Persian commanders decided that they could wait no longer and must hazard an attack into the Vrana Valley. This was the only way to clear the way to Athens before the Greek reinforcements could tip the balance of manpower.

Seeing the Persians approach, the Greeks arrayed into a phalanx facing east within the valley. Using a plan that Miltiades and others had worked out during the days of waiting, some 1,000 men of Leontis (led by Themistocles) and Antiochis (under Aristides) formed up four ranks deep along 250m in the center of this formation. The Plataeans and another 1,500 Athenians (three tribes, possibly including the Oeneis under Miltiades) set up on the left wing across just over 250m (up to the edge of the abatis) at eight deep. The remaining 2,500 Athenians (the other five taxeis, including the Aiantid tribe of Calimachus on the end) covered just over 300m at a depth of eight shields on the right wing, reaching all the way to the slopes on the south. The phalanx thus fronted along some 800m, with psiloi and attendants (the "slaves" of Herodotus) then manning the abatis up to the north edge of the valley.

The Persians would have marched toward the Greeks in battle formation. The hazarabam of ethnic Persians and the Sakae likely held the center, with the Medes divided between the wings and the Ionians on the far right. Once near enough to see their foes, it's probable that the Persians reduced files to only eight deep in order to match width of front. Their files had at least a shield-bearer or two in the lead, with sparabara carrying out multiple duties on this front wall and as both spearmen and archers among the Medes on either wing and in front of the Sakae bowmen in the center. This left the 50-meter stretch of Ionian hoplites on the extreme right as the only portion of the Persian line that had no backing archers. As for the Asians' cavalry, it doesn't appear to have participated in any preliminary skirmishing and probably took post in the far rear.

The Persians marched into the valley until within bow range at 150–175m from their rearmost rank. They then opened fire from behind a wall of spara in a reprise of the tactics that had been so successful in Ionia. This time, however, their hoplite opponents had no worry about cavalry; thus, well armored and facing arrows only from the front, they took little fright or real damage. Moreover, having learned from their defeat at Ephesos, the Athenians had no intention of remaining a static target. Therefore, on signal (possibly when arrow fire began to fall off), they charged, trotting the last 20–30m to launch a vicious spear assault.

This charge at Marathon marked a significant advance in Athenian tactics. Herodotus cites it as the earliest example known to him of attacking "on the run" (*dromo*). Indeed, those who fought at Marathon (the Marathonomachai) would later refer to the novelty of their assault in boasting of their presence at the battle with the simple phrase "I ran." Yet this seems to have already been common practice in the Peloponnese among all but the Spartans, who preferred a more measured pace to showcase their deadly intent and better maintain formation. At Marathon, any such concern for orderly advance lost out to a need to cross the killing ground of missile fire as quickly as possible. Persians archers were thus able to loose no more than a few volleys at the Athenian rush before it struck their front.

The Persian center held firm under this spear attack, as it had the best troops and faced only short Greek files that couldn't exert strong othismos. It was front-fighter against front-

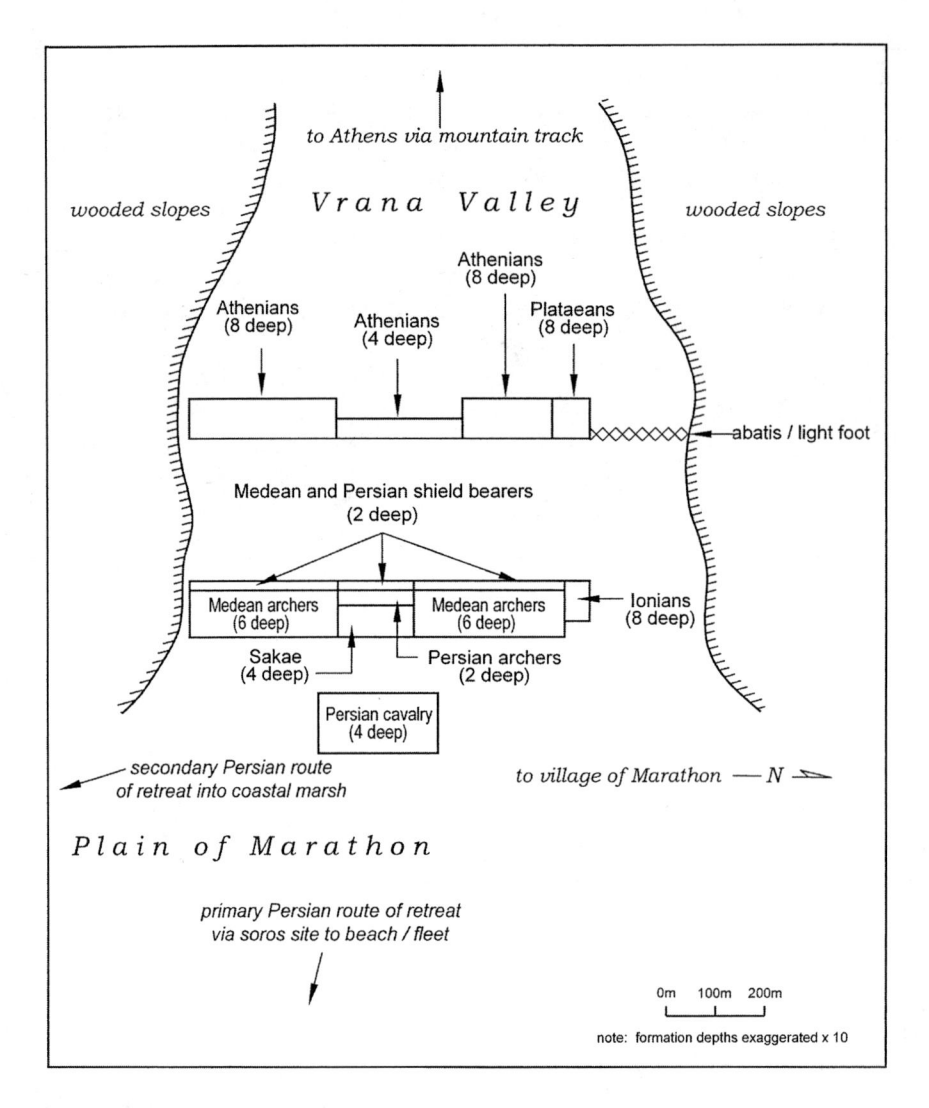

BATTLE OF MARATHON (490 B.C.)

fighter here and the sparabara forced their foes backwards. Herodotus said that the Persians went so far as to penetrate the middle of Athens' line, but this seems quite unlikely in light of the phalanx's ability to hold formation elsewhere. It's more probable that the Greek center merely fell back a bit and didn't actually break.

Things went very differently on the wings, where the deeper-filed Greeks managed to advance. There, the mainland hoplites took advantage of both the Ionians' relative inexperience in othismos and innate weakness of the thin Persian shield wall to push opposing frontfighters ever rearward. These had no choice but to give ground, doing so in a rising state of panic as they struggled awkwardly to even stay on their feet, let alone fight back. The Greek phalanx was soon able to turn both flanks. Fearing envelopment, the Asians on either wing took flight, with the less dedicated Ionians no doubt in the lead, but followed closely by the Medes.

The previous advance and near breakthrough by the Persians' center became a liability when their heavily pressured wings broke. Letting the routed men flee from each flank, the

Greeks held reasonable line order and folded in from both sides on the Persians, Sakae, and remaining Medes holding the center. Faced with attacks from three directions at once, the unarmored Sakae must have been first to lose heart and make a frightened run for the rear. The sparabara were made of sterner stuff, yet finally gave in as well, as their foes closed almost completely around and compressed them amidst a deafening din into a stunned and ineffective mass. The last of the imperial formation fell apart then, with its beaten warriors making with all possible speed for refuge with their fleet.

The initial pursuit was deadly and took a steep toll on the fleeing Asians, with Ctesias claiming that those lost included Datus. Confused and desperate, many Persians ran straight from the valley toward a swampy area along the coast to the south, rather than in the direction of their beached ships to the east. They stumbled into the marsh and mired down in the soft ground to let the frenzied Greeks catch and slaughter them. Meanwhile, the cavalry unit standing in reserve had lacked position and/or the opportunity to intercede. Caught up and swept along in the terrified rearward rush of such a large body of men, these horsemen had no real chance to rally their infantry, though they would eventually recover to screen the last stage of retreat.

The Greeks gave chase and engaged in a running combat from where the action had first turned. This was inside the valley proper, where a burial mound or *soros* sits that contains pottery dating to the period of the battle (Barber 1990, 237) and bodies that might include Plataeans and others who fell early on (though Lazenby [1993, 75] disputes this). Another soros lays some 3km (2 miles) farther out on the plain. This is an Athenian gravesite that probably marks the end of the Greek pursuit, where the last Athenian must have fallen in the chase. Hoplites were poorly suited for such work and the enemy's horsemen no doubt brought down a number of them at this point. The Greeks therefore stopped to catch their breath and regroup that they might prevent opposing riders from picking them off individually with bow or lance. Pritchett (1960, 159–160) reports the recovery of Asian-style arrowheads from this area, which are very likely souvenirs from the mounted effort made to cover the Persian retreat.

With ranks redressed, the Greeks advanced on the landing site and went into action against remnants of the Persian battle force and Punic marines protecting the fleet. A goodly number of men now fell in a fierce fight, including the polemarch Callimachus, the Athenian strategos Stesilaos, and Cynegirus, brother of the playwright Aeschylus (who was also present). Despite the Athenians' best efforts, their foes had gained enough time while the hoplites reorganized out on the plain to reboard most of their men and get clear. As a consequence, the battle on the beach resulted in capture of only seven vessels and a few horses. Nonetheless, Marathon was a great victory for Greece at very modest cost. A majority of Athens' meager losses on the day (said to be only around 200 men) must have come against horsemen at the end of the initial pursuit, with the rest split between the Persian anchorage and the engagement site in the Vrana Valley. These actions being so spread out, it makes a good deal of sense that the Athenians would choose to locate their burial mound on the plain. This put it between the battle's turning point inside the valley and its finish on the beach and thus central to where their men had fallen.

The Persians under Artaphernes most likely recovered their cached booty at this juncture and simply sailed home (Hippias dying along the way). Herodotus, however, said that they headed along the 90-kilometer sea route to Athens and, true or not, the Athenians moved to preempt any such threat from the sea. They sent a runner to warn Athens (the first "marathoner"—Thersippos if we follow Plutarch, but Eucles according to others) and then posted the strategos Aristides and his tribal levy to guard the spoils while the rest of the army set out for Athens, possibly with Miltiades now acting as polemarch in place of the fallen Callimachus. Delbruck (1990, 72) estimated that this forced march might have taken as little as eight hours. At any rate, it seems to have brought the army back well before the Persians could have arrived (Rogers [1937, 25] put sailing time from Marathon at 30 hours). Thus, even if a fleet was indeed approaching Athens, rapid Greek repositioning discouraged its landing. Arrival of a Spartan force of 2,000 hoplites the next day then firmly secured the city.

Whether they departed from Marathon on August 16 or a few days later from Athens, the Persians sailed away short of their goal. Early victories in the Cyclades and on Euboa had not led to success in the more important effort against Athens. It was a failed campaign that brought great national embarrassment. Worse yet, events at home would soon insure a long wait for any chance to erase this stain on Persian honor.

Reflections on Marathon

As one of the most famous battles of all time, Marathon has often been the starting point for discussions on the history of warfare. Yet many aspects of the engagement remain vague and their interpretation has led to a great deal of controversy. The foregoing reconstruction risks adding to these disputes, but is consistent with the most contemporary accounts that we have (those of Herodotus and Ephoros, the latter via Cornelius Nepos). It also owes a great debt to Hans Delbruck, whose detailed studies on ancient warfare were sometimes radical, yet always rich with logic. It's worthwhile at this point to discuss some of the major areas of debate in more detail and comment on the battle's historical impact.

SPLITTING OF THE PERSIAN ARMY • The presence of a huge Persian land force at Marathon has often been the subject of dispute. Clearly, if the invaders outnumbered their foes by two times or more then they would have used a portion of their force to pin down the Greek army as they moved with the rest to attack Athens by sea. This might explain why the Persian contingent that fought at Marathon was smaller than could fit on the 600 ships of Herodotus. In this light, a comment in the Suda (a Byzantine lexicon of the 10th century A.D.) that the Asian cavalry was "away" has fueled speculation that the Greeks faced only a modest rearguard.

Such a split-army scenario is both viable and consistent with a battle on the scale of the above reconstruction. If the invaders had divided for an alternate approach, then the Athenians would have turned about straight away to return home, refusing to risk their irreplaceable phalanx in a distant and now meaningless action. This would have forced the Persians onto the offensive in order to keep the Greek army from reinforcing Athens. And an attack into Vrana Valley to do this would have created just the match-up proposed here if it involved about half the landing force from a fleet of 600 ships.

Nevertheless, while the Persians could have parted their forces in the face of the enemy, it seems unlikely that they actually did so. First, we have no evidence that a Greek withdrawal prompted the Persian advance as called for in this scenario. If anything, ancient accounts paint the Greeks as the aggressors. Next, the invaders needed to defeat the Athenian army in the field, seaborne attack or not, yet would have been foolish indeed to seek this absolutely critical victory with only half their manpower. Finally, no classical account records the split-force tactic, while the lone later source is hardly reliable. The Suda tale derives from Ionian claims to have leaked Persian plans, which seems likely to have been a self-serving fiction fostered long after the fact to rationalize the Asian Greeks' unpatriotic role in so storied an event. Taking all of this together with valid arguments for a smaller fleet suggests that the Persians probably engaged with as much of their landing force as they could. If so, any move on Athens by ship came only after the engagement and in accordance with Herodotus's account.

CASUALTIES • The Persians' ability to seriously pose a threat after Marathon shows that their losses couldn't have been as high as claimed by Herodotus. It's proposed here that his casualty figure more reasonably reflects the size of the total force engaged. On the other end of the scale, the victors vowed to annually sacrifice one goat for each Persian killed, but initially offered up just 500 animals, with later celebrations involving only 300 victims. Just as Herodotus's tally was too high, these numbers are clearly too low and we need to rely on analogs for a better estimate. Based on an extended combat and hard pursuit, a good guess at Persian losses would be 2–3,000 men. In fact, such a 40 percent toll would have been unusually heavy by historical norms, even though it's less than half of Herodotus's figure.

By contrast to his death toll for the invaders, Herodotus's statement of Greek fatalities (192 Athenian hoplites plus some Plataeans and light-armed men) is sure to be much more accurate. After all, the names of the dead would still have been a matter of public record at the time (Pausanias noted their inscription at the battle site even in his day). But this understates the real damage. Hoplite deaths probably added up to more like 300 if we include Plataeans and those later succumbing to wounds, with total casualties (dead and injured combined) likely more on the order of 1,000. All the same, this remains a very modest butcher's bill, putting the victors' loses at only one man for every 20–30 among their enemy.

PERSIAN CAVALRY • The aforementioned Suda entry cites a signal that the invading horsemen were absent, and they play no role in ancient accounts of the battle. However, Herodotus hinted at their presence in reporting Persian surprise that their foes would charge without archers or mounted cover, which implied that the Asians had both these assets. Nepos, drawing on Ephoros, likewise assumed the presence of cavalry when he described using trees to shield the Greek flanks. Similarly, Pausanius said that ghostly sounds lingering at Marathon included the neighing of horses — something that made sense only if there was a tradition of cavalry taking part in the fight. The orator Aristeides reinforced this idea with his claim that a few horses were captured at Marathon. There are also two images thought to derive from the same painting of the battle on the Athenian colonnade that showed the Punic fleet (Santosuosso 1997, 33). One is a sarcophagus that portrays a horse among combatants before the sterns of two ships. The other is a frieze at Athens on the acropolis temple of Nike, which depicts a Greek warrior fighting a mounted Asian.

As a practical matter, the Persians had taken great pains to bring horsemen along and certainly would have used them in any plan of attack. It must therefore have been a combination of the Vrana Valley's wooded slopes and the Greek abatis that confined their deployment to a position at the far rear. Acting as a detached guard, these mounted troops could still serve to strike fear into the horse-wary Greeks. They might also provide stiffening to boost resolve among their fronting infantry. Most of all, they were in good position to come forward in pursuit or, as was the historical case, fall back to screen a retreat.

THE BATTLE SITE • Not only have the forces engaged at Marathon been controversial, but the exact spot at which they came to blows has also been in dispute. The present reconstruction differs from many accounts that assume the action began with a Greek charge onto the plain. The latter would put the Athenian soros along the initial battle line, rather than at the end of the pursuit as proposed by Delbruck (1990, 76) and endorsed by Gabriel and Boose (1994, 149).

In fact, a Greek advance out of the valley is dubious in view of previous Athenian experience with cavalry on open ground. The overwhelming message of these past actions was that challenging mounted troops without flank cover was to invite destruction. The Greeks took careful note of this maxim throughout their attempts to counter the Persian invasion. Indeed, a lone exception only served to underscore the concept when a hoplite column came to grief against cavalry on the plain at Plataea (479 B.C.). Also standing against a Greek offensive is that it made much better sense to wait for the Spartans. While it could be argued that the Athenians might have struck prematurely to avoid sharing the glory with Sparta, their earlier actions don't support this. They had actively sought Spartan aid, rather than tried to avoid it. It's far easier to imagine that the nervous men sitting above the huge Persian fleet were much less worried about Athenian renown than for their own survival.

The Greeks' need to ward cavalry, the logic of waiting for help from Sparta, pressure on the Persians to attack, and archeological support for combat within the Vrana Valley (Lewis 1984, 606–607) all point to the battle starting out in the hills. What then ensued was a running fight that stretched from just inside the mouth of the vale to the area of the Athenian soros and thence to the shore.

How important was Marathon to western history? While it's impossible to isolate the effects of this one action from the web of events it influenced, we can say that its claim to greatness rests on solid ground. True, the defeat did little damage to Persia's military potential (later battles at Salamis, Plataea, and Mycale were all more effective in this regard). Yet this was still a critical event for European civilization. The importance of what Athens achieved at Marathon lies in what it preserved, rather than in what it destroyed. The Athenians could easily have shared the fate of their neighbors at Eretria and ceased to be a major power. Without Marathon, there would have been no free Athens to build a fleet and bring the Persians down at Salamis, and no Athenian phalanx to hold the left flank at Plataea or fight to victory at Mycale. Without these later triumphs on sea and land, Greece might have become just another Persian satrapy, with all the consequences for western history that implies. The battle of Marathon saved Athens to fight another day and, in so doing, rightfully earned its lasting fame.

The Persian Invasion

The expedition to Marathon had certainly not been an all-out effort and Darius must have seen its failure as no more than a minor setback along the path to conquering Europe. He immediately began planning another campaign against the Greeks under his personal command. An uprising in Egypt delayed this work, and then came the death of the Great King in 486 B.C. Darius's eldest son, Xerxes, had to spend the next few years consolidating his succession. He had recovered Egypt by early 484 B.C., but a new effort against Europe had to wait again when Babylon went into revolt in 482 B.C. Once his general Megabyzus had quelled this last disturbance, Xerxes was finally free to complete preparations for a campaign of western conquest. He now stood poised to march into Greece at the head of the greatest army ever assembled.

The Host of Xerxes

How large was the Persian invasion force? Herodotus claimed that 1.8 million fighting men came from Asia—1,700,000 on foot and 100,000 mounted on horses, chariots, and camels. Moreover, this figure didn't cover support personnel, including tens of thousands in the fleet. The historian might well have derived his number from an official roster. In fact, he could have accessed such a document through his known acquaintance with Zopyrus, grandson of Megabyzus. If so, we can put some trust in his list of contingents, but their manpower is another matter. The huge force cited must have reflected availability of each troop type in its nominal entirety—far more men than could possibly have been committed to the Greek campaign.

Ctesias drew on Persian sources to claim 800,000 fighting men went with Xerxes. He used only about half the units of Herodotus, an approach that modern writers like Olmstead (1948) and Burn (1984) have also taken, yet still seems to have relied upon inflated "paper" strengths. Only a fraction of this potential could ever have gathered at one time and remained in the field. Many investigators have thus proposed fewer Persian combatants. These include Green (1970b) with 210,000, Burn (1984) with 200,000, Connolly (1981) with 187,000, and Nelson (1975a) with 149,500. Even lower figures have come from Lazenby (1993, with 70–80,000) and Delbruck (1990, with 65–75,000). These all fall within the bounds of General Sir Frederick Maurice's assessment of supply potential. He examined the route to Greece and claimed (Burn 1984, 328–329) that it could support only about 210,000 men and 75,000 animals. And indeed, if we examine the army's likely manpower unit by unit, we do seem to get totals very close to his limits.

The Persians built their host around sparabara in the army's first five corps (I-V). Each "Iranian" nation might have had nominal sparabara manpower for six baivaraba, but could likely mobilize no more than two per corps for a long foreign campaign. Corps I was an elite force among these. Known as the "Immortals" (possibly "Amrtaka" in Persian), this unit contained Persians, Medes, and Elamites, who formed a regular baivaraba as well as a separate hazarabam of 1,000 royal bodyguards from noble families. The other four corps (one each of Persians, Medes, Cissians, and Hyrkanians) each contained two full baivaraba. This force would have begun the march to Europe somewhat shorthanded and lost more men in route; thus, it was probably at no more than 80 percent of parade strength entering Thessaly, giving Xerxes some 73,000 sparabara in all.

Herodotus referred to the Immortals as "spear carriers" (*arstibara* in Persian), and they seem to have used both spear and bow, with 20 percent (two ranks in battle) likely bearing a shield as well. As noted, their numbers included royal bodyguards. Some believe that there was only a single, separate unit of these; however, a description of the army on parade suggests that there were two—one within and one outside the regular division of Immortals. This would have been parallel to the cavalry guard, which is known to have formed two hazaraba. Waterfield (2006, 2) has suggested that the term "Immortals" might have been a misinterpretation of the Persian word for "attendants," but it's more likely that it came from the practice of keeping the two guard hazaraba at full strength by drawing men as needed from other units. Sparabara that carried shields were elites that provided candidates for elevation to the Immortals when openings arose, with shield-bearers among the Immortals then being first in line to become royal bodyguards.

In addition to sparabara, there were about 40,000 auxiliary troops within another 25 corps (VI-XXX). Most of these troops were lightly equipped, with only the Assyrians, Chaldeans, Lydians, and Exiles (either Iranians of some sort or relocated Ionians) having gear heavy enough for use in the main line of battle. These levies were tasked with supporting sparabara in the main line of battle, but their main purpose was to make a political statement, since the presence of each contingent attested its nation's loyalty to the Great King. As such, these were probably smaller "token" units that were brigaded in pairs, with each corps consisting of around 1,600 men (two hazaraba at 80 percent nominal strength). Addition of these troops yielded a total infantry force of something like 76,000 frontline soldiers and 37,000 skirmishers.

Xerxes' cavalry arm consisted of twenty hazaraba in eight corps. The first three corps formed a baivarabam (ten hazaraba) of Iranian medium cavalry armed with a combination of spears and bows. The remaining mounted troops combined to make another baivarabam, this one of light cavalry armed solely with bows. This suggests some 16,000 troopers in all (nearly one for each five line infantrymen). Corps I had 3,500 Persians in four hazaraba, including two guard units at 1,000 riders each. The rest of Corps I, II (Medes), and III (Cissian/Kashite) provided replacements for these guards, which put their hazaraba at about 750 men each or 75 percent of nominal. Corps IV–VIII (Indian, Bactrian/Sakae, Caspian, Paricanian, and Arabian respectively) were each composed of 1,600 mounted archers, two hazaraba at 80 percent nominal strength. One note of special interest here is that half of Corps VII rode camels, though it's not known how many of these actually got to Greece, since they suffered inordinately from attacks by lions during the march from Asia.

These mounted forces brought the army up to some 129,000 fighting men. A huge crowd of attendants must also have been present. Assuming a reasonable 2 to 3 ratio of support staff to combatants, Xerxes would have had about 215,000 men in all — 113,000 infantry, 16,000 cavalry, and 86,000 others. If we put the beasts at around 70,000 (one pack animal for each four men plus 16,000 cavalry mounts), we get a total of nearly 285,000 men and animals. This closely matches General Maurice's assessment of maximum supply capability.

The Persians wintered around Sardis at the end of 481 B.C. before setting out in the spring along a route carefully prepared by their engineers. They transited the Hellespont in seven days over twin bridges built across the hulls of obsolete ships and then spanned and crossed the river Strymon in Thrace. They had cached stores along the route and distributed these by sea to points farther forward, a logistical feat carried out by a huge fleet (at least some 600 or so triremes plus a large number of lesser craft) that accompanied the advance. The Persians eased passage of this armada by boldly cutting a canal across the Mount Athos peninsula, which let them avoid the waters where storms had previously thwarted Mardonios. Xerxes' host thus moved relentlessly around the northern Aegean and descended through the plains of Thessaly in the heat of late summer.

Greece Prepares

As plans for the invasion advanced during the late 480s, the Greek states remained embroiled in inter-city warfare. Finds at Olympia show that the second-rank Peloponnesian poleis of Sicyon and Phlius fought a couple of battles in this period. Again, it's likely that eschatia lay at the core of the conflict, with the antagonists contesting farmland on their mutual border along the Asopos River. This seems to have been a triumph of the underdog, as Phlius, with only around 1,000–1,500 hoplites in its army, either defeated or at least traded victories with its larger neighbor, which could field up to 3,200 spearmen. (Yet numbers appear to have won out in the end, since the Sicyonians captured a decisive final meeting against Phlius c. 475 B.C.) Given the incomplete record for these years, this must have been only one of a number of traditional, small-scale conflicts that diverted Greek attention from the pending Persian threat.

The exception to such seemingly suicidal lack of awareness was in Athens. There, the general Themistocles had convinced the electorate to use proceeds from recently discovered silver mines to construct more warships. Promoted as a means to counter threats from nearby rival Aigina, there seems to be little doubt that the larger fleet was intended all along to oppose another seaborne Persian campaign. Soon, however, news began to filter in on the amazing scope of the Great King's preparations. Xerxes probably engineered these leaks, releasing captured spies so as to frighten and discourage his foes. But rather than daunting them, this finally energized the Greeks to act. They marshaled most of the mainland south of Thessaly (with the notable exception of Argos) into a league of resistance. The Spartans headed all land forces and held nominal command of the allied fleet, though as a practical matter, it was the Athenians who must have dominated naval operations.

Thermopylae (480 B.C.)

Seeking to block the Persian advance, the Greeks first sent a force of 10,000 hoplites to the pass of Tempe, north of Thessaly at the entrance to Greece proper, but found this position to be indefensible and quickly abandoned it. They then decided to make a stand farther south at Thermopylae and Artemisium. Thermopylae was a very slim passage between the mountains and sea that would be difficult for a large army to circumvent, while Artemisium was a strait suitable for blockade that lay between the mainland north of Thermopylae and the northern tip of the large island of Euboa. Coordinated defense of these "choke points" would stall the Persian host in a spot useless for cavalry and isolated from its fleet. At the same time, the Great King's ships would have to operate in confined waters where their numbers yielded little benefit.

It's likely that the focus of Greek strategy at this time was on the effort at sea. There seemed to be little hope for beating Persian land forces in open battle; however, a Greek naval success was much more feasible. Victory over the imperial fleet would disrupt Xerxes' line of supply and sharply reduce or terminate his offensive. Thus, the task of the Greeks at Thermopylae was not to defeat the Persians outright, but rather to hold them long enough for their ships to blunt or turn the invasion through action at sea.

Sparta's Leonidas (half-brother and successor to Cleomenes) moved to defend Thermopylae with an army that boasted close to 4,000 Peloponnesian hoplites of good quality. These included an elite bodyguard of 300 spartiates and (according to Diodorus and Isocrates) 700 other Lacedaemonians. The latter were probably perioeci, but could even have been freed helots. Other spearmen came from Tegea (500), Mantinea (500), Orchomenos (120), elsewhere in Arcadia (1,000), Mycenae (80), Phlius (200), and Corinth (400).

Besides his core force of Peloponnesians, Leonidas also picked up 4,000 hoplites from north and central Greece. There were 1,000 from Malis in Thessaly, 1,000 from Locris, 900–1,000 from Phocis, 400 from Thebes (led by Leontiades), and 700 from Thespiae (under Demophilus). The Boeotians from Thebes and Thespiae were by far the best men among these allies. In all, the Spartan king now had about 8,000 spearmen to defend the pass, as well as a modest force of psiloi (another 700–800 men drawn from a large group of attendants). This was not a small army by Greek standards, being nearly half again larger than the one fielded by Athens at Marathon ten years earlier. In fact, it was very likely the largest hoplite army to see combat in mainland Greece up to that time. Still, Greek strength paled in comparison to that of Xerxes' host, which held an edge in manpower of around 15 to 1.

Leonidas marched rapidly to arrive at Thermopylae several days ahead of the Persians in mid–August. He first set up a base in the village of Alpeni at the eastern end of the 6-kilometer-long, east-west-trending coastal pass and then moved on to station his army at the tightest point inside the pass. Known as the Middle Gate (between the West and East Gates), this was where the path between the Malian Gulf on the north and the mountainside to the south narrowed to only 15 meters (50 feet) wide. The Phocians had built a low wall here during the late 6th century as defense against intruders from Thessaly (McInerney 1999, 174–175). Leonidas immediately set his men to restore this now dilapidated field work.

As work proceeded on the wall, some locals brought word that there was a rough alternative path through the mountains. This was the Anopaia, named as per the highlands to the south, which, though little more than a goat track, might allow the Persians to bypass the Greek position at the Middle Gate. Leonidas quickly took the precaution of posting his Phocian hoplites to block this route and then raided north of Thermopylae to gather or spoil all foodstuffs and deny them to the fast approaching enemy.

When Xerxes arrived, he camped along the Spercheios River and took no action against the pass for four days. This delay was necessary to scout the Greeks (by riders per Herodotus, but possibly sending swimmers into the Gulf as well) and to gather up his huge army from its distended line of march. Moreover, delaying an attack gave him a chance to negate Leonidas's strong position by means of a naval landing farther south. Though the Greek ships off Artemisium prevented direct amphibious assault down the narrow channel between Euboa and the mainland, it was still possible to make an end run around this blockade along the eastern side of Euboa. However, bad weather came to the aid of Greece when a vicious storm wrecked a Persian task force before it could carry out this envelopment.

Frustrated at sea, Xerxes had no choice but to launch a direct assault against the Greeks inside Thermopylae. He chose the Medean sparabara of Corps III under the general Tigranes for this task, as they had extra motivation. The Medes thirsted for atonement of the defeat visited on their nation a decade earlier at Marathon, with many seeking revenge for relatives fallen in that battle. These determined warriors moved out of their camp in the early morning light to initiate what was to become an extremely fierce and costly three-day series of battles.

The First Assault/Medes

As Tigranes' men filed into the pass from the west, the Greeks assembled on a narrow front (some 50m across) just outside the Phocian wall. This forward stance would allow them to advance and use othismos. It also gave room for special Spartan tactics of false retreat and counterattack. Leonidas and his bodyguard moved out along the entire front (six men deep and 50 wide), while the rest of the hoplites would have followed in groups of 400 that were arrayed eight deep and 50 across. The Greeks must have used the long wait before the Persian attack to work out this order, taking care to place men into national units or compatibly mix them in the case of smaller contingents.

Depending on how much of the Greek army stood in front of the wall, its van extended anywhere from a few tens of meters up to as much as 300m toward the enemy forming up to the west. The leading phalanx of Spartans, with their king standing in the ranks, had one flank flush to the cliffs on the left and the other extending to the edge of the Malian Gulf. As a result of this natural anchoring for the hoplite formation, Greek psiloi didn't need to screen its wings, and must have gone to the rear after some preliminary skirmishing ahead of the battle line.

Assuming that both baivaraba of Corps III deployed for action, the Medes placed their front rank at least 700m into the pass from the West Gate. Their entire force could then set up behind it, arrayed to match both the terrain and Greek frontage. Each hazarabam stood 50 men wide and 16 deep, most likely with about 10m spacing between hazaraba. As the West Gate lay about 3km from the Phocian wall, the leading Persian elements set up no more than

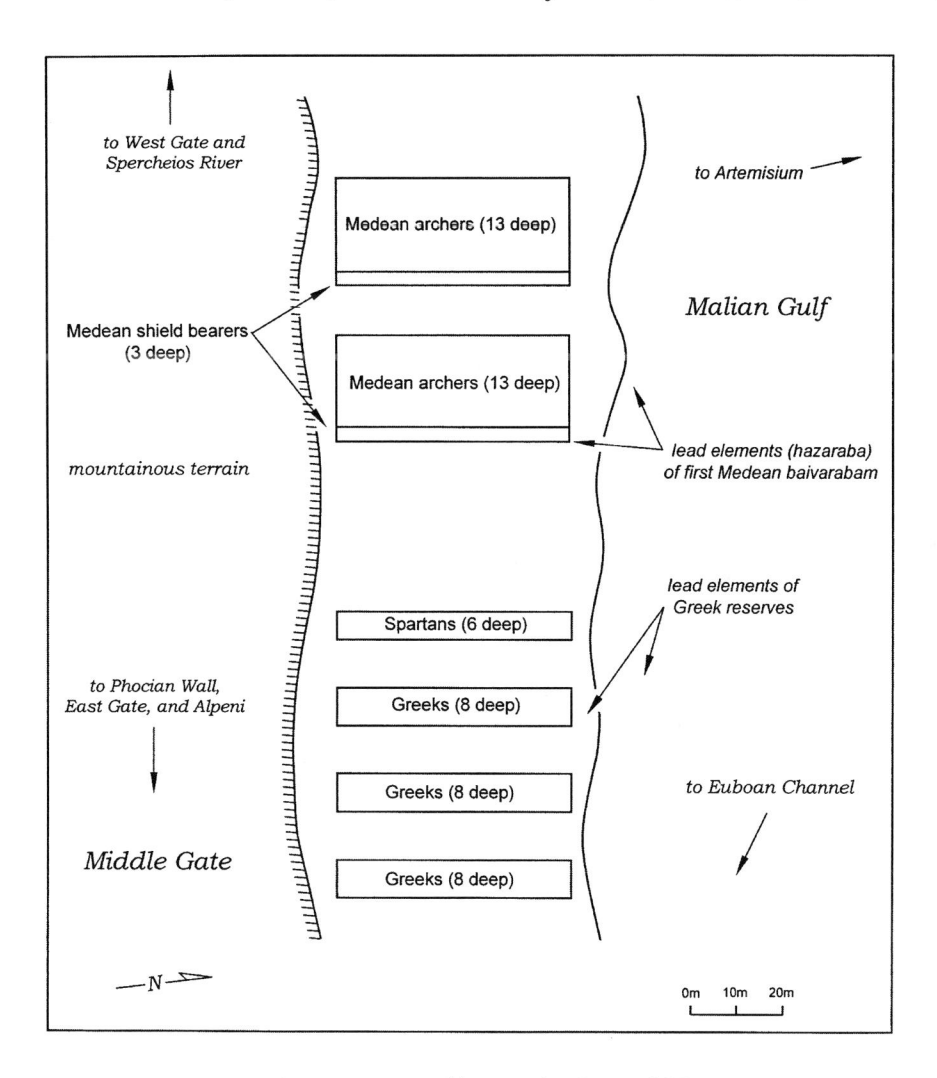

[Diagram: Battle of Thermopylae tactical map showing Medean archers (13 deep) in two formations backed by Medean shield bearers (3 deep), facing Spartans (6 deep) and three Greek units (8 deep) between mountainous terrain and the Malian Gulf, with Middle Gate at the south. Labels indicate routes to West Gate and Spercheios River, to Artemisium, to Phocian Wall, East Gate, and Alpeni, and to Euboan Channel. Lead elements (hazaraba) of first Medean baivarabam and lead elements of Greek reserves are marked. Scale: 0m, 10m, 20m. North arrow included.]

BATTLE OF THERMOPYLAE (480 B.C.) — DAY 1 / MORNING

2km from the first line of Spartans to the east. Some 20 percent of the Medes carried spara shield and spear (two men per dathabam) and these would have filled the first three ranks of each hazarabam in such tight quarters. Most of the sparabara in the next three rows had spear and bow, with the remaining ten men in each file carrying bow and sword.

Once in order, Tigranes' men marched forward to come within bow reach of the Greek phalanx (50–75m separation of the fronts would have moved the first three hazaraba into range of the Spartans). The lead hazarabam then set up its shield wall and the Medes laid down a barrage of arrows from their rear ranks. Heavily armored and shielded, the Spartans shrugged aside the falling shafts and, on signal from Leonidas, began a methodical advance. They crossed the relatively short zone of free-fire and smashed heavily into the line of wicker shields. Taking down a number of enemy front-fighters in this first powerful collision, the Spartans screened themselves from arrows behind the rear profile of the rest and reduced the battle to one of shock combat. Clearly, these conditions didn't favor the Persians' style of warfare, being closer to those they suffered under at Marathon than to the more open settings exploited in Ionia. The mainland Greeks, and especially the grim spartiate professionals, not only had sturdier equipment, but were also masters of phalanx tactics ideally suited to this kind of fighting.

Engaged hand-to-hand, the longer weapons and relentless othismos pushing from the Spartan files inflicted much greater damage on the lighter-equipped Asians than they could possibly return. The Medes must have been struggling valiantly to keep order and hold their ground in the confused crush of battle when, suddenly, the Spartans pulled back on signal and began to retreat. Sensing a quick victory, the Asian shield-bearers gave chase. Then, just as suddenly as they had withdrawn, the spartiates wheeled back on command. They once more rushed forward in a momentum-enhanced surge of muscle and metal that slammed into the now disordered Medean front. Their feigned retreat and countercharge not only made the hoplites difficult targets for any lingering arrow fire, but also broke up the opposing shield wall. By inducing the Medes into premature pursuit, the Spartans isolated many of their front fighters and inflicted hideous casualties on them with a new rush of spear points.

Heavy losses among those bearing lance and spara at the front now opened a path into the shieldless Medean mid-ranks. Thrusting and stabbing, the Spartans penetrated the shattered enemy van and quickly carried their attack past a few rows of Persians wielding spears. This assault then fell upon the archers beyond, pitting heavily equipped hoplites against men able to fight back with only a sword and armored with no more than a cloak wrapped around one arm. Such a physical mismatch goes far to explain the high death toll sustained by the Medes in this battle. Truly, it must have been more of a slaughter than a stand-up fight as Leonidas and his men punched deep into the opposing array. The first hazarabam of sparabara soon gave way, sending panicked survivors streaming rearward around the regiments still in formation to the west.

As the second hazarabam of Medes prepared to take up the fight, the Spartans charged to put this next group to the spear. They engaged and then repeated their tactic of false flight to the same deadly effect. (Herodotus claimed that this worked more than once, though just how many times remains speculative.) We don't know how long the spartiates continued at the front, but it might have been no more than half an hour. At this point, as a new hazarabam shed the confusion created by the retreat of its predecessor and readied for battle, the Spartans pulled out to be replaced by a fresh phalanx of around 400 hoplites at eight shields deep. In this way the Greeks were able to avoid exhaustion of their smaller force during the engagement, which was quite prolonged by the usual standards of hoplite warfare (battles normally lasting less than an hour). Leonidas had the manpower to field as many as 17 such 400-hoplite rotations behind his own spartiates, but it's more likely that only the most reliable of his mixed force (the 4,800 Peloponnesians and Boeotians, enough for a dozen rotations) actually got into the fight.

After Leonidas and his spartiates shifted out, their replacements (perhaps half of the Lacedaemonian perioeci, if actually present, or the ever-combative Thespians) advanced quickly to renew shock contact with the enemy. While these amateur hoplites lacked the skill to use a countercharge like the spartiates, their superior panoply and othismos still let them eventually rout the next hazarabam. Again, the Greeks would have taken advantage of temporary Medean disorder to move fresh troops into the front and resume the unequal fight. Finally, after two or three hours of combat and possibly half a dozen rotations by the Greeks, the Persians called off their assault. The Medes, having taken heavy loss without making effective headway against their foe, followed remnants of the latest broken hazarabam back through the West Gate under cover of arrow fire. The defenders of Thermopylae would not have pursued them far, preferring to resume their stance in front of the Phocian wall.

Persian losses were frightful. Even though it's likely that the second baivarabam never worked its way to the front, we can reasonably project that at least 800 Medes (10 percent) of the lead baivarabam fell on the field of battle. Another 4,000 would have struggled away wounded, with about 500 dying over the next few days. Thus, around 1,300 of the Great King's men probably lost their lives in the opening round at Thermopylae. On the Greek side, something like six rotations of 400 men each had followed the spartiates into battle, which would have put about 2,700 Greeks at risk. It's likely that no more than 100 (well under 5 percent) were killed in action or succumbed later to wounds — an order of magnitude less than the enemy's loss. It was an impressive performance by the hoplites of Greece, but it had bought them no more than a morning in the pass. A very long day still lay ahead for Leonidas and his command.

The Second Assault/Cissians and Sakae

Tigranes and Corps III had advanced into battle that morning just ahead of a second wave of troops that held back as the Medes tried to take the pass. Anaphes commanded this reserve force, which consisted of the Cissian sparabara of Corps IV and a hazarabam of Sakae archers (half of Corps VII) led by Hystaspes. Though the Sakae had no doubt been included in the arms mix to exploit their longer-ranged composite weapons, this was before the Greeks had administered an exacting lesson on close-order combat. It was perhaps beginning to dawn on the more astute among the Persians that shock capability, rather than weight of missile fire, was the real key to success in the narrow confines of Thermopylae. Nevertheless, Anaphes gamely prepared to advance with the men on hand. As defeated Medes streamed back through the West Gate and passed him, the Persian commander steadied his troops as best he could, gathered what intelligence was available on the situation that lay ahead, and arranged a battle formation accordingly. It was around midday when he was finally ready to resume the fight, leading the Sakae and at least one baivarabam of sparabara into action.

The Greeks within the pass had collected their casualties and then regrouped near the Phocian wall. Leonidas moved fresh troops forward in readiness for whatever would come next. Observing the Cissians filing through the West Gate, he must have placed either a lochos of his perioeci or some other choice Peloponnesian unit in the front ranks of a phalanx that was again arrayed 50 men across and eight shields deep.

Upon approach, Anaphes would have ordered his hazaraba much as the Medes had done earlier, adjusting to terrain and foe by deploying them at 50 men wide and 16 deep. It's likely that he posted the Sakae behind the third hazarabam, where they could add their greater-reaching missiles to the attack of his sparabara. If the second baivarabam of Corps IV came into the pass as well, it set up farther back in a manner similar to the first. The Cissians moved along the same path trod by the Medes that morning, but the scene had now taken on a grisly appearance. While Leonidas had cleared his own fallen from the field, hundreds of dead and dying Medes still littered a 300-meter stretch of blood-soaked earth above the Middle Gate. Bodies lay clustered in heaps, marking where the hoplites had overrun Median units during the fight. The Cissians had to march through and take station within this grim setting, stepping with care over discarded equipment and the mangled remains of former campmates. Thus, while the Greeks gained confidence from their initial victory, the sight and smell of defeat and death that surrounded Anaphes' command surely shook its morale.

The Cissians came within 50–75m of the Greeks, bringing the bows of the four leading hazaraba (three of sparabara plus the Sakae) into range. Once these archers opened fire, their fall of arrows must have been extremely dense, reflecting the combined efforts of over 3,000 well-trained bowmen. At a steady firing rate of five arrows a minute per archer, as many as 40,000 shafts could have come down on the Greeks during the two to three minutes it took them to move into shielding contact with the enemy's front rank. If directed solely at the leading phalanx of 400 men, this would have amounted to about 100 arrows per hoplite. It's no wonder then that Persian barrages were said to blot out the sun! Yet the shields and armor of the Greeks served them well amid this deadly rain and they were able to close into the Cissian front with only modest loss.

After the hoplites locked into shock combat and gained some protection from arrow fire, there would have been a virtual repeat of that morning's action. Again, the heavier weaponry and othismos tactics of rotating contingents pierced shield wall after shield wall as the Greeks put hundreds of nearly defenseless bowmen to the spear. In the case of the Sakae, it must have been truly terrifying once the first three hazaraba of sparabara had been cleared from before them. It's easy to imagine that these unarmored archers bolted for the rear as soon as this forward screen began to disperse, well ahead of actual contact with the enemy. In the end, the Cissians withdrew, having lost maybe 1,000–1,500 men in a couple of hours of combat. They had in turn killed no more than 100 Greeks. The defenders of Thermopylae had survived through to the afternoon, but an even greater challenge was still to come.

The Third Assault/The Immortals

Facing disaster, Xerxes and his counselors must have been nearly mad with frustration as the Cissians followed the Medes from the pass in defeat. Their physical loss was significant, with something like 2,500 of the army's core infantry dead or dying in the action so far and perhaps another 1,000 seriously wounded. Yet such damage was endurable, since it represented less than 5 percent of the host's frontline troops. Rather than these physical losses, it was actually harm to the morale of the Great King's army that was fast becoming an overwhelming concern. Veteran commanders among the Persians were well aware that the psychology of their soldiers was more vital to battlefield success than either sheer numbers or quality of armament; thus, the threat to the army's confidence that was currently emanating from the pass called for immediate and drastic action. After getting what information they could from Tigranes, Anaphes, and their subordinates on the nature of the fighting in the narrow defile, it was apparent that sending more bowmen into the fray would be a waste of time and good men. It would take hand-to-hand combat, not missile fire, to defeat the determined force of hoplites barring their way.

This situation called for commitment of Persia's most reliable shock troops — the crack division of Immortals (Corps I). Unlike other sparabara, these all carried spears for close-in fighting; moreover, they had the sort of soaring confidence that would not allow the day's earlier defeats to dampen their spirit. The Immortals therefore marched out under their general Hydarnes in the late afternoon at nearly full strength, being short only a unit of bodyguards for the king. These elite fighters advanced resolutely, fully determined to do what had so far eluded the best efforts of over 30,000 of their comrades.

The Greeks stood ready in the pass with equally firm resolve. Those who had fought in the morning again moved forward, with Leonidas and his Spartans once more fronting the phalanx. The hoplites redressed their lines to accommodate modest losses taken so far and then braced to meet the next challenge. They could see the Persians forming up some 2km to the west, once more arraying each hazaraba in 50-man ranks and files of 16 at maybe 10m of separation between the units. As the Asians came to order, there was a sound of horns and their formation began slowly and wordlessly marching toward the Greek position.

The highly disciplined Immortals kept their nerve as they silently advanced through bloody battlefield debris. This took them past hundreds of fallen Medes and Cissians; exposed for several hours in the hot summer sun, these lay as a gruesome tribute to the effectiveness of the enemy waiting ahead. The lead hazaraba closed within bow range of the Spartans and then stopped, as men behind the shield wall grounded their spears by the head and prepared to launch a flight of arrows. No sooner did shafts begin to fall than the Greeks followed their past pattern by sweeping across the interval between formations to smash brutally into the leading sparabara.

A desperate struggle ensued that matched up the most renowned warriors of two proud cultures. The Immortals had no doubt got warning on the Spartan retreat-and-wheel maneuver and would not have fallen for that ploy, but the longer spears, heavier armor, and pushing potential of the Greek phalanx still gave it a decided edge in shock combat. Hard-thrusting hoplites were thus once again able to breach their enemy's wicker-shielded front. The Persians responded with skill and courage, and when the Spartans had pierced the first hazarabam, it must have made an orderly, fighting retreat. As this van gave way and exposed the unit behind to attack, the Greeks would have taken the opportunity to move fresh men into their own front to avoid fatigue.

Rotation after rotation of hoplites pushed through facing shield walls, relentlessly driving ahead until dusk, when their foes at last gave up the fight. The Immortals' losses were no doubt significant — perhaps 500–600 men — but superior élan and weaponry had cut their fatality rate to about a third of that suffered by the Medes and Cissians. As for the Greeks, they likely paid around 150 men for their victory. This was well below damage done to the other side, but more costly than the previous fighting and strong testimony to the capability of their elite opponents. Night thus fell, with Leonidas's men having beaten back the best that Persia could throw at them, weathering three determined attacks to remain firmly in control of the pass.

It had been a bloody day, with some 3,000 of Xerxes' army probably losing their lives and maybe 350 hoplites doing the same. Yet on the surface, the basic situation didn't appear much changed: Leonidas still occupied Thermopylae and his much more numerous foes remained on the strategic and operational offensive. But this was deceptive, as each side now had to be seeing things in starkly different terms. Those defending the entry to Greece would have gained a great deal of confidence, while their attackers couldn't have avoided a rising sense of doubt. Above all, failure of the Immortals to carry the pass made it clear that the Greeks were likely to hold out as long as their courage endured — and that looked to be a long time indeed.

The Second Day/Fourth Assault

As dawn broke next day, a touch of panic had to be creeping into the hearts of Xerxes and his generals. Their navy had by now engaged the enemy fleet, but had gained no more than a draw. Thus, no amphibious solution to the challenge of Thermopylae was in the offing. Worse yet, results of the land offensive had shown that Persian tactical doctrine clearly wasn't up to the task at hand. As a consequence, morale of the imperial host must have been dropping fast.

To their credit, the Persians had adjusted tactics once they realized what was happening in the pass, de-emphasizing the bow and ultimately deploying their best spearmen. But this hadn't been enough to swing things in their favor. Though the Immortals' effort had resulted in fewer casualties than the earlier assaults, it had come no closer to breaking through. Stunned and facing an unimaginable defeat, Xerxes' generals decided to make yet another frontal assault, hoping perhaps to find the Greeks hurt, tired, and more vulnerable. And this time, they would strike with a formation specially designed for shock combat.

This seems to have involved assembling a picked division from elements of Corps III–V. Each sparabara dathabam included at least two shield carriers that were considered their unit's most steadfast soldiers. Drawing such men from the two Hyrkanian baivaraba in Corps V and the second baivaraba of the Corps IV Cissians and Corps III Medes could then make for the equivalent of eight hazaraba — all filled with troops of good quality that had yet to be bloodied. Finally, two more hazaraba might be formed by pooling a further 1,600 men with shields from the already battle-tested first baivaraba of the Medes and Cissians. This would complete a temporarily brigaded baivarabam of the best warriors from three corps. Most significantly, all stood fully armed with both spear and shield, making them as close as Xerxes' army could come to pure shock troops. It took much of the day to gather and organize this hybrid contingent, but by late afternoon it was ready for action.

The brevet division of shield-bearers advanced through the West Gate and took up combat formation (Diodorus says in a single mass, but more likely in national units). It then closed on the Greeks, passing through the previous day's battleground, where ghastly reminders lingered from the heaps of Persian dead that had littered the narrow field. Though most of the bodies must have been removed the night before, conditions would still have been most unpleasant, with effluents released after death decomposing to produce a foul miasma. Discomfiting as this was, mental stress upon the sparabara was sure to have been even worse. This reflected having to fight in a makeshift organization and unaccustomed, shock-dominant manner — unknowns guaranteed to raise anxiety among even the best of soldiers.

A final blow to the Persians' morale came as they neared the Greek line and saw crimson-clad Spartans at the fore. We know that even the proud Immortals had learned to respect these grimly efficient warriors from the Peloponnese, as they would later express relief on the Anopaia path when informed that their opponents were only Phocians, rather than the dreaded men from Lacedaemon. Tales of Spartan ferocity must have been rife around Persian campfires after the opening battles. While these may have served to rationalize and salve the experience of those defeated that day, they only painted the foe as fearsome bogeymen for everyone else. The hastily reorganized sparabara standing in the pass now faced these same opponents — merciless men, who were without peer in the kind of shock fighting that lay ahead.

There would have been no barrage of arrows to open the battle, as both sides advanced to meet more in the manner of a traditional hoplite engagement. Persian spears and shields notwithstanding, the Greek inventors of this style of warfare still held an edge in both experience and equipment. Smashing and lunging into their less heavily armored rivals, the Greek front-fighters cut steadily and deeply into the struggling Persian ranks, all the while benefiting from the tremendous forward momentum provided by othismos from the trailing files. This time though, the hoplites could no longer get at easier prey by breaking through a thin shield wall and the fight evolved instead into an extended penetration that drove ever deeper into the heart of a homogeneous Persian formation. Since the wicker shields of the sparabara were useless for othismos, the Greeks were able to push their foes awkwardly backwards. Those in the Asian van stumbled into comrades behind in a growing state of panic; however, with so many men bunched toward the rear, it was impossible to get away. Troops at the leading edge had no choice but to carry on. In fact, this was undoubtedly part of the Persian plan, removing the option for men up front to break and run.

The struggle must have been one of terrible desperation on the part of the sparabara along the front. Yet just as they had no choice but to face forward and fight or die, it was equally difficult in this unrelenting press for the Greeks to rotate their own men as they had before.

Diodorus claimed that Leonidas's hoplites fought with so much passion that those at the fore refused to relinquish their place to the men behind, but it's more likely that such replacement simply wasn't possible.

Quite a few Persians fell to Greek spears in the momentum of the initial crash of shielded lines. After that, othismos pressure toppled many more sparabara, who were slain where they fell as the phalanx rolled over them. At the same time, some Greeks dropped as well, but only a relative few. However, as the battle persisted and men had to labor without relief or retreat, forward pushing from the hoplites must have faded as they began to tire. Survival along the battlefront now became less a matter of aggressive penetration of the enemy array than one of conserving energy. Once the pace began to slow and Greek othismos fell off, perhaps within an hour, the action would have come to more closely resemble an old-style contest between front-fighters than a modern phalanx battle. Just the same, though the hoplites had lost most of the advantage from their formation tactics, they still had longer reaching weapons, better armor, and more experience at shock combat.

The battle dragged on toward evening, with exhausted warriors flailing wearily at each other like clinching prizefighters struggling toward the final bell. The casualty rate under these circumstances must have dropped quite a bit from that of earlier actions; still, it's likely that at least three Persians fell for every hoplite that went down. In the end, effects of this battle echoed those of the previous day, as the Greeks continued to inflict the greater harm and could not be broken. Finally, as darkness gathered, the Persian rear ranks began pulling out through the West Gate. This at last gave exhausted and badly battered sparabara along the front a chance to relinquish the field. The leading hoplites would have been equally spent and likewise more than ready to see the fighting come to an end.

Both Greek and Persian formations had stood their ground throughout this engagement and the latter's shields afforded improved protection. Thus, losses during the fourth assault were the lightest incurred by both sides so far in the contest for Thermopylae, with possibly less than 100 Greeks giving their lives to hold the narrow front and no more than 300 falling among their Asian opponents. Yet even though the use of better equipment and tactics served to cut their casualties, the Persians had again failed to generate the kind of offensive power necessary to dislodge Leonidas and his men.

Day Three/Last Stand

As the second day's battle was progressing toward another Persian defeat, events unfolded in Xerxes' camp that would finally give him victory. Unable to take the pass by main force, he was offered an alternative by a local man most commonly identified as Ephialties, who came forward to guide the Asians over the Anopaia track and down against the Greek rear. Ephialties' homeland of Malis lay undefended to the north of the pass and was being spoiled by the stalled Persian host; therefore, even though some of his countrymen were serving with Leonidas, leading the enemy away wasn't quite the act of treachery that it might seem. The Persians, a mountain people themselves, must have been searching for this alternative trail since their arrival in the vicinity. Without help, however, they hadn't found the correct route among the warren of faint paths that cut through the forested slopes.

At dusk, just as the shield-bearers were pulling back after the failed fourth assault, the Immortals marched out with their general Hydarnes to follow Ephialties on a difficult night climb around the Greek left flank. Reduced by the previous day's fighting and having detached Xerxes' personal bodyguard, they set forth in the deepening gloom at about 6,000 strong (ten hazaraba at 60 percent nominal strength). By daybreak they had reached the path's crest, where they came upon the Phocians that Leonidas had posted to guard his backdoor. These hoplites had more than enough manpower to block the Immortal's column, which couldn't have been more than a few men wide, but when alerted by the rustling of leaves, they took fright. Thinking themselves the focus of attack, they withdrew toward a safer position and left the path wide open. Reassured that the hoplites before them were not the much-feared Spartans, Hydarnes' men hastened the Phocians on their way with a few arrows and continued their trek. By late morning, they were descending near Alpeni and the East Gate of Thermopylae.

A deserter from the Persian camp (one Tyrrhastiadas, according to Diodorus) warned Leonidas of the Immortals' march, and a Phocian messenger arrived before sunrise to report the failure of his blocking force. Diodorus said that the Spartan king at this point realized he could no longer hold the pass, prompting him to launch a suicide attack on Xerxes' compound that resulted in the death of the last of the Greeks. This was reputedly an attempt to kill the Great King in hope that his loss would put an end to the invasion. The tale's fantastic elements and conflicts with Herodotus lead one to discount it as a later myth; nevertheless, it could hold a kernel of truth, since a failed commando strike by a small group of picked men is far from implausible.

Regardless of any raid on Xerxes, Leonidas acted quickly to dismiss most of his hoplites and all of the allied light infantry so that they might live to fight another day. These men hurried through the East Gate before the Immortals could block their escape. Yet the enemy's cavalry still posed a danger to the retreating Greeks should it catch them in open country below the pass. Only a delaying action could ward off this threat, a reality that prompted Leonidas to keep enough spearmen behind for a rearguard. Besides his spartiates (perhaps 250 remained), he retained the Boeotians, whose homeland lay just to the south and next along the Persian line of advance. These brave spearmen from Thebes (maybe 350) and Thespiae (another 600) brought the king's remaining command up to around 1,200 hoplites plus a few light-armed retainers.

Passing references in Pausanias suggest that the levy from Mycenae also stayed with Leonidas, yet Herodotus made no such claim and it would seem unlikely. Not only were the Mycenaeans too few to be of much value, but in contrast to the Boeotians, they were also too far from home to see a last-ditch fight at Thermopylae in terms of directly defending their farms and families. Throwing away their lives would just deprive Mycenae of its army and leave it helpless. We can therefore feel fairly confident that only the troops from Sparta, Thebes, and Thespiae remained at the Middle Gate on the third and final day of combat.

A fresh imperial battle formation moved into the pass from the west at mid-morning, with the sparabara of Corps II under Otanes at its front. Timing of this advance must have been meant to coincide with arrival of Hydarnes and his men in the Greek rear per a best guess at how long it would take to transit the Anopaia path. However, the Immortals were not yet on the scene, having had either a more difficult march than expected or some delay in chasing the Phocians out of the way. Otanes hastened to attack anyway. No doubt confident that Hydarnes would come to his support eventually, he seems to have been determined to clear Thermopylae as quickly as possible.

Seeing the Persians approach from the west and knowing that more foes were even now closing in from the east, Leonidas abandoned his previous stance near the Phocian wall and advanced toward the West Gate. Though the dead and wounded had surely been removed each evening, his men moved through abundant signs of the havoc they had already brought about as they steeled their nerves for one last confrontation. Leonidas finally halted to offer battle in a wider part of the pass that must have that allowed him to increase his frontage to around 100m for an array 12 shields deep. This put more of his troops at hazard, but gave them a chance to engage and kill a much greater number of the enemy in the brief time left before the Immortals would arrive. It's almost certain that the Spartans stood on the right, the Thespians at center, and the Thebans on the left. Xerxes' host could match this by forming up two hazaraba wide at a depth of 16 men. Three shield-bearers probably led each Persian file, followed by three or more shieldless spearmen and with archers making up the rear ten or so ranks. The other hazaraba would have arrayed similarly, with each pair separating from that ahead by about 10m until all of Corps II stood inside the pass.

Herodotus said that the Persian monarch was on the field of battle and, though no exact location is given, it's likely that Xerxes took post toward the rear with his bodyguard. Such participation by a Great King went all the way back to Cyrus, who died of combat wounds in 530 B.C. Likewise, both Artaxerxes II and would-be king Cyrus the Younger would later do battle at Cunaxa (401 B.C.), and even the last Achaemenid ruler, Darius III, took the field at Issos (333 B.C.) and Gaugemela (331 B.C.). Joining the fight not only allowed a king to inspire his men, but also let him claim direct responsibility for any success. Thus, Xerxes was astutely putting himself in position to gain a victory and great glory where others had failed.

It's interesting that Xerxes' presence in the pass lends greater credibility to the notion that there was a last-moment attempt on his life. Rather than a melodramatic suicide raid, it suggests that the mere act of advancing beyond the narrow Middle Gate had given the Greeks a chance to kill the enemy king and bring the war to an early end. Specific targeting of Xerxes might even have been a key part of Leonidas's decision to move forward and fight on more open ground. In this way, he could engage a thinner enemy formation and have a much better chance of breaking through to the royal position.

As in the first day's combats in the pass, the Greeks charged after coming under bow fire, closing through a rain of arrows to spear into the Persian front. Taking out the leading wall of shield-bearers with their initial rush and subsequent othismos, the hoplites thrust deeply into the unshielded ranks of the first two hazaraba. They routed the remaining spearmen to get at the backing archers and send them reeling in disorderly flight. Many Persians were trampled in the general panic to escape sharp death at the hands of the savage Greeks, while others stumbled into the sea to either drown or be cut down from the rear. This terrible scene repeated several times as Leonidas's men bashed through one shielded line after another to kill and scatter those ranked behind. Adding to the damage wrought was that this slaughter played out amongst the many notables that held posts in Corps II. As a result, men like Xerxes' brothers Habrocomes and Hyperanthes and his uncle Artanes were among the victims.

The battle raged for an hour, possibly two — so long and hard that most of the leading Greeks shattered their spears and had to fight on with spear-butts and swords. The deadly Spartan short-swords must have been especially effective at this stage for reaching around the large and awkward wicker spara of the enemy to stab or slash them down before taking an even greater toll among the unshielded men at the back. Still, the Persians were ultimately too deeply massed to be defeated in this way. Each time a fronting pair of units were broken, new ones moved up to take their place. Meanwhile, under the eyes of their king, the rearward hazaraba held steady and resisted any urge to give way. Throughout this ordeal, an occasional hoplite fell to Persian spear, sword, or arrow, with losses mounting over time and the rate of loss climbing as the Greeks tired and degraded their weapons. Finally, a turning point came when Leonidas went down. This ignited a vicious struggle over his body, which was recovered at last by his own men and carried from the fight. Even with the death of their commander, the Greeks battled on; yet the heart and strength must surely have been fading from their effort.

It was at this moment (about noon) when word arrived that Hydarnes and his Immortals were finally approaching. The surviving 600–700 Spartans and Thespians now chose to make a fighting withdrawal lest they leave their rear open to attack. As for the remaining Thebans (perhaps 200–300 hoplites), their position on the far left caused them to be cut off from this retreat. Facing an utterly hopeless situation, they had no real choice but to surrender. In truth, it's quite possible that diversion of the Persians in surrounding and subduing the Thebans was critical in buying time for the rest of the Greeks to escape for the time being. Some 200 hoplites and 1,000 sparabara were probably left dead or dying on the field as combat broke off.

The Spartans and Thespians pulled back in good order, but couldn't set up at the Phocian wall due to the certainty of being taken from the rear by the Immortals. Instead, they retired a short distance behind that barrier to make a stand atop the hill of Kolonos. This was a small rise (about 15m high) between cliffs and sea where they could circle to defend on all sides. Thousands of Corps II sparabara clambered past the abandoned wall as Hydarnes' men swarmed in from the other side, all converging on the final remnant of Leonidas's army to put it under relentless attack. Resisting to the end with whatever weapons remained, this small band was overwhelmed by missiles and killed to the last man.

Greek losses on the final day at Thermopylae likely numbered 900–1,000 spearmen killed and 200–300 captured. This added to the 400–500 fallen in the earlier fighting for a loss to the allied cause of at least 1,500 hoplites in all — more spearmen than most poleis had in their entire levy. Though this was well below the 5–6,000 slain among the invaders, it would prove a higher cost to the mainland Greeks than any other battle during their long-running conflict with Persia. And Thermopylae was a major defeat not only in terms of men killed, but also for loss of strategic position. All of central Greece now lay open before the host of Xerxes.

There has been a lot of speculation on just what happened that last day in the pass. It has been suggested (Bury 1900, 276; Grundy 1901, 308–309) that the Peloponnesians were not sent away, but assigned instead to block the Immortals. This proposes that they fled when presented with so daunting a task. Yet the terrain makes it unlikely that Leonidas would ever have ordered them to hold the East Gate, since bowmen descending the broad and forested slopes could easily have picked apart any hoplite force on the flats below. Moreover, our best ancient sources (Herodotus and Ephoros via Diodorus) are unanimous in stating that the Peloponnesians withdrew under orders. Likewise, it has been suggested (Delbruck 1990, 97) that the Thespians (and presumably the Thebans) were caught at the tail of the retreat as they too tried to get away. Again, this conflicts with our best historical accounts. It's also quite unlikely in view of the minimum needs of a delaying action. Leonidas could never have hoped to restrain Xerxes for long with only his spartiates, who by then were something less than 300 strong, and only by keeping the Boeotians with him could he have fielded enough soldiers to hold the rear.

Nor is there compelling reason to think that these allies were loath to stay. This was actually quite in keeping with heroic traditions among the Thespians. They displayed similar devotion to duty at Delium (424 B.C.) and Epipolae (413 B.C.), making valiant stands that turned looming defeats into victories, and would later pay heavily to hold their ground alone in a losing cause at Nemea (394 B.C.). Indeed, Thespiae had a reputation for stoic courage to rival even that of Sparta. But what of the Thebans, whom Herodotus said were reluctant participants? This could well be a libel based upon subsequent cooperation of their polis with the invaders and may well have come from Athens, where there was long-standing enmity against Thebes. Surrender of the Theban volunteers at Thermopylae much more likely reflected the tactical situation than any lack of courage or patriotism. The Thebans taken prisoner were branded before release and Plutarch wrote that they carried this mark with pride.

Even as Xerxes was forcing the pass, Artemisium was the site of a major naval battle which lasted all afternoon and ended only at sundown. Exhausted, both sides pulled back, leaving the Greeks still in charge of the Euboan straits, but only at great cost to ships and crews. News of the defeat on land arrived that night. The positions at Thermopylae and Artemisium were highly interdependent; just as Leonidas had required a secure Artemisium to prevent an amphibious turning of his position, so the fleet needed a barrier at Thermopylae to keep the Persian army from closing its line of retreat down the strait. In fact, this passage had been blocked in the past at its narrowest point (the Euripus Channel near Chalcis), where a chain had once been installed from shore to shore for the purpose of extorting tolls. With its escape route now at risk, the only prudent course for Greece's fleet was to abandon the blockade and sail south toward safer waters.

Xerxes proceeded to bury his dead in the pass, trying to hide the embarrassing extent of these losses from gawking onlookers, who now cruised offshore from the battlefield like tourists. Guided by allied Thessalians, the Great King then descended upon Phocis and Boeotia, bringing all of central Greece under his control. He met resistance only from Thespiae, which he destroyed in retribution. Xerxes next marched into Attica, where most of the Athenians had already evacuated their home city. Athens received no more than token defense and was quickly captured. Hoping still to protect the Peloponnese, the Greeks hastily threw up fortifications across the Isthmus of Corinth. Unfortunately, this position was like Thermopylae in that it could be bypassed at sea; thus, the focus of the war shifted inevitably once more toward naval action.

Psyttaleia (480 B.C.)

Having taken all of eastern Greece, Xerxes was eager to crush remaining resistance and complete his conquest. However, after absorbing the high cost of victory at Thermopylae, the thought of again engaging desperate hoplites in confined terrain at Corinth couldn't have been appealing. It was clear that he would be better off avoiding this strong position to bring about battle on open ground, where his cavalry had a chance to be decisive. It was now well into September and, with winter and the end of the campaigning season fast approaching, there was a growing urgency to decide the issue as soon as possible. Xerxes was well aware that the longer he remained in Europe the greater the danger that a political conspiracy might arise back home to bedevil him.

The best Persian strategy was an invasion of the Peloponnese from the sea that would threaten the Greek rear. This would also give access to potential local allies, with both the Argives and Messenians, long victims of Sparta, being likely to join in a fight against their tormentors in return for a promise of autonomy and power. Facing the loss of crops and homes, the Peloponnesians would have to either surrender or accept battle at a time and place unfavorable to their tactics. Only one obstacle stood in the way of this plan — the Greek ships now beached on the island of Salamis. This force posed a potent threat not only to any future landing operation, but to Xerxes' seaborne supply chain as well. If the king wanted to subdue Greece before the end of the campaign season, then he first had to eliminate its fleet.

As it turned out, the Greeks also needed a quick resolution. First, there was fear that the Persians would build a bridge and invade Salamis directly. In fact, such a causeway was already under construction (its remnants are still visible today) and seemed quite doable in light of the astounding engineering feats that had accompanied the march from Asia. Yet this imminent menace from without was still less urgent than problems building from within. Themistocles of Athens, architect of Greece's naval strategy, was well aware of the fragile nature of the anti–Persian alliance, which was at risk of falling apart should the current crisis persist for any length of time. Never strongly united under even the best of circumstances, the various poleis would soon seek separate deals with Persia toward insuring their own survival. Therefore, the only real hope for Greek victory was to precipitate a sea battle in a favorable setting before the allied fleet could disintegrate on its own.

Themistocles applied guile to bring about a timely confrontation at a place where his ships had the advantage. He sent a false message to Xerxes, telling him that the Greeks would escape to other anchorages if he didn't trap and defeat them immediately. As the Greek navy represented the greatest remaining barrier to his ambitions, the temptation was overwhelming for the Great King to move immediately to destroy these ships while they were still within easy reach. And it must have been readily believable that an Athenian might betray greater Greece in return for benefit to his own polis, as Xerxes had by now become well used to this kind of behavior from his fractious enemies. A number of turncoat Greeks (such as former Spartan king Demaratus) were among his advisors and yet another traitor had led the Immortals along the Anopaia path only a few weeks earlier. Focused on destroying his enemy in a great and glorious sea battle, Xerxes rushed into action. The plan was to attack the Greeks in their position north of Psyttaleia (modern Lipsokoutali), a small island bordering the main southern entry into the narrow strait between Salamis and the Attic mainland to the east.

In anticipation of victory at sea, Xerxes landed a force of sparabara on Psyttaleia. These were some 400 young men from the best families, who, in light of their high social rank, must have been members of the Great King's personal guard. These bodyguards among the Immortals were an elite within an elite that owed their positions not only to military ability, but even more to the prestige of their lineage (Xerxes himself had served in the bodyguard as a youth). Their mission on Psyttaleia was to assist friendly seamen forced onto the island, while dealing swift death to any Greeks attempting the same. We can suspect a strong political factor at work in this appointment. Though present with Xerxes among the rear ranks in the last engagement at Thermopylae, the proud men of his bodyguard had yet to display their prowess in battle and now there was every prospect that the Greeks would capitulate after a naval defeat. If so, this might well represent the last opportunity for these young heroes-in-waiting to gain glory. It's quite easy to imagine that both the ambitious guards and influential members of their families had lobbied fiercely to secure this plum assignment.

As events unfolded that day, the Persians fought the sea battle at great disadvantage. Having diverted their Egyptian squadron to block any attempt by their foes to flee around the north shore of Salamis, the rest of the Persian ships crowded together to pass through the strait's narrow southern opening. The Greeks waiting to the north were thus able to deploy on exterior lines around this tight entrance and attack with superior strength as the Asians emerged a few at a time into the more open waters of the strait proper (Nelson, 1975b, 69). Based on location of the Persian landing force and placement of a trophy on the adjacent Cynosura peninsula, most of the action likely took place just north of Psyttaleia, where Greek tactics negated Persian advantages in numbers and mobility at sea much as they had done on land at Marathon and Thermopylae. As a result, the imperial armada suffered a shattering defeat that left the sparabara on Psyttaleia stranded amidst waters completely under enemy control.

Seeing the strait cleared of Persian ships, Aristides of Athens gathered hoplites from idle men watching the fleet action and organized them for an attack on Psyttaleia. These were Athenians, who must have been seething to get into the fight not only to share the glory being won by their comrades offshore, but also to avenge the loss of their city. As Aristides was strategos of Antiochis, he most likely mustered the 500-man taxis of that clan for this operation, crowding it onto 12–15 triremes from the same tribe and adding their marines and archers to the effort.

The Persians must have taken station along the island's northeastern face so as to be close to the naval action. Now, seeing the ships of Aristides driving onshore to the west (proximal to Salamis and sensibly beyond enemy lines), they rallied toward the landing site to throw up a light barrage with their bows, but failed to discourage the enemy. Under cover of a hail of stones and arrows discharged by the crews of their ships, the Athenians gained a foothold ashore, with armor and shields deflecting the few shafts that came their way.

Aristides gathered his 600–650 hoplites and marines on the beach and must have put them into a deep phalanx with files of 12–16 shields over a 40–60m front. He then advanced on the thinner Persian array (no more than ten deep) that was hastily forming just to the east. The ensuing battle was short and extremely vicious as the Greeks rushed their enemy with a roar to use superior numbers, gear, and formation to slice through the hapless sparabara, carving their bodies "like butchers" according to Aeschylus, who was likely an eyewitness. The Persians, disheartened by their fleet's shocking loss and with nowhere to flee, were overrun and wiped out. The vengeful Athenians spared only a handful suitable for ransom, including three nephews of the Great King.

Salamis proved to be the turning point in the Greco–Persian conflict. While the Greeks had taken significant damage and were actually quite fearful lest the Persians make a second assault, Xerxes overestimated the strength of his foes and misread their immediate intentions. He thus rapidly retired to Asia with a major portion of his army, concerned that escape might be cut off by destruction of the bridge at the Hellespont. In fact, the king's fears may have been as much political as military. Defeat of his armada not only had potential to rekindle rebellion within the empire, but might also embolden his enemies at court in Suza. Considering that his own father had come to the throne via intrigue rather than birth, the primary motivation for Xerxes' return home may well have been fear of a coup.

Still, though out-maneuvered and embarrassed, the Persian monarch hadn't given up on his dream of European conquest. He left Mardonios behind in Attica with the most effective elements of the imperial army and a growing force of Greek allies. Having lost their bid at victory from the sea, the Persians now prepared to settle the issue ashore. Yet even as the war in Greece reached this pivotal stage during the fall of 480 B.C., events of great significance were also coming to a head farther west in Sicily.

Himera I (480 B.C.)

Settlers from Greece had come to overshadow the Phoenicians on Sicily. Unlike Punic traders, these farmers took the island's rich land for their own use, ousting the natives to effectively create three realms. Greeks held the eastern seaboard and Phoenicians the western, while local tribesmen (Elymians, Sicels, and Siculi) kept the less attractive interior. Grecian colonies spread ever farther along the shorelines until, by the early 5th century, they had reached Selinous in the southwest (bordering directly on the Phoenicians) and over half way along the north coast to Himera. The Punic domain now centered on just three cities in the west: Motya, Soleis, and Panormus. These trading posts operated as an administrative district of Carthage, the powerful Phoenician colony on the nearby shores of North Africa.

Sicilian Greek politics were notoriously unsettled and violent, with most of the city-states under ambitious tyrants that time and again intrigued against each other in bids to increase their territories. Gelon of Gela was foremost among these dictators. He had usurped rule from the young sons of his predecessor and then consolidated his position through a marriage of alliance with the daughter of Theron, leader of the strong nearby city of Acragas. Gelon's next triumph was to gain sway over Syracuse, which was the premier polis on the island. There, disgruntled hoplites had wrested power from the city's aristocratic class to set up a timocracy, causing the ousted men to approach Gelon in 485 B.C. for backing that they might reclaim their old authority. But instead of helping the Syracusan nobles, the tyrant took this opportunity to seize their polis for himself. Impressed by Syracuse's fine harbors and citadels, Gelon chose it for his capital and moved many of his other subjects there to boost the population. Theron of Acragas saw all of this and sought to emulate his son-in-law by extending his own holdings — in so doing, he set off a major crisis for all the Greeks of Sicily.

Tensions between Greek and Punic Sicilians had risen toward the boiling point as the latter found themselves ever more confined to the western corner of their triangular island. The Carthaginian leadership was sorely tempted to intervene, but remained passive in the absence of a clear pretense for such a drastic measure. This finally changed in 483 B.C., when Theron usurped control of Himera and expelled Terillus, the city's tyrant. Terillus had long enjoyed good relations with his Punic neighbors and fell back on these in an appeal for help from Carthage. This provided cover that allowed the Carthaginians to not only relieve Greek pressure on their Sicilian outposts, but also to expand their territory. Nevertheless, there remained a lengthy delay in their response and it wasn't until 480 B.C. that the Carthaginians finally moved against the island. It's hard to believe that the simultaneous timing of this with Xerxes' march into Greece was a mere coincidence. An embassy from the mainland city-states had sought aid from Gelon against Persia in 481 B.C., but when the tyrant agreed to help only if he could lead the overall effort, the Greeks rejected his offer and kept Sparta in command. Still, Xerxes clearly was aware that Sicily remained a threat to reinforce his enemies. A Punic invasion of the island in tandem with his own attack on Greece could solve this problem by tying down Sicilian and mainland Greeks on separate fronts. It's therefore likely that talks 483–480 B.C. via Phoenician intermediaries had led to the coordinated campaigns.

Hamilcar of Carthage set about gathering large land and naval forces to carry out his nation's part of the plan. Hamilcar was Greek on his mother's side and thus well suited to deal with the opposition as well as potential allies on Sicily. He led a military in the midst of an evolution that was transforming Carthage's citizen army into one more dependent on outside manpower. A corps of professional spearmen (the "Sacred Band" per our Greek sources) had come to front a much-reduced citizen element that made up less than a third of the army, which was then filled out by Africans of Punic culture (Liby-Phoenicians, akin to Greek perioeci) and mercenaries.

Much as for the Persian host, ancient authors have greatly overstated the size of Hamilcar's army; as a result, we can only roughly assess its true strength today. Both Herodotus and Diodorus put the land force at 300,000 men, with the latter adding support from a fleet of 200 warships. Warmington (1960, 46) accepted the naval figure, but creditably suggested that the old tales of army numbers might actually be high by an order of magnitude. If correct, this means that Carthage had only some 30,000 fighting men. Accepting Warmington's figures, we can use ratios among troop types from later campaigns along with Herodotus's list of units to paint a far better picture of the force that Hamilcar took to Sicily.

Hamilcar's army probably included shock troops to the tune of 18,000 men, with 3,000 members of the Sacred Band at the core. These latter had conical helmets, body armor, and round shields covered in white leather (both style and color likely copied from Carians employed in the past), wielding thrusting spears that were somewhat stubbier than those of the Greeks and straight short-swords. Libyan mercenaries with similar gear were present in numbers equal to the Sacred Band, as were hired hoplites from Italy (Etruscans, Corsicans, and Sardinians). Some 9,000 African militiamen — a mix of Carthaginians and Liby-Phoenicians — likely made up the remainder of the Carthaginian heavy corps. These were armored peltasts, who carried two light spears and a large oval shield.

Light infantry would have been on hand at a ratio of 1 to 2 with the shock troops. These might have included 3,000 citizen and Liby-Phoenician archers and 6,000 mercenary peltasts from Africa and Spain. As for cavalry, it must have made up about 10 percent of the army for a total of 3,000 riders. The mounted troops, all heavy peltasts with small shields, would have formed three 1,000-man divisions, one composed of upper-class citizens, another of Liby-Phoenicians, and the last of Libyan mercenaries. This brought the land force to 30,000 combatants, and if needed, Hamilcar could also call upon 2,000 or so marines (peltast militiamen with armor) at ten per warship. A very imposing host, this was in fact the largest amphibious deployment to that point in history (far exceeding the Persian landings on Cyprus and at Marathon).

Battle on the Beach

The invasion fleet set out from Carthage in August 480 B.C. It ferried supplies, noncombatants, and light-armed troops aboard a large number of wind-driven cargo ships (though far fewer than the 3,000 cited by Diodorus), leaving the faster, oar-powered triremes to provide an armed escort and carry the heavy infantry. At 30 passengers per ship, 200 warships could handle around 6,000 men at a time; thus, it took at least three sailings for the fleet to shuttle 18,000 shock troops to the chosen landing point at the harbor of Panormus (modern Palermo) some 60km west of Himera. The need for several trips to complete this transfer must account for a report that Hamilcar spent three days resting at Panormus before setting out for Himera. In truth, it took at least that long to fully relocate his army from Africa.

The cavalry sailed aboard older triremes that had special modifications to handle horses. Sadly for the Punic cause, the first voyage of these makeshift vessels also proved to be their last, as a severe storm overwhelmed them and other less seaworthy elements of the fleet. It's doubtful that there ever were enough transports to embark the entire cavalry force, but every one that was on hand went down. This cost Hamilcar about a third of his horsemen and stranded the rest in Africa, leaving him with an army composed solely of infantry. Undaunted, the Carthaginian general marshaled his remaining forces and set out for Himera, his warships keeping pace just offshore to provide support.

When the Carthaginians arrived near Himera, they beached their triremes and set up two bases. The city was located on high ground along the coast on the western bank of the Himera River and Hamilcar built an army post on an elongate, flat-topped ridge that stretched along the western margin of the city and down toward the sea. His landing area sat just below this ridge and became the site of a naval camp. The latter had a ditch and wooden palisade, which enclosed both the grounded warships and a depot for supplies that cargo vessels brought from Africa and Sardinia. Bury (1900, 302) has suggested that this facility lay immediately below the city heights; however, it more likely lay farther west, near the army base per Diodorus's claim that the invaders controlled the entire western side of Himera. Such a location was also more secure against sallies from the city's seaward gates.

Defending the campsites with his marines, militiamen, and archers, Hamilcar advanced the rest of his army along the beach to offer battle before Himera. Diodorus noted that he had selected the best troops for this action, these likely being the Sacred Band and mercenary contingents—all the men better fitted for shock combat. Standing ten deep over a 900m front, these troops stretched from the sea to the lower slopes of the highlands on the right, which provided topographic protection for both flanks in the absence of a cavalry screen. Some of the mercenary peltasts may have further secured the landward side, though most probably stayed rearward to provide limited missile fire over the heads of their heavy infantry companions.

The tyrant Theron personally commanded the defense of Himera. He could observe the enemy's movements from the walls and, apparently desperate to avoid a siege, sent his men out to accept engagement. Numbers are extremely speculative, but the Greeks probably fielded nearly the full strength of Himera and Acragas (Theron's home polis). Himera was a modest city that could muster perhaps 1,000 hoplites and a tenth that many horsemen with a screen of hamippoi. The levy from Acragas would have been much larger; maybe 3,000 hoplites (including some mercenaries), 300 archers and slingers, plus 300 riders (each with a hamippos). Having a mere 4,000 spearmen, the Greeks must have set up at a depth of no more than four shields so that their phalanx could match the approaching enemy front.

The thin line of hoplites likely stood with the mouth of the Himera River behind—ground chosen to keep the fight as close as possible to the city gates for a possible retreat. Here, they could hope to resist just long enough for their cavalry and light infantry to prove decisive in enveloping Hamilcar's landward wing. Yet if this was indeed the plan, it quickly came to naught, as rugged terrain and peltasts on the targeted flank combined to fend off the Greek horse and missile men. This allowed Hamilcar's heavy foot troops more than enough time to cut into the anemic files of opposing spearmen. Though fired by desperation, the defenders may well have been lacking in confidence against so numerous a foe, leaving them prone to panic when their cavalry failed to deliver quick success. Without sufficient depth for effective othismos, the Greeks jabbed and hacked at their foes in a frantic front fight, but it was hopeless and, as hoplites began falling in increasing numbers at the head of each file, their courage finally gave out.

Losses in the brief, initial action between the battle lines were no doubt minimal among the well-armored men on both sides. However, a fair number of Greeks must have died during the closing stampede to get away. Himera's own troops, on the right wing and farthest from the gates, undoubtedly took especially heavy casualties. Fortunately for those defeated, their cavalry was able to cover the retreat, while Hamilcar's lack of mounted troops and placement of his peltasts in the far rear abetted an escape. The Carthaginian's cavalry losses in transit had thus helped rob him of a quick total victory, allowing Himera to brace for a siege and send to Gelon for reinforcement.

Battle on the Ridge

Diodorus said that Gelon came with 50,000 foot soldiers and over 5,000 horsemen; however, these figures are surely too large. He likely had no more men than he'd offered against Persia just the year before and could call upon only 10,000 (Ephoros via Polyaenus) to 20,000 (Herodotus) hoplites, including the 4,000 already at Himera. This would have put 16,000 spearmen at most in his relief column. These included a large number from Syracuse (5,000) plus some local allies, but at least half of his troops were mercenaries brought in from the mainland in the mid–480s. Light support would have come from some 3,700 archers and slingers (half or more hired men) and 3,600 riders, with the horsemen a mix of Greeks (perhaps 1,600, each with hamippos) and Siculi.

After reaching Himera, Gelon set about building a fortified camp along the east bank of the Himera River and sent his cavalry to attack enemy troops looting the countryside. Appearing suddenly, these horsemen drove their foes from the field and captured a good number of them (though doubtless fewer than Diodorus's 10,000). Gelon then elevated Greek spirits by parading his prisoners into town.

Loss of his cavalry continued to handicap Hamilcar, leaving his foragers without a screen against mounted attack. Fearful lest he again have to engage without supporting horse troops, he sent an urgent appeal for mounted help to Carthage's lone Grecian ally — Selinous. In a stroke of luck for the Greeks, they intercepted the reply to this request and Gelon used the information to develop a stratagem that was to prove decisive in the battle for Himera. He had some of his own horsemen pose as the requested riders from Selinous so that they could make a sneak attack into the invaders' naval base. These false allies skirted around Hamilcar's lines during the night to approach the navy camp at dawn from the direction of Selinous.

Once inside the palisade, Gelon's riders shed their pretense and turned on the startled marines and bowmen within to push them aside and open the gates to a body of footmen from Himera. Hamilcar was at the sea base preparing for a ceremony to gain divine blessing for his own planned offensive. The raiders slaughtered him before the waiting altar and then spread terror and confusion by setting fire to the camp and the warships pulled up on the adjacent shore. It was said that only 20 overloaded vessels managed to flee this carnage, and even these were lost to a storm before they reached Carthage.

Gelon now led the main body of his men around the south side of Himera against the army base. The Greeks would have gathered on high, flat ground just south of the encampment to form a phalanx that spanned the narrow plateau at a width of no more than 800m. The hoplites had to mass in files of 20 to fit this setting, anchoring their flanks on the steep slopes on either side and placing their light foot troops behind the rear ranks. Caught off guard, the Africans rallied around the Sacred Band and scrambled into an even deeper array, with their 18,000 heavy infantry matching up well against the 16,000 armored men closing in on them. Like their Sicilian counterparts, the missilemen of Carthage took post at the back of their formation.

The opposing armies advanced into contact under a shower of javelins, arrows, and slingers' shot, with the fight in this confined space unfolding much like that between two phalanxes. Despite their surprise, the invaders fought back with desperate fury. Both sides were heavily armored, which lead to a lengthy duel in which neither could claim a distinct advantage. The clash was largely one of front fighters, with greater than normal depth of formation making flight impossible for those at the fore and frustrating othismos from the Greek files. Inevitably, the pace of combat slowed due to growing exhaustion and poor footing amidst a rising tangle of fallen bodies along the front. At this critical juncture, the Africans suffered a cruel psychological blow as smoke from the burning fleet appeared and news spread that their commander was dead. Despair worked its worst on the Carthaginian ranks, even as the Greeks took heart and redoubled their efforts. Tired, discouraged, and increasingly frightened, the invaders were staggering on the verge of defeat when another unexpected assault smashed into them from the rear.

Theron delivered the deciding stroke against the Carthaginians by leading perhaps 2,000 spearmen out of Himera while the foe was fully occupied with Gelon. Creeping around the eastern side of the battle ridge, his strike force skirted the enemy position unobserved and then negotiated the slope at a point known to his local men. Once atop the plateau, Theron's detail quickly came together for a charge into the invaders' left flank and rear. The Africans fell apart, their previous stubborn resistance evaporating before this sneak attack. With crowded deployment and terrain conspiring to make escape difficult, the Greeks mounted a merciless pursuit that slaughtered thousands and scattered the others into the hills. Most of the survivors were soon captured, either individually or by giving up in small lots, though one group managed to rally and dig in on high ground at Mount Calagaro to the west of the battle site. However, this position lacked water and these last holdouts surrendered.

The Carthaginians' defeat was a complete and devastating tribute to the tactics of surprise. Taking place about the same time as the combat off Salamis, this action surpassed even that storied engagement as a turning point, having taken out the enemy's land and naval forces in a single stroke. Most of the Punic losses were expendable foreign levies, but destruction of the Sacred Band and so many warships were severe blows. Carthage quickly sued for peace and it would be another 70 years before it found courage to again threaten Sicily.

Victory of the Dorian Spear

As 480 B.C. came to an end, the Sicilians had turned back the threat from Africa. Their kinsmen on the mainland, however, still faced great danger despite their victory at Salamis. Xerxes had fled to Asia with what was left of the imperial fleet and a portion of his mighty army, but Mardonios continued to menace the land from Attica. That Persian general was now satrap of Greece and eager to both better secure areas taken to date and bring others under his control. And he had a powerful command of picked troops to do this, men that he could maneuver and maintain with much greater ease than had been possible with Xerxes' huge host of the previous year. The original invasion force had suffered from a clutter of small contingents, which had gathered from around the empire to show political support for the king. Mardonios greatly simplified his logistics by shedding most of these token units. At the same time, he kept nearly all of the line troops best suited for taking on hoplites.

Iranian sparabara remained at the heart of Mardonios's army, numbering perhaps 35,000, including the Immortals of Corps I (about 7,000 after retreat of the king's separate unit of bodyguards), the ethnic Persians of Corps II (possibly 14–15,000 men), and the Medes of Corps III (maybe 13–14,000 strong). All of these units were now well below nominal strength due to losses in battle and other forms of attrition natural to a long stay in the field. Knowing the value of shield-bearers for fighting against Greek spearmen, the Persian general had retained most of them. Besides sparabara, these included the Lydians of Corps XXIII and all of the marines from the Egyptian fleet contingent. The latter amounted to some 6–8,000 men (30–40 from each of 200 ships) of the Hermotybian and Calasirian warrior castes, who carried large wooden shields of Assyrian design and spears, with small axes and swords for sidearms.

Mardonios also had nine hazaraba of light foot troops and ten of cavalry. The infantry were Corps VII (Bactrian light spearmen and Sakae archers), VIII (Indian and East Ethiopian archers), XX (Paphlagonian light spearmen and Matieni peltasts), XXIV (Thracian and Bithynian peltasts), and one hazaraba (Mysian peltasts) from Corps XXIII — perhaps a total of around 7,000 men at current field strength. The horsemen consisted of Corps I and II (4,500 Iranians) plus Corps IV and V (3,000 light horse-archers). All of these auxiliaries would have added to the 43,000 line troops to bring the army up to some 57,500 fighting men. While this number is quite a bit lower than that cited by Herodotus (300,000), it fits well with Burn's estimate (1984, 511) that 50–60,000 combatants would fit within known dimensions of the Persian camp later set up near Thebes. Still, while this was an impressive force, there was a clear need to add heavy foot troops. Mardonios therefore turned to the conquered Greek states to draft a division of hoplites that would boost his quota of shock troops. These new allies probably brought 9,000 spearmen and 3,000 skirmishers, with the latter including hamippoi attached to some 2,100 horsemen from Boeotia (600), Thessaly (1,000), and Macedonia (500). With these last additions, the Persian host rose to just over 70,000 fighters.

Mardonios stayed in Attica into mid-479 in an attempt to consolidate his position. All the while, he secretly offered Athens terms to change sides. Sparta and the other Peloponnesians had been reluctant to take the field against him and this was frustrating the Athenians to the point of driving them from the alliance. Fortunately for Greek independence, they rejected these proposals. Had Athens chosen to join an active Thebes and a passive Argos in the service of the Great King, the transfer of its fleet would have negated the last defensive position on the Isthmus of Corinth and doomed Greece to conquest.

The Athenians made these spurned offers known to the alliance's Spartan leadership and argued that it was time to reclaim Attica. The suggestion was clear that they would reconsider joining Mardonios if there were to be much more of a delay. Frightened by the prospect of losing Athens, Sparta's Pausanius (regent for his nephew Pleistarchus, the young son and heir of Leonidas) finally marched out with the allied army in late summer. He intended to engage the enemy on the plain of Thria, which was flat terrain amenable to hoplite tactics that lay just east of Megara along the route from Corinth to Athens. To help speed the Persians into such a battle on unfavorable ground, Sparta's King Leotychides also sailed a fleet against Ionia, a region that Mardonios might soon find himself compelled to fall back and defend. Mardonios chose to retreat northward onto the Boeotian plain, where he set up a camp with ditch and palisade above the Asopos River near Thebes. Pausanius followed and took a facing position to the south on the foothills of Mount Cithaeron and near the Athenian-allied city of Plataea.

Plataea (479 B.C.)

At possibly over 31,000 hoplites, Pausanius would have had the largest army ever gathered from the Greek city-states. He deployed this huge force in a phalanx that had four brigades spread across a common front. His own Spartans and the men from Tegea, a total of maybe 6,500 spearmen, took the post of honor on the far right. The Spartans probably amounted to 2,500 (5 lochoi) each of spartiates and perioeci (despite Herodotus's claim of twice this number, 5,000 was most likely a full levy, save for age reserves and a small royal bodyguard on the fleet). Next came something like 11,300 hoplites from the Peloponnese along the right-center. These were from Corinth (perhaps 5,300, including 300 from that city's colony at Potidaea), Sicyon (3,000), Troizen (1,000), Epidauros (800), Orchomenos in Arcadia (600), Mycenae and Tiryns (400 combined), and Lepreon (200).

In contrast to these sturdy Peloponnesians on the right, the men at left-center lacked high regard as phalanx fighters. These 7,300 or so spearmen came from the southeast and northwest of Greece as well as from some island states. Megara supplied 3,000, Euboa 1,000 (600 from Eretria and Styra and 400 from Chalcis), Leucas and Anactorium 800, Ambracia 500, Aigina 500, and Paleis 200. Recognizing their shortage of experience, Pausanius reinforced these troops with better seasoned hoplites from Phlius (1,000) and Hermion (300). This assignment had the added benefit of separating the men from Phlius and Sicyon, who had recently gone at each other in a bitter border war.

Pausanius filled the secondary post of honor on the left wing with perhaps 6,000 spearmen from Athens and Plataea. Including many veterans of Marathon, these men had already proven their worth in combat against the Persians and were worthy of respect. A few Thespians also stood on the left. These were less than 100 poorly equipped men mentioned by Herodotus and placed with the Athenians and Plataeans by Diodorus. They came from a pool of around 150 reservists not present at Thermopylae, who had survived the destruction of their polis to find their way into the Greek ranks. Their posting with the Plataeans put all of the still-loyal Boeotians in the same brigade. As for the Athenians, they seem to have taken the field with 5,400, out of what were probably 6,500 available prime-age hoplites, the rest being in Asia aboard the fleet.

Manpower proposed here for Athens is about half Thucydides' tally for the beginning of the Peloponnesian War. This matches the rate of growth needed to expand from 5,000 men in 490 B.C. up to that later peak force and also fits with an implication by Thucydides (Hornblower, 1991b, 56) that the combined strength of Athens and Sparta during the Persian invasion was less than that of Athens alone in 431 B.C. (13,000 prime hoplites compared to just under 12,000 for both states at Plataea and Mycale). Then there is Herodotus's claim of 8,000 Athenian spearmen at Plataea, which most likely reflects the city's full potential, including marines and reserves absent from the battle. Indeed, given a reserve content of 20 percent, Athens would have had just over 8,000 hoplites in all.

Greek attendants would have been more or less equal in number to the spearmen. Most of these were noncombatants, with javelin-armed psiloi amounting to no more than 4,000 men. The only other light infantry on hand were 800 archers from Athens. As for cavalry, Pausanius didn't have much of a mounted force as a result of the defection of the horse-rich northern Greeks. Athens could have provided 96 riders and Plataea maybe another 60 or so; however, these were a mere handful compared to the thousands of horsemen with Mardonios. Mounted and foot auxiliary contributions brought the Greek army up to nearly 35,000 fighting men. Strong in heavy infantry, this force faced a foe with only about two-thirds as many shield-bearers, but much richer in cavalry and with just over twice the total manpower.

Due to the sharp contrasts in opposing numbers and troop types at Plataea, a standoff quickly developed. Mardonios was reluctant to attack his hoplite opponents in a confined setting on the mountain slopes, while Pausanius didn't want to fight horsemen on the plain. As at Marathon a decade earlier, such an impasse favored the Greeks. This was because their naval offensive threatened to shift the focus of the war, driving Mardonios to initiate action before he found himself recalled to protect Ionia.

Cithaeron and the Greek Advance

Mardonios responded to his strategic dilemma by directing a mounted campaign against the Greeks on the facing slopes of Cithaeron. He apparently thought that this would either coerce or finesse his opponents out of their favorable positions in rough terrain. The assault's particularity threatened the Megaran-led brigade, whose right wing occupied the spot along the Greek front that was most open to cavalry attack. Heavily put upon, the Megarans sent for help from Athens's bowmen, who came to the rescue with the support of 300 picked hoplites under Olympiodoros (these forming a screen three-deep before eight-man archery files). The archers likely stood on the most exposed (right/west) end of the phalanx, with their fronting spearmen kneeling to clear the line of fire. The Greeks then hunched down behind their shields to weather the enemy's mounted missile strikes.

The horsemen flowed up and back in a series of assaults that allowed a few bolts to find their way past shield and armor to inflict cruel wounds. However, despite a valiant and persistent effort, the Asians couldn't turn the exposed flank, due largely to counterfire from Athens's archers. Those with lances among the Iranian horse troops then entered the fray, closing repeatedly in an attempt to get at the opposing bowmen. Athens's fronting hoplites met and turned back each of these attacks (De Souza [2004, 103] cites a record of this action on a late 5th-century Athenian vase, which depicts an archer-hoplite pair battling a Persian horseman wielding a spear). In the midst of this fight, Persia's cavalry commander Masistios was wheeling to launch yet another sortie when his mount took a shaft in the flank and threw him to the ground. Olympiodoros's men immediately ran forward to seize the wounded horse and dispatch its well-armored master, stabbing him in the eye with a sauroter. (Pausanius claimed that the Athenian cavalry slew Masistios, but since the action unfolded just in front of the hoplite line, it's much more likely that a spearman delivered the killing blow. Perhaps Pausanius confused the lochos of Olympiodoros with a later Athenian mounted unit of the same size.)

Seeing their leader go down, the Persian riders turned about and closed once again to initiate a fierce struggle for his body. Though able to hold their own at first against the small contingent from Athens, they finally gave ground and ceded Masistios's remains when additional hoplites began to move out against them. Dismayed by the loss of an officer second in acclaim only to Mardonios, and completely foiled in their attempts to turn the targeted flank, the Persian cavalry quit the field in a state of disorder.

This success seems to have lowered the Greeks' fear of mounted attack and they boldly advanced. In doing this, Pausanius maintained the same order for his brigades, but moved them onto the gentle Asopos Ridge along the south bank of the river and opposite the Persian camp. From here he could better threaten the enemy with a quick river crossing, but faced some major new liabilities as well. Exposure to cavalry was even greater than before and it would be much harder to protect supply lines that now stretched a good distance out of the mountain passes to the south. Ironically, defeat of Mardonios's horsemen had achieved their original purpose, leading the Greeks onto ground better suited to Persian tactics.

The antagonists kept vigil across the shallow late-summer flow of the Asopos, each spending the next few days trying to provoke its opposition into an ill-considered attack. Neither side was eager to take the initiative, since it would call for a contested stream crossing and then a fight on less favorable ground; they thus limited action to shifting around in their battle lines, jockeying to get optimum match-ups should the foe lose patience and strike across the river. This all came to nothing in the end, as the Greeks chose to resume their original positions. Mardonios's men then also returned to their initial posts so as to best oppose the various enemy units and support his battle plan.

The sparabara of Corps I and II set up against the Spartans on the Greek right. This reflected Theban advice that Mardonios pit his finest troops against the professionals from Sparta and count on superior numbers to tip the balance in his favor. And the manpower advantage was indeed significant. The Persians appear to have held a nearly 3 to 1 edge along this portion of the front, with over 20,000 sparabara against but 7,000 hoplites and psiloi. Mardonios quite clearly meant for this to be the key point of attack, where he would turn the flank and win the day. Not only a sound tactical plan, this had potential to give him a great moral victory as well. Defeating the Spartans would raise imperial spirits in avenging the casualties at Thermopylae, even as it discouraged the Greeks by destroying the red-clad heart of their army.

Mardonios had deployed the Medes of Corps III and Bactrians from Corps VII opposite the Peloponnesians of the Greek right-center. Numbers here (perhaps 14,000 sparabara and skirmishers versus some 12,000 hoplites and psiloi) show that he intended only a holding action. Likewise, he pitted his remaining Asian levies against the Megaran-led left-center of the Greeks, with maybe 8,000 or so Lydians and Egyptians assigned to fix 7,300 spearmen in place. Despite their past problems with hoplites, Mardonios was clearly relying on the sparabara of his left wing to deliver victory. He was no doubt quite comfortable with using these men from his own martial culture; after all, he was highly familiar with both their combat style and how to exploit it. Moreover, he planned to fight on terrain suited to his cavalry. Right or wrong, this mind-set led him into relegating his allied hoplites to a lesser role.

Persia's Greek allies took station on the right wing (a post of honor in their tradition, but of lesser importance in the current scheme). Here, some 9,000 northern hoplites confronted about 6,000 spearmen of the Athenian brigade. In spite of the raw numbers indicating a 50 percent edge in manpower for the imperial allies, this match-up was really more equal than it appeared, as only 6,000 of the northerners (the Boeotians) were up to their opposition's high quality. Thus, though there was a realistic opportunity for Mardonios's hoplites to turn this flank, he most likely didn't count on it. He would take a Boeotian victory as a bonus, but pinned his true hopes on carrying the day on the opposite end of the field.

Baiting each other from across the river, neither side would rise to the attack. However, after waiting some time for his foes to take action, Mardonios once again sent cavalry out to try to goad them into a rash move. Led by local Boeotian horse troops, it was Persian riders that did most of the damage as they closed to fire and inflict galling and cumulatively significant casualties among the Greeks. Pausanius and his fellow generals soon realized that their psiloi and handful of archers couldn't keep these attackers at bay. Their growing unease increased sharply as the Persians began interdicting vital food supplies coming through passes now too far to the rear. Then enemy riders succeeded in blocking the Gargaphia spring and cutting off the only water source with shelter from the fall of arrows. Pausanius now came to the grim realization that his army's advanced post along the Asopos had become untenable.

The veteran Spartan knew that his best strategy was to pull back to greater cover and more secure supply lines along the slopes of Cithaeron. Yet any attempt to withdraw would put the rear of his formation at the mercy of enemy horsemen. Even sacrifice of a trailing guard, as at Thermopylae, would prove useless in this case, since the Persians could easily bypass such a detachment in the relatively open country south of the river. The only answer to this dilemma was to relocate under cover of darkness, when the Greeks might be able to get onto safer ground before Mardonios had a chance to pursue. But what ended up happening instead was a very large and confused battle that involved at least three (and very likely four) separate engagements.

Moloeis River

Pausanias's plan required pulling the various brigades more or less straight back toward Cithaeron to reform in the same order on the slopes. While this was going on, he would detach a small portion of his force to reopen the passes that provided his army's logistical lifelines to the south. It must have seemed simple enough, but counting on carrying out such a maneuver at night without a major hitch was a serious miscalculation that very nearly cost Greece its freedom.

As the redeployment went into motion, the Peloponnesian- and Megaran-led brigades apparently took the line of least resistance along the main road from the river to Plataea. This allowed them to move out and quickly reach the slopes just below (the Peloponnesians) and northwest (the Megarans and others) of the town site. In fact, they had shifted too far west during their retreat, overlapping the intended post of the Athenian brigade on the left wing and leaving a dangerous gap in the Greek line between the Peloponnesian right and the targeted position of the Spartans and Tegeans along the slopes to the east.

Meanwhile, the two wing brigades had both met with unexpected delays. The Spartans had to deal with a hesitant division leader, Amompharetus, who refused to withdraw his men, arguing that it was cowardly to retreat in the face of the enemy (though he might simply have been confused about his orders). After extensive discussion, the rest of the Spartans pulled out near daybreak. They no doubt counted on their reluctant comrade and his unit coming along once they realized the army would abandon them, and they did indeed follow at last. The Athenians had likewise been slow to leave the river, seemingly waiting for the Spartans to move first. Informed by rider that Pausanius was finally retreating as dawn approached, the Athenian commander, Aristides, belatedly got his men underway as well. They then marched down the same road toward Plataea that had been used during the night by the other Greek brigades.

As the sun rose that day in early August, the Persians prepared to resume their mounted harassment of the Greeks only to find the enemy positions deserted. Alerted of this, Mardonios was finally able to put his battle plan into action. He ordered his right and left wings to cross the river and attack, while having the center of his line advance in support. Letting his Iranian and Sakae horse troops take the lead, Mardonios chased after the Spartans and Tegeans with his Corps I and II sparabara and the Lydians. These troops were able to advance rapidly due to good fords along their part of the front and clear passes through the hills on the south bank. Following Mardonios's example, the general Artabazus likewise crossed the Asopos with the remainder of the Asian levies from the Persian center. Having a more difficult fording point and facing rougher terrain on the opposite bank, Artabazus and his command struggled uphill, somewhat behind the right flank of Mardonios. At the same time, the northern Greeks were also moving over the river in swift pursuit of the Athenians.

The Spartans had wisely made their withdrawal across high ground, moving along the western slope of a limestone outcropping known as the Argiopia ridge. This let them take advantage of broken terrain to aid their defense when the Persian cavalry finally caught up. As his horsemen brought the Spartan brigade to a halt, Mardonios moved forward to engage it with his crack sparabara. Realizing that he would now have to fight it out, Pausanius immediately dispatched a courier with orders for Aristides to join him. He then formed up his men ten shields deep across a 600–700m front to rebuff the enemy cavalry and prepared to meet the Persian footmen that were now rapidly closing in.

The Spartans sat about 2.5km north of the Athenian border outpost of Hysiae, near the local temple of Demeter and just below the southern tip of the Argiopia Ridge. Pausanius was well placed here to repel a mounted attack. The Tegeans on his left wing anchored their flank along the eastern slope of a foothill spur, while the Spartan regent and his men rested their right flank against a streambed, that of the Moloeis. The latter was a tributary of the Asopos and had its headwater farther south on the same ridge that bordered the Tegeans. A steep rise, vegetation, and Greek psiloi along the far bank of this creek combined to discourage envelopment of that end of Pausanius's line. Upstream to the west, the Moloeis converged into the ridge spur at an angle that enclosed the Greek position within a protective, wedge-shaped pocket. Thus well ensconced, the hoplites stood their ground, presenting a solid front of shields and bristling spear points as the pursuing sparabara came into bow range.

Meanwhile, the Athenians had been moving down the road toward Plataea when the dispatch runner caught up to them with instructions to close on the Spartan left flank. They obediently turned toward the Lacedaemonian position to the east. Properly executed, this would have united the Spartan- and Athenian-led brigades to better receive the enemy pursuit; moreover, the other Greeks now on the slopes near Plataea would be in position to attack the unshielded and weakest flank of anyone moving against the Athenian left. All in all, this would have been a brilliant improvisational response to the mess that circumstances had made of Pausanius's original plan, but the difficulties of carrying out such a maneuver in the very face of the enemy were too much to overcome. Thus, sunrise found the Athenians and Spartans still well separated and under assault.

As Mardonios neared the Spartans, the lay of the land forced his infantry into an unusually deep array of up to 30 men per file. This formation likely had one baivarabam of Corps II on the right, the Immortals in the honored center position, and the other baivarabam of Corps II on the left, along with the men from Lydia. Diodorus's account of the Lydians' part in the ensuing action suggests that they took post on the eastern extreme opposite Pausanius himself. Once in order, the Persians closed as their fronting sparabara set up a wall of shields and the backing archers launched a deadly rain of arrows. In reality, the situation resembled that at Marathon, with bowmen operating behind a flimsy barrier of spara in the face of a terrain-secured phalanx.

The Spartans stood stoically under the falling shafts, waiting for their general to divine from sacrifices the correct moment to go on the attack. Their armor and shields gave good protection from this shower of missiles, yet it still claimed a few victims (the noted Spartan Callicrates, for one, took a fatal arrow in his side). Finally, the Greeks surged ahead and into the Persian front. Credit for triggering this assault has gone variously to an order by Pausanius following a favorable sacrifice (Plutarch), a response to attacks by the Lydians on Pausanius during his divinations (Diodorus), and a rash move by the Tegeans (Herodotus). The latter, older tale seems to have the ring of truth to it, since it's easy to envision the less-disciplined Tegeans breaking ranks to get at their tormentors. Regardless of what set them off, the hard-charging Greeks crashed into the enemy and, despite fierce resistance, began to drive them back. As had happened so often before, robust hoplite equipment and relentless othismos threatened to break through a sparabara shield wall. Faced by a Greek phalanx once more pushing its way to victory, the Persian Empire's finest troops made a supreme effort to fight back, with no man among them conducting himself more courageously than their commanding general.

Mardonios realized that the defining moment was at hand and personally led the spear-armed elements of his Iranian cavalry against the Spartan right flank (the Sakae horse troops were now detached elsewhere). Conspicuously mounted on a white charger, he hoped to inspire his men into regaining momentum and turning the tide of battle. But the rough ground, boulder-filled streambed, and enemy psiloi conspired to thwart this attempted end sweep by forcing his horsemen into an unequal melee at close quarters. Fighting furiously at the fore, Mardonios tried valiantly to rally his men as the Greeks speared and cut them out of the saddle all along the line. Fate turned against him at this pivotal moment when the Spartan Arimnestus picked up a heavy stone (probably from the bed of the Moloeis at his feet) and hurled it into the satrap's face. His skull crushed, Mardonios fell to the ground mortally wounded. The Persian riders, completely demoralized, gathered up their commander's body and pulled out of the fight. And as the mounted attack fell away, the Spartans turned an undivided effort against the badly battered and now leaderless Lydians and sparabara.

Herodotus's description of the fighting at this stage indicates that the Persians broke ranks in a charge, moving forward as individuals and in small groups of ten or less (a dathabam?). This required the Greeks to fall back and leave room for an enemy advance, which supports Plato's claim that the Spartans had once more executed a false retreat to induce premature pursuit. Whether it was by such a stratagem or simply through main force, the Greeks

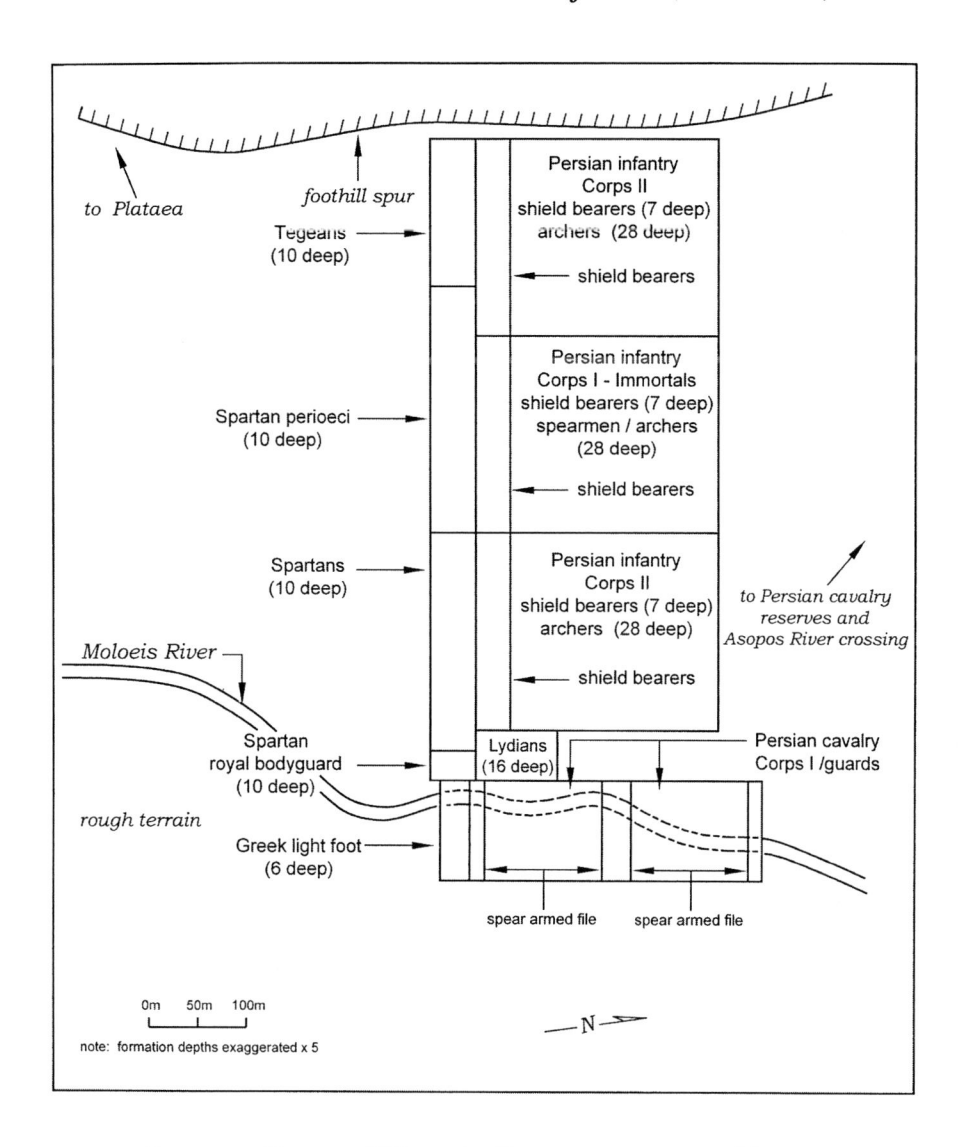

BATTLE OF PLATAEA (479 B.C.) — ENGAGEMENT ON THE MOLOEIS

finally broke past the ranks of shield-bearers in the enemy van. Heavily armored Spartans and Tegeans then lanced into the unshielded spearmen and archers of the Persian interior to initiate a horrendous slaughter. The proud and courageous Asians were driven into a frenzy of frustration at their impotence against the better-equipped Greeks, actually grabbing the longer enemy spears with bare hands in an effort to snap them and get close enough to use swords.

The men in the middle of the Persian array ultimately fled under the weight of unbearable losses. Panic then spread through the after ranks, causing a general stampede, with only the victors' lack of cavalry for pursuit preventing a complete massacre. In contrast, Persian horsemen provided a screen for their infantry's retreat, scattering psiloi and forcing the hoplites to stay in formation and advance very slowly. Many among those defeated were therefore able to recross the Asopos and seek safety within the walls of their camp. But this provided no more than short-lived refuge, since the Athenians, victorious on their own front, soon joined the Spartans in overrunning the stockade.

It's possible that no more than 1–2,000 Persians had fallen along the line of battle, but the remainder of infantry Corps I and II and most of the Iranian cavalry were also lost in the pursuit and fall of the camp. Imperial losses stemming from the engagement along the Moloeis therefore came to over 25,000 men. The Spartans and Tegeans left a reported 107 dead on the field, but this didn't include those lost to missiles before the phalanx attacked and men killed in the chase or at the stockade. Thus, the full toll of Greeks slain outright and succumbing over the next few days to wounds may have run closer to 250. Still, this falls well within the 3–5 percent range of cost that a victorious force might expect to pay in so intense an action. In addition, some 250–300 Spartans and Tegeans would probably have received non-fatal wounds. Yet even the most severe estimate of casualties among the Greeks pales in comparison to the near total annihilation suffered by their opponents.

Oeroe River

Failure of Athens's brigade to link with the Spartan left flank was the result of its having come to grips with the northern Greek cavalry while still moving laterally across the plain below Plataea. These horsemen had led their own hoplites at daybreak across a bridge over the Asopos and raced down the road toward Plataea. This let them close quickly on the rear of the Athenian column, which was still struggling across broken ground only about 1km east of the roadway.

The brigade commander, Aristeides, met this threat with an array that must have been ten shields deep and covered a 600-meter front between two branches of the Oeroe River. His position lay just downstream to the northwest of an area near Plataea known as "the island" for its location between streams. The Plataeans held the left (as at Marathon) and stood next to the tribesmen of Aiantis, with the rest of the Athenians spread out to the right and Aristides' tribal levy of Antiochis on the far end. As for the Thespians, they likely took post behind the rear ranks of their fellow Boeotians from Plataea. Though a case of making do, this was actually quite a strong position, with the flanking creek beds affording good protection from mounted attack. These stream courses would have held little or no water in late summer, but were strewn with cobbles and boulders treacherous for the fragile legs and unshod hooves of the enemy's horses. At the same time, fire from archers on the creek banks served to drive the opposition beyond javelin range.

Unable to get at Aristeides' men, the northern cavalry and their hamippoi withdrew out of bow reach and regrouped to the west. Their spearmen had now come on the scene and were forming to engage. The horsemen took up station behind this phalanx by national squadrons, with the Boeotians under the Theban Asopodoros on the left/southwestern flank, the Thessalians under Thorax in the center, and the Macedonians farthest to the northeast. Though unable to take direct part in the hoplite action, these mounted troops would play a major role later by driving off enemy reinforcements and screening a retreat.

The army that closed on the Athenians would have had a typical Boeotian organization, with city-state levies based on enomotai of 25 men (24 spearmen plus a leader) that were the building blocks for standard arrays eight shields deep. Four enomotai made a pentekostyes of 100, and ten of these yielded a lochos of 1,000. The 13 major cities of the Boeotian *koinon* or league (a late 6th-century foundation) had around 11,000 hoplites, but they never put that many into the field at one time. (Their largest mustering in the 5th century was some 7,000 spearmen at Delium in 424 B.C.) Thebes, the league hegemon, accounted for 4,000 hoplites, with the others coming from the principal poleis of Orchomenos, Hysettos, Eutresis, Thisbai, Tanagra, Haliartos, Lebadaia, Kiopai, Coroneia, Akraipphnion, Chaironeia, and Thespiae. These same sources also provided cavalry and hamippoi at one each for every ten hoplites. As the Thebans were fighting on their very doorstep, they must have been at or near their full force of four lochoi, while the rest of Boeotia probably sent enough men to put together at least two more lochoi. The Boeotian army thus likely totaled about 6,000 spearmen.

In all likelihood, it was only the Boeotians that advanced into contact with the Athenians and their allies that morning. Phocis, East (Opuntian) Locris, and Malis had (like Thebes and Thespiae) stood with Leonidas at Thermopylae; now, to avoid the same destructive fate as Thespiae, they were compelled along with the Thebans to deploy at full strength (about 1,000 spearmen each) in support of Mardonios to actively demonstrate their newfound devotion to the Great King. This also kept them away from the rear, where they might threaten the Persian line of retreat. While these troops probably had a military organization that was similar to that of their Boeotian neighbors, the resemblance stopped there. Their reputation as warriors was no match for that of the stalwart Boeotians and, indeed, Herodotus indicated that they made no effort to distinguish themselves on this occasion. These unenthusiastic and less-capable levies played no role in the battle, either remaining behind the river or staying in back of the Boeotians and well out of the fight. As it was, the men from Boeotia could equal the Athenian line on their own by massing ten shields deep, using enomotai not needed along so short a front to fill in the last two ranks. The Thebans took the honored right flank post, with their number including a forerunner of the 300-man elite unit later known as the Sacred Band (Hieros Lochos). Deploying three shields deep, the latter acted as lead strikers over a 100-meter stretch on the far right.

The armies sang their paeans as the Boeotians closed to within a few tens of meters of the Athenian brigade; then, with a sounding of shrill battle cries, the northerners rushed to the attack. Aristides' men stood in place to take the fearsome impact of this charge, holding steady between the streambeds as the momentum-enhanced rush took down a number of men among their forward ranks. Briefly staggered, the Athenians and their allies rebounded from this harsh, initial blow and fought back furiously. The encounter soon settled into a deadly scrum of thrusting and shoving as each formation labored to force the other backwards, with fighting being particularly vicious between the southernmost wings, where the Boeotians' picked men fronted the effort. The Plataeans and tribesmen of Aiantis took heavy losses in opposing these elites, but stood their ground (the Greeks later singled out the Plataeans for their valor). In the end, this match proved even in both strength and spirit, and neither side could gain the upper hand. Combat thus devolved into a grueling struggle of front fighting and othismos that began to slowly fade in intensity as exhaustion set in.

In the midst of this waning contest, it became apparent to the Boeotians that their Persian allies were in retreat. With no hope now for victory, the northerners disengaged on command to pull back beyond the river in an admirable display of discipline. Unable to pursue due to the danger of cavalry attack, Aristeides had no choice but to watch them withdraw, no doubt finding some comfort not only in survival, but also in having gained the battlefield and a technical victory. The Athenian general then quickly regrouped his men and led them northeast to the fords on the Asopos, which he crossed to join Pausanius in assaulting the enemy's camp. For their part, the Boeotians retreated all the way to Thebes, where they soon found themselves under siege. The turncoat city managed to escape devastation only by surrendering key Persian sympathizers for execution.

It was said that 300 Boeotians died on the battlefield. This suggests a total of 415 killed (7 percent, including those later lost to wounds) and nearly 700 injured—about one out of every five men present having become casualties. In contrast, Plutarch recorded only 52 slain Athenians. However, these were solely from the Aiantid tribe, which had faced the enemy's

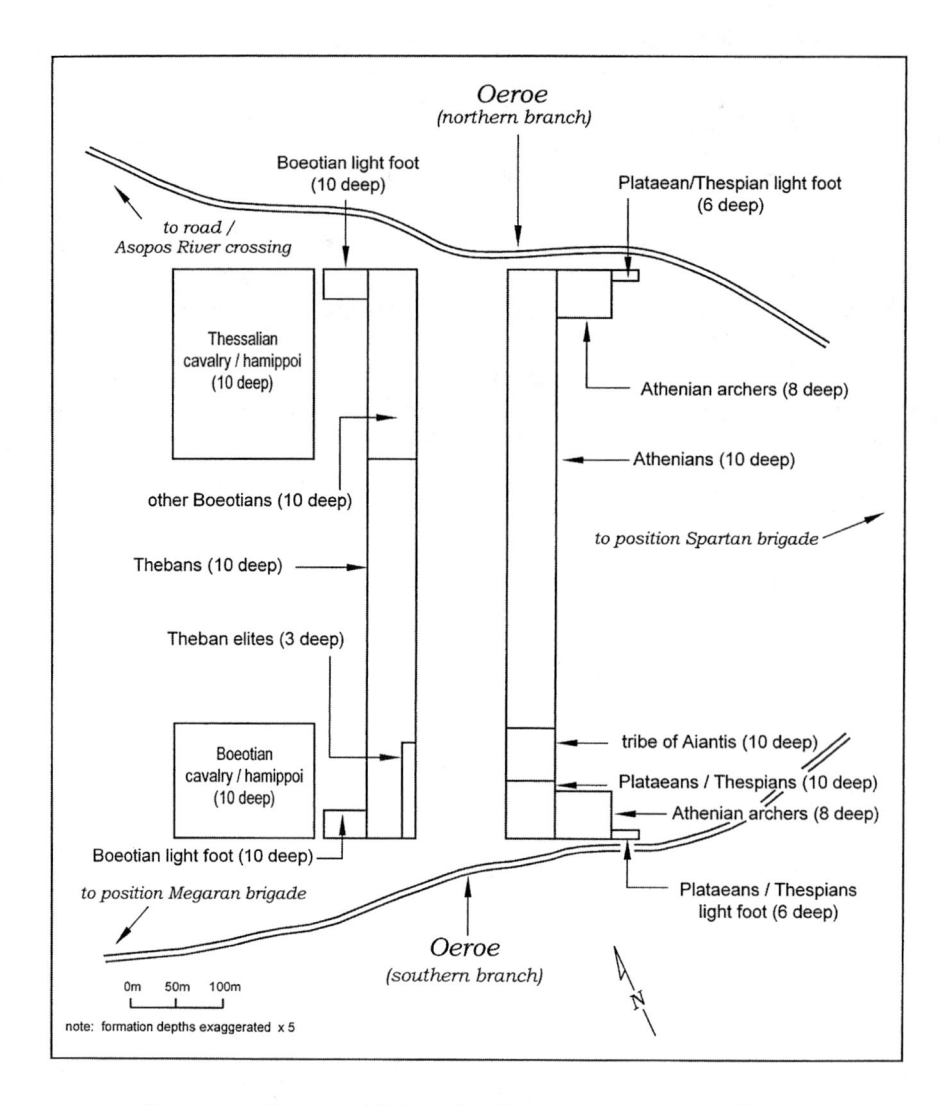

BATTLE OF PLATAEA (479 B.C.)—ENGAGEMENT ON THE OEROE

best troops and suffered disproportionately as a result. Though among the hardest hit, they wouldn't have been the only ones with losses that day. If we assume that the similarly positioned Plataeans took the same sort of damage, while the rest of the Athenians lost 3–5 percent in action, then the brigade likely gave up 250–350 hoplites on the field and another 100–270 to fatal wounds. Its final sum of casualties must therefore have approached or even modestly exceeded those of the enemy.

Asopos Plain

Leaders of the allied contingents on the heights near Plataea could observe the battle shaping up on the plain below as the Boeotians closed on the Athenians. More distantly, they saw dust rising above the low ridge of the Moloeis headwaters and could hear shouting that told that them the Spartans were also squaring off against pursuers. Quickly taking stock of the situation, they split their forces in an effort to support both developing engagements. The

Megaran-led group started downhill toward the northeast in an attempt to aid the Athenians. Simultaneously, the Peloponnesians, headed by the men of Corinth, moved laterally eastward along the slopes toward Pausanius's position.

Rushing down near the road from Plataea that lay west of the Athenians, the men of the Megaran brigade hastened to reach the side of their allies with all possible speed. Each hoplite in line on the slopes would have made a quarter-turn rightward to transform the phalanx into a column that was eight men wide. The Megarans, previously on the right wing, now stood at the van and swung about to head downhill, with the Phliasians, the western and island contingents, and the remaining Peloponnesians following in that order. Their intention must have been to descend and close across the Boeotian right flank before turning back into line for a charge into that unshielded end of the enemy formation. Such an evolution may have been easily doable for well-drilled elites, but was quite beyond clean execution by amateur militiamen struggling to keep a fast pace under the heavy burden of armor and shields. The result was that the Megaran brigade became quite disordered during its descent.

As the leading Megarans neared the south branch of the Oeroe, the Boeotian cavalry under Asopodoros noted their ragged approach. These 600 horsemen and their matching light foot troops had been holding station to the north, behind their phalanx's right flank. Asopodoros took quick action, charging to stop this poorly disciplined advance dead in its tracks. Thorax's Thessalians (some 1,000 riders with paired hamippoi) soon joined the fight, which left only the more distal Macedonian horse troops in reserve. Catching their opponents strung out and unprepared, the northern Greek riders wrought havoc upon them.

The cavalry and hamippoi would have closed on their foes in tight arrays (rectangular for the Boeotians and diamond-shaped for the Thessalnians), hurling clouds of javelins to devastating effect. The Megarans and Phliasians at the front of the hoplite column crumpled under this attack and fled in a panic, with most of them tossing their shields to run all the faster. Not only did these fleeing men make tempting targets, but their frenzied efforts at escape sent them crashing into comrades still coming up from behind. This rapidly spread fear throughout the entire hoplite column, sending it into confused and terrified retreat back toward the hills. As their opponents scattered, the northern riders burst after them, charging among the now nearly defenseless spearmen to strike them down from behind with javelin and saber.

Chasing the last of the broken Megaran brigade into the foothills, the northern horsemen finally turned from the slaughter to regroup once again behind their phalanx. That's where they stood when word arrived of Mardonios's defeat and death. They responded to this news by moving up to menace the Athenians, thus allowing their hoplites to pull out of combat and fall back across the river. Having now discharged their screening duties, the riders wheeled and followed their heavy foot troops to safety.

This action on the Asopos plain took a heavy toll on the allied Greeks. The Megaran and Phliasian levies left the bodies of 600 hoplites scattered between the Oeroe and the lower slopes of Cithaeron — a devastating 15 percent of their combined strength that confirmed the past wisdom of avoiding horsemen on open ground.

Holding the Center

As the Megaran-led contingent marched toward disaster, the Corinthian levy was leading its brigade onto the plain as well. This column seems to have come down somewhere between the Athenian right flank along the Oeroe and the eastern ridge that hid Pausanius's position. Opinion diverges widely on what happened next. Herodotus's account suggests that these Peloponnesians didn't engage the enemy and played only a passive role in the battle, but Plutarch strongly disputed this view and his argument has considerable merit.

There are several clues indicating that the Peloponnesians got into the fight. Simonides, a contemporary poet, composed verse honoring them for holding the center at Plataea (i.e., the ground between the Spartans and Athenians). They must have done this through force of arms, rather than by simply sitting on the position, otherwise it's unlikely they would ever have earned such elegant praise. Likewise, the Greeks awarded a cash prize to those that had displayed the greatest valor during the battle and, when politics ruled out Sparta and Athens, it was widely expected that the Corinthians would claim this honor. They deferred instead to the Plataeans in a very diplomatic and popular move. Nevertheless, anticipation that Corinth's spearmen might take the accolade shows that many felt them worthy of consideration and it's hardly creditable that this would have been the case if they hadn't actually come to blows. Finally, while Herodotus cited some 800 hoplites lost among the other Greeks, this doesn't fit with Plutarch's report of 1,360 dead. Even given the higher losses estimated herein along the Moloeis and Oeroe, about 250–300 victims remain unidentified. It therefore seems likely that the Peloponnesian tombs at Plataea were not just symbolic, but rather true monuments to fallen men.

What sort of fight evolved in the center at Plataea? It seems likely that it started with another confrontation between cavalry and Greek spearmen. The mounted archers of the Sakae stood somewhere behind the Persian wing that fronted the Tegeans on the Spartan left and, upon learning that the Peloponnesian brigade was approaching, they must have advanced to keep it from threatening Mardonios's flank and rear. As they did this, they also sent for help from Artabazus, whose division was still struggling up from the river.

The Peloponnesian column would have responded by turning right and marching until its leading half was deployed east to west. These men next made a quarter turn in place to form a north-facing phalanx eight shields deep that spanned the entire available frontage of about 700m between the ridge slope on the east and the nearest branch of the Oeroe on the west. Filling in behind, the rearward half of the column then doubled the formation depth to 16 shields. The ability of these soldiers to maneuver so adroitly would have been due to both their considerable experience and the presence of spartiate advisors in their ranks. With flanks now well anchored, the Greeks could channel the pending mounted assault into an unbroken line of sharp spears and gleaming shields. The Sakae must have pulled up short of this formidable barrier and laid down a barrage of arrows, striving to impede the enemy's advance long enough for Artabazus to arrive.

Sakae couriers likely found the Medean sparabara of Corps III advancing south at the end of Artabazus's left wing. Being the only infantry in position to offer immediate assistance, these troops must have rushed up into bow range, forming a shield wall as the Sakae relocated to their rear. Constrained by terrain features, the Medes would have massed their formation to about twice its normal depth (20-man files of two dathaba each), which let them match widths with the opposing phalanx and block its way forward.

Missile fire from the sparabara undoubtedly compelled the hoplites to reduce their exposure through a charge across the intervening killing zone that crashed heavily into the Medean front. A brief battle must then have ensued, which neither side proved able to control in the short time allotted for action. The Medes appear to have held the hard-thrusting enemy spearmen in check, while their archers showered the unusually deep after ranks of the phalanx with arrows. For their part, the Greeks would have begun the deadly process of pushing into the opposing shield wall. However, before othismos could do its work, the Spartans to the east managed to rout Mardonios's troops, and the Medes were obliged to follow them in retreat, with the Sakae coming once more into play in covering this withdrawal.

Losses on both sides in this short engagement had to have been moderate. Perhaps no more than 100–150 or so hoplites were killed in action among the Greeks, which falls well within the noted discrepancy between the casualty figures of Herodotus and Plutarch. The Medes probably took similar damage from their better-equipped opponents during the brief fight along the front, though it's likely that they also lost a few men during the difficult first moments of their disengagement. Such a low death rate for this encounter reflected the fact that neither side had broken ranks before combat came to a premature conclusion.

Both the Medes and Sakae joined with Artabazus, who then led his command across the river. Thoroughly shaken by the defeat of Mardonios, Artabazus wisely steered clear of both the Persian camp and the city of Thebes in his retreat, withdrawing instead all the way to Phocis on the other side of the Boeotian plain. From there, he marched the remnants of the once mighty host of Xerxes back to Asia.

Mycale (479 B.C.)

The strategic position of the Greeks had been desperate prior to the battle at Plataea. So long as Mardonios could sustain his army on their soil, there was an ever-growing danger that the union against Persia would fly apart due to internal conflicts, allowing the satrap to then isolate the various allied poleis and deal with them one at a time. While the prospect of Athenian defection had finally driven the Greek army into the field, there was no guarantee that its foe would accept combat in a timely manner. After all, Mardonios could simply pull back and wait for the opposing coalition to disintegrate on its own. Unless pressure could be brought to bear and force him onto the attack fairly soon, the alliance's hoplites would have to seek battle in an unfavorable setting on the Boeotian plain. But then, just as their situation was beginning to look desperate, a solution appeared.

An Ionian delegation arrived at the anchorage of the allied fleet at Delos in the Cyclades. This mission had come from the island of Samos to plead with Leotychides, Spartan king and fleet commander, for support in a revolt against the Persians. The Samians claimed that the Greeks of Asia Minor had grown restive under the yoke of the Great King and, encouraged by Salamis, were primed to again fight for independence. Xerxes' armada had already taken major battle and storm damage and given its Egyptian marines to Mardonios; now, it was on the verge of releasing the Phoenician squadron to cut costs as the naval phase of the European campaign came to an end. Thus, said the Samian representatives, Persia no longer had the strength to oppose an offensive into Ionia from the sea. Such an attack, if carried out in force, might well spark a general uprising that was sure to pull the imperial army back to Asia.

Leotychides knew a good opportunity when he saw it and, after consulting with the rest of the allied leadership, readied the navy for an all-out effort against Ionia. His fleet included some 175 triremes from Athens (110), Corinth (15), Aigina (10), Euboa (10), Megara (10), Troizen (10), Sicyon (5), and Epidauros/Hermione (5). These ships carried perhaps 3,700 hoplites (1,750 marines at 10 per ship and 1,950 as passengers at 30 on each non–Athenian vessel) and 440 archers (4 on each Athenian trireme). Accompanied by 300 bodyguards aboard the ships from Troizen, the Spartan King set sail with his entire fleet shortly after the Greek army marched for Boeotia.

Unaware that it was already a strategic success, the Greek fleet reached Asia to find the remaining Persian ships east of Miletus along the south shore of the Mycale peninsula. The imperials probably had no more than 100 triremes on hand, many of them Ionian Greek and of suspect loyalty. Badly outnumbered, the royal admirals (Mardontes, Artayntes and

Ithamitres) chose to avoid battle at sea and drove their ships ashore. Once on the beach, they fortified their position with ditches, stone walls, and sharpened stakes that blocked all landward approaches. They also provided for an offensive option by putting wide openings in both east and west walls that allowed them to deploy in either direction alongshore.

The satrapal baivarabam out of Sardis was responsible for Ionia and must have formed the backbone of the Persian defense with help from the fleet's marines. Though the latter were Greeks of questionable reliability, the sparabara were good quality troops. Tigranes, former leader of the Corps III Medes, had returned with Xerxes the year before and now had charge of the Sardis contingent. As this was a longstanding unit, its strength probably stood well below nominal at around 6,000 combatants. Herodotus again seems to have greatly exaggerated Persian manpower, in this case by an order of magnitude; still, the fighting men in camp appear to have outnumbered their Greek opponents by nearly 50 percent.

Leotychides sailed beyond the enemy base, hailing the Ionians and urging them to revolt as he passed. He finally beached well to the east near the island of Lade and opposite Miletus. The narrow plain between the sea and mountains here wasn't wide enough to array the entire Greek landing force at a reasonable depth, thus Leotychides and Xanthippos, his Athenian second in command, decided to form two detached wings of nearly equal strength. Xanthippos would make a direct assault along the beach with an estimated 2,000 spearmen from Athens (1,100), Corinth (600), Sicyon (200), and Troizen (100), plus half the archers. Meanwhile, the Spartan king would circle through the hills to the north with the intent of coming down on the left flank of any enemy sally. His force would have included 1,700 hoplites from Sparta (300), Aigina (400), Megara (400), Euboa (400), and Epidauros/Hermione (200), plus the remaining bowmen. The Greeks quickly organized and were ready to advance by afternoon, ignorant that their kinsmen had already won a crushing victory at Plataea that very morning.

Xanthippos and his men marched down the coastal plain to within sight of the Persian camp, while the other division made its way with considerably greater difficulty through the hills on their right. Seeing only the relatively small Athenian force approaching, Tigranes led his sparabara out to meet this threat along the beach. The Persian general must have used most of the men from Sardis for this, perhaps as many as 5,000, leaving only a small force of sparabara in the camp as a reserve and to insure loyalty from the local Greeks inside. (The Persians had already disarmed the Samians and sent the Milesians into the hills.) Tigranes advanced to do battle, not knowing that he was leading the last charge in Xerxes' doomed war on Greece, just as he had led the first a year earlier at Thermopylae.

As the sparabara drew near the Greek front, Xanthippos spread his men out to advance in a phalanx that stretched from the waterline on the left to rough ground in the foothills on the right, covering a front of 250m at a depth of eight shields. The Athenians would have held the right wing with their flank at the edge of the hills, while the hoplites of Corinth, Sicyon, and Troizen arrayed in that order on the left down to the sea. In response to this formation, the Persians set up at a depth of 20 men (two dathaba) along a similar frontage.

Taking their stance within bowshot of the enemy, the Persians dug a furrow in the sand to better seat their shields. Tigranes, having faced hoplites before, must have brought all his shield-bearers (some 1,200 at 20 percent of his command) and was able to file them nearly five deep at the head of his formation. The next five ranks contained spearmen/archers and the last ten ranks had men with bow and sword. The Persians likely opened combat with a heavy barrage of arrows from some 3,800 bows, which might have rained about 19,000 missiles on the Greeks in the first minute of fire alone. As this deadly shower of shafts pelted down, Xanthippos faced a choice of either holding station until help came or charging to reduce effectiveness of the missile fire and let his men get at the enemy hand-to-hand. Leotychides had obviously met some delay in negotiating the hills and it may have been some time yet before he would arrive. Given the damage that prolonged exposure to bombardment might cause, the Athenian decided in favor of attack, and signaled his phalanx forward.

With a shrill chorus of war cries, the Greeks moved swiftly across the relatively short distance between formations. They then subjected the Persian forward wall to a crashing assault of shield and spear. In the brutal fight that followed, the men from Sicyon had a particularly tough time of it, with their commander Perilaus and others going down in the vicious action along that part of the line. Yet despite an energetic effort by Tigranes' men and entrenchment of their shield wall, the determination and othismos-powered thrusting of the Greeks pierced their front. Driving furiously ahead over flattened spara and fallen foes, the hoplites cut through to the unshielded spearmen and archers behind.

As so often before in this war, once Greek shock troops got into after ranks with lighter gear, the contest turned from battle to rout. Terrified Persians in the front and middle of their formation tried to run, but the crowd still in place toward the rear slowed their flight. The rampaging Greeks speared and slashed down scores of these men with no thought of mercy. Finally, panic reached even the back of the Persian array and the last of it made a mad dash toward the east gate of the stockade. With no cavalry to fear and only a brief distance to be covered to the enemy palisade, the hoplites broke ranks in hot pursuit. Mixed among the disorderly mob of fleeing sparabara, Xanthippos's men raced through the still-open gate to breach the camp's defenses before they were ever used. The Ionians now turned on their Persian masters and a confused massacre followed.

Some Persians fled directly from the battlefield into the hills. Others, like the admirals Artayntes and Ithamitres, managed to escape from the camp through the western gate opposite the Greek penetration. (These officers had so badly bungled the defense that Xerxes' brother Masistes, who was also among the survivors, accused them in the most insulting manner of total incompetence.) A fair number of fugitives made it back to Sardis despite deliberate misdirection from their former Milesian allies in the surrounding highlands, these having now joined the other Ionians in changing sides. As for those Persians that remained within the stockade, they put up a valiant resistance, battling to the end, either singly or in small groups, as hundreds of hoplites swirled about them. Leotychides and his men finally reached the battle site during this final stand by the Persian remnants. They added the weight of their numbers to finally overwhelm and slaughter the last few defenders.

Perhaps half the Persians present at Mycale had been killed; furthermore, while two commanders had fled, two others (Tigranes and Mardontes) were among the dead. We can assume from reports on Sicyonian losses that casualties among Xanthippos's men were significant, yet were still only a small fraction of the damage inflicted upon the enemy. Even including victims of the melee inside the camp, only some 100–150 Greeks are likely to have lost their lives. But even this terrible discrepancy in casualties wasn't the most telling Persian disaster on the day, as defection of the Ionians and loss of the fleet trapped on the beach dealt even greater blows.

Xerxes' grand campaign of conquest was an utter fiasco, concluding with crushing defeats on both land and sea. It had begun with an imperial host marching into Europe against a motley collection of badly outnumbered hoplites, but finished with those underrated Greek spearmen standing triumphant on Asian soil. The Persians now had to defend their own territory, with resources in disarray and a once-fearsome martial reputation badly tarnished.

Tactical Patterns of the Persian/Punic Invasions

A great deal of mythology surrounds the invasions of 490–479 B.C. The failures of Persia and Carthage spawned a rich tradition that saw great glory in Greek triumphs against overwhelming odds. Legends grew that a handful of brave underdogs had bested swarming hordes of attackers through superior arms, leadership, and spirit. However, much of this doesn't stand up to close scrutiny. In fact, army sizes were rarely far out of balance and Asian weaponry was highly effective in the right settings. Likewise, Persian commanders were generally the more professional and most of their men had excellent esprit de corps.

What then were the real keys to Greek victory? The battles of the 5th century's opening decade had confirmed great benefits from surprise tactics and mounted superiority. These same factors remained major during the invasion period, though countermeasures were the important story in the case of cavalry. Sicilian Greeks proved quite adept at surprise, while their kinsmen in Greece got the most out of terrain and light foot soldiers to neutralize Persia's edge in horsemen. Each used methods best suited to their own unique situation to bring advantages held in heavy infantry and home positioning to the fore.

If earlier battles hinted that terrain could act as a counter to horsemen, then the actions of the invasion period proved it. Use of natural barriers (wooded slopes, cliffs, chasms, shorelines, and streambeds) and manmade impediments (abatis) as flank anchors was highly effective. Such tactics served on at least ten occasions to shield an army short on cavalry from attacks by mounted foes. In eight of these, the side weaker in horsemen was victorious, either repelling the enemy riders or preventing them from even taking the field. Moreover, the two times when armies with stronger cavalry did win, they did so solely with their footmen (on the last day at Thermopylae and in the finale at Himera). As if to confirm the value of favorable terrain, the lone fight in open country (the Megaran-led advance at Plataea) resulted in horsemen returning to their winning ways.

Light infantry also played important roles in keeping cavalry at bay. Bowmen drove off a mounted assault at Cithaeron, bringing down its leader, and then combined their efforts with supporting stream cuts to help fend off enemy riders on the Oeroe. These actions at Plataea foreshadowed the ability of Athens's foot archers to shield flanks from horsemen at Eion (476 B.C.) and Eurymedon (c. 466 B.C.). Cimon, son of Miltiades of Marathon fame, commanded both of these later victories. He would have been almost thirty years of age at Plataea and already a man of some distinction, as he gained election to the post of general the next year. Having seen the great effectiveness of his city's bowmen in that battle, he was to embrace them as cornerstones of his tactical style.

Yet while employment of optimum tactics might have rendered mounted troops less decisive, it didn't eliminate them as a force in battle. Thus, horsemen played major roles on no less than seven occasions during the invasion era. The first of these was at Marathon, where a mounted rearguard stung pursuing Greeks and forced them to halt and regroup. This robbed them of at least some of the fruits of success, cutting Persia's losses and saving its fleet from beachside destruction. Ten years later at Thermopylae, Leonidas's fatal holding action on the final day of fighting was necessary to forestall mounted pursuit of his retreating allies. Horsemen were therefore important to that epic clash, even though they didn't engage in combat. Just a few weeks after this, it was the riders of Gelon who opened the way to victory at Himera by infiltrating and burning the Carthaginian naval camp. Lastly, Persian cavalry confronted hoplites on five occasions at Plataea, most notably inflicting a thorough rout on the Megaran brigade, but also precluding Greek pursuit in all sectors at the end of that battle. Thus, though chosen terrain and missile counterfire kept horsemen from dominating these various engagements, they clearly remained very valuable assets.

While use of flanking barriers was a key to Greek success on the mainland, the shoe was on the other foot in Sicily. Here, it was the Grecian defenders who were stronger in horsemen and the foreign invaders who made use of topography and light foot troops to counter. Lacking a clear-cut edge in heavy infantry, the Greeks therefore found it necessary to dig into their bag of tricks toward generating surprise attacks. And between the clever infiltration and assault on the naval base and a flank/rear ambush in the climactic battle at the army camp, the Sicilians' talent for doing the unexpected proved crucial to their final victory at Himera.

Clever exploitation of the physical setting by both mainland Greek and Carthaginian generals in this period left their land campaigns to be decided by shock combat. The Greeks were clearly better at this sort of fighting, but their advantage was not just a matter of greater protection provided by hoplite armor and shield. In truth, while the Greeks might have had better helmets than most, the rest of their panoply wasn't all that marked an improvement over either Punic gear or that of shield-bearing sparabara. Rather than stouter protection on the defensive, it was actually the offensive use of spear and aspis in service of the phalanx that carried the Greeks to victory.

The Grecian spear was a bit longer than those commonly used by other nations. Though this made it less versatile (no good as a missile) and more fragile (prone to snap in two), it was without doubt the perfect weapon for phalanx fighting. The hoplite spear's great reach allowed men standing in the first three ranks to all strike at the enemy. Opponents with shorter weapons could retaliate in kind from only their first two rows, giving the Greeks a 50 percent edge in striking force along the battlefront. As for fragility, adaptation of this spear to the peculiar demands of phalanx warfare had produced a semi-standard length that offered the best possible compromise between range and durability. Spears might break on occasion, but they usually held up long enough to get the job done. Addition of a butt-spike (sauroter) compensated for breakage by allowing continued use of damaged weapons; this device served as a counterweight as well, extending more of the spear in front of its point of balance. Finally, the sauroter provided a means to ground the shaft, which was not only useful to free the right hand, but also let the spear act as a staff to push against and provide more powerful othismos.

The aspis shield was, like the Greek spear, perfectly evolved for phalanx warfare. Its size, concave shape, method of forearm suspension, and lipped edge all made it easier and more effective for a hoplite to press into the back of the man ahead and generate othismos. And this pushing, along with the aforementioned edge in striking capacity, lies at the very root of Greek shock superiority. Indeed, a brave and stalwart enemy might well take his lumps and endure in an unequal, give-and-take encounter with better armed and armored foes, as the Persians had done in Ionia; however, courage and individual strength weren't enough for a man trying to stay on his feet and fight while being shoved toward the rear by an entire file of opponents with only weak support at best from his own back-rankers. Thus, the Greeks used any means at their disposal (be it terrain, missile fire, or trickery) to bring their foes into shock contact and then applied their chosen equipment in support of phalanx tactics that they might drive to victory.

By favorably matching topography to their gear and martial style, the Greeks were able to gain an advantage from fighting on home ground. During the 15 actions detailed here during the invasion period, the side closest to its homeland won much more often than it lost (11 victories against only 4 defeats). And most of the failures were of a qualified nature, with Greek defeats on the last day of Thermopylae and in the first action at Himera largely a result of going against overwhelming numbers. Likewise, the Thebans' failure at Oeroe was more technical than real, since they withdrew voluntarily. In fact, only the Persian loss at Mycale stands as an outright beating taken near home against an enemy of comparable or lesser strength.

The foregoing record of success on native soil is a strong reversal of patterns during the century's first ten years, when invaders took 10 out of 15 engagements. Still, the overall sample of actions down to 479 B.C. doesn't give much of an edge to the local side (16 victories versus 14 defeats). Furthermore, the wide discrepancy between combat results in the first and second decades suggests that they had little to do with simple location. The real key to success seems to have been proper matching of arms and tactics to the lay of the land. Thus, any edge from fighting on home ground didn't come from mere proximity, but rather grew out of success in using aspects of the local terrain to force battle in a favorable setting. Any such advantage was physical and had to be actively pursued, rather than psychological and inherent.

* * *

Persia and Carthage went into temporary eclipse after their defeats. This shifted the focus of new conflicts toward competition among the victors for the spoils of leadership. Athens and Sparta had emerged stronger than ever, the former supreme at sea and the latter master on land. Their successes now set these rising powers onto a collision course, with Athens pursuing a policy of empire building that led to conflict with Sparta's vital allies. It was a clash of vaunting Athenian ambition against ingrained Spartan obsession with homeland security. The result was a series of wars that nearly tore the Greek world apart.

IV

Prelude to Collision: The Pentacontaetia (478–432 B.C.)

> "A succession of demagogues and warmongers arose, who proceeded to turn the Greek states against one another, and nobody could be found to separate or reconcile them before they met in the headlong collision of war."
>
> Plutarch *(Cimon)*

The era known as the Pentacontaetia covered a nearly 50-year span following the end of the Persian invasion. This was an ambitious time for the Greeks, when their leading states, no longer consumed by foreign threats, strove to gain sway over ever grander territories. Such fever for expansion was so widespread that it infected the entire spectrum of poleis, with an array of monarchies, tyrannies, oligarchies, and democracies all trying alike to grab ever more land and power. It seems that the intensely competitive nature that drove Greeks to excel at sports and trade was now pushing them with equal vigor to make warfare just another game, with hegemony as the victor's prize. Thus, in Italy and on Sicily there was fierce fighting for supremacy not only between colonists and native peoples, but even among the Grecian settlers themselves. And elsewhere, Sparta faced armed challenges to its leadership in the Peloponnese, while Athens turned toward empire, suborning its allies and spawning bloody wars of conquest.

Warfare in the West

The third decade of the 5th century gave rise to dramatic changes in leadership among major poleis in the Grecian West, where the deaths of Gelon of Syracuse in 478 B.C., Anaxilas of Rhegion in 476 B.C., and Theron of Acragas in 472 B.C. installed new regimes. Prominent among the new leaders was Hieron, who succeeded his brother at Syracuse. A suspicious and despotic man by nature, this tyrant suffered by comparison to his popular sibling, yet proved shrewd and well up to the task of leading his polis to greater glory. He not only expanded his base on Sicily by taking the last free cities along the eastern coast, but also came to terms with Acragas in the south and extended his influence into Italy.

Hieron allied with Locri, Sybaris, and Cume on the mainland, and married into Anaxilas's family as a tie to Rhegion, Syracuse's chief rival for the Sicilian Strait. However, upon the death of Anaxilas, the appointment of Micythus as regent at Rhegion for the tyrant's underage sons revived tensions along the strait. Micythus seems to have been an honorable man, who was genuinely concerned for the future of his youthful charges. He saw Hieron not only as a menace to Rhegion's outpost at Messana, but now had every reason to fear his intentions in Italy itself. The new regent thus moved to counter these threats through an alliance with the strong Spartan colony at nearby Taras. As this was transpiring in the north, Hieron's relations with Acragas in the south (again cemented by marriage) went sour. Theron's demise made the union with that ruler's daughter moot, as her brother Thrasydaeus came to power and set out to oppose Syracuse.

Hieron and the others were embarking on campaigns of self-interest at the expense of the fragile balance of power built by their predecessors. In doing so, they ushered in a new round of deadly hegemonic competition. Such turmoil not only set tyrants against each other, but also gave native peoples a chance to reclaim lost lands. The Iapyians of Italy as well as the Elymians and Siculi of Sicily all rose up at this time to strike back at the Greeks.

Taras II and III (473–460 B.C.)

Taras sat along the south Italian shore at the top of the Sallentine Peninsula (the "heel" of the Italian boot). From its foundation in the late 8th century, this city had contested control of the area's rich farmland with three native Iapyian tribes—the Messapians, Peucetians, and Daunians. The Tarantines had claimed a major victory (Taras I, c. 490 B.C.) over the Messapians, who lived to the south and east on the peninsula, which gained them a lengthy respite from serious warfare with the Italians. However, the conflict arose once more in 473 B.C., and this time it took on truly frightening proportions.

Diodorus claimed that 20,000 barbarians descended on Taras, and this might well have been the case. Judging by similar tribes at Rome (Sekunda, Northwood, and Hood 1995, 11–12), each Iapyian grouping could have had 2–4,000 shock troops, all carrying a short spear and oval shield and most with both a pectorale and a shin-guard on the left leg as well. Peltasts, slingers, and cavalry would have brought the Iapyians up to around 18,000 fighting men, while 2,000 allies (light foot troops and horsemen) might have then filled out their host in line with Diodorus's figure. It's therefore likely that the Italians closed on Taras with some 9,000 heavy footmen, 7,000 skirmishers, and 4,000 riders.

Taras was one of the most powerful states in the Greek west (only Cumae and Syracuse would have had greater resources) and could probably field an army on the order of 4,000 hoplites, 1,000 psiloi, and 400–600 horsemen. These were likely joined by another 3,000 spearmen from Rhegion, who also brought their own light foot troops and cavalry. (The proposed contingent from Rhegion equals Herodotus's report of Rhegian losses at Taras, which presumably reflects total manpower engaged for the polis at about two-thirds of its full capability.) The Tarantines could thus call on around 7,000 hoplite militiamen, just under 2,000 foot skirmishers, and 700–1,000 horsemen. In fact, though having fewer armored troops than the Iapyians, the Greeks were indeed strong enough to risk battle. If their phalanx could just hold fast, it had a chance to demoralize and defeat an excitable barbarian foe.

The Greeks must have marched out to take position on ground of their own choosing, probably just southeast of Taras. They now stood between the city and the enemy's point of assembly farther down the peninsula, blocking the best line of advance to Taras along the coast. As the leading barbarians came into view, the hoplites would have moved into a phalanx near the shoreline, forming at a depth of eight shields, with Tarantines holding the center and right wing and their Rhegian allies taking the left. The generals had no doubt carefully selected this ground as it was a good choke point between the sea on their right and rugged terrain and undergrowth on the left, yet still wide enough to deploy all of their spearmen. Posting light troops to further secure the landward flank, the hoplites now stood fast in their ranks as the enemy closed rapidly in a formation that probably was ten men deep to match width of line.

Both sides would have loosed a hail of slingers' shot and javelins as the barbarians made a screaming charge into the solid row of spears and polished shields fronting the phalanx. The fight went on for some time and, if Diodorus's brief account is accurate, took a high cost on both sides before reaching a resolution. In the end, the hoplites failed to break through the numerically superior Italians and were themselves penetrated and put to rout. This might have been due to either generally poor phalanx technique or collapse at a single point, but the latter seems more likely, in that the Tarantines and Rhegians fled in different directions. This suggests that the tribesmen split the Greek formation between its center and left wing. As enemy spearmen poured through this gap, the men from Taras must have broken northwest along the beach and toward their nearby city. They thus cut off their Rhegian allies on the left, landward side of the field, leaving them no choice but to flee into the interior in a desperate attempt to reach their much more distant homeland.

The Tarantines took a heavy hit, with the enemy's swift light foot and mounted troops spearing and slashing them down from behind. Characterized fancifully by Herodotus as being too many to count, Taras's losses on the day probably included nearly 900 hoplites killed — at least 20 percent of those engaged. Bad as this was, the Rhegians suffered worse still, not having a refuge close to hand. While we can discount Herodotus's claim of 3,000 slain and Diodorus's improbable story of fugitives being chased inside Rhegion itself, this was nonetheless a costly defeat that could have claimed the lives of around 1,000 citizens.

Micythus of Rhegion weathered this reverse (leaving office on his own terms in 465 B.C.), but the leaders of Taras weren't so lucky. The Tarantine royalty and aristocrats caught most of the blame and were replaced by a democracy. However, thorough as the Greek defeat appears to have been, it didn't have a lasting effect, since the barbarians had neither the mindset nor means to follow up with a siege, and Taras lived to fight another day. The city rebounded at Taras III (c. 460 B.C.) to inflict a decisive defeat on the Peucetians and their allies, taking the life of Opis, king of the Iapyians. Known only from dedications at Delphi, this battle likely was a fairly even match-up of armored troops, as the Peucetians had about 3,000 such men and could count on allies to equal the 4,000 or so spearmen on hand for the Greeks. The victory ended Tarantine conflicts with the Italian tribes for a full generation.

Acragas I (472 B.C.)

The victors at Himera vied for control of Sicily in the following years. Thrasydaeus of Acragas emerged at this time as a violent and ambitious man, who, according to Diodorus, gathered an army of 20,000 hoplites for a campaign of conquest. This figure looks to be badly inflated, since Gelon had shortly before been able to collect so large a host only by drawing on the resources of Syracuse and Acragas combined, plus a matching mercenary contingent. It's therefore likely that Acragas had a heavy militia that was no more than 3,000 strong. Adding twice as many hired men and drafting 1,000 spearmen from Himera, Thrasydaeus could thus have put no more than 10,000 hoplites in the field. Still, this was a huge force by the standards of the day, and one probably further supplemented by 1–2,000 archers and slingers as well as some 400 riders with hamippoi.

Preparations on such a scale didn't go unobserved. Hieron of Syracuse responded by gathering hoplites from Syracuse (perhaps 4,000), his allies (maybe another 2,000), and the mercenary community (4,000 or so, about all that would have remained available on the island). Though he likely had less than 1,000 archers and slingers, his legacy from Gelon gave him an edge in the form of around 2,000 excellent horsemen and a like number of hamippoi. Yet Hieron's greatest advantage lay in his genius for tactics. He displayed this by preempting opposition plans with a surprise march on the enemy assembly point near Acragas. Mustering in haste, an unready Thrasydaeus now had little choice but to meet Hieron on suitable open ground to the east of the city.

Once on the field, both sides likely lined up eight shields deep behind their skirmishers. Syracusans would have held Hieron's right wing, with allied troops in the center and the hired spearmen on the left. Meanwhile, Thrasydaeus must have had his locals and the men from Himera on his right, using his huge crowd of mercenaries to fill out at center and left. Note that professional hoplites were not preferable to citizen soldiers at this time, since, unlike the finer skills of archery or slinging, all Greek yeomen knew the basics of spear fighting. The militia's superior motivation and organization thus made it better qualified for the honored right-wing posting.

As their light foot troops retired, the hoplites on each side would have closed at a fast walk until less than a hundred meters apart and then raced to smash into each other with tremendous force. Yelling, stabbing, and slashing, men shoved and fought to deal out cruel wounds and death along a front that stretched over a kilometer wide. The battle was very hotly contested, but resulted in a clear-cut victory for Syracuse at the end of the day. Given Hieron's much superior cavalry, it's probable that this arm swept away the outmanned enemy cavalry, and either launched or threatened a flank attack that drove the opposing phalanx from the field. However, the battle's result must have hinged on psychological factors as well. Their surprise march would have given the Syracusans a decided edge in morale, boldly stealing initiative from a foe not fully prepared to fight. This had shaken Thrasydaeus's men, robbing them of the sort of confidence needed to persevere in a long and close-run shock action; thus, both mind and muscle played key roles in Hieron's success on the battlefield. Bested at last, the Acraganians withdrew, battered and bloody but still able to retreat in good order. They would have taken only modest losses to pursuers before they got to safety inside the city.

It seems that Thrasydaeus had absorbed a sharp, yet not ruinous defeat. Diodorus set his losses at twice those of the victors, which likely translates as 6–10 percent versus 3–5 percent for Syracuse. Nonetheless, the battle was decisive in that it profoundly altered the political landscape. Thrasydaeus had to flee a democratic uprising, but was quickly caught and executed. At the same time, Syracuse had become the leading state in Sicily.

Achradine I and II, Owl's Plain, and Crastos (466–455 B.C.)

Thrasybulus came to rule at Syracuse upon the death of his brother, Hieron. An unpopular despot, he held office less than a year before his abuses inspired a revolt. This uprising must have been apparent in its build-up, since the tyrant stood ready when it hit, having gathered a large mercenary legion that included both new recruits and numerous soldiers of fortune that his predecessors had brought into the city over the previous 20 years. These men followed the money and were more than willing to support a dictator still in control of the city's wealth. There undoubtedly were social factors at work as well, since the mercenaries were an underclass that had been denied true citizenship. They therefore not only had no reason to be outraged over Thrasybulus's treatment of those more privileged, but likely saw this as a chance to give their supposed betters some payback.

Diodorus put the tyrant's army at nearly 15,000, which could be true if he had engaged all of the available mercenaries. There might have been up to 12,000 such fighters in Sicily at the time, some 10,000 of them hoplites (per Diodorus and earlier deployments) and the remainder archers and slingers. Thrasybulus was also able to call upon local allies for another 2,000 spearmen (including 500–600 from Catana) and 200–400 horsemen (at one or two for each ten hoplites) plus a team of hamippoi. Some of these troops set up camp within Achradine, the northeastern sector of the central city, while the rest occupied Ortygia. The latter was an island just to the south that held both the palace and — critical to the hired help — treasury. A small harbor lay between these two sites, providing shelter for that part of the city's fleet still loyal to the dictator.

As Thrasybulus was digging in along the northern coastal district, the rebels moved to seize Tyche, the urban sector west of Achradine. From here they could control the rest of the city as well as the Great Harbor, which lay south and west of Ortygia. The militia of Syracuse formed the backbone of the rebel force, with what might have been 5,000 hoplites (including reserves) and 500 horsemen plus hamippoi. Help had also come from Gela, Acragas, Selinous, and Himera in the form of both ships and men. Acragas and Himera jointly supplied 4,000 spearmen, while Gela and Selinous each provided 1,000 for a grand total of 6,000 allied hoplites. These same cities sent mounted troops as well, lending perhaps 700–1,200 horsemen (200 from Gela, as per a later muster against Athens, and 500–1,000 from the others, at one or two for each ten hoplites). In addition to these Greek allies, the native Sicels also saw advantage in the uprising, and provided a mix of light horse and footmen. It's probable therefore that the insurgents were only a little inferior to their foe in spearmen and could actually field greater manpower overall. Most importantly, they held a huge edge in cavalry, which clearly dissuaded Thrasybulus from seeking a pitched battle in which horsemen might be the deciding factor.

The allied militias deserted Thrasybulus when the siege began to drag on and, having only his mercenary force now, he was more than ever unwilling to risk open battle. Instead, he sought to secure his seaborne line of supply and made a naval sortie against insurgent squadrons in the Great Harbor. The rebels dealt a sharp defeat to the tyrant in the ensuing action and loss of ships further degraded his logistics. As stores grew perilously short, Thrasybulus finally had no choice but to risk an overland breakout.

Thrasybulus made a morning sally into the poorly developed suburb just outside his wall to the west of Achradine, where he would have taken up formation eight shields deep across a 1,200m front. Shorn of allied cavalry, his phalanx had to use buildings and other man-made features on both flanks to help its light infantry defend against mounted attack. As the rebels saw their foe coming out to fight at last, they would have gathered into a facing array of roughly similar dimensions, with the Syracusans on the right side and their allies extending along the rest of the front.

After some minor skirmishing, the formations charged together into a vicious tilt of nearly even strength. Shouting and shoving, mercenary troops and militiamen struck at each other among the long shadows and harsh echoes thrown from surrounding walls and buildings. This urban setting precluded cavalry envelopment, making it the blood and sweat of the opposed spearmen alone that would decide the outcome. And though a close-run affair, the struggle came to an end by mid-morning, when the insurgents stabbed and pushed through the mercenary line to send it into flight.

Badly beaten, Thrasybulus and his surviving troops retreated into Achradine, with a likely 1,000–1,500 of the hired spearmen having lost their lives in the battle and pursuit. Beaten on both land and sea, Thrasybulus elected to negotiate terms that put him into exile at Epizephyrian Locri on the toe of Italy. His troops had the option to leave in peace as well, but most chose to remain. The decision to let these men stay would ultimately prove a costly mistake.

The mercenaries were resident aliens in Syracuse's new democracy; therefore, they weren't entitled to full participation in the government. Seemingly prone toward violent solutions, these men sought to improve their lot in 461 B.C. through open revolt. The 7,000 hoplites and a goodly number of archers and slingers that were still among their ranks retook Achradine and Ortygia, leading the local militia to build a counter wall that isolated these strongholds from resupply. The citizens then launched a futile series of assaults against Achradine, to which the other side replied with short raids into the city. Eventually, the mercenaries began to run out of food when their already poor situation grew worse after a reversal at sea cut off supplies from that quarter. They decided in desperation to settle the matter on the field of battle and attacked the Syracusans in front of the counter wall, perhaps setting up very near the same spot that they had contested five years earlier.

Diodorus claimed that the spearmen of Syracuse outnumbered their opponents. As their militia was made up of no more than 5,000 hoplites (prime and reserve), this suggests that help had come from a number of allies. Gela was closely tied to Syracuse and likely sent 1,000 spearmen, while other cities might have come up with another 1,500. The latter equals troops sent earlier to support the tyranny less the men from Catana, who were then at war with both Syracuse and the Siculi. Syracuse's resulting composite force of some 7,500 hoplites would have had light support from around 1,000 horsemen and a matching team of hamippoi to yield overall numbers in line with Diodorus.

The mercenaries probably marshaled a phalanx of eight shields in depth over a front of nearly 900m. They would have faced a similarly arrayed Syracusan formation of around 950m in width, with local militia standing from right wing through center and allies on the left. The former included a new lochos of 600 elite hoplites trained and maintained at state expense. These picked fighters might have filed eight deep along a 75m stretch on the far right, but alternatively could have taken post as the leading rank for the entire Syracusan contingent.

Once the opposing formations closed into contact, this second battle before Achradine apparently played out much like the first, with phalanxes of similar size engaged in an urban setting that neutralized the effects of light foot and mounted troops. Though both sides fought hard and took heavy casualties in the early going, it was the Syracusans who won the day. The elite lochos was crucial to this victory, likely pushing ahead in a compact mass on the right wing to break through and turn the enemy's flank. Unable to hold their position, the mercenaries pulled back to shelter behind the walls of Achradine. With no stomach for another fight, the hired men readily accepted a truce that let them leave with all their possessions.

A papyrus recovered from Oxyrhynchus in Egypt (Pearson 1987, 26) suggests that mercenary troops were involved in at least two other conflicts with citizen militias in the period 460–455 B.C. The first followed an attack by Omphace and Kakyros on Gela, which might have been seeking to reassert its sway over those nearby towns and the displaced foreign fighters that now controlled them. This led to a battle at a site called Owl's Plain, where the attackers advanced against a Syracusan column coming to relieve Gela. We have no details of this action, but it's likely that a couple of thousand mercenaries met defeat against a superior force from Syracuse.

The second action took place near Crastos. The Acraganians had marched against this former holding of theirs only to end up in a pitched action against the town's new mercenary masters as well as troops from Himera and Gela. The latter cities had probably joined in to check Acragas before it could threaten their own territory. The scope of this fight might have been fairly large, with each side fielding up to 3,000 spearmen. Again, we have no details, but continued ascendancy of Acragas suggests that its militia gained the victory.

Mazaros I (454 B.C.)

Syracuse had become the leading polis in Sicily; thus, its conflicts were the most noted military events on the island during the Pentacontaetia. Yet many other disputes between lesser states surely took place in this period as well. As these "little wars" rate only brief mention at best in our sources, we get no more than a glimpse at what must have been a common pattern of small-scale fights for eschatia that were much like those recorded in contemporary Greece. At least one such minor conflict can be pieced together from the murky data that has survived.

Diodorus reported a battle along the Mazaros River of far western Sicily in 454 B.C. that matched the Elymians of Egesta (Segesta) against the Greeks of Lilybaion. However, as Lilybaion had not yet been founded, this is obviously a case of confused info from older sources. Pausanius cited a war at this same time between Punic Motya and Acragas, while elsewhere, we hear that the Greeks of Selinous defeated an unnamed foe and that Egesta counted the Siculi town of Halikyai as an enemy. Freeman (1891–1892, vol. II, 338–41 and 549–57) sorted through this tangled story to suggest that there had been a land dispute that led Motya to join Egesta in a war on Selinous, which was the Greek outpost closest to Phoenician territory and thus in frequent conflict with Punic interests. Friction with the nearby Elymians was also common, dating back to 580–576 B.C. when Egesta defeated Selinous and its allies in battle. The outmanned Greeks looked for help to their powerful neighbors to the east at Acragas and also gained support from Halikyai, the latter being located within the contested area at the headwaters of the Mazaros.

The disputed territory lay between Egesta and Selinous and these must have been the primary antagonists, with Motya and Acragas playing more modest roles. We can estimate manpower for Egesta and Selinous on the basis of their strengths later in the century, which puts the Egestaean heavy foot troops at around 1,500, to which Motya might have added another 1,000. Light support would have come from a few hundred archers, slingers, and peltasts, plus 400 or so horsemen. (It's known that Egesta had at least 300 riders in 414 B.C., while the Phoenicians likely fielded 100 more at about one for each ten men in the heavy infantry.) The armored men from Motya were no doubt evenly divided per Punic custom between those with a thrusting spear and those with two javelins (one for throwing and one for close-in work). The Elymians used a mix of native Italian and adopted Greek gear and most had short spears suitable as either missiles or shock weapons. On the other side, Selinous could have fielded some 2,500 hoplites, with another 1,000 spearmen coming from Acragas. Greek light forces likely amounted to 200 horsemen (one for each ten hoplites), a matching number of hamippoi, and a few mercenary archers and slingers. The Siculi would have added several hundred footmen of various types and some light cavalry. Of no use in the phalanx, the Siculi infantry probably joined the Greek light forces in providing skirmishers and flank protection.

Meeting on a broad clearing near the river, both armies would have sent out advance screens of light foot troops and jockeyed into their battle formations along a front of more than 400m. The Greeks likely were in phalanx eight men deep, while the Phoenicians and Elymians took up a superficially similar but thinner and looser-filed linear array. As their skirmishers retreated, the formations moved into shock combat amidst much shouting and clashing of weapons on shield. Diodorus reported that the ensuing battle claimed heavy casualties on both sides before ending in a draw, but disputing this are commemorations that suggest Acragas and Selinous won the war. If this was, in fact, a closely contested Greek success, it must have featured a fierce and unusually lengthy melee between front fighters. Greater numbers, heavier gear, and othismos would then have allowed the Greeks to eventually claim the field and at least a marginal victory.

Despite being driven from the battle site, Motya and Egesta were still strong in light foot soldiers and horsemen. It's therefore probable that these recouped some glory by covering the retreat and inflicting damage on pursuing foes. Had the Greeks broken formation in giving chase, such retaliation by opposing light foot and mounted troops might well have forced them to pull back and regroup or even abandon the field entirely. This would have given both sides a measure of victory and given rise to the report of a drawn battle. In the end, Motya and Egesta would give up their land claims, perhaps doing so under pressure from much more powerful Acragas.

Greek Motya and Nomae (451–450 B.C.)

While the battle along the Mazaros was largely a Punic/Greek affair, the Elymians and Siculi had played supporting roles and, within a few years, the Siculi would unite on their own behalf to reclaim lands lost to the Greeks. Syracuse had ousted the tyrant Thrasybulus in 466 B.C., at which time Ducetius of Menae had been among the noble Siculi that came to the aid of the city. This natural leader later advanced his position with success in battle, including a joint campaign with Syracuse against Catana in 461 B.C. Driving the Catanans into exile at nearby Aetna, Ducetius regained land lost in Hieron's day and traded on this triumph to gather most of the tribesmen into a league under his leadership. He then used the strength of this alliance to push back the Greek frontier and recover portions of the southeastern coastal plain. The result of this aggression was open warfare with the Greeks.

After taking Aetna (formerly the Siculi town of Inessa) in 451 B.C., Ducetius next marched into Acraganian territory. His army would have been a little larger than the Siculi host at Hybla forty years earlier, as it represented a wider tribal unification. This suggests a total of around 3,000 armored men, the same in light foot troops, and some 300 horsemen. Ducetius invested the Greeks at Motya (not to be confused with the more famous Punic city of that name), pinning down a garrison from Acragas.

A relief column marched to Motya from Syracuse and Acragas under the Syracusan general Bolcon. The Greeks must have raised a formidable army despite having only short warning and could have put at least 6,000 hoplites into the field with light infantry and mounted support. The spearmen likely included 3,000 from Syracuse and local allies plus a contingent of equal size from Acragas. Cavalry would have numbered some 900, counting 500 from Syracuse and 400 from Acragas to the limits of their capability. Light foot troops consisted of hamippoi at one per horsemen and perhaps a few archers and/or slingers. Once this host neared the city, it broke into its separate levies, which then set up adjoining camps.

Heavily outnumbered in both armored infantry and horsemen, Ducetius seems to have realized that his best hope lay in a surprise attack on his enemy's camp — a choice that no doubt reflected knowledge of lax Greek encampment procedures gained during past service alongside the men of Syracuse. He thus led his forces out on a night march that put them in position to pounce at dawn.

Bolcon's men were startled out of their usual morning routines by the sound of bloodcurdling Siculi war cries and turned to see an enemy battle line sweeping down on them. Shock and fear would have raced through both camps and many of the badly shaken Greeks simply panicked and ran away without a fight. Others hastily prepared to resist, grabbing whatever gear was close to hand and attempting to get into some kind of formation. At best, these men could have gathered helmet, spear, and shield, since there was no time to struggle into body armor. Thus ill-prepared, the hoplites likely tried forming up to face the enemy at the camp perimeter, but must still have been desperately jostling into a semblance of rank and file when the Siculi attack struck home.

Withering under a barrage of javelins, the Greeks first took heavy casualties from these missiles and then were savaged all along their ragged line as a more coherent enemy formation smashed into them with momentum from a running charge. The tribal front washed over and through the defenders like a tidal wave, tearing the Greeks apart and driving survivors all the way into the woods beyond. Many Siculi, unable to resist the lure of piled armor and other booty, stopped at this point to sack the abandoned campsites. In fact, it was probably only this diversion that allowed many of the Greeks to escape.

Denied relief, Motya quickly fell. Meanwhile, Bolcon, who had managed to run from the battlefield with his life, was tried for conspiring with the Siculi to set up the ambush and defeat of his own expedition. Though this charge seems unlikely to have been true, he provided a convenient scapegoat for the incompetent performance at Motya and was promptly convicted and executed. Saving some face through this flimsy claim of foul play, the Syracusans regrouped over the winter and marched out in the spring to seek revenge with what must have been the city's full field army plus a few reserves, to the tune of 4–5,000 hoplites and 400–500 horsemen with hamippoi. While this army moved directly against Ducetius, the men of Acragas provided support with a simultaneous assault on his followers at Motya.

The Syracusans came upon Ducetius near the small village of Nomae and, alert to possible tricks, were able to bring him into open battle this time, gaining what Diodorus described as a hard-fought victory. Most of the defeated Siculi retired to hilltop strongholds, but a few remained on the run with their commander. With no hope now of defeating the Greeks, Ducetius was facing betrayal from his own disgruntled troops and fled to Syracuse that he might throw himself on the mercy of his enemies. Surprisingly, the people of Syracuse were in a forgiving mood and, without consulting their allies, let him go into exile at Corinth.

Himera River (446 B.C.)

Acragas and Syracuse soon resumed disputing hegemony over Sicily. And when Ducetius returned to found a colony on the northern shore, Acragas accused Syracuse of allowing this common enemy to go free without thought for the interests of their allies. It used the charge as a pretext to declare war and ignited a wide conflict that pulled most of the Greeks onto one side or the other.

Based on past deployments and losses to date, it's likely that Acragas had a modest edge in spearmen at 6–7,000 versus 7–8,000 for Syracuse. Yet the latter's mounted strength provided a telling advantage. Syracuse had the largest and finest cavalry force on Sicily and could put 700 citizen and allied horsemen into the field with a matching force of hamippoi. Acragas, on the other hand, had only about 500 riders of lesser quality. This must have influenced the Acraganians' final choice of a battle site, causing them to stay near home and let the Syracusans march against them in the summer of 446 B.C. The armies thus met along the Himera River (not to be confused with the stream in the north near the city of that same name) on Acragas's eastern frontier, where the Acraganians could make their stand on ground that was at least somewhat less favorable for the enemy's cavalry.

We have no description of this engagement, but Syracuse was able to claim the field, very likely with the help of its much superior cavalry. And regardless of their role in the main clash, those horsemen must have led a very deadly pursuit, accounting for many of the 1,000 Acrganian spearmen lost on the day. In contrast, the cost to Syracuse probably came to something less than 400 hoplites killed (below 5 percent). It would be more than a quarter of a century before Syracuse again faced a serious challenge, though not from local rivals this time. Instead, the threat came from mainland Greece, where decades of strife had led to the rise of other, equally powerful states.

The Spartans Eaten Raw

The Peloponnese saw a great deal of upheaval during the Pentacontaetia, hosting several conflicts that would prove of considerable consequence in the future. And Sparta was at the center of all this turmoil, engaged in desperate struggles to preserve its hold on both the helots at home and the more reluctant among its allies abroad.

Sparta's system of serfdom posed a constant internal problem. The helots had a hard life, with little personal freedom and burdened by dedication of a substantial portion of the fruits of their labor to support the spartiate elites. This gave rise to such great hatred that it was later said the helots would be willing to eat the Spartans raw. Sparta responded to this menace by eliminating the more aggressive and independent serfs. Though sometimes executed on a wide scale, these purges were mostly carried out on an individual basis through a constant campaign of nighttime terror and assassination called the *krypteia*, which was a task for youths in the final stages of spartiate military and social training (the *agoge*). The threat of a helot uprising was always foremost in the minds of the Spartans and dissuaded them from sending troops out of the country; and when their armies had no choice but to operate at a distance, a strong force stayed behind as a safeguard.

There were, in fact, practical limits to how much territory a small ruling class could control through such methods. Sparta therefore took a different tact during its subjugation of Arcadia in the early 6th century, since this mountainous region to the north was too distant, too large, and too populous to control in the same brutal fashion. After the Spartans gained Tegea, they thus permitted it to remain separate in return for an agreement that the Tegeans would provide a levy of troops in times of war. This set the pattern for all of Sparta's future relationships in the region, which formed a network of one-on-one pacts that would eventually extend hegemony over most of southern Greece within what is known today as the Peloponnesian League. Yet despite this system's potential for mutual benefit, it's clear that much of Arcadia remained allied only under threat of armed reprisal.

Tegea (470 B.C.)

The Tegeans revolted in 470 B.C. and, seeing an opportunity to hurt its old rival Sparta, a resurgent Argos quickly came to their aid. These states put an army into the field that might have had around 5,000 hoplites and 750–1,000 psiloi. This would have been an all-out, 2,000-man effort for Tegea that committed about 80 percent of its full levy (the 1,500 spearmen at Plataea having likely been two-thirds). As for Argos, a force of 3,000 hoplites is consistent with its later effort nearby at Mantinea I (418 B.C.), though minus reserves in this less urgent case. There would have been an irony here in that that these troops probably took the field in 500-man lochoi that mimicked the organization of their enemy, reflecting both the Tegeans' long service in the Peloponnesian League and post–Sepeia reforms at Argos that copied many such Spartan practices.

As the rebel army was mustering near Tegea, it suddenly found itself facing the Spartans, who had assembled a strong force of their own and marched out to strike first. Sparta could have closely matched opposition manpower by mobilizing all ten of its lochoi (five each of spartiates and perioeci). Pausanius (of Plataea fame) probably commanded this host, having returned from Asia earlier that year and still being regent for the young son of Leonidas.

Once in sight of each other on the plain south of Tegea, the armies formed up in phalanxes that would have had eight men per file to square off along a front just over 600m wide. The Tegeans must have held the honored right side of their array, with the Argives on the other wing. The local men were thus opposed to perioeci on the Spartan left, while the troops from Argos faced the spartiates and their general on the opposite end of the field. Following some preliminary skirmishing, psiloi on both sides retired to provide flank support, allowing their hoplite companions to begin moving forward for the main engagement.

The Spartans marched at a slow pace, in time with the strains of battle poetry (Castor's song) set to the deep, oboe-like sound of flutes. Few things in classical warfare were more unnerving to an anxious opponent than a Spartan phalanx's deliberate rate of advance. While the patriotic singing, hot-blooded shouting, and final rush to battle of other Greek armies created an enthusiastic atmosphere much like that in a modern athletic contest, the methodical approach of the Spartans smacked of cold-blooded killing. It struck mortal fear into their enemies. Still, the Arcadians and Argives apparently moved out bravely to meet this fearsome display of murderous intent, their front no doubt drifting a bit as each man instinctively sought the shield of his mate on the right. The Spartans must have likewise slid rightward as they closed, in their case consciously enhancing the natural drift of their formation. As separation shrank to less than 100m, the allies vented their battle cries and charged at the run to smash into the Spartans.

The leading ranks now stabbed and slashed all along the front, as men behind shoved into the backs of those before them that they might drive through the enemy. The Tegeans seem to have put up a good fight against the perioeci opposing their wing, with an epitaph later claiming that their bravery in the battle ultimately spared Tegea from the torch. In the end, however, the action seems to have turned on the allied left, where the Argives took the worst losses that day. This appears to have been a classic case of envelopment by the opposing spartiates. While their perioeci stalemated the Tegeans on the left, these elite troops must have used an enhanced rightward drift to overlap, partially encircle, and roll up the Argive flank. Set upon from side and back, the men from Argos on the far left would have broken away in terror, sending a wave of panic surging along the line to tear the rest of their phalanx apart.

The Tegeans seem to have held their own on the west side of the battleground, which let them withdraw in fairly good order and with only modest loss. The Argives on the other wing took a great deal more damage, having lost heavily among those surrounded and cut down on their flank. This defeat would remove Argos from Arcadian affairs for the next half century; therefore, though the battle didn't end unrest in the region, it did limit the Arcadians to only those forces they could draw from their own fractious poleis.

Stenyklaras (c. 465 B.C.)

Sometime 469–464 B.C., a powerful earthquake rocked Sparta. The epicenter, which lay beneath the valley of the Eurotas, sent out an initial tremor and strong aftershocks that tumbled major structures and killed many Spartan citizens. This disaster set off a fateful chain of events that would play out over a decade to not only threaten Sparta's hold on the Peloponnese, but also forever alter its relationship with Athens. Of course, the first to exploit this tragedy were those bitter enemies of Sparta already on the scene — the helots.

Many helots rose up against their masters in the chaotic aftermath of the quake, gathering to menace the metropolitan area. Archidamus, one of the Spartan kings, rallied his people to form a defense and cause the mob to flee from Laconia. The helots crossed the mountains on the west to collect in great numbers in Messenia, traditional heartland of their people. Local serfs joined the revolt there, as did Messenian perioeci from the towns of Thuria and Aethaea. Such support from perioeci must have been of particular concern to the Spartans, since it not only provided the rebels with hoplites (likely a lochos of 500 prime and 100 reserve spearmen), but also men who had served in Sparta's phalanx. This gave the helots knowledge of Spartan field tactics that would increase the danger to any force sent against them.

The spartiates responded by pulling together an under-strength lochos of 300 picked men from the earthquake's survivors and sending it into Messenia. This contingent marched under Arimnestus, slayer of Mardonios at Plataea, who likely had support from a party of still-loyal serfs, with 50 or so of these serving as psiloi. Given the small size of this force and that the Spartans weren't insanely foolhardy, Arimnestus probably didn't intend ending the uprising alone. Rather, he must have meant to persuade the perioeci spearmen to join him in a joint attack. As he had fought alongside these same Messenians at Plataea, Arimnestus might have been relying on that old bond and his wide renown to win them back.

Advancing rapidly into hostile territory, the Spartans encountered an army of helots and their hoplite allies somewhere northwest of the mountain stronghold of Ithome. This was on the plain of Stenyklaras, possibly just south of the village of that same name. Whatever Arimnestus's hopes had been for detaching the perioeci, neither his reputation nor the menace of his spartiate warriors was enough to turn them from revolt and they took the field in an array that most likely stood eight shields deep over a 75m front. With old-age reservists holding the last rank and youths enclosed in the center, the Messenian hoplites must have had a huge swarm of helot psiloi posted along each flank.

It would have been prudent at this point for Arimnestus to back down from what was clearly shaping up to be an unequal fight. Perhaps the large numbers of opposing light foot troops made escape impossible; more likely, an excess of honor and/or confidence led him to meet the challenge head on. After all, he had won battles against long odds before, and no spartiate wanted to turn his back to the enemy. It thus appears that the Spartans moved to match the opposing front by forming up only four deep, standing on the plain with their flanks screened by a mere handful of helots whose loyalty had to have been in doubt. Once organized for action, the two formations must have closed together with a minimum of preliminaries to lock into a vicious fight to the death.

The battle at Stenyklaras was both short and bloody. Desperate spartiates would have fought with grim determination and skill all along the line, either holding their ground or giving way only very grudgingly to their deeper-filed foes. But rebel numbers and skirmishing on the flanks quickly proved decisive. Chasing away the light screen from either end, vengeful helots apparently enveloped the thin Spartan line from both sides, folding it in on itself to be completely encircled and overrun. Herodotus's remarks on the death of Arimnestus indicate that his entire command was wiped out. Most of the spartiates must have died where they stood, trying in vain to hold their hopelessly surrounded position. In truth, there might have been no chance for escape, as a mob of pursuers could have quickly downed anyone trying to flee.

Decisively triumphant in this first clash, the helots retired to Mount Ithome and spent the next summer raiding the countryside in a guerrilla war. An ever-increasing number of Messenians joined this effort, being equipped and trained in shock combat and phalanx tactics by both their perioecian kinsmen and mercenary adventurers from nearby Arcadia. The Spartans now found themselves in dire straits, devastated by the earthquake and with an economy ravaged by the effects of both raids and the loss of so many helot workers. It wasn't long before others among their enemies sought to make use of this growing weakness.

Dipaea (c. 464 B.C.)

While the Spartans were occupied to the east, Tegea saw a chance to once more assert its independence. Though the Argives weren't involved this time (having taken serious damage on Tegea's behalf in 470 B.C. and already exploiting Spartan woes nearer home in the Argolid), this didn't dissuade the Tegeans. They were able to find plenty of support in the form of an alliance with all of the other Arcadian states save Mantinea. The latter was the second-leading polis in Arcadia, whose heretofore cool relationship with Sparta was as much as anything a case of gainsaying the more favorable one of its southern neighbor and arch rival. The Mantineans were thus content to remain neutral if it might derail Tegean ambitions.

This was, in fact, an opportune time for the Arcadians to rise up. In contrast to Sparta, which was depleted and overextended, they had gained additional manpower. A large number of Arcadian mercenaries had come back from Sicily following the defeat of their employer, Thrasydaeus of Syracuse. After a few prosperous years abroad, these men were now once more stuck on their hardscrabble farms and would have been in a foul mood. Such veteran fighters not only boosted raw troop strength, but undoubtedly lifted the courage of their fellow hoplites as well.

The Arcadians began to collect near the small town of Dipaea, which lay in west-central highlands within the upper valley of the Helisson River. Central to the many poleis involved, this site was also farther than Tegea from the enemy and across the mountains from prying eyes in Mantinea. The gathering here had potential to reach as many as 5,000 hoplites, with perhaps 3,000–3,500 from Tegea and Orchomenos and the rest from a mix of smaller hamlets. Returned mercenaries might have composed from a third up to half of this heavy force, while light support came from poorer men to the tune of 750–1,000 psiloi.

The hard-pressed Spartans learned of this assembly (perhaps via Mantinea or from a friend among their former allies at Tegea) and scrambled to respond, cobbling together what strength they could and sending a makeshift army north under Archidamus. Based on the reduced size of the lochos fielded at Stenyklaras, only about 60 percent of the Spartans were in shape to take up arms, which suggests that less than 4,000 hoplites were available nationwide following the earthquake, including reserves. Given perioecian defections, the losses at Stenyklaras, and forces stretched to cover security at home as well as in Messenia, it's likely that no more than 2,000 of these spearmen (perhaps half of them spartiates) and a few light foot troops could be spared for the column that marched to Dipaea.

Sparta's king took a bold risk by moving so deep into foreign territory, since his men would face a long and costly pursuit should they lose. Yet by meeting the Arcadian host before it was all together, he could not only tackle a smaller phalanx, but deal it a psychological blow at the same time. In fact, it's likely that only about 4,000 (80 percent) of the Arcadians had reached the muster point when Archidamus arrived. The orator Isocrates said that the Spartans fought at Dipaea in a single rank, implying that they were outnumbered by at least 8 to1 at normal formation depths. Given that this surely reflects some dramatic liberty, we can more reasonably project that the manpower discrepancy was closer to 2 to 1. While still significant, this wasn't overwhelming in light of superior Spartan fighting abilities.

The surprised Arcadians would have drawn up eight shields deep on the plain south of Dipaea, with Tegeans likely holding the right wing, the men from Orchomenos on the left, and the smaller levies filling in at center. This must have forced Archidamus to file his own men at four in order to create a matching front of 500m. As this was the practical minimum depth for a phalanx, it might well have inspired the later claim of a single rank (Cawkwell has alternatively suggested [2002, 240] that Isocrates meant that there was only one rank of spartiates).

The phalanxes would have closed slowly amid the sound of the clanking of armor and Arcadian battle hymns until only tens of meters apart; then, with a shout, the Arcadians would have rushed to meet a Spartan front that had maintained a deliberate pace all the while. What followed was the first heroic feat in a day that surely saw many, as the thin line of red-clad warriors withstood the awful concussion of this charge. The Spartans might have bent a little, but they didn't break, and fought back with desperate fury, even though their short files had no real hope of piercing the facing line by othismos. Indeed, despite their great martial skills, it's doubtful that they could have resisted penetration of their own formation for very long. Still, the battle would end in a Spartan triumph.

How did the Spartans pull this off? Most likely, Archidamus and his spartiates holding the right wing were able to overawe the opposing Orchomenians, chasing them from the field within a few minutes. Intimidated by Spartan repute from the start and further shaken by their foe's cool and assured advance, these troops must have verged on panic even as the fronts were closing. And once they saw their fearsome foes pivoting adroitly to wrap around and begin rolling up their flank, they simply broke and ran, causing the rest of their city's levy to soon follow suit. Of course, once its left wing had fled, the rest of the rebel formation had to withdraw as well. Such a collapse at first contact with the Spartans is well documented elsewhere and is as plausible an explanation as any for the upset at Dipaea. Sparta's clear victory brought the Arcadian uprising to a quick end.

Mycenae (c. 464 B.C.)

Another local conflict was brewing at this time that pitted Argos against Mycenae. Once among the greatest of citadels, Mycenae and its sister city Tiryns had gone into decline at the end of the 13th century to become no more than minor poleis subject to the Argives by the start of the 5th century. The rise of Sparta gave these states an opportunity to reclaim some of their old independence through an alliance that saw them fight beside the Spartans against Persia, even as Argos kept neutral. Mycenae then went on to reassert control of both the Nemean Games (a regional festival) and the Heraion (a shrine along the Argive frontier). The proud Argives bristled under these challenges, but stayed cautiously in check until the earthquake of c. 465 B.C. put Sparta on the sidelines.

The Argives now marched out to seize the Heraion and ravage the southern reaches of Mycenaean territory — and one thing is sure: they weren't looking for a fair fight. The Argive army likely counted some 4,000 hoplites, including 3,000 citizens and another 1,000 from their vassals at Orneai and Cleonai. The field force of Mycenae and Tiryns, in contrast, probably numbered no more than 600 spearmen (based on the 400 sent to oppose Persia being a two-thirds levy), and even calling up the reserves would have added but 200 more. Thus, it must have been with a strong sense of doom that the defenders formed on the broad western plain below Mycenae's hilltop citadel.

The shallow-filed hoplites from Mycenae (who would have been on the right) and Tiryns were facing a foe able to deploy eight shields deep and still cover a wider front. It's likely then that the right-wing Argives quickly took advantage of natural drift to envelop the Tirynian flank, while the rest of their phalanx used greater depth to shove forward across the entire front. The disparity in manpower here was much worse than that set against Sparta at Dipaea, and there would be no repeat of that heroic upset. Outflanked and stumbling backwards, the men from Tiryns must have been first to give way, but the Argives then pushed through at several other points to complete the rout.

The Mycenaeans seem to have withdrawn in some semblance of order. This kept their manpower sufficiently intact to permit adequate manning of Mycenae's walls after the battle. Tiryns was less fortunate. Nearly encircled, its ranks were overrun and devastated, leaving the city's defense in the hands of no more than those few remnants that managed to flee the debacle. The Argives settled in to besiege both cities. Tiryns quickly fell, but Mycenae held out until either starved into submission or (per Diodorus) taken by storm the following summer. Argos went on to completely absorb these poleis, much as Sparta had done with Laconia and Messenia.

Battle of the Isthmus (c. 463 B.C.)

The Messenian revolt entered a second summer that saw the rebels striking from a fortified safe haven on Mount Ithome. Short of men and powerless against helot defenses, the Spartans called upon the old anti–Persian league for help, and close allies Mantinea, Corinth, and Aigina responded to this appeal, as did Plataea and Athens. Cimon, son of Marathon's Miltiades, was an advocate of joining this mission, and Aristophanes claimed that he got command of 4,000 hoplites (probably including Plataeans) for the effort. Despite this, the helots continued to hold out; thus, by fall, the spartiates found their own depleted numbers spread widely in defense of the homelands just as harvest season began pulling perioecian and allied militia from the field. Before long, only a small contingent of Spartans and a much-reduced corps of allies (supported at Spartan expense) were left to prosecute the war.

The rebels chose that moment to sortie from Ithome and seek battle at a site known as The Isthmus. This might have been the Skala Ridge (Cartledge 2002, 188), which forms an east-west divide across the Messenian plain. By going on the attack then, the Messenians no doubt hoped to face not only a reduced foe, but also one likely to include quite a few poorly motivated non–Spartans. Nevertheless, Sparta must still have had 5–6,000 hoplites, counting a mora of its own (perhaps 500 perioeci and 300 spartiates), nearly the full levy from Athens, and some token units from the other allies. Psiloi would also have been present (at around one per ten hoplites) along with at least a few Athenian horsemen.

The Messenians probably fielded a mix of spearmen composed of the lochos of perioeci that had fought at Stenyklaras and a few disaffected Arcadians plus a huge force of newly armed and trained helots. The latter could indeed be effective as hoplites. This is attested by Sparta's own later success with the use of helot spearmen (*neodamodeis*), which confirms that basic hoplite skills were not that hard to acquire. In fact, that the rebels took the initiative on this occasion suggests they had hoplite manpower comparable to that of the enemy, in addition to a superior host of light-armed skirmishers.

We can never know what took place on the battlefield, but the action at The Isthmus was most likely a triumph of experience over enthusiasm. While patriotic fervor and hatred of the enemy might often lure men into war, it was generally confidence (in their leaders' abilities, in their own skills, and in their companions) that got them through a fight alive and victorious. Such a winning attitude could best be acquired through successful combat experience, and the Spartans and their allies must have had the edge in this regard. Some of the neophyte hoplites among the Messenians probably lost their nerve in the terrible press of battle, running from the fight and costing their side critical formation integrity. Fortunately for the rebels, their numerous light troops allowed them to cover the withdrawal and preserve enough manpower to continue running Ithome. Cimon and his men now returned home with victory in hand, leaving the small force of Spartans and other allies to contain the insurgent stronghold through the winter.

When the Messenians persisted in their resistance, Sparta again called for allied help in 462 B.C. Once more Cimon got leave to march an army to their support; however, during the campaign that followed, the Spartans took the controversial step of discharging the men from Athens. This might have been because they were uncomfortable with having a democratic contingent in such close contact with rebels seeking the same freedoms. Yet there could have been an economic motivation as well, since paying to keep so many men in the field was probably more than Sparta could readily afford. Moreover, though the Athenians had gained a reputation as siege experts in storming the Persian camps of 479 B.C., they had failed against Ithome, making it hard to justify their continued expense.

This dismissal deeply wounded Athenian pride and disgraced Cimon, whose unpopularity outside his own clan got to such a state that it led to exile. A rise in anti–Spartan sentiment then sent the Athenians into alliance with Argos and led them to support peaceful relocation of the Messenians as a solution to their uprising. Athens thus settled the rebels sometime 461–455 B.C. at Naupactus, which it had recently annexed on the north shore of the Corinthian Gulf. This not only allowed a measure of revenge for Sparta's insult by frustrating punishment of the Messenians, but also created a loyal base on the Gulf that would prove invaluable in future conflicts.

The Athenian Empire

Greece's confrontation with Persia continued into the mid 5th century, with the Athenians taking the lead in pushing the Great King's forces back into Asia. In the course of this campaign, Athens became hegemon of a far-flung maritime domain rivaling that of Sparta on the Greek mainland. Hoplites were an element in this rise to power, as success in battle raised both expertise in phalanx tactics and the confidence of the troops using them. Yet it was really the signature use of naval mobility and battlefield terrain that made Athenian warfare so effective. Athens spent the Pentacontaetia fine tuning these tactics and building an empire in the process. However, like Sparta, it would find that controlling a vast territory in the face of outside competition, reluctant allies, and contrary native peoples was no easy task.

Eion (476 B.C.)

The Grecian alliance set out after its dual victories at Plataea and Mycale to retake the north Aegean from Persia. The renowned Spartan general Pausanius led this campaign and, though he had subdued most of Cyprus and captured Byzantium, this harsh and arrogant man took a high-handed approach with his allies, who also thought he was far too cozy with the enemy. The Athenian commanders in the field (Aristides and Cimon) exploited these character flaws to have Pausanius recalled. His replacement was then rejected and Athens moved to take over the Greek counter-offensive by popular acclaim.

The Athenians now formed the Delian League (named for its treasury on the island of Delos in the Cyclades) as a formal alliance of the poleis actively engaged against Persia; they then sent Cimon out with a 300-ship fleet to attack enemy remnants still holding Thrace. We can make a fair estimate of the fighting strength on hand by assuming that 200 of his vessels were Athenian (as used later at Eurymedon) and the rest from League allies. The triremes from Athens had been built in the 480s under Themistocles and normally carried ten hoplite marines and four archers each, while the other ships would have been crewed in the old style with 30–40 spearmen apiece. This gave Cimon a total of 5–6,000 hoplites and 800 bowmen that he supported with skirmishers drawn from among the oarsmen. The Athenian general landed this force in Thrace and marched on the city of Eion, which lay on the east bank of the Strymon River. The Persian general Butes had his headquarters here, likely manning it per a typical satrapy with a baivarabam of sparabara (3–6,000 men), a hazarabam of Iranian horsemen (300–600 riders), and some local light foot troops (perhaps 1,000 peltasts).

Butes must have sorted to meet Cimon under the south-facing walls of Eion, hoping by taking the field to prevent his enemy from investing the city. The Greeks likely stood above the beach at eight men deep across some 625–750m (a front that might have been a bit wider than that of the Persians, who tended toward deeper files). Pitted against a foe strong in cavalry, it was critical that Cimon find a way to secure his flanks. Plutarch cited an inscription that describes the combat at Eion as taking place beside the swift current of the Strymon and, if not mere poetic contrivance, this suggests that Cimon anchored his left, western flank against the river. This would have allowed him to use his entire force of bowmen to protect the right side of the line, where he stood with the men from Athens. That he employed such tactics is no surprise, given that his father had used terrain masterfully at Marathon, and Cimon himself had seen the effectiveness of his city's archers against horsemen at Plataea just three years earlier.

Opening the fight with flights of arrows, the Persians probably stood their ground as the Greeks shed the missiles, and advanced to launch a spear attack on the facing shield wall. There is no reason to doubt that Butes' men put up stiff resistance, but they were doomed when the river and Athenian archers conspired to foil their best attempts at turning a flank. As so often in previous years, hard-driving hoplites must then have used their heavier gear and othismos to bully through the thin Asian shield front and put light-armed after ranks to flight. The Persians were badly mauled and chased back inside the city behind a screen of horsemen and peltasts. Cimon next set his men to scattering the local population, thus cutting Eion's main source of supply and rapidly reducing Butes to dire circumstances. The Persian eventually torched the city, choosing to die in the holocaust that he might deny his enemy an even greater victory.

Cimon went on to lead Delian League forces in a series of fruitful campaigns over the next decade, capturing the island of Scyros in the Aegean, prosecuting a war against Carystus on Euboa, and putting down a revolt on allied Naxos. If operating against fellow Greeks at Carystus signaled that the Athenians might be doing more than simply fighting Persians, then the attack upon Naxos confirmed more sinister ambitions. This was the first time that a member tried to break from the League, and Athens's brutal response told one and all that the alliance and its treasury were no more than Athenian assets. The contributions of funds and/or warships required of League poleis had effectively become tribute.

Eurymedon (c. 466 B.C.)

As Athens tightened its grip on the Delian League, Persia was marshaling resources for a counterstrike under the admiral Tithraustes. This commander began to gather a fleet off the mouth of the Eurymedon River in Pamphylia (on the southern coast of modern Turkey), where a small army under the general Pherendates guarded his anchorage from landward attack. Reports put Persian naval strength at between 350 and 600 ships. The higher number is certainly much inflated, yet even the lower figure may overstate the case for a fleet that would soon fare poorly against a Greek force only about 60 percent this size. Nevertheless, it was still a powerful armament that offered a real threat to Lycia and Caria, which Cimon had just recently seized for Athens. The Persians actually had good reason to like their chances on the open sea; after all, their Punic squadron was of the highest quality, reinforcements on their way from Cyprus would give them overwhelming numbers, and their naval defeats to date had all come in confined waters.

The Greeks moved to preempt Tithraustes by sending Cimon and a 200-ship task force to Eurymedon. This was a potent fleet — smaller than the force at Eion a decade earlier, but all its ships of the latest generation. It seems that the active-duty life of a trireme hull was only 15–20 years (Casson 1991, 88; Morrison and Coates 1986, 155); therefore, the older vessels in service at the time of Salamis and Eion had by now been entirely replaced with Themistocles' more modern designs. Raw numbers aside, the superior quality of these Athenian ships and the skill of their crews alone boded ill for the Persians. Cimon arrived ahead of the enemy squadron expected from Cyprus and wasted no time in defeating the Asian fleet already gathered, driving its battered survivors onto the shore.

The beached imperials were now under the protection of their army, which was most likely made up from the local satrapal garrison. At 60 percent of nominal strength, this gave the Persians 6,000 sparabara and 600 horsemen plus some local light foot troops (perhaps 3,000 Cabelee peltasts). Encouraged by the continued enthusiasm of his men, Cimon was not daunted by this Persian force and chose to take the fight onto land; nor was this a rash move, as his fleet carried a strong hoplite component. Plutarch noted that these new vessels could carry more troops due to special structural modifications — most likely an extension of the ships' decking — and we can assume that they had a full load of both Athenian and allied spearmen at 10 marines and 30 passengers on each trireme. This let Cimon come ashore with about 8,000 hoplites, 800 archers (four per ship), and a swarm of crewmen skirmishers.

Cimon disembarked at a distance and then marched in phalanx down the shore toward the remnants of the Persian fleet. Spread across coastal flats, his formation might have been a kilometer wide at a depth of eight shields. As at Eion, Cimon was using terrain to anchor one flank while securing the other with archers and light foot. Pherendates had rushed to get his men ready to fight as well. The exact form of his array can only be guessed at, but he could have matched the enemy front at something like the Persian norm of ten ranks deep by employing men drawn from his grounded ships. He would have had sparabara in the center of this formation and shielded peltasts on his wings behind a few rows of more shock-capable marines, with cavalry stationed either rearward or on the landward flank to threaten the unanchored side of the Greek line.

The setting here carried echoes of Mycale, where sparabara had tried in vain to fend off hoplites bent on destruction of an imperial fleet. But the Persians might well have been counting on improved equipment to yield a more favorable result this time. At some point before 460 B.C., they had outfitted the archers in their rearward ranks with a small, crescent-shaped shield called a *taka*; and while we can't be entirely sure that this innovation was in place at Eurymedon, it seems highly likely. Just a bit larger than the similar Greek pelta, the taka not only provided an increased measure of protection in shock combat, but also gave great comfort to the psyche of a man facing the awful stress of a hand-to-hand action. The latter meant that, though the taka was essentially a defensive device, it would have improved Persian offensive potential by boosting morale and the will to fight aggressively.

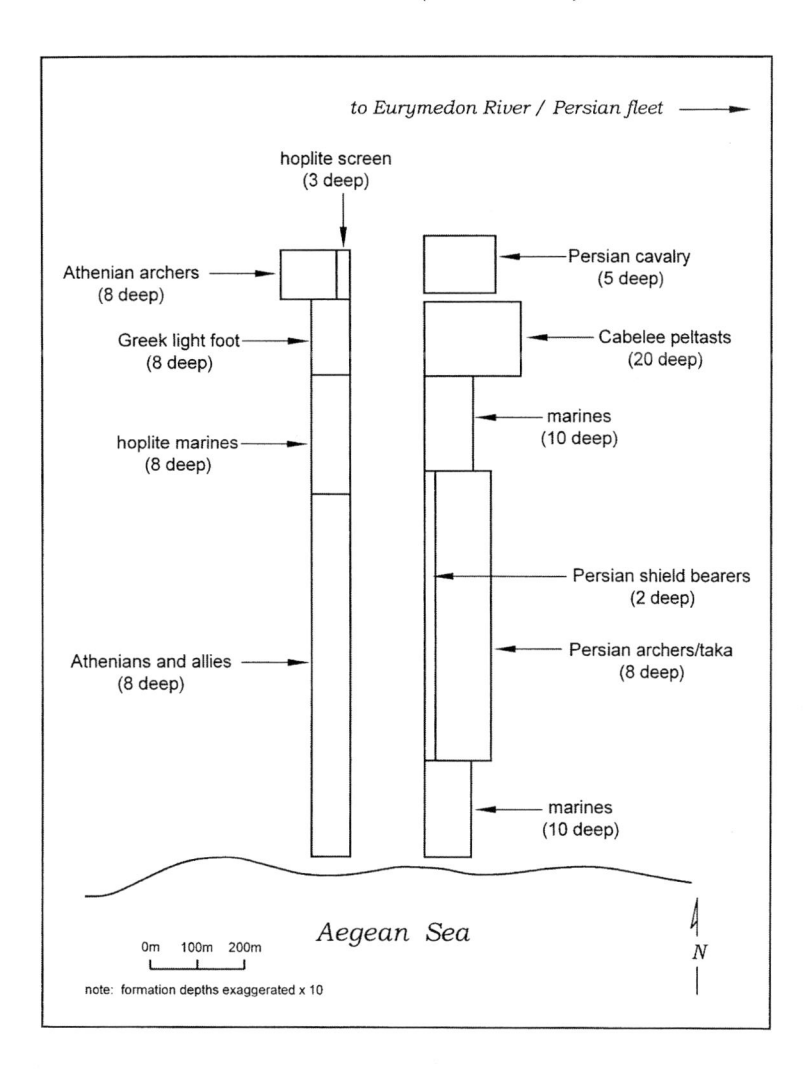

[Diagram: Battle of Eurymedon troop formations, labeled with:
- to Eurymedon River / Persian fleet
- hoplite screen (3 deep)
- Athenian archers (8 deep)
- Greek light foot (8 deep)
- hoplite marines (8 deep)
- Athenians and allies (8 deep)
- Persian cavalry (5 deep)
- Cabelee peltasts (20 deep)
- marines (10 deep)
- Persian shield bearers (2 deep)
- Persian archers/taka (8 deep)
- marines (10 deep)
- Aegean Sea
- Scale: 0m, 100m, 200m
- note: formation depths exaggerated x 10
- N (north arrow)]

BATTLE OF EURYMEDON (C. 466 B.C.)

The armies closed, and when the Athenians came under arrow fire, Cimon charged his hoplites into the facing wall of spara. The ensuing melee must have been intensely contested by both sides, but the longer it lasted the more the Greeks seized the upper hand. The Persians' lighter battle line had no ability to penetrate the opposing phalanx and their hopes therefore hung on successful cavalry envelopment of the landward flank before their shield wall gave way. When their horsemen were unable to get past the Greek light foot soldiers posted there, the action thus turned into a line-against-line affair that the Asians had no real prospect of winning. Still, Persia's front fighters gave a good account of themselves, battling fiercely and inflicting numerous casualties on the fronting Athenians. But the overmatched sparabara and marines couldn't keep this up for long, and relentless forward pressure from the Greek phalanx eventually breached their front. The now-exposed Persian rear ranks, with or without shields, were no match for hoplites and quickly broke into flight, allowing the Greeks to sweep ahead and destroy the grounded fleet.

Note that this account follows Plutarch, who probably drew from Ephoros. Diodorus's version differs, tracking Callisthenes in attributing Persian naval command to Arimandes. It poses that Cimon defeated the enemy fleet and seized most of its ships on the beaches of Cyprus; if so, the Persians had linked with the tardy Cypriots and engaged the Greeks far from Eurymedon. The story that follows then was that Cimon put his deckhands into Persian dress and used the captured vessels to infiltrate the imperial encampment at night, killing Pherendates and routing his army. Full of fantastic elements, this tale is hard to credit and seems far less likely than that of Plutarch.

The Greeks lionized Cimon's victories on sea and land as having duplicated the glories of both Salamis and Plataea in a single day. And, indeed, though smaller in scale, these triumphs did carry similar significance, since Cimon went on to defeat the tardy naval force coming from Cyprus and drive the Persians out of Asia Minor. This forced the Great King to recognize Greek dominance in the Aegean, perhaps even formally, as some hold that he signed a treaty to that effect in the spring of 465 B.C. Yet this didn't prove a lasting solution, with any such agreement falling into disregard upon the death of Xerxes in the fall of that same year.

Drabescus (465 B.C.)

While Eurymedon had put an end to foreign threats for a time, Athens still faced challenges with uprisings among subject allies; at the same time, barbarians within the city's expanded territory gave rise to another menace. In Thrace, a mix of 10,000 colonists from Athens and its allies (including Decelea, Aigina, and Argos) had set up along the Strymon River some 8km upstream from Eion. This had been the site of a Thracian town called Nine Ways (Ennea Hodoi) and lay on a flat-topped hill about 3km north of the later city of Amphipolis (Pritchett, 1995, 94–121). It seems that the locals very much resented this settlement and were ready to do it harm at the first good opportunity.

The colony at Nine Ways lay along the important route to Asia Minor and oversaw a land rich in precious metals and timber for ships. The barbarian Edonians already occupied the region, but it appears that this new batch of Greek settlers had enough manpower to suppress these warlike tribesmen, at least when operating near the coast. Flush with their initial success, the Greeks next advanced an armed force some 40km inland under the command of the generals Leagrus of Athens and Sophanes of Decelea. Their intention was to seize the gold mines known to exist in that area.

Nine Ways might have had around 3,000 hoplites at most (half the adult male population) and may have sent as many as 2,500 of these on the inland campaign along with an equal number of attendants and psiloi. This would have been a powerful force, but the Edonians and their allies were set to resist it and had more than enough men to do so. In fact, by gathering a coalition army of horsemen and peltasts from all the tribes thereabouts, the barbarians very likely outnumbered the Greeks in fighting men by a considerable margin. The Thracians descended on the Greek column at Drabescus (somewhere near the modern site of Drama at the upstream confluence of the Strymon and Angites rivers) and swarmed to the attack.

This was a battle on open ground, where success didn't depend on greater weight of armor but rather on superior mobility. Pritchett inspected the area around the probable site of Drabescus and described it as immense and dominated by rolling hills (1995, 109), making note of its great suitability for cavalry. This was critical in that the Thracians had good horsemen, much like those of their Scythian neighbors to the north. Thus, the action at Drabescus pitted a highly mobile attacker (fielding perhaps 30 percent of its strength in mounted men per a known Thracian deployment in 429 B.C.) against slow-moving infantry.

The Thracians took the colonists by surprise, catching them after making a very close approach, perhaps under cover of a thunderstorm (per Pausanius's comment that lightning struck the Athenians). Storm or no, the Thracians hit their foe with thunderbolts of the figurative kind, charging at speed to launch a devastating missile strike. Caught out of order and mentally unready, the hoplites were barely able to scramble into a ragged and unsteady formation as the enemy engulfed them. Thracian peltasts and horsemen hurled their javelins from beyond reach of the Greek spears and then hurried back to safety before their slower opponents could touch them. Any psiloi who tried to remedy this situation by giving chase fell quick prey to their more numerous and shield-equipped Thracian counterparts. The tribesmen would have bled the hoplite line with repeated sallies; then, having taken the inferior measure of the light-armed Greeks guarding the phalanx's flanks, they charged down to drive them off. Stung by heavy missile fire and with both flanks exposed, the embattled line of spearmen crumpled under unanswerable pressure, giving way at both back and sides as a mob of barbarian cavalry and light foot soldiers swept the field.

Once scattered in frantic retreat, individual hoplites made clumsy and inviting targets for the Thracians. The tribesmen pursued and cut them to pieces, with their victims including both Greek generals. The colony at Nine Ways, having lost its leaders and much of its militia, couldn't survive, and shortly thereafter either fell to assault or was abandoned. It would be nearly 30 years before the Athenians found heart to return and found Amphipolis.

Papremis (460 B.C.)

Any formal peace between Athens and Persia either died with Xerxes or didn't apply to Africa, since the Athenians now supported an uprising in Egypt. Amidst the turmoil of Artaxerxes' rise to the Persian throne, Egyptians used mercenaries from Libya under the general Inaros to expel the Great King's overseers. Inaros then seized power and hired more fighters even as he sought help from Athens. The Athenians (now led by Pericles) were keen to secure African grain and deal more harm to Persia, and they thus sent Charitimides to Egypt with a 200-ship fleet from Athens and Samos (Hornblower 1991, 163) that had been readied for use on Cyprus.

Artaxerxes seems to have responded by amassing an army from his satrapal garrisons, which he dispatched to Africa in the summer of 460 B.C. under his uncle Achaemenes (per Diodorus, while Ctesias held that Achaemenides, the king's brother, got the posting). Our best sources diverge on what then took place. Ctesias described a naval encounter, which fits with Thucydides' report of a fleet action on the Nile, but Diodorus's history provides convincing detail of a land battle near the Nile delta at Papremis. The latter does seem quite reasonable; after all, Athens had demonstrated its naval superiority against Persia at Salamis, Mycale, and but a few years before at Eurymedon, all of which had left the empire very weak at sea. It's therefore unlikely that the Persians had either the assets or confidence to again challenge the Athenian navy. Moreover, only a victory ashore against the insurrection could settle the sort of land-control issue at stake. This all makes it more likely that the Persian host moved overland against Egypt, as that route was more secure and better able to support a large force.

The Persians would never have stripped their satrapies in such uncertain times; thus, the troops sent to Africa might have included no more than 18,000 sparabara. This was half the garrison strength (at 60 percent nominal) of the six western provinces. They also would have taken a strong contingent of light archers and peltasts (4–5,000 men) plus nearly 2,500 horsemen, all 50 percent levies from the same satrapies at 80 percent nominal strength. Though well below the 300,000 of Diodorus or 400,000 of Ctesias, this army of 25,000 fighting men was still more than large enough for the task at hand.

Inaros prepared to meet the imperials with what must have been a somewhat smaller force, perhaps fielding around 20,000 men in all. He could probably muster a main battle line of some 16,000 armored spearmen — half mercenaries and Egyptians, and the rest Greek (at 40 hoplites for each ship in Charitimides' task force). His light support came from Egyptian archers and peltasts, 800 Athenian bowmen (four per trireme), and some mounted Libyans. Though the Persians had a little more manpower, the rebels had big advantages in both numbers of armored men and the proven superiority of Greek hoplites. If the Asians were to have any hope for victory, they thus had to offset their weakness in shock troops by relying on a considerable edge in cavalry.

The rebel forces likely picked their ground carefully, waiting for the enemy host at a suitable spot along the Nile. This would have let the Athenians anchor their flank on the riverbank and thus secure one wing of Inaros's formation from mounted envelopment. Meanwhile, the full rebel complement of light infantry and cavalry could have taken post on the landward flank to heavily screen that end of the line as well. As for the Persians, they must have fielded as many spara-bearing spearmen as possible in an attempt to match up against their heavily equipped foe, which left only the last few ranks of their formation to be filled by men with taka and bow. At ten men deep for Persia and files of eight to ten for the rebels, both sides presented fronts nearly 2km across as they faced off and prepared to close for battle.

The armies would have crashed into each other all down the line beneath a shower of arrows and javelins from their flank screens and after ranks. Diodorus said that it was a particularly hard fight and it's likely that neither side could claim an advantage for some time; but in the end, the othismos of the Athenian phalanx must have finally let the Greeks overcome the sparabara facing them. As hoplites pushed and lanced through the forward shield wall to get at the lighter-equipped men behind, the Asians took to their heels. And once having inflicted heavy casualties on the fleeing enemy wingers, the Greeks wheeled about and rushed the now exposed tip of the opposing line, rolling it up to rout the rest of the Persian army and bring to a close what would prove to be the last major shock action between hoplites and sparabara. A hot pursuit now slaughtered many among the Great King's men, including their commander, whose body was sent to Artaxerxes as an insult. The royal troops that survived fled to Memphis, where they regrouped inside a fortified garrison facility known as the White Wall or White Fortress.

Most of the Athenians withdrew after the battle, leaving only 40–50 ships and 1,500–2,000 hoplites behind to help besiege Memphis. This investment didn't turn out well for Athens. Following defeat of their Egyptian allies in 456 B.C., the remaining Greeks fell back with their fleet onto Prosopitis, an island formed by a canal connecting two branches of the Nile delta near Papremis. Here they held out until Persian engineers found a way to drain the canal and strand the Greek triremes in the mud. Persian forces then poured over the defenses and finished the siege by killing about half of the Athenians and burning their ships.

The victors allowed the remnants of the Athenian expedition to depart in peace; still, most of these men perished trying to make their way home. And Athens's losses didn't end there, as it suffered further when a relief fleet of 50 vessels, ignorant that it was too late, met destruction attempting to land at the mouth of the Nile. Yet despite these setbacks, the Athenians' steady rise to power continued and they grew ever more aggressive, expanding their realm until finally checked on the Greek mainland itself.

The First Peloponnesian War

Athens emerged from the struggle with Persia as the Greek world's leading sea power. Its navy had helped transform a league of allies into an Aegean empire, but maintaining this vast hegemony made great demands on the city's human resources. While Sparta had responded to a similar challenge by replacing direct rule over new lands with a system of alliances that could be administered with less manpower, the Athenians took the opposite tack, expanding their military to meet the widening scope of external interests. Fueled by tribute plus its own booming economy and population, Athens built the largest and most diverse war machine in Greece. And once possessed of such great strength, the Athenians found ways to use it, doing so with ever increasing arrogance. This put them on a collision course with Sparta and its allies that would lead to a series of conflicts sometimes referred to as the First Peloponnesian War.

When Sparta denied the Athenians a role in the Messenian conflict in 462 B.C., they had petulantly exiled pro-Spartan Cimon and then struck back more tellingly by allying with the Argives, Sparta's most bitter rivals. The Spartans now feared that an Argos fully recovered from Sepeia and flush with Athenian aid might once more threaten their security. They addressed this in typical Spartan fashion by mounting a punitive expedition.

Oenoe (461 B.C.)

Sparta's response to the Argos/Athens alliance was by necessity modest, with ongoing commitments at home and Messenia limiting its field force to only about the size of that sent against Arcadia three years earlier. This would have put some 2,000 spartiate and perioeci hoplites plus retainers in the army that now marched north toward Argive territory along the road through Mantinea. While adequate against a surprised and less capable foe at Dipaea, the Spartans had to have known that such resources were insufficient to challenge Argos. They must therefore have intended no more than a demonstration, hoping to dissuade the Argives from holding to their agreement with Athens by spoiling assets close to hand in the western Argolid.

The Spartan column moved into Argive territory around the north flank of Mount Artemisius and along the track that ran between Mantinea and Argos. However, if the Spartans had planned to catch their enemy unaware with a rapid march, they mistook the quality of either Argive intelligence or anticipation. Not only had Argos learned of the invasion and moved quickly to intercept with a hoplite contingent of its own, but it also found time to acquire help from Athens. This led to quite a shock for the Spartan commander, who suddenly found his advance challenged at a point just east of the Argive border town of Oenoe on the Charadrus River.

The blocking force likely had a twofold edge in hoplites, with 3,000 from Argos and 1,000 from Athens. And it probably held an even greater advantage in light troops in the form of 300–600 Argive psiloi plus teams of Athenian archers (a few hundred) and horsemen (up to 300). These allies stood facing west on the north side of the Charadrus, where they could span the road to Argos at eight shields deep along a 500-meter front. The Argives would have held the right and center, allowing the Athenian spearmen to anchor far left on the river. This presented the Spartan generals with a stark choice to either retreat or fight on ground where their preferred maneuver — wheeling from the right to roll up an opponent's left flank — simply wasn't possible. To make matters worse, the vastly superior light foot troops and cavalry guarding the enemy's right wing made turning that side of the field equally unfeasible. Though the Spartans were facing no greater deficit in numbers than they had overcome just a few years earlier at Dipaea, the terrain tactics, strong light-infantry support, and mental preparedness of their present foe made another such upset extremely unlikely. Despite this, the Spartans' pride and soaring confidence seem to have driven them to accept battle.

Matching the opposition's frontage, the Spartans likely aligned only four shields deep, placing spartiates on the right and perioeci on the left. They then would have closed in their characteristic slow march timed to baleful flute music. As they met the enemy front, the Spartan hoplites lunged forward in a violent effort to break its will and gain a quick, nearly bloodless victory. This time, however, their foe didn't give way. Failing to intimidate, too thin to breach by othismos, and denied envelopment, the Spartans struggled doggedly against relentless pressure from the deeper opposing formation. Inevitably, the allies were able to slowly shove ahead until they gained control of the field. It's probable that this came as a result of a threatened turning on the unanchored inland wing. Allied cavalry, archers, and psiloi on that side of the field must have eventually dispersed a weak helot screen to bring the perioeci under flank attack and force them to withdraw.

There's no tradition that the Spartans took a heavy defeat at Oenoe, suggesting they got away with only minor losses. With their left wing in retreat, the spartiates had to back off as well, but were able to do so on command and in good order. A well-practiced maneuver for these elite soldiers, much like the false retreats men of their class had executed at Thermopylae and Plataea, this was a tribute to their professionalism, since no other army of the era could have done this without triggering a rout. As for the Argives and Athenians, they eschewed pursuit. Seemingly content with a low-cost triumph over the dreaded Spartans and reluctant to risk either this success or more lives, they chose to let their beaten foe move back toward Mantinea unmolested.

Oenoe is a controversial event, with some doubt that it ever took place (Pritchett, 1994, 1–26). Yet evidence at Delphi and on the painted colonnade at Athens (both described by Pausanius) is persuasive that it did happen. There was certainly adequate political motivation (Meiggs 1992, 469–472 and Badian 1993, 209–210); then too, the battle's relatively small scope might well have led to its obscurity outside of Argos and Athens. Most notable to contemporaries as a rare victory over the Spartans, Oenoe resonates stronger today as the opening round in a running conflict that would profoundly affect the history of Greece.

Halieis (459 B.C.)

Within a year of Oenoe, Athens was at odds with Spartan interests again, this time clashing with Corinth. Joining with other Spartan allies, Corinth had decided to dispute control of the Saronic Gulf and its surroundings, something the Athenians were pursuing as a first phase of extending their empire landward into Greece. This "Saronic War" would last three years and trigger several major hoplite engagements.

The roots of this confrontation lay in a treaty between Athens and Megara that impacted an ongoing fight between the latter and Corinth for land along their common frontier. Suffering from raids and skirmishes, the Megarans had soon realized that their more powerful neighbor was coming out on top, prompting them to seek Athens's help toward evening the odds. Undeterred, the Corinthians continued their aggressions in belief that Athens could give little aid on account of its many foreign adventures. But this proved a false premise. Instead of sitting idle, the Athenians sent a task force to seize the Saronic port of Halieis in the territory of Corinth's ally Epidauros. Though its resources were indeed being stretched at this time by the war in Egypt and various other commitments, Athens could still spare some 50–60 ships for the campaign. A squadron of this size would have carried 2,000–2,400 hoplites, with an archer for every ten spearmen and plenty of oarsmen from which to draw skirmishers.

The Athenians appear to have landed unopposed at Halieis, but soon ran into stiff opposition. Corinth and Epidauros had been alert, and swiftly deployed a force that was most likely quite a bit larger than that of the invaders. Epidauros could field around 800 hoplites (as at Plataea) and Corinth probably sent 2,400 more (about half its field army), while Sicyon (Hornblower, 1991, 165) supplied another 300. These hoplites and their backing light foot troops must have come upon the Athenians near their anchorage and ordered into an eight-deep phalanx across some 400–450m. Hustling into an array with only five or six men per file that it might match fronts, the landing force would have moved to engage this advancing enemy formation.

Thucydides claimed that the Athenians took a defeat in the subsequent action and, given the defenders' apparent advantage in manpower, this isn't surprising. The thinly filed Athenians likely made no progress with othismos and finally had no choice but to fall back to their ships. Lacking horsemen and high quality light infantry, the Peloponnesians couldn't then mount an effective pursuit, and their opponents were able to retreat in good order and re-embark with the loss of something less than 10 percent of their men. Of course, Corinth and its allies suffered more lightly still, with losses perhaps running below 3 percent killed. Despite this rebuff, the Athenians remained potent, and shortly thereafter gained a victory at sea off the nearby island of Cecryphalia.

Historical accounts of this action are not in agreement, with that of Diodorus dissenting from the version of Thucydides followed here, by claiming a pair of victories for Athens at this time. Diodorus said that the first was the result of an overland campaign in the Peloponnese and the second came after a landing near Halieis. However, he identified the engagement around Halieis as the battle of Cecryphalia, which is quite impossible, given that Cecryphalia actually lies offshore. This seems to be a clear case of the historian misinterpreting land and sea phases of the same campaign to create two separate engagements ashore.

Cimolia I and II (458 B.C.)

The Saronic conflict soon grew when the island polis of Aigina also joined in against Athens, with the Athenians then winning a major sea battle over the islanders to put them under siege. Noting that Athens was now fighting on two fronts (in Egypt and on Aigina), and buoyed by its victory at Halieis, Corinth decided that it was time to seize the disputed frontier area that had first ignited the war. The Corinthians therefore marched out in strength to occupy Mount Geraneia at the Megaran border and then move deeper into their neighbor's territory. However, while Athens did indeed refuse to divert troops from other theatres, it had the general Myronides march into the Megarid with a force made up from home front spares.

The Athenians at this time likely had 8,000 citizen spearmen in their field army and another 3,000 assigned to the fleet. (Hoplite marines served on 100 triremes normally on active duty, with another 200 in reserve to meet the needs of major campaigns such as those now going on in Africa and in the Saronic Gulf.) The city's remaining hoplites were resident aliens (*metoikoi* or metics) and old-age/youth reservists. As we know that 3,000 metic spearmen were on hand in 446 B.C., we can project that there were 2,000 or so at this earlier date; indeed, this is close to the one for each six citizens at the time of the Persian invasion cited by Howatson (1991, 456). As for the age-reserves, they were roughly 20 percent of total citizen manpower or about 3,000 hoplites. Given an 80 percent muster of reservists and metics, Myronides could thus have had up to 4,000 Athenian spearmen and might then have added another 3,000 hoplites from Megara (as at Plataea), who surely would have taken the field to support their new ally in a battle on and for their own land. Participation of both prime-aged metics and Megarans in this campaign isn't on record, but this is most likely because the tale of youths and old men fighting alone made for a more dramatic tale, thus it's probable that both resident aliens and local allies were indeed present to give Myronides some 7,000 spearmen in all. Modest contingents of archers and horsemen as well as several hundred Megaran psiloi would have been present to back this hoplite force.

Myronides met the enemy near Megara at a place called Cimolia. His opponents must have numbered around 4,800 spearmen from Corinth (eight lochoi) plus 300 allied hoplites (noted by Diodorus and probably the Sicyonians cited by Thucydides at Halieis and as going later to Aigina). The Athenian general would have used his greater manpower to file eight deep across a front of 875m, placing the Megaran troops on the left wing and his own men at right and center. The metics and a leavening of older veterans probably made up the Athenian front ranks, which put the youths in the middle while the most elderly men provided a steadfast presence at the rear of each file. No doubt startled by such strong opposition (probably expecting to face only the Megarans), the men from Corinth had little choice but to deploy for battle, equaling the enemy front by setting up at a depth of five or six shields.

The opposing lines swept forward, drifting rightward prior to crashing together for a fierce engagement that Thucydides said ended in a draw. Though this might signify that the fight went on until dark, it seems more likely that each army claimed victory on opposite ends of the field. This means that the Athenian right wing used its numbers and drift extension to outflank the Corinthian left, while the men from Corinth on the opposing right took similar advantage of natural drift to envelop and best the Megarans. Neither side then had time to regroup before night fell and ended any chance for a resolution.

The older men on the triumphant Athenian right wing must have exercised restraint in foregoing pursuit of the broken Corinthian left, thus keeping their formation intact and in place. But the right wing of Corinth, though equally successful in the main action, seems to have let their bloodlust get the better of them and chased after the Megarans. They probably assumed amidst the dust, noise, and confusion of combat that their left was doing the same to the Athenians. Therefore, at the end of the day, it was the men from Athens who held the field and the Corinthians had to ask for a truce that they might recover their dead. This gave a technical victory to the Athenians under the conventions of classical Greek warfare, which could well have prompted Thucydides' comment that Athens had the better of the fight.

Myronides' soldiers headed home after setting up a trophy, but news of this insulting Athenian monument soon reached Corinth and led to considerable criticism of the city's hoplites. One can imagine the kind of ridicule dished out to these proud men, not the least of which were accusations of youthful incompetence cast by their own old-age reservists. Stung by this scorn, the Corinthians marched out again after a dozen days in order to set up their own commemorative at the spot where they had turned the Megaran wing. Myronides and his reservists somehow learned of this and once more linked up with the Megarans to confront the invasion. Finding a few Corinthians working on the new trophy, they launched a surprise attack that quickly drove them away. Myronides then advanced against their nearby encampment.

If the first Athenian mobilization to Cimolia had found the army of Corinth somewhat unready, then this second one must have come as a shock indeed. Nevertheless, the Corinthians gamely formed up to fight. With an apparent edge not only in numbers, but in morale as well, the men from Athens and Megara charged into a pitched battle that would have been very similar in scope to that fought 12 days earlier. This time, they scored a decisive victory over the Corinthians in all quarters, with manpower, leadership, and confidence combining to let Myronides' unlikely host defeat the best that Corinth had to offer.

Corinth's losses were severe, compounded due to many of its defeated hoplites having blundered during the pursuit into an enclosure surrounded by a deep ditch. This let Athenian spearmen seal off any escape as a crowd of their light footmen and attendants stoned the hapless Corinthians to extinction. Such a vicious action lacked honor and was far out of step with Grecian martial etiquette, being more like the noted atrocity visited on the Argives after Sepeia, and goes far to show an increasingly heartless set of mind among Athenians.

Events at Cimolia joined with Athens's reduction of Aigina by siege to put an end to the Saronic War. The Athenians now held Megara (including its port of Nisaea), Aigina, and Troizen (another Saronic port gained at the time of the campaign around Epidauros) to give them a stranglehold in and around the gulf.

Tanagra I and Oenophyta (457 B.C.)

After besting Corinth and absorbing Aigina into the Delian League, the Athenians turned their ambitions northward and formed an alliance with Thessaly. This was quite disturbing to the Boeotians, who suddenly found themselves being squeezed between Athenian allied territory along both southern and northern frontiers. It was the latter that troubled them most. The famed horsemen of Thessaly were far too close at hand and well suited for aiding an Athenian incursion onto the open Boeotian plain.

At this tense juncture, the Phocians along the upper fringe of Boeotia seized one of the towns of Doris, reputed home of the Dorian race. Sparta reacted strongly, trading on its Dorian origins to send an army north under the regent Nicomedes. Ferried across the Corinthian Gulf, this was a huge force of 11,500 hoplites from Sparta (1,500, likely a lochos of spartiates and two of perioeci) and its allies. The allied troops were a mix from the northern Peloponnese, with 4,000 spearmen from Arcadia, the same from Corinth and Sicyon combined, and the rest from Phlius, Pellene, and Epidauros. These hoplites undoubtedly had support from an equal number of attendants, including at least 1,000 psiloi. Both Plato and Pausanius claimed that local men swelled Nicomedes' ranks once he got ashore and these may have included spearmen from Thebes (2,000, about half its full muster) and Tanagra (1,000 or so), which were the leading states in the vicinity. The Boeotians would also have supplied horsemen (maybe 300) and matching hamippoi. Considering that Phocis could field no more than a thousand hoplites in opposition, there was obviously much more afoot here than the rescue of some small village, and it seems likely that Nicomedes' show of strength was really focused on warning off Athens by demonstrating support for Spartan ally Thebes. The Phocians paid a dear price for getting in the path of these machinations, being chased from the field in a very brief and perfunctory action.

Nicomedes turned about for the Peloponnese upon completion of his stated mission, but the Athenians sent a force of 50 ships to preclude his return across the Corinthian Gulf. Unable or unwilling to challenge Athens at sea, the Spartan commander next tried to take the most direct route overland, but found it blocked by an Athenian-led army in the Megarid. Nicomedes then turned east and marched to Tanagra on the Asopos River just north of the Attic frontier, which put him in position to launch his powerful army directly into Athens's territory if need be. Realizing that a threat was now developing to their homeland, the Athenians abandoned their post in the Megarid and rushed to intercept.

The Athenian force that drew up near Tanagra had some 14,000 spearmen. About half of these were from Athens itself, including all the non-reserves not in Egypt or with the fleet, while the allied hoplites came from the Argolid (likely a forerunner of the elite Argive "Thousand" per Tomlinson 1972, 182–184), Cleonai, Plataea, Megara, Euboa, and elsewhere in the Delian League (including some Ionians). Modest contingents of Athenian archers and allied psiloi would also have been on hand. This army matched up well against Nicomedes' men in numbers, though there must have been some question about quality among the islanders and Ionians. In truth, it was only in their mounted arm where the Athenians held a clear edge, having 300 riders of their own, a few from Plataea, and perhaps as many as 1,000 from Thessaly with hamippoi. All of these were as good as or better than the horsemen from Boeotia on the other side.

Breaking from their camps in the morning, it wasn't until late afternoon that the many diverse elements present could get into order to do battle. (It's notable that preparing for a fight in this era seems to have always taken much longer than the combat itself.) The armies drew up on the plain before Tanagra and faced off along a front that might have been about 1,750m long, with each contingent filing according to their own custom (the bulk at eight shields deep). The Spartans and most of the Athenians likely held their respective right wings, the former opposing the Argives and the rest of the men from Athens and the latter facing the Boeotians on the other end of the line.

Cavalry and light foot soldiers on each side would have skirmished before retiring to the flanks, with the Boeotian horse troops splitting onto either wing of their phalanx, the Athenians taking post beside their city's hoplites on the opposing right wing, and the Thessalians moving next to the Argives on the left. The long lines of spearmen then advanced, slowly at first, but finally breaking into a trot to collide with much shouting into a deadly shock contest. Being evenly matched, the two armies struck and shoved at each other in a protracted melee (but not the two-day ordeal cited by Pausanius), which took a terrible toll in energy and blood from all involved. It's probable that the Athenian right wing, though hard pressed, finally broke through their opponents and put them to flight as their cavalry scattered the small force of enemy horsemen on that side and moved out in pursuit of the defeated infantry. However, this Athenian success was offset on the other end of the field. Here, a story of treachery played out as the Argives were holding their own against the much-hated Spartans, when the Thessalian horse suddenly deserted, peeling off to attack the Athenian supply train camped in the rear. This had a devastating moral effect on the always excitable men of Argos and allowed the Spartans to envelop and rout the Argive wing.

Most of the casualties on the day (and Thucydides noted that both sides took heavy losses) must have come on the broken left wings that had suffered pursuit. The fired-up Athenians seem to have chased the Boeotians far from the battle, their horsemen bringing down many and the hoplites finishing off any brought to bay. At the same time, epigraphic and archaeological evidence (Tomlinson 1972, 183) suggests that between 129 and 400 Argives (up to 40 percent of the total) went down in the fight and flight on the other side of the field. Athenians from Cimon's tribe of Oeneis had held post beside the Argives and were also hit hard.

The Spartan hoplites, having kept their place on the battlefield, swung about at this point to face the Athenians returning from the chase. With night now coming on, the men from Athens — tired, emotionally drained, and badly in need of reorganization — chose to withdraw rather than fight another round. They were also now dangerously short of cavalry, reflecting both defection of the Thessalians and diversion of their own horsemen to keep those turncoats from doing further damage. Combat thus ended with each army claiming success on one wing, prompting Ephoros (via Diodorus) to describe a draw. Yet the Spartans had managed to seize the field when all was said and done, justifying Thucydides' opinion that they had been victorious.

The Spartans were evidently happy enough with these results, especially the bloodying given to Argos as payback for Oenoe. They therefore made a truce with Athens that was good for four months, allowing them to return to Laconia in triumph. The Athenians were obviously satisfied with the turn of events as well. Though denied a victory, they had removed the threat of an invasion and hurt the Boeotians at the same time. Moreover, the truce now let them move directly against Boeotia without fear of Spartan intervention.

Only sixty-two days after the fight at Tanagra and well within the armistice period, the Athenians threw another army into the field under Myronides to take the Boeotians by surprise. They marched this time without Delian League support (Diodorus said that they fought single-handed), though it's likely that at least their old friends from Plataea were present. This should have given them some 6,500 hoplites, even with losses from the recent battle and a decision to leave behind "malingerers" (those opposed to the campaign). Small numbers of bowmen and cavalry would also have come along.

Myronides' men crossed over the frontier and began spoiling the countryside just southeast of Tanagra around the polis of Oenophyta. Gathering hastily in response, Thebes and Tanagra could themselves field no more than 3,800 hoplites—those lacking serious wounds from the previous battle (likely 60 percent of those engaged) and another 2,000 called up fresh from Thebes. A two-thirds mobilization from the rest of the newly restored Boeotian League likely provided another 4,000 spearmen, while some 800 cavalrymen and a matching force of hamippoi must have been on hand for light support. Therefore, in spite of Diodorus's claim that the Boeotians were much more numerous, it's probable that their edge in manpower was actually rather modest.

The Boeotians found the invaders massed on a broad plain outside Oenophyta and would have formed up in opposition at eight shields deep. This created a phalanx almost 1km wide that had the troops from Thebes and Tanagra on its right side. Myronides assessed this formation and must have countered it with a slightly thinner array (six to seven men per file) that he might present a matching frontage. The Athenian general then walked up and down his line to encourage the men, stressing the importance of standing firm, despite having lesser depth, lest they fall prey to a devastating pursuit from the host of horsemen supporting their enemy. The Athenians steeled their resolve with these words and, on signal, marched across the flat to meet the similarly advancing Boeotians. The phalanxes closed at a final sprint into a massive collision, which both sides absorbed as they pressed together in a vicious trial of spear-fighting and othismos. Well enough matched, the armies battered each other for some time, with neither side willing to buckle under the opposing pressure.

Myronides, knowing that the longer this fight lasted the more it would favor his foe's greater manpower, became concerned when he saw that his men were making no headway where he stood on the right wing. He therefore resorted (per Frontinus and Polyaenus) to a clever stratagem that he might break the stalemate, shouting to those about him that their comrades at the other end of the field had already beaten the enemy's best (though they were, in fact, also stalled in place). Inspired by this, the men on the Athenian right gained the courage needed to surge ahead and carry the day. Not only did Myronides' troops now assert a more effective physical attack, but their cheering of victory on the far wing must have undercut their foe's psyche as well. The dust, press of men, and cacophony of battle made it impossible to see or hear what was taking place elsewhere, thus the Boeotians believed what they heard and gave in to mindless panic and flight. This exposed their right wing to envelopment and quickly transformed the Athenians' faux success on that end of the front into the real thing.

Only the Thebans, who were farthest from the initial point of collapse, managed to withdraw in good order. Thebes' lighter losses and strong defenses allowed it alone among the Boeotian states to resist falling to Athens in the battle's aftermath. Myronides went on to march his army about Boeotia. He cowed the Phocians and brushed aside the Opuntian Locrians on the Euboan strait (with no more than 1,000 hoplites they couldn't really oppose so strong a force). He even toyed with the idea of invading the Thessalians to repay them for their treachery at Tanagra, but turned back instead, content with the successes already in hand. His victory was so thorough that it would hold Boeotia in thrall to Athens for a full decade.

Sicyon I and II (457–454 B.C.)

Buoyed by their triumph in the north, the Athenians now set out to hit the enemy heartland in the Peloponnese. They played to their strength at sea with plans to mount a series of amphibious raids against Sparta and its allies, hoping to keep them occupied at home and far from Athenian assets in Attica. At the same time, this would deal a serious blow to opposition morale. Spartan allies would now have to pay a steep price for staying loyal, while the Spartans might well lose their reputation for invincibility if they proved powerless to stop the raiding.

The general Tolmides set the pattern for this sort of campaign in 457 B.C., sailing clockwise around the Peloponnese with 50 triremes. Fully loaded, these could carry 2,000 hoplites and 200 archers, all crack troops distilled from the best of Athens's army. (Diodorus claimed that Tolmides took twice as many men, but this ignores normal ship capacity on such a long voyage.) Yet though he had plenty of manpower, the Athenian commander apparently planned to rely more on speed and surprise than strength, seeking to strike and withdraw before any serious opposition could develop. He burned a Spartan arsenal in Laconia using this low-risk approach and captured Chalcis, which lay west of Naupactus on the north side of the Corinthian Gulf. However, it seems that the longer such a voyage lasted, the more likely that future targets would become alert. This appears to have happened at Sicyon on the southern shores of the Gulf to the northwest of Corinth, where Tolmides came ashore to a hot reception from local forces.

Sicyon's army was drawn out of four tribes, three Dorian and one from the pre–Dorian population known as the Aegialeis ("men of the coast"). These clans had sent 3,000 spearmen to Plataea and another 200 on five ships to Mycale, suggesting that each could field around 800 hoplites, which means that, in an all-out effort on home soil, Sicyon should have had half again more hoplites than Tolmides as well as a superior force of psiloi. Advancing on the landing site, these defenders would have formed a phalanx that faced the beach at eight men deep over a 400m front. Tolmides then had no choice but to file at only five shields if he was to avoid an overlap.

Overcoming their surprise, the Athenians dealt the Sicyonians a sharp defeat, perhaps, in light of their lesser manpower, by enveloping a flank. A startling result, it's easy to see how this short-handed victory might have prompted Diodorus to recast the odds and credit Tolmides with a larger force than he actually had. In fact, it was more likely the greater skill and confidence of Tolmides' men that won the day. Regardless, this was an impressive victory, and Tolmides went on to complete his campaign and return to Athens in triumph.

Pericles (son of Xanthippos of Mycale fame and future leader of Athens) commanded another such raid on Sicyon three years later. Setting out from Megara's port of Pegae on the Corinthian Gulf, he had 1,000 hoplite passengers aboard what Diodorus said was a fleet of 50 ships. These were probably the same triremes that had blocked the Spartan return from

Doris and set up the battle at Tanagra. (Note that Plutarch's alternative count of 100 ships appears unlikely due to both ongoing operations in Egypt and a starting point on the gulf). Even adding in the normal 500 hoplite marines, Pericles' vessels were well short of their full load of 40 spearmen each, which suggests that he meant to embark another 500 hoplites at some point. Athens already held most of the gulf's northern rim and now intended to take the facing shore and convert this waterway into another "Athenian lake" like the Saronic Gulf. Counting on initial success to bring more of this southern coastal area into line, it must have been there where Pericles was looking for new allies that could top off his ships.

By striking from nearby Pegae, Pericles kept Sicyon from getting any advance warning this time, allowing him to ravage the coast before advancing inland. There, in the area of Nemea, he finally ran into some opposition. Caught flat-footed, the Sicyonians had likely been able to gather only about 1,600 hoplites (half their full levy), which let them do little more than match enemy manpower. The ensuing engagement ended up being a brief one, with Plutarch claiming that Pericles' men carried the fight through main force. In truth, already fearful of the growing reputation of Athens's hoplites and unsettled by their previous loss to Tolmides, the Sicyonians must have faltered early on and fled after no more than minimal contact.

Diodorus reported that many Sicyonians were killed while running from the battle and this indicates that they fled in such a tight and confused press that even the slow pursuit of hoplites was effective. Pericles followed up with an attack on Sicyon itself, but had to eventually withdraw in the face of a Spartan relief effort. Nonetheless, Athens had once again shown an ability to strike at any site within reach of its fleet, something not lost on the Achaeans of the coastal area west of Sicyon, who volunteered to fill Pericles' ships to capacity. Pericles now sailed against Oeniadae in Acarnia, a Spartan ally that commanded the northern promontory where the Corinthian Gulf opened on the Ionian Sea to the west. His siege of that citadel would prove fruitless; nonetheless, overall results of this latest naval campaign had put Athens in a strong position around the entire Gulf.

Having proven that they could hurt Sparta and its allies from the sea, the Athenians were able to negotiate favorable terms to end the war in 451 B.C. The resulting five-year truce stopped the fighting for the moment, but did nothing to reduce the ambitions and deep-seated hatreds that had kindled the conflict in the first place. This First Peloponnesian War had lasted a full decade, yet would prove no more than a bitter foreshadowing of the greater conflict that would engulf nearly all the Greek world within 20 years.

Empire in Retreat

Athens took advantage of the end of its long duel with the Peloponnesians to once again indulge a hunger for foreign adventures. Thus, when Cimon's ten-year exile ended in 451 B.C., the Athenians eagerly put his returning talents to use, outfitting him with a fleet that he might resume the attack on Cyprus that had diverted to Egypt a decade earlier. Oddly, some 60 ships from this new armament soon went off to Africa as well, detaching to support another uprising in the Nile Delta. Nevertheless, Cimon still retained a powerful force of 140 triremes, and he now sailed out to besiege the Punic Cypriot stronghold of Citium. This campaign would prove Cimon's last, as he died of natural causes during the investment. Mourning their leader and low on supplies, his men headed for home, but ran into a challenge off Cyprian Salamis from the combined Phoenician and Cilician fleets.

Cyprian Salamis II (449 B.C.)

The Athenians would have prepared for action at sea by landing most of their hoplites near Salamis and retaining only the normal complement of marines and archers aboard ship. This could have put some 4,000 spearmen ashore on the assumption that losses at Citium (mostly to disease) had not exceeded 5 percent. These troops joined local Greeks from Salamis, Soli, and Paphos, who might have mustered about half the strength of their heyday during the Ionian Revolt. Greek forces therefore might have totaled some 7,000 hoplites with modest light foot and mounted (chariot?) support. A coalition of Punic Cypriots from Citium, Lapethus, and Amathus gathered in opposition, no doubt eager to pay back the attack on Citium and fearful lest a defeat at sea strand these invaders on their island. The Punic forces probably had around 5,000 shielded spearmen and heavy peltasts plus contingents of light foot troops and chariots.

The opposing armies met on the plain near Salamis even as their ships moved likewise to engage. The Greeks had the edge in numbers and would have deployed eight shields deep across nearly 900m, with light forces on the flanks. Their opponents were able to match this only by forming up at about six deep, with spearmen at the fore, heavy peltasts behind, and light infantry and horsemen screening the ends of the line. Though we lack a creditable account of what happened next (Diodorus seems to have confused this action with the earlier one at Eurymedon), it's likely that the Greeks applied othismos to drive their deeper phalanx all the way through the Punic ranks. Bowled over and cut down, the Phoenicians could only scatter and run as their array disintegrated under the relentless pressure of spear and shield. Moreover, this penetration must have taken place with such great rapidity that any Punic advantage on the flanks in light-armed troops had no real chance to come into play. The day then turned into a total triumph for the Greeks when word arrived that their fleet had also been victorious.

The Delian League and Persia agreed on a peace after the fighting at Cyprus, with the pact either renewing a lapsed treaty from 465 B.C. or setting entirely new terms for coexistence. As it turned out, while this accord clearly set Athens up as the dominant power in the eastern Mediterranean, it also marked an apex for the city's drive to empire. Events in Greece would soon reverse the fortunes of the Athenians, dealing them a major defeat in battle and ultimately robbing them of most of their mainland holdings.

Megara, Coronea I, Taras/Thurii, and Thurii/ Lucanians I and II (448-c. 433 B.C.)

The years following the Athenian triumphs at Cyprus saw growing unrest on the Greek mainland. There were alternating interventions by Sparta and Athens at Delphi during this period (so-called "Sacred Wars"), and though no direct confrontations took place, these leading powers clearly were set on adversarial courses. Yet rather than Sparta, it might have been the Megarans that first challenged Athens face-to-face. Diodorus claimed that Megara tried to break from the Delian League in 448 B.C. and the Athenians responded with a punitive expedition. Per this account, the Megarans sallied to confront Athens's army before the walls of their city.

If Megara did indeed revolt, it could have made an all-out effort with some 3,000 hoplites in five lochoi, one from each of the city's five tribes (three Doric and two of non–Dorians). The Megarans would likely have faced an Athenian counterstrike of equal strength. We know from inscriptions (Meiggs 1992, 177) that Athens sent hoplites to the Megarid in 446 B.C.

from three of its tribes: Pandionis, Cecropis, and Antiochis. These men marched from scattered districts in Attica (their homelands not being those closest to Megara), very likely rushing to rescue kinsmen garrisoned in the crisis area. Should Diodorus's account be right and there was an uprising in 448, it's probable that the response at that time was similar, with perhaps even the same three clans being involved (thus accounting for their men still being there on guard two years later). This indicates a force from Athens on the order of 3,000 hoplites (1,000 or two lochoi per tribe in this era).

Diodorus said that a pitched battle took place, with the Athenians driving their foe back into town. If true, this must have led to a return of the Megarans to the Athenian fold, since Thucydides reported that Megara was again in revolt in 446 B.C., when the five-year truce between Athens and Sparta expired. It's quite possible that Diodorus confused his sources and was actually referring to the same uprising mentioned by Thucydides. Certainly, his accounts of a Megaran pact with Sparta in 448 and a Spartan raid into Attica the following year make more sense if we place both in 446 B.C., after Athens lost its treaty protection. The lone argument in favor of an earlier date for the revolt is that it would have justified the strong Athenian presence that we know was already in place by 446. These static troops would seem to be more useful for ensuring local loyalty than for stopping an attack from Sparta.

But even had the Megarans made an early stand, it was the Boeotians who struck the first telling blow. Athens had spread democracy across Boeotia in the decade since their takeover, which led to exile for many oligarchs. These outcasts banded together in 447 B.C. to take over Orchomenos, Chaeronea, and a few lesser towns in the northwest. Tolmides led Athens's response to this challenge, taking 1,000 hoplites (many of them young firebrands), perhaps 1,000 allied spearmen, and some light support into the troubled area.

Despite his modest numbers, Tolmides captured Chaeronea and left some hoplites behind as a garrison before turning toward home. He was then met somewhere on the road from Coronea to Haliartus by a contingent of oligarchs from Orchomenos and elsewhere, who had the backing of allies from Opuntian Locris and Euboa. Their army might have numbered around 3,000 hoplites, with 100–150 horsemen, a matching band of hamippoi, and several hundred psiloi—a force much larger than Tolmides' small column.

The Boeotians engaged Tolmides in what Diodorus described as an ambush; and though probably more of an unexpected mobilization (given size of the forces involved and open country during daylight hours), this assault took the Athenians quite by surprise. Outnumbered in spearmen on the order of 2 to 1, Tolmides did what he could and must have doggedly got his troops into formation. Out of necessity, he would have had to file at only half the depth of his opponents so as to most nearly match the width of their phalanx. But even his best effort was in vane, as the Boeotians and their allies closed to use their great advantages in manpower and morale to claim a swift victory. Just how they did this isn't recorded, but in all likelihood younger and more volatile Athenians simply gave way to othismos at several points, sending their entire formation into panicked flight. Tolmides and many others were killed, while the rest had no choice but to surrender.

The exiled oligarchs made the most of their prisoners, which included a number of Athens's most prominent young men. Eager to get these youths back, the Athenians cut a painful deal to secure their release, giving up all claims on Boeotia. This didn't entail any loss of revenue, as the area paid no tribute, but was still a bitter blow to Athenian prestige and ambition. As it turned out, the reverse at Coronea proved to be a major turning point and Athens would lose even more of its holdings before another year was out.

Having been among those that fought Tolmides at Coronea, the Euboans rose up against Athenian control of their island in 446 B.C. Pericles collected an army and started out to put down this revolt, only to learn that Megara had also broken away, isolating many garrisoned Athenians. Troops from Corinth, Sicyon, and Epidauros had already joined the Megarans, while Sparta, free now of the five-year truce, was gathering an invasion army under its king Pleistoanax (son of Pausanias). Pericles turned about to meet this greater crisis and met Pleistoanax near Eleusis on the Attic frontier. An epic hoplite battle that might have decided the fate of Greece for many years was then avoided at the last moment, when Pericles negotiated a truce with the young Spartan monarch and his advisor, Cleandridas.

The agreement reached on the field at Eleusis was later formalized into a 30-year peace treaty. And in spite of the fact that the more warlike in Sparta criticized this deal and caused both Pleistoanax and Cleandridas to go into exile, the terms were in reality quite harsh on Athens, rolling back most of its gains on the mainland by taking away Megara and its ports plus Troezen and Achaea. It's unlikely that a more costly victory in the field could have gained a better result for the Spartans, though it might have better suited their martial tastes.

The Athenians had lost their bid for dominance on the mainland, but remained free to deal with their offshore allies as they saw fit. Pericles therefore invaded Euboa with a 50-ship fleet and a force of 5,000 hoplites to regain that island in short order. He then focused Athens's efforts away from expansion in the waning years of the Pentacontaetia, seemingly content to maintain the territory already in hand. To be sure, other threats to the city's hegemony arose over this time frame, most notably a long and fierce revolt by Samos in 440–439 B.C., but the Athenians successfully met each challenge. In the end, the treaty with Sparta served to keep peace for nearly half its nominal term — the longest period without a major land battle in mainland Greece during the 5th century.

Though the Greek mainland was now relatively calm, this didn't extend to the south of Italy, where Athens had helped to set up a colony at Thurii around 443 B.C. On the old site of Sybaris (destroyed in 510 B.C.), this was near where the Crati River emptied off the front arch of the Italian boot. Thurii drew settlers from throughout the Grecian world (including the exiled spartiate Cleandridas and the historian Herodotus), but faced difficulties from the very start. First, there was an internal dispute with a few lingering Sybarites, who were quickly expelled. Then came friction with the Spartan descendants at neighboring Taras, which lay around the other side of the arch to the northeast. This rivalry between Thurii and Taras seems to have been more of a local contest for eschatia than a proxy war for their distant parental poleis. Thurii sought to match greater Tarantine resources by allying c. 440 B.C. with the Messapians on the Adriatic coast at Brundisium, a people likewise hostile to Taras. Violent conflict was nigh and archaeological finds (Woodhead 1962, 86) indicate that it wasn't long in coming.

The forces of Thurii and Brundisium appear to have met the Tarantines in battle somewhere on or near their disputed borderlands. Composition of the Thurian army is speculative, but it probably had no more than 1,000 hoplites backed by a couple of hundred psiloi and about 100 horsemen. The Messapians might have marshaled half their tribe, amounting to around 2,000 armored men plus 1,000 skirmishers and the same in mounted nobles and retainers. The barbarian heavy foot troops wore open-faced helmets, pectorales, and greaves, each carrying an oval scutum and either a thrusting spear or two lighter, multi-purpose ones. Secondary weapons included either a slashing sword or hand-axe. Their skirmishers were mostly javelinmen, but some used axes instead, while a few carried slings. With respect to the Messapian horsemen, they had gear much like their heavy infantry and fought with javelins.

Taras probably took the field with 4,000 hoplites, 800–1,000 psiloi, and a mounted force of 400 riders. Its overall edge in manpower was thus modest, but there was a substantial advantage in armored men, both in terms of numbers and in having more uniform arms and shock tactics. The only glaring weakness of the Tarantines lay in their cavalry, but they were past masters at using terrain to offset horsemen and must have done so here. This brought their superior infantry to the fore and, though we have no details, a dedication (Pritchett 1971–91, Part III, 291) shows that Taras claimed the victory, most likely using heavier equipment and othismos to break the barbarian left wing.

Sometime after this, Thurii came to blows with others of its neighbors. This time it was the Lucanians, an Oscan hill people who posed a threat by descending on the Greeks' lowland holdings. Calling once more on their alliance with Brundisium, the Thurians could have gathered in strength similar to that sent against Taras. Significantly, this force must have had a renewed sense of confidence due to the leadership of Sparta's Cleandridas. As for the Lucanians, Polyaenus reported them to have had a third fewer men than the Greeks, which presumably referred to line troops only and suggests that they fielded about 2,000 armored fighters — from half to two-thirds of a total tribal pool of 4,000–6,000 men. Outfitted in typical Oscan style, these would have ranged from wealthy warriors with spear and/or javelins and scutum (wearing helmet, a harness for the chest with one to three small metal plates, and at least one greave) to poorer men with only a portion of this panoply. There probably were some 200 highborn cavalrymen on hand as well, having armor like the best equipped among their footmen (but no shields) and javelins.

Both Frontinus and Polyaenus reported Cleandridas to have bested the Lucanians by disguising his greater strength with a deceptively narrow formation. He likely did this by filing deep and hiding a reserve behind one wing, probably the left. The logical choice for such duty was a 500-man lochos of his best Thurian hoplites that had been drilled intensely in this single maneuver. As the Lucanians moved up to initiate battle, Cleandridas sent forward the cavalry and light foot troops from off his left flank to scatter the opposing light-armed screen on that side of the field. Meantime, his reserve contingent would have moved out in column (each man turning to convert ranks into files) and rounded the fronting line to advance unseen behind cover of their charging auxiliaries. These hoplites swept across the now-exposed end of the Lucanian heavy formation and wheeled back into line to launch a devastating flank attack as the rest of their army charged into contact all along the front. Falling into disorder on their doubly assaulted right wing, the Lucanians couldn't hold position and gave way to suffer a crushing defeat.

Cleandridas later toured his troops across the abandoned battleground to point out the high price that their foes had paid for failing to stand fast. This soon paid dividends when the Lucanians regrouped. Marshalling at full strength, the tribesmen could have sent 4–5000 infantry and 4–500 horsemen against two-thirds as many Greeks and Messapian foot troops and 600 riders. Cleandridas countered by emulating his countryman Leonidas's feat at Thermopylae and setting up to fight in a narrow place that discounted the enemy numbers. Taking to heart their recent lesson on holding firm despite opposing pressure, the Thurian and allied troops then persisted and finally broke the tribesmen's will, driving them from the field in a pursuit that inflicted heavy losses.

Athens, Corinth, and War

Any calm after the face-off at Eleusis proved to be no more than a brief lull before the storm, as a wealth of unresolved issues and lingering hatreds soon triggered renewed conflict. This largely reflected the same sort of strategic tensions that had sparked the First Peloponnesian War, but also had roots in the old tradition of competing for eschatia. Indeed, the border fight between Corinth and Athens that culminated in the twin battles at Cimolia had left deep and lingering enmities that exacerbated a natural rivalry between two of Greece's greatest sea powers. And when a similar dispute arose over control of Corcyra, it set off a powder train of events that would lead to bitter fighting across nearly the entire Greek world.

Corcyra was an 8th century foundation of Corinth on the northernmost island in the Ionian Sea. This distant colony along the lucrative western trade route competed with its founder and became very prosperous, powerful, and independent. As relations between Corcyra and Corinth grew increasingly strained, they led to open warfare in the mid 7th century. This poisoned family tie continued to fester, keeping the islanders neutral during the Persian invasion and then flaring once more into armed conflict in 435 B.C. At this time, the Corcyran colony of Epidamnus (near modern Durres in Albania) expelled its ruling elite only to have the exiles try to reclaim their polis with the aid of local barbarians. When Corcyra refused assistance to the rebels, they got it from Corinth instead. Angered at this, the Corcyrans promptly went to war against Epidamnus and its allies from the mother city.

Corcyra boasted a navy second in size only to that of Athens and did well at first, taking Epidamnus and besting a fleet from Corinth. But when faced with a more powerful Corinthian effort in 433 B.C., the Corcyrans sought a pact with Athens. The Athenians were undoubtedly drawn to this conflict by the thought of adding the island's ships to their alliance and thus denying them to Corinth. Athens therefore sent a modest flotilla to Corcyra and, when the Corinthians gained a tactical victory over the Corcyran fleet, intervened to save the islanders. This inflamed old hatreds and set off a deadly sequence of events that led Thucydides to cite it as the first cause of the second (or Great) Peloponnesian War.

Frustrated at Corcyra, Corinth sought a suitable revenge, finding it soon enough at Potidaea, an Athenian allied polis on the Pallene peninsula of Chalcidice. Like Corcyra, this city sat on a vital trade route, this one feeding grain into Athens from what is now the Ukraine. The Corinthians, who had founded Potidaea, offered to help it break away from Athens. Further support for this came from nearby Macedonia, where the Athenians were interfering in a civil war. Still, Potidaea didn't take up arms until Athens imposed punitive measures in an ill-advised attempt to discourage any thoughts of independence. Instead, this pushed the Potidaeans in 432 B.C. to finally join alliances in Boeotia and Chalcidice that were hostile to Athens. The embers of a widespread conflict that had begun to glow at Corcyra now burst into full flame.

Potidaea (432 B.C.)

The Athenian general Archestratus was close to hand when Potidaea went into revolt, having recently sailed 1,000 hoplites aboard 30 ships to Macedonia. Hearing of the uprising, he marched to Chalcidice, but saw that he had too few men and turned back. Athens then crowded 2,000 spearmen onto another 40 ships and sent them north under Callias. The Corinthians had meanwhile dispatched some reinforcements of their own to Potidaea with Aristeus, well known as an advocate for that colony. These included a 600-man lochos of militia personally loyal to Aristeus and 1,000 mercenary hoplites (likely Arcadians serving under a few veterans from the fighting on Sicily) plus perhaps 400 psiloi.

First quelling the civil unrest in Macedonia, Callias then moved on to Potidaea with some 3,000 hoplites from Athens plus a few allies that had probably joined in transit at Chalcis on Euboa. Chalcis had historical ties to Chalcidice and could have supplied some 400 spearmen. Light support for this effort was in the form of 600 cavalry with hamippoi from Macedon,

280 archers, and a crowd of skirmishers drawn from the ships' crews. Callias set up camp with this army along the coast northwest of the city.

Aristeus and the men from Corinth had taken post around Potidaea, which stood at the narrowest point of the Pallene peninsula. Having been joined by 800 or so local hoplites, they had around 2,400 spearmen in all and had added some local psiloi as well. Though this force was still smaller than its opposition, Aristeus was counting on help from other allies in Chalcidice. The population of this region opposed Athens and had united and centralized around the city of Olynthus, which lay due east of the Athenian camp and was well sited for an attack against the rear of any advance on Potidaea. There were also some 200 Macedonian horsemen at Olynthus that were hostile to the faction partnered with Athens. In the end, however, this split defense proved a failure. Callias was able to occupy the Chalcidians to the east with his cavalry and a few hoplites (perhaps half the Euboans) as he marched the main body of his army on Potidaea. Once Aristeus became aware that the enemy was on his doorstep, ready to ravage the territory and put him under siege, he sallied to engage in a pitched battle. The phalanxes confronted each other to the immediate north and west of Potidaea near the western shoreline of the isthmus.

Callias would have used his superior numbers (some 3,200 hoplites against only 2,400) to form in files of eight over a width of 400m. He claimed the right wing himself, placing his small band of allies on the far left with the light foot troops on the flanks. We know that Aristeus's men heavily engaged both Athenian wings, thus they must have deployed along the full front at only six shields deep. The Corinthians and the best of the mercenaries took station on their right wing, with the remaining Peloponnesians in the center and the Potidaeans on the left. Like his foe, Aristeus would have divided his light infantry to screen both flanks.

The two phalanxes advanced into shock combat, with each side drifting rightward to slightly overlap the enemy's left wing. Using their extended flank to good advantage, the Corinthians and picked mercenaries enveloped the Athenian left, breaking it down to be driven from the field before its greater depth could have an effect. Meanwhile, the Athenian right wing had lost Callias, but still achieved similar success against the overlapped Potidaeans. With the results on the wings offsetting each other, it was action in the middle of the field that proved decisive. Here, hired men once more came up short against militia, as the Athenians used depth and élan to force the mercenaries rearward until they broke and ran. Keeping passions under rein, the victors then limited pursuit and held onto the battleground. But this wasn't the case with the Peloponnesians on the other side of the field, who chased their beaten foes for quite a distance. They then turned about, only to find the enemy blocking the way back to Potidaea.

Unlike his Athenian counterpart, Aristeus had survived and now came forward to lead his isolated troops to safety. He swung west along the seashore, keeping the enemy on his left (shielded) side as he rushed his men toward the city in a compact body. The Athenian hoplites couldn't maneuver fast enough to stop this end run, but their archers pelted the fleeing men with arrows and some got past upraised shields to find fatal gaps in the Peloponnesians' armor. However, there weren't enough bowmen to exact too high a price and Aristeus made it into Potidaea with most of his division. Nevertheless, the battle was costly for all involved. Athens lost Callias and 150 hoplites (5 percent of those engaged) plus a few allies (perhaps 30 or so), the majority going down in the collapse and pursuit of the Athenian left, which likely suffered around 15 percent killed. The Corinthians lost nearly 300 spearmen (12.5 percent), with casualties heaviest among the hired men and Potidaeans defeated at center and on the left wing.

The Athenian army now moved to put Potidaea under siege, setting up along its north wall and Phormio soon arriving from Athens with another 1,600 hoplites to allow operations against the south side as well. (Notable among those with Phormio were the philosopher Socrates, 37 years old at the time, and his pupil Alcibiades, ward of Pericles and future general, who was seeing his first combat action.) Surrounded ashore, Potidaea was also cut off from the sea by patrolling Athenian ships. Their desperate situation seems to have crushed the defenders' morale and, though he had hoped to remain in the city with 500 militiamen, Aristeus could find no support for this among his Corinthian troops, who chose instead to escape by sea at an opportune moment. Aristeus, however, remained in Chalcidice to pursue a guerrilla war and later managed a successful ambush near Sermylium to the east of Olynthus. Many of his mercenaries stayed as well and enlisted with the Chalcidians. Abandoned by their allies, the Potidaeans did their best to resist, but finally had to surrender in 431 B.C.

The Corinthians turned to their hegemon at Sparta in a bid to get even for their humiliating reverses at Corcyra and Potidaea. The Spartans clearly had concerns about the Athenian resurgence, but they must have been even more worried that Corinth would leave their alliance if they did nothing to curb Athens. Corinth was a key member of the Spartan league, its army second only to Sparta's and its fleet far and away the league's best. Fearful lest they lose this valuable partner, the Spartans accused the Athenians of violating the current 30-year treaty.

Sparta met with its allies in late 432 B.C. to discuss the issue, with Corinth arguing for a declaration of war on Athens. Most of the allies were in support due to heavy lobbying by the Corinthians prior to the meeting. It was therefore decided to provoke a conflict by deliberately making unreasonable demands. Thus, Athenian refusals to raise the siege of Potidaea, free Aigina, and remove a trading ban on Megara were used as pretexts for war and the Peloponnesians marched on Attica in force during the next summer campaign season. Most expected a quick and decisive victory, never dreaming for a moment that they were embarking on what would become a 27-year ordeal that no Greek would truly win.

Tactical Patterns of the Pentacontaetia

Combat results during the Pentacontaetia clearly show that doing the unexpected worked very well. There were four surprise attacks or maneuvers during this period: the Thracian ambush at Drabescus, the Thessalian desertion at Tanagra I, the Sicel assault on the camps at Greek Motya, and Cleandrias's subterfuge in his first fight against the Lucanians. Every one of these delivered victory. Furthermore, there were six other times when an army arrived with little or no advance warning and all but one of these actions (Athens's draw at Cimolia I) likewise proved a complete success. The element of surprise thus nearly guaranteed a win regardless of any other factors present.

Battles in this era also strongly reinforce the idea that there was great advantage in having more hoplites than the opposition. Armies holding a significant edge (+33 percent) in numbers of spearmen scored 12 victories against a single draw and only four defeats. Furthermore, all four losses (Dipaea, Drabescus, Sicyon II, and Greek Motya) can be attributed to an overriding element of surprise attack and/or mobilization.

Another pattern was that hoplites did well against barbarians. Just as during the Persian invasions, this was the reverse of what had happened in the Ionian revolt, confirming that it was fighting on open ground unsuited to the phalanx that had caused those earlier losses. The Greeks now avoided such combat sites (they weren't common in Greece anyway) or warded their flanks well with skirmishers and/or terrain, which left them free to defeat lighter-armed foes with the mass power of their battle array. Yet it would be wrong to think that such formation weight only impacted engagements with barbarians, since things were much the same when hoplites fought each other. Phalanxes with significantly more spearmen won seven battles versus just two defeats (both affected by surprise tactics). Therefore, while morale and troop quality were without doubt major factors in Greek warfare, raw numbers were also very important.

Light-infantry support became stronger in mainland Greece during the Pentacontaetia, with the ratio of psiloi rising from one per ten hoplites at the beginning of the period to as high as one per five or six in later years. This was a response to the growing threat that light foot troops and horsemen were now posing to the traditional phalanx and resembled deployments already common in the Grecian west and Asia. However, since psiloi tended to neutralize each other and leave a battle's decision to the heavy infantry, their increased numbers went largely unnoted. Engagements like Stenyklaras and Drabescus, where they played a major role, were scarce and looked upon as anomalies. Thus, though light footmen were vital to screen formation flanks and could be dangerous to hoplites when not countered by adequate numbers of their own kind, they garnered little comment and remained lost in the background of Greek battle.

Nonetheless, psiloi did play an important part along with terrain tactics against mounted troops. The Greeks thus fared well in fights with barbarian horsemen, defeating them in no less than six battles during the Pentacontaetia. With one tribal victory (Taras II) gained by foot soldiers, only the ambush at Drabescus and loss of the battlefield at Mazaros I count as reverses against foreign cavalry during this period. And though Greek armies with a mounted advantage were undefeated over the same interval, this isn't so impressive when examined in detail. Indeed, in spite of being present in greater mass on the winning side, horsemen likely had little or no effect at Achradine I/II, Cimolia I/II, and Coronea. Instead, it was their infantry comrades who carried these actions. There were, in fact, but two battles in Greece (Oenoe and Tanagra I) and two more in Sicily (Acragas and Himera River) where superior cavalry and skirmishers might have been decisive. In this light, we can say that horsemen did actually decide a few engagements, but were rarely an overwhelming factor.

What about the effect of doing battle on home soil? Armies fighting near home won 11 battles during the Pentacontaetia, but also suffered 13 losses and two draws. And the home record is no better if we consider only actions between hoplite armies, with invaders winning eleven times against eight defeats and one draw. This doesn't lend much support to the concept of a "home field advantage" in hoplite warfare. Moreover, the argument gets even weaker when we filter out other major factors. In actions with no mismatch in hoplite manpower, local forces posted only three victories to seven defeats; and when strength in horsemen was near equal, those fighting at home prevailed just twice against nine losses and a draw. Finally, where numbers were on a par for both spearmen and cavalry, local men were winless in all five matches.

This contrasts strongly with results during the Persian/Carthaginian invasions. Then, the Greeks used knowledge of local topography to great advantage, but such settings were unusual in the Pentacontaetia. If anything, data for this later period suggest a bias *against* those defending their homeland. This might reflect how important confidence was to troops facing the ordeal of shock combat, since men marching aggressively into enemy territory were generally more self-assured than those being targeted. Actively taking the offensive could therefore give a moral edge over defenders standing reluctantly near home. Such aggression and confidence, when channeled by discipline within an entire unit, was often more critical in the heat of battle than the more passive concepts of home and family. Marching to meet invaders at the border was thus better than waiting for them to arrive, as Thucydides said Pagondas of Thebes pointed out to his troops before the battle of Delium (424 B.C.).

Given that controlled aggression could be vital to combat success, how did some poleis achieve superior development of this martial virtue? Simply put, winning begat more winning. When not fighting each other, the leading poleis of Sparta, Athens, and Syracuse claimed victory (at least on their side of the field) in 18 of 23 engagements during the Pentacontaetia. What was the secret of this success? These states had to fight often in seizing and holding their hegemonies, which gained them combat experience and enhanced military prowess. Their initial success, regardless of whether due to innate ability or just pure luck, then served to breed more of the same. An honored history of triumph thus conditioned warriors of these powers to not just seek victory, but to expect it, making them deadlier than ever on the field of battle. This frequently led to opponents lacking in such a winning tradition being cowed and defeated before the first blow was even struck.

It needs to be stressed that, while repetitive combat honed physical skills, it was its mental rewards that counted most. An army that was always losing was unlikely to become formidable no matter how often it fought. Of course, any strength carried to extremes can become a weakness. While the Spartans were able to overcome long odds to win at Dipaea, their martial hubris led to predictable defeat at Stenyklaras and Oenoe. Likewise, the Athenians charted a course to disaster at Coronea in a fog of overconfidence. Nevertheless, the best phalanxes won as much as anything simply because they were used to doing so.

Such controlled aggression seems to have been easiest to build within a body of militia, whose members shared origins, experiences, and values. But what of the several units of mercenary hoplites that fought during the Pentacontaetia? It appears that no matter how effective these hired men could be against their own kind (as at Acragas), they rarely defeated citizen soldiers at this time, strongly suggesting that patriotism usually trumped pay as a motivating factor (at least, when all else was more or less equal).

All the same, there was a growing appreciation in this period for troops trained beyond the level of militia. One had only to look at the success of Sparta's full-time soldiers to see the value of such men. Therefore, a few states formed units of picked hoplites (epilektoi) at public expense, filling them with their finest men. These were hybrid contingents that sought to combine the best qualities of both mercenary professionals and militia patriots. Such elite lochoi appeared at Syracuse (600 men), Elis (300 men), Argos (a forerunner of The Thousand), and in Boeotia at Thebes (300 men, the model for the Sacred Band of 4th-century fame). These provided well-trained bodies of troops that could either stiffen the ranks of a phalanx or separately execute difficult maneuvers on one wing. Also, much like the French Foreign Legion in recent times, they could tackle distant and hazardous duty with less political trauma than would be the case with militia drawn from the general population. Argos appears to have used its elite troops at Tanagra I in just this kind of dangerous foreign campaign.

The Athenians didn't develop true epilektoi in the 5th century, yet this didn't signal distaste for innovation, since they adopted many other new military practices. These innovations included adding decks to their triremes, expanding light-armed capabilities on several fronts, and developing advanced terrain and amphibious tactics. Known for contributions to the fine arts, Athens seems to have been no less inventive when it came to the art of war. And this creativity was tied to another trait: not trying to do more with less. Indeed, the record shows that Athens not only modernized its military through the years, but also greatly expanded it to meet the demands of empire. This stood in stark contrast to Sparta, which held to the status quo on all fronts by stressing quality over quantity and expert execution of tried-and-true tactics. There were, of course, both economic and demographic aspects to the Spartans' tact, since they lacked the wealth and population growth of Athens, yet such an approach was very much in keeping with the rigid nature of their society as well. If controlled aggression was truly the key trait that physically beat and mentally cowed an enemy, then Sparta could best cultivate this quality among its conservative citizenry by sticking to old methods that were the bedrock of its past success in combat. Still, in the end, neither the Athenians nor Spartans could be said to possess the superior system, as both methodologies worked well in their different ways.

* * *

Athens and Sparta followed different routes to reach their positions as Greece's leading states. One had developed democracy and looked outward, building up capability in all types of arms and using its seafaring skills to seize a far-flung empire. The other stuck to monarchy and turned inward, maintaining traditional land forces within a system of alliances that secured hegemony close to home. But Athenian expansion had triggered conflict when it threatened allies vital to Sparta's defensive league, and as summer opened in 431 B.C., these deeply contrasting powers stood poised to test their unique strengths in an all-out war

V

Danger and Glory: The Archidamian War (431–422 B.C.)

> "It must be thoroughly understood that war is a necessity ... and that out of the greatest dangers communities and individuals acquire the greatest glory."
> — Pericles (Thucydides: *The Peloponnesian War*)

Athens found itself once again at war with Sparta and its league of allies in 431 B.C. and most of the Greek world was ultimately forced to take part in this epic contest, which would not reach a conclusion for 27 years. Often called the Great Peloponnesian War to distinguish it from the first struggle between most of the same opponents (461–451 B.C.), the initial phase of this dispute lasted a full decade. Known as the Archidamian War after the Spartan king most prominent in its prosecution, this opening round of hostilities was, in its own right, the widest conflict up to that point in Greek history, with theaters ranging from Italy to Asia. It became clear early on that the fight would involve a different type of warfare than any seen in Greece's past. Rather than being the sole means of resolution, a state's phalanx was only one asset used among many within a much broader economic and political struggle. The differing natures of the Athenian and Spartan military machines thus led each side to take very different approaches to the war.

Sparta had Greece's most formidable army. A Spartan general could call upon at least 5,000 hoplites from his homeland and up to 40,000 more from allies. And though Athens itself had an even larger militia, with some 16,000 prime-aged citizen and metic spearmen, its allied manpower was much smaller. Long-time Athenian allies had sent less than 3,000 hoplites to Plataea in 479 B.C., while new partners on the islands of Chios, Lesbos, Samos, and Corcyra could add no more than 9–12,000 more based on the size of their fleets. Besides being short on numbers, many of the spearmen among Athens's allies were also less adept at phalanx fighting than their Spartan-aligned counterparts. Accepting these realities, the Athenians knew that they would have little chance in a conventional hoplite engagement. However, they had a huge margin in naval resources, being able to deploy 500–600 triremes (including up to 300 of their own) against no more than 150 ships and crews of generally lesser quality from Sparta's allies. Athens therefore sought a way to make its advantage at sea decisive against a foe intent on pursuing a land-bound war.

Confident in the superiority of their army, the Spartans initiated this current conflict much as they had the smaller scale wars of the past, marching out to ravage farmland in an open invitation to pitched combat. The Athenians under Pericles didn't take the bait. Instead, they harassed the invaders with cavalry and avoided a set battle in favor of seaborne assaults on the Peloponnese and elsewhere. By using their superb fleet to raid enemy territory, they hoped to lure Sparta's great host from Attica and cause it to disperse among many small defensive efforts at home. Rather than seeking a quick decision between phalanxes, the plan was to outlast Sparta in a longer and murkier struggle of economic attrition. To be sure, hoplites were still the primary tactical tool in this kind of warfare, but their use was now subordinated to the needs of higher strategy. Warfare among the poleis would never again be simple and decisive.

Cavalry Clashes and Sea Raids

The first act of war had come in the spring of 431 B.C., when Thebes tried to take over Plataea by sneaking a party of men into that city on a moonless night. The Plataeans rose up to best these intruders in a confused fight that swirled through the streets, but then came under siege from the rest of the Thebans waiting outside. It was shortly after this opening clash that the Spartans moved against Attica in force. Archidamus of Sparta planned to settle the war in one mighty battle and had gathered an army of some 20,000 spearmen for this purpose by calling up a two-thirds draft from selected allies. His hoplites included 4,000 from Sparta, 9,500 from elsewhere in the Peloponnese, 1,500 from Megara, and 5,000 from Boeotia. He also fielded 5–6,000 light footmen, including hamippoi attached to horsemen provided by Boeotia (600–700) and Phocis/Locris (200). The Spartan king began his campaign by crossing into Athenian territory at the start of summer to invest Oenoe, a border fort and local refuge that was manned by a lochos/taxis of about 500 reservists (Munn 1993, 29–32, 169). He hoped that a threat against this outpost would serve to goad the enemy into coming out to do battle with their full citizen levy of 13,000 hoplites.

Athens's leader, Pericles, elected to counter the invasion without fighting a pitched battle. He left Oenoe to defend itself and readied for a siege at Athens as well, relying on the city's fleet and long walls connected with the port of Piraeus to insure a seaborne line of supply. Yet Pericles couldn't simply abandon the countryside, lest he incur the wrath of a host of landowners. This led him to launch mounted attacks against Archidamus. After all, cavalry had proven effective the last time that a Spartan army had closed on the city (in 510 B.C.) and he must have known that Gela's riders in Sicily had foiled similar plunderers during the Punic invasion.

Rheiti and Phrygia (431 B.C.)

Archidamus soon realized that it would be difficult to take Oenoe and, when the Athenian phalanx didn't show, shifted his attack to the nearby plain around Eleusis. After spoiling this region and still not getting a response, he next decided to advance southeast toward Athens itself. The first serious opposition appeared at Rheiti ("The Brooks"), which lay at the foot of Mount Aegaleus some 12km west of the city. Cavalry from Athens (probably a squadron of 500 javelinmen plus 100 mounted-archers) essayed an attack there that the Spartan countered with his allied cavalry. Their screen of mounted bowmen should have given the Athenians a modest edge, yet they were unable to hold the field. In view of the setting, this was more likely a failure of raw manpower than of courage. The defenders could take full advantage of the greater reach of their weapons only by yielding ground as they fought, staying beyond javelin range while still able to use their bows to telling effect; however, rugged terrain behind them to the south and east must have eventually put an end to their ability to withdraw. The riders from Athens then came under fire from 1,600–1,800 horsemen and light foot troops closing from the northwest, who held a better than 3 to 1 advantage in missilemen. This forced the Athenians to retire, likely moving southwest along the mountain front toward the coast and the nearest pass to Athens as their archers trailed to forestall pursuit.

Still hoping to flush out the phalanx of his foe, Archidamus turned northeast to pass into the Attic province of Acharnae, an area with a large population that might convince Pericles to come out in defense of the land. But the Athenian leader stuck to his strategy and, rather than offering up his smaller army for destruction, sent out an even more powerful force of horsemen. This time, an Athenian squadron (again, probably 600 strong) sortied along with cavalry from Thessaly. The Thessalians would have had 700 riders, with each of the seven commanders present (two from Larissa and one apiece from Pharsalus, Cranon, Pyrasus, Gyrtone, and Pherae) leading 100 mounted men and the same number of hamippoi. The Athenian horsemen caught Archidamus northeast of Athens (Spence 1993, 131) at Phrygia and charged into battle with his Boeotian cavalry.

Riders from Athens and Thessaly used different formations (rectangular and diamond-shaped respectively) and screening methods (mounted archers versus hamippoi) and thus must have operated as distinct units, either closing along slightly separated fronts or alternating their attacks. Putting greater numbers and the skill of their horse-savvy allies to good use, the Athenians fared well in a back-and-forth skirmish that inflicted a beating on their foes, knocking some of them from their saddles and scattering others. But when hoplites from Boeotia came up to support their mounted comrades, the tide of battle shifted. How did slow moving heavy infantry do this? It's likely that the spearmen anchored their flanks using terrain and/or psiloi and then channeled their more mobile foe against a line of shields and deadly spear points. Pressed toward this bristling barrier by the weight of the opposing cavalry and a hail of hamippoi javelins, the Athenians had to break from the fight. As it developed, they got away with little damage, since the enemy's cavalry didn't dare give chase lest it risk further losses from mounted archers screening the retreat.

Though bested for the moment, Athens's mounted force remained potent, and prospects of its regrouping for another attack led the Boeotians to abandon the ground. Thus, while the victors would later erect a trophy on the site, the Athenians were able to return and recover their dead without arranging a truce. Nevertheless, it must have now become clear to Pericles that his cavalry couldn't drive Archidamus from Attica. His attention thus turned toward launching a campaign from the sea against the enemy homelands.

Pheia and Alope (431 B.C.)

Athens sent out 100 ships to attack the Peloponnese even as Archidamus's army spoiled the Attic countryside. Carcinus, Proteas, and Socrates (son of Antigenes and not the philosopher — son of Sophroniscus — who was at Potidaea at the time) led this effort. Traveling light so as to be ready for action at sea, they must have embarked only the usual complement on each ship — sailors, rowers, hoplite marines (ten), and archers (four). Nevertheless, this was more than enough men to make good a series of quick strikes similar to the ones visited on Halieis (459 B.C.) and Sicyon (457–454 B.C.). They next sailed to join 50 ships from Corcyra, and take on some Messenian hoplites from Naupactus, and then turned back to land near Methone on the southwest coast of Messenia.

Athens's armada must have made an impressive sight, its triremes beached stern-first with 30m or so between them to stretch along 4–5km of seafront. Each ship was pulled to rest onto dry land atop wooden rollers before being wedged into place with external supports. Once so grounded, the vessels formed a temporary camp from which the raiders swarmed forth over the near-defenseless countryside. The local Spartan commander, Brasidas, kept the Athenians from sacking Methone in the first of his many notable actions in this war, but couldn't stop them from pillaging the rural area before moving up the coast. Landing next in the territory of Elis near the port city of Pheia, the Athenians ravaged the land for two days before meeting resistance from a contingent of 300 picked hoplites. Elis maintained these epilektoi at state expense as a quick reaction force for just such emergencies. The plan must have been to delay the raiders long enough for the Elean army to gather, yet there simply weren't enough men to pose any real threat to an Athenian host with more than 3,000 hoplites. Indeed, the raiders no doubt needed but a fraction of their strength (a lochos?) to chase the Eleans away in a minor combat (though their lack of horsemen meant that most of the beaten men escaped unharmed).

The Athenians took Pheia and weathered a storm in its harbor before departing upon arrival of a full Elean levy of some 3,000 spearmen. This underscores the Athenians' campaign strategy of carrying out hit-and-run operations over a wide range and avoiding any hoplite army that could match their numbers. The expedition had enough men to easily overrun local garrisons that could be called upon with short notice, while its ships allowed it to avoid larger musters that took days to gather. There was no effective shore-based defense against this approach in a land that lacked cavalry or standing armies of any size; thus, facing no challenge at sea, the Athenians were free to strike at any coastal target they chose. They therefore went on to hit northwestern Greece (taking Sollium and Astacus) and along the Ionian Sea (capturing the island of Cephallenia), all while suffering but little loss in the course of dealing out some real harm to Sparta. Later that same year, Cleopompus of Athens led 30 ships on a similar campaign to strike at allies of Sparta in eastern Greece. Operating far from enemy naval bases, he didn't have to be concerned with being trim for a fight at sea, which would have allowed him to add a full load of hoplite passengers (900) to his marines (300) and archers (120). He sailed to Opuntian Locris (onshore of northern Euboa), raided the coast, and captured Thronium before the now alerted Locrians intercepted him at Alope.

Unlike in Elis, the Athenians seem to have been confident enough of victory here to stay ashore and fight a hoplite battle. Yet a full Locrian muster of around 1,000 hoplites plus some psiloi and a few horsemen (perhaps 100) with hamippoi wouldn't have been much smaller than what Cleopompus could land. This means that his decision to engage probably rested more upon disdain for Locrian prowess than on any upper hand in manpower. He presumably counted on the greater experience of his men in shock combat to overcome a foe already shaken by his unexpected arrival. Moving confidently inland with hoplites likely aligned eight deep over 150m, the Athenians came to action near the beach.

It's probable that the Locrians matched the facing front with slightly thinner files, but couldn't hold the field and eventually gave way. Casualties would have been quite light on both sides, the victors taking little hurt in so brief an action and the losers having horsemen and light foot soldiers to cover their retreat from opponents weak in such arms. Just as at Pheia, Athens's shortage of quality light troops allowed most of a defeated army to escape for the paltry price of a few tossed shields.

Despite being unable to properly pursue and finish the fight at Alope, Cleopompus could still claim considerable success upon his return to Athens; after all, he had spoiled enemy territory, taken a city, and gained at least a modest battlefield victory. His campaign and that against the Peloponnese had thus repaid the Spartan alliance in kind for the destruction being visited on Attica and must have had a salving effect on the temper of the besieged Athenians. This helped them bear their losses in service of Pericles' policy of victory through attrition. However, if meant to trigger a recall of Archidamus (as per Diodorus), these sorties failed, since Thucydides claimed that the Spartan king stayed in the field until he had used up his provisions.

The Athenians made one brief overland offensive after the Peloponnesians disbanded in the fall of 431 B.C. Pericles led 9,000 citizen and 3,000 metic hoplites into Megaran territory, where he was joined by another 1,000 spearmen from the fleet just returned from Cephallenia. At 13,000 hoplites, this was the largest army ever fielded by Athens and it thoroughly ravaged the Megarid before marching home. Why use so powerful a force for a mere raid? One reason is that a majority of Athenians had been unable to strike back in defense of their land. By leading out as many of these men as he could, Pericles provided an outlet for pent-up rage that might otherwise threaten his strategy. There were also operational reasons for deploying in great strength. Using a more powerful army than nearby Spartan allies could gather meant that any real response would have to originate deep in the Peloponnese, giving plenty of time for retreat.

What was emerging at this time was a new style of war that struck less at an opponent's army than at its economy, focusing on damaging property and avoiding major hoplite battles. This was a complete reversal of the past pattern in Greece, which had minimized economic harm by seeking out decisive phalanx engagements. The Athenians, like most Greeks, had always sacrificed lives to preserve their land holdings. They now abandoned this very same property in order to husband manpower for a sustained war effort.

Cranae and Lycia (430 B.C.)

Archidamus again invaded Attica the following summer and the Athenians once more refused battle. But a new menace arose in the form of a virulent plague that began infecting those shut up for so long in Athens under crowded and unsanitary conditions. At the same time, the Corinthians mounted a more distant threat, moving to emulate Pericles with a seaborne raid of their own into northwestern Greece.

A fleet of 40 ships sailed from Corinth to land 1,500 hoplites at Astacus and quickly retake the town. As it turned out, this initial success proved to be the expedition's last, as, striking at a number of other sites along the coast of Acarnania, it failed to capture a single one. The fleet's commanders turned back in disappointment, but decided to make one last attempt and landed on the island of Cephallenia to assault the town of Cranae. This final effort proved the worst failure of the lot when the landing party fell into an ambush against a defending force of half or less its size. Apparently catching their more numerous foes strung out in column, the islanders sprang from hiding to rout the would-be raiders and chase the survivors back to their ships. This put a dismal end to a frustrating campaign, yet the Peloponnesians weren't ready to give up on amphibious operations altogether and launched a second fleet that same summer in an attack on Zacynthus, an Athenian allied island off the coast of Elis. However, despite deploying 100 ships and 1,000 hoplites under the spartiate Cnemus, the effort failed and did no more than confirm Athens's edge in this kind of warfare from the sea.

As 430 B.C. unfolded and plague continued to wound their city, the Athenians once more struck at the Peloponnese to raise their spirits and deal some payback to Sparta. They put 40 hoplites aboard each of 100 of their own triremes and joined up with 50 more ships from Chios and Lesbos that were likewise fully loaded. This gave the combined fleet some 6,000 spearmen—twice the number sent against the Peloponnese a year earlier. Since the Athenians seem to have been careful to board only marines on that previous expedition so as to be configured for action at sea, their inclusion of so many hoplite passengers here indicates a growing contempt for enemy naval forces. And there was a new element present in this effort — 300 horsemen and mounts aboard ten older triremes reconfigured as cavalry transports. Inclusion of mounted troops gave the landing force capability to scout inland, more securely screen flanks, and better provide for either post-battle pursuit or retreat. This force hit the Peloponnese and then its Athenian component sailed far up the eastern coast to deal with the Chalcidians and give aid to the ongoing siege at Potidaea. Sadly for the Athenians, these ships carried the plague and over a thousand of the embarked hoplites died over the next few months, taking many others already at Potidaea with them.

At this juncture, a minor but painful battlefield reverse added to Athens's terrible losses from pestilence. Melesander had set out in late 430 B.C. on a mission to collect tribute in Asia Minor with six triremes full of armed crewmen, two dozen archers, and up to 240 hoplites. His expedition ran into trouble in Lycia, a former Persian ally that appears to have been only a reluctant member of the Delian League. Having joined with some locals for a march into the interior, Melesander suddenly found himself under attack from a superior force of Lycian rebels.

The infantry force that confronted Melesander would have been well equipped to oppose his spearmen. Like their Phoenician neighbors, Lycian line troops carried two javelins and wore body armor (corselet and greaves) similar to that of the Greeks (though fitted with a soft headdress instead of helmet); however, the Lycians didn't carry the small shield favored by Punic fighters, but substituted a bow instead. This mix of weapons let each man fire arrows and then advance to hurl one javelin before finally closing with the other to use it as a short spear — all while those behind continued to use their bows. It's also possible that the Lycians emulated Persian tactics by providing shields of some sort to their leading ranks that they might harden their front in shock actions. As for cavalry, the Lycians, like others long subject to Persia, relied on their imperial masters for this arm and probably had few horsemen of their own.

Melesander would have set up a small phalanx, placing his own and allied light foot troops on the wings (archers outboard), and then advanced through a heavy fall of arrows. The goal was to get his hoplites within spear reach so that their sturdier gear might carry the day. What happened next is unreported, but enemy firepower might have combined with terrain and/or a lack of discipline to fatally disrupt the Athenians, causing them to lose heart and flee well short of the opposing front. What we know for sure is that the Lycians inflicted a thrashing that took the lives of Melesander and a number of his men. Still, this was but a minor setback for Athens, and the year would end on an upbeat note when Potidaea finally surrendered.

Spartolos (429 B.C.)

The Spartans changed their approach the next campaigning season, diverting Archidamus and his army from Attica to send them against Plataea instead. They might have been hoping that Athens would deploy its phalanx rather than face loss of its lone Boeotian ally; if so, they were disappointed. Pericles seems to have been no more tempted to fight an unequal battle for Plataea than he had been for his own croplands, perhaps relying on Spartan ineptitude at siege warfare to save Plataea. And despite being defended by only 400 citizens and 80 Athenian volunteers, the town did indeed manage to hold out until the bulk of the invading force had to disband in the fall.

Meanwhile, the Athenians sought to subdue the area around Potidaea, a region recently turned hostile within a new federal union, the Chalcidian League. The major goal of this campaign was to secure the route for Athens's shore-hugging transports, which had to pass close along the coast of Chalcidice in carrying vital grain imports from the Black Sea region. It was an effort that would spawn the largest phalanx battle of the war to date. That an action on this scale didn't take place until the third year of the conflict and in such a distant arena shows just how far the Greek way of war had shifted from its past pattern of quick hoplite clashes fought close to home. Moreover, events on the field would show an evolution in tactics as well.

Xenophon (son of Euripides and not the historian, son of Gryllus) and others led an army from Athens toward northern Greece. A seasoned general, Xenophon had served at Potidaea and now held chief command of a strong force that boasted 2,000 hoplites, 200 cavalrymen, and some light foot troops (perhaps 500 archers and/or psiloi). Quickly crossing a hostile Boeotia, the Athenian column reached friendly territory in Thessaly and continued on to Spartolos, a Chalcidian League stronghold along the coast northwest of Potidaea. Xenophon set up a camp for his baggage and, putting a few men on guard (at least 200 spearmen and some archers), moved against the city. Here he met frustration. Xenophon had arranged for friends inside the walls to betray a gate, but the recent arrival of enemy reinforcements from nearby Olynthus had ruined his plot.

Spartolos reacted to Xenophon's approach by rushing its army out to form up on level ground under the city walls. This array would have had 1,600–2,000 spearmen in all, including 600–800 mercenaries left from Corinth's expedition to Potidaea in 432 B.C. Hoplite numbers were thus about equal on either side. However, the locals had a strong advantage in light-armed troops, with hundreds of peltasts from the adjacent coastal area of Crusis, at least 500 horsemen (all those from Olynthus — half of total League strength), and a hamippos for each rider.

Both armies likely set up eight shields deep along a front of around 225m in length. On the Chalcidian side, the mercenaries must have formed the left wing, leaving the center and honored right-wing stations to local men. Next, the light foot troops skirmished and then retired to the flanks of each army as cavalry moved outboard onto the wings (two squadrons of 250 riders each for the Chalcidians and two of 100 each for Athens). Finally, the phalanxes closed with a crash into close combat. It must have soon become apparent that the Chalcidians were no match for their more experienced and confident foes, with the Athenian hoplites pushing and stabbing through the northerners to send them into battered and bleeding flight. As for the hired Peloponnesians, though they had no doubt done better along their end of the line, they too fell back when the others gave way. Spartolos's phalanx was badly beaten and done for the day, but events now unfolded that would turn the battle around. This began when the local peltasts and cavalry moved up to cover the retreat and succeeded in routing their Athenian counterparts.

The more numerous northern horsemen had played a key role in these victories at the edges of the fight, killing the opposing cavalry leader and chasing off both his riders and light infantry to denude the Athenian flanks. At this crucial juncture, the Chalcidians were fortuitously joined by a large contingent of peltasts that had just marched in from Olynthus. Boosted by these reinforcements, the Chalcidian light forces now turned against Athens's spearmen where they still stood on the battlefield, charging to loose a hail of darts at the unsupported hoplites and threaten the perilously exposed flanks of their phalanx. Accustomed to having a clear field after driving away an enemy's heavy troops, the Athenians must have been truly shocked as showers of javelins began finding fatal openings through shield and armor. Unable to reply effectively, they attempted to back off toward their encampment. Their opposition then closed repeatedly to further wound and kill with their missiles, able to speedily draw back to safety each time their foes mounted a slow and cumbersome counterattack. Xenophon's men must have felt helpless, with a sense of panic rising as each new fall of darts thinned their ranks. Before long, their battle array began to unravel, a victim of both the enemy and its own hurried rush toward the rear. Eventually, those men at the back and closest to camp simply could take it no more and began to flee pell-mell.

When the Athenian rear ranks gave way, they abandoned those still resisting at the fore to be overwhelmed by swarms of peltasts. Nearly all of these front fighters were surrounded and killed, including Xenophon and his fellow generals (Hornblower 1991, 361). Pursuing cavalry and light foot troops then struck down many of those in flight. Thus, even though most of the Athenians gained their base and a temporary respite, they left the bodies of nearly a quarter of their comrades strewn along the battle front and in the wake of their retreat. The survivors now lost little time in abandoning the campaign to head home.

Stratus (429 B.C.)

Not long after Spartolos, another hoplite army suffered a defeat against light-armed fighters. The leaders of Ambracia on Greece's northwest frontier had come to Sparta seeking assistance for a war on their neighbors in Athenian-allied Acarnania, the region just above the opening of the Corinthian Gulf. They suggested that such a campaign could drive Athens from all western Greece, and the Spartans agreed, dispatching Cnemus with 1,000 spearmen aboard a flotilla that probably had 25 ships. His was to be an advance party, with a larger fleet to follow in due time. Cnemus eluded Athenian patrols in the Gulf and sailed north to the isle of Leucas, a Corinthian foundation, where he added more ships and men before moving on to enter the nearby Ambracian Gulf. Landing here, Cnemus joined troops that had come overland from Ambracia, Anactorium (allied to Leucas and another Corinthian colony), and various non-Greek tribes. (A contingent of Macedonian peltasts had also set out secretly to join the campaign, but didn't arrive in time to take part.) Now the Spartan general marched south, moving at last into Acarnanian territory as his ships kept pace offshore in support.

Cnemus likely had nearly 6,000 Greeks in his army. These included hoplites from the Peloponnese (1,000), Leucas and Anactorium (1,000 or so — they had fielded 800 against Persia), and Ambracia (a two-thirds levy of 3,000). Only the Ambraciots and Anactorians arrived on foot and brought psiloi (maybe 350–700 in all), but there were enough barbarians on hand to compensate. The tribesmen represented both the area onshore from Corcyra (Chaonians, Thesprotians and Antintanians) and the adjacent interior (Parauaeans, Molossians, and Orestians). Orestis and Macedon had sent 1,000 men and the other tribal levies must have been of like size, which suggests that Cnemus had as many barbarians as Greeks, for a total of almost 12,000 men.

The tribesmen with Cnemus were highlanders that lived north of Greece and south of Illyria. Though racially mixed with the nearby Greeks, their military style was likely closer to that of the Illyrians. If so, they wore no body armor beyond an open-faced helmet and carried a light, round shield of wood or leather with a central bronze boss for offensive strikes. They fought primarily with a long, heavy spear (*sibyna*) that was fitted with a massive head, but also used a downward-curving saber similar to the Greek machaira as a secondary shock weapon. Most also brought along a couple of javelins, and there were probably some slingers in their ranks as well. Missile weapons of this sort let them open battle from a distance, fighting from ambush and skirmishing in open order actually being their preferred methods of attack. These barbarians were poorly suited to form part of a phalanx and were of most use for screening hoplites from light-armed opponents as well as detached duty like raiding, reconnaissance, and siege work.

The Acarnanians were in awe of the might being brought against them and refrained from moving out against it, holding instead to strong defensive positions as their own forces continued to collect. Cnemus therefore quickly moved against the Acarnanian capital at Stratus, seeking to strike before his foes gathered their full strength. He split his army into three columns so as to speed his advance. This common tactic recognized that the sort of narrow tracks that ran through rugged and heavily wooded country would overly string out a single body of men and greatly slow its rate of march. In dividing his men, Cnemus put the barbarians in the center, between his own Peloponnesians and the Ambraciots to the left (landward) and the men from Leucas and Anactorium to the right (along the coast and closest to their homelands). Placing all the tribal skirmishers into a single column clearly shows that he didn't intend to attack on three fronts, but planned to reunite prior to battle toward achieving a proper mix of arms. Though this scheme was sound enough, it was a bit complex and soon fell victim to an uncooperative enemy.

As the Chaonians led the central column of tribesmen close to Stratus, they got out well in front of the more heavily equipped hoplites on their flanks. These barbarians, confident in their numbers and prowess, were eager to engage the enemy before their fellow attackers could arrive. Perhaps they sought greater glory from an independent action (as suggested by Thucydides), but more likely they were simply after a larger share of the spoils. Unfortunately for them, their foes had scouted the situation and were apparently well aware that these lighter-armed men were now exposed and unsupported. Rather than waiting for the rest of their army to muster, the Acarnanians decided to take advantage of this golden opportunity and strike first.

The Stratians hid at opportune sites near their city and unleashed a surprise assault upon the leading elements of the tribal column just as it arrived. As groups of spearmen charged from ambush to take them at close range, the Chaonians in the barbarian van panicked, losing all order and bolting for the rear as the aroused defenders gave chase and slaughtered them from behind in great numbers. Fleeing northward, the Chaonians now spread fear among other tribesmen still approaching from that quarter and, before long, the entire barbarian division was on the run, with vengeful Acarnanians following in hot pursuit. Meanwhile, Cnemus and his left-flank column of spearmen were ignorant of the disaster that had befallen their allies, only becoming aware of the situation when a few of the barbarians, having spread out in their direction, ran past with shouted warnings that the enemy was close on their heels. Thus alerted, Cnemus sought the closest relatively open ground and formed a battle line along a short front.

Stuck in a clearing along his marching route, Cnemus was on ground ill-suited for phalanx tactics—a fact not lost on the increasing number of Acarnanians arriving on the scene. Though these were soon present in some strength at perhaps 2,000 spearmen with a host of light foot troops, they didn't seek close combat; instead, they set up on surrounding hillsides and sent down slingers to bombard the invaders. These agile troops could stay just beyond javelin range and hurl bullets with deadly effect, responding to any enemy sally by retreating back upslope to reach safety behind the shields of their heavier-armed comrades. The modest number of Ambraciot psiloi with Cnemus lacked the range to protect against slingers and had neither the manpower nor gear to contest the hills with hoplites. Loss of the defeated barbarians and tardy Macedonian peltasts was now proving a severe handicap. And Cnemus couldn't rescue the situation by leading his spearmen against their opposite numbers on the high ground. He would have been foolhardy indeed to advance against a foe whose true strength was hidden by tree cover, while that same vegetation and the rugged slopes before him would have destroyed integrity of his formation long before it could have pressed home a shock attack.

Cnemus and his men remained stalled in place to suffer under a steady shower of lethal shot until dusk finally brought an end to these assaults. They then quickly pulled out under cover of night, which ceded the battlefield and forced them to seek a truce next day in order to recover their dead. Electing not to return north, Cnemus now swung south, going around Stratus to join with reinforcements coming up from Oeniadae, his lone local ally. He went on to take refuge in that city, being unwilling to face the full force of the Acarnanian host now rushing to the defense of Stratus. It was a sad finish for an ambitious campaign. It seems that Cnemus, like the Athenians at Spartolos, had been undone by a shortage of light-armed support for his superior force of hoplites. The real tragedy was that he actually had enough auxiliaries on hand, but hadn't utilized them well, failing to prudently disperse them evenly among his columns of advance.

Coupled with a subsequent defeat at sea, Sparta's efforts in the northwest had gone badly on all counts and 429 B.C. would end with the Athenians still firmly ensconced in the region. The year did deal Athens a severe blow, however, when Pericles died of plague to rob the city of its most far-sighted strategist.

Malea and Antissa (428 B.C.)

The fourth year of the war saw the Spartans again march an army into Attica, but the Athenians remained defiant and continued to avoid pitched battle. Yet even as this now-familiar pattern was repeating, Athens suddenly found itself faced with a more distant, yet even greater challenge to its security. The isle of Lesbos off the Ionian coast rose in revolt from the Delian League as the oligarchs of its leading polis of Mytilene openly defied Athenian authority by seeking local hegemony, with the three other major oligarchic cities on the island (Pyrrha, Antissa, and Eresus) joining their cause to leave the north-coast democracy of Methymna standing in lone opposition. Anticipating Athens's response, the rebels built fortifications and expanded their fleet, while at the same time importing stores of grain and mercenary archers from the Black Sea region.

Events on Lesbos were call for genuine alarm, as a successful uprising would cost the island's navy and might spread to enough tribute-paying states to bring financial ruin and defeat. Athens took swift action, seizing ten Mytilenian ships with its fleet and diverting a task force to Lesbos that had been set to raid the Peloponnese. Cleippides and two other generals sailed to put down the rebellion with 40 triremes that likely carried a full complement of 1,600 hoplites and 160 archers. Chasing off some Lesbian ships, the Athenians landed and set up a fortified camp around their beachhead at Cape Malea, just south of Mytilene (Hornblower 1991, 387). A few allied triremes from Imbros and Lemnos (perhaps 10 ships with 300–400 hoplites) and some men from Methymna (maybe 200–400 spearmen and less than 100 psiloi) joined them there. Cleippides then proceeded to carry out a round of half-hearted peace talks that only made further conflict inevitable.

The rebels elected to risk a decisive engagement and massed their forces late in the day to march out in battle order against the Athenian landing site. Cleippides and the others quickly deployed their full complement of around 2,200 hoplites in front of the camp, with the Athenians likely holding the right wing and center and the allies the left wing of an eight-shield deep phalanx. Fleet archers and the local psiloi on hand would have taken post on the flanks. A few oarsmen might have joined the flank screen, but most probably remained with their ships, where they formed a last line of defense for the invaders' only means of escape in the case of defeat.

An estimate of islander manpower rests on knowing that Lesbos had a fleet of 70 triremes, which would have required 2,800 hoplites to fully man at 40 per ship. Adding 700 old-age/youth reservists (25 percent as many as the prime levy) would then have brung the island-wide force up to some 3,500 spearman. However, Methymna and its 750 hoplites (15 triremes-worth plus reserves) stood with the enemy, and another 400 spearmen were being detained with their ships at Athens. This means that the Lesbians could at most have fielded 1,800 prime-aged hoplites (800 from Mytilene itself) along with 500–600 reservists, giving them no more than a very small advantage in heavy manpower. One factor clearly in their favor, however, was light infantry, as they could call upon the lower classes of four cities to the tune of at least some 400–500 men. They had also recruited mercenary archers and could field several hundred whose composite weapons at least equaled, and likely far exceeded, the range of their Athenian counterparts.

The phalanxes confronted each other just above the beach and closed into a vicious shock combat that proved long and somewhat indecisive. The Mytilenians on the rebel right were well matched against fellow islanders on the Athenian left and easily held their own. It was along the rest of the line where things took a surprising turn as the other Lesbians managed to fight their more experienced foes to a standstill and even drove them back a bit. Action dragged, with neither side giving way until darkness began to fall, then the heroic insurgent effort finally bore fruit when the exhausted Athenians were first to quit the field. Still, the victors were too worn out themselves to pursue and allowed their foes to retire behind the landing-site barricades. In truth, such success didn't encourage the islanders, as they refused to attack the enemy camp and wouldn't even stay on the field long enough to set up a trophy. Rather, the men of Lesbos meekly pulled back inside their walls and, seemingly convinced that they couldn't drive the Athenians away, sent to Sparta for help.

The Athenians took advantage of opposition timidity after the clash at Malea by sending for more men from regional allies and setting up positions on either side of Mytilene that they might invest its defenders. However, these isolated outposts failed to prevent egress from the city. A Mytilenian contingent was thus able to sneak out to join with allies in launching an assault on Methymna, which they hoped to gain by treachery. When this didn't work out, the army went on to march around to various rebel cities, where it worked to improve defenses. The rebels disbanded upon completing these tasks and those from Mytilene returned home, once more getting past the woefully inadequate siege barriers with ease.

As the host that had threatened them dispersed, the men of Methymna decided to take revenge and forestall future attacks by means of an offensive of their own. They set out against Antissa (10km down the coast to the southwest) with a few psiloi and perhaps 400 hoplites — all they had, save those serving with the Athenians. This modest force met a defending army that must have been of similar size, and under the walls of Antissa both sides deployed into phalanx formation to fight it out. It seems that in addition to their native levy, the defenders also had some bowmen recruited from the Black Sea region and these must have taken a toll on the closing foe and then kept up a withering fire throughout the battle. Perhaps this arrow fire proved decisive, or maybe the courage of the men from Methymna simply failed; either way, the Antissans carried the day and inflicted heavy losses.

The reverse at Malea combined with defeat of their allies at Antissa to raise doubts among the Athenians as to the adequacy of their forces on Lesbos. Their efforts to date had gained little, as the insurgents still held the entire island save for a few campsites and Methymna. Athens adjusted by sending Paches to Lesbos with another 1,000 hoplites (who rowed their own ships, underscoring that the city's assets were falling low). With these fresh troops in hand, the Athenian command now set about a serious siege of Mytilene, building a wall with fortified strong points around the town.

Nericus and Sandius (428 B.C.)

While the action on Lesbos was extending through the summer of 428 B.C., the Athenians sent Asopius (son of Phormio) to raid the Peloponnese with thirty ships. After striking at Laconia, he continued with a dozen vessels to Naupactus, gathered an army of Acarnanians, and then launched an assault on Spartan-aligned Oeniadae. However, when he failed to reduce the town, Asopius dismissed his allies and sailed off in search of a softer target. This led him to the island of Leucas, where he set up camp and marched inland to spoil the area around the city of Nericus.

Having dealt out enough destruction for the day, Asopius and his men were returning to their anchorage when they ran into serious trouble. A unit of border guards had crossed over from Leucas's mainland territory (*peraia*) and these men caught the Athenians by surprise. Though Asopius had most of his hoplites and archers with him (perhaps 400 and 40 respectively) plus some light-armed oarsmen, he was facing poor odds against as many as 600 hoplites (a lochos of guards with some locals) and assorted light foot troops. Still, there was nothing for it but to try and fight through to the beach. This proved futile. The islanders took full advantage of surprise and numbers to shove through and chase off the Athenians, killing Asopius. Those who survived to reach camp joined with the men there to negotiate a truce next day that let them recover their dead before sailing home.

The modest size of Asopius's command shows that Athens was reducing the magnitude of deployments in an attempt to conserve its dwindling funds and manpower. The Spartans noted this frugality and saw it as a sign that their foe was losing the ability to continue the war, which led them to mount yet another invasion of Attica (the second that year) and accept an alliance with the rebels on Lesbos. The Peloponnesians even prepared a fleet for relief of that island in defiance of Athenian sea power. Aroused by this series of developments, the Athenians made a supreme effort to counter the impression that they had grown weak and scraped together the money and troops to launch an impressive 100-ship raid against the Peloponnese. The effort marked a high point in Athenian naval activity, with some 250 vessels operating across all theaters — more than at any other time in the city's history. Yet while this demonstration of strength strongly attested a continuing will to fight and did cause the enemy to pull out of Attica, it strained resources to the limit. Never again would Athens be able to put so many ships and men into action.

The Athenians sought to heal their ailing finances not only by raising taxes on citizens, but also through an increased effort to collect tribute owed by subject allies, including some very reluctant vassal states on the Asian mainland. Melesander's earlier defeat in Lycia had taken that province out of the income stream, but neighboring Caria was still nominally part of the Delian League, and Lysicles and four other commanders set out in the closing days of 428 B.C. with a twelve-ship task force to collect the Carian dues. Sailing into the mouth of the Meander River, the Athenians came ashore at Myos and marched north into the interior, where they then hit serious trouble near the hill of Sandius almost 40km inland. Here, Samian exiles from the nearby coastal town of Anaia joined with a force of Carians in launching an attack on the landing party. Lysicles had probably set out with around 480 hoplites, 48 archers, and a team of armed oarsmen/attendants, but the opposition must have out-massed him by at least 2 to 1 in spearmen and would have held an even greater edge in light foot troops.

Likely enveloping an Athenian flank, the attackers killed Lysicles and many others to clear the way for a Carian break from the Delian League.

Corcyra (427 B.C.)

As the war entered its fifth year, the Peloponnesians readied a fleet of 42 ships to break the siege at Mytilene and sent the Spartan Salaethus ahead to take command on Lesbos. He arrived to find the town critically short of food and, when the relief force proved overlong in coming, he decided to take aggressive action. Salaethus ordered an assault on the surrounding enemy positions in hope that he could breach them and create a supply route into the city. He prepared for an all-out effort by directing that armor and weapons be given to the general population to boost manpower for this attack. In so doing, Salaethus badly misjudged the volatile political atmosphere within Mytilene. The common people were starving and, once armed, became belligerent and demanded that the oligarchs either distribute all remaining stores of food or come to terms with the enemy.

Unable to resist this uprising and aware that rapid consumption of supplies would destroy their ability to further withstand the siege, the oligarchs of Mytilene sued for peace. Athens accepted their surrender and, shortly thereafter, took Antissa as well. The commanders of Sparta's relief fleet learned of these events upon arrival in Ionia and elected to run rather than attack, escaping back to Greece just ahead of Paches. Though he failed to catch the fleeing flotilla, Paches was able to turn about and capture both Pyrrha and Eresus — the last rebel strongholds on Lesbos.

Paches stayed to administer the island's affairs, but sent most of his troops back to Athens with Salaethus and the rebel leaders. The Athenians executed these prisoners as an object lesson to any other states that might be contemplating a break from the Delian League, and it was only by the slimmest of margins that the entire male population of Mytilene avoided the same fate. Years of brutal war were making the Greeks increasingly callous and violent, ever more prone to the harshest means for meeting their ends. Indeed, shortly after the narrow aversion of atrocity on Lesbos, such horrors were carried out in full at the fall of Plataea, where the small defense force was put to death and their women sold as slaves.

The sort of killing rage vented on foreigners at Lesbos and Plataea could come to the fore within a polis as well. This happened on Corcyra, where class tension exploded into an orgy of internal violence. Corcyra had done little since the opening year of the war to support its pact with Athens, a neutral leaning that Corinth sought to exploit in 427 B.C. by releasing 250 captives taken during the fighting at Epidamnus six years earlier. These were upper-class Corcyrans who favored oligarchy and were willing to work against the Athenian-allied democracy in their homeland. The freed men joined with a group of sympathizers upon their return and tried to persuade the general population to abandon Athens for an alliance with Sparta. However, their politicking failed, coming to naught just as a Corinthian trireme sailed into harbor to monitor the situation. Unable to get what they wanted by talking and perhaps aware from the newly arrived ship that help was on the way, the plotters now sought to take over by force.

Likely numbering something over 600 hoplites (400 plus others from five ships), the oligarchs launched a surprise attack on the main market (*agora*). In less of a formal battle than a massacre, ordered ranks of spearmen put most of the poorly armed crowd to flight and slew anyone standing their ground. Those beaten found refuge in the higher parts of the city and retaliated with skirmishes the following day. This bought them time to gather weapons from both private homes and city's temples (votive arms were traditionally used in emergencies to outfit the lower classes). Based on their later ability to man 60 ships, these democrats must ultimately have been able to equip 1,800–2,400 hoplites as well as a large host of light-armed men. The oligarchs had meanwhile imported 800 mercenaries from the mainland. Given the short notice for mobilization, these new troops were probably Greco–barbarians from the coastal area adjacent to the island, perhaps the same ones who had worked with the oligarchic camp a few years earlier during the civil war at nearby Epidamnus. Armed in the Illyrian style, these tribesmen wore helmets and carried round shields, heavy spears, and swords. Though unfamiliar with phalanx tactics, they were armed more heavily than Greek auxiliaries and well suited for less formal shock combat.

The next day saw a series of chaotic struggles rage through the wider avenues and public squares. With combatants crowding into deep files along narrow fronts, there was little room for either maneuver or retreat. Fighting would have been evenly matched in those areas where armored spearmen confronted each other, but it no doubt varied starkly when barbarians were at the front, these faring poorly when facing hoplites and much better against makeshift weaponry. The battle ebbed and flowed through the streets, with the oligarchs and their mercenaries suffering all the while under a rain of debris hurled from the rooftops by women, children, and the elderly. By nightfall, a combination of high ground, greater numbers, and pure grit had given the democratic faction control of the city. Falling back, the oligarchs set smoky fires around the agora to cover a retreat behind temporary ramparts as both their barbarian hirelings and the Corinthian ship in the harbor fled.

At sunrise, the Athenian general Nicostratus arrived with 12 triremes carrying a force of Messenian hoplites from Naupactus. He brokered a truce and then put back to sea, leaving his Messenians and five ships behind to help keep the peace. His departure would prove a bit premature. The armada that Corinth had pledged in support of the oligarchic uprising finally showed not long after Nicostratus left and, though tardy for its original mission, it dealt a sharp defeat to some poorly led Corcyran ships. In fact, it was only timely intervention by the small Athenian flotilla that saved the islanders from complete disaster. Yet this success yielded little profit, as Eurymedon soon sailed in from Athens with a strong fleet to chase the Corinthians off without a fight. The democrats now turned their fear and anger against the surviving oligarchs, killing many and driving the rest to suicide.

Athens Takes the Offensive

Patience with the cautious style that had been prevalent under Pericles had begun to grow thin by late summer 427 B.C. and the Athenians began to question the concept of standing on the defensive while wearing down the enemy. Though still loath to face the Spartans in open battle, they looked to a bolder, more offensive approach in hope of hastening their foe's economic and political collapse. This new scheme sought to inflict mortal wounds on Sparta by striking deep into the territory of its key allies. It was a strategy with considerable merit that would bring them near to total victory; yet it also exposed Athens to large-scale defeat in the field and would ultimately inspire Sparta to retaliate in kind.

Mylae II (426 B.C.)

The first chance to apply the new strategy came that fall, when Leontini on Sicily asked for aid to counter a Syracusan threat to itself, Naxos, Rhegion, and Camarina. Already suffering blockade, the Leontines hoped that Athens would intervene on their behalf; after all,

Syracuse not only shared Dorian heritage with Sparta, but was also a colony of chief Spartan ally Corinth. Cultural bonds aside, the Athenians saw this as an excellent opportunity to advance their economic war on Sparta, since Sicily was a major source of grain for the Peloponnese. They thus sent Laches and Charoeades out with 20 triremes, which landed at Rhegion to pick up more men and then descended on Sicily in a series of raids. One of these resulted in a minor sea battle just north of Syracuse (Pearson 1987, 27 and Hornblower 1991, 495), costing Athens one ship and dealing a serious wound to Charoeades. Laches now took sole command and led an attack against Syracusan interests on the Aeolian Islands north of Sicily. Unable to capture the islands, he wasted the countryside and then retired into winter quarters at Rhegion, Charoeades dying there that spring.

Laches opened the campaign season in 426 B.C. with a strike at Locri, a city on the toe of the Italian boot that was an ally of Syracuse and posed the closest threat to Rhegion. After capturing five Locrian ships, the Athenian commander then decided to cross onto Sicily, where he made the Messanian colony of Mylae his first target. Given that he had 40 ships, half of them Athenian, he must have landed around 1,600 hoplites, 80 archers, and at least a few armed crewmen. This was enough to give him numerical superiority, since his opposition amounted to only two Messenian tribal lochoi with but 1,000–1,200 hoplites and 200–300 psiloi. Facing such a shortfall in manpower, the defenders sought assistance from an ambush. For some reason this ploy didn't work, probably because scouts revealed the trap before it could be sprung. Exposed, the Messanians could either run or fight. They chose to fight.

Laches would have deployed his hoplites in standard fashion, stacking them eight deep over a front of 200m, with the troops from Athens on the right and their allies on the left. The Messenians seem to have taken an irregular approach in opposition. Instead of equaling the Athenian front with thinner files, they apparently elected to form a shorter line at matching depth. This was a terrible mistake. Following a storm of arrow fire, charging Athenian hoplites must have quickly dispersed the psiloi guarding the Messenian flanks and then folded around both ends. Troops caught along the flanks by this pincher movement died where they stood inside a half-circle of lancing enemy spears; and men ranked at the front faired no better, being overrun and slaughtered after those behind tossed shields and bolted.

Diodorus claimed that Messana lost 1,000 hoplites in the fight at Mylae and that another 600 gave up later, but it's more likely that no more than 1,000 spearmen were engaged (two 500-man lochoi), with only 400 dying in battle before the rest surrendered. Even this less sanguinary reading of the historian suggests a staggering 40 percent fatality rate among the Messenian hoplites. Since they had a nearby refuge and didn't suffer mounted pursuit, such casualties are quite shocking and a gruesome tribute to the effects of double envelopment. Losses must have included nearly all of the 375 men in the three leading Messenian ranks— those actually engaged at the front— plus a couple of dozen more from the flanking files. The Mylaeans quickly capitulated and agreed to join in an attack on their mother city of Messana, just across the strait from Rhegion. Messana surrendered without a fight and Laches withdrew once more to Italy.

Locri, Inessa, and Caicinus River (426 B.C.)

Laches made his next attack against Epizephyrian Locri on the underside of the Italian toe. He landed at the fringe of that polis's territory, but didn't catch the Locrians completely unprepared, as they rushed out to meet him near the landing site. It's probable that a second-tier city of this sort could put only some 1,500 heavy infantry in the field on such short notice. This represented just over half of Locri's total strength and matched the enemy's hoplites in number, though not in terms of combat experience. The one real advantage for Locris lay in its having superior light-armed support from sizeable contingents of cavalry and foot skirmishers; however, as it turned out, these wouldn't play a significant role in the fighting.

What followed appears to have been a fairly typical hoplite battle in which Athenian spearmen on the right wing of their formation swiftly defeated the Locrian left. The remainder of the Italian phalanx then simply disintegrated, though a lack of horsemen or sufficient light foot troops on the other side meant that this didn't cost the Locrians too much and their city walls remained safe from assault. Still, they did surrender a fortification at Peripolion, which sat on the Halex River that marked the Rhegian frontier. The Athenians were thus able to retire, having gained both greater security for their base and a somewhat expanded territory for their hosts at Rhegion.

Laches again crossed to Sicily in fall 426 B.C., landing east of Leontini to join Siculi and others that had risen up in revolt from Syracuse. He led this combined force on a Syracusan garrison in the former Siculi stronghold at Inessa. Finding that he couldn't take the city's citadel by direct assault and being ill prepared for an extended siege, Laches gave up and retired toward his ships. As he did so, the Syracusans saw that his Siculi contingent had lagged behind as a rearguard and quickly launched an attack on these barbarians in what must have been a small action with less than 1,000 men on either side. Taken by surprise and without hoplite support, the tribesmen suffered a heavy defeat as a hard-driving phalanx of Doric spearmen smashed through and scattered their much less coherent battle array. The victors briefly dealt out punishment to the fleeing Siculi and then fell back on Inessa ahead of any possible counterattack. Laches had no choice at this point other than to accept his losses and return to Italy.

As winter began, Laches shook off any lingering effects from his failure at Inessa and struck again from the sea at Locri. By besting the Locrians the previous summer, he had shifted the Rhegion frontier eastward from the Halex and he now sought battle within this new boundary. Laches met Proxenus of Locri and a likely 2,000 or so hoplites along the Caicinus River. And though his foes would have had a modest edge in heavy manpower, the Athenian once more carried the field, beating men who, despite their numbers, were short on past combat success and the confidence that went with it. Yet lack of quality support troops must again have muted this triumph, with the opposing hoplites getting clear at a cost of no more a few men and some discarded arms. Laches collected these modest spoils and once more sailed back to Rhegion.

Tanagra II (426 B.C.)

Sicily wasn't the only theater where the Athenians put their more aggressive new strategy into action. They also sent Demosthenes and Procles on a 30-ship raid around the Peloponnese and detailed Nicias with 60 triremes against Melos, Sparta's lone ally among the Cyclades Islands. When this effort failed to bring quick results, Nicias looked for another opportunity, getting it when the usual summer invasion of Attica turned back after a series of earthquakes. With the Spartan army all the way back home, Nicias was suddenly clear to lead an expedition into Boeotia.

Nicias landed on the Boeotian coast at Oropus and moved inland to just above the Attic border at Tanagra, where he met an army from Athens. Though the city had lost some 4,000 hoplites to plague and had another 2,000 on duty elsewhere, it could still field around 7,000 spearmen for this enterprise. As for light-armed troops, these would have included at least

600 foot archers and 600 horsemen (100 with bows). Nicias attacked the countryside and soon drew the expected response, with the Tanagrans calling up what must have been a full levy of about 1,500 hoplites and their hegemon Thebes adding perhaps 3,000 more (most of its field army). Likely supported by some 400 horsemen and matching numbers of both hamippoi and psiloi, the Boeotians marched out onto the Tanagran plain.

Nicias no doubt deployed eight shields deep, creating a phalanx that was a little more than 800m across. His contingent of foot archers and its 300 fronting hoplites must have split in two to cover both flanks as cavalry took up station off each wing in rectangles that had mounted bowmen at the fore. The Tanagrans and Thebans could match the Athenian front only by filing some lochoi at six deep and others only five. Their light foot and horsemen would have posted at the edges of this thin array to mimic the enemy's flank screen.

Each army sang its paeans and closed with a final rush into deadly shock combat. Regardless of their disadvantage in heavy manpower, the Boeotians, widely known for their athleticism, put up quite a fight. The men from Thebes and Tanagra must have used pure physical strength to resist their foe's deeper files, giving as good as they got in a vicious melee all along the front. Yet these Athenians were themselves hard men, battle-wise and aware that the longer they fought and shoved the weaker their outmanned opponents would become. And, indeed, the numbers finally did begin to tell. The Boeotians started to gradually lose ground and, finally at the very limits of their courage and muscular endurance, had to break off the fight and take to their heels. The fleeing men littered the field with shields and other gear, but most reached safety at Tanagra with help from cavalry and light foot troops. Their Athenian victors harvested the abandoned equipment, set up a trophy, and went home.

Ellomenus and Aegitium (426 B.C.)

Beyond Athens's success in Boeotia, Demosthenes and Procles were doing well in their campaign as well. They had put in at Naupactus to add 900 Messenian spearmen to the 300 marines and 120 archers already aboard their 30-ship fleet before sailing toward Leucas. Apparently intent on avenging the killing of Asopius two years earlier, they prepared a surprise attack on the very outpost garrison responsible for that defeat.

The Athenians came ashore on the mainland territory of Leucas, where they feinted toward the town of Ellomenus with a party that might have been composed solely of marines. As planned, this small group quickly fell back upon approach of the local guard unit, whose 600 or so spearmen took the lure and pursued right into a trap. Here, the roles of predator and prey reversed as the Messenians charged from hiding to turn the odds on end. This ambush left no easy route for escape and cut down the guardsmen from every quarter. Demosthenes and Procles then crossed over against the city of Leucas at the north end of the island. The nearby isles of Cephallenia and Zacynthus sent aid for this effort, supplying perhaps 10 ships and 400 spearmen, and Acarnania sent help as well in the form of hoplites (maybe 1,000) and some light forces. More surprisingly, support even arrived from Corcyra, that sadly strife-torn island somehow managing to send 15 ships and 600 spearmen.

The huge force arrayed against Leucas was intimidating and kept its troops walled up as their outlying cropland was destroyed. Demosthenes chose at this point to ignore the advice of his Acarnanian allies to reduce the town by siege, preferring instead to heed the Messenians, who urged him to redirect his efforts against the Aetolian tribes of the interior north of Naupactus. They claimed that a victory over these primitive and light-armed villagers would not only remove them as a threat to that vital port, but also allow for wider conquests. Indeed, besting the tribesmen might clear the path for an advance into northern Boeotia via Phocis.

If Demosthenes could coordinate such a backdoor invasion with a march from the south by the main Athenian army, he might well regain the entire region for Athens. With this grandiose scheme in mind, the daring Athenian talked his cohort Procles into an attack on Aetolia.

Most of Demosthenes' allies didn't share his wider vision and saw no gain for their cities in the proposed campaign. Thus, all but the Messenians and a few western islanders pulled out of the operation when informed of the new plan. Loss of the Acarnanians was particularly costly to Demosthenes, as their light foot troops would have been of great value against the targeted tribesmen, who were mostly peltasts. Nevertheless, Demosthenes sailed out with his remaining task force to land just east of Naupactus at Oineon in the territory of Ozolian Locris (Pritchett 1991, 60), where he set up base for the campaign into Aetolia.

Demosthenes now made a grave error in his eagerness to get underway. The Locrians, who were well versed in both the terrain and Aetolian style of warfare, had pledged their light infantry to his expedition. However, when these troops proved slow to gather, Demosthenes decided impetuously to set out anyway and drafted a Messenian named Chromon as his guide into the interior. Demosthenes had plenty of hoplites (300 of his own, 900 Messenians, and 400 islanders), but no more than 120 bowmen for missile support; thus, for all his tactical wiles, he clearly hadn't absorbed the light-infantry lessons of Spartolos. He was about to receive a painful refresher course.

The Athenians captured three enemy villages with little or no resistance. Buoyed by easy victory and assurances from the Messenians that he was in little danger from so lightly armed a foe, Demosthenes pressed ever deeper into the rugged interior. He soon reached Aegitium, which the locals had abandoned much like the sites taken earlier. However, this time they hadn't simply run away, but had gathered instead on the surrounding hills to join a huge host from other tribes. Swarming all around, thousands of peltasts now descended on Demosthenes and his men, who formed up to meet the threat by anchoring their phalanx on the roughly karsted terrain thereabouts. Despite being taken by surprise, Demosthenes used the given ground skillfully, fixing his flanks as well as possible and putting his back against secure topography and/or the rude structures of Aegitium itself. Having done all that he could to restrict the foe to only frontal attacks, he assigned his archers to the ends of the hoplite line that they might keep the enemy out of javelin range.

The Aetolians charged raggedly through the arrows to launch their own, shorter-reaching missiles and then fell back as the opposing spearmen attempted to bring them within spear-length. Thus began a deadly dance of charge and retreat in which the hoplites had no chance to catch their swifter foes. Throughout, Demosthenes' men took ever more wounds as a few darts struck home through shield and armor with each round of attack. As this damage slowly mounted, only the efforts of their bowmen kept the opposing peltasts at bay, forcing them to spread out and hurl their javelins from a distance. However, bow fire began to fall off as the supply of arrows dwindled, and the Aetolians then closed to kill several archers and scatter the remainder when their commander went down. Exhausted by vain attempts to close with their enemy, bloodied and humbled by a hail of missiles that were now coming from point blank range at both front and sides, the last of the hoplites' courage finally gave out and they broke ranks in a run for their lives. Making matters worse, their Messenian guide fell at this point to end all hope of finding a path to safety.

The defeated men fled through the rugged and unfamiliar countryside as fleet-footed tribesmen exacted a fearsome toll. Doom came for the routed Greeks in many forms: some ran up box canyons and died under the javelins of their pursuers, others succumbed to misadventure in the treacherous terrain, and one group, hopelessly lost in the woods, was wiped out by a fire set by the enemy. Demosthenes escaped, but the Athenians lost Procles and 120 other spearmen — a full 40 percent of those who had marched so boldly into Aetolia. This suggests that total hoplite casualties included more than 600 killed, with around 500 Messenians and western islanders also falling victim.

Demosthenes regrouped at Oineon and recovered the bodies of his men under a temporary truce before retiring to Naupactus with the sad remnants of his army. He had paid a steep price in blood for the folly of advancing without adequate light-infantry support, as his final death toll was half again higher than that exacted at Spartolos. Fortunately for Athens, he was a highly intelligent man who emerged from the disaster as a much wiser general.

Olpae and Idomene (426 B.C.)

Demosthenes elected to stay at Naupactus, knowing that he faced disgrace and likely punishment if he returned home. He sent five of his ships back with the surviving Athenian hoplites, but kept the other 25 in hope of finding some way to atone for his costly defeat. Meanwhile, an Aetolian embassy had gone to Sparta seeking help in mounting a reprisal against the Messenians. The Spartans were so eager to deal harm to these old foes that they lost little time in sending 3,000 hoplites to aid the tribal effort. Eurylochos led this force and, with fellow spartiates Macarius and Menedaius as subordinates, he marched overland to stage near Delphi for an assault on Naupactus. His troops were mostly Peloponnesian, including a large contingent from Mantinea, and also boasted a 500-man lochos from the new Spartan colony of Heraclea in eastern Greece.

Eurylochos descended from Delphi to Ozolian Locris, which he compelled to supply light infantry to his expedition. In an ironic turn, many of the same troops that Demosthenes had failed to take to Aegitium now stood in the ranks of his enemy. Eurylochos arrived near Naupactus to join his Aetolian allies for an assault that captured both outlying portions of the city and the nearby Athenian-allied polis of Molycrium. Demosthenes still held the fortified port area of Naupactus, resisting with 60 archers, the remaining Messenian hoplites, and other armed townsfolk. Unable to properly guard the perimeter, he used his triremes to bring in another 1,000 spearmen from Acarnania. Apprised of this, Eurylochos realized that a successful investment was now impossible. Without a fleet, he had no hope of cutting the port off from resupply by sea, and should he try to take it by storm, not only would his light-armed men be of little use, but Demosthenes' now well-manned walls would claim far too many hoplites. Faced with these hard realities, the Spartan commander chose to abandon the siege.

Rather than heading home, Eurylochos led his men westward into Aeolis. Here, above the mouth of the Corinthian Gulf, he sought other opportunities to attack enemy interests before winter set in. And his chance was not long in coming, as the Ambraciots soon approached for aid in a campaign against Amphilochia and Acarnania, Athenian-allied states that lay in that order to the south of Ambracia along the western coast above Aeolis. Eurylochos agreed to join their effort and, dismissing the Aetolians, set out against the nearest target at Amphilochian Argos.

Argos soon found itself menaced not only by the Spartan-led force moving up from the south, but also by the Ambraciots, who descended from the north with 3,000 of the region's best hoplites and a force of light spearmen hired from their barbarian neighbors. The Ambraciots marched to Olpae, a fortified coastal hill that lay just north of Argos, and stopped there to send for the rest of their polis's troops. Eurylochos and his men also arrived at Olpae, having eluded a blocking force of Acarnanians by means of a night march from Aeolis. The invaders now had a combined force of some 6,000 hoplites plus auxiliaries (perhaps 500 Locrians still serving under duress with Eurylochos and 1,000 barbarians). Argos was cut off at this point from most of Amphilochia to the north and could rely for its defense on only local men and Acarnanians called up from the south. Becoming aware of their peril, the Argives sent for help to both Demosthenes and an Athenian fleet that was operating in the Corinthian Gulf.

Demosthenes saw a chance for redemption at Argos and got leave to come to the aid of the city with his archers and 200 Messenian hoplites. Sending his ships to stand off Olpae in a blockade, he took charge of the defense forces and marched out to camp across a deep, stream-carved ravine that lay just south from the enemy. His army was quite a bit smaller than that of Eurylochos, having no more than 4,000 hoplites (a mix of Acarnanians, Amphilochians, and his own Messenians) and less than 1,000 light foot troops (60 bowmen and some local javelinmen). Knowing that any phalanx he could field at a reasonable depth would be at great risk against a much longer opposing line, Demosthenes came up with a plan of action built around surprise. He scouted inland to the east and found open country for fighting along the south side of the same stream that had cut the gorge separating him from Olpae (Pritchett 1992, 27–29). A rough footpath ran alongside the creek bed, whose course was sunken and heavily overgrown with brush. It was the perfect spot to conceal an ambush and Demosthenes hid 400 Acarnanian hoplites and a few psiloi some ways upstream. He then deployed the rest of the men in plain sight across the nearby field, with his right wing facing north and standing closest to the concealed contingent. The enemy would have to cross the creek bed to get at him, giving his hidden force a clear shot at their unprotected backs.

Demosthenes must have set up his hoplites six deep over a 600m front, personally taking post on the extreme right with a few men from Athens and the Messenians to act as bait for his trap. This left the Acarnanians to hold the center of the phalanx and fill in toward the smaller number of Amphilochians on the far left. These men held firm as Eurylochos and company crossed onto the field and formed a line that was likely some 750m long at a depth of eight ranks. The Spartan generals took post on the far left among their kinsmen from Heraclea and a few others, with the Mantineans completing that wing to the tune of 2,000 hoplites. It was clearly Eurylochos's intention to put his best men on the left, where they could confront the much-hated Messenians, whom he no doubt considered the other side's best fighters. His remaining Peloponnesians alternated by units with a like number of Ambraciots in the center so that they could stiffen that part of the front. The balance of the Ambraciots thus held the right wing, facing the spearmen from Amphilochia.

Action opened with some preliminary dueling between light-armed troops as the hoplites on each side made final adjustments to their formations. The skirmishers then retreated: Acarnanians to join Athens's bowmen on the eastern flank, Amphilochians moving beside their men on the western flank, and the opposing light foot troops splitting to cover both ends of their own phalanx. With the field ahead clear at last, the heavy spearmen moved to take center stage, giving vent to shrill war cries and closing to smash into contact all along the line. The fight seems to have gone on for a while, with both sides taking heavy losses. The ambushers moved out once their lookouts saw that combat was in full progress, but having hidden at some distance to avoid detection during the enemy's stream crossing, it took a bit of time to reach the battlefield. Thus, their charge into the rear of the Spartan-led wing didn't come until it had nearly enveloped the Messenians.

Eurylochos and those around him were taken completely by surprise to be scattered in utter confusion and dread as enemy spearmen cut them to pieces from either end. Panic spread like wildfire through the remaining Peloponnesians and Ambraciots, tearing their phalanx apart from left to right as men broke from the battle in terrified flight. Only the Ambraciots

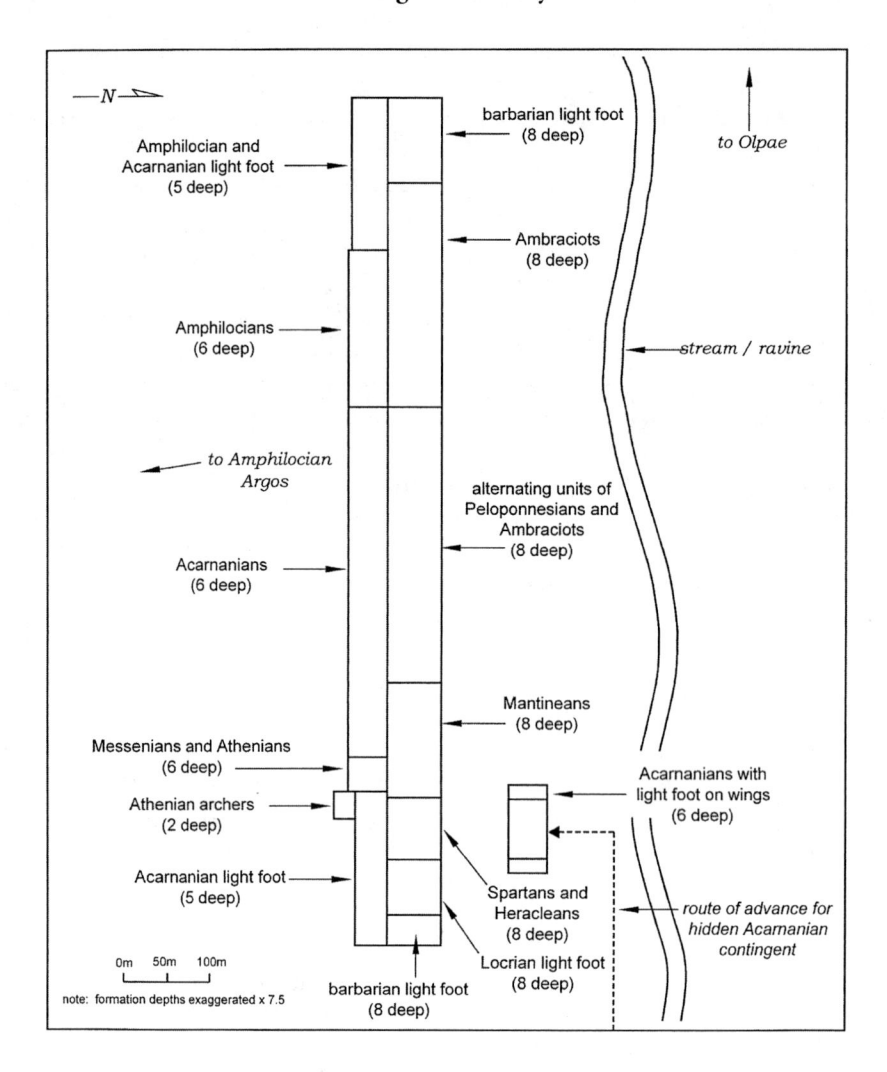

BATTLE OF OLPAE (426 B.C.)

on the far wing escaped immediate defeat. Having taken advantage of a longer line and rightward drift during advance to quickly best the opposing Amphilochians, they had chased those beaten men well off the field before the wave of panic had a chance to ripple down to their position. Most of their comrades, however, were routed and thoroughly mauled as they ran for Olpae. The Mantineans alone kept their heads in this helter-skelter retreat as, managing some semblance of order, they withdrew in a compact body and thus encouraged pursuers to pass them by in favor of easier prey.

When the victorious Ambraciots of the right wing returned after breaking off pursuit, they discovered that the rest of their army had fled. Coming under attack from the Acarnanians that had taken and held the center of the battlefield, these men were able to cut their way back to Olpae only with the greatest difficulty and heavy loss. In the end, the engagement cost the lives of Eurylochos and his fellow general Macarius and killed as many as 1,000 of their hoplites (an estimated 650 Peloponnesians and 350 Ambraciots at 25 percent of the ambushed left wing, 15 percent of the center division, and 10 percent of the more successful right). Demosthenes lost around 180 or 15 percent from his defeated left wing and 5 percent of the rest of his phalanx for a total of 300 spearmen killed. Certainly, these were light casualties compared to those among the losers, yet high enough to show that the fight was very hotly contested right up until the surprise attack struck home.

Menedaius had taken charge following the death of his spartiate colleagues and now found himself under siege on Olpae hill. Demosthenes secretly offered a deal that would allow him, his subordinate officers, and the men from Mantinea to abandon the other defenders and flee unmolested. For his part, the Athenian must have hoped to not only get rid of a still dangerous foe without a fight, but also to expose a lack of loyalty that might well ruin Sparta's reputation in the region. Seemingly heedless of any diplomatic risk, Menedaius agreed to this intrigue. Having thus made arrangements to neutralize the Peloponnesians and put the remaining defenders at Olpae in a hopeless fix, Demosthenes prepared to deal with the rest of his opposition. He had learned that more troops were on the way from Ambracia and sent out scouts to find them, readying his full army to march as soon as the enemy's whereabouts were known.

Menedaius and his fellow plotters emerged from their defenses in due course, accompanied by some of the Ambraciots and others that they might gather firewood and the like under truce. As arranged, all the Peloponnesian officers and Mantineans began to slip away in small groups as the afternoon wore on; however, the rest of those that had come out saw what was going on and quickly joined in the flight. The Acarnanians were now let in on Demosthenes' scheme and moved to attack their much-loathed Ambraciot foes, who had no leave to run off. There was, of course, considerable confusion and difficulty in sorting out nationalities among so many fleeing men. Thus, though some 200 of the Ambraciots were slain, many more made good their escape, running toward the south as darkness fell to cut off further pursuit.

Even as the Peloponnesians and others were getting away, a reinforcement of perhaps 2,000 Ambraciot hoplites was approaching nearby Idomene. This was a place along the coast about 13km north of Olpae (Pritchett 1992, 37–49) that featured two hills separated by a sloping saddle. The Ambraciots chose a night camp on the lower of the rises, unaware that enemy scouts had spotted them. These observers sent for their army and took up position on the other hill after dark so that they could mark the best spots for setting traps along all avenues of escape from the area. Once alerted, Demosthenes wasted no time in marching to Idomene, dividing his men into separate columns for a speedier advance and assigning his ships to take post offshore. Upon arrival, those on watch guided some of the Athenian's troops to selected ambush sites and then led a main strike force directly against the unsuspecting Ambraciots.

While it was still dark, Demosthenes closed on the enemy position in company with a strong force of Acarnanian spearmen and local psiloi and having the Messenians in front. His plan was for the men from Naupactus to fool any sentries they might meet in the dark by using their Doric accent to pass for Ambraciots. Thanks to this trick, his troops got right in among their foes without being detected and, on signal, struck just before dawn to catch them abed and totally unprepared. The massacre that followed was hardly a battle. Screaming out of the dark, Demosthenes' men cut down many of the Ambraciots before they could even get to their arms and speared others from behind in the midst of flight or slaughtered them within the prepared ambushes. Some of those defeated slipped free only to meet with fatal accidents in the rugged terrain, while a few ran to the nearby beach in despair and threw themselves into the sea, preferring death from the Athenians offshore to being killed by their local rivals.

Less than half of the men routed at Idomene managed to get away. Thucydides related that the Ambraciots who had fled from Olpae the day before sent someone to seek a truce for recovering the bodies of those killed in the course of their escape, and this poor fellow was the first of his countrymen to learn of the new disaster. Expecting to see arms and armor of around 200 men lost the previous afternoon, he went away in shock and mournful anguish with his task forgotten upon being shown the gear of over 1,000 others that had died that morning.

Sensing an easy conquest, Demosthenes sought to follow up his smashing victories at Olpae and Idomene with an attack on Ambracia, which had lost most of its army. The Ambraciots were, in fact, so depleted that they pulled in 300 hoplites from Corinth in a frantic effort to man their walls. However, the Acarnanians proved less keen to deprive beaten rivals of freedom than to safeguard their own, fearing that further cooperation might well put the Athenians too much in control of local affairs. Faced with the reluctance of these key allies to mount an invasion, Demosthenes had to settle for his gains to date, which were actually quite considerable. He could now return safely to Athens with more than enough success in hand to compensate for his disastrous misstep in Aetolia.

Athenian High Tide

The seventh year of the war saw the Athenians' daring strategy of attacking deep into enemy territory reach its height of success. They suffered another invasion of Attica and met mixed results in Sicily, but struck hard at the Peloponnese from the sea. Moreover, the leadership at Athens took a new approach that significantly increased the effect of these attacks. Eschewing their normal hit-and-run tactics, they now began setting up outposts in the Spartan homelands, these being placed at the shoreline to gain protection and supply from the sea, and well fortified to resist assault from the land. The Athenians could raid the countryside from such safe havens as well as use them as escape points for local helots. By drawing off disaffected serfs, these modest footholds drained agricultural laborers vital to Sparta's way of life. Both economic damage and Spartan losses in trying to retake these outposts would carry Athens to the very brink of total victory.

Halex River, Naxos, and Messana (425 B.C.)

Laches ended 426 B.C. with another successful raid, joining his Siculi allies for an assault on the territory of Himera on the north coast of Sicily. He then returned to Rhegion, where the general Pythodorus met him fresh out of Athens with authority to take over the western campaign. The new commander had only a few ships at present, but they were no more than a vanguard from a fleet of 40 triremes that was still on its way from Greece. His orders were to combine these reinforcements with the ships already at Rhegion and embark a landing force of overwhelming strength. The prospect of fielding such a powerful armament seemed to promise ultimate success in the Sicilian theater; however, an uncooperative enemy soon put a crimp in these carefully laid plans by forcing Pythodorus into action before the bulk of his fleet had arrived.

The Locrians moved in spring 425 B.C. to take back the fort along the Halex that they had lost to Laches. This threatened the southern Rhegian boundary and Pythodorus led a seaborne sally with intent to preserve that expanded frontier. He landed near the contested outpost at Peripolion to confront the Locrians, but met defeat in a battle about which our sources give no details. While it's possible that this was only a minor action, subsequent signs of a significantly weaker Athenian presence in the region strongly imply that Pythodorus suffered a major reverse. Since the Locrians took the initiative, they could achieve a fuller mobilization, likely putting around 3,000 hoplites in the field — twice as many as they had thrown against Laches the previous year. Pythodorus could counter with only some 2,000 spearmen and 120 archers from 50 or so ships, which must have let the Locrians anchor against the Halex at eight shields deep and compel their foes to file at five or six to avoid being outflanked. The Italians then gained victory, most likely by pushing through the thinner opposing array, with their superior light forces (maybe 1,000 psiloi and horsemen) then allowing for a thorough pursuit.

While our surviving description of the battle doesn't indicate that the Athenians were badly hurt, losses were heavy enough to dissuade them from meeting another challenge that summer. This was when the Locrians took advantage of factional strife at Rhegion to despoil land around the Athenian base. Pythodorus stood idle as this unfolded, in stark contrast with his reaction to the much more distant threat that had been posed along the Halex. Despite having sent most of his fleet on a mission to Sicily, he still had 16 ships on hand and might reasonably have been expected to make a defensive sortie. His failure to do so suggests not only that civil unrest had reduced his pool of allied manpower, but also that the defeat on the Halex had cut his own strength sufficiently that it was now spread too thin for a proper response.

Messana made the most of Pythodorus's weakness and, upon arrival of a flotilla from Syracuse and Locri (ten ships from each), renounced its involuntary ties to Athens. The Syracusans then sailed home, but the Locrians remained to support the city's restored regime, which was spoiling to go on the attack. The Messenians quickly gathered all their land and sea forces and struck at Naxos, an ally of Leontini and Athens that lay nearby along the northeastern coast of Sicily. The attackers forced the Naxians behind their walls and raided the country until a large force of Siculi arrived to try to break the siege. This brought the army of Naxos out into the open under the mistaken belief that other allies were also on the way.

Messana probably fielded about 2–3,000 hoplites and 500–750 psiloi, putting its strength on a par with those of similarly-sized Rhegion and Locri. The Naxians must have been much fewer in number, but their sudden appearance outside the walls took their foes by surprise and scattered them in fear. Thucydides said that 1,000 Messanians died on the spot, with the Siculi butchering most of the rest as they fled for home. Even if we take his report to mean that about 1,000 hoplites from Messana were killed in all, this would have been a shocking loss of over 30 percent.

The Leontines quickly followed up their ally's success at Naxos with a march on Messana, investing the city from landward while the Athenians cut it off from the sea. However, Demoteles of Messana rallied those hoplites still in shape to fight (perhaps 1,000–1,500) and sallied with the help of some 400 spearmen from the Locrian ships yet in the harbor. In a reversal of Naxos, it was now the Messanians who abruptly charged out of their gates to catch a besieging army milling around and unready to fight. Though likely outnumbered by better than 50 percent, the defenders slew scores of Leontines and chased the rest from the walls under hot pursuit.

Those on the Athenian fleet saw this disaster developing and rushed to aid their allies. Having some 25 ships (Laches' old command plus the ones that came with Pythodorus), it was possible for them to land around 1,000 hoplites and 100 archers, who formed a modest phalanx near the beach and advanced to catch Demoteles and his troops out of order as they chased the defeated Leontines. The Athenians must have swept against these men before they could properly redress, striking them in the flank to initiate a rout. This last-minute action gained Athens the field and salvaged a victory despite heavy losses among its allies, allowing Pythodorus to set up a trophy before returning to Rhegion.

The back-and-forth fight at Messana was the last significant action in Sicily during the Archidamian War. Syracuse, Leontini, and their local allies came together during summer of the following year and agreed upon terms for a general peace. The presence of the Athenians in the region was a major motivation for this rapprochement, since both sides had come to see them as potential conquerors. Nor were they wrong. Athens actually prosecuted the leaders of its Sicilian expedition on suspicion that they took bribes to leave instead of staying to capture the island.

Spaectaria (425 B.C.)

Commanders of the Sicilian campaign received a poor reception upon return to Athens in part due to unfavorable comparisons to successes gained elsewhere over the same period. Demosthenes had delivered the first of these. Among leaders of the fleet sailing to meet Pythodorus in Italy, he held authority to strike in passing at the Peloponnese. He sought to take full advantage of this opportunity by setting up a fortified outpost in Spartan territory and circumstances soon came to pass that let him do just that.

Bad weather struck as the fleet was rounding Messenia and it came ashore on the western coast of that region on the narrow, southward extending peninsula of Pylos. This was an ideal spot for Demosthenes' outpost, surrounded by the sea on three sides and having both spring and harbor. The Athenians reinforced this naturally strong site by erecting stone barricades at a number of key points. When the fleet eventually resumed its journey for Sicily, it left Demosthenes behind to hold Pylos with five ships, 200 hoplites, and 20 bowmen. However, even with the later addition of 40 Messenian spearmen from Naupactus, there were too few regular troops to properly secure the place. Demosthenes solved this problem by arming the thousand or so crewmen from his ships and incorporating them into the garrison.

The Spartans had been slow to respond to the incursion at Pylos, but one of their kings (Agis, son and successor to Archidamus) finally abandoned Attica to meet this new threat. The Spartans invested the peninsula on its landward side as ships arrived from their allies to seal the coast, and a force of Spartan hoplites even landed just south of Pylos on the island of Spaectaria that they might complete an encirclement. Despite all this, Demosthenes was able to use the great natural strength of his position in repulsing every attack.

The fleet bound for Sicily turned about at Zacynthus upon learning that Pylos was in peril, with other Athenian and allied triremes joining to create a 50-ship armada that first reinforced Demosthenes and then handed Sparta a decisive defeat at sea. The Athenian naval triumph not only secured a route of supply into Pylos, but also cut off the troops on Spaectaria from the mainland. The Spartans were now greatly concerned, in the short term that their men on the island might be starved out or otherwise overwhelmed and in the long term that the enemy outpost on Pylos might wound their economy by serving as a portal for escaping helots. They thus offered to settle the war on terms that would leave the dignity of both sides intact by returning to a prewar status quo. Led by the demagogue Cleon, the Athenians spurned this proposal, which they saw as reiterating the unfavorable settlement that ended the last conflict with Sparta in 446 B.C. Feeling that their success at Pylos put them on the brink of total victory, they made a harsh counteroffer that would have restored much of what they had lost back then. This was tantamount to demanding surrender and patently unacceptable to the Spartans; therefore, the talks broke down.

Epitadas led the troops stranded on Spaectaria. His was a composite unit of 420 hoplites that had been assigned by lot from available Lacedaemonian lochoi, with 180 of them spartiates and the rest most likely perioeci ("allies" per Diodorus), drawing on a team of perhaps

200 helots for support. Composition of Epitadas's command suggests that the contemporary Spartan army had about three agoge-trained citizens to each four of perioecian rank. Spaectaria was a small place, only 4km in length from south to north and less than 1km wide, but it had a spring near its center with potable water, about which Epitadas arranged his main camp. The Spartans also set up two sentry points on the otherwise uninhabited island, placing a small outpost to the north in a ruined fortification that faced the Athenian positions across the channel and a somewhat larger one at the more exposed southern end. The marooned men remained vigilant and survived 71 days of siege, subsisting at first on supplies received openly during the period of peace negotiations and then making do with what they could get from small boats running the blockade.

The Athenians hesitated to attack Spaectaria, as the island's thick vegetation hid the enemy's true strength and dispositions. This all changed when a stray party of Athenians sought relief on the island from crowded conditions at Pylos. They set off a wildfire while cooking their evening meal, burning away enough cover to reveal the Spartan positions, which were actually stronger than assumed. Demosthenes studied this new information and planned an assault that would make use of his hard-won knowledge of light-infantry techniques.

Though Demosthenes must have designed the tactical plan for Spaectaria, he shared command and credit with Cleon. This fellow was not a soldier of repute, but had made a bold claim before the assembly in Athens that he could capture the island within 20 days. His political foes met this boast with derision and demanded that he go out and back up his words. Perhaps Cleon already knew that his cohort-to-be had come up with a sound plan of action; if so, he may merely have been setting up his opponents with a staged show of false bravado. Then again, he might simply have been militarily naïve. At any rate, he duly set out for the front with 20 ships, which he used (in two or three trips) to shuttle in fresh troops for an assault on Spaectaria, taking care to place an emphasis on bringing missilemen well suited to a strategy of light-armed attack. Combining these new arrivals with men already on hand at Pylos, Demosthenes was able to create a strike force of 800–1,200 hoplites (Athenians, Messenians, and islander allies), 400–600 archers, and 800–1,200 Thracian peltasts. He also planned to press thousands of oarsmen (the upper two banks from 50–75 triremes) into service as makeshift psiloi.

The invasion team sailed from Pylos in the dark to approach Spaectaria from both seaward and landward sides. Demosthenes had gained victory a year earlier at Idomene by infiltrating enemy positions at night and seems to have used the same approach here. As their ships ground into the shallows just before daybreak, his hoplites leaped into the water to wade ashore at several points around the opposition's southern outpost. These spearmen rapidly overran 30 Spartans on guard there, cutting them down as they arose in surprise from their beds.

Having secured a landing site, Demosthenes brought the remainder of his men ashore at first light. He then demonstrated his skill with light troops by organizing the peltasts and armed oarsmen into 200-man teams and sending them to take all of the high ground around the main Spartan camp. Demosthenes next advanced northward with his hoplites to form up within sight of the enemy, assigning bowmen to back and flanks and deploying his spearmen perhaps 8–12 deep to cover a 100m-wide front. The movement of so many men alerted the Spartans and, seeing the Athenian phalanx taking position in the distance, they got into battle order and moved to close on the opposing line of shields.

The Spartan hoplites were outnumbered by two or three to one, thus they had to file no more than four shields deep in order to match their enemy's frontage. They were certainly in a tough spot, but the spartiates at least must not have felt the situation was hopeless. These men had learned from early youth to disregard numbers going into battle, believing that they and their system were superior to any opponent. If anything, they were likely thinking of how their fathers had prevailed over long odds at Tegea some 45 years ago. Their king Agis the Younger would characterize this attitude with the remark (per Plutarch) that "Spartans do not ask how many the enemy are, but where they are." However, there was to be no repeating of past heroics on this day, as Demosthenes had no intention whatsoever of engaging the Spartans shield-on-shield.

Demosthenes' spearmen held fast as the enemy advanced, refusing to come forward and meet them. Instead, their light-armed men swarmed down from the surrounding hills onto the attack, pelting the Spartans from a safe distance and then retiring well ahead of clumsy pursuit by their heavily equipped opponents. Having far too few psiloi for an effective screen, the Spartans were unable to advance on the Athenian hoplites for fear of exposing their flanks and rear beyond endurance. Caught in a situation where their vaunted skills at close combat had no value, they soon began to tire as the unequal contest dragged on, with futile attempts to fend off the encircling light foot troops only serving to further sap their strength. The Athenians saw the enemy's plight and, losing their dread of the Spartans' fearsome reputation, picked up the pace of attack. Charging forward with piercing war cries and raising clouds of ash from a landscape blackened by fire, they hurled javelins and rocks as their archers rained a deadly fall of arrows all the while. The nearly helpless Spartans were exhausted, blinded by ashen dust, and suffering ever more casualties.

Giving up at last, the Spartans pulled close together and withdrew under fire. They reached the fortified northern tip of the island, but not before losing a number of stragglers to a spirited pursuit. Once beside the old stronghold and its backing cliffs, the retreating men joined with the small garrison there to line up and again face their foe, better able now to hold the Athenians at bay with flanks secure and having a rock wall and high ground at their backs. The opposition could only attack from the front, which made it much easier to ward off showers of arrows, darts, and rocks. However, the Spartans' stance also precluded a counterattack, as it would disrupt their defensive front and open them to being scattered and overwhelmed.

By late morning, the battle on Spaectaria had settled into a stand-off that threatened to go on until thirst and exhaustion brought an end to Spartan resistance. Comon, commander of the Messenians, now came forward with an idea that might bring the fight to a faster conclusion. He led a small force of archers and other light troops out of sight, taking them on a difficult climb along the island's steep eastern shore face to reach high ground behind the enemy position. Comon then directed missile fire down on the Spartan rear to devastating effect. The defenders had been fully focused to the fore and this new attack from an unwarded quarter took them completely by surprise. Under assault from both front and back, the Spartans were cut off without food or water and outnumbered by better than 40 to 1 with no hope of relief. Desperate, the less than 300 effectives remaining pulled into a tight body to make a last stand. Demosthenes and Cleon intervened at this point and held back their men. Hoping to make victory more complete by taking valuable hostages, they offered their foes a chance for survival.

Epitadas had died in the fight, while his second in command lay badly wounded and presumed dead on the field to leave a third officer, Styphon, to negotiate terms. After contacting the mainland and being told to do what he thought was best, Styphon agreed to surrender. Thus, Demosthenes' plan of attack had worked to perfection, decisively defeating a Spartan phalanx and killing a quarter of its men at minimal cost to his own forces. Basking in the glow of his comrade's triumph, Cleon erected a trophy on the island and proudly sailed his prisoners (120 spartiates and 172 perioeci) off to captivity at Athens.

The battle on Spaectaria was a stunning blow to Spartan prestige and the cherished memory of Thermopylae. A force close in size to that of Leonidas's bodyguard had failed to fight to the death, giving in this time when the enemy got around its natural defenses. The defeat also put restraints on Spartan strategy, as any new invasion of Attica would now endanger the lives of captives from the island. The Athenians were actually quite familiar with exploiting this kind of leverage, since the Boeotians had used hostages taken at Coronea against them in much the same way back in 447 B.C. Of more immediate concern to the Spartans, the action at Spaectaria helped secure Athens's hold on Pylos, which would remain an open wound on the Spartan economy. In fact, the foothold at Pylos proved so effective at bleeding Sparta that it kicked off a campaign to set up other such garrisoned fortifications or *epiteichismoi* (singular *epiteichismos*) around the Peloponnese.

Solygeia (425 B.C.)

Cleon's victory on Spaectaria pressured his detractors to match it. Nicias responded by joining two colleagues to lead a fleet across the Saronic Gulf and land at dawn some 10km southeast of Corinth at the headland of Chersonesos. This was near the village of Solygeia in the foothills of Mount Oneion, revered as site of the area's first Doric settlement. Nicias probably had some 3,200 hoplites and 200 archers on his 50 Athenian and 30 allied ships (Milesian, Andrian, and Carystian) and had also brought cavalry, with 200 riders and their mounts sailing on special transports.

The Corinthians knew of Nicias's plans through Argive informants and had responded by dispatching an army under Lycophron. His forces included 4,800 hoplites from all eight of the city's lochoi, likely having ranks filled out by veteran reservists as replacements for younger men posted to Ambracia (300) and Leucas (200). (Thucydides, however, claimed that the older troops remained in the city until summoned later.) There were also 1,000–1,200 psiloi, but no horsemen, as Corinth still had a typical Doric disdain for cavalry at this time. Two sling bullets found at Corinth with the name "Lycophron" (Hornblower 1996, 198) suggest that slingers might have been present among the light foot troops as well. As the exact site of the pending attack was not known, Lycophron set up half of his host at Cenchreae, poised to counter any move on Corinth's outpost at Crommyon on the Megaran frontier. He then marched the rest of his men southward and, as luck would have it, came upon the Athenians just as they were making landfall.

While splitting his army had allowed Lycophron to cover more area and quickly intercept the enemy, it also left him with a smaller command to meet the immediate threat. He had no more than 2,400 hoplites (four lochoi) and some psiloi to oppose a force that was a third again larger. This strength went down further when Battus split off with a lochos to guard an unfortified and highly valued Solygeia. Lycophron sent for the rest of his army at Cenchreae and then moved out with what he had on hand — some 1,800 hoplites and 500 or so light foot soldiers. Timing of his advance proved fortunate in that the Athenians were as yet driving aground from Chersonesos toward the stream of Rheitos in the south, and had only about half their men ashore. These formed the right wing under Nicias himself, who held the northernmost stretch of beach with 1,400 spearmen (1,000 from Athens and 400 from Carystus on Euboa) and 100 archers. As the Corinthians closed, their march kicked up a cloud of white, limey dust to give notice that trouble was on the way. Nicias reacted by hurriedly forming a phalanx and marching to engage as far inland as possible.

When Lycophron came within clear view of the Athenians, he deployed out of column into an array that would have been eight shields in depth and a little over 200m in width.

Nicias sent his skirmishers forward as he thinned files so as to match the enemy front. He likely reduced the men from Athens on his right and center to only six deep, thus putting the greatest burden on these dependable veterans while keeping the less experienced Carystians in safer, eight-man files on the left wing. The skirmishers withdrew as final shifting of ranks on both sides came to an end and the formations advanced to collide in a stubborn shock combat. Neither side seems to have gained the upper hand in the fighting that followed, but it was the Corinthians who pulled back first, which must have been a response to approach of the rest of the invaders, who had finally gotten ashore and moved up from the south to join battle. Nicias and company hadn't driven the enemy off by force of arms; nonetheless, it was an impressive performance. They had overcome their initial surprise and held out against superior numbers until their left wing could come to the rescue.

Lycophron and his men had kept formation in the opening round of fighting and taken but few casualties; therefore, they were more than ready to go back into action. Having retreated behind a wall on nearby high ground, they hurled rocks at their pursuers and regrouped to take on the enlarged enemy host now on the field. Still waiting for his reserves to arrive from Cenchreae, Lycophron called for immediate help from Battus's lochos at Solygeia and then took post on the right side of his reorganized phalanx to once more lead an attack. With arrival of the Athenians left wing, his foes had something like a 2 to 1 advantage in hoplites, which forced him to reorder once on the plain, filing only four deep to equal the width of the opposing line.

The Corinthians made at most a short advance and then strove heroically to contain the surging enemy as their leading ranks moved into deadly shock contact. Battus soon rewarded this valiant effort by coming up from behind with his lochos to act as a sort of inadvertent tactical reserve. Seeing that the greatest peril came from the Athenian right, he swung around that end to threaten a flank attack. The few archers (100 or less) screening this wing had no chance against heavy infantry and they scattered, allowing Battus and his spearmen to smash into the Athenians on their unshielded side. Startled and terrified, Nicias and his entire right wing bolted toward the rear, seeking safety among their beached fleet as the Corinthians followed close behind. Though a few of the fleeing men fell to psiloi during this disorderly retreat, Nicias and most of his troops got to the shore well ahead of slow pursuit from the hoplites that predominated among their opposition. They were then able to rally with aid of the ships' crews to drive back the Peloponnesians and chase them inland.

Even as action flowed back and forth on the north, crucial events were unfolding on the other side of the field, where the Athenians had somehow held formation despite desertion of their right wing. This left Lycophron and the Corinthian right struggling to stave off a deeper-filed foe and keep sacred Solygeia from harm. It was a desperate effort that might have borne fruit had the success of Battus and company on the other end of the line been enough to carry the fight; instead, it was Athenian cavalry that turned the tide. Unloading their mounts had caused these horsemen to be last ashore and they had landed at the far south end of the beachhead, the most distant point from the site of battle. Once in the saddle, however, they galloped toward the din of combat and came to grips with the enemy, charging in to disperse psiloi guarding the opposition's right side and sweep around that flank. Lycophron's men had no choice but to give way and retire toward the same hillside from which they had launched their advance. Many fell in this retreat, accounting for a majority of 212 spearmen from Corinth lost on the day, Lycophron among them.

It seems that the Athenians didn't pursue as hard as they might have, probably an effect of having suffered such a bad mauling on their own right wing. This let the surviving Corinthians (including those on the left coming back from the beach) regain high ground and rally once more within a defensive perimeter. Their losses hadn't been crippling (around 9 percent) and they now prepared to sell their lives dearly. As for the Athenians, they had lost less than 50 hoplites and their allies perhaps another 30 for a total of only 2.5 percent killed among the entire landing force. Yet Nicias, having barely escaped disaster on his end of the field, was apparently in no mind to push things any further and limited his men to stripping the enemy dead of their gear and setting up a trophy.

Reinforcements coming from Cenchreae must have anxiously watched the dust of battle rising in the distance as they marched to aid Lycophron. As these men finally came near, the Athenians and their allies made haste to take up their dead and re-embark, thinking that a large army was approaching. When Nicias realized that this was only the rest of the Corinthian levy finally coming on the scene, he promptly sailed north and ravaged the area around Crommyon that these very troops had just abandoned. He then turned about to land on the small peninsula of Methana near Epidauros and set up a fortified outpost on the eastern side of the Peloponnese to complement that on the west at Pylos. This gave Athens a stronghold from which it could raid at will along the Saronic seaboard to further pressure Sparta's alliance. It also let Nicias sail home with success that compared with that of Cleon, having won a major battle and set up an epiteichismos.

Cythera and Cotyrta/Aphrodisia (424 B.C.)

The Athenians had hurt Sparta in 425 B.C. with their outposts at Pylos and Methana and they set out the following year to put another one on the isle of Cythera, which lay just off the southern coast of Laconia. The Spartans had acquired Cythera from Argos in the 6th century and it was the piece of their core territory most at hazard to seaborne conquest. Capturing this island would do much to highlight Sparta's impotence against Athenian fleets, hitting hard at its morale. Beyond its propaganda value, such a seizure had great practical potential as well, since Cythera not only guarded the least rugged portion of the Laconian shoreline best suited for amphibious operations, but was also entry point for African trade goods. By launching strikes from Cythera and cutting off imports, Athens could heap yet more harm on an already struggling Spartan economy.

Sparta was certainly aware of Cythera's vulnerability and had backed up the local perioeci (probably 500–600 hoplites of prime age and 100–150 reservists) with a force of spartiates (perhaps 300 spearmen). This should have been proof against a typical raid, but the Athenians had something much grander in mind. Nicias and two other generals sailed with 60 ships (50 Athenian and 10 allied) carrying 2,000 of their own crack hoplites, 400 more from Miletus and elsewhere, and 200 archers. As had been the case at Solygeia, care was also taken to bring cavalry along in the form of one transport filled with riders and mounts.

Nicias chose to use his less-seasoned allied troops for a diversion. He sent their 10 triremes against Scandea (located near Cythera's primary harbor on the eastern side of the island) and, as that town fell to the surprise assault, landed farther north with his main force. Nicias's use of a feint likely reflected his experience at Solygeia, where rapid interception had nearly dealt him a costly defeat. (This became a regular part of his repertoire, as he would use a similar ruse a decade later to land uncontested near Syracuse during an invasion of Sicily.) He was no doubt counting on his foe being distracted as he marched directly against the eponymous city of the island, which lay inland just to the east of Scandea. However, upon arriving near the lower portion of the city, Nicias found an army encamped there. His diversion might have insured a safe landing, but it hadn't tempted the Spartans to split their forces.

Both sides would have deployed into phalanx as they got set to do battle. The Athenians had quite an edge in numbers (2,000 versus around 1,000 spearmen), allowing them the luxury of forming at a depth of eight shields over a 250-meter front as they split the archers and mounted men evenly off their wings to screen the flanks. This gave the Spartans little choice but to file only four deep if they were to match formation widths, placing the small band of spartiates on the far right and filling out the rest of the line with Cytheran perioeci. Albeit short on hoplites, the Spartans would have had secure flanks, with their 200–250 psiloi not only being at least equal in number to the opposition's cavalry and bowmen but also superior in shock fighting ability. With light forces so well matched, it must have been a clash of spears along the main battle line that decided the issue.

The Spartans might have been counting on reputation and skill to once more let them beat long odds when the formations closed into contact. However, on this day they faced veteran spearmen whose own spirit was strong and who had fighting abilities that were well up to the challenge. The men from Sparta might have held their front for a while, valiantly resisting the press of deeper Athenian files, but it was a brutal, draining effort and they soon tired, gradually losing ground to finally break and flee from the field. With the city being very close by and the enemy's pursuit force small, most of the Spartans reached safety in the upper town. Still, there was no enthusiasm for risking another pitched battle and the Cytherans chose to surrender, submitting to Athenian occupation and expelling the surviving spartiates.

Nicias and his companions now used the Cytheran port of Scandea as a base for raids along the southern enemy coast, landing at night to camp and ravage the countryside at daybreak. The Spartans were in disarray, as the staccato series of body blows at Pylos/Spaectaria, Solygeia/Methana, and Cythera had sent them reeling. Feeling extremely vulnerable to attack from Athens's epiteichismoi, they fell back on the defensive, dispersing their hoplites into a network of small garrisons and forming a unit of archers and 400 horsemen as a rapid-reaction force. However, the raiders always brought so much strength that thinly spread garrisons feared to even take the field. At the same time, the Athenians' ships allowed them to pull out well before the flying squad of bowmen and riders could come into play. Only one outpost, that near the villages of Cotyrta and Aphrodisia (otherwise unknown sites along the Laconian coast), braved the odds to strike back. The Spartans sortied there to drive off light-armed crewmen put ashore to spoil the land; yet their triumph proved brief, as Athenian hoplites soon arrived to rescue their comrades. This must have been a modest action, probably resembling a small-scale version of the earlier engagement on Cythera. As in that battle, the small force of Spartans present (a few hundred spearmen) couldn't keep the field for long against a much larger opponent. It's likely that only a few of the losers paid with their lives, since most must have shed shields and other gear to get clear. Still, their quick defeat underscored shortcomings of such small garrisons against the kind of raids in force that Athens was mounting.

There was a great loss of prestige and confidence for Sparta during this period and its army became increasingly dispirited. This crisis of morale is well shown by reaction against a raid on Thyrea, where men from Sparta and Aeginian exiles were putting up fortifications along the western shore of the Argive Gulf. Outnumbered by 4 to 1 or better, the Spartans declined battle and retreated to high ground outside the city, leaving their allies behind to hold Thyrea's acropolis. The Athenians then sacked the lower portion of the town and carried off prisoners. The latter included a number of Aeginians and no less a person than the Spartan commander, who, unlike his men, had stood fast against the foe and fallen wounded. Any boast that Spartans cared not about enemy numbers must have now rung hollow indeed. In reality, their garrisons weren't adequate to contend with large Athenian landing parties, yet had too many spartiates to be sacrificed in forlorn hopes. Spartan options thus shrank to an

Athens Stumbles

The Spartans grew ever more concerned as the eighth summer of warfare neared its close. They had found no effective way to fend off escalating attacks against their homelands and could no longer continue their strategy of striking directly at Attica lest harm come to the captives from Spaectaria. Sparta had lost all initiative in the war and stood on the verge of defeat. However, Spartan fortunes were destined to revive before the year was out.

Nisaea and Antandrus (424 B.C.)

Emboldened by its run of success, Athens launched another offensive in late summer 424 B.C. Hippocrates (a young firebrand and nephew of Pericles) and Demosthenes invaded the Megarid, with the former landing 600 hoplites on the Megaran island of Minoa and the latter marching overland to set up in hiding near Nisea, Megara's Saronic port. Demosthenes led a force of border guards (*peripoli*, about 1,000 hoplite reservists from the fort at Eleusis, likely in two lochoi/taxeis as per Munn 1993, 7, 28, 169) and some psiloi from Plataea. Using these men and with help from local conspirators, he made a night attack that captured the long walls linking Nisea with Megara. An army of 4,000 spearmen and 600 riders now came up via Eleusis to join an attempt on Megara, but its defenders exposed a plot to open their gates and were able to save the city. Casting about for an easier target, the Athenians now turned against Nisaea, where a small Spartan contingent had fled when the long walls fell. It soon proved that there were too few men to secure the port and its garrison gave up, unaware that help was actually close at hand.

Brasidas of Sparta happened to be nearby gathering an army for a campaign in Thrace. Hearing of events at Nisea, he marched out with 100 of his countrymen and 3,700 other spearmen from allies nearby at Corinth (2,700), Sicyon (600), and Phlius (400). The Boeotians came to his aid as well, bringing another 2,200 hoplites and 600 horsemen with hamippoi. This made for a total of 6,000 spearmen, 600 cavalry, and some light foot troops that more than matched Athens's strength (5,600 hoplites, 600 horsemen, and a few psiloi). Surprisingly, Megara didn't join in the effort. It seems that a stalemate between supporters of Athens and Sparta had put that city on the sidelines, with both sides now waiting to throw in with whomever should come out on top of the pending fight. Brasidas must have been aware of this tipping point and closed on Nisaea in hope of gaining a victory that would secure Megara for Sparta. Chasing off those spoiling the countryside, his Boeotian riders fought an inconclusive skirmish against the Athenian horsemen as he formed up his infantry to offer battle. The Athenians then mustered before the long walls as if to take up the challenge.

As it turned out, the forces arrayed at Nisaea never came to blows, both being willing to accept limited gains rather than risk a battle where neither could see clear advantage. The men from Athens had already captured Megara's port and long walls and could profit little by taking on a greater number of hoplites that were also more experienced (most of the peripoli being youths). Likewise, Brasidas couldn't gain much by fighting. Beating the Athenians would inflict only minimal damage on them, given a nearby safe haven at Nisaea, and would regain neither harbor nor walls. At the same time, he knew that a defeat might well push Megara into the enemy camp. Risks inherent in a battle thus outweighed potential rewards for all involved and both armies retired from the field, having satisfied the demands of honor by publicly offering combat and privately relieved that their opponent hadn't accepted. Yet this turned out in the end to be a bloodless Spartan victory, as the Megarans interpreted Athens's refusal to engage as a sign of weakness. They therefore pledged allegiance to Sparta and allowed Brasidas into their city.

Looking back, it's now possible to see this turn of events in the Megarid as, if not a reversal of Athenian fortunes, at least a slowing of their advance. The Athenians wouldn't have perceived this at the time, since capture of Nisaea and the long walls seemed to offset their failure to best Brasidas and take Megara. In fact, things likely still looked to be on the upswing, as Athens soon gained another battlefield success. The Asian port of Antandrus, just inboard of Lesbos, went into rebellion and set itself up as a refuge for men on the run from Mytilene. The Athenians responded to this by sending some 20–25 ships, 200–250 Athenian hoplites, and 500–800 allied spearmen (drawn from the same poleis that had lent support four years earlier to the Lesbian campaign). This gave them a fair advantage in manpower over the Mytilenian exiles and Antandrans, who might have had no more than 300–400 hoplites of their own. With these odds, the battle couldn't have been in doubt for long and Athens's superior force must have enveloped a shorter phalanx to put the rebels to flight and regain Antandrus.

The Athenians seem to have taken their modest victory at Antandrus and an optimistic reading of developments in the Megarid as indications that their star was still on the rise. They now prepared to lash out even more aggressively, no doubt feeling that ultimate triumph was only a matter of time and continued avoidance of the Spartan phalanx. However, Sparta's allies, who were butts of this strategy, would soon expose the transitory nature of Athens's recent ascendancy.

Delium and Sicyon III (424 B.C.)

Athens decided in fall 424 B.C. to attack Boeotia, and prepared an ambitious and complex operation. The scheme called for Demosthenes and Hippocrates (the same command team as at Nisea) to take advantage of democratic uprisings to invade Boeotia from the west by sea in parallel with an overland thrust into Tanagran territory to the east. On this occasion, it was Demosthenes in charge of the seaborne effort, starting from Naupactus with 40 ships and 1,600 spearmen (marines, Messenians, Acarnanians, and others). At the same time, Hippocrates led the land force from Athens with 7,000 hoplites that included prime-aged citizens as well as a good many older men, some metics, and a few allies. He also brought along cavalry (likely 600 riders) and a large body of attendants. Yet even as this column set out, the plot on which its mission depended was coming apart. Revolts at coastal Siphae and inland Chaeronea, both crucial to the western feint, had fallen victim to betrayal, causing Demosthenes to turn back almost immediately. This warned the Boeotians and allowed them to marshal all their strength against the remaining threat in the east. Ignorant of all this, Hippocrates forged ahead to set up a fort at Delium, a border shrine near the coast northeast of Tanagra.

Hippocrates posted a garrison to Delium (likely 300–600 hoplites) and stayed with his cavalry to finish the fortifications as the rest of his army marched off. The main force moved south until just inside Attica and then split up, with the spearmen stopping on the northeast slope of the Paliokhani plateau (Pritchett, 1969, 32) to wait for their leader while most of the others kept on for home. As it turned out, delaying at the border gave the Boeotians time to prepare a response with 7,000 hoplites gathered from Thebes (2,500), Tanagra (1,000), Orchomenos and Hysettos (1,000), Thespiae (500), and Haliartia, Copaea, Coronea, etc.

(2,000 combined). There were also 1,000 horsemen with hamippoi and 500 peltasts (likely Thracian) as well as thousands of light-armed men. Staging at Tanagra, this host marched out to catch up with the invaders late in the day, approaching from the west behind the plateau's crest. The Boeotians were at first reluctant to attack, given the hour and the fact that the foe was already out of their territory. However, the elderly general Pagondas talked his men into fighting and they formed up just behind the ridgeline, where they were still hidden for the most part from the enemy below. Alerted by dust and noise that they had been found, the Athenians sent for their general and readied to defend themselves. Hippocrates left half his cavalry to guard Delium and rushed to join his spearmen.

Pagondas arranged his phalanx with the men from Thebes holding 100m along the far right wing at 25 deep — each file being made up of an entire enomotia. Picked hoplites 300 strong filled the first three ranks that would come into striking range of the enemy front. This was the same elite prototype for the Sacred Band that had fought at Plataea, its members called *heniochoi* (charioteers) in homage to their origin in a past tradition of aristocratic horsemen. Spearmen from Orchomenos and Hysettos, Tanagra, and Thespiae stood on the left wing from left to right, with the remaining federation hoplites filling in the center. Unlike the deeply massed Thebans, all of these other levies must have formed up at a depth of eight to give the entire formation a width of just over 650m.

Some of Pagondas's cavalry and skirmishers took post on his flanks, but steep ravines on either side narrowed the field to a little over 900m (per Pritchett [1969, 32] plus allowance for some erosion over better than two millennia) that couldn't accommodate all of the light troops present. This most affected the cavalry, as it normally stood outermost and was also the arm least able to handle rugged terrain. The Theban thus had to post at least two 100-horse squadrons in his rear, forming a tactical reserve that, as events unfolded, would play a decisive role in the battle. Once in order, Pagondas marched his men to the ridge crest to confront the enemy.

Hippocrates moved quickly to meet this challenge. He set up his hoplites on the slope below in files eight shields deep, over a front of around 875m, with metics stationed in the center/interior and himself on the right wing. Simultaneously, he split his modest cavalry and light foot off both flanks. Just as for Pagondas, rough ground at either edge of the field frustrated proper cavalry deployment and kept the tips of Hippocrates' wings out of engagement.

It's probable that the men from Athens initially thought they were facing only about 5,000 enemy hoplites on the basis of the foe's line length and assuming a depth of eight shields. Having an advantage in formation width, they must have intended to hold against the Thebans on the left, while using their overlap to envelop the other end of the enemy line. Pagondas was clearly aware of these traditional tactics and apparently planned to counter by using his deeply filed right to overpower the enemy on that side for a quick victory before his left could fail. He therefore moved to open battle by advancing downhill in the afternoon sun, revealing his overly deep wing in the process. It was far too late at this point for Hippocrates to adjust to the unusual Boeotian array, and trying to withdraw in the face an attack would only trigger disaster. He thus decided to try and fight through the situation and charged uphill so that he didn't cede all momentum to his enemy.

The advancing lines crashed together into bitter shock fighting that quickly evolved into a race between competing strategies — the Theban right wing trying to push to victory as the Athenians strove to wrap around the other end of the Boeotian front. Early on, it was the men from Athens that took the upper hand. Though their left did indeed come under great pressure from the deeply-filed Thebans shoving down the slope, it summoned forth an all-out effort, pushing back fiercely to grudgingly give ground only very slowly. This stubborn

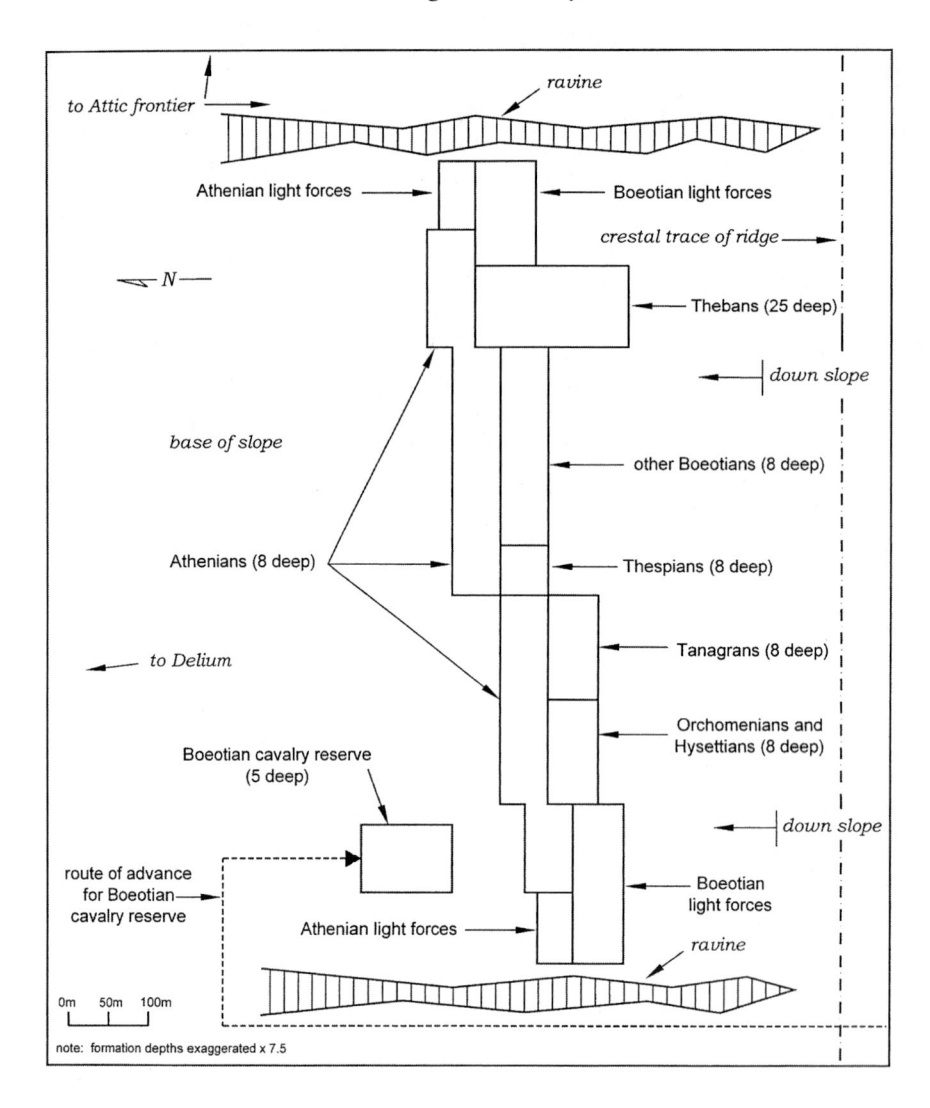

BATTLE OF DELIUM (424 B.C.)

and heroic stand bought enough time for their comrades on the right to begin turning the enemy's overlapped flank. The Athenian horsemen knocked back the more numerous Boeotian riders on that side of the field, which let their hoplites engage and rout the northerners' screen of light foot troops. Driving forward, the Athenians were then able to curl their longer line around the opposing flank to devastating effect. Most of the Boeotians on that wing broke and ran amidst the growing encirclement, leaving only the steadfast Thespians holding to their post. Spearmen closed around these stubborn fighters and slaughtered many in a killing frenzy so heated that some Athenians cut down their own men. Yet just as determined opposition against the Thebans gave time for Athens's right wing to pursue victory, so the tenacity of the men from Thespiae bought a chance for Boeotia to still carry the day.

As the Thespians struggled in desperation, the two squadrons of horsemen holding behind the Theban ranks went into action. Either on signal or on previous orders, they looped left behind the northeast-trending Mandra salient off that flank (Pritchett, 1969, 36) and came around undetected to strike the Athenian right rear. (Hanson has proposed [2005, 130] that this maneuver was much shorter, hooking just around the Theban line and then straight over the crest to hit an Athenian front that had reversed its facing in surrounding the Thespians.) The hoplites from Athens had fought to the verge of victory on that side of the field only to now face a sudden and complete reversal of momentum. Believing that they were under attack from another army, they took fright and ran. Hippocrates fell at this crucial moment and his death further fueled the panic. On the other side of the battleground, the Athenian left wing now stood with an exposed right flank, which put a rapid end to its dogged resistance. The deep Theban files now pushed through at last, as all opposition to their advance simply disintegrated. Within minutes, the Athenian army had split into three disorderly mobs, with the right wingers heading back to Delium, those in the center making eastward for Oropos on the coast, and the left-wingers going south toward Mount Parnes.

Just as things turned against Athens, a force of cavalry from Opuntian Locris arrived to support the Boeotians. Seeing the enemy running from the field, these horsemen joined with the riders from Boeotia to carry out a deadly pursuit of the broken army. This vicious hunt took many Athenian lives, but was mercifully cut short by the fall of darkness, since the battle hadn't begun until late and sunset was almost upon the combatants when a final decision came. Athens nevertheless paid a high price for its effort at Delium, with nearly 1,000 hoplites killed (around 15 percent of those engaged). This was the city's greatest loss in a single action during the Archidamian War. Most of these casualties came during the final chase; still, many kept their wits about them and got away. These included the philosopher Socrates and his comrade Laches (the general from the Sicilian campaign), who were among those making for Parnes. They were able to preserve both life and honor by holding onto their shields and putting up a good front that discouraged pursuit. Socrates' student Alcibiades, a cavalryman at the battle, aided this escape. The youth rode to his mentor's rescue, thus repaying gallant assistance received from the older man at Potidaea.

The victors also took heavy losses at Delium, with almost 500 (7 percent) of their spearmen going down. But distribution of this pain was by no means uniform, as it was men on the nearly defeated left wing that took most of the damage. And the Thespians, who bravely stood their ground when everyone else fled, were hardest hit among these, losing some 300 hoplites (Hornblower 1996, 306) — a shocking 60 percent of their total levy. (Sadly, Thebes later exploited this noble sacrifice to further exert dominance over Thespiae.) The men from Tanagra on the Thespian right faired better, but still lost 63 spearmen (just over 6 percent, including some Euboans fighting in their ranks). Most of the other fatalities were among troops from Orchomenos and Hysettos that held the enveloped left flank, where close to 100 hoplites (10 percent) might have lost their lives. In contrast, the Boeotian right and center got off light, suffering less than 50 (1 percent) of their spearmen killed.

Delium wasn't the only bad news for Athens at this time, as its western task force met defeat as well. Demosthenes had turned from his failure in Boeotia to direct an assault on the northern coast of the Peloponnese at Sicyon. It must have seemed a relatively safe venture, given past Athenian success in raiding this area from the sea. Though his 40 ships and 1,600 hoplites were less than resources brought against Sicyon by either Tolmides (457 B.C.) or Pericles (454 B.C.), they were still more than enough for a hit-and-run attack. But as happened during Tolmides' campaign, the Sicyonians got wind of the scheme in time to prepare a hostile reception.

Sicyon had long ago recovered from its losses against Athens and could now field an army of something over 3,000 hoplites and 500–1,000 psiloi. This force likely attacked before all the raiders had a chance to beach and unload, not unlike what had transpired at Solygeia a year earlier. However, Demosthenes faced an even more menacing situation than had Nicias, as he was heavily outnumbered. If no more than half his men were on shore, he had but a quarter of the opposition's manpower and no chance to hang on long enough for reinforcements to land. Sicyon must have gained or threatened envelopment to quickly drive the invaders back to their ships for a harrowing escape out to sea. Demosthenes fled with his life, yet likely lost around 100 men (a tenth of those ashore).

Pagondas was following up on his victory in the field with a siege of Delium even as Demosthenes retreated from Sicyon. His ranks had grown as hoplites arrived from allies closest to hand at Corinth (2,000, including 500 from the former Spartan garrison at Nisaea) and Megara (500–1,000) and he had also secured the services of more mercenaries (both slingers and peltasts). Delium's garrison held out for just over two weeks against this assault, fleeing only when the Boeotians set fire to its wooden walls. Many Athenians escaped by ship, but the enemy killed some and captured 200 others (perhaps a rear guard). Athens's attempt on Boeotia thus ended without a single success to show for the loss of some 1,300 lives.

Reflections on Theban Tactics at Delium

The battle of Delium is of great interest as the largest hoplite action of the Archidamian War and because of novel Boeotian tactics. Pagondas's stratagems included an initial hidden deployment, forming unusually deep files on one wing, and use of a mounted reserve. Though some of these ploys worked better than others, all deserve a closer look.

HIDDEN DEPLOYMENT • It was normal for Greek armies to form up in full view of their enemy, which allowed both sides to adjust formation toward creating a contest between battle lines of similar length. Pagondas chose here to hide his phalanx behind a ridge and didn't reveal its frontage until after beginning his final advance into combat. This clever approach allowed him to disguise his true strength from the foe (who no doubt thought they were in the majority, when they were actually slightly outnumbered) and kept his ploy of filing deeply on one wing a secret until the opposition was irrevocably committed to fight.

DEEPLY MASSED OTHISMOS • Use by Pagondas of 25-man files on his right at Delium foreshadowed stacking of spearmen by Thebes at similar (Stylianou 1998, 402–403) or even greater depth on the opposite, left wing during its period of military supremacy in the 4th century. This ran counter to common practice, which dictated optimum files of eight men. Other Greeks had deployed at greater depth only within restricted topography, with Thermopylae a prime example. Limiting terrain was not a factor at Delium, since the Athenians had been able to file a force of similar size at eight deep on the same field. Why then did Pagondas choose to mass his hoplites at 25 shields? As a deeper formation would allow more men to contribute to othismos (pushing), it might be that he was attempting an overwhelming offensive. Was this indeed the case?

The most cost-effective variants of the Doric phalanx had developed through trial and error during the 7th and 6th centuries B.C. A four-man file was the practical minimum, allowing for the first three ranks to reach the enemy with their spears while the fourth rank provided replacements for losses at the front. However, this shallow array had two major shortcomings: it was hard to keep together during maneuver and it could exert very little pressure through othismos. Adding more ranks improved formation cohesion on the move, but rapidly reached a point of diminishing returns for concerted pushing. It was clear that shoving ahead became less effective the farther it took place from the front, perhaps providing no real help beyond 16 shields deep (as per Polybios on Macedonian experience). Furthermore, since they had to shorten ranks to deepen files, they increased the risk of envelopment. The action at Delium clearly demonstrates the limited benefits and significant risks of overly extended depth. The Thebans initially met with the greatest difficulty in inching ahead against an Athenian left wing that was less than a third as deep, while at the same time nearly suffering defeat due to a turning of their own shortened line.

It's reasonable to propose that Pagondas might have deepened his files to 12 or even 16 in hopes of maximizing othismos and securing a quick victory. However, given common knowledge that files deeper than this were of little if any help to forward momentum, it's unlikely that he filed at 25 men to further enhance othismos. Why, then, did he do this? We must look for our answer not among offensive considerations (i.e. those meant to harm the enemy), but rather from the opposite side of the combat equation — the effort to protect one's own men.

DEFENSIVE FILING • Two engagements in 480 B.C., on the second day at Thermopylae and in the finale at Himera, illustrate the defensive value of exceptional file depth. These battles featured very lengthy shock combats where both sides were better able to protect themselves than hurt their foe. This to a large degree reflected the use of very deep files, whose benefits stemmed from both psychological and physical aspects of massed battle.

With regard to psychology, normal signals of stress and defeat transmitted back from the front never affected distant after ranks (those actually able to break and run). It seems that men in the rear couldn't sense a negative turning at the unseen head of the battle and be panicked into flight because the huge central mass of their formation absorbed all such energy long before it was able to reach them. As to physical effects, not only did anchoring terrain prevent turning of flanks, but there was also no way to break through the front as long as everyone stood fast in back. With no way out at either side or rear, those in the leading ranks had little choice but to fight on. Yet the longer they fought, the more tired they became, with exhaustion further reducing the offensive effort in favor of a defensive stand. In essence, unusually deep files, like anchored flanks, boosted the ability of formations to hold their ground. This caused the subject battles to go on until either darkness (Thermopylae) or a surprise attack (Himera) broke the stalemate.

The dynamics of these marquee battles and lesser engagements of like aspect must have been familiar to most Greek generals. Thus, it's highly likely that Pagondas was keying on an improved defense when he deployed his Thebans in such deep files at Delium. However, unlike Leonidas at Thermopylae or Gelon at Himera, he wasn't facing an opponent massed at a similar depth; therefore, he must have been hoping to render his own ranks invulnerable to othismos while fighting an opponent still thin enough to be pushed from the field. If so, he misjudged the situation and/or badly underestimated his foe. In the end, this approach nearly undid his hoplites and only timely intervention by their cavalry snatched victory from the jaws of defeat.

MOUNTED TACTICAL RESERVE • The Theban cavalry strike at Delium is of special note not only for its outstanding results, but also as a rare 5th-century use of reserves in battle. Though not the sole example of horsemen turning the tide of a hoplite engagement, this might have been the first time that such an action came from a designated reserve. Even if posting horsemen to the Theban rear was more due to terrain than planning, someone in the chain of command certainly put it to decisive use. The Boeotian mounted maneuver here stands with the charge of Battus's lochos at Solygeia and the ambush at Olpae as early testaments to the potential of tactical reserves.

Lyncestis (423 B.C.)

Stymied in the Megarid and repulsed from Boeotia, the Athenians also saw their fortunes take a turn for the worse in the far north. Brasidas had lost little time in launching his Thracian campaign, taking a hoplite army of 700 picked helots and 1,000 mercenaries through Thessaly into northernmost Greece, where he soon claimed a major success with the capture of Amphipolis. Loss of this key outpost dealt Athens a hard blow, which was buffered only by quick action from Thucydides, who saved the city's port of Eion from a similar fate. (Though he had preserved the coastal route for critical grain shipments from the Black Sea region, Thucydides found himself the focus of anger over loss of Amphipolis, and the Athenians banished him. This would become a blessing for history, since his writings in exile are our best source on this period.) Brasidas went on to inspire revolt within his foe's alliance. By striking at key allies rather than Athens itself, he was copying recent Athenian strategy and turning it back on its creators. Stung by their defeat at Delium and Brasidas's success in the far north, the Athenians agreed to a one-year peace with Sparta in spring 423 B.C.

While this cease-fire gave both sides a much needed break after eight years of war—yielding a chance to husband flagging resources, mend wounds, and reassess strategies—it didn't stop all fighting, as the area north of Thessaly continued to seethe with conflict. Brasidas was still active in that region and, while keeping within the peace accord by avoiding direct attacks, he spread discord among Athens's supporters. He also assisted Perdiccas II of Macedonia, who was mounting an expedition against rebels in his northwestern province of Lyncestis. Such internal strife was typical of Macedonia at this time, setting eastern coastal lowlands loyal to the monarchy against one of the fiefdoms of Upper Macedonia. The latter was a valley-cut highland that stretched eastward toward Illyria in a rugged setting that inspired local nobles to independence. Nowhere was this better shown than at Lyncestis, where the warlord Arrhabaeus sought to hold onto a defiant autonomy.

Macedonian lowlanders were largely peasant farmers who yielded military service to their king in times of crisis, forming a militia of skirmishers organized by tribe (*ethnos*). These commoners were poor folk, who mostly carried inexpensive javelins and small shields and fought using a "charge and retreat" style of open-order combat. There were, however, some exceptions. A few of these men carried bows for longer-range work or had spear, sword, and a large wicker shield to provide some very modest shock capability. Macedonian foot soldiers in this era were of little value in close combat, unable to stand up to hoplites despite being available in great mass. Their most useful function was to screen for cavalry drawn from the aristocracy.

It was horse-breeding nobles (*hippobotai*) who actually formed the backbone of the Macedonian army. These wore some body armor and carried a thrusting spear (*xyston*, wielded overhand with butt-end resting on the right shoulder), saber, and a light shield. Following in a long tradition of mounted fighters, these elite warriors bonded to their king as his "companions" (*hetairoi*). Since the Macedonian heavy cavalry consisted exclusively of wealthy aristocrats, it lacked large numbers but was the most shock-capable cavalry in Greece and a force worthy of respect.

The various districts in Upper Macedonia used military systems much like that of the coastal region. They thus had small numbers of mounted nobles taking the field with support from a horde of commoner foot militia, which, like its lowland counterpart, was of poor quality. Still, there were some significant differences in detail between highland and lowland arms. Instead of bowmen, the mountaineers deployed slingers, since herdsmen familiar with the sling were common in their region. Also, though they fielded peltasts, many of their skirmishers used sturdier gear as per the neighboring Illyrians. These men wielded a long and heavy-headed sibyna spear, which was much better adapted for shock combat than javelins. They also wore helmets and carried small, round shields, each of the latter having a bronze boss for offensive strikes. Though still preferring to engage in open order, such fighters were more comfortable with hand-to-hand action than their lowlander counterparts. This was a characteristic that Arrhabaeus sought to exploit, fitting out some of his Illyrian-style spearmen as hoplites. His hope was that opposition skirmishers would be powerless against a heavy-infantry phalanx — even one with very little training and no experience.

It's highly speculative as to how many converted hoplites were present for Arrhabaeus. Our only clue is that upon Brasidas's first arrival in the region he had tried to negotiate with the highland warlord rather than directly engaging his makeshift phalanx. We can thus infer that it posed a serious challenge to the Spartan's 1,700 spearmen, which suggests 1,500–2,000 armored men. This also helps explain Brasidas's subsequent move to augment his army with more hoplites from local allies. As a practical matter, it seems unlikely that Arrhabaeus would have risked a trial by phalanx unless he had a heavy force of at least this size to put him at a ratio of no less than two spearmen to three for his opponent. Beyond his tyro hoplites, Arrhabaeus had 300–600 horsemen of the heavier, Macedonian type, with a screen of hamippoi. Other light footmen came from a regional population of some 30,000 adult males. If a third of these were available to the rebel leader, either directly or as allies, he might have fielded some 4–5,000 skirmishers.

The royal army included 1,200 southern hoplites (the helots plus half the hired men, all others having stayed behind on garrison duty), 1,800 allied spearmen (Chalcidians, Acanthians, etc.), and large contingents of both cavalry and light foot troops. There would have been 500 Macedonian heavy cavalry and a like number of light riders that comprised half the Chalcidian League's mounted contingent, with one hamippos for each horseman regardless of category. The king also brought peltast militia at a strength at least equal to what he expected to meet among his enemies. Yet for all its size, this host didn't intimidate Arrhabaeus. He moved to engage and the opposing forces soon faced each other from hillsides separated by a narrow plain well suited to hoplite combat.

Action began with a cavalry engagement. Given that hamippoi would have limited participation by the vulnerable and shorter-ranging Chalcidian light cavalry, this contest came down to a brief duel between heavy horsemen that might have seen Arrhabaeus and Perdiccas personally involved. It appears that the highlanders, despite having fewer men, held their own and were able to stay on the field until their heavy infantry got to the scene. These neophyte hoplites now prepared to square off against the more seasoned spearmen of Brasidas.

It's likely that Brasidas had advanced with his mercenaries on the right and northern allies on the left, nestling less experienced men (helots, et al.) in between. Having an edge of 50 percent or more in manpower, he would have filed eight shields deep over a width of around 375m. This forced his foes to either line up at equal depth along a front of but 200–250m or match widths at only five shields deep. Either way, the Lyncestians faced a crisis of confidence. Being not only short on manpower, but also new to the phalanx, they couldn't avoid having serious doubts about both the savvy of their leaders and their own ability in this unfamiliar kind of fighting. The impact of these physical and psychological factors didn't leave the battle long in doubt and Brasidas's phalanx looks to have routed its jerry-built counterpart shortly after making contact. The rebel spearmen must have run from the field amidst a vigorous pursuit that cut down perhaps 20 percent or more of their number.

Arrhabaeus and his surviving men set up in the hills and readied a defense as their foes stood by for several days in separate camps to await reinforcement by Illyrian mercenaries that

Perdiccas had contracted. When the Illyrians finally arrived, however, they surprised the king by defecting to Arrhabaeus. Faced with such an unexpected reverse, Perdiccas and Brasidas agreed to support each other in retreat. But this pact came to naught. Overcome with panic, the Macedonian lowlanders lost all discipline and made a premature run for home that left Brasidas in the lurch.

The Spartan general rose to this challenge and organized a brilliant fighting withdrawal by forming his men into a moving rectangle. Fleeter young spearmen sallied out to confront smaller-scale flank attacks, while Brasidas led a 300-man flying squad of picked hoplites against more substantial threats against his rear. Possibly standard Spartan practices, these were sound tactics and Arrhabaeus's assaults failed. He reacted by sending men ahead to block the escape route and, after dispatching a few stragglers at the tail of Perdiccas's fleeing mob, this advance party took up position in a key pass. However, Brasidas and his select team of spearmen answered by moving to the front of their column, where they cleared a path to safety. Enraged at the cowardly behavior of their erstwhile allies, the retreating Greeks took revenge against any local asset that fell in their path. This ended Sparta's brief partnership with Perdiccas, who shortly thereafter sought a new alliance with Athens.

Mende and Scione (423 B.C.)

The sea-lane skirting the three-fingered Chalcidian peninsula was of critical concern to Athens, as it remained the path for imports from the Black Sea region. Brasidas had established a menacing position onshore of this strategic route just as the temporary truce was being negotiated and signed. He had first campaigned across the easternmost lobe (Acte) to take several villages along the Aegean coast and then got inside help to expel Athens from Torone, a key site near the southern tip of the central landmass (Sithonia). Scione, an outpost with Peloponnesian roots, was his next target and it revolted from Athens at Brasidas's urging to give him a toehold at the point of the third, westernmost promontory (Pallene). Finally, Brasidas went after Athens's remaining strongholds on Pallene at Mende and Potidaea, which lay northward along the western coast. These efforts met with some success when oligarchs at Mende, egged on by supporters in nearby Scione, gained control of the city and took it out of the Athenian camp. However, Brasidas's triumphs at Scione and Mende were, in fact, mistimed. Both poleis had broken away after the cease-fire had gone into effect and Athens was eager to take them back.

Brasidas failed to recognize the immediacy of the threat to Mende and Scione and provided poorly for their defense when he left for Lyncestis. He had posted his Spartan subordinate Polydamidas with only 500 spearmen and 300 peltasts to assist the locals in holding all of his recent gains in the north, and this simply wasn't enough to cover so many sites. At Athens, Nicias and Nicostratus loaded 40 of the city's ships and 10 more from Chios with 1,000 hoplites and 600 archers and set out for Potidaea. There they added some peltasts to their force, including 100 Thracian mercenaries, at least 120 Macedonians, and other allies for 400–600 in all. Having fully filled their ships, they headed south to make Mende the first target.

When Nicias and company arrived at Mende, they found an army under Polydamidas atop a hill near town. The Spartan not only had Mende's hoplites with him (200 or so), but also spearmen from Scione (300) and probably half his mercenaries (250—the rest being at Scione). He also had some 200 peltasts (from Mende and Scione) and 150 Chalcidian psiloi (half those available). Splitting his forces between Mende and Scione had let Polydamidas make a quick interception, but as per Lycophron at Solygeia two years earlier, this undercut resources on hand at any single location. The Athenians therefore moved to attack with a fair edge in hoplite strength (up by about a third) and an overwhelming superiority (better than 3 to 1) in light foot troops.

Polydamidas saw that he was outnumbered and kept to the high ground, occupying a rise that would limit the width of any phalanx brought against him while allowing him to still file eight or more deep. In concert with his hoplite deployment, he must have placed peltasts in his rear to defend all back and side approaches. Nicias assessed the situation and decided it best to dislodge his foe from the exposed hilltop with arrows. He led his archers into range up a path along one flank and opened up from behind a screen of peltasts and hoplites — but Polydamidas and his spearmen weren't impressed. They shrugged off the missiles and stood firm as their javelinmen charged forward to return fire and wound some of the attackers, including Nicias.

Nicostratus now swung into action with his main force of hoplites, advancing in a bid to maintain momentum and take the hill. His phalanx was restricted to a fairly narrow front and he likely had to file at a depth of 10 shields or more, with all remaining peltasts spread off each wing as flank cover. However, a steep slope and stalwart defense by his thinner-arrayed foe combined to spoil this attack. Stalemated, Nicostratus finally withdrew, being fortunate to get down off the hill in sufficient order to avoid a rout. The Athenians returned to their landing site and spent the night encamped; the garrison of Mende, meanwhile, retired behind the nearby city walls.

The Athenians sailed around south of Mende next morning to capture suburbs on that side of the city and raid outlying farmland. This went unopposed due to turmoil among the Mendeans. The men from Scione saw this growing political unrest and, fearing for their own lands, left for home that evening. Things came to a boil the following day when Polydamidas tried to organize a sally against the Athenians who had raided as far as the border with Scione and come back to draw up for battle just north of the city. Most of the populace suddenly turned on the Spartan, his mercenaries, and their oligarchic backers, taking them by surprise and killing many on the spot. Polydamidas and his remaining supporters fled to the local citadel and the rebels opened their gates to the Athenians. Nicias and Nicostratus couldn't stop their men from looting, but did save most of the townsfolk. Putting Polydamidas under siege, the Athenians now moved on to Scione.

Events at Scione opened much as they had at Mende, with the garrison taking post on a nearby hill. Here, however, similarities ended. Scione had even fewer hoplites than Mende, with perhaps only 300–400 locals and 250 mercenaries; furthermore, Nicias seems to have learned from his earlier failure. This time he wasted no effort on a bow attack and immediately launched his phalanx at the enemy. Once more a smaller force sought the aid of elevation, narrow deployment, and moral grit to hold off deeper-filed opponents. But it was a doomed effort, as the Athenians were simply too strong to be denied and their charge drove the defenders from the hilltop and into town.

The mercenaries trapped in the citadel at Mende made a nighttime escape to Scione shortly after this battle. There they could help fend off a direct assault, but were powerless to prevent a wall of circumvallation from being completed by summer's end. Nicias now had everything under control and, having accepted an alliance with Macedonia's Perdiccas, returned with his ships to Athens. He left behind sufficient force to finish the siege, including local peltasts, some archers, and around 500–600 hoplites (all save enough marines for the fleet). Mende would hold out until summer 421 B.C., but when it finally fell, the Athenians executed its men and sold their families into slavery (exiles from Plataea would later settle the site).

Laodocium (423 B.C.)

While southern Greece remained free of fighting between Athens and Sparta during the truce of 423 B.C., this didn't mean an end to all conflict in the region. A minor war broke out at this time in Arcadia — a district under Spartan control since the mid 6th century. Mantinea had long been second there to its older southern neighbor and bitter rival, Tegea, but had set out to change this by absorbing smaller communities and now felt ready to challenge for area leadership. This was not unlike the situation that had unfolded five years earlier on Lesbos, where nominal Athenian ally Mytilene made a similar bid for local hegemony.

With a cease-fire in effect, Spartan partners Mantinea and Tegea saw no disloyalty to their hegemon in pursuing selfish ambitions. Nor was Sparta, unlike Athens, opposed to lesser hegemonies within its larger system of alliances. The Spartans thus made no move to interfere in this purely Arcadian affair. Tegea and Mantinea gathered support from other Arcadians and met to settle things at Laodocium in the territory of Oresthis. Though this site is otherwise unknown, it must have been somewhere within the scant 15km stretch between Tegea and Mantinea, probably southwest of the latter on the Alcimedon plain.

A pandemic effort by the Tegeans would have mustered some 2,000 of their own hoplites and perhaps 1,500 more from allies. This latter represented about half the Arcadian hoplites available outside of Mantinea. Tegea probably organized its heavy foot troops much like Sparta, and formed four lochoi of 500 men each. As for the Mantineans, they could call upon 1,500–2,000 citizen spearmen and draw another 1,500 from elsewhere in Arcadia. Hoplite organization at Mantinea is likely to have been five lochoi of 300–400 men each, consistent with the city's mid 6th-century to early 5th-century union from five villages. Allied lochoi in both camps varied from 300 to 600 men after the custom of each community, while there would have been about one psiloi for every six spearmen. It was a fair match, with Tegea having an edge of less than 10 percent in hoplites.

The Tegean phalanx must have approached from the south at eight shields deep, with allied troops posted from left wing to center. The Mantineans probably assumed a similar depth of file and assignment priority, placing their own men on the right side and allies to the left. Initial set-up and final adjustments appear to have taken quite a while; thus, it was only very late in the afternoon when both sides were finally ready for battle. Signals sounded and skirmishers retired to the flanks as the phalanxes closed on each other to execute a final charge amid a chorus of war cries. Crashing together, the hoplites engaged in a lengthy and vicious shock combat, yet neither side could sweep the field and a draw ensued.

Given such great similarity in strength and background of these armies, it's probable that each enveloped the other's left flank. This would largely have come as a consequence of rightward drift during their initial advances that caused mutual overlaps of allied troops on those ends of the field. When the men being outflanked fled, the Tegeans and Mantineans threw away a chance to wheel against each other and gave in alike to pursuit. Hoplites from Tegea had shown similar lack of discipline in a premature charge at Plataea (479 B.C.) and such behavior was undoubtedly common among Arcadian troops (and most other Greek militiamen). Since the fight had begun quite late, time lost in the chase meant that darkness must have been falling before the successful wings got back to the battlefield. All concerned were by now exhausted and content to quit for the day.

The Tegeans remained on the field that night, while the Mantineans withdrew to a nearby village. As for their allies, they apparently left for home in some haste after the battle. Having absorbed most of the punishment, these men must have felt that they had rendered all the service that honor required. Next day, it became apparent that neither Tegea nor Mantinea had the stomach for another fight, something that speaks volumes for the physical and mental toll exacted by shock combat, even among units that had avoided serious casualties. In the end, both sides simply declared victory and set up trophies, though these claims were but half-truths at best.

Mantinea seems to have been reluctant to go it alone after this and gave up its hegemonic quest, apparently content to bask for the near term in the modest and incomplete success gained on the right at Laodocium. The Tegeans actually had a better claim to victory, not only carrying their own wing in combat, but also having remained on the battleground at day's end. More importantly, they had managed to frustrate Mantinean ambitions and therefore preserved a status quo favorable to their cause.

Amphipolis (422 B.C.)

The Athenians once more took up arms against Sparta when the brief truce ended in 422 B.C. With things seemingly in hand on their southern front, they strove to regain key points along their northern trade route. Cleon instigated his own assignment to this mission and led out a fleet that had 30 triremes with 1,200 hoplites and 120 archers aboard. He also took 10 transports carrying 300 horsemen and their mounts, while 50 ships from Aegean allies joined him to add 1,600 islander spearmen from Lemnos and Imbros. Cleon landed first at Scione, where the siege was still in progress, and picked up a few more hoplites (most likely 400 — a majority of those on hand and equal to remaining cargo capacity of the fleet) before sailing against Torone. Taking that city quickly, Cleon left a garrison (perhaps 200 spearmen from Scione) and moved on to Eion to set up a base camp and then hit some small, local objectives even as he made preparations to assault Amphipolis.

Brasidas had been on the way to Torone when its fall sent him back to Amphipolis in correct anticipation that it would soon become a target. He had but 2,000 hoplites (700 helots, 500 mercenaries, and 800 locals) to defend against some 3,000 among the enemy, but did, however, hold a strong edge in both light foot troops and cavalry. Though Cleon had sent for more skirmishers from Macedonia and Thrace, he currently had only some poorly armed retainers and 120 archers for light support. These were no match for Brasidas's peltasts, who included 1,500 hired Thracians, 1,000 from Myrcinus (Edonian) and Chalcidice (Greek), and others from Amphipolis and neighboring tribes for a total of 4–5,000 in all. As to mounted forces, the Spartan could call on 300 Chalcidian and 200–300 Edonian riders — up to twice Cleon's strength. However, despite his greater overall manpower, Brasidas appears to have been loath to chance a pitched battle. Such a contest would swing on hoplite combat and his phalanx might not be up to the challenge; not only did he have fewer spearmen, but he also must have doubted the quality of his helots and local recruits.

Cleon was eager to exploit his superiority in hoplites before Brasidas could get help. (This was a realistic concern. In fact, though he didn't know it, 900 spearmen were even now on their way from Sparta.) He wanted to delay an assault on Amphipolis until reinforcements arrived from Macedonia and Thrace; still, it seemed that scouting the city in force was a safe way to speed things along. He set out on this task without cavalry, apparently thinking it unnecessary, but took the precaution of bringing all of his hoplites. At this point it must be noted that while Thucydides described what happened next in some detail, his story seems rather confused. At the same time, our only other account, from Diodorus, is quite general and strongly conflicting. As a result, the following reconstruction owes much to the keen field observations of Pritchett (1980).

As Cleon scouted Amphipolis from a hill about 1.5km north-northeast of town, his heavy infantry formed a line of battle that stretched from just below this observation post to reach along the city's eastern walls. Brasidas noted these dispositions and saw an opportunity. He devised a double assault timed to strike when Cleon began to withdraw south toward his base at Eion. In accordance with this plan, the spartiate Clearidas grouped most of the garrison (1,850 hoplites and a mass of peltasts) for a charge from a northern portal (the "Thracian" gate) that lay nearest to the enemy line. Meanwhile, Brasidas mustered 150 picked spearmen at a second opening farther west along the north wall, which exited onto a short road just north and west of the highway to Thrace. Events soon played out to the Spartan's benefit when Athenians near the Thracian gate noted the activity within and informed their leader that Brasidas might be preparing a sally. Cleon, seeking to avoid a fight, then ordered the very withdrawal for which his opponent was waiting.

The Athenian phalanx made a quarter-turn to the left and started toward Eion. There seems to have been some delay in carrying out this evolution, but Cleon came down to join his men and helped expedite matters. As usual during such a maneuver, gaps formed at several points along the line as men naturally divided up into city-state and tribal contingents to begin their trek for home. After Cleon finally got his troops underway, he took the general's traditional station with the former right wing, which now formed the rear of the column. This trailing segment was composed of spearmen from his own city, since the islanders of Lemnos and Imbros would have stood on the less prestigious left side of the original array. Brasidas kept still until the center of this marching formation came across the road running from his station at the northwestern portal. He then signaled for a charge from both gates.

Brasidas and his 150-man company trotted out with all the speed possible for men burdened by hoplite gear (perhaps 10km/hr), moving in a tight grouping that was probably eight men wide. They rushed up the strait road toward the middle of the Athenian line, which lay some 1,500m away. It would have taken about nine minutes to cover this distance — enough time for their foes to pivot and face the charge, but not to adjust formation or steel their nerves for this unforeseen assault. The more forward Athenian elements (the allied spearmen) had by now come under fire from peltasts leading the simultaneous rush of Clearidas out of the Thracian gate. This all added to a general state of alarm that now spread throughout Cleon's command.

Upon nearing the enemy, Brasidas seems to have aimed his charge at an opening near the center of the opposing shield front. This was where a slight separation existed between the last group of islanders and Athenians following next in line. The gap couldn't have been very large, yet it still allowed Brasidas and his fast moving wedge of men to slice completely through Cleon's formation. Quickly rolling up the foe on either side, the attackers then wheeled northward to strike the leading Athenian unit on its left flank. Cleon's startled men struggled to regroup and fight back, but couldn't drive off the determined team of elite fighters opposing them. Brasidas had thus split his foe in two and held the northern portion back from Clearidas's left flank as he moved up to take on the other half of the Athenian army at favorable odds.

Clearidas had emerged from the Thracian gate on signal, leading his hoplites out along the city wall in a column eight abreast. Assuming a pace of around 6km/hr, it would have taken him nearly three minutes to get all of his troops through the portal. He then pivoted them a quarter turn to form a phalanx eight shields deep and 230m wide. As this deployment unfolded, the Spartan's peltasts had raced at top speed (12–15km/hr) toward Athens's islander allies standing some 700m away straight down the road toward Thrace. These swift skirmishers closed and began launching their weapons while Clearidas led his now tightly arrayed spearmen forward. The peltasts then peeled off around the flanks of their approaching phalanx as it charged across the final meters and into the islander front. Spear-on-shield contact probably came within seven minutes of Clearidas starting his final advance — a scant 10 minutes after clearing the city gate and shortly after Brasidas had cut through to provide a vital flank screen on the left/north.

Taken by surprise, the men from Lemnos and Imbros bolted in terror toward the south. Clearidas left these beaten foes to flee under pursuit from fresh peltasts and horsemen coming from the city and spun his hoplites about to face north (speaking well of his control over them in the heat of battle). He then advanced quickly to aid Brasidas's tiny holding force, which by now must have been coming under growing pressure from the recovering enemy right wing.

The Athenians saw Clearidas's men closing and, outnumbered now by 50–100 percent in heavy infantry, prudently fell back toward high ground on the north. They succeeded in carrying out this retreat despite a virulent rain of missiles from masses of opposing light footmen and cavalry coming onto the scene. Ironically, Nicias's men now suffered siege atop the same peak from which their general had earlier scouted his own planned investment. Both armies had by this time lost their leaders, Brasidas having gone down with a mortal wound during his initial assault and Cleon succumbing to a javelin shortly thereafter. Several times the Athenians courageously repulsed enemy spearmen swarming from below, but it was a forlorn hope. Falling victim at last to relentless missile fire, they broke apart and scattered downhill in a run for Eion.

Amphipolis was a key victory for the Spartans at a time when they badly needed something to counter losses all around the Peloponnese. Some 600 of their enemy's hoplites had been killed in the action (20 percent of those engaged, mostly native Athenians) at a scant cost of only seven of their own spearmen. This lopsided body count stemmed from the ability of Brasidas's hoplites to hold formation plus the deadly effectiveness of his light troops in overcoming the Athenian last stand and in pursuit. Yet these numbers don't tell the full tale of Sparta's loses. Commanders like Brasidas were rare and his demise was a considerable blow by any measure.

The deaths of Cleon and Brasidas removed two strong advocates of continued warfare and a formal treaty, the Peace of Nicias (brokered by that Athenian general), was agreed upon in spring 421 B.C. Both sides were hurt and exhausted, but Sparta seems to have been the more desperate party. The Spartans wanted to recover their hostages, were suffering from enemy strongholds dotting their coast, and remained fearful of helots and fractious allies alike. In addition, they now faced pending expiration of a 30-year armistice with Argos. Sparta therefore took cover behind its face-saving triumph at Amphipolis to accept a settlement that actually favored Athens. Had the agreement held up, the Athenians would have gained a minor victory in the war, keeping at least a few of their territorial gains while recovering all of their losses. However, neither this initial understanding nor a mutual defense arrangement that followed were to endure. As it turned out, there was little real peace during the truce's brief term in effect.

Tactical Patterns of the Archidamian War

The most telling physical edge that an army could hold during the Archidamian War was to field a superior number of hoplites. Those with significantly more spearmen than their foe (+33 percent) came out on top better than 70 percent of the time. Moreover, there were extenuating factors (sneak attacks, surprise maneuvers, terrain) in all the defeats suffered by larger phalanxes. Thus, though efforts at the strategic level had come to focus on economic and psychological attrition, actual combat central to those longer-term goals was still very much the domain of armored spearmen. Recognizing that hoplite strength was vital to success on the field of battle, some states hired heavy foot troops when local manpower came up short, or where they didn't want to risk their citizens in distant lands. This was especially true of Sparta, which used mercenaries, mostly from Arcadia and Achaea, on its far northern fronts. So closely did phalanx size track with victory in pitched battle that Lyncestis even went so far as to convert some of its light troops into hoplites in an attempt to become more combat effective.

The record of armies stronger in cavalry was also outstanding in the Archidamian War, winning 8 times against only 4 losses. This, however, is deceptive. In fact, larger mounted forces often came along with a superior phalanx that actually carried the day. Greater impact by horsemen was really more a case of certain states and regions rich in cavalry (Athens, Boeotia, Thessaly, Macedon, Chalcidice, etc) being prominently involved. The Peloponnesians, in contrast, still relied almost exclusively on heavy infantry and remained weak in mounted forces throughout the war. Nevertheless, appreciation for cavalry was widely on the rise and even the Spartans saw fit to raise a few mounted units (albeit of dubious quality) by the later stages of the conflict.

Horsemen played critical roles in defeating hoplites at Spartolos, Solygeia, and Delium — some of the era's most important engagements. There were also actions waged largely or solely between mounted forces at Rheiti, Phyrgia, and Nisaea. All the same, the greatest impact of cavalry on pitched battle remained in either screening to limit losses among defeated friends or pursuing to inflict higher casualties on a beaten foe. And nowhere were these traditional roles more valued than at Athens. Athenian horsemen not only limited the deprivations of invading armies, but also contributed to offensive operations. Of particular note with regard to the latter is Athens's eventual use of purpose-built cavalry transports to enhance even its seaborne campaigns.

Much as per horsemen, light foot soldiers only rarely dominated on the field of battle in this period. In fact, armies who significantly outnumbered their opposition in foot skirmishers ended up losing nearly as often as they won (18 victories and 17 defeats). Nor do considerations of hoplite manpower negate these results, since larger forces of skirmishers fared little better in actions where heavy spearmen on each side were about equal in number, winning but 5 times in 9 tries. Still, though skirmishers usually played only a supporting role, they were decisive on a few occasions. Peltasts, bowmen, and slingers — alone or in combination — were key to besting phalanxes at Stratus, Aegitium, Spaectaria, and Mende, and helped cavalry to a landmark victory at Spartolos.

Actions carried mainly by light forces were relatively few and tend to get lost within overall results, but they do show growing influence of such troops on mainstream Greek warfare. The most astute among the era's generals certainly took note of this trend and made efforts to incorporate more horsemen and skirmishers among their troops. They often did this by hiring expert foreign fighters and we see a wide array of these taking part in battles of the period, including horse-archers (Scythians), peltasts (mostly Thracians), foot bowmen (Black Sea region), slingers (both Greek and foreign), and other auxiliaries from the barbarian northwest. Therefore, while hoplites remained very much at the core of Grecian tactical thinking, any commander worth his salt now took hard account of his capability in light arms.

Of course, generals of the Archidamian War did much more than rely on the physical advantages of their armies and also employed a wide variety of special tactics. Corinth and especially Athens pursued amphibious operations, while use of terrain, both man-made and natural, was widespread. Of particular note among the latter were hidden deployments, with armies forming up behind a hill at Delium and within the walls of Amphipolis. Also, employment of tactical reserves came into play a few times.

Yet the most effective stratagems continued to involve the element of surprise. The subject era saw surprise attacks and trick field maneuvers deliver 11 victories at a cost of but two defeats. (Losses came at Mylae, when an ambush was exposed before it could be sprung, and at Solygeia, where Corinth's use of a tactical reserve was trumped by Athenian cavalry.) Doing the unexpected was so effective that six of nine losses taken by armies with hoplite superiority were to opponents employing surprise tactics. It's notable that the use of surprise attacks and maneuvers during the ten-year span of the Archidamian War exceeded that of the preceding seven decades combined. This is true not only in terms of absolute number (13 times versus 10), but as to rate as well (32 percent against only 15 percent). It's clear that generals of this era had grown more familiar with such ploys and were much less restrained in exercising them.

Whether making better use of light forces or exploiting surprise, Greek commanders of this period showed themselves to be a new, more creative breed. This in part reflected a broadening of the leadership franchise to meet the demands of a more enduring and widespread conflict than those of times past. In Sparta, the traditional role of kings and regents was to lead major campaigns, while selected members of the spartiate class undertook lesser efforts. Thus, Archidamus and then his son Agis conducted their polis's main levy into Attica and left smaller expeditions for others. But royal commanders saw little combat in this war when their attempts to come to grips with the Athenian phalanx proved futile. At the same time, the long term and wide scope of the conflict gave plenty of opportunity for commoner generals like Brasidas to gain fame and glory (or, per Cnemus and Eurylochos, prove wanting).

Nor was Sparta the only state with noteworthy generals during the Archidamian conflict. Demands brought on by broad campaigns over a long period also caused Athens to spread command among an unusually large number of men. While none would win the sort of universal praise that Cimon had enjoyed earlier in the century, an array of competent leaders did emerge. These were quite varied in their talents and approaches. Thus, we see unimaginative but sound officers like Laches; men like Nicias, who was cautiously effective; and still others like the creative and risk-prone Demosthenes. As for Spartan and Athenian allies, these too had some outstanding generals, including Lycophron of Corinth and Pagondas of Thebes. More than their predecessors, these men displayed distinctive styles with strengths and weaknesses that could significantly affect battlefield results.

As a final set of observations, the Archidamian War's many battles yield a sizeable database that allows for informed observations on the combat value of home ground. Among actions involving sovereign defense, the local force won about as often as it lost, with 19 victories and 18 defeats. Where neither side had a significant edge in hoplites, the home record was evenly balanced at 4 victories and 4 defeats. This all goes to support the idea that engaging on one's own soil was a neutral element; indeed, armies of the 5th century down to 421 B.C. did little more than break even on native soil (46 wins and 45 loses). Yet a closer look actually shows two patterns present—one favoring homeland fighting and the other putting it at disadvantage.

Local forces did well exploiting intimate knowledge of their own land to set up sneak attacks and ambushes, or to gain support from architecture or landscape. Armies using such tactics won 12 times and lost only twice. These results are much like those during the Persian and Carthaginian invasions, which saw defenders exploit terrain to inflict some stunning defeats on invading armies. Clearly, when the Greeks could choose favorable sites for engagement, they truly did derive an edge from fighting near home. But there was another side to homeland defense. If combat didn't involve an ambush, sneak attack, or terrain features, then it usually was the foreigners who prevailed, coming away with 16 victories in 23 engagements — a nearly 70 percent rate of success. It seems that during this era, just as for the Pentacontaetia, those sitting on the defensive near home were at considerable psychological disadvantage against an aggressive invader. Detailed knowledge of contested ground was undeniably of great benefit; nonetheless, it was still a very damaging thing to have a soldier's vulnerable property and family too close to hand.

* * *

With fundamental frictions that led to the Archidamian conflict unresolved by the Peace of Nicias, Greece was destined to once more descend into the maelstrom of war. Both Spartan and Athenian armies soon took the field to fight for the same old causes — Sparta to preserve its hegemony and Athens to extend its empire. Although the peace accord would stagger along for eight years, it never evolved into anything with lasting effect.

VI

Daring and Destruction: The Peace of Nicias and the Sicilian Invasion (421–413 B.C.)

> "They were beaten at all points and altogether ... everything was destroyed, and few out of many returned home. Such were the events in Sicily."
> Thucydides (*The Peloponnesian War*)

The Peace of Nicias had no real chance to succeed. Many of Sparta's supporters refused to accept the terms and this resulted in troops from these balking states refusing to return important properties to Athens as agreed. Each among Sparta's allies had its own reasons for obstructing the settlement. Elis and Mantinea were embroiled in land disputes with Sparta in the Peloponnese and neither wanted to deal with an opponent no longer distracted by war. Corinth was equally hostile to an accord that would leave its colonies at Corcyra and Potidaea in Athenian hands, while much the same was true for Megara, as the treaty wouldn't recover its port of Nisaea.

Even well outside the Peloponnese, prospects for peace weren't good. Thebes had made gains in central Greece as Spartan offensives into Attica and its own success at Delium kept the Athenians at bay. The Thebans therefore rejected terms that would leave Athens free to once more pursue its ambitions in Boeotia. The Chalcidians took a similar stance in the far north, where their federation had gained greater independence as Athenian influence waned. They quite sensibly had no desire to see Athens getting a chance to rest and rearm, fearing that it would again move to take a stranglehold on their land. This led them to strike hard at the proposed terms by refusing to abandon Amphipolis, therefore insuring that the route for Athenian grain supplies remained at hazard. Of course, after Sparta failed to deliver Amphipolis, Athens retaliated by holding fast to Pylos.

The Spartans saw that it was hopeless to force their rebellious allies into line and offered an alternative to Athens. They proposed a defensive pact that was to last for 50 years. This would allow each great power to pursue selfish interests without fear of attack by its strongest foe; in fact, they could now proceed in expectation of help from that other dominant force should their homeland come under threat. Athens was just as tired of fighting as Sparta and, under the influence of Nicias and others, accepted this surprising alliance. Greece passed then into a mode where smaller disputes were dominant as lesser poleis continued to contest eschatia. Yet this was to prove no more than a brief interlude, since the same frictions that had triggered the Archidamian War were still very much in play.

A Bloody Peace

Because our surviving documents covering the late 5th century tend to concentrate on issues surrounding the major struggle between Sparta and Athens, we have but a hazy and incomplete view of other events in the Greek world. Clearly, the petty fights over borderlands that so typified Grecian culture were still going on, as were disputes between Greek colonists and native tribes. These formed a background chatter of violence that our surviving sources largely take for granted and rarely bother to note. We know that the Greeks engaged in at least three such traditional contests in central Greece and southern Italy during the early years of the Peace of Nicias. However, there surely were many other "little wars" in this period of which no record survives.

Phocis/Locris, Heraclea, and Cumae (421–419 B.C.)

Phocis lay above the Gulf of Corinth and west of the Boeotian plain, a mountainous land sandwiched between Opuntian Locrians to the north and settlers from that same race to the southwest in Ozolian Locris. The Phocians were a collection of pastoral tribes that lived in small villages scattered along valleys north and south of Mount Parnassos. These people had come together by the end of the 6th century to form a federation, allowing them to function as a unified state that could concentrate the efforts of its widespread communities for the welfare of all. Perhaps most important of these group projects was pooling of the various tribal levies into a national army.

Though we have very few details on the nature of the Phocian army, it does appear to have been like most others among the Greeks in its strong hoplite orientation. We know that Phocis sent 900–1,000 spearmen to Leonidas at Thermopylae in 480 B.C. and 1,000 to Mardonios at Plataea a year later. Supposing that these likely were partial (two-thirds) levies, the federation might have had around 1,500 prime hoplites and some 400 more in old-age and youth reserves. There was also a group of wealthier landowners that supplied cavalry. A good guess at Phocian mounted strength, using Boeotia as a model, is that something like 100 riders could normally be put into the field. Yet spearmen and cavalry were only part of the story. Phocis was not a rich land and its dominant population of herdsmen could afford neither cavalry nor heavy panoply. Skirmisher manpower might therefore have rivaled or even surpassed hoplite numbers. While most of these poorer men used the javelin, some also carried a sling, a popular weapon among pastoral peoples.

Land disputes with the Locrians along both upper and lower frontiers were common for Phocis, with one such clash leading to open warfare in 421 B.C. Some particulars cited by Diodorus show this to have been a typical fight for eschatia that climaxed in a test of phalanxes. Our sources fail to reveal which Locrian group was involved, but it seems most likely to have been Ozolian Locris to the southwest (McInerney 1999, 193–194). In that case, the contenders waged war for control of grazing land on the slopes of Mount Parnassos and must have fought the decisive engagement on a plain below those rugged pastures.

We know little about military potential among the southern Locrians beyond their provision of 500 light footmen to the campaign against Amphilochian Argos in 426 B.C. Since this muster was made under duress, it's reasonable to assume that it represented only part (perhaps between a third and half) of available light-armed men. An estimate of hoplite strength for Locris is even more speculative. Diodorus claimed that more than 1,000 Locrians (presumably all hoplites) died in the pitched battle of 421 B.C. This is an impossibly high figure for an action that couldn't have been of more than modest size. Given that the population of Locris was probably no larger (and more likely somewhat smaller) than that of Phocis, the number that Diodorus pulled from his sources is best seen as being the full levy of spearmen and not just those killed. If so, we might reasonably put the phalanx of Ozolian Locris at 1,000–1,200 men. As for mounted troops, the northern (Opuntian) Locrians had cavalry and it seems fair to assume that their kin in the south developed this arm as well, though perhaps to a lesser extent than in Phocis.

Neither Phocians nor Locrians were fierce phalanx warriors; in fact, the hoplites of Phocis had a reputation for timidity — running from the Anopaia path above Thermopylae and avoiding action at Plataea. Therefore, once the contending armies came into shock contact, efforts along the main line of battle were probably not very intense and might well have featured more posturing than actual violence. Yet despite their lack of martial fame, the Phocians came away with victory, a result best attributed to othismos from superior heavy manpower. While the casualty figure given by Diodorus is not reliably precise, it does suggest a tradition that those defeated suffered grievous loss. This implies a hard pursuit that might have taken down 20 percent or more of those in flight.

Central Greece hosted one other documented battle for land during the Peace of Nicias. This took place near Heraclea, Sparta's settlement on the east coast, which came under attack from some of its neighbors. Heraclea was a late foundation (426 B.C.) along the Malian Gulf south of Trachis and lay just above the Asopos River on a northern spur of Mount Oeta. As the colony sat only 8km below Thermopylae, it was well positioned to guard that important pass and so give its founding polis a greater say in regional affairs. Unfortunately for Heraclea, it faced a troubled life from the very start due to strong resentment among locals of longer standing, especially those to the north at Aenis, Malis, and into lower Thessaly. These enemies finally came together in winter 420–419 B.C. for a joint effort to drive out the newcomers.

Heraclea had sent 500 spearmen on the ill-fated expedition of Eurylochos only a short time after its settlement and this must have been a fully manned lochos similar to those of the colony's Spartan founders. As the city was already under threat from neighboring states, it would not have totally stripped its defenses to support such a distant venture. It's therefore likely that a second lochos, the other half of a mora-sized army, stood guard at home. The colonists might then have massed something like 1,250 spearmen (1,000 of prime age and 250 reservists) in a pandemic effort against the invasion. This Doric outpost would have had little or no cavalry, but could have supported its phalanx with a few hundred javelin-armed footmen from the poorer classes. Beyond simple manpower, the Heracleans could call upon the storied traditions of their Spartan ancestry to inspire discipline and confidence. They had to look no further for an embodiment of those martial virtues than to their commander, Xenares, a seasoned spartiate who had come directly from the homeland to serve as governor (*harmost*).

The attackers descending on Heraclea would have held no more than a very modest edge in heavy infantry. Malis could field around 1,000 hoplites (per the levy it sent to Thermopylae in 480 B.C.) and Aenis must have brought several hundred more. And numbers aside, these men were for the most part of lesser quality than their opponents among the Spartan colonists, thus any real advantage they held lay in light-armed forces. A large contingent of Dolopian skirmishers from the highlands west of Thessaly had come down to join with the lowlanders to give them great superiority in light foot troops. Even more important, the invading army had the services of several hundred Thessalian riders. Backed by hamippoi, these were the best horsemen in Greece and posed a grave threat to an opponent sorely lacking in cavalry.

We have no detail of what took place on the field between the Heracleans and their northern opponents, but known tactical preferences and the mix of forces combine with recorded general results to suggest a likely scenario. Faced with a foe filed at eight shields deep, Xenares would have deployed his spearmen in phalanx over a front of equal width. He might have had to thin his files a bit to achieve this match, but was probably not unduly concerned about doing so, as he counted on the greater skill and grit of his hoplites to prevail over a formation manned by spearmen of lesser reputation. This was the sort of traditional approach to phalanx warfare that worked well in the horse-poor Peloponnese, where Xenares had learned his trade; however, it was a tactic steeped in hubris against opposition rich in cavalry on open ground. Once closed into shock combat, the hoplites from Malis and Aenis must have held fast just long enough for their edge in cavalry and light footmen to sweep the Heraclean right flank. The Spartan governor and his best men went down in the subsequent collapse of that wing, tearing apart the rest of their phalanx at an ultimate cost of perhaps 40 percent of those in its ranks. Heraclea was so devastated that it had to call in aid from Thebes to man its walls.

While the colonists at Heraclea had faced fellow Greeks, the settlers at Cumae in Italy had only a few months earlier come under attack from a competing wave of barbarians. Cumae was the oldest Greek colony in Italy and one that had been a dominant force in the west during the late 6th and early 5th centuries, though at this time it was somewhat past its prime. Located well up the shin of the Italian boot in coastal Campania, it served as forward post for the Greek presence in the west and now faced barbarian Samnites, who were sweeping down from the central highlands to conquer most of Campania. These warlike Oscan tribesmen had taken nearby Capua from the Etruscans in about 425 B.C. and were basing from there to threaten Cumae with the same fate.

The Samnites formed a federation of four tribes (the Pentri, Caudini, Hirpini, and Caraceni) and were the largest Oscan national grouping. Documented 5th-century manpower for similar Iapyian tribes suggests a field force in excess of 20,000 warriors. Each tribe might therefore have mustered something like 6,000 footmen (all heavy-armed, as skirmishers were not common among the Oscans) and a few hundred mounted nobles and retainers. Livy said a 4th-century army of 40,000 Samnites and Polybios gave them nearly 80,000 fighters in the late 3rd century, with 10 percent being cavalry. However, these numbers reflect the growth in population and greater access to pastures that came from long residence in Campania. The Samnites were still poor hill people in 420 B.C. and must have been lower in manpower at that time as well as poorer in horses than their lowland neighbors.

Samnite infantry relied on the javelin as its primary weapon, using it as both a missile and a short spear, though some men followed personal preference in carrying a longer, counter-weighted spear as well. A downward-curving saber similar to the Greek machaira was the secondary weapon of choice. Protective gear varied widely with a man's wealth, but always included helmet and center-grip shield (the oval scutum, sometimes trimmed flat on top to improve visibility). Livy indicated that Samnites used a single greave on the left leg that protruded beneath the shield in combat, but it's likely that most wore a full pair. Many could afford light armor for the breast as well, wearing a leather harness fitted with between one and three metal disks. Samnite horsemen also wielded javelins and a saber like their infantry comrades; however, though normally helmeted, they didn't use shields and rarely wore much body armor.

Cumae likely had a field army that was no larger than the one it mustered in the late 6th century, which Dionysius of Halicarnassus put at 4,500 foot (presumably all hoplites) and 600 horsemen. Some Cumaean light infantry must have mobilized as well in the current crisis, there being perhaps 1,000 skirmishers on hand (one for each five mid/upper-class spearmen and riders). Such a force was a bit smaller than even a single Samnite tribe and tiny compared to the entire tribal coalition. Despite this, the men of Cumae came out to fight a pitched battle, perhaps desperate to avoid a siege they had no prospect of enduring. Whether it was a calculated act of valor or merely a forlorn hope, their sortie ended in utter defeat.

Oscan warriors preferred fighting in open array, yet could engage effectively in close order when it suited them. Emboldened by massive superiority in numbers, they must have closed in a tight body on the Greeks standing before Cumae. Samnite shock formations were at their best when operating over rough ground, where internal division into small war bands of 400 men each allowed them to adjust for irregular terrain. Countering, the defenders of Cumae no doubt chose flat ground for their stand, since this was better suited to the stiffer ranks of their Doric phalanx. Other factors were that the Oscans had no specialist light foot soldiers and their horsemen were focused on shock combat (Head 1992, 41, 62). By taking advantage of both topography and their skirmishers, the Greeks likely were able to secure their flanks and focus on fighting along the front, where their hoplites could make optimum use of othismos. Still, the barbarians must have been too deeply filed for even the most ardent pushing attack to win through. The Samnites seem to have absorbed any opposing pressure, bled and exhausted the fronting hoplites, and then triumphed through main force, going on to then capture Cumae in short order.

Rising Conflict in the Peloponnese

The close of the Archidamian War came just prior to expiration of a treaty between Sparta and Argos. The Argives were eager to reassert their authority in the Peloponnese, but knew that this would be difficult if the Spartans were no longer hamstrung by a war with Athens. Argos therefore enlisted help from a league of allies that included Mantinea, Elis, and Athens. In early summer 419 B.C., this fresh alliance set about provoking Sparta. The campaign began with Alcibiades leading a small Athenian army into the Peloponnese to defame his city's still extant pact with the Spartans and flaunt the new tie with Argos. To their embarrassment, the Spartans didn't respond. Meanwhile, the Argives geared up for an attack on Spartan-allied Epidauros under the pretext that it had failed to pay an agreed fee for certain grazing rights. Sparta took action this time, sending out its army under Agis, one of the kings. However, having reached the border of Laconia, Agis determined that auguries weren't favorable and marched home, asking his allies to gather again at the end of the next month. This allowed the Argives to ravage Epidaurian territory, something they then repeated when Agis subsequently dismissed yet another army after failed sacrifices at the frontier. The Spartans were now in a tough spot. Their deal with Athens having clearly gone sour, they were facing a crisis of confidence among their allies. If they didn't take strong action and take it very soon, Sparta would lose all credibility as hegemon. Agis therefore marched out once more, determined this time to bring about a decisive trial of arms.

Agis set out for Phlius, which sat above the Argive plain, planning to join there with allied troops coming down from the north. His army counted around 8,000 hoplites from Sparta (a levy of over 4,000 plus 700 freed helots) and Arcadia (including 1,500 Tegeans) backed by a couple of thousand psiloi. Strong as this force was, Agis planned to boost it at Phlius with another 12,000 hoplites. Boeotians made up the largest group standing by in the north (5,000 spearmen and a large host of light foot troops, including 500 hamippoi alongside a like number of horsemen). Other hoplites came from Corinth (2,000), Sicyon and Megara (1,500 apiece), Phlius (1,000), Epidauros (800), and Pellene (200), each levy with a few psiloi. Adding these troops would give Agis an army such as Greece hadn't seen since Plataea more than half a century earlier.

The Argives were aware of the magnitude of the forces that Sparta was bringing against them, if not their exact numbers. Desperate to keep Agis from his rendezvous at Phlius, they hurried with local allies to cut off the Spartans before they got out of Arcadia. If they could overcome Agis's column, then there was every reason to believe that the larger army in the north would disband upon learning that its hegemon had been defeated. Arriving at Methydrium (about 20km west-northwest of Mantinea), forces of the Argive alliance set up on high ground, where they had a good view of every approach and could sweep down to block any Spartan advance.

Thrasyllis headed the Argive army as part of a team of five generals, leading an impressive host that drew a majority of its spearmen from Argos (4,000) and its subject territories (1,000 from Orneai and Cleonai as well as 400 or so from Mycenae and Tiryns). Allied hoplites came from Elis (3,000) and Arcadia (2,000 from Mantinea and others). These totaled over 10,000 spearmen, who joined with several thousand light foot troops to give Argos a slight edge in manpower. An additional force of 1,000 hoplites and, more importantly, 300 horsemen was on the way from Athens. As it turned out, these troops wouldn't arrive in time to be of any value.

When Agis saw the Argive position, he directed his troops onto a facing hill. It was clear that Argos had greater numbers and that it would be foolish to engage without taking advantage of reinforcements already at Phlius. Agis thus waited for sundown and escaped under cover of darkness, no doubt having his spartiates lead the way since they were accustomed to operating in poor light (Cartledge 2003, 71). The Argives didn't discover this ploy until dawn. Agis was by then well away to meet the rest of his allies and Thrasyllis could only follow in frustration.

Upon joining his allies in the north, Agis immediately prepared for a descent on Argive territory. He anticipated that the Argives would rush to intercept along the road that ran south past Nemea and thence through the Tretus Pass to Argos, which was the only direct path suitable for his allied cavalry. Agis prepared for this response by splitting his army into three columns for another night march. He assigned the Boeotians, Megarans, and Sicyonians to meet the Argives near Nemea, where they were to avoid battle and hold the foe by threatening any withdrawal with mounted attack. As this was happening, the men from Corinth, Pellene, and Phlius were to move south down a more rugged western route near Mount Kelussa, while the king took his Spartans, Arcadians, and Epidaurians along a path even farther west.

The Argives reached Nemea in the morning only to discover that they had once more been out-maneuvered. Recovering with surprising speed, they got back through the Tretus Pass quickly enough to keep ahead of the Boeotians in their rear. They then brushed passed the Corinthian column that was just now closing in on them from the west, killing a few Phlians in the process. Meanwhile, Agis had emerged well to the south and was ravaging the countryside above Argos in the vicinity of the village of Saminthus. This put the Argive army in trouble. Though it had broken clear of the enemy's northern divisions, it was now trapped between all three opposing elements. The Argives decided to move south on Agis as their best chance to break through to home.

Events soon revealed that leaders on both sides were uneasy about fighting such an important action under the circumstances at hand. Failure of his holding force on the Nemean road had left Agis and his lone column at severe numerical disadvantage and he was sensibly loath to risk his nation's army (and hence its future) at unfavorable odds. On the other side, Thrasyllis (if not all of his fellow generals) also harbored grave doubts about the wisdom of accepting combat, as there was great danger in the Argives' position despite their superior numbers.

While an edge in manpower gave a fair chance to defeat the foe now before them, it in no way guaranteed that this could be done swiftly against the notoriously stubborn Spartans. And any extended engagement would run the risk that other enemy forces still closing from the north might have time to come into play. Absence of the Athenians must have further fueled this concern, since it denied cavalry vital to scouting and screening key rearward approaches.

Thrasyllis concluded that discretion was called for in the current setting and thus made the first move by approaching Agis through an intermediary just as the armies were preparing to engage. This resulted in a four-month truce that let the Argives pass safely and freed the Spartans to release their allies and go home as well. However, while the opposing commanders had avoided an engagement neither wanted, they had done nothing to resolve hegemony in the Peloponnese. In fact, many in Sparta and Argos bitterly criticized the pact, with both sides bemoaning a lost opportunity for victory. Moreover, Spartan and Argive allies alike came forward to angrily question legitimacy of an agreement made without their consent or even consultation.

As a result of widespread condemnation of the truce made with Agis, the Argives and their allies returned to the attack near the end of summer. They launched an assault on the Spartan-allied polis of Orchomenos, northernmost of three major cities on the plains that coalesced along the eastern edge of Arcadia (Mantinea and Tegea lying in that order farther south along this same trend). Taking this town, they next marched on Tegea — a move not backed by Elis, which pulled its troops from the campaign. Sparta was aware by now of this growing threat and Agis led out an army to intercept the Argives. Prevailing attitudes left no room for either side to back down from a fight that would assign dominance in the Peloponnese for decades to come.

Mantinea I (418 B.C.)

The Spartan army that marched forth in August 418 B.C. was on a scale that Thucydides claimed had never been seen before. It had four of Sparta's five regular mora, with seven 512-man lochoi and one of 600 perioecian Sciritae from the northern frontier. (Chrimes [1949, 376] has made a sound argument that this Sciritae unit's size allowed for an extra team of lighter-equipped scouts.) Others present were Agis's bodyguard of 300 picked troops and a sixth mora (two lochoi) of reservists, which brought total Spartan heavy foot troops to just over 5,500. (Note that the claim of unprecedented size for this deployment is consistent with projections of 5,000 hoplites at Sepeia and Plataea, but doesn't fit Herodotus's 10,000-man count for the latter.) There was also a unit (likely 700 strong) of helot spearmen — neomodeis, who had taken up arms in return for freedom. Finally, Agis had 1,000 mercenary hoplites, these being called "Brasidians" due to some having served under Brasidas.

Our sources are somewhat unclear on details of movements leading up to the battle of Mantinea I. However, Kagan (1981, 109–123) has proposed a likely ordering of events that began with the Spartan host moving north along a route that went up the Eurotas River to Orestheum, which lay southwest of Tegea. Local allies joined at this point, including 2,000 Tegeans (a full levy) and perhaps 1,000 others from the rest of Arcadia. Learning that Elis had left the enemy camp, Agis decided to reduce manpower and limit exposure for his own polis by sending his Spartan reservists back to reinforce the mora standing guard at home. He still had over 9,000 hoplites plus thousands of psiloi; furthermore, word had gone out via Corinth for some of his northern allies to muster at Mantinea. Linking with these would double Agis's hoplite force (adding at least 2,000 Corinthians and 7,000 or so from Boeotia, Phocis, and

Opuntian Locris) as well as provide horsemen and more light foot troops. The Argives, however, moved swiftly to bring Agis to action before he could amass such an overwhelming force.

The Spartan king marched to make camp just southeast of Mantinea and set about spoiling the area, but the enemy countered rapidly and he was soon facing a hostile army aligned for battle on the slopes of Mount Alesion above his camp. Spearmen from Argos led the opposing phalanx with 1,000 elites (a unit formed in 421 B.C. and trained at state expense), five 500-man lochoi of regular militia, and a sixth lochos of reservists. Other hoplites came from Orneai and Cleonai (1,000 Argive perioeci), Athens (1,000, half being settlers from Aigina), and Arcadia (2,000, mostly Mantineans). These 8,000 heavies had support from 300 Athenian horsemen and about 1,500 light footmen.

Agis raced to draw up his phalanx and then advanced within stone's throw of the enemy, but then hesitated when a veteran on his staff cautioned against an uphill attack. Agis must also have realized that it would be reckless to fight without the rest of his allies, and thus pulled back to retire south onto Tegean land. The Argive League generals made no move to dispute this retreat, a lack of action that many disparaged. Yet their reluctance to attack seems entirely reasonable, since rushing against Agis would have pitted them against a larger opponent on neutral ground.

Still hoping to settle matters on the field of battle, Agis sought to entice his enemy onto the plain with a very unusual ploy. Mantinean territory sat on low ground at the north end of an enclosed basin, where even today rivers and streams cannot remove winter rain from the valley; instead, water drops into limestone sinkholes and escapes eastward below the surface into the Gulf of Argos (Higgins 1996, 70–73). Agis could plug or divert flow around a series of these natural drains just inside the border of Tegea, which would cause water to collect downslope to the north and flood Mantinean territory. (These sinkholes would see just such use in 385 B.C., when Sparta captured Mantinea by washing away its walls.) Disrupting the drainage posed no immediate danger, as there was little water about at end of summer, but it would eventually cause serious trouble and was sure to goad the opposition into action.

And, indeed, the Argive generals marched onto the plain with surprising speed once word arrived on these activities. Their advance was so swift, in fact, that it seems to have caught Agis unprepared as he returned from the work sites. It's likely that he thought it would take a day or two for the enemy to learn about what he was doing and a bit longer to formulate a response, but when his troops emerged from a wooded area just south of his former camp, they saw the Argives and their allies already grouped in fighting order. Agis hurriedly prepared for combat, passing word down his chain of command to deploy out of marching column into a north-facing line of battle.

Standing before Agis was a phalanx eight deep that stretched over a kilometer wide. Mantineans stood far right in their own country, with their fellow Arcadians and then the elite Argive "Thousand" completing the right wing. At center were the five regular lochoi from Argos plus their older men, which left the Argive perioeci and Athenians to fill out the line, with Athens's troops holding the far end. After some skirmishing, all light forces retired to the flanks of this heavy array, with the Athenian cavalry taking post beside their own hoplite levy.

Agis scrambled behind his skirmisher screen to form his own phalanx to a depth of eight shields, making it more than 100m wider than that of his enemy. Withdrawal of his light troops onto the flanks revealed that Agis had his small bodyguard far right with the Tegeans next in line; therefore, with the Tegean troops set to match the opposing enemy left, his elite Spartans were outboard and in position to guide an envelopment. Inside these men were the other Arcadians and then seven Spartan lochoi, making up a formation center that, at some 4,500 spearmen, was half again larger than its opposite number. Agis stood with the most rightward Spartan lochos, which included the Hippeus (best of the young spartiates) and their older mentors. Having dispatched his guardsmen to lead a flank attack, he must have chosen this spot to be close to the rest of his countrymen. Finally, the Spartan left was 2,300 hoplites strong, with the Sciritae on the outside and the Brasidians and neodamodeis in some combination toward the middle. Agis's left wing was thus the only element of his phalanx with fewer men than its opposition (the Argive right having 3,000 spearmen). It would soon develop that he meant this imbalance to be only temporary.

It must have been obvious to Agis that he held only a small edge in numbers and he sought to better his chances by exploiting unique Spartan talents for field maneuver. Well aware that both formations would naturally drift rightward, he sent an order around that his left-wing units should do all they could to keep in front of the enemy's right. At the same time, he instructed that the two lochoi immediately left of his own should wheel out of line during advance and shift westward along the rear. These could then swing back to fill between Brasidians and helots bearing left and the phalanx mid-section pulling right. It would then fall to Agis to mend his proximal line before making contact with the Argive center. He hoped by these maneuvers to eliminate any overlap of his left, remain favorably outboard on the right, and put all three parts of his phalanx (right wing, center, and left wing) at superior manpower to their opposition.

Each army must have closed in its distinct fashion — Argives and allies at speed with much clamor and passion, Spartans at a slow pace set by flute players. The entire Argive front drifted right and the Sciritae, Brasidians, and neodamodeis mirrored this movement, keeping directly before the opposing right wing. As expected, their leftward pull opened a gap within Sparta's phalanx as its main body kept on fading the other way. It was at this point that Agis's plan fell apart when commanders of the lochoi meant to fill this opening failed to respond. Understandably fearful of carrying out their instructions in the very face of the enemy, they continued charging ahead. Once realizing that his orders were being ignored, Agis sent word for those on his left wing to shift right as fast as possible that they might mend the rifted line, but it was too late and the Spartan formation lay in two pieces when its hard-driving foe smashed into contact.

The Mantineans and other Arcadians charged into the isolated Spartan left, fixing it as their elite Argive allies rolled through the gap and made a natural swing toward their right, pulling toward the shields of their line-mates and against the now exposed mercenary/helot flank. Both hired men and neodamodeis quickly gave way, taking the Sciritae with them to be chased rearward as far as their baggage train. However, it was quite a different story in the middle of the field and on the Spartan right. Argos's regulars and older men at center had put up but a brief fight before breaking apart. And once the always volatile Argives tossed shields and raced for safety, the men from Athens on their left were left struggling in desperation to avoid a deadly double envelopment. They broke clear at last, but with heavy losses that included the general Laches. In truth, escape of Argive and Athenian alike owed much to Agis's ability to keep his victorious army under discipline and turn it around so that he could rescue his own defeated left wing.

Agis swung his right wing and center about to face the Arcadians and Argives returning from their pursuit. Advancing in lock step, this reordered phalanx then struck the exposed right side of what was more of a celebrating mob than a coherent enemy formation. The Mantineans and other Arcadians were still badly out of order when this attack utterly shattered them; however, Argos's select troops fared much better, keeping together to make a fighting withdrawal. Heeding wise advice, the Spartan king avoided further injury by not pressing after these still-dangerous men.

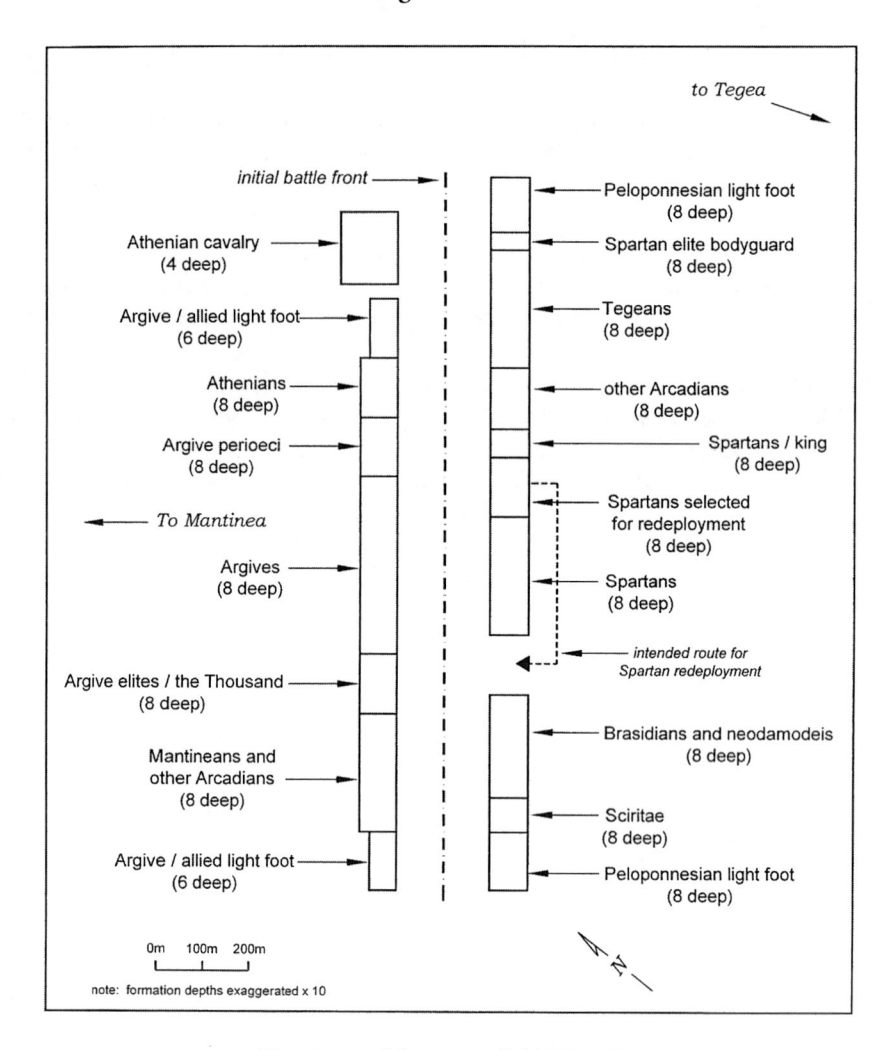

BATTLE OF MANTINEA I (418 B.C.)

Agis had been fortunate to escape his bungled initial maneuver with so solid a victory at small cost. Only 300 of his countrymen had fallen; mostly perioeci and helots, these added to loss of a few mercenaries and allies for a fairly modest butcher's bill. The Argives, on the other hand, had suffered heavily, leaving 700 citizen and perioeci spearmen (14 percent of those engaged) dead on the field. Their Arcadian allies got off a bit lighter at 200 hoplites killed (10 percent), but counted their general among the slain. Yet it was the Athenians who took the most severe damage, losing 200 spearmen (20 percent) from their small contingent. Such heavy casualties despite little pursuit reflect the terrible harm that even a partial encirclement could inflict.

Mantinea had clearly taken a harsh physical toll on the losing side. Yet psychological damage to Argos might have been even more telling, with the Argives feeling that they had neither the strength nor martial skill to compete with Sparta. This became evident when Spartan ally Epidauros invaded Argive territory shortly after the fight at Mantinea. Wounded and dejected, the Argives did nothing, leaving a response to Elis and Athens. Some 3,000 Elean and 1,000 Athenian hoplites marched on Epidauros during a religious celebration that sidelined the Spartans, but before they could invest the city, Argos came to terms with Sparta.

This put paid to the attack on Epidauros as well as the entire anti–Spartan league. Argos even went so far as to then help Sparta promote oligarchy in the Peloponnese.

Argos/Phlius, Mazaros II, and Melos (417–415 B.C.)

Oligarchic control at Argos proved short-lived when members of the popular faction gathered that summer under cover of a festival and fell upon the oligarchs at an opportune moment. After a fight in the streets, the democrats recovered their polis and set about putting some opponents to death and banishing others. Many of the latter took refuge nearby in Phlius. Sparta was slow to react, but finally took action after learning that Argos had again allied with Athens and was building long walls to secure its seaward supply line from siege. Agis moved out in winter 417–16 with an army of Spartans and allies that tore down these walls and took outlying Hysiae before withdrawing. Too weak to strike back at Sparta, Argos instead raided Phlius that same winter, looking to punish the harboring of exiles.

The Argive army that marched on Phlius must have been smaller than the one that fought at Mantinea, which was a result not only of casualties, but also of losing oligarchic manpower. Some 1,000 Argive hoplites had supported the Spartan campaign to boost oligarchy and at least that many must have died or gone into exile during the democratic coup to reduce the militia to something like 2,000 veteran spearmen. Calling up youths now of age and promoting men from the lower classes would have brought the hoplite count up to no more than 2,500–3,000 (five lochoi of 500–600 men each). Still, Argos likely held a considerable advantage in manpower, since the Phlians and exiles could at best field only 1,500–2,000 heavy foot troops.

The Phlians sensibly took a defensive approach to warring against an enemy that had a much more powerful phalanx. They avoided pitched battle at bad odds and kept behind their walls, with the pain of invasion lessened due to this being a winter campaign with no crops exposed. Truth be told, this strategy probably wasn't all that displeasing to Argos; after all, risking a heavy defeat in the field, no matter how improbable, was poor policy in light of the ongoing threat posed by Sparta.

The Argives seem to have split up their army upon meeting only passive resistance, the better to essay a series of hit-and-run assaults at widespread points. Phlius replied to these attacks by awaiting safe opportunities in the months that followed to strike back in kind at Argive assets across the frontier. This led to a desultory war of raid and counter-raid, with the Argives gathering to invade again in force that following summer. However, this time the defenders were able to make a stronger response. When Argive lochoi separated to once more spread damage about the countryside, one of them walked into a well-laid ambush. A force of Phlians and exiles took these invaders by surprise, routing them and killing 80 hoplites (13–16 percent). Costly as this defeat was to Argos, it didn't put an end to the conflict, which was to drag on for another two years (a last Argive incursion coming in 414 B.C.).

The Argos/Phlius affair was a minor clash that grew directly out of the broader struggle between Sparta and Athens. Yet in Sicily, which had stayed out of the fighting since departure of the Athenians in 424, a contrasting sequence emerged where a small war sowed the seeds of a greater conflict. This all began with an eschatia dispute during summer 416 B.C. that brought Selinous and Egesta in western Sicily once more to blows over land along their common border on the upper reaches of the Mazaros River. The Selinutians had crossed from the south to claim territory held by Egesta and then gone on to greatly expand their foothold. When diplomatic efforts had no effect, the Egestaeans marched out in force and ejected these interlopers. This soon led to a pitched battle on the contested ground, which Selinous won at steep cost to those defeated. The work of Diodorus, our main source on this incident, offers little tactical detail, but the action likely featured a strong Selinutian army of around 2,500 hoplites routing no more than 1,500 armored footmen deployed by Egesta. The unusually heavy casualties inflicted on the losers suggest a very thorough pursuit.

Reeling from their losses, the Egestaeans appealed in vain for help from Acragas and Syracuse, and an embassy to Carthage did no better. Egesta then found common cause with the Leontines. Syracuse had taken over Leontini and driven many from the city. Eager to win back their polis, those ousted joined Egesta that winter in sending to Athens for aid. The Leontines traded on the Ionian heritage that they shared with the Athenians and asked that Athens lead a crusade against Syracuse on behalf of all Ionians on Sicily. They sweetened the proposal by offering to pick up most of the cost of this campaign. The Egestaeans then pooled what they had and borrowed from their neighbors to dazzle Athenian representatives with a phony display of wealth. Deceived by this show and prompted by a desire for Sicilian conquest, the Athenians agreed after only brief debate to launch an invasion in summer 415 B.C.

Athens had grown more vaunting than ever in its imperial ambition and greed as a decade and a half of deadly war had served to harden, rather than humble, these dangerous drives. The arrogance and high-handed approach of the Athenians are nowhere better seen than in the ruthless treatment given at this time to the Spartan colony on Melos in the Cyclades chain. Athens sent out a fleet to ferry a large expedition against this island during the summer of 416 and the force that came ashore was overwhelming, possibly having more than 3,000 hoplites backed by archers (both mounted and on foot). Dismissing all appeals to fair justice with an argument that "might makes right" (famously documented in the fifth book of Thucydides' history), Athens besieged the badly outmatched islanders in what can only be described as a display of naked aggression. After gallant resistance (twice breaking through enemy lines for supplies), the Melians suffered treachery inside their walls and finally chose to surrender. The Athenians showed no mercy, slaughtering all the island's men and selling the women and children into slavery. If nothing else, this shameful episode gave fair warning to Syracuse of what a defeat would likely hold in store.

Assault on Syracuse

Athens swiftly mustered a powerful armament for Sicily. This began with a fleet that had 100 Athenian triremes — 60 of the best new hulls fit for combat plus 40 older ones as transports and another 34 warships from allies. In all, these vessels carried 5,100 hoplites, with 2,200 from Athens (mostly middle class, but including 700 marines drafted from among the poor), 2,150 allied militiamen, and 750 soldiers of fortune (500 from Argos — likely epilektoi — and the rest from Mantinea). Hired troops were also at the core of the expedition's light infantry, which made up 20 percent of all dedicated combatants. These were 480 archers from Crete, 700 Rhodian slingers, and 128 Megaran exiles with javelins. A small cavalry unit was present as well. Having embarked only 30 riders and their mounts aboard a single horse carrier (a 60-oared *hippagogos* or *hippegos*), the Athenians were clearly restricting this arm in light of both carrying capacity and travel distance. Yet they don't seem to have been concerned about a lack of horsemen, no doubt planning to make up any shortage with local recruits.

Nicias, Alcibiades, and Lamachus held joint command when the expedition first set out from Athens. This trio was highly diverse in ideology. Alcibiades was a bold proponent of the Sicilian enterprise, while Nicias had openly opposed it. Lamachus served to mediate between these two, voting with one or the other so as to prevent deadlock. As it turned out, this curious and potentially volatile leadership structure didn't last long. A charge of sedition (likely trumped up by political foes) caught up with Alcibiades shortly after arriving in Sicilian waters and he fled into exile at Sparta.

The Athenians met a number of disappointments early on in their Sicilian campaign. First, there was a general reluctance among most local cities to join into alliance (Rhegion, Messana, and Camarina remained neutral, while Catana had to be forced into cooperation). Then it became apparent that the promised wealth of Egesta was a fraud. Finally, initial raids along the eastern coast of Sicily cost a number of light-armed men when Syracusan cavalry arrived to drive off a landing party. The subsequent departure of Alcibiades did nothing to improve this frustrating situation. Nicias and Lamachus now decided to split up, the former working with the Egestaeans in the south as the latter sortied along the island's northern shore. Neither gained much success, with Nicias coming up short in an assault on Hybla and Lamachus taking a minor port, but failing to gain Himera. The generals reunited near Catana in the fall, where they set up camp, added some Sicel allies, and worked to devise a better plan of action.

Anapus River (415 B.C.)

The problem for Nicias and Lamachus was how to strike against Syracuse without taking unacceptable losses during the initial approach. They hadn't done well recruiting horsemen and their enemy's vastly superior mounted forces could have exacted a costly toll from any overland move. Trickery and naval mobility provided the solution to this dilemma. A man from Catana took on the role of double agent by going to Syracuse and making a false offer to betray the Athenians. As this fellow claimed to speak on behalf of known and trusted men, the Syracusans imprudently took him at his word and marched by night to prepare a dawn assault on the Athenian stockade. Meanwhile, Nicias and Lamachus sailed out with all their forces to land unopposed at daybreak just south of the Anapus estuary, below the main harbor and near the coastal road that ran down to Helorus. Syracusan horsemen had reached Catana by this time, only to discover their foes long gone. They quickly rode back to their approaching infantry with this startling news and then joined the van in a race for home. The wayward army got back late in the day to find its missing opponents not only disembarked, but having already destroyed the main bridge across the Anapus, built a camp with palisade, and erected a stout fort. The Syracusans regrouped, spending the night on the north side of the river in position to launch an attack next day that would drive the invaders into the sea.

Morning light revealed that the Athenians had chosen their ground well. They had negated Syracuse's cavalry by anchoring against a slope on the landward side and amongst a mixture of man-made structures, trees, and marshland to shoreward. The Athenians had put all their hired hoplites nearest the beach, some of their own militia spearmen (1,200 strong) at center, and the best of their allies (600 hoplites) on the inland left. Since a variety of barriers already provided flank protection, their javelinmen (both Greek and Siculi), archers, and slingers took post at the rear, where they could arc missiles over onto an enemy approach. Deploying on such a short front let Athens's spearmen array at eight shields deep using only half their number. This freed the rest of their heavy corps (1,000 Athenian and 1,550 allied hoplites) to shield the camp and fleet from cavalry, while at the same time standing ready to back any part of the phalanx that might falter, or form a final redoubt should the entire front give way.

The Syracusans had some 5,000 hoplites, equal to Athens's entire invasion force and twice those now in formation across the Anapus. Expecting the foe to remain in their current defensive position, the Sicilians arrayed in files of 16 and prepared to ford the stream. Once across, their phalanx could match the enemy front of just over 300m at a double depth that promised a decisive edge in othismos. Syracuse's own spearmen held post from right wing through center at about 4,000 strong (a full levy sans reservists), while allies filled out to the left at a strength of a bit over 1,000 spearmen, the largest allied contingent being from Selinous. Because terrain across the river denied a normal flank deployment, all mounted troops stood at the right rear, including riders from Syracuse (about 1,000), Gela (200), and Camarina (20). Narrow ground would also keep light footmen off the flanks and these were therefore set to open action at the front, but then retire to await a decision between the heavy divisions.

Since the Syracusans anticipated making the first move, they seem to have been in no great hurry to get into order; thus, many were still arriving at posts in the rear when the Athenian phalanx suddenly began to advance. The Sicilians scrambled to respond and must have sent skirmishers out to meet their opposite numbers and buy some time. Meanwhile, Nicias and Lamachus led their hoplites aggressively forward, keeping their right flank anchored on coastal marshland while abandoning the shelter that high ground had previously given to the left end of their line. They no doubt covered this risky move by assigning all their missile troops to shield the lone exposed flank. Easily out-ranging enemy javelins, Athens's bowmen and slingers would have screened the left side of their phalanx as it crossed the Anapus (shallow and easy to ford in October) to close into shock combat with the Syracusans.

Allied spearmen on the Athenian left wing held their own against Syracuse's best men in the early stages, which gave the Peloponnesians on the right and Athenians at center a chance to carry the day. In fact, having been taken off guard by their enemy's sudden advance, it's a tribute to the toughness of those standing for Syracuse that they didn't swiftly break contact; instead, they put up a long and determined fight. Stabbing and shoving, they were able to take advantage of superior numbers to offset both their initial surprise and the foe's greater combat experience. Nevertheless, allies on the Syracusan left must have been near the very limit of their courage and panicked when a violent thunderstorm unexpectedly burst overhead. The Argives and Mantineans drove through these terrified men, and Athens's hoplites soon did the same to the now-exposed Syracusans in the center. Finally, with most of their army running away, the Sicilian right wing pulled out as well.

Despite suffering a crushing defeat along the line of battle, Syracuse took only modest losses thanks to its cavalry—the victors being unable to break ranks in pursuit lest these horsemen isolate and cut them down. The retreating hoplites even managed to rally along the road to town and got back into good order before making their final withdrawal. Thucydides set Syracusan losses at a mere 260 hoplites (5 percent of those involved), and even Diodorus's higher estimate of 400 killed (8 percent) would have been far from crippling. As for the Athenians, they lost just 50 spearmen (2 percent), but their lack of mounted forces had denied a decisive victory. This left Nicias and Lamachus outside the walls with little gained beyond temporary bragging rights. The Syracusans still had plenty of men to hold their city and could look upon the Anapus fight as no more than a minor setback.

The Athenians now faced the need to invest Syracuse; however, the same lack of horsemen that had prevented them from exploiting success in battle also forestalled a siege. Blockading the city required building a lengthy wall to cut off its landward side at the same time that the fleet sealed seaward approaches, but Athens's missile troops, though adequate for pitched battle, couldn't protect widespread work parties from mounted attack. This needed a strong counterforce of cavalry, something that could be obtained only through a lengthy process of local recruitment and/or importation of riders from home. Nicias and Lamachus therefore had little choice but to re-embark and find a safer campsite, where they could regroup and come up with a plan for launching an effective assault on Syracuse in the spring. They therefore sailed north to Naxos and set up for the winter.

Terias River and Euryelus (414 B.C.)

Winter 415–414 passed with both sides preparing for another round of fighting. The Syracusans used this time to reinforce their defenses, while the invaders made a failed attempt on Messana and sent to Athens for more horsemen and cash. Some Siculi from the interior rallied to the Athenian cause and a few in the coastal area were coerced to join in as well, though most lowlanders remained neutral with help from Syracuse. However, it turned out that the most critical developments for Sicily at the moment were taking place back on the Greek mainland.

Corinth was eager to aid its colony at Syracuse, yet the Spartans were slow to take an action that might reopen festering wounds from the Archidamian War. Weakening its forces at home was always a concern for Sparta, and there was extra peril in doing so at present due to a fresh dispute with Argos. The Spartans might have to go into action in the Argolid and wanted to husband their manpower for that possibility. Still, though Sparta was unwilling to commit its own troops, it did agree to send a military advisor. The man chosen was Gylippus, son of the exiled Cleandridas, who set off with a fleet that eventually reached 18 triremes, including 12 from Corinth and two each from Leucas, Ambracia, and Sparta itself (perioecian ships). Fully loaded, these would have carried some 720 hoplites.

Meanwhile, Nicias and Lamachus had found Naxos to be less than ideal as a winter camp and moved back to Catana. They then sailed out in early spring for an attack on Megara Hybla, just southeast of Syracuse, hoping to turn it into a forward base. This assault failed when it couldn't dislodge the Syracusan garrison of a key fort. Giving up, the Athenians retired northward toward Catana, with a substantial contingent marching along the beach and the rest keeping pace offshore aboard the fleet. When the land column reached the mouth of the Terias River, which divided the territories of Syracuse and Catana, it sent a party of retainers and skirmishers upstream to burn enemy grain fields on the south side of the border. The invaders apparently took care to support this sortie with a potent escort (most likely a 500-man lochos of either Athenians or Argives backed by all available horsemen), which soon went into action against a detachment that had come up to protect the crops. Unlike the earlier mounted interception, it seems to have been foot soldiers who responded here — perhaps part of the garrison that had just prevailed at Megara Hybla. A combat ensued along the Terias that must have been a modest affair involving no more than 1,000 hoplites on both sides combined. A fairly even match in terms of numbers, this engagement likely turned on the greater experience and confidence of those fighting for Athens. After killing a few Sicilians and running off the rest, the victorious escorts set up a trophy and then returned to the beach, where everyone boarded for Catana.

The small body count among those defeated along the Terias reflects the same lack of adequate cavalry for pursuit that had reduced the value of Athens's victory on the Asopos. This problem was probably endemic to operating in so distant a theater, since it was impractical to ship large numbers of mounts over that great a distance and recruiting of local horsemen was an inefficient process. In the end, Nicias had to combine what local cavalry he could find with riders imported from home, with 250 Athenian cavalrymen landing at Catana in the spring of 414 B.C. under Callistratos, who brought enough silver to buy mounts. A Scythian contingent of 30 mounted archers arrived at the same time to provide a critical missile screen for the regular, javelin-armed riders. Unlike their Athenian counterparts, these mercenaries came with their own horses aboard what might have been the same transport used in 415. A fine mounted force was finally taking shape, but was not yet ready for action. It therefore fell to Athens's hoplites to deliver the next major blow against Syracuse, moving to once more catch their foe by surprise with an amphibious landing under cover of darkness.

Epipolae ("Overtown") was a low, sparsely populated plateau that ran above the northern wall of Syracuse and extended for about another 4km inland. Nicias and Lamachus had realized that these heights would be of great use in the coming siege and developed a plan for seizing them. But some hint of their scheme must have leaked out, as the city's leadership suddenly became concerned for the first time about security for this high ground. A team of three elected generals (Hermocrates, Heraclides, and Sicanus) now had charge of the garrison and they called for a morning review of hoplites on open ground along the Anapus. A major aim of their meeting was to choose 600 men for an elite reserve lochos to defend Epipolae and other essential points. Diomilus, an exile from the Greek island of Andros and probable mercenary, was to lead this picked unit.

There seem to have been few secrets in either camp and the Athenians apparently got wind of the planned gathering on the Anapus in much the same way that their own plans for Epipolae had become known. Nicias and Lamachus took preemptive action by making a night landing with their entire host at an inlet just above Epipolae. They ran to climb paths on the northern side of the plateau at Euryelus, which stood where the tableland narrowed toward the west, and then marched to take post atop slopes to the south. These had a scaleable grade that provided an approach for men in formation to assault the heights. Having delivered its army, Athens's fleet retired nearby to the north, beaching along the Bay of Thapsus and throwing up a protective palisade.

When the Syracusans found out that their enemy was on Epipolae, they rushed toward Euryelus with Diomilus and his freshly chosen lochos in front. Though caught off guard and somewhat winded by rapid marching, the Syracusans gamely prepared to go into action. Having some 5,000 spearmen, they started up the rise with the hoplites of their new elite unit in the leading rank of a phalanx that must have filed eight shields deep. Meanwhile, the Athenians waited patiently on the crest in a similar array of about the same number of spearmen. As Syracuse's formation moved uphill over irregular ground, it grew increasingly disordered, which likely reflected not only a hurried march and difficult climb, but also an unstable mental state. Natural confusion inherent to such an unanticipated confrontation must have combined with discomfort over the unfavorable ground and shaken confidence from the Anapus defeat to deal a heavy blow to morale.

A wall of Athenian hoplites met the struggling Syracusan charge just as it reached the top of the slope. No doubt assured in their superior prowess by past success against this same opponent, the invaders lunged into battle, using elevation and tighter order to drive down and through the ragged ranks of their enemy. Many at the fore for Syracuse must have fallen victim to spear thrusts, with their bodies slipping downslope to further disorder the files behind. It would have taken mere minutes of such punishment to force back the attackers and fill them with fear, shattering any remnant of cohesion and sending the Syracusans stumbling downhill in a frenzy to escape. The Athenians now rolled over the enemy front fighters, slaughtering all who tried to hold their ground. Standing in the first rank, Diomilus and others from his picked lochos made up a hefty share of the 300 or so Syracusans slain that day. Without encirclement or extended chase, the Athenians couldn't have killed 50 percent of their opponents regardless of relative manpower, and it's more likely that the reported deaths represent 6 percent lost from the entire Syracusan army — a rate typical for a defeated phalanx that had suffered little or no pursuit. As for the victors, our sources don't preserve a figure, but their loses must have been very modest.

Having taken a reverse every bit as heavy as that dealt them on the Anapus, the defenders withdrew behind their horsemen, who had been holding station below on the flats. The Athenians set up a trophy and briefly descended to flaunt their victory before the city walls. They then retired to set up camp on Epipolae, building a fort on the north side at Labdalum, from where they could signal their fleet at Thapsus. Rather than the wasted effort a year earlier on the Anapus, Euryelus was really the first critical engagement in the fight for Syracuse. Poor initial planning had delayed things for nearly a year, but a siege was now finally underway.

Syca and the Lysimeleia Counter Wall (414 B.C.)

The Athenians planned to isolate Syracuse with a wall and it was vital that men working on this barrier remain safe from mounted attack. And while hoplites and light infantry were of use for this, a counterforce of cavalry was the real key. It had taken much longer than expected, but Nicias and Lamachus had at last gathered enough horsemen to shield their construction crews, fielding 280 riders from Athens plus 300 allied horsemen from Egesta and 100 (Thucydides) to 250 (Diodorus) more from the Siculi, Naxos, and elsewhere. With these mounted assets in place, the Athenians erected a circular fort (*kylos*) on eastern Epipolae near Syca ("The Fig-tree"). This strong point was to form a central hinge for siege lines that would extend both north and south, curving to meet the sea on either side of the city for a complete landward seal.

The Syracusans didn't sit by idly as their foes worked. Desperate to stop or at least slow construction, they sallied with all their hoplites and riders through the nearest gate, which led to the main road along the southern base of Epipolae. They gained the heights along some nearby paths that included at least one suitable for horses. However, once before Syca, the Sicilian generals grew reluctant to accept battle after seeing that their men were both slow to order and poorly arrayed. Having already come out the worse in two major engagements, they seem to have decided against risking a third beating and withdrew. Syracusan cavalry covered this retreat and a portion remained on the heights to harass the laborers.

A 500-man tribal lochos of Athenian spearmen advanced with some of their own horsemen against the Syracusan riders, dispersing them and inflicting a few casualties. We have no record of just what role spearmen played in this action, but it's likely that they closed on the enemy as their cavalry provided flank cover and missile fire. Steady encroachment by the hoplite line pushed the Syracusans back at spear-point, denying them open ground in a drive toward the plateau edge. The horsemen had no choice in the end but to flee before their opposition could cut off all routes down slope. Victorious again, the Athenians set up yet another trophy—their fourth since landing on Sicily—and pulled back to resume building their wall.

The Athenian commanders set out to first run their rampart around the north end of Syracuse (blocking the way toward their anchorage at Thapsus). The lower arm of the siege line seems to have been a lesser priority and they extended it no farther than the south rim of the plateau. The Syracusans saw opportunity in this and began to throw up a stone counter wall; building their barrier from the city at a right angle, they intended to cut the path for future southern investments at a point just below Epipolae. This structure started out of a minor gate and was double-walled so as to be defendable on either side and allow builders to work with greater safety from within. A tribal lochos of spearmen protected the narrow open

216　　　　　　　　　　VI. Daring and Destruction

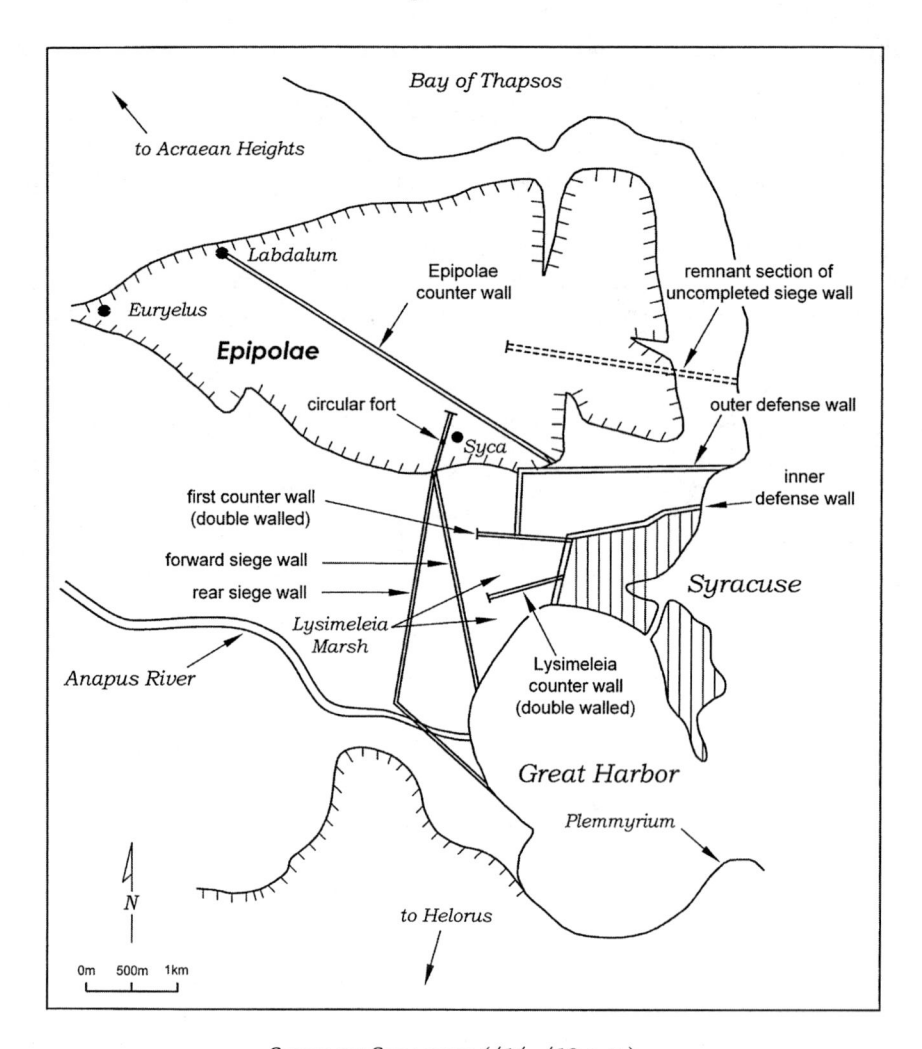

SIEGE OF SYRACUSE (414–413 B.C.)

end of this work, using a temporary wooden stockade that could be shifted forward as construction advanced.

Syracuse's first counter wall failed when a picked band of 300 Athenian and Argive hoplites stormed it. These spearmen and a few light-armed men chased off the stockade guards with ease, though they then suffered some minor casualties in unwisely trying to press a pursuit. The Athenians promptly began to tear down the stoneworks and carried off wooden stakes from the stockade for their own use. Nicias and Lamachus now realized that counter walls to the south posed a paramount threat to their plans and shifted all effort onto the previously neglected branch of the siege barrier below Epipolae. But the enemy started a second wall even farther south, where the wetlands of Lysimeleia would make approach difficult for an attacker. The marshy ground in this sector was far too soft to support the same kind of stone structure attempted earlier, so this new barrier consisted of a pair of ditches backed by wooden palisades. As before, a detachment of hoplites manned a moveable stockade set across the construct's open end.

The Athenians reacted swiftly to this latest menace, ordering their fleet into the Great Harbor and marching out before sunrise to assault the Lysimeleia counter wall. With their army standing by, the same select team of hoplites and light-armed troops that had led the successful attack on the first Syracusan barrier did the same for the second. These men stole up in predawn gloom, getting across swampy areas by laying down planks and old doors to provide firmer footing. They achieved complete surprise and quickly captured not only the terminal stockade, but most of the ditch-line as well. When daybreak found the enemy holding their new works, shocked and angry Syracusans overrode their generals' reluctance to risk battle.

Syracusan and allied hoplites sortied onto the road around southern Epipolae and deployed into phalanx formation, likely at eight shields deep. Their front would have covered some 500–600m, fixing its unshielded right against the plateau and its left along swampland to the south. Skirmishers and horsemen probably screened forward as this array was forming up and then fell back to secure the flanks and cover any retreat. But anchoring terrain on either side precluded a major role for Syracuse's cavalry and most of the horsemen therefore took up position across the marshes and near the Anapus River to picket southern approaches to their city. As these riders must have used the lowermost gate, the Athenians might not even have known that they were in play.

Watching the opposition organize, the Athenians would have adjusted behind their skirmishers to align 4–5,000 spearmen into a phalanx of similar proportions. Nicias had fallen sick and remained on Epipolae at the circular fort, which put Lamachus in sole command on the battlefield. He likely took post with the mercenaries and some Athenians on the left wing, his flank resting next to Epipolae and allowing him use of his crack troops against the enemy's best men on their right wing. This relegated his marines and allied troops to the center, with the remaining Athenian militiamen extending toward the marshes on the right. Athens's cavalrymen and light infantry had to have been in the rear of this formation, yet our sources are silent about them and it seems safe to say that they played no significant role in the day's events. Meanwhile, the detached squad that had taken the counter wall held its position on the captured stockade.

Channeling terrain would have joined with relatively short separation to eliminate any profound drift as the armies charged into violent contact and ground together along the entire front in a shock action dominated by othismos. Numbers were on a par, but the more seasoned men fighting for Athens undoubtedly held the upper hand in confidence; after all, they had bested these same spearmen at every opportunity to date. And it doesn't seem to have taken long for this differential in morale to have its effect, as the Syracusans quickly lost heart and gave way. Based on what happened next, Athens's center must have achieved a frontal penetration that sliced the opposition phalanx in two. Troops on the Sicilian right reacted by running straight toward the nearest city gate. Unfortunately for those on the Syracusan left, they couldn't follow, since the enemy's center division had pushed into the middle of the field to block their way. Their only escape lay toward the river, and they ran that direction with men from the Athenian right wing close behind.

The team holding the counter wall had watched all this unfold and saw the large body of Syracusans hastily making for the Anapus. They decided to try to reach a key bridge ahead of this crowd so as to cut off its retreat. This proved a serious mistake, as most of Syracuse's cavalry and hamippoi had responded at last to the mounting signs of battle and come up from monitoring arrival of the Athenian fleet at the Great Harbor. These horsemen suddenly fell upon the select team, which was strung out and exposed in its race to the bridge. Cutting down some of the startled footmen, the Syracusans chased the rest northwest and cleared the way for their infantry to escape across the Anapus. Desperately fleeing survivors from the picked team soon reached their comrades pursuing from the battlefield and rushed among them in a panic. The tribal lochos that had been leading the pursuit became badly disordered, and this confusion threatened to spread as the Sicilian riders arrived to press an attack.

Things were just as fluid on the northern end of the battlefield. Lamachus and his left wing had followed behind the retreating Syracusans, eager to inflict some real damage on them before they could get back inside their walls. But learning of the cavalry assault in the south, the Athenian general broke off with the hoplites from Argos and some archers to remedy that situation, leaving the rest of his troops to continue the chase. The Sicilians, seeing their foe split up and no doubt also aware that their cavalry was joining the fray, rallied to confront their pursuers with help from a few horsemen that had held the rear. At the same time, a portion of their force scaled Epipolae in hopes of destroying the siege works there. However, though a stretch of the outlying barrier fell victim to this attack, Nicias and a small band at the circular fort held firm until help could arrive. Down below, good order kept by the veteran Athenians during their pursuit allowed them to crash into the reorganized Syracusans for another victory. This forced the twice-beaten men to join those returning from Epipolae in fleeing back inside the city.

Even as his left wing put final touches on victory to the north, Lamachus and his scratch force of Argives and bowmen were going into action on the other side of the field. All was chaos there. During the rush to put his men to good use, the Athenian general and a few others crossed a ditch to find themselves cut off and under attack from horsemen. This isolated group died to the last man, with Lamachus taking his killer with him in a mutually fatal single combat. Despite their leader's death, the other Athenians recovered and their foes decided to back off, carrying away the bodies of Lamachus and his comrades. The victors set up a trophy and recovered the corpse of their general after the Syracusans asked for a truce to claim their own dead (who numbered 350 or so).

Now in sole command, Nicias rushed to complete two walls along the southern side of Syracuse. His men quickly carried these near the shoreline, with the inner/northern barrier running just below the Lysimeleia marshland and the outer rampart dropping down to where their fleet now lay repositioned on the southwest side of the Great Harbor. They also gathered stones to finish the northern stretch of their investment. An arrogant confidence seems to have taken hold among the Athenians at this point. Shrugging off the loss of Lamachus, they must have taken comfort in having soundly beaten their foe in three major battles and a couple of minor actions; thus, with circumvallation nearly complete, they felt that they were on the verge of final victory. Others were of the same opinion and food began coming in from Sicilians keen to curry the invaders' favor. Etruscans from Italy also arrived to support the campaign, with 150 of their hoplites rowing in aboard three small galleys.

As for the Syracusans, their morale had plummeted. New leaders had replaced their former trio of generals, and these began openly discussing surrender with Nicias. It was at this crisis point that help suddenly appeared, as a Corinthian trireme sailed in to announce Gylippus's expedition. This welcome news was as yet fresh when word came that the Spartan had already landed at Himera and was even now fast approaching overland. Reinvigorated, the city's defenders eagerly made plans to join him and go on the offensive.

Changing Fortunes

Gylippus had begun setting up a second line of defense in Italy. This reflected a false report that the siege walls at Syracuse were complete, thus cutting him off from joining the defenders. However, once he learned that the city was actually still open on one side, he sailed for Sicily in great haste. Landing at Himera, Gylippus had only the lead element of his fleet — four triremes carrying the Corinthian general Python and some 160 hoplites. The rest (14 vessels and 560 spearmen) had trailed him to Italy and were now to head directly to Syracuse. Indeed, it was the first of these ships that brought initial news of the relief effort. Gylippus picked up some local Greeks and Siculi and marched out with a force of 3,200 men. He had around 2,200 Greeks, with 700 from his fleet (all the hoplites plus some light-armed crewmen), 1,300 out of Himera (1,000 spearmen and 100 each of psiloi, horsemen, and hamippoi), and 200 from Selinous and Gela (riders with hamippoi). Some 1,000 Siculi footmen with gear ranging from light to heavy completed this small army.

Gylippus reached the western end of Epipolae without detection and led his men up the north side of Euryelus. Passing through the incomplete siege works, he then joined with the Syracusans, who had emerged with all their forces to meet him. This left the Athenians scrambling to get into combat array, the sudden appearance of the relief column and coordinated Syracusan sally having caught them unprepared. As the armies faced each other just in front of the investments across eastern Epipolae, Gylippus sent a herald to propose that the Athenians depart in peace. Nicias, having won every battle to date, treated this offer with contempt and readied his men to fight. Gylippus, however, saw that his local troops were having trouble getting lined up for combat and chose to retire eastward onto clearer ground. Nicias refused to follow; perhaps feeling that his horsemen would be no match in the open for the cavalry of Syracuse, he elected instead to hold close to his siege wall. Since Gylippus must have remained unsure about Syracusan moral and had yet to fully integrate his army, he was equally reluctant to force matters and cautiously descended to the city, where he spent the night consolidating his command.

Gylippus led his army out the next day to again confront the Athenians, taking care to keep his distance as he once more set up a phalanx at the more open eastern end of Epipolae. But this was merely a diversion. While Nicias and his men were watching Gylippus, a detachment from the city infiltrated their lines to capture the fort at Labdalum. Having secured this strongpoint behind Nicias, Gylippus then put his men to work on yet another counter wall.

Gylippus's counter work differed from its predecessors in being single-walled. This allowed for a much faster rate of fabrication, which was further accelerated by use of the Athenians' own building materials, these having been left strewn along the unfinished siege line. It was clearly intended that the new counter wall cross to Labdalum so as to cut off the Athenians on the southwest half of the plateau and put an end to their circumvallation. This construction's simpler design precluded defense from behind its own walls and a terminal stockade as before. The entire army therefore had to take the field to keep the Athenians at bay, standing in battle array on the northeast side of the advancing wall (inside its projected path and with a clear route back to the city). The Syracusans must have held post just behind the leading edge of the stonework and edged forward in pace with its progress.

Rather than attacking, Nicias chose to speed up his own works, building northward from Syca on a course that would run his barrier across the counter wall's path and render it useless. The two sides now raced to be first to extend their line past the projected point of intersection. It was a contest that would make or break the siege of Syracuse.

The Epipolae Counter Wall I and II (414 B.C.)

The wall-building race on Epipolae was a close-run affair, with neither side having a clear-cut advantage in the beginning. This seems to have led Gylippus into more aggressive tactics, attempting an armed intervention by leading his men in a nighttime assault on the still-rising enemy works. However, the Athenians were camped close by and able to quickly come to the defense of their wall. Gylippus was apparently unwilling to hazard a major battle in the dark and promptly pulled back. Nicias reacted to this aborted attack by raising the height of his barrier and taking care to put his best men at all of the most critical points along his perimeter.

Nicias seems to have remained confident of success on Epipolae and felt free to divert some of his resources elsewhere. Looking to support the maritime portion of the siege and further secure his seaborne line of supply, he fortified Plemmyrium, the headland opposite Syracuse to the south across the mouth of the Great Harbor. He then shifted his fleet to Plemmyrium, where it could better guard the enemy's anchorage across the way and counter any attempt to sail goods into the city. Rather less logically, he also decided to move most of his supplies there as well. This kept his stores at a hardened site near both fleet and landing point for resupply, but dangerously separated them from the army. Nor was this the only drawback. Plemmyrium lacked adequate fresh water, forcing supply teams to bring it in from afar under frequent mounted attack. It seems that despite having superior numbers, Athens's horsemen had been unable to contain their Syracusan counterparts — a third of whom (300–400) held station south of the city.

Gylippus led his army out on a daily basis to protect the counter wall even as the enemy lined up opposite in readiness to pounce should he then try to withdraw. The formations appear to have faced off across a 650m stretch that angled northeast from near the end of the counter wall toward remnants of the old siege works. Gylippus must have stacked his spearmen in files of eight, taking the right end of the line himself with 200 Corinthians (from his original four ships plus the one recently arrived at Syracuse). The best of some 4,000 hoplites from Syracuse and its allies could then stand at his side and on the far left, while the other locals and 1,000 spearmen from Himera filled in the center. The Athenians would have been opposed at six shields deep, having only about 4,000 hoplites after their losses to date and above garrisoning needs. The hired Peloponnesians and Athenian militia likely held the wings with their marines and allies at center. The long lateral barriers relegated the cavalry and skirmishers for each side to the rear.

Apparently sensing that the time was right, Gylippus signaled his phalanx forward. With both flanks anchored, the ensuing contest must have been one of front fighting and othismos that the more willful Athenians eventually carried despite their shallower array. It's likely that the Syracusan middle gave way first, with troops of lesser quality in that sector falling prey to fear in the claustrophobic press of battle. Soldiers striving for Syracuse on that part of the field would have had no reason as yet to trust Gylippus and surely took little stock in native leaders that had thrice led them to defeat in major engagements. Thus, as frightened comrades fled from their rear, the defending front fighters probably broke down in the center to send a wave of collapse out toward their wings. The Athenians surged ahead, overwhelming anyone attempting to stand fast and spearing down others as they tried to run. Fortunately for the Syracusans, the men about Gylippus and along other portions of their formation seem to have been able to pull back in some semblance of order, which kept loses down until cavalry and light foot troops could interpose and cover retreat. Though denied an extended pursuit by these light forces, the invaders were still able to claim the field, tearing down a section of the counter wall and erecting a trophy to mark their latest victory. Gylippus had no choice in the end but to pull back inside the city walls and seek a bitter truce that he might recover his dead (some 200–300 spearmen).

Gylippus now proved his worth by recognizing and moving to correct his tactical mistake of failing to exploit Syracuse's advantage in cavalry. He was also aware of the crisis in morale that his defeat had engendered and went before his army to confess personal shortcomings in planning the battle. Speaking openly and honestly, he won over the Syracusans, who were undoubtedly more accustomed to hearing a litany of excuses from their previous failed commanders. Gylippus laid out things in a light that favored their strengths and highlighted enemy weaknesses, all of which went far to restore confidence within an army that never lacked for good fighters, but only sound leadership.

Gylippus marched his reenergized troops out at the first good opportunity. This time he seems to have set up his phalanx beyond the terminus of the counter wall, which the enemy had partially dismantled and trimmed back toward the city. He would have deployed behind his skirmishers, likely arraying just under 5,000 spearmen in files of eight over a 600m front to anchor his left flank above the southern cliff face of Epipolae and stretching out his right toward the north. Showing an improved appreciation of their value, he took care to post horsemen and light footmen off the open end of his line, extending them for some distance in front of the gap between the butt of the counter wall and Athens's unfinished siege works.

Nicias came out to meet this new challenge and undoubtedly formed up much as for the first battle at the counter wall. His 4,000 or so hoplites would have had to file six deep to match the enemy front, with their horsemen and light infantry retiring from initial skirmishing to guard the open north/left flank. It's likely that Gylippus then charged first, as he had earlier, letting his deeper line strike the enemy in a hard-driven rush of spears. The Athenians and their allies met and held this initial assault, stabbing and shoving back all across the front. However, their light troops, who had already proven no match for good cavalry in detached combat, now failed against horsemen in pitched battle as well. The more numerous Syracusan riders and light footmen drove off their opposite numbers and fell on the enemy's now-exposed left flank, causing the Athenian phalanx to fall apart from left to right and send its hoplites scurrying for their camp under hot pursuit.

Athenian losses in the second engagement around the Epipolae counter wall probably amounted to several hundred spearmen—a relatively modest price that owed much to close proximity of a safe haven. Still, this was a pivotal engagement that now threw the Athenians back on the defensive. Gylippus had gained free reign over the eastern plateau and took full advantage to work through the night and extend his wall past the abandoned outer siege works. This dashed all hope for a quick circumvallation; and with winter fast approaching, Nicias sent word to Athens of his defeat. He pointed out that the enemy had now turned the situation upside down, capturing the initiative to invest him and his men within the southern siege walls and the base at Plemmyrium. Nicias offered to resign and, invoking his poor health, asked to be either rapidly reinforced or allowed to withdraw.

The Athenians weren't ready to quit and elected to reinforce Nicias, sending two new generals with fresh troops. Eurymedon (who had fought on Sicily during the Archidamian War) promptly set sail for Syracuse with a few ships and a store of cash that he might deliver the assembly's decision to Nicias and join him as strategos. Meanwhile, the other general, the wily and capable Demosthenes, stayed at Athens to outfit the rest of the expedition.

Mycalessus and the Enna Road (413 B.C.)

Athens's decision to send more resources overseas flew in the face of current events on the mainland, as it was already clear that renewed hostilities with Sparta were pending. The clouds of this conflict had begun gathering in earnest as early as the summer of 414 B.C., when Athenian ships raided the eastern Peloponnese in open support of the Argives against Spartan interests. Since then, continued occupation of Pylos and the rising enmity of Spartan ally Corinth had made another war all but inevitable. Thus, when the Spartans saw the tide turn in Sicily, they marched into Attica in the spring of 413. They ravaged the countryside and, advised by Alcibiades, turned the tactic of the epiteichismos back on its creators by setting up such a fortified enclave just east of Athens at Decelea. But in spite of this continuing threat, Demosthenes still set off for Sicily with a powerful armament. He had 60 Athenian ships and five more from Chios, which held 1,200 hoplites from Athens and another 1,400 subject Aegean islanders at 40 spearmen per trireme.

Though renewed war with Sparta might not have prevented the task force from departing, it did inspire one diversion along the way, as Demosthenes descended upon the Laconian coast to set up an epiteichismos onshore from Cythera as an offset to Decelea. With this task out of the way, he was then free to sail around to western Greece, where he intended to collect more ships and men before finally moving on to Syracuse.

Meanwhile, it seems that some 1,300 mercenary peltasts from Thrace had arrived too late to make Demosthenes' hurried sailing. The Athenians couldn't afford to waste scarce funds on keeping these troops further in service, so they arranged for the general Diitrephes to take them home by sea along a route that ran up the Euboan channel. Diitrephes had orders to attack Sparta's Boeotian allies in passing and opened with a raid near Tanagra before putting ashore at the channel's narrowest point to attack the small inland polis of Mycalessus. The Thracians struck this unprepared and poorly fortified site at dawn to initiate a horrific slaughter. Nearly unopposed, they cut down townsfolk without mercy, taking an especially bloody toll among children. Yet the barbarians soon paid for these atrocities when a force of horsemen and perhaps 1,000 hoplites came to the rescue of Mycalessus from Thebes.

The Greek spearmen ran the Thracians out of town and their cavalry gave chase. However, being from a horse-rich country, the retreating peltasts apparently knew how to keep a tight formation for fending off riders and took few casualties in their race to the beach, though they did have to abandon their booty. It was only at the coast that a real problem arose— their ships were standing offshore and few of the barbarians could swim. Waiting for these transports to row closer proved costly, as it gave the hoplites time to catch up with their horsemen and launch an attack. Trapped between a phalanx and the sea, some 250 Thracians (19 percent) died before the rest got away, all at a cost of but 20 Thebans.

Back on Sicily, Gylippus had received his remaining 13 ships, adding 520 more hoplites and around 2,500 crewmen to his host. These men boosted a work force that now took the Epipolae counter wall all the way to Labdalum. This ended the siege, raised Syracusan morale, and was a great propaganda victory. With the Athenians now keeping for the most part inside their walls, Gylippus next devised a scheme to capture Plemmyrium, using a naval attack on the enemy fleet in the Great Harbor as a diversion to cover a land assault against the headland. While the Athenians were winning the sea battle, their foes overran the ill-defended forts at Plemmyrium, killing many in the garrisons and capturing vital supplies. The Syracusans then manned the site on their own behalf to the great discomfit of Athens's fleet. Nicias chose to relocate his ships to their old anchorage near the Anapus, thus giving away the harbor entrance and his seaborne line of supply.

Syracuse's control of entry into the Great Harbor soon proved useful, as more help arrived aboard a fleet of merchant vessels. These brought spearmen from Thespiae (300 elite volunteers led by two Thebans and a Thespian), Sicyon (200), and a 500-man lochos of Corinthians and hired Arcadians. Gylippus also made a drive to recruit locally, which netted him 500 hoplites, 300 peltasts, and 300 archers from Camarina plus a Gelan force of five ships, 400 peltasts, and 200 horsemen. Also, his envoys enrolled 3,000 men in western Sicily, mostly spearmen from Himera and Selinous.

Almost the entire island was now supporting one side or the other in the fighting at Syracuse. The main exception was at Acragas, which remained neutral and refused to allow troops from either side to cross its territory. This ended up playing a role in events when the above-mentioned recruits from western Sicily moved through the central highlands so as to avoid Acragas on their way to the front. Somewhere along the road toward Enna, this column fell prey to a Siculi ambush that seems to have struck without warning from left and right to cut the marching column apart. In the wake of this disaster, only about 1,500 hoplites (half the intended reinforcement) ever reached the city. Led by a surviving envoy from Corinth, these men had fought their way through, but left 800 dead strewn along the path and the rest of their column (some 700 men) scattered and effectively lost as well. Though serious, this reverse really had little strategic effect. Even with his losses on the Enna Road, Gylippus still had around 8,000 heavy spearmen — nearly twice the number available to Nicias — and could support them with large contingents of light infantry and cavalry.

The conflict now turned out to sea, where the Syracusans slowly gained the upper hand through a series of engagements with the highly regarded Athenian fleet. Their key to victory lay in an innovative ship modification based on a Corinthian design. A fleet from Corinth had recently had some limited success using ships with reinforced bows that could deliver devastating blows in headlong collisions. Taking little damage themselves in such attacks, they were able to neutralize their foe's greater ability to maneuver. While such an approach was of little value on the open sea, where Athenian triremes could easily avoid head-on contacts with the modified vessels (which were heavier and slower), it was perfect for use in a confined setting like the Great Harbor. When the Syracusans learned of this new ploy from their Corinthian allies, they immediately set about replacing their ships' bow timbers or "catheads" with sturdier material. (The trireme employed an outside beam resembling an outrigger along each side to brace its uppermost bank of oars. The catheads were the bow extensions of these outlying structures.) They then took on the Athenians in a sequence of battles within the harbor as their army sortied to keep them occupied ashore. Though results were inconclusive in the early going, the Syracusans were eventually able to use their more rugged vessels in concert with a host of small craft (and a declining level of maintenance within the opposing fleet) to deal out a great deal of punishment. They managed with these tactics to sink or disable a number of Athenian ships and drive the rest onto the shore.

As all this was unfolding, Demosthenes was making his way westward at a slow pace that allowed him to recruit in route. In this way, he added some peltasts and slingers from Acarnania (perhaps 150 of each); spearmen from Zacynthus, Cephallenia, and Naupactus (1,000 or so); and 15 ships with 600 hoplites from Corcyra. But after a trireme arrived from Syracuse bearing Eurymedon with news of the fall of Plemmyrium, he gained a sense of urgency and rushed to join Nicias before the situation got any worse. Obliged to lend 10 ships for ongoing operations in the Corinthian Gulf, he packed their fighting men onto his remaining decks and set off. Still, even in such haste, Demosthenes took time to pick up more men in Italy, subscribing some Messapians (150 peltasts) and Greek colonists from Metapontum (300 peltasts and two triremes) and Thurii (300 peltasts and 700 spearmen). His fleet now numbered 73 ships in all (Diodorus cited 80, but seems to have missed those detached in Greece and addition of Eurymedon's and the two Italian vessels). Fighting men aboard this armada would have totaled about 4,900 hoplites, 900 peltasts (if there were 150 from Acarnania), 150 slingers, and 200 archers (four on each Athenian ship, save the one with Eurymedon).

Gylippus had by now completely turned around the situation at Syracuse. He had broken the siege on both land and sea, forcing the Athenians to stay within their walls southwest of the city. Nicias found himself heavily outnumbered, having lost most of his stores and with opposing cavalry and ships cutting off all routes of resupply. Yet just as everything seemed to be sinking beyond hope for the ailing general, he and his men looked up to see a powerful new armament from home rowing boldly into the Great Harbor. This was a truly ostentatious show, with scores of freshly outfitted triremes parading grandly past the enemy-held headland. Fairly bristling with warriors, each ship carried about twice its normal load of troops. Bracing as this sight would have been for Nicias and company, its impact on those watching from Syracuse had to have been equally profound in the negative, leaving them in fear for their future.

Epipolae (413 B.C.)

Athens's generals conferred on their next course of action. Demosthenes was set on exploiting the psychological effect of his sudden arrival by making a bold night attack on the Epipolae counter wall, but Nicias proposed a less daring daytime assault from the existing Athenian toehold on the plateau at Syca. Demosthenes, perhaps feeling that there would be time to use his own approach later, agreed to try Nicias's plan. The Athenians emerged from their lines next morning to charge at the counter wall, trying to scale or smash it with aid of wooden ramps and ladders, towers, and battering rams (Marsden 1969, 150). The defenders could clearly see these threats coming in broad daylight and easily beat them back, showering their attackers with missiles and setting fire to any devices placed against or near the wall. Demosthenes must now have felt more than ever that only cover of darkness would give his men a decent chance for success.

It was around the end of July when Demosthenes and nearly his entire army emerged under either a full or gibbous moon. Passing behind their lines, they were hidden from lookouts atop Epipolae and able to move undetected around the western end of the plateau to scale the north side of Euryelus. The force that moved up the slope contained something over 9,000 hoplites. (Diodorus listed 10,000 spearmen, but this is clearly the total brought to Sicily—5,100 in 415 B.C. plus 4,900 in 413 B.C.—and does not account for casualties, sickness, and detached garrisons.) A host of light foot troops must also have been present, but not cavalry, as it was unsuited to the rough terrain and weak lighting.

Thucydides' description suggests that the attack force made its climb by divisions. This would have allowed for brigades corresponding to positions in the normal line of battle—right wing in the lead, followed next by the center, with the left wing coming last. Each division on its own could form a modest phalanx once atop the hill, or should there be no initial opposition, all could combine into a single formation. (Such partitioning was undoubtedly meant to compensate for the poor communications common to any nighttime operation by letting officers command fewer men across a smaller area.) It was thus the right-wing brigade (hoplites from the Peloponnese and Athens, including Demosthenes) that went into action first.

Demosthenes and his men quickly captured the fort at Labdalum and then apparently fanned out northeast into battle array on the backside of the counter wall. This let them anchor their right flank and use the wall as a guide in marching southward toward campfires that marked the remaining enemy positions. If Demosthenes' division held about a third of his spearmen, it could have had a little over 3,000 hoplites lined up at eight men deep along a front some 400m wide. These attackers worked their way up a slight incline (the mesa being highest along its southern edge) with only moonlight to show the path. Meanwhile, most of the garrison from the fallen fort had escaped to spread the alarm and raise resistance.

Gylippus seems to have given defense of Epipolae top priority and deployed most of his army near the counter wall. These troops occupied three camps: Syracusan, allied Sicilian, and Peloponnesian from north to south along the front. The Spartan general had also set up the city's 600-man elite unit (reconstituted after its defeat at Euryelus) as a quick-reaction force. It was this picked regiment that responded first, moving to engage an enemy that had suddenly arisen to the north, silhouetted against the low-hanging moon. It was a brave but futile act, as Demosthenes' men took full advantage of their vast superiority in numbers (perhaps 5 to 1) to overrun this lone lochos. Nonetheless, the brief resistance of these select hoplites bought time for their countrymen and the other Sicilians to come up from the south and throw their weight next into the enemy. Gylippus led this fresh assault, which held all the men from the two northernmost camps. However, despite having equal or greater manpower, his phalanx couldn't hold its ground. The Athenians must have made the most of any advantage in morale that their sudden appearance had created and pushed through to rout this second wave of defenders. Fortunately for Gylippus, the victors weren't well equipped to pursue in the dark and he was able to withdraw with only modest losses. Nevertheless, Demosthenes now threatened to clear the field and restore the siege of Syracuse, with his drive picking up ever-greater impetus as it rolled across the plateau.

Yet the rapid initial success and advance by Demosthenes and his lead division had left their second brigade struggling to catch up from the north. The third division was even farther back, perhaps still climbing onto the crest near Euryelus on the far side of the counter wall. The effort was actually moving too quickly. It not only left reinforcement behind, but had also sacrificed a great deal of formation cohesion in a rush to crush all opposition and preclude a rally. And disorder among the Athenian ranks probably grew greatly after the defeat of Gylippus and the main body of Sicilians, which might have mistakenly been seen as a final triumph. However, one major obstacle still remained — the Peloponnesian encampment. These mainland Greeks had actually reacted poorly to the surprise alert and were having problems getting ready to fight, with only the small Thespian contingent having come forward under arms by the time the enemy arrived. Had these 300 hoplites not kept their composure and coolly hurried into battle array, it's likely that the Athenians would have struck upon a totally unprepared camp and easily driven the last of Epipolae's defenders from the field. But it would instead be the men from Thespiae who caught their foe less than ready for battle.

The Thespians must have deployed with the counter wall fixing their left flank and whatever light infantry had gathered covering right. Even at a minimum depth of four shields, they spanned a scant 75m, which was less than 20 percent of the advancing Athenian front. It thus took a lot of courage for these men to hold steady as they heard (more than saw) the enemy closing. Perhaps they were thinking of their forefathers, who had stood gallantly against fearsome odds two-thirds of a century earlier at Thermopylae; more likely, they thought of Delium, just a little over a decade before, where men of their polis held out against an Athenian onslaught to buy victory with their lives. However motivated, the Thespian hoplites charged with a fierce war cry once their foe got into range. Their rush smashed into the right side of the Athenian line, finding an opposing formation that lacked good order and knocking it backwards. This small success seems to have rippled through the Athenian host in a way that amplified its effect, with front fighters along Athens's right wing falling back among their after ranks to spread confusion and terror. Beaten at the fore and unable to properly assess its foe in the dark, the entire wing bolted in a shower of discarded gear.

When the Athenians near the counter wall broke away under light-armed pursuit, the victorious Thespians wheeled about to charge against the unshielded right flank of the opposition center. They drove this attack home to devastating effect and it was at this very moment that some of their allies finally came on the scene to threaten the stalled Athenian front and further fill it with fear. Demosthenes likely stood on the left wing, where his most trustworthy troops held the unanchored flank, but neither he nor they could really see what was going on in the surrounding darkness. Judging the flow of events largely by sound and feel, the general and his men could hear frightful cries coming from companions on their right and, increasingly, toward their rear. The enemy then began cheering victory all about. Ominous as this was for the Athenians, things got infinitely worse when they became aware of their fellows flinching and fleeing along the line to the right. It was now clear that their array was falling apart and they tossed shields to run for their lives.

As the leading Athenian brigade fell rearward, it couldn't help but blunder into the unengaged second division that was still moving up toward the front. Panic must have spread like wildfire, and the fresh brigade, a mix of Athenians and islander allies, lost its nerve to break without a blow being struck. Much the same undoubtedly happened when a portion of the fleeing mob mingled with and carried away the final Athenian division near the top of the slope north of Euryelus. The attack had gone down to utter defeat and chaos ruled. Terrified men scattered all over the plateau, with some losing their way in the dark and plunging to their deaths off the northern cliffs. Others, unable to tell friend from foe in the gloom, killed their own men or themselves fell victim to friendly fire. Amidst all this, Syracusan hoplites and light foot troops kept up a steady chase that took hundreds of lives. Defeated Athenians continued to pick their way down from Epipolae all night long, yet morning still found a few wandering lost on the plateau. Horsemen rode down and dispatched these last unfortunates.

Demosthenes' personal luck had held once more and he survived to fight another day, but many of his men weren't so fortunate. Estimates of the Athenian slain range from 2,000 (per Plutarch) to 2,500 (per Diodorus), with an even heavier loss of equipment noted in all sources. In particular, many of the beaten men had discarded their shields in a panic to escape. Syracuse suffered modestly by comparison, perhaps losing only 300–400 spearmen among some 6,000 engaged. This was easily the worst defeat ever suffered by the Athenian army, with a death toll that might have surpassed the previous high at Drabescus (465 B.C.) at a much greater strategic cost. Epipolae ended the Athenians' dreams of conquest and cast doubt on their very survival.

Defeat and Destruction

The Syracusans set out to exploit their great victory, trumpeting it around Sicily in hopes of gaining more allies. And though he couldn't persuade Acragas, Gylippus did enjoy a very successful recruiting campaign that yielded an especially pleasant surprise when he came upon some troops from Laconia. Apparently a 500-man lochos of neodamodeis hoplites and 100 helot psiloi under a spartiate officer, these men had failed to reinforce him earlier when storms drove them all the way to Africa. Doric Greeks at Cyrene had aided them in setting sail once more and they had traced an adventurous course along the African coast before crossing to western Sicily, making their way to friendly Selinous just in time to encounter Gylippus. The Spartan general must have been overjoyed to gain some fighting men from home and marched back to Syracuse more eager than ever to go on the attack.

Demosthenes had by now taken stock of the situation and joined with Eurymedon in advising Nicias to sail home while they still had naval superiority. Fearing political reprisal and/or simply too proud to accept defeat, Nicias wouldn't agree. The other generals then pleaded for him to at least pull back from Syracuse and find a base more secure from mounted and seaborne attack. This too Nicias refused. The impasse left the Athenian host stuck in camp close below the Lysimeleia swamp, where mosquitoes and unsanitary conditions afflicted the tightly crowded men, and it wasn't long before malaria and dysentery began taking a heavy toll. As Nicias watched his troops fall from disease, he saw the enemy getting stronger and bolder each day. Realizing at last that he must act soon or risk complete disaster, he finally relented and ordered a full-scale retreat.

It was at this critical juncture that mechanics of the solar system and religious piety conspired to doom a quick withdrawal. On the night of August 27, with the Athenians loaded to depart, there was a total eclipse of the moon. Shaken by this omen, many of the men hesitated to leave, prompting Nicias to consult soothsayers and postpone sailing for a full lunar cycle. This went down poorly with many in camp and a number of men deserted, bringing word to Gylippus of the planned retreat and its mandated delay, prompting him to attack by both land and sea.

The Helorus Gate and Lysimeleia Marsh (413 B.C.)

Gylippus set out against the south side of Athens's lines. Some 300–400 riders from Syracuse, who had long held post below the enemy camp, joined with their hamippoi and some hoplites (maybe a lochos of 500–600 men) to launch a morning assault, apparently hoping to take a portal that opened on the coastal road running toward Helorus. No doubt seeing their foe's small numbers, and having a portion of their own cavalry on hand, a band of Athenian hoplites (perhaps an under-strength lochos of 300–400) responded with a sally. But the Sicilian cavalry prevailed, breaking up this charge and cutting off some of the opposing spearmen. Most of the beaten Athenians then tried to escape via the Helorus gate, but were slow to get through. The pursuing horsemen soon caught up to take down a few spearmen and capture 70 precious Athenian mounts left behind when their masters found it easier to squeeze past the narrow gate on foot. As it turned out, this foiled counterattack marked the last Athenian land offensive at Syracuse.

Focus of the struggle turned out to sea the following day. The opposing fleets fought a fierce battle in the Great Harbor, which saw the Syracusans drive through their foe's center and cut off Eurymedon, who was sailing with his right wing. The general would lose his life after going aground near Plemmyrium. Badly battered, Athens's armada fled to shore just northeast of its own lines. This was in plain view of Gylippus, who had been standing below the city with his army to menace the enemy wall in hopes of provoking another ill-advised sortie.

Gylippus set out to capture or destroy the beached enemy ships, and those leading his assault (likely a tribal lochos) eagerly rushed ahead to get at what appeared to be a soft target. But a too hasty advance seems to have put their formation into disorder. This was much the same mistake that the Athenians had recently made upon Epipolae and it had a similar consequence as, once again, overconfident troops with poor cohesion ran into a small force of determined defenders—the 150 Etruscan hoplites that had arrived shortly after the death of Lamachus. These troops had been guarding the seaward end of the Athenian position and, being close to where the fleet ran aground, had moved up in a tight array to meet the fast approaching Sicilians.

The Etruscans had the Lysimeleia swamp to their left and a high beach berm on their right to secure their flanks from mounted attack, which let them stand fast and turn back a ragged infantry charge, rolling up their opponents from shoreward to drive them into the marsh. By the time that Gylippus and the rest of his army arrived, more men had come up from the Athenian camp to help defend their ships. In a second phase of battle, the Athenians and their allies appear to have had the better order and motivation (desperate to preserve their seaborne lifeline to home) plus support from grounded crewmen on their most open (right/seaward) flank. Their combined efforts eventually repulsed the Syracusans and saved most of the triremes. But this minor Athenian success was of little consequence compared to Syracuse's' naval triumph; something that became clear a few days later when Gylippus used an array of small boats, merchant vessels, and old triremes to build a boom across the mouth of the Great Harbor and deny any escape by sea.

Recognizing the enormity of this threat, the Athenians threw every ship they had at the harbor barrier, sailing out with over 100 triremes and a strong force of hoplites. They pierced through the boom with their initial attack, but then fell back to meet an all-out effort by the smaller Syracusan fleet. First one side and then the other gained the upper hand, sending emotions rising and falling among those watching from shore as the fight became so crowded that dueling triremes often became entangled to spew bloody, hand-to-hand combats across adjoined decks. In the end, such a battle without sophisticated maneuver favored Syracuse and allowed its fleet to drive the Athenians onto shore and deal a mortal blow to their already shaky morale. Once supremely confident in their prowess at sea, they were now so cowed that they not only refused to row out again, but didn't even seek to recover their dead.

The Retreat from Syracuse (413 B.C.)

The Athenians now elected to retreat overland and set some of their ships on fire to prevent their capture. Though this served to alert Gylippus that his foes planned to make a run for it, he couldn't get Syracuse's political leadership to interrupt victory celebrations and bar an escape. Hermocrates of Syracuse reacted to this by sending out riders posing as Athenian sympathizers, who gave false warning to Nicias that troops were already guarding all exits. Whether due to this deception or mere lack of readiness, the Athenians ended up postponing their departure until a full two days after the sea battle. The fictional blockade had by then become all too real.

The Athenian army that mustered to retreat was a far cry from the one that had menaced Epipolae only weeks earlier. The 9,000–9,500 hoplites with the invaders at that time had shrunk to only about 5,000. (This assumes 2,000–2,500 lost on Epipolae, 350 or so in the first two days of the Syracusan offensive, some 1,000 in the last engagement at sea, and the rest from disease and crippling wounds.) Likewise, losses to men and horses left only 200–250 Athenians and Scythians in the saddle plus a like number of allied Greeks—the Siculi horsemen having already gone home. The light infantry had fared better, but still mustered no more than 2–3,000 men (a mix of peltasts, slingers, archers, and dismounted troopers). There were also some 13,000 armed rowers from the grounded fleet—enough to crew at least 60 ships after the battle at the boom. The grand total under arms was therefore 20,000 men, who had to protect an equal number of camp followers and walking wounded. Given that the spearmen had replaced lost gear from captured stores or the fallen, their strength remained on a par with the army of any single polis in Greece save Athens itself, but the opposition boasted an even greater host.

The Syracusans had fielded around 8,000 hoplites against the Epipolae attack and, though losing perhaps 400–500 then and since, had added others from both Sicily and Greece and could now put at least 8–9,000 spearmen into action. Large contingents of cavalry (more than

1,200 riders with hamippoi) and light foot troops (2–3,000 peltasts and slingers) were also on hand, as were over 10,000 drafted men from the fleet for use on land. Gylippus placed some of these troops at river crossings in groups of perhaps 600–1,200 hoplites and a few hundred skirmishers. He also scattered mounted patrols about the area, but seems to have kept most of his troops within the city. This main body of at least 6,000 spearmen, 1,500 light footmen, and 1,000 horsemen was set to strike at any attempt by the Athenians to leave, or to invest them should they stay.

The Athenians finally emerged from the back/southwest side of their encampment. They marched out on a heartbreaking note, leaving behind their unburied dead and, much more distressing, the sick and wounded who couldn't travel. Thucydides must have drawn his vivid description of this awful leave-taking from men who were there. It details how the cripples clung pitifully to friends and relatives and even crawled along behind, pleading not to be abandoned. The column gradually distanced itself from these mournful scenes, but they could only have inspired deep sorrow and apprehension. Still, it's unlikely that any among the departing men foresaw the true scope of the trials yet before them. They would spend the next eight days fighting an increasingly desperate series of engagements on the way to their own tragic fate.

Days 1–2: The Anapus Crossing

Nicias and Demosthenes led separate brigades during the retreat, having divided combatants and dependents more or less equally between them. This gave each general some 2,500 hoplites, 7,500 light-armed men, and 10,000 noncombatants. We know little about specific units, save that Demosthenes got the islanders — men from the Aegean and western Greece that had sailed with him to Sicily. It seems likely that most of his troops came from such allied states, while Nicias had most of the native Athenians. These divisions formed up into two rectangles, which had lesser width than length toward easing through any narrow passages along the way.

Spearmen held station in some depth at front and back of each array (maybe an understrength lochos of 300 across 100m, three deep), with the remaining hoplites lined alongside and the other men in between with the animals. If the lateral guard formed a double file, there would have been about 475m between front and rear units of each formation, which would have allowed for just under 3 square meters per man in the interior. The fittest spearmen would have been in the van of Nicias's lead formation and rear-guarding the trailing one of Demosthenes. All of the bowmen must have stood inside their hoplites at front and rear, while horsemen, peltasts, and slingers would have been set to sally from the flanks. As these divisions moved ahead, one close behind the other, they formed a single, kilometer-long column.

The Athenians marched away unopposed while the enemy was busy hauling off the abandoned remnants of their fleet. They made their way westward at all possible speed, though their actual destination lay to the north at Catana. This undoubtedly recognized that it would be tough to reach that old base by the most direct path (around Epipolae and up the coast), where the enemy's cavalry and ships had open access. They thus sought to move inland toward the Acraean Heights, a broad, north-trending plateau above the Anapus plain that was a grander version of Epipolae. Once atop this upland, they would be safer from mounted attack and among friendly Siculi that could provide men and supplies for a swing across to Catana.

Nicias and Demosthenes meet no real resistance until they got to a crossing on the Anapus that was about 6km upstream from Syracuse; here, troops had set up on the far bank to bar their way. The enemy force would have included Syracusan and allied spearmen (perhaps a lochos of each, totaling 600–1,200 men) flanked by horsemen and foot skirmishers. They held a strong position that required any attack to come through a stony riverbed that held little water at this time of year. The bulk of Nicias's hoplites moved up to join their van and, once in combat array, picked their way across the ford to spear into the defending phalanx. Strongly motivated and holding a likely 4 to 1 edge in heavy manpower, the Athenians pushed through and routed their thinly filed foes. It must have been a quick action in which the victors, having easily carried the fight, took little hurt. Nor was their opposition much harmed, since the retreating column had no time for pursuit.

The Athenians struggled on under harassment from enemy riders and light infantry, including not only those that had been at the river crossing, but also others fresh from Syracuse. Nicias and Demosthenes ended up only about a kilometer past the crossing before halting to set up a night camp on high ground. And things went no better next morning when the march resumed, as progress slowed to a crawl under countless light-armed attacks and the necessity of foraging for food. The column was so distressed that it stopped early, camping on some flats after having advanced only about 3km. The rest of the day was spent gathering supplies from nearby farms, something that the enemy light-armed men on hand apparently couldn't yet prevent. However, Gylippus's vanguard arrived that night in the form of a large body of horsemen and skirmishers.

Days 3–5: Anapus Plain and the Acraean Bald Rock

The third day of the retreat saw Nicias and Demosthenes approach the Acraean Heights, which lay before them across the open plain of the Anapus. Their objective was a prominent cliff face, whose white limestone outcrop had been dubbed the Acraean Bald Rock. Approach to the Bald Rock was up a deep streambed that ended in two gorges that sliced up either side of the cliff, with the larger of these erosions providing a suitable pathway onto the plateau above. However, the Athenians had hardly begun their advance across the plain when they came under attack from cavalry backed by light foot troops. Action soon escalated from harassment into full-scale battle.

It must have quickly became clear that the Athenian hoplites couldn't close against their more mobile opponents, who rushed in to discharge a cloud of missiles and then rode or ran to safety. There were too few archers (or arrows) on hand to fend off such assaults, and sallies by horsemen and skirmishers offered no better solution, as these would have wilted against the large numbers available to the other side. Suffering rising casualties and unable to break free, the Athenians gave up and limped back to the previous night's campsite. Yet even here the dynamic had changed. Though the enemy didn't move against the camp itself, their horsemen had free rein over the surrounding area and prevented foraging for food. Making matters even worse for the beleaguered army, this last delay had finally allowed Gylippus and a portion of his heavy infantry to catch up.

The Athenians seem to have realized that it was now or never to gain the Acraean plateau and set out before sunrise, bypassing unready light-armed opposition in the weak light of false dawn to reach shelter within incised terrain trailing up to the Bald Rock. Leading the way inside this narrow passageway, Nicias and his brigade approached the cliff only to find that Gylippus's men had thrown up a low wall ahead. A deep phalanx stood behind this crude fieldwork, which likely reached to just below the waist — protecting the legs and too high to step over, but low enough to allow use of spear and shield above. Archers and slingers were on high ground either side of the ravine to lend fire in support of their hoplites. Undeterred,

Nicias and his spearmen charged through a deadly rain of missiles to shove into both the wall and front fighters standing beyond. It's possible that they pushed through the flimsy stone barrier at several points, maybe even all along its narrow front, but the deep enemy files behind didn't yield. Both sides were in a position much like that of the close-packed combatants on the second day at Thermopylae, with neither able to advance nor receive relief from the rear. Making no headway and utterly exhausted, the Athenians finally retired.

While Nicias was regrouping for another go at the barrier in front, rearguard troops with Demosthenes discovered that Gylippus was trying to wall off the mouth of the passage behind them and quickly rushed to break up the construction before being sealed in. Alerted to this new danger, the Athenian commanders withdrew their entire column as night fell, moving well out onto open ground before setting up a new camp. It must now have become apparent that they couldn't scale the plateau here and needed another way up.

The Athenians elected next day to go around the enemy blocking force by skirting past the Acraean Heights along the Anapus. They started northwest, marching with the river on their left and hoping to find an alternative path up the cliff face to their right. Gylippus followed with his hoplites in battle formation, blocking any opportunity to double back on the pass at the Bald Rock. He seems to have been determined to bleed the enemy at minimal cost to his own forces, falling back every time they sallied, only to close again as soon as they returned to formation. Meanwhile, the Syracusan cavalry and light infantry kept up a steady fire from all directions, causing their foes to suffer greatly. A shower of javelins, shot, and arrows took a particularly nasty toll among the unarmored, killing a few and injuring many. So fierce was this missile assault that the retreating men spent most of the day cowering behind the shields of their hoplites and had advanced less than 1km by sunset. Syracusan attacks broke off at dusk, and the wounded column settled down for the evening without leaving the river plain. Gylippus and his men appear to have been confident then that they had the situation under control, and withdrew some distance to set up their own encampment.

Day 6: Cacyparis River and the Estate of Polyzelus

Nicias and Demosthenes surely knew that their men couldn't long endure such constant pounding, especially without replenishing food supplies. They therefore came up with a bold scheme to break away at night and move eastward toward the sea. Once free of opposing cavalry and light infantry, they hoped to turn back up one of the many river courses of southeastern Sicily to met their Siculi allies and resume their march through the interior to safety. It has been logically suggested (Green, 1970a, 327) that a messenger was dispatched to the Siculi advising them of this change of plan. The Athenians heavily stoked their fires when darkness fell and slipped off quietly for an arduous 18km hike to the coast. Though not mentioned in our sources, a goodly number of the injured must have been unfit to travel and stayed to keep up the fires and make noise so as to mimic a fully occupied camp. Stealing away just before dawn, a few of these men might then have escaped to the nearby uplands.

Nicias and his brigade again took point for the Athenian column as it worked its way through the dark toward shore. This division pressed ahead and before long became separated from its trailing counterpart; as a result, though it was well before sunrise when the Athenian vanguard reached the coastal road that ran down to Helorus, it wasn't until dawn that Demosthenes and his men finally got there. Joining once more, the generals then marched against a fortified crossing on the next river to the south, the Cacyparis.

The guard contingent at the Cacyparis must have been similar to that seen earlier on the Anapus — a couple of lochoi with 600–1,200 spearmen plus several hundred skirmishers and a few horsemen. Having more time (and perhaps keen to improve on what their comrades did at the Anapus), these men had thrown up field works before the north side of the crossing that consisted of a stone wall with wooden wings. The wall was probably a low frontal work much like the one across the pass at the Acraean Bald Rock; if so, it was not so much a barrier as a device to aid their phalanx by stiffening its front rank. The wooden section of this defense was a higher palisade manned by light foot troops that screened the flanks, angling from each end of the rock wall down to deeper water on either side. Yet strong as this position might have been, it was no match for the desperate Athenians, who likely threw 2,000 or more hoplites into pressing through the stone and human obstacles blocking their escape. Shoving and spearing the outmatched Syracusans into the streambed behind, the attackers bloodied and broke them to secure the ford.

The retreating army might have planned to move upstream along the Cacyparis, but arguments against this by Kagan (1981, 346) seem sound. More likely, its Siculi guides had recommended a route along the next river to the south (the Erineus) and it was down this path that Nicias led his point division and most of the available cavalry. He intended to take this crossing before it could be fortified in order to hold it open for the rest of the column coming up from behind. Nicias and his men made good time along the 10km to the Erineus, crossed without opposition, and set up on high ground about 1km beyond to await Demosthenes.

As for Demosthenes and his men, they had barely gotten underway before coming under attack from cavalry. This was the main body of Syracusan horsemen, which had raced after the Athenians that morning upon finding their empty camp. The retreating brigade tried to inch ahead under withering fire from both riders and hamippoi, but was soon full of wounded men and barely able to hold formation, let alone make forward progress. Thus, when Gylippus came on the scene around noon, he found Demosthenes' division crawling along in agony no more than 1km from the Cacyparis.

Aware that enemy spearmen were fast closing in, Demosthenes prepared to make a last stand, forming a square just off the Helorus road. This was on a country estate that had belonged at one time to Polyzelus, brother of former Syracusan tyrants Gelon, Hieron, and Thrasybulus. The Athenian formation had shrunk greatly since leaving Syracuse, with combat and a difficult march reducing it to perhaps fewer than 12,000 men. These survivors gamely arrayed once more, putting the road on one side and an olive grove on the other. Gylippus surrounded the estate, but didn't send in his hoplites, choosing to employ missile fire instead. Suffering horribly from a steady fall of darts and shot, the brigade of Demosthenes faced destruction.

It must have been obvious to Gylippus that his enemies were on the verge of collapse and he craftily offered separate terms to their weakest link, the islanders. Some of these accepted and their betrayal broke the back of any remaining opposition. When the Spartan then asked for surrender from the rest, Demosthenes had little choice but to agree. Having done his best to secure survival for at least some of the others, the demoralized Athenian then attempted suicide only to have his sword wrested away and be taken prisoner.

Days 7–8: The Erineus River and the Assinarus Crossing

Nicias was encamped on a hill just south of the Erineus River on the morning of September 17 when a large body of Syracusan cavalry appeared and announced the surrender of Demosthenes. Dubious at first, the Athenian commander soon confirmed the shocking news through his own representatives. Though no doubt shaken by this turn of events, he rejected an offer to surrender and stood his men fast in their current camp on high ground. Gylippus had already arrived with his heavy infantry to encircle this position and, when the enemy refused terms, he put them under the same sort of missile attack that had so devastated Demosthenes. However, Nicias's native Athenians were of sterner stuff than the mostly allied troops that had failed his comrade. Though the assault took a terrible toll, they held out until darkness brought a halt to the action.

Undoubtedly aware that his men couldn't endure this kind of punishment for long, Nicias tried to repeat his stratagem of sneaking away after dark. However, Gylippus was not to be deceived a second time and had kept his men alert to just such a move. Hearing those in camp preparing to depart, the Syracusans took up arms and began singing battle songs to raise their spirits and strike fear into the foe. Having lost the element of surprise, Nicias called off the escape. This order was either not received or simply ignored by 300 Athenians (perhaps a select vanguard set to lead the breakout) and these continued on to pierce the enemy cordon and scatter into the dark.

As sunrise approached to begin the eighth day of retreat from Syracuse, the remaining Athenians must have been in desperate straits. They not only faced another attack, but also, sitting a kilometer from the Erineus, had been cut off from water for more than a day and a half. Combat was thirsty work and without something to drink they couldn't repeat their heroic resistance of the previous day. Knowing that he had to somehow fight his way through to water (and apparently preferring to move forward, rather than retrace his steps), Nicias gathered his men for one last desperate effort. He prepared to strike out near dawn, perhaps hoping to catch the enemy less than alert after keeping vigil all night. Leaving behind anyone who couldn't keep up, the Athenian commander led out the remnants of his brigade, likely now having no more than a few thousand combatants. Moving in a compact body, these men cut through the enclosing lines and made for the next river southward, the Assinarus.

Gylippus reacted to this escape by sending his cavalry and light foot troops on ahead to hinder the enemy's advance while he followed with the hoplites. Nicias raced for the Assinarus under constant harassment from these light forces, finally making it to the river crossing only to find a strong force in place to oppose him (from a position that must have been reinforced with field works). Seemingly reluctant to attack amidst a swarm of enemy horsemen and skirmishers, and with a hostile army closing on his rear, Nicias turned westward up the north side of the Assinarus. Green has suggested that he immediately headed inland from the Erineus to trace an old track that only later crossed the Assinarus [1970a, 343].) All the while, Syracusan cavalry and light infantry must have kept up a steady sniping against his flanks, shepherding him away from the river and its precious water.

The fleeing men huddled behind their shields and staggered ahead, weak from dehydration and dogged by missiles every step of the way. Before long, Gylippus and his spearmen had caught up with them. The pursuers split into two groups: one (under the Spartan general) following behind and the other moving parallel to the Athenian left flank (keeping pace across the streambed). The situation approached crisis point as the afternoon wore on and the Athenian formation melted away both in manpower and vitality. Things finally came to a head when the retreat approached another crossing on the Assinarus.

Clearly near their limit of endurance, Nicias's men charged the ford. Their numbers and speed yielded enough momentum to sweep past opposing light forces all the way to the river, but there could have been no hope of holding any kind of order during such a rush. Sicilian hoplites keeping pace to the south, perhaps 3,000 strong, wheeled out of column into a phalanx along the far bank of the stream and, as their enemy piled down into the water, advanced to the attack with lowered spears. Meanwhile, Gylippus and his men on the other side of the river menaced the Athenian rear, even as their riders and skirmishers rallied to renew fire into the jumbled ranks crowding toward the crossing. What followed was little more than a massacre. Nicias had too few hoplites (maybe only about 1,000 at this point) to have any chance of cutting through the larger enemy formation atop the bank, especially given the state of physical weakness and disorder of his men. Thus, the Athenians died by the hundreds as they pressed ineffectually against the enemy front, broken bodies falling back among the mob still surging from behind. Even more than the enemy spears at their rear, it must have been a desperate need to drink that kept driving these men ever forward into the river. Many already caught in the deathtrap at the crossing were so thirsty that they dropped in the very midst of battle to lap up churned and muddy water turned crimson with blood.

With no way out, Nicias offered to yield that his men might avoid complete annihilation. As a Spartan, Gylippus was no doubt well disposed toward the man who had brokered peace between his polis and Athens to end the long Archidamian War, and he therefore seems to have moved quickly to call off his troops. Of course, it was easier to issue such an order than get compliance from soldiers caught up in slaughtering a much-hated foe; as a result, there were only 1,000 Athenians left to be herded into official custody when the killing finally stopped. This count encompasses those rounded up later that day from the 300 Erineus escapees, but not others hidden by some of the victors for their own profit.

There were actually survivors of the Athenian expedition beyond those taken captive. Cavalry commander Callistratos led some of the best-equipped troops (including a number of hoplites and some of his riders) through a weak point in the closing enemy ring. Breaking free into the interior along the north side of the river, this small force reached Catana, from where it would ultimately mount raids against Syracuse and gain sufficient booty to ransom at least a few prisoners. However, Callistratos wouldn't take part in this later effort. Apparently seeking atonement for his role in the failed campaign, he rode alone to the old siege camp below Syracuse; there, he found looters and charged to slay five before dying with sword in hand.

Nicias and Demosthenes suffered execution despite the best efforts of Gylippus to take them into captivity at Sparta. Nor would many of those imprisoned ever see home again, with thousands dying under hideous conditions within a quarry. The Athenians were reluctant at first to believe that their magnificent expedition had come to such a disastrous end; ultimately, however, they accepted the truth with surprising stoicism. Quickly shedding any sense of panic, they set about the task of recovery with grim determination. Often flighty and excitable, the people of Athens could also endure the most daunting circumstances with a great tenacity. And so it was in the winter of 413–412 B.C. that they resolved to resist Sparta with all their remaining might.

Tactical Patterns of the Peace of Nicias and Sicilian Invasion

War in the Grecian west dominates our battlefield records from close of the Archidamian conflict in 421 B.C. through Athens's Sicilian expedition. Of 28 engagements in this interval, 23 (82 percent) took place in either Italy or Sicily. In fact, all but two of the latter (Cumae and Mazaros II) occurred at or near Syracuse between October 415 and September 413. Waging war here didn't differ all that much from contemporary practices on the Greek mainland, but it did employ greater numbers of horsemen and light foot troops on a regular basis. This was largely due to the western region's more open terrain, which encouraged use of these sorts of light-armed and highly mobile fighters. Moreover, the leading role that Athens played in this period served to further the trend toward such troops, since the Athenians were among Greece's more ardent advocates of both archers and cavalry.

In the struggle for Syracuse, that city's horsemen far outdid their counterparts from Athens. Yet despite great strength and nearly universal presence, Syracusan cavalry dominated only two battles (Epipolae Counter Wall II and Helorus Gate) and combined with light infantry to decide just two more (on Anapus Plain and at the Estate of Polyzelus). Still, the influence of Syracuse's mounted forces went far beyond these meager statistics, since they forced the Athenians to counter with special defenses on numerous occasions. A more accurate summary of their impact can thus be found in the fact that there were a full dozen battles (just over half the total on Sicily) in which these horsemen were either decisive or drove their foes to use of terrain barriers or cover of night. This contrasts strongly with what was happening in Greece proper. Of five battles there during this same period, there is only one (Heraclea) where cavalry might have been the dominant factor; nor are there examples of terrain or darkness being used to ward off mounted assault.

Light infantry had been going up over time as a component in Greek armies. Athenian skirmishers at Syracuse, for instance, equaled 25 percent of their hoplite count—well up from the 10 percent or so that had earlier been common. Perceived value of light-armed foot soldiers was clearly on the rise and inspired generals to lay out hard cash for well-trained men; we therefore see employment of mercenaries from Crete (archers), Thrace (peltasts), Rhodes (slingers), etc. Of course, there were also hired hoplites, as at Mantinea I and on Sicily, but it was specialist missilemen that really dominated the ranks of paid fighters. These professionals, along with even more numerous amateur light foot troops, were generally effective in neutralizing similarly armed opponents. This made them an important factor in combat, even though they rarely were prime instruments of decision.

The ability of light-armed troops to offset their counterparts let hoplites continue their tradition of ascendancy. Armies with a substantial heavy infantry advantage (outnumbering their foe by a third or more) won 11 of 16 combats in the subject period. At first glance, this might not seem much better than the success rates of those with a similar edge in horsemen or light foot; however, other troops usually operated only at the periphery of battle and thus dominated much less often than heavy foot (seven times versus 19). Hoplite phalanxes therefore continued to play the most important role in pitched combat.

A tactic of particular note in its aid to hoplite fighting was use of temporary fieldworks to stiffen phalanx fronts, with low stone barriers thrown up to protect the legs of spearmen standing on defense and hinder charging opponents. These both physically blocked the path of advance and limited the effect of othismos. The Syracusans championed this device, using it first at the Acraean Bald Rock and then again at Cacyparis River. All prior examples of field works in 5th-century Greek battle are confined to the Persian invasions, with the Athenians building an abatis at Marathon, Leonidas repairing (but not actually using) a low wall at Thermopylae, and the Persians digging a shallow trench in front of their leading rank at Mycale. Yet while such constructs strengthened the defense, they did so at the cost of all forward momentum; furthermore, the more effective Greek versions were practical only where materials were abundant (rocky passes or stream crossings) and flanks secure. As a result of these limitations, fieldworks didn't find common use during the 5th century.

Combat results in this era show that the element of surprise continued to be a potent factor in battle. Ambushers at both Argos/Phlius and Enna Road were highly effective, and surprise mobilizations produced five victories in seven actions. Even Demosthenes' surprise march on Epipolae had produced early success before it fell apart amidst a welter of confusion in the dark. Also, while not involved in the sort of open fighting that is the subject here, it's worth noting that surprise attacks worked well against fortified sites around Syracuse. The city's defenders had good luck with this approach against Labdalum and Plemmyrium. Likewise, the Athenians used similar tactics to capture palisades at the first and second counter walls and to briefly retake Labdalum.

In contrast to the use of surprise, fighting on home ground in this period doesn't seem to have given an overriding tactical advantage, as those in action on or near native soil lost 15 times while chalking up only nine victories. Nevertheless, there's no denying that there was real value in being familiar with the landscape on which one was engaging. Forces battling near home continued to be more effective in setting up traps (local men sprung both ambushes named above) and terrain-related defenses. Physical factors therefore still favored armies operating in familiar territory, with Syracuse's ultimate triumph over the Athenians showcasing long-run strategic benefits as well. Yet the poor record of defenders in this era's pitched combats makes the case once again that it was their opponents that more often than not held the winning edge in battlefield morale.

* * *

Athens, the world's first and greatest democracy, had launched a vicious attack on equally democratic Syracuse, something that casts grave doubt on the fashionable modern idea that states sharing such popular rule are unlikely to ever go to war with each other. In fact, inter-democracy warfare was a reality among the classical Greeks and avoiding it doesn't seem to have figured in any way into their martial decisions. It was therefore only a brutal defeat in the field, and not consideration for fellow democrats, that finally turned the Athenians from their dream of Sicilian conquest. Creasy (1987, 36) hailed this failure as a pivotal event in Western history. But while certainly a major turning point for Athenian fortunes, it was hardly so grand in the broader scheme of things. Athens was, after all, unlikely to have held Syracuse (much less all of Sicily) in thrall for very long. Defeating an opponent in the field and overcoming its defenses is one thing, while maintaining an occupation among a large and hostile populace is something else entirely. Indeed, Sparta would experience this bitter truth just a few years hence, when unable to sustain its hold on an otherwise beaten Athens. Win or lose at Syracuse, the Athenians were destined to eventually fall back on their core bases of power in Attica and around the Aegean. This was where the true strength of their empire lay, and it was here where the conflict with Sparta would ultimately have to play out.

VII

A World at Spear's Length: The Decelean/Ionian War to the End of the 5th Century (413–401 B.C.)

> Asked once how far Sparta's boundaries stretched, he brandished his spear and said, "As far as this can reach."
> Plutarch *(on Agesilaus, King of Sparta, 400–360 B.C.)*

Sparta's Agis renewed hostilities with Athens by leading an army into Attica in early spring 413 B.C. He destroyed crops and, on advice from Alcibiades, built a fort about 20km northeast of Athens at Decelea, a site between the city and the Boeotian frontier. This outpost allowed him to strike at will against surrounding farms and served as safe haven for runaway slaves and other deserters from the Athenian cause. There was minimal resistance to this Decelean campaign. After all, Athens had committed 3,400 hoplites to its effort at Syracuse as well as tens of thousands of other troops (cavalry, skirmishers, sailors, oarsmen, etc.), some 160 triremes, and most of its treasury (Kagan 1987, 4). Thus, though their city remained inviolate, the Athenians didn't have the strength to match Agis in pitched battle and chose to stay within their walls. Nevertheless, loss of a harvest combined with the steady drain on slave labor to quickly put them under great pressure, which was compounded when word came of the disaster in Sicily.

With Athens reeling from such a crushing defeat, most in the Greek world assumed that it would fall before the summer of 412 was out; neutral states therefore moved to join Sparta and many in the Delian League now dared to think of open revolt. The Athenians rose resolutely to this challenge. They created a committee of elders to oversee the assembly's decisions and pulled resources together to gain greater security for food imports by fortifying Sunium (at the southern tip of Attica) and building more warships. This restoration of the navy was also key to keeping skittish members of their alliance in line. The Spartans moved to create a larger fleet as well, assigning shipbuilding quotas to their seafaring allies as they also opened talks with Persia toward arranging for a combined effort in Asia Minor. Having finally accepted the vital role of sea power in this conflict, and vicariously savoring the benefits of a naval victory in the Great Harbor at Syracuse, Sparta was ready at last to come out and challenge the Athenian fleet.

Warfare at the Ocean's Edge

Several Delian League states approached Sparta in early 412 B.C. to seek aid in making a break from Athens, among the supplicants being representatives from Euboa, Lesbos, and

Chios. At the same time, Persia asked that the Spartans send ships to the Hellespont to back an uprising in that strategic province, through which Athenian grain moved from the Euxine (Black Sea) region. Agis weighed his options and chose to put a bid for Euboa on hold, perhaps feeling that the strong Spartan position at Decelea made that nearby island a bird in hand. This allowed him to make a more concentrated effort in Asia Minor, and the plan that now emerged was to first promote rebellion at Chios and then move on to Lesbos and the Hellespont.

Sparta gathered forces for its Asian campaign by shifting 21 triremes from the Corinthian Gulf (nearly half the vessels recently levied from allies around that region), which went by portage across the isthmus to the Saronic port of Cenchreae. After delaying for a religious festival, Corinth provided its share of manpower and the fleet finally set out for Chios; however, alert to just such a move, the Athenians twice intercepted this sailing. Deploying a superior force, they first turned it back and then drove it onto shore, capturing one ship in the process. The Peloponnesian admiral, Alcamenes, had gone aground to buy time for another breakout attempt. What he ended up accomplishing was instigation of the first land battle in what is known today as either the Decelean or Ionian War.

Spiraeum, Mytilene, and Chios (412 B.C.)

Alcamenes and his 20 surviving vessels lay at Spiraeum, an abandoned port about 17km southeast of Cenchreae. Sending for help to Corinth (26km away), the cornered admiral made ready to defend his beached fleet with some 800 hoplites (40 or so per ship) supported by armed oarsmen. The Athenians moved to attack with 30 ships of their own and seven more, ironically, from their still loyal allies on Chios. Leaving maybe a dozen triremes offshore to prevent escape by sea, the Athenians could have put 1,000 hoplites on the beach from the rest of their fleet. These spearmen would have advanced along the strand toward their enemy's landing site in company with some archers and a crowd of light-armed crewmen. We don't know whether the troops standing on defense came out to meet this assault or stayed close by their ships, but Thucydides painted the action that followed in terms of great violence and confusion. Orderly battle lines must have quickly broken down to send combatants swirling around the stranded vessels in a riot of bloodshed. Alcamenes and a number of his men met their deaths in this fierce melee and the other defenders promptly fled, freeing the Athenians to then turn their attentions onto the grounded hulls left behind.

Smashing at the enemy's triremes, the victors disabled most of them before shoving off. Failure of the Athenians to utterly destroy or haul away the enemy vessels shows that they were in a great hurry to be gone, no doubt fearing that a large enemy column was on its way. It's even possible that a dust cloud on the horizon had revealed advance elements of an opposing force actually closing in. In fact, Alcamenes had sent for aid by mid-morning and his request had likely gotten to Corinth within three hours. This would have allowed ready forces in town to gain Spiraeum well before dark, though the rest of the army couldn't reach the scene until early next day.

Their setback at Spiraeum heavily discouraged the Spartans, serving as a painful reminder of the challenges their overseas campaign faced against Athens and its mighty fleet. Alcibiades nevertheless persuaded them to continue supporting an uprising in Asia and they sent him off with the spartiate Chalcideus and five Laconian ships. The famous exile and his comrade arrived safely at Chios and arranged for that island and other nearby poleis to revolt. After operating out of Chios for a time, they replaced their oarsmen and ship handlers with more skillful islanders and sailed to the nearby mainland along with 20 Chian ships. They came ashore at Miletus and had no problem inspiring rebellion there as well. Chalcideus followed this success by making a tentative alliance with Tissaphernes, Persian satrap of lower Asia Minor.

Even as Chios, Miletus, and others split away, Athens avoided a similar rising on Samos in the northern Aegean through the brutal action of local democrats. Abetted by crews from three Athenian ships, the Samian popular party killed 200 oligarchs friendly to Sparta and banished 400 more, paving the way for Samos to become the main Asian base for Athens's fleet. News then came that an insurrection had sprung up on Lesbos. This island lay off the Asian shore north of Chios and its leading city of Mytilene was promoting a break from the Delian League. In truth, unrest at Mytilene wasn't all that surprising given the ferocity of that city's revolt during the Archidamian War.

Athens's Diomedon and Leon led out 25 triremes to retake Lesbos, carrying 1,000 hoplites for this enterprise, all of good quality from the regular list. They could also deploy at least 100 bowmen and a large number of other skirmishers drawn from over 4,000 oarsmen in their fleet. Potential opposition on the island would have consisted of some 3,500 prime and reserve spearmen and perhaps 500–700 light infantrymen. The Lesbians thus had a decided advantage in manpower, but it was spread thinly among at least five cities and the Athenians saw a chance to draw first blood by striking quickly at one of these population centers before a pandemic effort could be gathered. However, for an attack like this to be telling, it had to both damage major enemy assets and spread fear among other insurgents, and the objective needed to have a high profile in order to accomplish these twin goals. Diomedon and Leon therefore chose the highest visibility target available — Mytilene.

The Athenian task force sailed into harbor at Mytilene to chase away a few Chian ships and catch the city off guard as Diomedon and Leon marched their phalanx up from shore to challenge the defending militia. Given that the Mytilenians could likely muster less than a third of their island's men under any circumstance, and even fewer on the short notice then in effect, they likely took the field with no more than 800 hoplites. Surprised, outnumbered, and outclassed, the rebels appear to have suffered a rapid defeat, sending them running for the nearest city gate with their vanquishers close behind. Though most of those beaten escaped, the victors demanded and got Mytilene's surrender by threatening to impose a siege, and it wasn't long before all Lesbos was back under their control.

Diomedon and Leon sailed on to Chios, where they landed at several points, apparently seeking to again put their men into action at favorable odds against only a portion of the opposition. Chios was a rich island that had enjoyed a long era free from attack within a propitious relationship with Athens and its strength at this time must have been near that at century's turn, when great prosperity allowed for a 100-ship fleet. This suggests some 4,000 prime hoplites, with another 1,000 reservists and some light foot troops; however, about 1,000 spearmen were not on the island at this time (a portion being in custody at Athens, while others were serving at Miletos). Since at least a third of the isle's forces resided at its chief city of Chios (along the east-central shore), only about 2,000 prime and reserve hoplites would have been available to defend other sites.

Once more exploiting a widely dispersed opponent, Athens' fleets assaulted the mountainous northern end of Chios. The lesser cities of Cardamyle and Bolissus in that part of the island could do no more than match Athenian manpower, having scarcely a thousand spearmen between them. Moreover, though these defenders might have equaled their foes in raw numbers, their troop quality was poor and the men from Athens handed them a costly defeat. Two more victories soon followed against what must have been even weaker opposing forces (perhaps lone 500-hoplite lochoi) at Cape Phanae (on the island's southern tip) and Leuconium (location unknown). Reeling from three bloody reverses in the field, the Chians refused to again risk battle, letting the invaders plunder and set up a blockade at sea. The Athenians began to fortify Delphinium as a long-term base. Near Chios's main city, this was a well-suited site with multiple harbors and strong natural defenses.

Panormus and Miletus (412 B.C.)

While the Chian campaign was developing, another Athenian fleet sailed via Samos to begin operating from the small island of Lade just off the Milesian coast. Of modest size at only 20 ships, this was actually a reconnaissance-in-force ahead of a major expedition still in preparation. Strombichides and Thrasycles led the squadron at Lade, intending to use their fast triremes against vessels trading with Miletus. They also planned to probe that city's outlying defenses with an embarked force that probably numbered 800 hoplites and 80 bowmen. Pursuing the latter objective, they dropped down to come ashore at Panormus, which lay on a headland about 21km south of Miletus.

The assault on Panormus saw yet another amphibious force of modest size strike within a broad area held by an opponent with greater numbers. The Athenians at Lade couldn't have had much more than a quarter of the hoplite strength that was available to Miletus, but by taking advantage of their seaborne mobility, they were able to mass against a thinly spread defense to achieve local superiority. No doubt alerted by coastal scouts, Sparta's Chalcideus moved to oppose the landing with what Thucydides characterized as a few men, probably a flying squad for point defense similar to those that guarded Laconia in the closing years of the Archidamian War. If so, Chalcideus met the invaders with some Persian-supplied horsemen and a 500-man lochos of hoplites.

Chalcideus seems to have come upon the raiding party from seaward. Had he approached from inland, his foes would simply have pulled back to their ships without a fight; instead, he must have blocked their escape to the beach and forced an engagement. The Athenians were able to form ranks despite any surprise that the appearance of Chalcideus and his men might have created, and appear to have taken advantage of deeper files to push through the opposing array and regain their ships. The Spartan general lost his life at some point in these proceedings, turning an otherwise minor action into a more significant victory for Athens.

Not long after the raid on Panormus, a large fleet arrived at Miletus from Athens by way of Samos, bringing 3,500 hoplites aboard 48 ships that included some troop transports. Like horse carriers used on Sicily, the transports were converted triremes, with the upper two banks of oars replaced by passenger space, making it probable that each had about 150 spearmen aboard in replacement of 110 oarsmen and a normal load of 40 passengers. This indicates that the fleet had 14 transports and 34 triremes full to capacity. With over 300 bowmen and numerous skirmishers drawn from their crews, Athens's hoplites set up camp before the beached fleet at a site near Miletus, from where they could threaten landward access to that site at the same time that their ships cut off supply from offshore. Clearly fearing the kind of siege that had devastated their city during the Ionian Revolt, the Milesians elected to fight a pitched battle.

Miletus's defenders marched out to form their phalanx, which likely stood eight shields deep at a strength of about 2,800 spearmen. Their hoplites included 800 Milesians, most of 200 Peloponnesians from the five triremes of Chalcideus, and 800 Chians from 20 other ships. There were also perhaps 8,000–1,000 mercenary spearmen who had arrived with the Persian satrap; "barbarians" per Thucydides, these were probably Carians. Some 400–500 peltasts would also have been on hand to back up the heavy infantry. Tissaphernes himself rode with his cavalry, which might have been a 600-man hazarabam (at 60 percent nominal strength). Hoplites from Miletus held the phalanx's right wing, putting the Peloponnesians with Alcibiades at far left and the Chians and mercenaries in the center.

The Athenians advanced into combat along a front that probably matched that of their foe at some 350m wide. Their failure to spread out in an attempt to outflank and turn the smaller opposing formation must have been due to terrain limitations — yet it's not clear whether it was the defenders or the Athenians that chose to fight on a restricted field. In fact, both sides could have seen benefits in such a setting, and its selection may have been one of mutual consent. Just as a shortened field precluded an enveloping move by the larger army from Athens, so it also protected Athenian flanks from mounted attack. It thus seems reasonable that the engagement took place at a predetermined site where each side sacrificed an obvious physical advantage toward reaching a decision on the basis of courage and skill along the battlefront.

Adjusting to terrain, the Athenians had 1,000 of their own hoplites on the right wing, with 1,000 Delian League allies at center and 1,500 Argives on the left. The right and center divisions stacked eight deep to oppose enemy units of similar number and depth, but the troops from Argos had to file at 12 shields due to the narrow field. The Argives actually had only 1,000 veteran hoplites (likely epilektoi), as their other 500 were men who normally fought as peltasts, but had on this occasion borrowed heavy gear from the Athenians. Of course, skirmishers with the invading force couldn't take their usual flank positions and all must have stood at the rear on the left, well positioned to either pursue or protect a retreat as needed.

The deeply filed Argives on the right surged ahead in a burst of overconfidence as their phalanx closed range. These men might have assumed that Ionian spearmen like the opposing Milesians would be no match, especially when heavily outnumbered. If so, they got quite a nasty surprise. The hoplites from Miletus withstood the collision along their front and then went on to exploit disorder that a wild charge had created among their enemy. The best spearmen from Argos no doubt lined the first four to six ranks of their phalanx, leaving steady, older men to hold the last two to four rows and keeping the inexperienced former peltasts enclosed within. Thus, when the Milesian assault carried well into the leading Argive ranks, it sent a tremendous thrust of momentum into the tyro hoplites stationed in that formation's center. Panic exploded through these green troops, sending them scrambling rearward. More seasoned warriors at Argos's rear had no choice but to give way before a flood of men being driven from the front by the enemy and from the interior by fear. The Dorians fled with their Ionian conquerors close behind. Argive loses were heavy at 300 hoplites (20 percent), indicating that cavalry and peltasts joined in the chase.

Fortunately for the Athenians, allied spearmen in the middle of their line held up better than the more highly regarded Argives. These troops stood their ground long enough for the Athenian right to shove around end of the facing Peloponnesians and roll them up. The left wing of the defending phalanx broke apart under this flank attack and, with their left now exposed, the Carians battling in the center of the field also gave way toward the nearest city gate. Peltasts and horsemen holding post near the city apparently moved up at this point to cover the developing retreat, and were so effective that the Milesians returning from pursuit were able to safely pause under their walls to ground spears in haughty defiance before finally retiring.

Athens had gained a major victory at the price of perhaps 350 hoplites, most of them Argive. It's interesting to note that the losing side might well have taken even lighter casualties (maybe only 200–250 spearmen killed), but had ceded the field to put themselves at risk for a siege. The victors set up a trophy and began planning an investment; however, word soon arrived that a large Peloponnesian fleet was drawing near. Phrynichus, one of a trio of Athenian generals, decided that it would be foolhardy to engage this armada, which had 55 triremes to his 34. Nor would it be any better waiting to fight on shore, since hoplites aboard the approaching fleet (likely over 2,000) could join those in the city for an overwhelming advantage in heavy infantry. His colleagues were still set on a sea battle, perhaps thinking to square the numbers by pulling in ships from Lade, but Phrynichus was able to convince them that it was wiser to orchestrate smaller attacks at favorable odds than to put their city's fleet and future on the line in a single battle at even strength. The Athenians therefore returned to Samos, where the men from Argos, shamed by their poor showing and denied hope for quick redemption, sailed for home.

Rhodes and Delphinium (412–411 B.C.)

The Peloponnesian fleet arrived at Miletus and its leaders conferred with the satrap Tissaphernes, who got them to join an attack on Iasus. This was a Delian League city that lay on a narrow-necked peninsula along the coast of Caria about 45km southeast from Miletus. Iasus was the stronghold of Amorges, a Carian leader and Athenian ally who had risen up against the Great King. This rebel used the city's wealth to sustain his efforts and had even hired some hoplites from Arcadia, Achaea, and other poor areas of the Peloponnese. The fleet sailed to Iasus in parallel with an overland march by Tissaphernes. Those in town thought at first that these new arrivals were Athenian, but then panicked when they realized that the ships in their harbor were hostile. The city fell in short order and Amorges was taken into custody for delivery to the Persians. Though they looted Iasus, the Peloponnesians offered no harm to its mercenaries, absorbing them instead into their army.

About the time of the expedition against Iasus, Alcibiades bolted the Peloponnesian camp and attached himself to Tissaphernes. He did this in fear for his life, having seduced the wife of Agis to incur the Spartan king's wrath. The wily Athenian now worked against his former allies by having the satrap exchange one-sided support of Sparta for a more balanced program that would prolong the war and exhaust both sides. Meanwhile, a movement arose at Athens to recall Alcibiades and replace the democracy with an oligarchic regime. The idea was that Alcibiades could then persuade his Persian friends to back this new government with him at its head.

As Athens drifted toward oligarchy, Leon and Diomedon took charge at Samos and promptly sailed against the Dorian island of Rhodes (about 170km to the southeast off the coast of Caria), which had also revolted against the Delian League. Their landing party might have had around 2,800 hoplites and 100–200 archers, including men who had fought at Miletus (minus those returned to Argos) plus troops drawn from Lade. If transports had been used to take the Argives home (eight filled with 150 men each), then there were still six such vessels on hand for this action, leaving some 48 triremes to carry the rest of the army.

The Peloponnesian fleet had sailed out from Miletus, but fled upon arrival of the Athenian task force in Rhodian waters. The Peloponnesians drove ashore to take up a defensive stance, probably along the northwestern coast near Camirus, a spot where they had based before. Leon and Diomedon were thus easily able to sail past their grounded enemy and make an unopposed landing. It's likely that they put in either to the south near Lindus or on the northeast cape at Ialysus. Both were prime targets, the former being the island's leading polis and the latter home to the rebellion's leader, Dorieus. Regardless of exact landfall, the Athenians had split their foes so as to engage a Rhodian army bereft of mainland allies.

While fixing a size for Athens's armament is very much an exercise in guesswork, doing so for the other side is even more speculative. Herodotus cited Rhodes as sending 150 triremes to fight for Xerxes in 480 B.C., but his figure came from a gross overestimate of Persian resources meant to magnify Greek heroism. It's probable that actual Rhodian strength was only about half the historian's claim. This would mean that there were some 3,000 prime spearmen (enough to man 75 ships) and 750 reservists on the island, and a pandemic muster at 80 percent could have at best roughly matched Athenian manpower. Any substantive advantage for the defenders would have come from their light-armed forces. Whereas Athens might land 100–200 archers and some armed rowers to support its heavy troops, the Rhodians could call upon a large body of javelinmen and the finest slingers in the Greek world — perhaps 500–750 light-armed men in all.

We know little about tactical aspects of the fight on Rhodes, but the Athenians were able to deal their island foes a sharp defeat. Given a Rhodian advantage in skirmishers off the wings, the battle-savvy invaders must somehow have been able to secure their flanks to then carry the center of the field. The death toll was likely modest on both sides, what with the winning formation staying intact and taking little hurt and the losers having a strong light force to screen their retreat. With an enemy fleet and still potent Rhodian army around, the Athenians sailed to the nearby isle of Chalce.

Even as events were unfolding on Rhodes, Pedaritus, Spartan commander on Chios, decided to attack Delphinium. Athens's troops there were tightening a siege from their now completed harbor-side fort and dealing out a great deal of harm. And of all the wounds that they inflicted, the taking in of runaway slaves might have been most damaging. Unique among Greek states, Chios used slaves as oarsmen; thus, their loss hit hard not only at the economy, but at the polis's fighting ability as well. Needing to address this threat quickly and apparently despairing of reinforcement, Pedaritus prepared to attack with whatever troops he could muster locally. His hoplites probably consisted of about 1,000 militiamen from the city of Chios and 300–600 mercenaries (those who had been with Amorges at Iasus). This would actually have given him the larger force, since Athens likely had something less than 1,000 spearmen in camp after three previous battles.

Pedaritus launched a two-pronged assault, sending his Chian contingent against the fortified main encampment while he and the mercenaries broke through at the harbor to seize some beached triremes. But then, an Athenian counterattack crashed into and routed the Chians. There was a brief pursuit that inflicted heavy losses on the fleeing islanders before their attackers turned back toward the harbor. Arriving in full strength, the Athenians overwhelmed the small force standing with Pedaritus in a sharp action, the Spartan commander falling as the last of his men bolted. Chios, having lost many of its hoplites and even more battle gear, now faced a tighter siege that threatened to starve the city into surrender.

The Athenians were performing superbly at the tactical level, yet their ship losses at Syracuse continued to haunt them strategically. Time and again they had to back down lest they risk the precious remainder of their fleet. And the signing of a treaty that winter between Persia and Sparta made this situation worse still, raising the specter of an enemy able to acquire new ships with imperial funds while the Delian League coffer was nearly empty. Amidst all this, oligarchs in Athens continued their efforts for a change of government, but now without reference to Alcibiades, since they no longer believed that he could deliver Persian aid.

Lampsacus, Athens I, and Cyzicus I (411 B.C.)

Rebellion within Athens's empire crept much closer to home when Oropus, on the mainland coast just opposite Euboa's Eretria, went over to the enemy through treachery. Both natives and Eretrians had betrayed an Athenian garrison there, with the Euboans hoping to spread this revolt across the channel onto their island. Meanwhile, in Asia, the Chians had some success at sea, but still couldn't capture Delphinium. Going on the offensive, Dercyllidas of Sparta marched a small force from Miletus that inspired Abydos on the eastern edge of the Hellespont to break from Athens. He then continued northeast along the Asian shoreline to Lampsacus and gained that city as well, bringing the entire eastern side of the strait under Spartan control. Seeing its vital route for grain from the Euxine region in deep peril, Athens dispatched Strombichides from Chios with 24 triremes and transports. This force bypassed Abydos to land at Lampsacus.

The Athenian landing party probably boasted 1,400–1,600 spearmen (from 18–20 triremes and 4–6 transports) along with ships' archers and armed oarsmen. Such an armament offered a powerful threat to the unfortified city, which could muster less than 1,000 hoplites in defense, including both local militia and possibly a few men left behind by Dercyllidas to stiffen and lead the resistance. Lacking strong walls, those in Lampsacus had no option to resist a siege and therefore set up their phalanx on open ground for a desperate attempt to drive off the Athenians before they could reach the edge of town. It was a doomed effort. Badly outmanned, the defenders fell back in defeat on their city, which then gave way at the very first assault. Athens spared Lampsacus only after claiming its slaves and portable wealth as booty. Strombichides next moved to reduce Abydos, but was unable to gain surrender from that better-provided site. He withdrew after a number of failed attacks and retired to Sestos, which lay on the European side of the strait across from Abydos.

Wealthy citizens at Athens rose up at this time to overthrow the democracy. Coordinating their effort with a campaign to establish oligarchy across the Delian League, they assassinated many opponents and gained Athens, but met with mixed results elsewhere. The victorious oligarchs installed a secretive 400-man ruling committee to replace the council of 500 and sought to treat with Agis at Decelea. Unwilling at first to negotiate, the Spartan seems to have taken these contacts as a sign of weakness and, adding fresh troops from the Peloponnese, marched on Athens. He must have hoped to find his enemies in disarray, but they proved both calm and alert. They even sallied to the attack when the king's vanguard got too far out in front.

The 600-man perioecian lochos of Sciritae, which normally held point for Sparta's army, appears to have come under fire from archers backed by both spearmen and cavalry. The attackers likely comprised a full division of 800 bowmen and its frontal guard of 300 hoplites supported by a few skirmishers (Thucydides' account suggests some light foot troops other than archers), 500 mounted troopers, and 100 horse-archers. The Sciritae took rising casualties and couldn't get close enough to bring their foe into shock combat; therefore, with horsemen menacing their flanks, they had no choice but to retreat. Agis didn't yet have his main force ready for action and couldn't stop Athens from claiming slain men and arms left behind by his bloodied vanguard. With all hope for an easy victory now gone, the chastened monarch went back to Decelea, sent his excess troops home, and reopened peace talks.

Meanwhile, though oligarchy continued at Athens, it didn't take hold within the fleet. Oarsmen from the lower, *thetes* class dominated the navy and were steadfast supporters of a broad-based democracy that had always favored their interests. Nor did other Athenians at Samos feel differently, joining the rowers in forming their own ruling council of 500 and inviting Alcibiades to return. Alcibiades hastened to Samos and was named a general by election. Assessing the situation, he gained agreement not to sail against the rebel government at Athens. He thus kept the city's naval power concentrated on the vital eastern trade routes, perhaps being well aware that other factors were at work and the situation back home would resolve itself.

And indeed, the regime in Athens soon started to unravel as many hoplites vital to army strength became increasingly hostile to rule by wealthier men. The spearmen wanted a council of 5,000 (representing those who could provide hoplite gear) to take charge, thus giving power to the middle, *zeugitai* class. Facing growing resistance, the oligarchic cabal suffered great loss of prestige after a modest naval defeat in the Euboan channel. This reverse triggered widespread revolt on Euboa and ultimately lead to a hoplite uprising at Athens that killed a few of the more extreme oligarchs and drove the rest into asylum at Decelea. Theramenes, who had backed a more moderate oligarchic scheme, now led the city to reconcile with its fleet. This restored Alcibiades along with a number of other exiles, and though a select council held sway at first, the full citizenry would return to power within a year.

The new council sent Thrasyllus and Thrasybulus to Samos, with the latter holding supreme command (Kagan 1987, 218). These generals joined Alcibiades and others to campaign in the Hellespont region, where they won two notable sea battles (Cynossema and Abydos). While the most important action took place offshore in these engagements, each saw late-stage skirmishing along the strand. In both cases, ship-borne Athenians failed against crews fighting from shore to protect their grounded hulls with help from Persian allies. Though these major naval events didn't evolve into set battles on land, one smaller clash off the south coast of the Propontis (the modern Sea of Marmara above the Hellespont) did precipitate a significant combat ashore.

Eight ships from Byzantium (which had joined in the revolt against Athens) ran from 18–20 triremes out of Sestos and beached near the wealthy polis of Cyzicus. The Athenians landed and routed the Byzantines in a pitched fight. Byzantine forces were clearly the smaller in this action, probably having only about 300 hoplites and some 1,600 light-armed crewmen. The Athenians, on the other hand, had brought an assault force for use against breakaway outposts like Cyzicus that included perhaps 700–800 spearmen. It's likely that with plenty of light support from its ship crews, this embarked force prevailed by enveloping the flank of a thinner and shorter Byzantine formation. Turning then on Cyzicus, the victors were able to extort a large ransom before sailing away.

Shifting Fortunes and the Fall of Athens

It must have been growing obvious to Athens's leaders that their hit-and-run campaign along the Asian shore wasn't producing decisive results. Despite a host of tactical successes, many key sites remained in enemy hands and there was no sign of an end to the rebellion wracking their overseas empire. As long as Sparta and its allies had a strong navy, they could back uprisings among island poleis and threaten critical trade routes, putting both tribute-paying territories and vital grain imports in jeopardy. The obvious remedy was for the Athenians to completely destroy opposition naval capability with their superior fleet. Of course, Sparta had come to a similar conclusion in devising its own strategy: it could cut Athens's supply lines and win the war only through victory at sea. The conflict thus came to focus increasingly on fleet actions.

Cyzicus II and Athens II (410 B.C.)

Mindarus, who had been Peloponnesian admiral in the defeat off Abydos, spent the winter assembling another 60 ships (per Xenophon, though Diodorus claimed he had 80). Fearing that this armada would attack Sestos, the Athenians pulled in triremes from all around the Aegean, 86 in all, to make a preemptive strike. Mindarus ducked immediate confrontation by sailing up the Hellespont to put in just below Cyzicus on the southern shores of the Propontis. He must have felt secure here, as the satrap Pharnabazus was present with cavalry and mercenary spearmen to shield his landward side. At the same time, lookouts along the Hellespont were ready to give advance warning of any developing seaborne threat. However, the Athenians foiled this early warning system by rowing up the strait under cover of night, taking advantage of a heavy rain to further mask their passage as they made close approach to the opposing fleet without detection.

The Athenian commander, Thrasybulus, made a landing on the south side of the peninsula jutting northwest from Cyzicus (which lay on a narrow neck connecting to the mainland) and then sent the general Chaereas overland toward the city with an assault force. Chaereas likely led around 1,700 hoplites, comprising half those aboard the fleet if each trireme carried about 40. Meanwhile, Thrasybulus split his ships into three groups and sailed against Mindarus. His sub-commanders, Alcibiades and Theramenes, each had 20 ships, leaving over half the fleet (46 vessels) under direct control of the admiral-in-chief. (Plutarch's account gives 40 ships to Alcibiades, but the most complete battle description from Diodorus favors Thrasybulus having a larger share. This is also consistent with his higher rank. The 40 triremes of Plutarch were thus more likely a total for both subordinates, rather than Alcibiades alone.)

Alcibiades led his small flotilla forward as bait, enticing Mindarus to sail out for a battle against a foe he appeared to outnumber by 3 to 1. While continuing foul weather (Kagan 1987, 241) might have hidden size of the opposing force at first, Mindarus soon made out its true strength and realized his peril. Fearing both enemy seamanship and numbers, the Spartan ran for Cleri, a northeast-trending beach south and west of Cyzicus. Mindarus lost a few ships to hot pursuit, but got most of his fleet ashore, where Pharnabazus's men came up to help fend off Alcibiades' attempts to grapple and tow off the grounded vessels.

Assuming that 50 of Mindarus's triremes survived, they would have beached as close together as possible (10m or so apart from prow to prow) along a half-kilometer stretch. This crowding let their spearmen (probably 2,000 at 40 per ship) front the entire anchorage at three shields deep, putting all within spear's reach of a seaward attack. Mindarus also set up a reserve of 500 hoplites under Clearchus, Spartan governor of Byzantium, who was to back up the main line as well as respond to any landward threat. Many of the fleet's spearmen were Ionian, while others came from Syracuse (volunteers and/or epilektoi) and the Greek mainland (Peloponnesians likely made up the elite reserve unit). The satrapal mercenaries, probably a hazarabam of 800–1,000, supported the defense by joining Clearchus.

Alcibiades' marines made a spirited attempt to drag away some of the stranded ships. Though few in number (there would have been no more than 400 hoplites left after manning the column of Chaereas), they could strike with superior strength at select sites along the thinly stretched enemy line. Dashing in to throw their grapples, the Athenians took full advantage of opponents that had to stay in place if they were to guard all their ships. No doubt very sporadic in pace, this action must still have been intense at times, taking a toll on both sides to scatter dead and dying men along shore—some staining the sand with their blood as others reddened the shallow surf. The Athenian assaults would surely have succeeded at a few points if it had not been for Clearchus and his reserves stepping in time and again to prevent a breakthrough. But Alcibiades and his men persisted, falling back to regroup after each failed attack under protection of a deadly screen of arrows from their triremes.

Thrasybulus saw that Alcibiades was making little progress from offshore and sent Theramenes to find Chaereas so that they might then bring their combined strength overland against the enemy position. Meanwhile, the admiral took his own troops ashore to launch an assault that would provide more immediate help. Thrasybulus led what must have been just over 900 hoplites and nearly 200 archers in a bold advance on Mindarus's northeast perimeter. As he approached, the Athenian would have fixed his right wing on the sea and spread out sufficiently to anchor his left in rough terrain; all of his bowmen could have then set up to further secure the landward flank. Mindarus reacted by sending his reserve up to confront this new threat before it could reach his embattled anchorage. Clearchus marched on Thrasybulus with 1,300–1,500 hoplites. This gave him a 50 percent or better edge in manpower, which would have allowed for files at least 12 deep versus only eight on the other side.

Thrasybulus undoubtedly sought to delay engaging for as long as he could. He would have done this by making as if to attack, but actually holding back in expectation that Theramenes would arrive soon and tip the numbers in his favor. The Athenian likely stood as per tradition, near the front and on the right side of his formation, putting him in all likelihood directly across from Clearchus and his picked lochos. While such a left-wing post was unusual for a Spartan commander, it made sense here, not only positioning him closer to the ships he was protecting, but also allowing him to face the best enemy troops with a secure anchor on his flank. The riskier and less prestigious job of holding the center and right thus fell to Pharnabazus's hirelings.

As minutes passed without action, Clearchus couldn't have helped but sense his opponent's reluctance. He therefore decided to take the initiative and signaled his phalanx to advance into shock contact. The Spartan himself sought to push through on the left side, while mercenary hoplites extending out onto his right wing tried to turn the inland flank. Their opponents put up stiff resistance as, killing and being killed, they gave as good as they got in holding fast against superior depth and othismos. However, the satrap's paid men eventually began to make gains as Thrasybulus's troops tired and their fire fell off due to a dwindling supply of arrows. The mercenaries were soon on the verge of wrapping around an ever more exposed Athenian left.

Just as the Athenians were losing all hope, Theramenes finally arrived from northward with just over 2,100 hoplites, which let Thrasybulus and his exhausted men pull out of contact. They retreated through the approaching line of their comrades to then form ranks in back as fresh soldiers replaced them at the front (the account of Diodorus implies that Theramenes now led). Clearchus didn't contest this rotation, apparently seeking instead to reform for another round of battle. But his opposition didn't allow time for such adjustments, advancing to renew combat and take advantage of a phalanx that would have been filed at 24 shields against one at but half that depth. Clearchus and his troops seem to have given a good account of themselves in a stubborn contest of othismos and front fighting that lasted for some time. Eventually, however, the deeper Athenian files took their toll. The satrapal troops on Clearchus's unanchored landward wing broke first, their flight exposing fellow mercenaries in the center of the field to trigger a collapse there as well. When these hired men fled, Clearchus and his elite reserve lochos had no choice but to also quit the field, falling back in reasonable order toward their anchorage.

As Theramenes and Thrasybulus redressed their ranks for a final advance on the grounded fleet, runners alerted Mindarus of Clearchus's setback. Though still engaged in a chaotic duel with Alcibiades and his marines, the admiral reacted coolly by again splitting his hoplites, sending half of them (700 or so) up to reinforce his faltering right flank. Clearchus rushed to incorporate these men into his line for another effort against an enemy whose advantage in heavy infantry now approached 3 to 1. While both sides got ready to go at it again on the north, there was a lull in the action on that part of the field. But no such pause took place along the seafront, where pressure from offshore may even have picked up in pace. Alcibi-

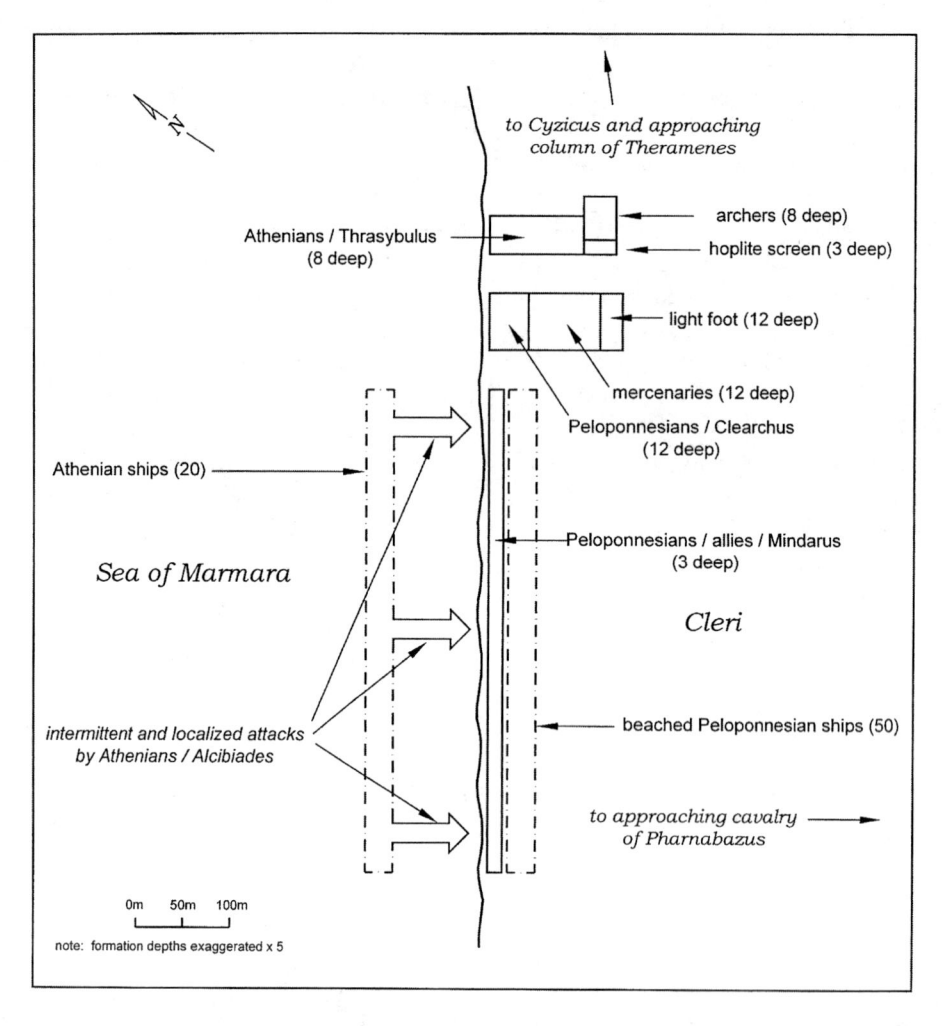

BATTLE OF CYZICUS II (410 B.C.)

ades' men were able to strike with increasing effectiveness as the opposing force shrank to meet threats elsewhere; and now, with their foes standing no more than two deep, they finally cut through to the beached ships.

Some among the stranded crews must have jumped into the fray in an effort to save their vessels, but had little chance of stopping the heavily equipped Athenians. Mindarus soon went down and his death put an end to the defensive stand. The Syracusans set fire to their triremes and joined other beaten men in a desperate race for the interior and safety. With black smoke rising, Clearchus witnessed the chaotic flight of those protecting his rear and sensibly withdrew as well, managing to get away before Theramenes could close into contact and fix him for an attack from behind by Alcibiades. There was little pursuit, as the victors were more concerned with securing abandoned ships and moving on Cyzicus. As it turned out, though they ultimately looted the city, they then had to put back to sea in order to avoid Pharnabazus, who had come up with his cavalry to support survivors from the battle.

Cyzicus II spurred the Spartans to propose a peace that would freeze territory held by each side at its present extent. Predictably, this was unacceptable to the Athenians, since it would cede much of their overseas empire. Ending hostilities now would also give Sparta time to replace its ships with Persian aid. Athens thus preferred to press its current naval advantage and recapture as much territory as possible before seeking a settlement. The Spartans countered by getting to work on rebuilding their fleet and sending Agis out from Decelea in the meantime to once more menace the walls of Athens. This last move proved rash. Thrasyllus was in the city at the time, exploiting victory at Cyzicus by asking for more resources for the Asian campaign. He took command of the garrison and led his troops out to marshal near the Lyceum (a gymnasium on the outskirts of town) that he might meet the enemy advance. Such boldness was a marked reversal of earlier Athenian reluctance to engage Agis, which strongly suggests that Thrasyllus held substantial superiority in numbers. If so, the Spartan king must have brought his modest Decelean contingent without waiting for a major mobilization from the Peloponnese.

Though sometimes recklessly aggressive, Agis was no fool; therefore, when he saw the sort of overwhelming manpower that Athens was sending out, he lost no time in turning about and marching back to Decelea. However, in his hurry to be off, the king left his rearguard exposed without adequate cover from either cavalry or light foot troops. This was likely one of his hoplite lochoi, perhaps the Sciritae if the column had retreated after a simple 180-degree turn. Thrasyllus's light-armed troops took advantage of this mistake by charging in to repeatedly launch their javelins and arrows from short range, pulling back beyond spear-reach each time their slower opponents tried to close. Agis finally got away, but only after losing a number of men from his trailing unit. This sorry performance served to confirm the wisdom of concentrating on denying food and funds to Athens though action closer to its source of supply—in Asia.

Oeta/Heraclea and Ta Kerata (409 B.C.)

Though strategic focus of the war was now firmly fixed overseas, the next year saw a couple of significant actions take place on the Greek mainland. The first involved Sparta's outpost at Heraclea on the northeastern edge of Boeotia, which was resurgent under a new governor, Labotas. The colony now got involved in a clash with Oeta over rights to nearby land along the northwest border of Doris and its forces marched out to secure this territory by force of arms.

Manpower for the Oetaeans must have been much like that of other minor powers in their region (Phocis, Malis, etc.) and they would have had about 1,000 spearmen, a couple of hundred skirmishers, and a few horsemen. The Heraclean levy was no larger and of similar composition. Labotas sought to improve his odds by joining with Phthiotan Achaea, which lay just north of Doris across the Malian Gulf. This would let him deploy something like 1,500 hoplites along with a much larger light support force. But Labotas's choice of allies proved poor indeed, as the Achaeans switched sides once on the field of battle—a betrayal no doubt worked out with Oeta toward splitting the spoils of victory. The turncoats on Heraclea's left wing made a flank attack on the colony's center division at the same time that the Oetaeans made contact all along the front. Fixed by thrusting spears both ahead and alongside, the Heracleans appear to have been caught within a deadly double envelopment. Almost completely surrounded, they fell in shocking numbers, with Xenophon citing 700 slain, including Labotas. If all of these reported casualties were hoplites, then very few in Heraclea's forward and middle ranks escaped with their lives.

Disappointing as it might have been for Sparta, the setback in Doris was very much a minor affair, a colonial sideshow that had little effect on the course of the war. Of much greater concern was defeat of Spartan ally Megara in a pitched battle against the Athenians.

This was of potential import because Megara sat astride a bottleneck in the route from Laconia to Decelea, and there was a risk that any reversal on this front might very well isolate Agis and overturn the favorable strategic situation in Attica. In fact, the Megarans' defeat had come as a result of their own aggression. They had struck first, retaking the Saronic port of Nisaea (lost to Athens in the Archidamian War) and inviting a counterattack. A Megaran force had then sortied to confront the Athenian overland advance just below some hills called Ta Kerata (The Horns) on the Attic border opposite Salamis.

Athens mustered 1,000 hoplites, 400 horsemen, and a couple of hundred light footmen. This armament must have been quite a bit smaller than that sent out by Megara, despite the latter having several other commitments. Not only were Megaran troops in the Hellespont, with two tribal lochoi (1,200 hoplites) at Byzantium, but polis reserves were busy as well, guarding their home city and Nisaea. Nevertheless, the Megaran army could still take the field with about 1,800 spearmen in its other three regular lochoi. It also had some skirmishers and 300–500 additional hoplites that had marched in from Sparta to help stiffen the Attic frontier. The latter were freed helots that had served with Gylippus in Sicily, whom Sparta's leaders had taken care to post to distant Megara as a precaution against their inspiring unrest among their still subjugated brethren at home. With all of these troops combined, the Megarans would have had more than twice the heavy infantry of their Athenian opponents.

Yet despite this manpower discrepancy, the Athenians seem to have deployed boldly for battle on open ground. And indeed, though they couldn't have filed at more than four shields deep against foes standing at perhaps double that depth over a slightly longer front, it was the men from Athens who came away with a resounding victory. Athens's cavalry must have been the key to this success, since it was the one arm that the other side couldn't match in kind. Likely massing most heavily on the Athenian left, these horsemen would have charged to scatter the opposing light infantry before turning to break the enemy right. With their premier wing running away, the remaining Megarans had little choice but to collapse into a mad flight for safety as well.

The action at Ta Kerata ended with the victors mounting a hot pursuit that inflicted heavy damage on the Megarans, maybe raising their death toll to as high as 350–550 hoplites (roughly 20–30 percent). Sparta's helots faired much better in contrast. Sitting farthest from the engagement's turning point, these men largely escaped notice during the retreat. Their opponents appear to have been intent on avenging loss of Nisaea by punishing the Megarans, and this let the helots get away at a cost of only 20 (5–7 percent) of their spearmen. Still, though having exacted a fearful price in blood, the Athenians gained little from their victory. They hadn't hurt Megara enough to make it vulnerable to either intimidation or assault, nor were they able to regain the lost port, which remained firmly under enemy control behind its stout walls.

Pygela and Ephesos II (409 B.C.)

At Athens, Thrasyllus had parlayed his success against Agis into approval of reinforcements for the eastern campaign. He mustered 1,000 veteran hoplites (two lochoi), 100 horsemen, and 50 triremes; also, besides sailors, his ships carried 500 additional spearmen (young marines at ten per vessel) and 9,000 rowers. Each trireme normally held four bowmen, but it was apparently necessary to leave half of these behind in order to provide space for all the hoplites. Spearmen thus filled all 900 passenger slots on 30 ships and displaced the archers on 25 of these as well. Thrasyllus compensated for these lost bowmen by outfitting 5,000 oarsmen as peltasts. Cavalry took full cargo space on the other 20 triremes at five riders and their mounts each (room usually allotted for five men accommodating only one horse). This armament sailed via Samos to strike first at Pygela, which sat just south of Ephesos and was the main enemy harbor in that region. Thrasyllus sent out armed crewmen to lay waste to nearby fields as he moved with the rest of his landing party to attack the city walls.

A force that included about 200 spearmen arrived from Miletus during the Athenian operation at Pygela. These men were intent on helping the embattled town and, seeing the enemy spread about, they gave chase. When Thrasyllus became aware of this, he hastened to aid his exposed men, leading out every rider, his remaining light infantry, and the two lochoi of embarked hoplites (1,000 strong, leaving behind what was effectively a third lochos of marines). This rescue party overwhelmed the Milesians, finding them to be much fewer in number and standing without good order due to their pursuit of widely scattered targets. The Athenians used their cavalry and peltasts to deadly effect in running down and killing nearly all the intruders as they tried to escape. Thrasyllus set up a trophy and then shifted focus of his effort. He now moved up the coast and even made a brief sortie into the interior; as it turned out, this brought only modest success, leading him to seek greater impact by dropping back upon Ephesos.

Thrasyllus arrived at Ephesos after dark and, keeping his marines aboard, landed the other hoplites just below the harbor under cover from the hill of Coressos. He then offloaded his remaining men near the marshes that dominated on the other side of town. Thrasyllus's strategy seems to have required advances on Ephesos from two directions at once, yet his logic remains elusive. Certainly, splitting his resources so close to the opposition was fraught with risk should he meet an aggressive counterattack. Perhaps the Athenians believed their Ionian foes lacked the necessary combat experience and martial spirit to be a real threat. However, if this kind of thinking lay behind Thrasyllus's curious plan of attack, then it soon played him false.

The Ephesian militia was no doubt smaller than earlier in the century, but it still probably boasted 1,500 spearmen, equal to the invaders' entire hoplite force. Nor was this the only military resource available. Tissaphernes, area satrap, had urged regional forces to rally at Ephesos and some other Ionian spearmen, a few heavily equipped Lydians, and a large number of peltasts must have been present as well. Furthermore, a fleet of 27 triremes had come in from Sicily (25 from Syracuse and two from Selinous) with over 1,000 hoplites. Most of these were veterans from the siege at Syracuse and it's likely that they included all of that city's epilektoi. The Sicilians not only brought much-needed experience in phalanx fighting, but also an air of confidence — they had taken down a great invading army in their homeland and were now set to do the same here.

Thrasyllus began his offensive at sunrise, when he had enough light for marching and might still catch his foes unprepared. As it turned out, it was he who was taken off guard. The Ephesians must have been aware of the landings and had set out before dawn to preempt any assault. Though the Oxyrhynchus text (Lazenby 2004, 209) suggests that the Athenian advance penetrated town to trigger a response, it's more likely that defenders were already in place south of the harbor, hiding behind high ground near shore. Thrasyllus and his hoplites thus would have fallen into an ambush just as they rounded the upper end of Coressos hill. All of a sudden, the Athenians found themselves facing an opponent with something like a 3 to 1 advantage in heavy foot troops.

Our meager information on the opening round at Ephesos II indicates a spirited fight. This suggests that the landing party held out for a while, most logically by anchoring its flanks against the nearby hill and other terrain. Able to then array along a short front at eight shields deep or more, the Athenians dampened the effects of greater opposing manpower by forcing it into extremely deep files with less efficient othismos. There was, however, a limit to how much such tactics could accomplish, and the troops from Sicily eventually won a prize for valor by breaking through on their end of the battlefront. Defeated on that wing, the invaders gave way and raced toward their ships. Their retreat drew no more than brief pursuit, since the victorious army was more intent on regrouping so as to move on the other enemy assets across town. Still, Athens's loses were steep, with 100 hoplites killed (10 percent of those engaged) at what must have been very little cost to the opposition.

Rounding the city, the Ephesians and their allies now dressed ranks and closed on the marines, armed rowers, and horsemen near the marshes. What followed wasn't much of a contest. With only about 500 hoplites, the Athenians had no real chance against a force that might have included nearly 3,000 spearmen. Nor did they have enough archers and horsemen to impact the outcome. A rout and pursuit therefore ensued that took down around 200 Athenian marines as well as some 40 riders and 60 light-armed footmen that were too slow to escape over the swampy ground.

Thrasyllus negotiated a truce the next day, that he might recover his dead, and then sailed off to meet other Athenian forces in the region and camp for the winter at Lampsacus. While he had survived a costly reverse, the same can't be said for his reputation; in fact, there was widespread reluctance within Athenian ranks to associate with anyone beaten and thus shamed at Ephesos. Thrasyllus and his men would have to make a strong show of bravery if they were ever to restore their honor.

Abydos, Chalcedon, and Byzantium (409–408 B.C.)

The Athenians narrowed their strategic focus after the defeat at Ephesos. Instead of ranging throughout Asia Minor in an effort to recover all of their overseas empire, they now concentrated solely on securing their route of grain supply. This meant clearing the enemy from key Hellespont and Bosporus passages into the Euxine Sea. Thrasyllus sailed out with what remained of his command to strike the first blow in this northern campaign, descending on Abydos, which sat along the Asian shore near the southwest entry to the Hellespont.

Thrasyllus had 30 triremes capable of carrying 900 spearmen passengers, 300 marine hoplites, a few archers (less than 100), and 60 or so horsemen (all that remained from Ephesos). The riders and their mounts would have taken up all cargo space and displaced bowmen on a dozen ships that sailed under Alcibiades. This latter flotilla kept on after the rest of the fleet put in near Abydos, thus putting Alcibiades at a distance when he landed to begin raiding the countryside. Menander accompanied this effort and had command of the 120 marines, whose apparent assignment was to guard Alcibiades' foragers. This reflected lessons learned at Pygela, where unescorted crewmen had nearly come to grief.

Pharnabazus, the local Persian governor, sent troops to rescue Abydos. This column likely consisted of satrapal cavalry (some 600 riders at 60 percent nominal strength) and a hazarabam of local peltasts (perhaps 800 men). Reaching Abydos that afternoon, these troops descended to rain missiles down on Thrasyllus and drive him into a defensive phalanx. Moving into bow range, the Persians could loose their shafts and then withdraw far ahead of their slow-moving hoplite opponents; at the same time, their javelinmen were proof against less capable enemy skirmishers. Yet they couldn't quickly break so well armored a force and the Greeks held out until reinforcements arrived. Alcibiades and Menander had marched with all possible speed to join their embattled comrades, charging onto the scene to take the satrap's men completely by surprise. The Asians panicked and scattered beneath a hard pursuit that lasted until dark. Though the Athenians would fail in the end to take Abydos, this victory did allow them to collect a great deal of booty from surrounding areas.

Late arrival of reinforcements at Abydos had yielded considerable tactical advantage, though this seems to have been more a matter of luck than planning. As fate would have it, something very similar took place in the next significant engagement. This was at Chalcedon, which lay just east of the southern entrance to the Bosporus passage. Having defected to Sparta, this polis had accepted a garrison from its new ally along with a Spartan governor, Hippocrates — a survivor of Cyzicus II, where he was second in command of the lost fleet. Theramenes sailed 70-ships against Chalcedon in spring 408 B.C., joining there with Alcibiades and Thrasyllus.

A mighty armament now menaced Chalcedon. Athenian strength included perhaps 190 ships (Kagan 1992c, 277) and as many as 5,000 hoplites (if manpower reported by Diodorus was only for heavy infantry). In truth, given the likelihood of 40 hoplites on each of Theramenes' ships, ten marines on the others, and 900 spearmen with Thrasyllus, there must have been at least 4,900 hoplites. Some 60 horsemen were again present, along with archers (nearly 800) and a huge crowd of crewmen (over 30,000). Even as their fleet set up to cut off supply to Chalcedon from the sea, the Greeks ringed its landward side with a wooden stockade that ran from the Propontis on the east to the Bosporus on the northwest, with the only break a minor one across a stream. The barrier was double-walled in order to be defendable both front and rear; a design that soon proved its value when Persia's Pharnabazus arrived with an army to relieve Chalcedon.

The satrap targeted the weakest part of the siege line, the modest gap at the streambed. The Greeks flowed to meet this threat, with spearmen supported by archers and a few javelin-armed rowers moving into the creek's shallow waters and setting up along the walls coming down on either side. Troops from his 70 ships plus half of all remaining marines and bowmen would have given Theramenes 3,400 hoplites and just over 500 archers to man the defense. Alcibiades and his cavalry backed up their infantry, ready to pounce should opportunity allow.

Forces advancing on the palisade included both cavalry and infantry that likely represented the local satrapal complement. If so, they were probably cored by a standing hazarabam of 600 riders and a more recently raised 800-man regiment of mercenary hoplites. At least two more 800-man hazaraba of peltast levies (one Thracian and the other from elsewhere in the satrapy) would have brought total combatants up to something like 3,000. Even so, the Athenians were a good bit more numerous — especially in armored men — and they could fight from behind a stout wall. This suggests that the Persians might really have been trying to draw attention from a sortie by allies in the city. Yet the Athenians were well prepared for any such sally from town, having Thrasyllus watch the gates with perhaps 1,500 spearmen — 900 from his own command of long standing and 600 marines (half those that had arrived with Alcibiades). He also likely had some 200–300 bowmen and a host of armed crewmen. Thus, when a breakout attempt did indeed come, it ran into firm resistance. Sparta's Hippocrates led this sortie with a few psiloi and what must have been three lochoi of 500–600 hoplites each. One of his heavy units was made up of foreigners (Cyzicus II survivors and others from the Hellespont via Byzantium), while local militia manned the other two. The Spartan veteran quickly saw that he was going to have a tough fight on his hands and must have filed his men at eight shields deep across 200m to face an enemy array of similar size and shape.

The phalanxes closed to smash into each other, initiating an evenly matched duel of thrusting spears and pushing shields in which neither side could gain advantage. Resolution came only when Alcibiades arrived late in the action (much as he had done at Abydos) with his cavalry and a few hoplites spared from the stockade. Falling upon the enemy right flank, these new arrivals cleared away any screening psiloi and drove into the unshielded side of the opposing line. Results of this strike were devastating. Hippocrates, who had apparently taken his place on the right with his foreign spearmen, was among the first to fall, causing those standing with him to break away. When these men fled, the locals at center and left also fell back, joining in a terrified rush toward Chalcedon. The aroused Athenians followed close behind and exacted a heavy toll that took the life of no small number of those in flight and wounded many more. Despite this, most of the beaten men got back to town and managed to keep their pursuers from entering.

The satrap's troops eventually withdrew from the siege wall and conceded victory on that front to Athens as well. Alcibiades departed shortly thereafter to raise funds in the Hellespont, which left Theramenes and Thrasyllus to conclude the investment. They proceeded to settle with Pharnabazus, agreeing to bypass Chalcedon and his other holdings in return for payments in cash and his promise not to threaten Athenian interests.

Action in 408 B.C. closed on one last triumph for Athens. With the eastern side of the Bosporus now calm after the agreement at Chalcedon, focus had shifted onto Byzantium, which commanded the western side. The Athenians landed to pit their full strength against this key site, moving to erect an encircling wall and then launch a series of direct assaults. Clearchus of Sparta, still governor of the polis, was able to repulse these attacks with a combination of local militia (including perhaps 2,000–2,500 heavy-armed), mercenaries (800–1,000 hoplites), and allied spearmen from the Greek mainland. He had brought in the latter himself on troop ships — a dozen having survived his daring run past the enemy fleet. These men were a mixed lot from Laconia (perioeci and freed helots), Megara (Byzantium's mother city), and Boeotia. Originally 1,800 strong (at 150 per transport), some of the mainlanders had gone to Chalcedon, leaving 1,500 or so with Clearchus.

Though there were 4–5,000 spearmen on each side of this confrontation, more than half of the city's hoplites were lesser-quality locals and Megarans who would be of questionable value against the seasoned opponent camped outside. A wary Clearchus thus refused pitched battle, preferring to base his defense on the famously sturdy walls of Byzantium. Sound as this strategy might have been, it visited considerable hardship on the populace, with looming starvation sparking envy and anger against Clearchus and his well-fed garrison, whom most in town came to see as foreign occupiers. This led some citizens to conspire with the enemy, agreeing to betray a gate while Clearchus was out of town trying to secure ships and more money for his troops. For their part in the plot, the Athenians sailed away, making a showy pretense of abandoning the siege only to return that night. Secretly landing its hoplites in darkness near the targeted entrance, the fleet then rowed back into harbor at dawn to make a diversionary attack with light-armed men. As the garrison rushed dockside to meet this unforeseen menace at full strength, Athens's spearmen marched to the appointed gate where their agents let them inside.

Regardless of any attempt at stealth, there was a major commotion as the Athenians came spilling in, and defenders at the harbor, who had forced their skirmisher opponents to reboard, saw that they had been tricked. They quickly prepared to meet this new threat by dividing their force more or less in half, setting the local men to safeguard the docks while the mercenary and allied troops marched back to town. Helixus of Megara and Coeratadas of Boeotia led the foreign contingent and put their 2,300–2,500 hoplites in order for a battle in tight quarters.

The returning garrison came to blows with the Athenians, possibly within the "Thracian Square," which lay on the street the invaders used for entry. Alcibiades commanded on the right wing against the Megarans and Theramenes did the same on the left against the Boeotians, leaving the other Athenians and mercenaries to fight it out at center. Both sides must have filed very deeply in such a restricted setting, which most hurt the Athenians, who couldn't take advantage of their greater numbers to outflank the enemy. As a result, the contest turned into a long and stubborn stalemate, with neither side able to push to victory in the close press of so many men. It was the Byzantines who then came forward to break this deadly impasse. Taking heart from assurances that no harm would come to them, the townsfolk changed sides. Their former allies suddenly found themselves among an openly hostile populace, with Byzantine spearmen moving up from the harbor to menace their rear and threaten their route of escape. Some of those surrounded chose to resist to the last, while others turned and ran for their lives through the streets.

There must have been a great slaughter of the garrison at Byzantium, and hundreds perished in a final stand. As for those who broke ranks, long-held enmity of many in town for these foreigners now came to the fore as citizens denied refuge to the fleeing men and even helped to cut them down. No record survives of how many Peloponnesians died in the aftermath, or how many got away altogether. Our sources indicate only that the Athenians took a mere 300 alive at the battle site, while but 500 more gained sanctuary in temples that they might surrender next day. Athens had finally secured both sides of the Bosporus and could now turn full attention upon remaining enemy strongholds on the Hellespont, in Thrace, and around the Aegean basin.

Thasos, Gaurium, and the Surrender of Athens (407–404 B.C.)

Thrasybulus sailed out in early 407 B.C. with 30 ships (per Xenophon, 15 according to Diodorus) in order to attack sites along the Thracian seaboard that had gone over to Sparta. This campaign eventually led him to the isle of Thasos, which famine and internal turmoil had made ripe for retaking. Thrasybulus landed on the northern shore to muster his phalanx of perhaps 1,200 hoplites before the island's eponymous main city, likely filing eight shields deep across 150m and having archers and armed crewmen screening his flanks. Thasos answered with no more than 750 hoplites, probably filed at five deep. This reflected manpower for the polis' 20 triremes plus reserves, yet was down 25 percent from peak strength due to local supporters of Athens having gone into exile. So small and relatively inexperienced an army had no real prospect for victory against a larger host of battle-hardened veterans, and it must not have taken long for Thrasybulus's phalanx to push back the thinly filed islanders until their rear ranks broke away in panic. This left those at the Thasian front to be butchered, with some 200 losing their lives. The survivors were now in no shape to face a siege and gave up, agreeing to an Athenian garrison and return of their exiles.

Alcibiades made a triumphal return to Athens at this time, and though still controversial in some quarters, again won election to generalship. Alcibiades then sailed from the Piraeus with a fleet of 100 ships that held 2,500 hoplites (counting 1,000 marines) and 150 horsemen. His first target was rebellious Andros in the Cyclades chain, which was now home to a Spartan garrison (likely a 500-man lochos of perioeci and/or neodamodeis).

Even as Alcibiades departed, Sparta's Agis marched once more upon Athens at the head of a full levy. He commanded a huge army that had (per Diodorus) some 14,000 hoplites, a like number of light foot troops attendants, and 1,200 horsemen (900 of them from Boeotia). Seeing this massive armament arrayed against them, the Athenians refused to deploy their hoplites, since most were only reservists. Their cavalry, however, did risk a sally. Being about equal in number to their opposition, these local riders soon proved a match in prowess as well, winning a fierce mounted clash just beneath their walls. They followed this initial success with a hard pursuit. However, when hoplites advanced on them from the Spartan line of battle, Athens's horsemen finally fell back, being more than content for now to savor a victory gained at little cost.

The Athenians put up a trophy the next day, so provoking Agis that he lined his men up to fight for its possession. Changing tactics, the Athenians sent out their spearmen this time and formed a phalanx tight upon the city ramparts. Astutely, these men held fast, keeping close to their bowmen and peltasts, who had an extended range from high up on the walls. Agis must have quickly realized that his troops would come under heavy and unanswerable missile fire should they get any closer, and he chose to march away without a fight. After thoroughly plundering Attica, the bulk of the king's army went home and he returned to Decelea.

Alcibiades was by this point busy on Andros, where he had come ashore near the island's chief city and captured an outlying stronghold at Garium. The wily Athenian further walled this site and waited for his opponents to attack in a bid to avert investment. And it wasn't long before he found himself facing an army that was likely made up of the 500 spearmen from Sparta's garrison lochos plus perhaps half again as many local hoplites. The islanders would have formed both left wing and center of a four-deep phalanx, while the foreigners held the right wing post of honor and light-armed troops guarded the flanks. Alcibiades and his men advanced at a likely eight shields deep against their game foes, who must have held stationary to preserve formation integrity.

Reports of casualties from Garium indicate that the Andrians suffered by far the heaviest damage, suggesting it was their end of the line that collapsed first. This was probably due to Athens's archers thinning opposition light infantry on that side prior to a devastating cavalry charge. Spearmen on Alcibiades' right wing would then have pushed through the islander front as it softened under this side assault. The men from Andros scattered toward town, running in stark terror as pursuers speared them down from behind. Only the modest size of Alcibiades' cavalry force allowed many Andrian troops to get away. Meanwhile, most of the Laconians managed to escape, as their right-wing post lay favorably farthest from the point of formation failure.

Alcibiades put up a trophy, assigned the general Conon to Garium with 20 triremes and enough troops to prosecute a siege, and then set out on a raiding cruise that led him in late 407 B.C. to Notium. This Ionian city served as port for Colophon, the only friendly polis close to the enemy fleet lying southeast at Ephesos. Leaving most of his ships here, Alcibiades sailed north with maybe a dozen transports full of troops to join Thrasybulus in besieging Phocaea. He wanted the rest of his command to avoid action and gave orders to that effect to Antiochus, whom he had put in charge of the fleet in his absence. Unfortunately for Athens, this man foolishly provoked a battle with Sparta's Lysander and the resulting reverse cost the city 22 triremes. This debacle coupled with Alcibiades' ill-advised plundering of allied territory to send him into exile.

Garium was the last significant land engagement of the war between Athens and Sparta and attention now turned completely onto naval operations in what would prove to be the final stage of the Peloponnesian War. Action in this closing round of fighting began just off the island of Lesbos, where an Athenian squadron was bested and ran into harbor at Mytilene. Athens responded to this in grand fashion by launching a huge fleet to the rescue. This great armada bested the Peloponnesians in the northern Aegean near the islands of Arginusae in the largest naval battle ever fought between Greeks. Though stormy seas prevented a proper follow-up, Arginusae was a major tactical success for the Athenians; all the same, steps taken by both sides in the aftermath of this battle were destined to lay the seeds of Athens's ultimate defeat in the war.

Sparta and its allies had suffered grievous losses, but were able to swiftly rebuild their fleet with Persian financing (Lysander using his cordial relationship with Cyrus, younger son of the Great King and now satrap of Ionia, to gain all necessary funds) and were thus ready to fight again in a matter of months. As for the Athenians, they unwisely accused their victorious generals of a crime, blaming them for not recovering shipwrecked men after the fight — a questionable claim in light of terrible weather at battle's end. Two of the accused fled, but six others returned to face this charge and were tried, convicted, and executed. Coupled with the earlier loss of Alcibiades, such waste of the city's best military minds set the stage for disaster.

Any hope for final victory came to an end for Athens in 405 B.C. at Aegospotami in the Hellespont region. There, an incompetent set of new commanders allowed Lysander to catch and destroy their fleet onshore while many crewmen were away foraging for food. Only nine triremes managed to escape destruction and Athens could no longer defend its route of grain supply. The Athenians were soon starving under siege by both land and sea. They surrendered in March 404 and found themselves reduced to being unwilling allies of Sparta, with their fabled democracy outlawed and a foreign garrison in place to prop up a ruling council of pro-Spartan oligarchs.

Carthaginian Aggression and the Rise of Dionysius I

While war had raged throughout Greece and the Aegean, other events were making their mark to the west. Sicily was not only torn by strife between its city-states, but also faced a grave external threat from the Carthaginians. This turmoil would give rise to Dionysius I, who came to power at Syracuse to lead the effort against Carthage. Dionysius proved up to the task of preserving his city's independence and ultimately gained tyranny over most of Sicily to become one of the longest-ruling and most successful dictators in Grecian history.

Mazaros III, Selinous I and II, and Himera II (410–409 B.C.)

The Greeks of Selinous and Elymians of Egesta in western Sicily had been in conflict over their common border since at least the early 6th century. They had twice come to blows along the bounding Mazaros River in the mid-to-late 5th century, with the last clash leading to Athenian intervention and the siege at Syracuse. Yet this did nothing to settle the old acreage dispute, and it was destined to once more explode into violence and trigger an invasion.

Selinous declared war on Egesta in 410 B.C. and moved to seize frontier territory. The Egestaeans were significantly the weaker side in this confrontation (likely having only about 60 percent as much heavy infantry) and chose to give up the contested ground. However, the Greeks, flush with easy success, threatened further annexations and Egesta now decided to resist with help from Carthage. The Carthaginians were sympathetic to Egesta and hostile to its Grecian foe, something in no small part due to the leadership of Hannibal, grandson of that Hamilcar lost at Himera in 480 B.C. So great was this man's hatred of the Greeks that he now sought revenge even against Selinous — his grandfather's only Greek ally and later home for his father in exile. This animosity must have had its roots in Selinous's role at Himera, since it was failure of that city's cavalry to arrive as requested that left Hamilcar open to the sneak attack that took his life and initiated Gelon's great victory. Thus, when the Selinutians refused to arbitrate this latest land issue, Hannibal arranged for a force of mercenaries to aid their enemies.

Carthage contracted 800 Campanians (Oscan Samnites from Italy) and 5,000 Libyans on behalf of Egesta. The Italians had originally come to Sicily in support of Athens, remaining thereafter to back other foes of Syracuse. Diodorus claimed that Carthage equipped these men with horses, yet they appear to have fought as heavy infantry. Most likely they were mounted infantry, riding on the march and performing the sort of detached tasks usually assigned to cavalry, but dismounting for pitched combat. This made sense in light of their modest equestrian skills, which limited their ability to maneuver in formation. As for the African troops, they had likewise arrived in connection with the Athenian invasion and stayed (Caven 1990, 24, 27), but had gone home by 410 B.C. only to return now for another tour. Their numbers likely included 3,000 heavies (per other Punic divisions in this era), who were Phoenician-style shock fighters with large shields and short spears. The other 2,000 men would have been archers and peltasts, which gave the hirelings about one light-armed fighter for every two armored men, much as in Hamilcar's earlier force.

As the mercenaries moved out, they joined men from Egesta. These locals probably amounted to 300 riders (per mounted strength in 414 B.C.), 1,500 heavy foot troops (five for each horseman), and 600 skirmishers (half of them hamippoi). This made for over 8,000 combatants marching against no more than half that many opponents. Selinous likely had a levy of only about 2,500 spearmen, representing around 10 percent of its populace if we add up Diodorus's figures. Light support for these line troops came from 500 horsemen (one for each five hoplites), a matching team of hamippoi, and 500 other skirmishers. Bad as this was, their lack of numbers wasn't the only problem facing the Greeks along the Mazaros — they were also unprepared for battle.

The Selinutians had arrived in battle order, but had then scattered to spoil the countryside. Egesta's sudden strike caught them by surprise. Our lone surviving account by Diodorus suggests that the startled Greeks might not have been able to set up a phalanx, which would have let their attackers serially engage small groups of hoplites and defeat them in detail. A reputed 1,000 Greeks lay slain along the Mazaros at day's end, suggesting at least partial encirclement and a very thorough pursuit. If this number should pertain solely to fighters from the upper classes (hoplites and cavalrymen, who were the usual focus for ancient Greek casualty reports), then Selinous lost a full third of its social elites.

The Selinutians thirsted for revenge and got help from Syracuse; meanwhile, Egesta, fearful that the Grecian cities would band against them in just this manner, sought and received aid from Carthage. Hannibal took command of the latter effort and set about recruiting troops, culling the best men from both his citizenry and the Liby-Phoenician perioeci and then adding Iberian mercenaries from southern Spain. The Iberians were mostly heavy troops (sporting leather helmets and large, center-grip shields of oval shape) that fought with throwing spears and a variation on the machaira saber called a *falcata*. A lesser number of Spaniards were light foot troops, these being peltasts, each equipped with a small, leather buckler. A huge naval force gathered at Carthage that winter in preparation for transporting Hannibal's army to Sicily.

How large was the Carthaginian armament? Ancient Greek accounts of its manpower are outrageously high. The most realistic number we have is that of Diodorus for warships, which he pegged at sixty. This would represent a 70 percent reduction from the previous fleet of Hamilcar. Tellingly, the historical figures for troops, though still astronomical, also show sharp declines compared to similar exaggerations made about the first invasion, making it apparent that this Punic expedition was much smaller than the one of 480 B.C.

Ephoros set Hannibal's army at 200,000 foot and 4,000 cavalry, while Timaeus said that it had no more than 100,000 men in all. These numbers range from just over two-thirds down to only a third of the strength credited to Hamilcar, with Diodorus's figure for the war fleet favoring the latter. This makes it likely that there were only about 10,000 combatants, most of them within three infantry divisions of 3,000 men each. Shock troops would have made up two of these units — citizens and perioeci in one and Iberians in the other — while light-armed Libyans would have formed the third. As a lack of cavalry had cost his grandfather dearly, Hannibal must have piled 1,000 horsemen and their mounts into all his other billets, with the riders probably being Africans who carried javelins and small shields. Hannibal's subsequent pursuit of fairly limited objectives supports the idea that he had an army of only modest size. Still, some modern writers have proposed that he fielded many more fighters — Warmington (1960, 76) says 50,000 and Caven (1990, p. 32) 40–50,000 (including 8,000 already on the island).

Hannibal landed on western Sicily in spring 409 B.C. and paused briefly to collect troops from that region. Recruits would have numbered something like 5,000 mercenaries, including some Greeks (per Griffith 1984, p. 209), 2,000 Egestaeans (1,500 armored and the rest light foot troops), and 1,000 others. The Carthaginians rolled over a fortified outpost and marched on to Selinous, which lay on the southern coast between the mouths of two rivers (the Selinous and Hypsas). Hannibal occupied hills west of town (Freeman 1891–1892, Vol. III, 460–461) and broke his men into four groups for a two-pronged attack. He could have created two of these brigades by splitting his embarked light infantry between the African and Spanish heavy units; the Libyans from Mazaros III then formed a third grouping, while Sicilian troops and the Campanians made up the fourth. This teamed men who had compatible fighting styles and were, in many cases, familiar from past campaigns.

Hannibal's two African divisions moved against Selinous from the west, while his Sicilian and Iberian troops skirted the northern end of the city to attack from the east. Teams with iron-tipped battering rams led both assaults, their efforts being covered by bowmen mounted on half a dozen mobile towers of wood. Tarn was of the opinion that these siege devices derived via Phoenicia from Assyrian originals (1930, 102). Hannibal's towers were, in fact, so tall as to loom above the city walls, which were not only of modest height, but also suffered from poor upkeep. The twin attacks beat upon Selinous and finally achieved some success in the eastern sector, where the Sicilian brigade breached the outer wall to initiate a fierce urban battle.

The mercenaries from Campania were eager for plunder and led the way into Selinous, having dismounted to form a heavy-armed vanguard. They penetrated easily at first down the tight, stone-paved passages of the city, since most of the garrison was still battling on the upper ramparts and those few men trying to hold the streets were in disarray. However, as more Greeks — many of them hoplites — poured down from above to form a defense, the Italians found they could make no more headway and soon began to lose ground. Selinutian spearmen were able to file at unusual depth in the close, city confines and they shoved back in a powerful wave of othismos. The Campanians had no choice but to give way, pushing rearward and spreading panic throughout the entire assault force. All the attackers fled back through the breach and the men of Selinous cut down a good many mercenaries in retaking their perimeter. Having lost this opening engagement in the narrow streets, Hannibal called off his men as darkness fell. It had been a hard-fought and very close-run affair, but the city's defenders had survived their first test. Fearing further assaults, they sent out their swiftest riders to seek aid from other Greeks at Acragas, Gela, and Syracuse.

In spite of the desperate note of Selinous's plea for help, its allies were slow in marching to the rescue and Hannibal remained free to continue his siege. While assaults pressured the town's entire outer circuit, action was fiercest on the east at the old breach in the wall. The Greeks had stopped this gap with rubble and manned it heavily; still, it remained a glaring weak point in their defenses and came under persistent attack. Hannibal's men hammered at this sector with rams, rotating paired brigades so as to relay well-rested troops into the fight. There must have been only about 2,500 hoplites within Selinous — counting survivors of Mazaros III, reservists, dismounted aristocrats, and some from the lower classes armed with temple stores — and it was these men who bore the brunt of fighting at the barricade. Their foes did push through more than once, yet they never got very far inside or stayed for very long, as the desperate Greeks battled back each time to reclaim their posts. However, the defenders were tiring even as casualties cut their numbers. Thus, on the ninth morning of siege, Hannibal's forces finally smashed into town for good.

The Iberian division drove inside Selinous amid cries of alarm from women keeping lookout on rooftops. This brought townsmen rushing from the walls to mass in the streets that they might put their lesser numbers to best advantage in these manmade canyons. And indeed, their opponents suffered heavily in the early going. Hoplites standing deeply filed within the maze-like cityscape threw up impromptu barriers at key choke points and stalled all enemy progress on the ground. At the same time, women and children rained rocks and tiles onto the invaders from above. Still, despite these heroic efforts, the battle began to turn in Carthage's favor by early afternoon. That's when those on high ran out of missiles as their men below became seriously degraded by wounds and exhaustion against a foe that kept on throwing fresh troops into the fray. Hannibal's men now carried the streets to flush their remaining opposition into the open. Action came to an end on a gruesome note, with a vicious fight in the town's main market, where a battered band of defenders made a defiant final stand and died to the last man.

Selinous became a cavalcade of horrors in the battle's aftermath as the victors celebrated with an orgy of murder, rape, and looting. Hundreds had died defending the city and many thousands more lost their lives once it fell. The Carthaginians captured most of those who survived, but some 2,600 inhabitants (perhaps including 500 hoplites and horsemen) escaped to Acragas. Hannibal quickly tore down the walls of Selinous and marched north toward Himera. Eager to boost his manpower and gain local support, he picked up Sican and Siculi allies as he advanced. Our sources give large numbers for these additions, but most must have provided only logistical support. Nevertheless, we can reasonably project that there were at least 2,000 warriors of various sorts among the new recruits.

What were the island's other Greeks doing as Carthage's war machine rolled toward its next overmatched victim? Though it was far too late to save Selinous, Syracuse had finally put a force into the field under Diocles. His column included 3,000 hoplites, which are referred to as epilektoi (picked men), but more probably represented most of the spearmen available within the polis, since many men were serving in Asia at the time. Diocles picked up another thousand hoplites (volunteers from Acragas and Selinutian refugees) and rushed to Himera, which was already under attack. The relief force just barely got inside by slipping through the siege lines at an opportune moment. This could have happened at daybreak, when there was enough light to show the way, but before most of those carrying out the investment had arrived at their scattered outposts (having spent the night on more suitable ground). What these new arrivals found inside was a populace already bloodied in combat and desperate for help.

Hannibal had cautiously set up one division (perhaps the handpicked brigade of citizens and perioeci) and most of his cavalry as a reserve on the long ridge west of Himera (near Hamilcar's old army camp). He then spread his remaining host around the town. The plan must have been to encircle and isolate Himera, yet limited manpower, rugged terrain, and supply requirements made this difficult (as Diocles' entry would shortly suggest and subsequent escapes serve to confirm). A round of assaults had followed, but Himera's walls proved much sturdier than their dilapidated counterparts at Selinous. The defenders threw back each attempt on their positions, though the Carthaginians did manage at one point to briefly create a breach. This happened when they dug a mine beneath the city's outer wall and burned away its supports to collapse the overlying ground and structures. However, once inside, the invaders couldn't sustain their foothold and fell back at dusk. Himera's rebuff of this opening thrust was a remarkable feat in that there might have been no more than 3,000 hoplites in town, including reservists, men armed from temple stores, and a few allies. It's clear that strength of the city walls, constriction within the mined opening, and efforts from some 2,000 light-armed regulars and a throng of others with makeshift weapons had trumped manpower in favor of the defense.

Hannibal's men now seem to have fallen into a dangerous nighttime routine. Though they had surrounded Himera, their lines appear to have been but lightly manned after dark, likely being at no more than one third of full strength. Cutting the guard allowed most of the besiegers to retire into camp on or near the beach north of the city. This would have been purely a matter of convenience. An encampment near shore made for more secure sleeping arrangements and eased the offloading of supplies brought by sea (since it was necessary to ship in food for so many men, they could pick it up near the landing point before returning to their widespread daytime posts). Hamilcar had done something similar in 480 B.C., setting up a naval base to support his siege operation. However, he had recognized risks inherent to this arrangement and thus located his camp some distance from the city and provided it with a palisade. Hannibal took no such precautions and this carelessness coupled with inattention to enemy movements to very nearly bring him to grief.

Though Himera had repelled the enemy's first attempt, its defenders must have had few illusions about their chances to withstand the sort of sustained assault that had overcome Selinous. And while a counterstrike held some promise of saving the polis, a lack of heavy-armed manpower precluded that strategy. This all changed with the arrival of Diocles, who restored an offensive option by adding enough hoplites and light-armed troops to bring those fit for a sortie up to around 10,000 men.

Leaving a smattering of irregulars on guard, Diocles and the other defenders struck at first light next day. Bursting from the gates on command, preassigned contingents must have rapidly ranked eight shields deep into a phalanx that extended across a front of nearly 900m. The hoplites advanced in lock step toward the beach and, with light infantry horsemen at their side, seem to have caught their foe completely by surprise. Assuming that the Sicans and Siculi slept elsewhere, it's likely that there were 10,000 combatants in camp. These Punic soldiers dropped what they were doing in a frenzied scramble to get into formation, but were apparently still milling about in a state of great disorder when the attack hit. Slamming into its startled enemies like a hammer of bronze, the Greek phalanx swiftly penetrated, panicked, and routed them.

Ancient reports on the Carthaginians' casualties at Himera are just as out of line as estimates of their manpower; nevertheless, we can find useful clues about the truth within these figures. Timaeus put barbarian losses at 6,000 men. If we assume that the equivalent of two divisions were on hand (two-thirds of the heavy infantry before the city), then the historian's claim might very well correspond to a full count of the defeated armored force. Likewise, the tendency to overstate Carthage's strength by at least an order of magnitude suggests that Ephorus's tally of 20,000 dead more likely reflects 2,000 fatalities (20 percent–33 percent if from only heavy infantry). The beaten men must have taken severe losses from pursuit as some units fell back in good order and others broke apart in terror; and without doubt, all would surely have been lost had Hannibal and his select reserve not now descended to join the fight.

Hannibal did a masterful job in rallying the more coherent elements of his retreating host, forming them up around his picked division for a counterattack. Just as the first strike from Himera had exploited disorder among those camped on the beach, so the back-thrust of Hannibal's redressed army found its foe in disarray. The Greeks had probably flowed to their left in the chase, with both light-armed men and hoplites from that side of their phalanx leading the way. Sensing total victory, they had lost order in the heat of pursuit — a fatal error against an opponent that maintained a tactical reserve. This pell-mell Greek charge ran into the advancing front of Hannibal and disintegrated against an orderly wall of shields. It was now Himera's defenders who fell back along the strand in panic, racing to regain the city gates. A large portion of the retreating force (Diodorus cited 3,000 men) made a stand. This effort bought some time for others to escape, but in the end, despite putting up a valiant fight, the Greek rear guard met utter destruction.

The mood inside Himera was grim. Having lost a third of his manpower, Diocles had no hope of mounting another sally. He also must have known that a passive defense was sure to fail before long against the fearsome siege engines of Carthage. Adding to these worries was fear that Syracuse, bereft of its best troops, might soon come under attack as well, with rumors to this effect already rife among his men. Diocles thus decided to abandon Himera. The city's natives complained bitterly, yet really had no choice but to accept his decision. The Greeks once more took advantage of their enemy's poor nighttime staffing of the siege lines and a large body of them slipped out after dark to make a clean getaway. A fleet of 25 triremes had arrived from Syracuse (Caven 1990, 35) to assist this escape; thus, some refugees left aboard ship to reach safety at Messana, while others (perhaps 1,000 hoplites and their families) went overland with Diocles.

A large number of citizens remained behind in Himera to keep the besiegers occupied. Though the plan was for ships to return in shifts and evacuate these people, Carthaginian forces stormed and broke through the defenses before this rescue could take place. Hannibal's men slaughtered thousands in their subsequent sack of the city, the victims including 3,000 captured men, who were tortured and sacrificed where Hamilcar had died in 480 B.C. Hannibal razed the town and sailed home after setting up some garrisons and dismissing his allies. He had come near to disaster on the beach at Himera, but his leadership and skillful use of reserves saved the day and he could return to Africa in triumph, having secured western Sicily and avenged the past failure of his grandfather.

Punic Motya, Sicilian Panormus, and the Syracuse Marketplace (409–408 B.C.)

Hannibal's withdrawal brought only a brief pause in warfare on Sicily, as the return of Hermocrates that same summer served to spark yet another round of bloodshed. This Syracusan officer had been an important leader early on in the fight with Athens, but faded from the limelight after Gylippus arrived. He had then sailed as part of the command team for a flotilla sent to aid Sparta's campaign in Ionia. That endeavor had not gone smoothly and Hermocrates had suffered exile. He now returned to land at Messana with a private force of five ships filled with Greek mercenaries — all paid for with Persian funds. Hermocrates subscribed more men once ashore, bringing his hired contingent up to 1,000, and added an equal number of refugee warriors from vanquished Himera. After seeking and being denied restoration to his homeland, he marched to Selinous instead, setting up a base there for operations against nearby Carthaginian interests.

Hermocrates gathered a capable army at his western outpost; perhaps 6,000 strong, it likely contained some 4,000 hoplites, 1,500 skirmishers, and 500 horsemen. Besides the mercenaries and Himeraens he had brought from Messana, there were a great many Greeks from western Sicily. These latter included displaced men from Selinous itself as well as others who had come to resent Punic dominance of their land. There were also a number of political allies from Syracuse. Hermocrates had the backing of a sizable faction among his compatriots in the upper-class community and some of these had hastened to join him, no doubt making up most of his cavalry.

Motya was first to come under attack. Staging point for the last Punic invasion, the city was a fitting focus for Greek wrath, and while well sited on an island off the western tip of Sicily, its onshore territory was quite vulnerable. These holdings were open to assault from both land and sea, with the latter a significant factor in that Hermocrates was concentrating against coastal objectives. Basing out of Selinous, his triremes could not only provide tactical support for the army, but also transport supplies and booty and even carry out independent raids.

With farms at hazard on the mainland, the Motyans rushed to save their crops. However, it's likely that they had no more than 2–3,000 heavy infantry, half again as many light footpen, and a few hundred horsemen — a combination of militia and garrison troops, with the latter having stayed behind upon Hannibal's departure. The odds were therefore daunting against a foe that was not only more numerous, but also better equipped with both heavy gear and cavalry. And sure enough, these factors combined with sound leadership and a strong thirst for revenge in allowing the Greeks to drive all before them in the battle. A good many of Motya's defenders lost their lives and the rest took shelter behind barriers on the causeway leading to their island.

Hermocrates now moved up the coast, swinging around the western end of Sicily against Panormus (modern Palermo). This was another coastal site that had served as a staging point for past Carthaginian aggressions. Though even less capable than Motya of challenging the Greeks in open combat, the Panormans were under pressure to put an end to devastation of their croplands. Facing a tough choice between fighting at bad odds and starving that winter, they chose to do battle. Panormus would have had only some 2,000 armored men plus 500–600 light foot troops and cavalry. With a foe about twice their strength, these must have formed very thin files in order to match the opposing front. This left them highly susceptible to the Greeks' hard-driving othismos, and Hermocrates' phalanx appears to have smashed through in short order to claim an easy victory. Around 500 Panormans (20 percent of those in action) probably lost their lives on the spot as their comrades fled the field. Fear now mixed with practicality to discourage another sortie, leaving the victors free to pillage at will.

Following his successes against Motya and Panormus in the later half of 409 B.C., Hermocrates sought the following year to weaken his political foes at home and boost his own stock through a grand, patriotic gesture. He marched to Himera and recovered the bodies of those fallen against Hannibal, which included many Syracusans that his rival Diocles had abandoned in the course of a hasty retreat. Hermocrates returned these to their homeland with great ceremony. He hoped by this act to restore some of his past acclaim, while at the same time sparking widespread denunciation of Diocles. This ploy met with only partial success.

While an aroused populace did indeed force Diocles from the city, Hermocrates' supporters failed to gain his recall. Yet they kept on encouraging their hero to return and, based on their overly optimistic reports of his rising popularity, Hermocrates decided to march on Syracuse that he might take through force what he had failed to gain by consent.

Hermocrates set out with a force of some 3,000 men, which must have been all his mercenary troops and such others as were staunch political backers, including most of the cavalry. Half of his army remained at Selinous, likely representing most of the Himereans, Selinutians, and other western Sicilians — men who would have seen little profit in aiding a coup at distant Syracuse while their own lands were still under threat from Carthage. The exile pressed on with all possible speed, striving to meet at an appointed hour with conspirators in town, who had agreed to pass him through the northwest gate and into the suburb of Achradine. He found his advance going much slower than anticipated and decided to leave the infantry behind, pushing ahead with only his mounted men. Hermocrates' friends did open the gate for him, but had yet to collect all of their strength. Having left most of his army on the road, the exile was now short of manpower and had little choice but to wait for the rest of his urban support to gather. Unfortunately for his ambitions, this delay also allowed his political opponents — who composed a majority in town — to mass as well, a large force of them coming together at the main market.

Hermocrates took quick action once he learned of the opposition gathering and marched to the marketplace. It's doubtful that he had more than 1,000 hoplites, while his foes probably fielded at least twice as many heavy foot troops as well as a huge crowd of light-armed men. The two sides must have filed deeply and come to blows in the plaza. Despite crowded conditions that would have extended the action, this turned out to be no real contest, as those standing against the coup carried all before them to take the lives of Hermocrates and many of his followers.

Acragas II (406 B.C.)

Carthage was slow in responding to Hermocrates, but by late 407 B.C. began to gather an attack force. The city's leaders again tapped Hannibal to take command of the expedition; however, in deference to the old war-horse's age, they also assigned his younger cousin Himilco as an advisor and alternate. Our Greek sources once more vastly inflate troop strength in describing this enterprise and it's unlikely that Hannibal embarked more than 15,000 fighting men. Such a figure fits well with both estimates herein for previous Carthaginian efforts and ancient claims that manpower was as much as 50 percent above that for the invasion of 409 B.C. Further evidence comes from Diodorus's report of a fleet with 90 triremes, which would also have been half again greater than for Hannibal's first campaign.

Hannibal based his army around units of African spearmen. Both citizens/perioeci and subject Libyans, these most likely deployed in two divisions of 3,000 men each. There also would have been about 4,000 heavy-armed mercenaries in the form of a division of Iberians and 1,000 Campanians, with Hannibal probably supplying the latter with mounts just as he had done for their countrymen in 409 B.C. Light support for the frontline troops likely numbered 1,000 horsemen and 4,000 light infantrymen, with the later including African javelinmen and archers plus Iberian peltasts. There were also slingers from the Balieres Islands off southern Spain.

Hannibal sailed in spring 406 B.C. and, despite losing a modest sea battle on the way, landed safely in western Sicily to join his local allies. Between local men and their foreign garrisons, these latter would have provided some 4,000 heavy foot troops along with 2,000 skirmishers and horsemen. Sican and Siculi tribesmen likely chipped in another thousand fighters with armor plus an equal number of light-armed men and cavalry. Hannibal thus could have had 20–25,000 combatants in all when he finally marched on the Greeks. Note that Warmington (1960, 46) and Caven (1990, 81) again have suggested that he had much higher manpower, estimating from something in excess of 35,000 men up to 60,000.

Hannibal seems to have been intent on expanding Punic control along the southern coast, making first for Acragas. This city was not only a rich prize in itself, but also might threaten the rear of any march on Syracuse. The Acraganians wouldn't surrender, and Hannibal deployed for a siege by first setting up a camp on the city's western side to hold his citizen/perioecian and Sicilian divisions. He also sent the Iberian and Libyan contingents to take post on hills northeast of town, where the Campanians joined them to provide mounted support. In the meantime, Acragas got ready to resist, its resources including a probable 3–4,000 spearmen plus thousands of skirmishers (many from among the city's poor folk). There were also some mercenaries under Dexippus, a Spartan soldier of fortune, who led 1,500 hoplites and nearly 800 heavy-armed Campanians. The latter had left Punic service three years earlier and now served Acragas.

Hannibal opened with the same weapons that had proven so effective at Selinous — siege towers. He sent these toward the most vulnerable part of the city perimeter so that bowmen in their heights could cover an assault by battering rams. However, the Acraganians beat back this thrust and sortied after dark to set the engines on fire. With his towers in ashes, Hannibal next decided to build a ramp that would top the opposing walls. It was while this stratagem was being pursued that a plague struck the invaders' camp, claiming the elderly general as one of its victims to leave Himilco in sole command.

Seeing Acragas as a useful outer line of defense, the leaders of Syracuse sent out a large army under Daphnaeus to help the beleaguered city in mid–December. Diodorus put this host at 30,000 foot troops and 5,000 horsemen plus an escort of warships, but his figures are assuredly greatly inflated, much like those he cited for Gelon's army in 480 B.C. In fact, only the proportions reported offer truly useful clues as to the actual strength of the force that marched to Acragas. The claim for infantry in 406 B.C. is 60 percent of that given to Gelon and, based on a realistic estimate of that army, we can propose that Daphnaeus probably had only 9–10,000 hoplites and 4,000 light foot troops. The latter would have included hamippoi attached to some 2,000 horsemen, at one rider for each five spearmen. All this fits well with likely strengths for the component contingents. Syracuse could have fielded no more than 3,000 hoplites and 600 horsemen — half again more of each than in an apparent two-thirds levy sent to Gela the next year. This reflects both fleet demands and the exile of some of those that had backed Hermocrates. Gela, Camarina, and other allies plus some Siculi would have supplied another 2–3,000 spearmen along with a fifth as many riders. Finally, a major part of the relief column was from Messana and Grecian Italy (perhaps Locri and Rhegion). No doubt fearful that Carthage would turn on them next, these might have sent 4,000 hoplites and 800 horsemen.

Daphnaeus approached from southeast and crossed above the mouth of the Acragas River, where enemy forces in place farther north on that side of the city moved swiftly to engage him. He faced about to form a phalanx that must have been eight shields deep across 1,200m, with Syracusans on the right and northern allies on the far left wing. Iberian and Libyan heavy spearmen undoubtedly cored an array of similar width for Carthage, though, at less than 6,000 strong (having taken some losses to disease), they could line up only six deep. After dueling in no man's land while their heavy formations took shape, light-armed troops on both sides would have retired onto their respective wings as cavalry came up outboard. With horns blaring, the lines then started toward each other, first at a walk and then gathering speed to dash into brutal shock combat.

Diodorus's account of the battle makes it a long one. If true, this stands as a tribute to the spirit and fighting capabilities of those opposing the phalanx, since superior Greek manpower and othismos should have been quickly telling. And however long the action might have remained in doubt, it did end in a decisive Grecian victory. Carthaginian forces gave way and fled around the northern wall of Acragas in an effort to reach Himilco's camp beyond. Daphnaeus and his men declined to give chase, seemingly mindful of what had happened at Himera three years earlier, when Hannibal had employed a tactical reserve to butcher hard-chasing Greeks. Nor did those inside Acragas sally; therefore, the barbarians got away with only modest losses. (Diodorus's report that more than 6,000 died can be discounted. Much like the figure of Ephoros for Punic losses at Himera in 409 B.C., this likely reflects total heavy-armed manpower defeated — two 3,000-man divisions plus the Campanians.)

Daphnaeus and his men took station in the hills east of Acragas and then sought to unite with the city garrison for an assault on Himilco's camp, but problems in the city delayed this. Townsfolk there were enraged that an opportunity had been missed to strike at the retreating barbarians to put an end to the siege, and their anger boiled over into a riot that slew four of the five generals. It was thus a new team of officers who belatedly led out local forces to join Daphnaeus in a probe against enemy lines. As it turned out, Himilco's position proved strong enough to discourage any such direct assault.

There were only about 12,000 heavy foot troops in Himilco's command at this point, and he seems to have been understandably reluctant to risk pitched battle against an army of some 15,000 better-armed hoplites. Yet there also proved to be danger in simply sitting tight and avoiding combat, as the Carthaginian host soon began to suffer from a shortage of food, some men even starving to death. It got so bad that mercenaries in camp threatened to defect if not properly fed as per their contract. This crisis compelled Himilco to seek rapid relief. As luck would have it, an opportunity soon arose that allowed him to pull off a masterstroke against his foe — one that not only solved the immediate supply problem but also led to ultimate victory over Acragas.

Himilco had learned that the Greeks were bringing in foodstuffs from Syracuse by sea and, realizing how vital these were to both sides, he sent out his fleet to intercept. This naval attack was a complete success and captured most of the Syracusan convoy. The logistical situation at Acragas was now totally reversed, enriching the invaders and impoverishing the defenders. Facing starvation, Acragas's Campanian mercenaries deserted and the large contingent from northern Sicily also departed, its members being far from home and loath to stay all winter under any circumstances. Outnumbered and dangerously short on grain, Daphnaeus had little choice but to order a general retreat. Most of the population fled that night, following their withdrawing allies. It was a painful yet prudent move, as the enemy stormed inside at dawn and slaughtered anyone that had remained behind, even those that sought refuge in the temples. Himilco then settled in to savor his victory and use what was left of the city for winter quarters.

Gela (405 B.C.)

Failure of Syracuse's leadership to save Acragas emboldened its political foes and led to a change of government. Dionysius, a former follower of Hermocrates, was a young man who had performed well in the failed campaign. He soon proved not only capable, but enormously ambitious as well, a trait that came to the fore when others were slow to act, allowing him to seize center stage in the debates that followed upon the army's return. His bold words struck just the right chord with the common people and, after deposing their generals, they elected him as one of the replacements despite his being only 24 years of age.

Dionysius got his first independent command that spring, moving to assist Gela, which sat next on the path that Himilco was blazing along the southern coast. Syracuse's leaders rightly saw this town as the last good choke point before their own walls and dispatched Dionysius to strengthen its defenses. The young general marched out with what was probably two-thirds of his city's available manpower, having 2,000 hoplites, 400 horsemen, and a likely 1,500 skirmishers. Upon arrival, however, Dionysius didn't rush to improve Gelan security, but instead exploited local class disputes for selfish ends. He pandered to the majority by accusing wealthy men of disloyalty so that he might confiscate their property. He then put these riches to use in buying off the town's mercenaries (Dexippus and company back from Acragas) and enriching his own troops before finally departing with a promise to return soon.

Dionysius arrived home carrying ample words of praise from the Gelans, even though he had not actually made them any safer. One can only assume that he had taken care in his dispensation of booty to reward key local voices that would favorably influence opinion back in Syracuse. His next major step in the quest for power called for playing upon his own polis's fear of a Carthaginian attack. Dionysius cast doubt on the loyalty of his fellow strategoi, suggesting that all but he were ready to turn traitor for Himilco's gold. This propaganda proved highly effective. The common folk again rose up to depose their generals, this time ceding sole command to Dionysius, who used his new authority to call for an army muster at Leontini. This distant site was chosen in part to hide his next moves from political enemies in Syracuse. Free from oversight, the aspiring dictator further secured his position through guile. Faking an assassination attempt, he got approval to form a bodyguard. Dionysius recruited over 1,000 men for this elite unit, the final count perhaps composed of 600 hoplites (as per the actual authorization) plus a matching number of light-armed troops and 100 horsemen. Feeling safe now from interference, he was ready for the last step needed to gain tyranny over Syracuse–usurping allegiance of the army.

The secret to personal control over Syracuse's army appears to have lain in its expansion. Dionysius could insure majority support from the ranks by adding large numbers of men who owed their primary loyalty to him alone. A mustering station near Leontini was perfect for this scheme, as that city was filled with banished Syracusans and other homeless souls from Acragas and elsewhere. He recruited heavily among this pool of unfortunates and swelled his host with soldiers who regarded him as their savior from destitution and/or exile. Dionysius also called up the mercenaries from Gela, though he saw Dexippus as a threat and lost no time in sending him packing for Sparta. There were now some 6,000 hoplites in the army, of whom it's probable that two-thirds or more would back their young leader without question. Nor did Dionysius stop there, as he moved to further supplement his host with 1–2,000 loyal allies from the interior. He now had in hand the very tool needed to reshape his temporary position as commander-in-chief into a dictatorship for life.

Dionysius had thus gone a long way toward becoming tyrant of Syracuse by summer 405 B.C., when his first great test of leadership arose. Himilco had finally departed Acragas, torching it as he left, and marched on Gela to set up a strong position with ditch and palisade before the western end of the city, his lines running from shore onto the plain north of town. Himilco then struck against the walls in front of his camp, which were the ones most accessible for his siege engines. Despite facing superior numbers and several breaches of their walls, the defenders held firm and even came out at night to hit back at their besiegers. Seeking a preemptive strike, Dionysius rushed to Gela with an army of his Syracusans plus troops from Messana and Grecian Italy.

Diodorus claimed that Dionysius had about the same amount of infantry as Daphnaeus had at Acragas II, which suggests 9–10,000 hoplites. A reasonable breakdown of his spearmen would be 3–4,000 Syracusans and local allies, 2,000 hired men (including bodyguards), and 4,000 northern allies. The historian also said that 1,000 horsemen were present and these would have been 600 from Syracuse, 100 mounted guards, and 300 allies. There must have been some 4–5,000 light foot soldiers on hand as well, making for a grand total of around 15,000 combatants. But these were not the only fighting men coming to the aid of Gela. More missilemen and some 2,000 Syracusan hoplites sailed beside the land forces aboard the city's fleet, filling 50 triremes that were meant to insure control of all seaward approaches. Dionysius was clearly bent on avoiding the sort of naval reverse that had cost his predecessors so dearly at Acragas.

As the relief force neared Gela, it stopped to set up camp on the eastern bank of the Gela River. This stream entered the sea east of town and a campsite near its mouth was well placed to serve both ground and naval contingents. Dionysius and his officers assessed the terrain and came to the conclusion that it was unwise to fight a large-scale battle on the plain north of the city. Any such grand action on open ground would leave their flanks vulnerable to an opponent that held considerable advantage in mounted strength. It was obvious that they would have a much better chance of success if they could get Himilco to make a disadvantaged attack on their own strong position along the river, where they could anchor one flank on the sea and have a large enough mobile force to screen the other, at the same time forcing their foe into a dangerous river crossing. The Greeks therefore set their light foot troops and cavalry to harassing opposition foraging parties. If successful, this would starve the besiegers much as Daphnaeus had done at Acragas, goading them into an ill-favored offensive; however, the Carthaginians were well stocked and refused to take the bait. After 20 days without effect, Dionysius knew that he had to try something else lest his allies get impatient and go home. Wracking his agile brain for a suitable ploy, the youthful Syracusan now seems to have fallen prey to his lack of experience.

Dionysius devised a complex plan that involved a three-pronged attack. He planned to send his Syracusan militia and its southern allies against the landward end of the enemy lines at the same time that his northern allies joined the fleet in an assault along the beach. This sought to pit superior numbers against lone divisions posted at either extreme of Himilco's front. In concert with these flanking attacks, Dionysius would pass through town and strike with his mercenaries and guards at the enemy center. This would be a diversionary action meant to occupy the remaining Carthaginian divisions holding that vital area (the siege engines being there). These would have no choice but to heavily oppose any threat to their sector and might well fail to then send timely help to the embattled outposts to north and south. It was a bold and clever strategy; unfortunately, it was also very unlikely to succeed.

Dionysius appears to have seriously misjudged how difficult it would be under existing circumstances to make three simultaneous assaults. He needed five contingents (three afoot, one mounted, and one at sea) to move for some distance along four different paths (across open plain, down city streets, following the beach, and through the water). Every one of these divisions would have to reach its staging area and get into battle order in time to strike at the assigned moment. Action had to take place at a set time, rather than upon signal, as neither horns nor visual methods of signaling were suitable here. The former lacked sufficient range and distinction, while only the beach and offshore divisions had line of sight for use of the latter. It was naïve to think that all of these component attacks could actually come off together.

And synchronized actions were critical, since widely staggered assaults would inevitably leave the enemy free to concentrate upon and defeat each isolated effort in turn.

Whether ignorant or uncaring of these dangers, Dionysius deployed his army at first light, with the various divisions crossing the river and splitting up in accordance with instructions. The men from Messana and Italy dropped down to pass south of town, moving easily along the beach below limestone cliffs topped by Gela's seaward walls. Meanwhile, the cavalry fanned out in a screen ahead of the Syracusans and southern allies, who struck out across the plain on the city's north side. Though this latter route was not rugged, there must have been just enough terrain features (minor hills and gullies) and culture (buildings, walls, ditches, etc.) to slow the advance and put it far behind schedule. As for Dionysius, he entered town with both his bodyguard and mercenaries (some 2,000 spearmen and 600 light foot troops in all). He meant to cross swiftly and launch an opening assault from Gela's western gate, but it was impossible to move quickly down narrow and sometimes crowded city streets. As it developed, only the naval and northern allied contingents were in place when it was time to attack.

Syracuse's triremes swooped into shallow water below the enemy encampment and landed a deadly cargo of 2,000 fighting men. Mostly hoplites, these troops waded in under cover from archers offshore and formed up on the beach to come to grips with Carthage's Sicilian allies. Overcoming their initial surprise, the defenders arrayed for action, no doubt looking to carry the day through superior numbers. However, action had barely gotten underway when the Messanians and Italians charged down the strand from the east, their phalanx taking the defenders in the left flank. It was the Greeks who now held the advantage in both manpower and position. The men in camp quickly gave way, falling apart as they backed up under unbearable pressure from both front and side. Sensing victory, the Greeks followed, though their ranks now became somewhat disordered amidst a riot of campsite clutter. All seemed to be going well at this point for Dionysius's plan, but the tide of battle was destined to turn.

Sadly for those Greeks fighting near the shore, their comrades inside Acragas and on the northern plain had yet to make an appearance. There were thus no visible threats to other sections of Himilco's position and he was free to send as many reserves as needed to the area under attack. His Iberians and Campanians moved down to bolster the hard-pressed Sicilians. Having 4–5,000 heavy-armed men in their ranks, these newcomers once more swung the numbers in Carthage's favor; moreover, their sudden appearance and orderly advance must have had huge impacts on what had become an increasingly chaotic fray. Unprepared for this counterattack, the Greeks turned and fled, the marines struggling to get back aboard ship as their northern allies raced toward Gela. Fortune smiled on this retreat, as missiles from the fleet and a brief Gelan sortie from the nearest city gate allowed most to escape. Nevertheless, Himilco's men had cut down hundreds before they could get clear, adding to a total of 1,000 Greek dead on this part of the field.

The fight down by the sea was finished before Syracusan and allied militias on the north had formed up in phalanx to menace that end of the enemy camp. The Libyan brigade holding this sector promptly moved out to meet the threat. At 3–4,000 strong, the Greek hoplites must have advanced eight deep across a front of better than 400m, forcing the less than 3,000 Libyan heavies on the other side to align at a depth of only six men. And this imbalance seems to have proven telling once the formations closed into shock combat, the Africans, fewer in number and pressured by othismos, being unable to stand their ground long enough for any advantage they held in cavalry or light infantry to have much effect. The Libyans gave way in desperation, taking heavy losses from hot pursuit as they pulled back inside their ditch and palisade. However, just like on the beach, Greek success proved short-lived.

Dionysius and his division of guards and mercenaries had yet to get across Gela, let alone carry out their assignment of pinning down the opposing center. Himilco therefore had no problem in dispatching more troops to the inland front and sent his elite brigade of citizens and perioeci to aid the similarly armed Libyans. This combined force charged out to strike back at the Greeks, who nevertheless seem to have held their own for some time. Himilco's men had a fair edge in manpower, but lacked the cohesion and othismos that a Doric phalanx gave their foes. Still, once the Iberians and Campanians came on the scene as well, Greek flanks became untenable and the Syracusans hastily withdrew with their allies to trigger a pursuit. In the ensuing chase, though their light troops must have provided some cover, the Syracusan brigade lost 600 hoplites.

By the time that Dionysius and his men reached the western side of Gela, the battle was already over. Opening attacks to north and south had met with considerable success, but failure to pull them off simultaneously and pin enemy reserves had spelled doom as counterattacks defeated the Greeks in detail. At over 1,600 spearmen killed (nearly 15 percent of all those in action), this was one of the costliest defeats ever suffered by a Greek army. Worse yet, the northern allies, having been badly mauled, now wanted to declare the campaign over and go home. This would combine with combat losses to cut the hoplite force in half, making further resistance impractical. It must have been a bitter pill to swallow, but Dionysius found himself forced to give up the city. He retreated that night, leaving 2,000 light-armed men behind to cover escape by maintaining a pretense of occupation until dawn. Moving eastward through Camarina, Dionysius ordered that unfortified site abandoned as well.

Fallout from the defeat was immediate. Dionysius's tardiness in reaching the battlefield had left the Syracusan cavalry stranded on the northern plain to suffer along with their hoplite militia. These aristocratic riders were doubtless already resentful of an appointed leader that had gained authority and approval of the wider populace at expense of their class, and this new setback seems to have elevated that anger and given them the perfect opportunity to express it. The horsemen raced ahead of the retreat, reaching Syracuse after dark with intent to raise a revolt that would return them to power. They looted Dionysius's house and abused his wife so badly that she took her own life. Yet the conspirators couldn't rouse a majority to their cause and soon paid for this failure.

Dionysius had also made a rush for Syracuse, abandoning his hoplites to cover the last stage with only 100 horsemen and 600 light footmen from his bodyguard. Arriving late that night to discover the horrors perpetrated in his home, he hurried to the marketplace, where some of the insurgents had begun to gather. The vengeful leader and his men slaughtered this handful of plotters and went on to pull others from their houses for similar execution as the remaining rebels fled to Aetna. Once the rest of his army arrived next morning, Dionysius deployed it (or, at least, mercenary and guard elements that he could trust) to take full control of the polis.

It was as sole ruler that Dionysius set out to negotiate with Himilco for his city's survival in the weeks that followed. As it turned out, he found his foe quite willing to cut a deal. Disease had hit hard at the Punic army after its victory at Gela, and Himilco clearly was aware that he would need major reinforcement before he could tackle a well-fortified position like Syracuse. He was therefore open to a peace accord, so long as it preserved his gains to date. Dionysius proved more than willing to concede this if he got what he wanted as well — recognition of his own sovereignty. Himilco thus returned to Africa, leaving the Campanians behind to act as a garrison within Punic territory. With the Carthaginian threat out of the way for now, Dionysius turned to consolidating his tyranny.

Neapolis (404 B.C.)

Dionysius worked to bolster his power throughout the winter and into the summer of 404 B.C., bringing in more mercenaries and fortifying Ortygia as an island refuge. He also extended citizenship to sections of the lower classes and passed out a great deal of wealth taken from his exiled opponents. With this done, he mustered the city militia for a campaign to firm up control over nearby Sicel territory. It was the first time that the full army had massed since returning from Gela and proved a volatile event. Great resentment of Dionysius's rule had spread among the hoplites, who had never actually endorsed tyranny and felt, quite justifiably, that it had been imposed upon them through trickery. They also no doubt resented both the presence of foreign fighters in their city and sharing their rights as citizens with poorer men. The militia was therefore more than ready to revolt and that's just what it did once gathered under arms.

The Syracusans killed Dionysius's proxy commander and marched on the city to threaten the tyrant himself, calling upon the exiles at Aetna to join their cause. Dionysius fled ahead of the rebels to reach safe haven on Ortygia, which he now defended with his guards and mercenaries against all attempts by the citizenry to storm this citadel. Triremes from Messana and the Italian Greeks soon arrived in support of the rebellion and their offshore patrols tightened the siege. The insurgents had requested this help and the northerners seem to have readily complied, perhaps hoping to prevent Dionysius from extending his influence into their own territories.

Dionysius probably had 2–3,000 hoplites and around 1,000 skirmishers plus most of his original 100-man squadron of cavalry. This was adequate to staff the defenses, but nowhere near enough to have any real prospect for success in open battle. The rebels were simply too numerous, likely having 4–5,000 hoplites (regular militia, reservists, and returned exiles), 2–3,000 in light footmen, and 300–500 horsemen. Any sortie from Ortygia would thus find itself outnumbered by half again or more. And this imbalance only got worse as the investment wore on and many hired men changed sides, choosing to accept amnesty rather than face starvation and defeat at the side of their autocratic paymaster. Dionysius soon had no more than 1,500–2,000 spearmen left, making even manning his walls a daunting task. Yet just then, the young tyrant got a chance to turn things around.

A reversal of fortunes began with the arrival by sea of another 300 mercenary spearmen. Dionysius was shortly thereafter able to secure the services of the Campanians left behind by Himilco, which further boosted his strength even as he made a show of negotiating abdication. In reality, he was merely waiting for the moment when his increasingly confident foes would feel safe in reducing their levy to tend the needs of an approaching harvest. In fact, the rebel cavalry had already gone home, and he must have known that many rural hoplites would soon do the same to work their farms. Nor was he wrong, as the insurgents before long allowed much of their strength to bleed away into the countryside. The rebels probably didn't see this as all that risky, since they could still deploy perhaps 2–3,000 hoplites to deal with any attempted breakout. Events would soon prove them sadly mistaken.

The Campanian mounted infantry got things started by riding at night through what appears to have been some very laxly manned siege lines. Numbering 1,200 or so, these Italian hoplites brought Dionysius's heavy foot troops up to around 3,000 strong, giving him a potent shock force to put into the field next day. Emerging at the head of his cavalry guard, he launched a fierce assault at first light, catching the besiegers slightly outnumbered and, more importantly, unready for a fight. The Syracusans were encamped west of Achradine in the suburb of Neapolis ("New City"), and it was through this district that a running battle now raged. The rebels seem to have been too disorganized to take advantage of available choke points and gave way rapidly. At this point, Dionysius forbade pursuit, correctly thinking that such mercy would ease later reconciliation with the townsfolk.

The defeated citizens rallied at Aetna and once more gathered those who had scattered onto their farms, which brought their numbers back up to around 7,000 footmen of all classes plus several hundred riders. They still had a much more powerful force than that backing Dionysius, but it was one largely separated from both home and family, these being hostage in the city under the tyrant's control. Thus, though a few rebels continued to resist out of Aetna, most accepted an offer of peace in return for the safety of their goods and kin. Having learned his lesson, Dionysius now marginalized his citizen troops by hiring more mercenaries, eventually taking on some 7–10,000 of them. With this remodeled army and an augmented fleet, he would then go on to conquer all of eastern Sicily.

Tyrants, Democrats and Mercenaries

Sicily wasn't alone in seeing mercenary hoplites fuel turmoil after the close of the Peloponnesian War. These now began to gather under various freelance commanders, with each man seeking an escape from poverty through pay and/or booty gained by force of arms. So common did these hired soldiers become that they can be found serving one or both sides in an overwhelming majority of all battles recorded through the end of the century.

Pharsalos and Porus (404 B.C.)

Thessaly in the northeast had long been a hotbed of tyrants that ruled in league with a few wealthy men. The latter owned the land, working it with peasant labor in a system that precluded rise of a yeoman class of populist hoplites; thus, conflicts here didn't feature the oligarchy versus democracy dynamic so common elsewhere in Greece, but centered instead on attempts by one or another chieftain to take land from his despotic rivals. Lycophron was one of these dictators on the rise. He had come to power in 406 B.C. at Pherae, a polis in east-central Thessaly that controlled much of the coastline to dominate that region's seaborne trade. Such an economic edge elevated Pherae and set Lycophron on a collision course with Medius of Larissa, whose own city, inland to the northwest, had previously been preeminent. Medius set out to raise a coalition against Lycophron and brought about an engagement in 404 B.C. at Pharsalos in southwestern Thessaly, a major crossroads that was hostile to Pherae. That events unfolded near a polis opposed to Lycophron suggests that he had taken the initiative, marching out to force his foes into a decisive combat before they were fully ready to fight.

Cavalry had traditionally dominated Thessalian armies and remained an important part of the regional military equation well into the mid 4th century B.C. Pherae could field up to 6,000 riders at its height of power at that time and might have deployed at least 3–4,000 at Pharsalos. Each horseman rode with a hamippos at his side and a matching force of other light footmen provided further support. What was new in Lycophron's arsenal for this action was a large contingent of hoplites, mercenaries recruited from southern and central Greece that might have numbered about 1,500. (This figure for Pherae's heavy infantry derives from its roster in the early 4th century, when Jason could field up to 6,000 hired spearmen. These included an elite force of 1,500 hoplites that the tyrant might well have inherited from Lycophron.)

The opposition also fielded paid hoplites, likely about 1,000–1,500 in number. (Support for this comes by way of a passing note from Aristotle regarding severe losses by Medius's hirelings at Pharsalos.) Of course, cavalry would have been an important element in any Thessalian army. Medius and company probably put around 2,000 horsemen into play, reflecting figures from early 4th century Thessaly, which had 2,000 riders apart from those of Pherae. Just as for the opposition, matching contingents of both hamippoi and other light infantry would also have been on hand.

The two sides met on an open plain and it was Lycophron that came away with victory. Hired spearmen at the core of both armies would have held their ground against each other as large contingents of cavalry and light infantry off the wings decided the battle. Using their numerical superiority to full advantage, the Pheraean riders no doubt were ultimately able to chase screening troops from at least one flank, more likely both, turning inward against the enemy's spearmen to shatter their formation and cut down most of Medius's mercenaries as they tried to escape.

Tyranny was also raising its ugly head to the east, where Sparta had dispatched Clearchus to help Byzantium against hostile Thracian tribes. But this man soon began to transform his appointed position into something that much more resembled an independent dictatorship. He had taken advantage of factional strife as an excuse to raise an army of mercenaries, paid for with funds seized from wealthy citizens accused of treason; then, instead of fighting the Thracians, he used this hired force to establish himself as tyrant. We have no record of the size of Clearchus's mercenary corps, but it may have been similar to the one that he later led on behalf of the Persian prince Cyrus. If so, there were some 1,000 hoplites along with an equal number of light infantry. The latter would mostly have been Thracian peltasts, yet could also have included a couple of hundred archers from Crete. When the Spartans back home learned of this abuse of their authority, they sent representatives to ask the renegade governor to stand down, but he refused. Therefore, in 403 B.C., Sparta sent out the general Panthoedas to rectify the situation by force.

Clearchus couldn't count on getting any support from the local people, whom he had victimized in his rise to power; therefore, when he learned of the expedition coming against him, he relocated westward along the south Thracian shore to Byzantium's sister city of Selymbria. Shortly thereafter, Panthoedas arrived with 25 triremes, landing at least 1,000 hoplites (a Spartan mora) and a contingent of light-armed crewmen. Perhaps adding a lochos of hoplites and more skirmishers from Byzantium, the Spartan general then set out for Selymbria.

Clearchus met Panthoedas at a place called Porus. He was an experienced and capable combat commander and must have carefully selected this spot for his stand, its name suggesting a restricted passage. By staking his position in what was probably a narrow stretch between the sea and rough or heavily vegetated inland terrain, Clearchus could negate most of the effects of greater enemy numbers. Ideally, he would then have set up his phalanx eight or ten shields deep across a front of some 100–125m, placing peltasts to cover any passable ground on his upland left flank, with any bowmen present taking station at the rear.

Panthoedas would have arrayed to match Clearchus's line, likely by ranking half his Spartans in front and the rest at the rear to sandwich the less reliable Byzantine hoplites in the middle, where they would add weight to his formation at minimum risk to its integrity. Panthoedas then led his men forward through a limited killing ground of missile fire, advancing at a deliberate pace until smashing with great violence into an enemy front that had to remain fixed on its chosen ground. Clearchus and his mercenaries probably withstood this initial blow, shoving and spearing back to make a hard fight of it. With both sides at or above optimum file depth, their othismos was very nearly equal in strength and the contest must have evolved into a lengthy affair. Still, Clearchus's files weren't so deep that they could hold out indefinitely — or even long enough for rearward archers to carry the day. Quantity might not have been able to dominate in this setting, yet that just made quality all the more important, and Sparta had the finest spearmen in the Greek world. Fighting and pressing ahead with indomitable fury, these superbly skilled and conditioned warriors seem to have simply outlasted their opponents, breaking down their will to resist and finally driving them into panicked flight. Clearchus escaped to eventually find refuge in Persian-held Ionia.

Acharnae, Munychia, and Halae Marsh (404–403 B.C.)

Athens fell under sway of an imposed council after its surrender. The city's conquerors named 30 Athenians for this duty, selecting them on the basis of an oligarchic bias, with many having suffered exile under the old regime. These picked men set about designing a new constitution that would replace broad-based democracy with a government under sole control of the wealthy. A Spartan governor, Callibius, backed the council's decrees with 700 hoplites (Bury 1900, 510), these likely being freed helots per other deployments at just this strength. Eager to establish its power, the ruling body killed or drove off other citizens, both democrat and oligarch alike. In fact, most of these men suffered for no better reason than that the council wanted their wealth. Such pirated funds provided at first for upkeep of the foreign garrison; later, as noted by Diodorus and implied by Xenophon, this same money purchased mercenaries. It wasn't long before Athenians began bitterly referring to their new rulers as the Thirty Tyrants.

The councilors allowed no part in governance by the rest of the populace, though they did extend some judicial privileges and the right to bear arms to the cavalry (perhaps 600 strong at this time) and 3,000 picked hoplites. The latter came from those among the zeugitai class that the leadership regarded as being most sympathetic to its narrow form of oligarchy. Meanwhile, the government confiscated all other weapons and armor to take firm control of the city as the winter of 404–403 set in. However, a small group of democratic fugitives was about to turn this situation on its head.

Thrasybulus had fled to Thebes at Athens's fall, where he had organized a band of 70 fellow exiles from the hoplite class. Ready to take action that winter, he led these men down along the route from Tanagra to Athens, transiting a narrow pass on Mount Parnes. A natural strongpoint existed within the pass at Phyle (possibly at the site of a 4th-century fortification; Munn 1993, 9), which lay only 20km north of Athens. The outcasts set up at this citadel and began collecting a modest army of their countrymen toward raising a rebellion. The Thirty, under the leadership of Critias, responded to this challenge by calling out their cavalry and select citizen spearmen. Leaving the Spartans and a growing body of mercenaries behind to control the city, they marched out to preempt any uprising. This effort failed when Phyle proved too strong to overcome by direct assault, with harsh winter weather then driving the expedition back to Athens.

Though they now ruled out an actual siege on Phyle, the councilors still hoped to limit rebel access to supplies. They therefore sent out most of the Spartan garrison (perhaps some 600 hoplites) along with 200 horsemen (two squadrons) to patrol below the enemy position on the plain of Acharnae and cut off foodstuffs from area farms. This force made camp in a flat, brushy area near the pass. But Thrasybulus didn't wait to be starved out and gathered his men for a nighttime sortie. He had by this time collected about 700 hoplites (per Xenophon), whom he stealthily moved into position near the enemy camp for an attack at first light. This sudden assault caught the Spartans and their cavalry escort completely unprepared, with most of them still being abed as their attendants went about early morning chores. The surprised hoplites managed only a brief resistance before abandoning the camp. As for Athens's aristocratic riders, they did little more than mount and gallop home, losing only three men in the process. It was much worse for the Spartans, who took heavy casualties (about 120 or 20 percent going down). The rebels collected much-needed arms from their victims and then retired back into the Panres pass.

Acharnae left the Thirty badly shaken. Fearing now that they might lose control of Athens and need Spartan reinforcement, they moved with their cavalry and mercenaries to capture Eleusis as a possible refuge on the western Attic frontier. And this soon proved a prudent precaution, as Thrasybulus marched from Phyle with a force that Xenophon claimed had grown to include about 1,000 hoplites. This column moved by night into the port district of Piraeus, which lay along a peninsula that projected southwest along the lower side of Athens's main harbor. Piraeus was home to the populist fleet faction and would provide a friendly base for the rebels. Thrasybulus camped atop Munychia, a hill near the base of the peninsula, and began recruiting more men until he had 1,200 spearmen (per Diodorus) plus a host of light foot soldiers. The Thirty reacted swiftly to this growing challenge. Calling up their full levy, they set out for Munychia with some skirmishers and what must have been about 6,000 hoplites (3,000 militia, 2,500 mercenaries, and 500 left from the Spartan garrison).

Critias led his council forces into the market of Hippodamos northwest of Munychia and formed up in a very restricted setting. It appears that various urban structures narrowed the route toward the enemy-held hill so much that his phalanx could rank no more than 120 men wide. This not only led to files at an extreme depth of 50 shields, which would have offset much of Critias's edge in heavy infantry, but also have taken his cavalry almost entirely out of the picture. With no room to deploy on the flanks, his horsemen had to keep to the rear, where they could do no more than watch in frustration as the battle developed.

Thrasybulus observed Critias's array and then set up his own spearmen in a phalanx similar in width to that of his foe, but much shallower at only 10 shields deep. The veteran Athenian clearly knew that if he held fast upslope, both gravity and excessive file depths would allow his men to largely negate othismos and draw things out into an extended bout of front fighting. His javelinmen and slingers might then decide the battle. Standing behind their phalanx, these men could use superior elevation to bombard a static opposing formation — one with great depth that would make for a large and inviting target. At the same time, their counterparts at the enemy rear would face significant disadvantages. They would not only be a bit farther from their targets and need to fire uphill, but would also run a significant risk of hitting their own deeply filed men.

Once engaged, the slope and lack of efficiency of their deep files soon brought charging council forces to a grinding halt. With the hoplites thus stalemated along the front, Thrasybulus's missilemen now had a golden opportunity to dispense a deadly rain of darts. This took a heavy toll in blood that the council troops couldn't long endure, finally forcing them to break off and run for cover. Thrasybulus's men briefly gave chase, but pulled up once out on level ground, probably in deference to the opposition's still intact cavalry reserve. The rebels then wisely limited themselves to stripping the enemy dead of much needed equipment before retiring back atop Munychia. Elite citizen hoplites had stood at the front of the losing phalanx and it was these men who suffered the most, losing over 70 of their number, including Critias and one other from the council.

Failure at Munychia brought down the Thirty, whose survivors fled to Eleusis with their mercenaries as Athens's oligarchic hoplites installed a new council of 100 from their own ranks. Meanwhile, thousands of disenfranchised citizens and metics rushed to Thrasybulus.

In fact, so many men now joined the rebel army that there wasn't enough stored, donated, and captured gear to arm them all. Thrasybulus solved this problem by putting artisans to work making new equipment. Spears proved simple enough to fabricate from wood and iron; however, shields were different, requiring a thin covering of bronze that was both costly and took a lot of time to apply. Workmen overcame this by foregoing a final metallic layer on their constructs of wood and wicker, replacing the bronze with no more than a coating of paint. The resulting "soft" shields were not suitable for the front line, but would serve well enough in the after ranks, where the chore was generating othismos rather than deflecting weapons. Within ten days of the fight at Munychia, Thrasybulus began making forays with at least 3,000 hoplites, 300 of them hired men (Parke [1933, 19]), a large body of light foot soldiers, and some 70 horsemen.

The Athenian oligarchs did little as the revolt continued to grow, mostly relying on their cavalry to harass foragers from the Piraeus and spar with the main rebel force. Seeing a lack of progress in all of this, Lysander of Sparta took action. First, he hurried to Eleusis and gathered an army of 1,000 Peloponnesian mercenary hoplites (with most perhaps coming from among those that had fled with the Thirty) and then had his brother block the Piraeus with a fleet of 40 triremes. Lysander was now poised to march on Athens, but just then, politics intruded.

Sparta's king Pausanius seems to have grown concerned that Lysander was infringing on his royal authority and persuaded his council to place him in charge of the expedition to Athens. This let him lead out an official levy that included at least two morai of Spartans (some 2,000 spearmen in four lochoi) and maybe twice as many allied hoplites. (Corinth and Boeotia did not approve of or participate in this effort. Still, Pausanius would have had nearly half the 14,000 spearmen credited to Agis five years earlier.) The king added Lysander and his hired troops and then marched to set up camp on the plain of Halipedon — a marshy area along the south-facing coast that stretched east of Munychia. This campsite mirrored intended dispositions within the invading phalanx, putting Lysander on the west/left (closest to the enemy), both Spartan morai on the other wing, and allies in between. Counting garrison and militia, Pausanius could probably call upon something like 10,000 hoplites that had the support of a third to half that many skirmishers plus 500–600 horsemen.

When the insurgents refused battle, Pausanius decided to invest them, planning to wall off their peninsular location while he used the triremes of Lysander's brother to cut supply from the sea. In order to scout positions for his siege works, the king set out with a Spartan mora (1,000 spearmen) and 300 Athenian horsemen. He skirted Munychia to get as far as an inlet known as the Still Harbor, but this sortie didn't go undetected and drew fire from rebel missilemen during the return march. Responding angrily, Pausanius sent his cavalry and light foot soldiers after these attackers, having a team of the youngest and fleetest hoplites follow close behind, as the king then brought up the rear with his remaining spearmen. Some 30 rebels fell in the course of this chase, which carried all the way to the theater of the Piraeus. Here, however, the situation changed dramatically. It seems that Thrasybulus and his entire army were at this moment standing in the theater district, where they had gathered for an armed review. Skirmishers in the milling rebel host, seeing their comrades fleeing under duress, dashed to the rescue and initiated what would prove to be the century's last grand hoplite battle on the soil of mainland Greece.

The pursuing horsemen recoiled from a storm of javelins, arrows, and slinger's shot issuing from the charging rebel light infantry. They fell back in disorder among the young hoplites at their heels and all then retired hastily to rejoin the rest of their troops in the far rear. But this provided no refuge, as the attackers advanced to boldly engage the entire Spartan column. Hopelessly outnumbered, Pausanius made a desperate, fighting withdrawal toward his camp, his men suffering horribly all the while under a cloud of missiles. Spartan losses were heavy, with both lochos commanders and many others going down. Meanwhile, Thrasybulus had managed to get his hoplites into order at the theater and marched them out to join the fray.

Pausanius was nearing his camp when the opposition spearmen caught up and began forming for battle in front of their light-armed troops. The king saw that he could retreat no farther and led his surviving men onto some high ground near Halae (a stretch of marshland along shore between Munychia and Halipedon). From there, he sent a rider ahead with orders for the balance of his army to join him post haste. Pausanius held fast until this help arrived, then formed a phalanx and advanced that he might take the fight to his foe. The setting here was not as pinched as that at Munychia, yet it still somewhat constrained deployment between the coastal swamp and inland urban development. Thus, while Thrasybulus's smaller force could file at an optimum eight shields (his 3,000 spearmen facing northeast across some 375m), the Spartans would have had to array their 7,500 or so hoplites to a depth of 20 or more. The king must have taken post with his countrymen on the right while allied troops held the center, Lysander lined up his hired men far left near the salt marsh, and all cavalry and light foot troops gathered at the rear.

The phalanxes met with a crash to initiate a fierce contest of stabbing spears and othismos. Crowded conditions no doubt prolonged the action; yet free from excessive missile attack and given plenty of time, superior Spartan depth eventually began to tell. Lysander's hired troops on the seaward wing might have scored first, breaking through the rebel right at a point well inside its anchored flank. The mercenaries then rolled to push the now isolated end segment of the opposing line into adjacent marshland. Meanwhile, other insurgent contingents gave way to enemy pressure all along the front and the rout was on. Thrasybulus and his beaten men ran toward Munychia and most got away. This escape was largely due to Pausanius, who called off any pursuit and directed instead that his men set up a trophy and return to camp. As a result, rebel losses came to only about 150 dead (5 percent), which most likely saddled the victors with a higher cost in blood on the day due to heavy casualties during their initial retreat.

Restraint shown by Pausanius in the aftermath at Halae Marsh reflected traditional Spartan distaste for risking men when a battle was already won. It also signaled his intentions with regard to the rebellion in general. Seemingly eager to avoid getting bogged down far from home in a vicious civil war, he arranged a reconciliation between the Athenian factions. Democracy thus returned to Athens, and though restricted at first, it soon regained its earlier broad basis.

Elis (402 B.C.)

Byzantium and Piraeus weren't the only crises that led to an armed response from Sparta in the closing years of the 5th century, as a long-simmering problem also came to a violent boil at Elis. This polis in the northwestern Peloponnese had allied with Athens during the Peace of Nicias and then barred Sparta from the games held in Elean territory at Olympia. The Spartans decided to retaliate and made a series of unreasonable demands of Elis before declaring war upon its refusal to comply. They then sent Pausanius out in late summer 402 B.C. with a levy of 4,000 hoplites (four morai), to which he added allies in equal strength. Corinth and Boeotia had again refused to join what they saw as an unjust campaign, thus rendering the allied contingent very similar in composition and size to that at Halae Marsh a year earlier.

Elis had only around 3,000 prime-aged hoplites and couldn't really engage Pausanius in the field, which left the king and his men free to overrun an outpost on the Arcadian frontier and enter Elean territory. They quickly won over several small towns, captured another, and then marched on the city of Elis itself. Though the Eleans had by now hired 1,000 Aetolian peltasts and called up their reservists, they still lacked the strength for a pitched battle and kept within their walls. Denied combat, Pausanius began to prepare a siege, but got careless in setting about this work, letting some of his units become isolated as they spread around the city's perimeter. The Aetolians saw this and made a sudden sortie with a few Eleans against what appears to have been a 500-man lochos, wreaking havoc on this surprised, outnumbered, and less mobile foe to take down 30 Spartans and force the rest to withdraw. Pausanius then seems to have realized that an investment was sure to prove a long and costly undertaking; therefore he withdrew, though doing so in an aggressive fashion by plundering the countryside on his way out.

Cunaxa and Calah (401 B.C.)

The final year of the 5th century saw a dispute arise over succession to the Persian throne when Darius II died in 404 B.C. and his eldest son came to power as Artaxerxes II. It seems that Artaxerxes had been born prior to his father's kingship and supporters of his brother Cyrus, who was the first male child after Darius gained the crown, challenged legitimacy of the older son's ascension. Cyrus was summoned to the capital at Persepolis, where he faced a capital charge of treason, and it was only through intervention of Parysatis, mother of both royal claimants, that he escaped execution. Allowed to return to his satrapal post at Sardis, Cyrus was obviously aware that he remained at hazard and, if he hadn't earlier, now began to plot a coup in earnest. He quickly called in some favors from allies in Sparta to help find mercenary hoplites and then engaged the exiled Spartan Clearchus to command them.

Clearchus created a fighting division for the Persian prince and trained it in Thrace. By the time he marched to join Cyrus, this force numbered 1,000 hoplites, 800 Thracian peltasts, 200 archers from Crete, and 40 horsemen. That these men had been collected in Europe, where Persian authorities were less likely to notice them, was typical of Cyrus's stealthy approach to building a mercenary army. He likewise paid for upkeep of a contingent in Thessaly, giving Aristippus of Larissa money to hire 4,000 fighting men. Back in Asia Minor, Xenias (Arcadian commander of the prince's personal bodyguard) similarly collected a large number of hoplites. These ostensibly were to combat renegade tribesmen within the satrapy; however, this was little more than a cover story that gained Cyrus another 4,000 hoplites for use in his coup attempt. Cyrus was also at this time fighting supporters of the former satrap Tissaphernes, who was leading a resistance movement in southern Ionia. The prince used this as an excuse to gather yet more mercenaries for a siege at Miletus — a combined 1,800 spearmen and 300 skirmishers under three different Greek commanders. Nor did Cyrus stop here, sending out other recruiters to engage additional soldiers from throughout the Greek world

Naturally, Cyrus didn't depend entirely on Greeks for his army, and he put together an even larger body of Asians. Our sources greatly exaggerate the total for this part of his host; still, their count for mounted troops appears sound at 3,000 cavalrymen and 20 scythed chariots. If we assume that Cyrus's cavalry was about one-tenth as large as his infantry and that Greeks made up a third of the latter, then we get a figure for Asiatic infantry much like the 20,000 proposed by Anderson (1974, 99–100). Most of these lacked armor, but there must have been at least a few heavy spearmen from Lydia and Caria (most likely a myriad/baivarabam of 8,000 men at 80 percent nominal strength).

Cyrus gathered his forces during spring 401 B.C. at his satrapal capital in Lydia, but didn't let on that his plan was to attack the Great King, saying instead that he was intent on a campaign against tribesmen in the interior. Most of his local troops were already on hand, as were a force of Grecian mercenaries that included 5,800 hoplites and 300 light foot troops that had come with Xenias and from Miletus, as well as 1,500 spearmen and 500 skirmishers under Proxenus of Thebes. Once his army was fully assembled, Cyrus marched southeast, crossing the Meander River and pausing at Colossae to gather a local Carian contingent and meet another group of Greeks. These were a portion of the men hired by Aristippus of Larissa, who was still busy in Thessaly, but had sent his friend Menon with all the troops he could spare (1,000 hoplites and half as many peltasts).

Cyrus next proceeded northeast, moving along the southern side of the Meander until reaching Celaenae. Clearchus and two other mercenary commanders joined the column here with 2,300 hoplites and 1,000 light infantry (the Spartan's peltasts and archers). The army then continued along its northeasterly track for a while before eventually swinging south to Issos on the Cilician coast. Cyrus met a convoy of triremes at Issos that delivered the Spartan general Cheirisophus and some hoplites (700 per Xenophon, 800 according to Diodorus), who were probably neodamodeis sent in semi-official support. The mercenaries now began to question their paymaster's actual intent. After all, they not only had many more men than needed to tackle a few tribesmen, but were also far off course for such a campaign. But Cyrus was not yet ready to reveal his plans; instead, he claimed to be marching against the satrap Abrocomas, whose realm of Phoenicia lay farther south. However, awareness of the truth must have been seeping in, as Xenias and Pasion (one of the mercenary generals who had been at Miletus) chose this moment to desert with some of their troops. Undeterred, Cyrus led on eastward toward the Euphrates River and Abrocomas.

The invading column lost 100 hoplites before it reached the Euphrates, but more than compensated by adding 400 Greek spearmen who had deserted from Abrocomas's bodyguard. When Cyrus reached the river, which provided a path into the heart of his brother's realm, he finally announced for the Persian throne. Persuaded by financial rewards, the Greeks agreed to join his plot. Marching along the Euphrates, they expected to meet Artaxerxes' army at the Babylonian frontier. When this didn't happen, Cyrus's men relaxed a bit, but kept pushing down river. It was then, as they made a mid-morning approach to the small town of Cunaxa about 80km northwest of Babylon, that their scouts found a large royal host standing before them.

Tissaphernes had seen Cyrus's real intent early on and warned his monarch in time to gather a powerful counterforce. Our sources tend toward gross exaggeration of Persian numbers, but reports of mounted strength at 6,000 riders and 150–200 scythed chariots seem reasonable. This suggests that the infantry probably came to around 60,000 (again, as per Anderson 1974, 100), which was nearly twice Cyrus's strength. It's likely that two-thirds of the king's force were frontline troops in five 8,000-man baivaraba. Soldiers in the first three myriads derived from the old sparabara type and carried short thrusting spears and large wicker shields. There would have been one division of Persians and Medes, another of Elamites, Cissians, and Hyrkanians, and a third of elite guards from all these "Iranian" peoples. The fourth unit of the line was Egyptian and the fifth Assyrian and Chaldean/Babylonian — all spearmen with chest-to-toe shields of wood. The remaining 20,000 footmen were peltasts and archers in a variety of small contingents.

Artaxerxes had set up his host facing northwest, with Tissaphernes and a third of the cavalry (2,000 horsemen) flanking the riverbank. Light footmen stood next in line, with an Iranian unit and then the Egyptians completing Artaxerxes' left wing. Massed at a depth of ten men across a width of just over 2.5km, the heavy infantry contingents had spearmen in the lead and half the king's chariots a short distance farther forward. Another force of 2,000 cavalrymen held post rightward from the chariots, in position to front for their king and his elite guard in the formation center. The bodyguards stood ten deep over a span of 800m. Next right from Artaxerxes and his men were the Assyrian/Babylonian division and the last Iranian myriad in that order, together making up the royal army's inland arm. This wing had all remaining chariots at its front and more light infantry alongside, with the final third of the cavalry pacing far right.

The sudden appearance of Artaxerxes' army had caught Cyrus and his men strung out in line of march along the river. A third of their cavalry was in the van, followed in sequence by the Greeks, the prince and his companion horsemen, the Asiatic infantry, and Ariaeus (Cyrus's uncle) bringing up the rear with the remaining riders. Cyrus's men began moving up into the line of battle, but it was a long process from such a distended column. When the enemy formation finally began to advance in late afternoon, only the Greek mercenaries (flanked by their own light foot troops and cavalry, the latter next to the river) and the 600-man mounted guard under Cyrus were in place on the battlefield. And though Ariaeus and his following contingent of horsemen were coming up fast, the prince's Asian foot troops remained hopelessly far to the rear.

Xenophon claimed that he and his countrymen waiting in phalanx came to 10,400 hoplites and 2,500 skirmishers, while the cavalry on their right was 1,000 strong. (These figures add 200 more light infantry than his various earlier tallies and 1,200 fewer spearmen. The lower hoplite number likely reflects men that left with Xenias and others posted with the baggage train, while the additional light-armed troops might have come along with Abrocomas's bodyguard.) The Greek spearmen were able to match their enemy's left-wing front by filing only four deep, as they had at a recent review in Cilicia. They then put their light footmen and horsemen along the river, where they were in position to match up with Tissaphernes and his cavalry. Clearchus and the troops from Thrace held the far right, with Proxenus next in line and Menon standing far left beyond all the other mercenaries. Cyrus and his guard took up center position next to the Greek left flank. But unfortunately for him, the barbarian infantry and Ariaeus's cavalry, who should have been there to form the left wing and flank screen, were not yet in place when the battle began.

Already stretched to the practical limit, Clearchus couldn't extend his ranks farther left and cover for Cyrus's absent Asian troops. Likewise, any mass relocation away from the river could prove a serious liability, since it would give the enemy room to outflank his line on the right. Clearchus therefore took the only reasonable course open to him and ordered a charge directly ahead at the opposition's left wing. His phalanx moved out on signal, a bit raggedly at first, but quickly evening up to present a fearsome image to its nervous foe across the field. The helmets, shields, and greaves of the Greeks shone golden bronze in the late afternoon sun, their gleam complimented by red tunics adopted by the mercenaries as a common uniform in imitation of Spartan custom. Clearchus's hoplites sang war hymns and clashed spear on shield to raise a frightening din as they came on at the double. Though it has been proposed that the facing Asians at this point gave way on command to deliberately draw the Greeks away from the battle (as per Waterfield, 2006, 18), it's much more likely and widely accepted that holding firm before the charging phalanx was simply more than the king's men could endure. Panicking, the charioteers broke first, some abandoning their vehicles and others turning back against their own troops; the infantry then quickly followed suit, making a pell-mell run for the rear before Clearchus and his men could even reach them. The Greeks gave chase with a care to keeping good order.

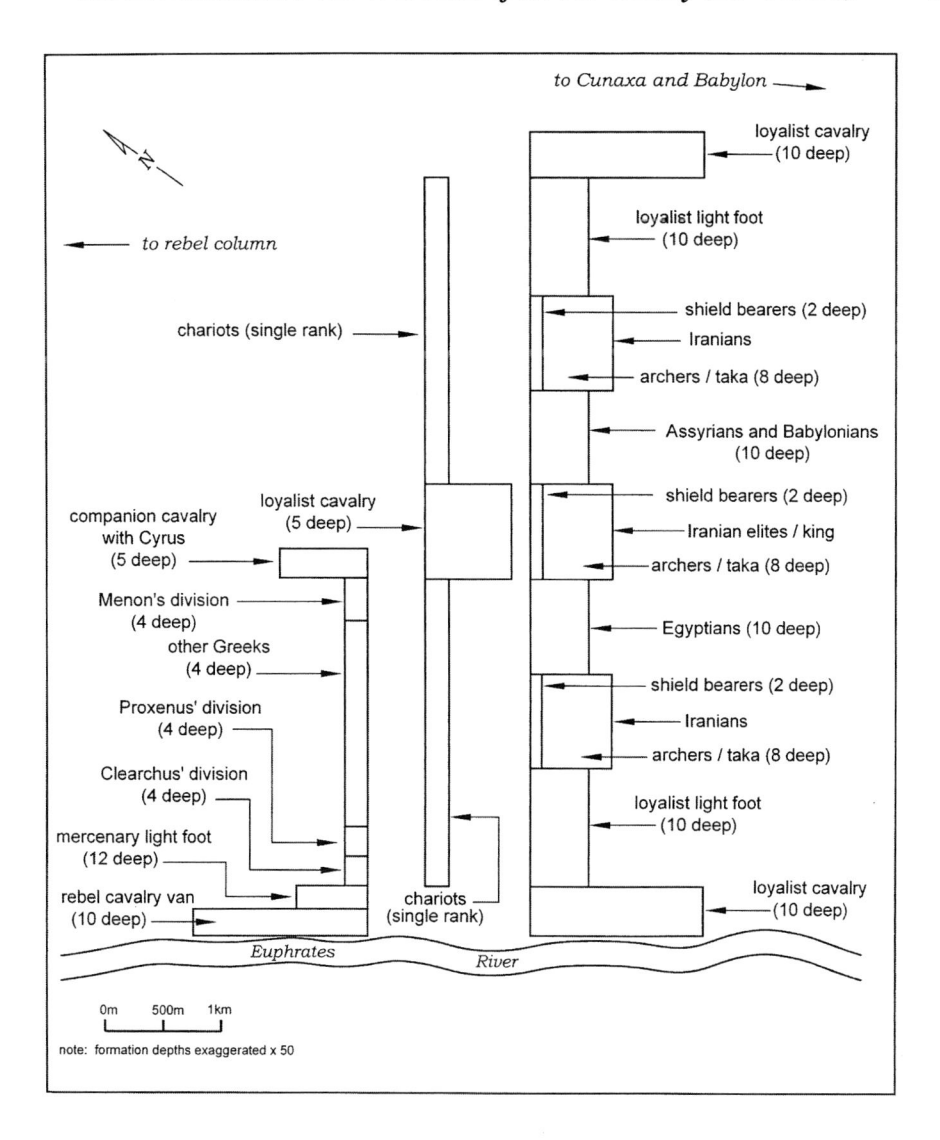

BATTLE OF CUNAXA (401 B.C.)

Tissaphernes seems to have been alone in keeping his wits about him on the royalist left, matching the Greek assault with a mounted thrust of his own. This drive along the riverside scattered the opposition horsemen and carried beyond the skirmishers on that flank. The Greek peltasts loosed a telling shower of javelins at the Persians as they swept past, and Tissaphernes, stung by this fire, decided not to turn back and fight. Instead, he led his men on to the northwest in an attack on the enemy baggage train. Cyrus, meanwhile, had held firm in the center with his guard cavalry, waiting for Ariaeus to come up with the left wing as the mercenaries carried out their successful foray on the right. However, Ariaeus and his horsemen were only just now approaching, while the Asiatic infantry was nowhere to be seen. The Greeks thus left Cyrus and his small command terribly exposed when they took up their pursuit. On the other side, those holding the king's right wing prepared to take advantage by swinging around and wrapping across a still naked enemy left flank. At least a portion of the royal chariots and cavalry on that side of the field went into action at the same time, engaging to turn back Cyrus's mounted rear guard before it could reach his side.

Cyrus could have retreated at this point in hopes of fighting another day on better terms. Yet such a move would have been fraught with political risk, appearing timid and costing him the trust and loyalty of many supporters. Moreover, it seems to have been contrary to this young man's proud and aggressive temperament. He therefore elected to make a risky, high-profile charge into the enemy center, seeking to find and kill his brother in personal combat. Our ancient sources have painted what followed in highly romantic terms, with Cyrus cutting through the opposing cavalry screen to wound his rival only to be unhorsed by a blow to the head and killed once on the ground. Regardless of whether such colorful details are accurate, the daring pretender lost his life in the fight, as did most of his closest companions. This effectively put an end to the rebellion, even though the battle of Cunaxa had yet to run its full course.

With Cyrus slain, Artaxerxes pushed on to join up with Tissaphernes. His men then pillaged most of Cyrus's supply train, though a small guard of hoplites managed to protect a modest portion. Eventually, the Great King reordered his troops and turned back south so that he could deal with the still intact division of Greek mercenaries. Clearchus and his men had by this time learned of the assault on their baggage and that the king's men were forming up in their rear. They quickly executed a countermarch, a parade-ground maneuver that changed their facing 180 degrees by opening ranks so that each man could pivot about face, thus inverting file order and placing the men previously on the right wing now on the left. Men at the front of the reversed files then held fast as those behind followed their original file leaders forward to resume their initial front-to-back order (though the wings remained exchanged).

As the armies again closed, the Persians swung away from the Euphrates to skirt eastward across the right side of the Greek formation. Fearing an attack on his unshielded flank, Clearchus again skillfully maneuvered his phalanx, this time rotating each man 90 degrees to turn line into column. He next marched in a right turn until this column was fully deployed on a southward facing and then pivoted his troops 90 degrees left, putting them back into line of battle with the river at their back and enemy in front. As before, the Greeks chorused battle songs and advanced with intent to engage in shock combat. And once more, their foes gave way before contact was made, collapse coming at an even great distance of separation than in the opening bout.

The victorious mercenaries chased after the Persians, but came to a halt before a rise that hid what lay ahead and took the precaution of scouting the far side for an ambush. By the time that they had precluded a trap, the sun was dropping below the horizon, which prompted them to call off further pursuit. The Greeks fell back to set up a trophy and returned to their ravaged camp. Though Clearchus had gained two essentially bloodless tactical victories on the day, he didn't know what had transpired elsewhere on the field. Indeed, the news that Cyrus was dead and the rest of his army (under a wounded Ariaeus) had withdrawn didn't arrive until dawn, just as he and the other Greeks were gathering for a fresh offensive against the king's host.

Artaxerxes had no desire to fight again, the succession dispute having already been resolved. Instead, he entered into an agreement to let Clearchus and his men join Ariaeus in a peaceful march back to Ionia. This, however, proved to be a ruse, as his general Tissaphernes followed with an army and successfully intrigued to separate Ariaeus and his Asiatic troops from their Greek allies. Tissaphernes then tricked Clearchus and most of the other mercenary commanders into attending a conference at his camp, where he seized them for delivery to the king and eventual execution. At the same time, the Persians also cut down some lesser Greek officers and 200 hoplites that had come along with their generals in hope of securing supplies. Only one badly wounded man got away from this slaughter, staggering back to report the treachery.

Having lost most of their leaders, the mercenaries briefly gave way to despair, yet soon recovered to select another set of commanders. Chief among these was the Spartan general Cheirisophus. Steeped in Greece's most respected martial tradition and with a long record of senior service, Cheirisophus's election was no surprise. However, the fresh list of officers also included Xenophon, an Athenian with no prior experience of military command. He had come along as a friend of Proxenus of Thebes (who had been among those captured) and it was his ability to remain calm and eloquently dispense sensible advice that earned him a command slot. Fortunately for his companions, this untested young man's soldierly skills would soon prove up to the challenge.

The reconstituted Greek leadership decided to withdraw northward toward Grecian communities along the Euxine (Black) Sea. They formed their men into a rectangle for the long trek, surrounding baggage, camp followers, and light infantry with hoplites in line at fore (under Cheirisophus) and aft (under Xenophon and others) as contingents of spearmen in column moved along either flank. This formation proved only a limited success, having difficulty adapting to terrain variations, and the first day of retreat saw the Greeks fall prey to a string of minor attacks from mounted bowmen and supporting light infantry. These enemy troops served under Mithradates, a former associate of Cyrus that Tissaphernes had set upon the retiring army.

The mercenaries had trouble responding to Mithradates' harassment. This was due to a lack of cavalry (all 40 horsemen and 300 of the peltasts that came from Thrace with Clearchus having deserted) and because their javelinmen and archers couldn't match range with Persia's bowmen and slingers. A sally by rearguard spearmen and peltasts under Xenophon brought only brief relief, since they could do no more than chase their tormentors back, being far too slow to catch and punish them. Moreover, even a short absence of the rearguard had endangered the formation, making it clear that a better answer was needed. In the end, the Greeks found solutions within their own ranks, fielding 50 riders (with mounts culled from draft animals) and 200 slingers. The latter were Rhodians drawn from the various mercenary contingents, islanders known as the best slingers in the Greek world. Highly effective, their lead bullets carried twice as far as Asian stone ammunition and could even outdistance Persian arrows. Now equipped with an adequate light-armed screen, the Greeks set out for the Tigris River, which would act as their initial guide toward the sea.

The mercenaries' route passed near the ancient Assyrian city of Calah, whose ruins sat beside the Tigris. They were still a few hours march from Calah when their first major challenge arose in the form of a deep gorge that had to be negotiated. Fearful at first of suffering an attack here, the Greek commanders saw an opportunity once their men had gained the far side. They put on a show by marching on for about 1.5km and then readied a surprise assault on their pursuers, who were still struggling across the troublesome chasm.

Mithradates had some 1,000 horsemen plus 4,000 archers and slingers in his command. A large portion of his cavalry must have started in front, but soon fell behind at the ravine, since each rider had to dismount and lead his horse down and back up at the most advantageous points on either side. This left them still in the rear carrying out their difficult passage when a wave of Greeks swept back toward the crossing. Several thousand of the younger and more agile hoplites led this charge at the double, trying to maintain a loose line as teams of peltasts and cavalry kept pace off each wing. The startled Persian foot soldiers that had already transited the chasm were taken completely by surprise and fled in a desperate attempt to outrun their more heavily armed foes; however, they had to slow down at the gorge, where many lost their lives as the pursuit caught up. Nor did Mithradates' cavalrymen go unscathed, since 18 of them were still struggling to get out of the ravine when the Greeks arrived to effect their capture. Stung by this action, Tissaphernes now seems to have given up any thoughts of a pitched battle; and though he did go on to mount some missile assaults from a distance, even these eventually ceased under pressure from the Greeks' slingers.

Calah was the last real battle of the 5th century. The Greeks finished 401 B.C. by marching out of Mesopotamia, going on to reach the sea in spring the following year after many adventures. This famous "Retreat of the Ten Thousand" was a masterpiece of discipline and improvised tactics that exposed profound weaknesses in the Persian Empire and would help inspire the Asian conquests of Alexander the Great in the later half of the 4th century.

Tactical Patterns at the End of the 5th Century

A review of combat 412–401 B.C. reveals that the Greeks remained as reliant as ever on hoplites to fashion success on the field of battle. And even when Grecian spearmen weren't themselves driving to victory, they were usually forcing the enemy to counter with their own armored fighters. As a result, just over 80 percent of the period's actions featured heavy infantry in a decisive role — the same percentage as when Greek fought Greek during the century as a whole. Certainly, cavalry and light footmen were generally present at greater strength at this time, but commanders had adjusted and continued to confine such troops to supporting roles. This led to light arms being elements of decision on only eight of 42 occasions, making it clear that hoplites remained the best single gauge of an army's prospects in battle.

Quality was one element in the dominance of shock infantry. Not only were seasoned and therefore highly trained hoplites much less prone to yield the field by breaking prematurely from a fight, but they were also much more likely to intimidate and morally break a less experienced opponent. Thus, we find such men scoring numerous victories against foes of lesser caliber. Superbly skilled spartiates, for example, won nearly three-quarters of their 5th-century actions, and the combined record of success for the century's three most active, well-trained armies (those of Athens, Syracuse, and Sparta) soared to 80 percent when facing less-veteran opposition.

Numbers were another major factor in hoplite dominance, since they had a profound effect on a phalanx's width and depth of file. In actions during the closing years of the 5th century where one side held a significant edge (+33 percent or better) in heavy-armed manpower, it claimed the field 25 times against only six defeats — a success rate of 81 percent. It therefore obviously behooved a general not only to come up with the best men he could find, but also to field them in quantity. The statistic that shows this most clearly is the battle record of Athens, which was by far the century's most combat-active polis, having engaged in 95 battles (more than twice those of Syracuse and more than three times as many as Sparta). Athenian armies won 83 percent of the time when fielding significantly superior manpower, yet just 70 percent if odds were even and only 42 percent when outmanned.

The advantages of outnumbering an opponent in hoplites led to widespread employment of paid spearmen in the late 5th century. Indeed, such heavy-armed hirelings took part in 70 percent of engagements from close of the Peloponnesian War through century's end (versus being present in no more than 13 percent of all Greek armies during the 5th century as a whole). One popular supposition about this is that spoiling of the countryside related to the

Peloponnesian War drove many of these men into the mercenary trade. Yet it seems that few actually took up arms for money in order to escape ravaged homelands; in fact, they came for the most part from Achaea and Arcadia in the north-central Peloponnesian highlands, where there had been precious little combat of any sort. They thus were simply after money, much like those who earlier had gone off to fight in Sicily for tyrants' pay. This latest breed of mercenary did, however, differ from its predecessors in one important aspect — it had superior training. This was what permitted the sort of complex maneuvers recorded at Cunaxa. Thus, though three decades of war might not have actually forced men into a mercenary career, it had without doubt schooled them well for it through years of drill and combat.

Regardless of the make-up of an army with regard to mercenary content or ratios of troop types, its most reliable route to success always lay in exploiting the tactics of surprise. Nearly 80 percent of the surprise attacks launched 412–401 B.C. delivered victory, consistent with an 88 percent rate of success throughout the entire century. In fact, the only effective counter for such unexpected assaults was a fairly sophisticated use of tactical reserves. This was something quite foreign to most Greek generals and it's notable that the two failed surprise attacks recorded in this period were against Carthaginians — Hannibal at Himera II and Himilco on the beach at Gela. The Africans in both instances wielded reserve forces to counterattack and reverse the course of those battles, rescuing hard-fought victories from the brink of defeat. Conversely, every surprise attack targeting Greeks (who usually had no provision for tactical reserves) was an unqualified success.

And direct assault wasn't the only form of surprise that consistently brought victory. Those using unexpected mobilizations did well too, going undefeated in the century's closing years. The Athenians were leading practitioners of this tactic, employing their fleet to make rapid deployments against selected targets that gave an edge in both manpower and moral. So effective was this approach that the Athenians won 92 percent of the amphibious engagements they undertook during the 5th century. Of course, surprise mobilizations could be executed on land as well. However, an overland march did raise the risk of detection and worked best on targets either focused elsewhere (per Mazaros III) or very close to hand (as at Neapolis).

Use of terrain features to gain an edge on the battlefield was a prominent ploy during the waning years of the century and there are no less than eleven examples of this tactic 412–401 B.C. To a large extent, this reflected a rise in urban warfare, as per the street fights at Selinous, Syracuse, Byzantium, and Athens. Such settings favored defenders by channeling opponents into tight confines where much of their manpower couldn't reach the front. Though often not enough of a help to allow underdogs to overcome extremely long odds, such artificial restrictions did contribute to victories at Selinous II and Munychia. Along similar lines, there was the beach action at Gela, where an initially successful Greek attack became fatally bogged down in campsite clutter. This period also saw a few uses of natural features in attempts to counter either greater opposing manpower (without success at Cyzicus II, Porus, and Halae Marsh) or superior cavalry (with good results at Calah).

Unique formations weren't a big factor in late 5th-century combat, with the only real example being the rectangular array used by Greeks retiring from Cunaxa. Many aspects of this tactic mirror the marching order adopted by Sparta's Brasidas after Lyncestis. Perhaps Xenophon did, as he claimed, come up with this ploy, or maybe he got it from Brasidas's adventure via one of the many Spartans with the Ten Thousand. It actually seems more likely that the marching box technique had been designed at Sparta as an alternative to the sort of rearguard action that had proven so costly at Thermopylae.

Finally, what effects did fighting on home ground have at century's end? Armies coming to action on or near their own territory during the century's last dozen years met defeat 24 times in 36 battles. This disappointing 33 percent success rate drops to only 25 percent in those cases where heavy-armed forces were about the same size. And such results fit well with those for the century overall, when invaders won 55 percent of all their engagements and 60 percent where neither side could claim a significant edge in numbers of hoplites or the equivalent. This all lends strong support to the idea that a variety of psychological negatives associated with engaging close to home usually more than offset any physical advantages that such a setting might provide.

* * *

The Greek formation that advanced across the plain at Cunaxa was strikingly similar to that of Argos at Cleonai 100 years earlier. Though Doric phalanxes were now better drilled and possessed superior light-armed support, they hadn't really changed their primary function. Heavy spearmen remained closely ranked and bore aspis shields that they might march against their foes and drive them from the field in a wave of bronze-sheathed pressure and thrusting steel. Yet while the tactics of set combat had largely held true, broader strategy had undergone profound changes. Hoplites no longer fought for small stretches of bordering farmland, but for wider conquest and plunder, and often for a tyrant's pay. The concept of decisive pitched battle had slowly given way to that of total war. Rather than loss of a few volunteer soldiers, a defeated polis might now face massive casualties, widespread destruction of property, and even utter extinction.

Conclusion

"Warfare is the greatest affair of state, the basis of life and death, the way to survival or extinction. It must be thoroughly pondered and analyzed"
Sun-Tsu (*The Art of War*)

Pitched battle in classical Greece took place within a tactical system that restricted a man's options in combat. Confined to rank and file by his phalanx, a soldier's entire being — physical, intellectual, and emotional — was focused on survival through besting the enemy in a grueling shock action. This experience colored his entire concept of war. Much of the martial sensibility that this created in the ancient Greeks has filtered down through the millennia to us today, the latest inheritors of their western cultural traditions. Thus, by grasping the detailed reality of Grecian battle, we can hope to gain insight into classical views of warfare and how they might affect our modern perceptions. The foregoing has attempted to contribute to this goal by taking a hard look at what actually happened on battlefields of the formative 5th century B.C., with the results dispelling a number of myths about ancient Greek warfare.

Among the largest misconceptions exposed is that Grecian arms and tactics were innately superior to those of barbarians like the Persians. It appears instead that terrain conditions dictated which fighting style was best suited for any given engagement. Similarly, it's a common assumption that Greek warriors did better on home soil; yet the record clearly shows that they actually performed more poorly when engaging near home. It has also been said that the Greeks shunned surprise attacks, when, in fact, this tactic seems to have seen rather frequent use. Another major fallacy is that democratic states have always tended to avoid making war on each other. But such conflicts did happen, even at this early date, with two of the world's first and foremost democracies (Athens and Syracuse) battering each other in some of the bloodiest actions of the entire 5th century. The truth is that democratic Athens initiated more battles during the subject period than any other Greek state, while no army ducked battle more often than that of authoritarian and supposedly warlike Sparta. Indeed, it appears that the Spartans usually went to war very reluctantly, and frequently avoided combat so as to preserve their precious citizen manpower. Still, even this high degree of caution and the undeniable prowess of their magnificent spartiate spearmen didn't render them as invincible in battle as legend would have it. Despite posting outstanding results in major engagements, a number of poor showings in lesser actions left 5th-century Sparta saddled with nearly as many defeats as victories.

Such myth-busting aside, there is one figure that emerges from this study with reputation fully intact — the common hoplite. Ordered in strict formation, these amateur militiamen fought front and center in every significant engagement. And in doing so, they battled their own fear as much as the enemy in all-out efforts to literally spearhead victory. Each man carried the middle-class values of his native city with him into action, which combined with a sense of élan and community to provide the courage needed to endure the horrors of shock combat. Every citizen was or had been a soldier. Therefore, when ancient Greeks voted or otherwise agreed to go to war, they did so with full knowledge of the true nature of combat and the terrible sacrifices that it was likely to require.

Things are very different today. We live in a time when increased military professionalism has insulated the average person from personal exposure to battle and its deadly realities. Awash in a seductive, multimedia sea of stirring martial fictions, citizens of our era are at risk of being uninformed in their war-making decisions. We would therefore do well to fill this crucial gap in our experience by seeking out accurate accounts of real combat past and present. It's only by appreciating these that can we begin to approach the Greek hoplite's hard-won awareness of war's potential merits and ultimate limitations.

Table 1: Combat Factors in Greek Pitched Battles (500–401 B.C.)

See Key on page 292

BATTLE	HI	HS	HO	CV	CS	CO	LI	LS	LO	SA	SM	MV	FM	TR	HM
500 Argos/Corinth	W	–	–	–	–	–	–	–	–	–	–	–	–	–	W
500 Cleonai/Orneai	W	–	–	–	–	–	–	–	–	–	–	–	–	–	–
500 Cleitor/Heraia	W	–	–	–	–	–	–	–	–	–	–	–	–	–	–
500 Lemnos	–	W	–	–	–	–	–	–	–	–	–	–	–	–	L
500 Region/Gela	W	–	–	–	–	–	–	–	–	–	–	–	–	–	L
498 Ephesos I	–	–	–	–	–	W	–	–	W	–	–	–	–	L	L
498 Cyprian Salamis I	–	L	–	–	–	W	–	–	W	W	–	–	–	–	L
497 Marsyas	–	L	–	–	–	W	–	–	W	–	–	–	–	L	L
496 Labraunda	–	L	–	–	–	W	–	–	W	–	–	–	–	–	L
496 Pedasos	–	–	–	–	–	L	–	–	L	W	–	–	–	W	W
494 Hollows Chios	–	L	–	–	–	–	–	–	–	W	W	–	–	–	L
494 Malene	–	–	L	–	–	W	–	–	W	–	W	W	–	–	W
494 Sepeia	W	–	–	–	–	–	–	–	–	W	–	–	–	–	L
492 Helorus River	–	–	–	–	–	W	–	W	–	–	–	–	–	–	L
491 Heraian Hybla	–	W	–	–	–	W	–	L	–	–	–	–	–	–	L
490 Taras I	–	–	–	–	–	L	–	–	–	–	–	–	–	W	W
490 Marathon	–	–	W	–	–	L	–	–	L	–	–	–	W	W	W
487 Mylae I	–	W	–	–	–	–	–	W	–	–	–	–	–	–	L
485 Sicyon/Phlius I	–	–	L	–	–	–	–	–	L	–	–	–	–	–	–
480 Thermopylae 1	–	W	–	–	–	–	–	–	L	–	–	–	–	W	W
480 Thermopylae 2	–	W	–	–	–	–	–	–	L	–	–	–	–	W	W
480 Thermopylae 3	–	W	–	–	–	–	–	–	L	–	–	–	–	W	W
480 Thermopylae 4	–	–	–	–	–	–	–	–	–	–	–	–	–	W	W
480 Thermopylae 5	–	–	–	–	–	–	–	–	–	W	–	–	–	L	L
480 Psyttaleia	–	–	W	–	–	–	–	–	–	–	W	–	–	–	W
480 Himera I-Beach	–	–	W	–	–	L	–	–	W	–	–	–	–	W	L
480 Himera I-Hill	–	–	–	–	–	–	–	–	L	W	–	–	–	–	W
479 Plataea-Cithaer.	–	–	W	–	–	L	–	–	W	–	–	–	–	–	W
479 Plataea-Moloeis	–	W	–	–	–	L	–	–	L	–	–	–	–	W	W
479 Plataea-Oeroe	–	–	–	–	–	–	–	–	–	–	–	–	–	W	W
479 Plataea-Asopos	–	–	L	–	–	W	–	–	W	–	W	–	–	–	L
479 Plataea-Center	–	–	W	–	–	L	–	–	L	–	–	–	–	W	W
479 Mycale	–	W	–	–	–	–	–	–	L	–	–	–	–	W	L
476 Eion	–	–	W	–	–	L	–	–	–	–	–	–	–	W	W
475 Sicyon/Phlius II	–	–	W	–	–	–	–	–	W	–	–	–	–	–	–
473 Taras II	W	–	–	–	–	W	–	–	W	–	–	–	–	L	L
472 Acragas I	W	–	–	–	–	W	–	W	–	–	W	–	–	–	L
470 Tegea	W	–	–	–	–	–	–	–	–	–	–	–	–	–	L

289

Table 1

BATTLE	HI	HS	HO	CV	CS	CO	LI	LS	LO	SA	SM	MV	FM	TR	HM
466 Eurymedon	–	W	–	–	–	L	–	L	–	–	–	–	–	W	L
466 Achradine I	W	–	–	–	–	W	–	–	–	–	–	–	–	L	W
465 Drabescus	–	–	L	–	–	W	–	–	W	W	W	–	–	–	W
465 Stenyklaras	–	–	W	–	–	–	–	–	W	–	–	–	–	–	W
464 Dipaea	–	–	L	–	–	–	–	–	L	–	–	–	–	–	L
464 Mycenae	–	–	W	–	–	–	–	–	W	–	–	–	–	–	L
463 Battle Isthmus	W	–	–	–	–	–	–	–	L	–	–	–	–	–	L
461 Oenoe	–	–	W	–	–	W	–	–	W	–	W	–	–	W	W
461 Achradine II	W	–	–	–	–	W	–	–	–	–	–	–	–	L	W
460 Owl's Plain	–	W	–	–	–	–	–	W	–	–	–	–	–	–	L
460 Crastos	W	–	–	–	–	–	–	–	–	–	–	–	–	–	L
460 Taras III	W	–	–	–	L	–	–	–	–	–	–	–	–	W	–
460 Papremis	W	–	–	–	–	L	–	–	–	–	–	–	–	W	W
459 Halieis	–	W	–	–	–	–	–	W	–	–	L	–	–	–	W
458 Cimolia I	–	–	–	–	–	–	–	–	–	–	–	–	–	–	–
458 Cimolia II	–	W	–	–	–	–	–	W	–	–	W	–	–	–	W
457 Tanagra I	–	–	–	–	W	–	–	W	–	W	–	–	–	–	W
457 Oenophyta	W	–	–	–	–	–	–	–	–	–	W	–	–	–	L
457 Sicyon I	–	L	–	–	–	–	–	L	–	–	W	–	–	–	L
454 Sicyon II	W	–	–	–	–	–	–	–	–	–	W	–	–	–	L
454 Mazaros I	–	W	–	–	–	–	–	–	L	–	–	–	–	–	–
451 Greek Motya	–	–	L	–	–	L	–	–	W	W	–	–	–	–	L
450 Nomae	–	W	–	–	W	–	–	–	L	–	–	–	–	–	–
449 Cyprian Salamis II	–	W	–	–	–	–	–	–	–	–	–	–	–	–	W
448 Megara	W	–	–	–	–	–	–	–	–	–	–	–	–	–	L
447 Coronea I	–	–	W	–	–	W	–	–	W	–	W	–	–	–	W
446 Himera River	–	–	–	–	W	–	–	W	–	–	–	–	–	–	L
440 Taras/Thurii	–	W	–	–	L	–	–	–	–	–	–	–	–	W	–
433 Thurii/Lucania I	–	W	–	–	–	W	–	–	–	–	–	W	W	–	L
433 Thurii/Lucania II	–	L	–	–	W	–	–	–	–	–	–	–	–	W	L
432 Potidaea	–	W	–	–	W	–	–	W	–	–	W	–	–	–	L
431 Phyrgia	–	–	W	–	L	–	–	–	–	–	–	–	–	W	L
431 Pheia	–	–	W	–	–	–	–	–	W	–	W	–	–	–	W
431 Alope	W	–	–	–	–	–	–	–	–	–	W	–	–	–	L
430 Cranae	–	–	L	–	–	–	–	–	L	W	L	–	–	–	W
430 Lycia	–	–	W	–	–	–	–	–	W	–	L	–	–	W	W
429 Spartolos	L	–	–	–	–	W	–	–	W	–	–	–	–	–	W
429 Stratus	–	–	L	–	–	–	–	–	L	W	–	–	–	W	W
428 Malea	W	–	–	–	–	–	–	–	W	–	–	–	–	–	W
428 Antissa	W	–	–	–	–	–	–	–	W	–	–	–	–	–	W
428 Nericus	–	W	–	–	–	–	–	–	W	–	W	–	–	–	W
428 Sandius	–	–	W	–	–	–	–	–	W	–	–	–	–	–	W
427 Corcyra	–	W	–	–	–	–	–	–	W	–	–	–	–	W	–
426 Mylae II	–	W	–	–	–	–	–	–	W	L	–	–	–	–	L
426 Locri	W	–	–	–	–	L	–	–	L	–	W	–	–	–	L
426 Inessa	–	–	W	–	–	–	–	–	L	W	–	–	–	–	W
426 Caicinus River	W	–	–	–	–	L	–	–	L	–	W	–	–	–	L
426 Tanagra II	–	W	–	–	W	–	–	–	–	–	–	–	–	–	L
426 Ellomenus	–	–	W	–	–	–	–	–	W	W	–	–	–	–	L
426 Aegitium	–	–	L	–	–	–	–	–	W	–	W	–	–	L	W
426 Olpae	–	L	–	–	–	–	–	L	–	W	–	–	–	–	W
426 Idomene	–	W	–	–	–	–	–	W	–	W	W	–	–	–	W
425 Halex River	–	W	–	–	–	W	–	L	–	–	–	–	–	–	W

Combat Factors in Greek Pitched Battles (500–401 B.C.) 291

BATTLE	HI	HS	HO	CV	CS	CO	LI	LS	LO	SA	SM	MV	FM	TR	HM
425 Naxos	–	L	–	–	–	W	–	L	–	W	–	–	–	–	W
425 Messana	–	–	W	–	–	–	–	–	W	L	W	–	–	–	L
425 Spaectaria	–	–	W	–	–	–	–	–	W	W	–	–	–	L	L
425 Solygeia	–	W	–	–	–	W	–	L	–	–	L	L	–	L	L
424 Cythera	–	–	W	–	–	W	–	–	W	–	W	–	–	–	L
424 Cotyrta-Aphrod.	–	–	W	–	–	–	–	–	W	–	L	–	–	–	L
424 Antandrus	–	–	W	–	–	–	–	–	W	–	–	–	–	–	L
424 Delium	W	–	–	–	–	–	–	–	W	–	–	W	W	W	W
424 Sicyon III	–	W	–	–	–	–	–	W	–	W	–	–	–	–	W
423 Lyncestis	–	W	–	–	W	–	–	–	–	–	–	–	–	–	L
423 Mende	–	L	–	–	–	–	–	–	L	–	–	–	–	W	W
423 Scione	–	W	–	–	–	–	–	–	W	–	–	–	–	L	L
423 Laodocium	–	–	–	–	–	–	–	–	–	–	–	–	–	–	–
422 Amphipolis	–	L	–	–	–	–	–	–	W	W	–	–	–	–	W
421 Phocis/Locris	–	W	–	–	W	–	–	–	–	–	–	–	–	–	–
420 Heraclea	–	–	–	–	–	W	–	–	W	–	–	–	–	–	L
419 Cumae	–	–	W	–	–	W	–	–	W	–	–	–	–	–	L
418 Mantinea I	W	–	–	–	L	–	–	–	–	–	–	L	W	–	L
417 Argos/Phlius	–	W	–	–	–	–	–	W	–	W	–	–	–	–	W
416 Mazaros II	–	W	–	–	W	–	–	W	–	–	–	–	–	–	L
415 Anapus River	–	–	L	–	–	L	–	–	L	–	W	–	–	W	L
414 Terias River	W	–	–	–	–	W	–	–	–	–	–	–	–	–	L
414 Euryelus	W	–	–	–	–	–	–	–	–	–	W	–	–	W	L
414 Syca	–	–	W	–	–	–	–	–	–	–	–	–	–	W	L
414 Lysimeleia C.W.	W	–	–	–	–	–	–	–	–	–	–	–	–	–	L
414 Epipolae C.W.I	–	L	–	–	–	–	–	–	–	–	–	–	–	W	L
414 Epipolae C.W.II	–	–	–	–	W	–	–	W	–	–	–	–	–	–	W
413 Mycalessus	–	–	W	–	–	W	–	–	L	W	–	–	–	–	W
413 Enna Road	–	–	L	–	–	W	–	–	–	W	–	–	–	–	W
413 Epipolae	–	W	–	–	–	–	–	W	–	–	L	–	–	–	W
413 Helorus Gate	–	–	L	–	–	W	–	–	W	–	–	–	–	–	W
413 Lysimeleia M.	–	–	L	–	L	–	–	L	–	–	–	–	–	W	L
413 Anapus Cross.	–	–	W	–	–	–	–	–	W	–	–	–	–	L	L
413 Anapus Plain	–	–	L	–	–	W	–	–	W	–	–	–	L	–	W
413 Acraean Bald R.	–	–	–	–	–	–	–	–	–	–	–	–	–	W	W
413 Cacyparis River	–	–	W	–	–	–	–	–	W	–	–	–	–	L	L
413 Est. Polyzelus	–	–	L	–	–	W	–	–	W	–	–	–	–	L	W
413 Erineus River	–	–	W	–	–	L	–	–	L	–	–	–	–	W	L
413 Assinarus Cr.	–	–	W	–	–	W	–	–	W	–	–	–	–	W	W
412 Spiraeum	W	–	–	–	–	–	–	–	–	–	–	–	–	–	L
412 Mytilene	W	–	–	–	–	–	–	–	–	–	W	–	–	–	L
412 No. Chios	W	–	–	–	–	–	–	–	–	–	W	–	–	–	L
412 Cape Phanae	–	–	W	–	–	–	–	–	–	–	W	–	–	–	L
412 Leuconium	–	–	W	–	–	–	–	–	–	–	W	–	–	–	L
412 Panormus	–	W	–	–	–	L	–	W	–	–	W	–	–	–	L
412 Miletus	W	–	–	–	–	–	L	–	–	–	–	–	–	–	W
412 Rhodes	W	–	–	–	–	–	–	–	–	–	W	–	–	–	L
412 Delphinium	–	–	L	–	–	–	–	L	–	–	–	–	–	–	L
411 Lampsacus	–	W	–	–	–	–	–	W	–	–	W	–	–	–	L
411 Athens I	–	–	L	–	–	W	–	–	W	–	W	–	–	–	W
411 Cyzicus I	–	–	W	–	–	–	–	–	W	–	–	–	–	–	–
411 Cyzicus II	–	W	–	–	–	–	W	–	–	–	W	–	–	L	–
411 Athens II	–	–	L	–	–	W	–	–	W	–	–	–	–	–	W

Table 1

BATTLE	HI	HS	HO	CV	CS	CO	LI	LS	LO	SA	SM	MV	FM	TR	HM
410 Mazaros III	–	W	–	–	L	–	–	–	W	–	W	–	–	–	W
409 Selinous I	–	–	W	–	–	–	–	–	W	–	–	–	–	W	W
409 Selinous II	–	–	W	–	–	–	–	–	L	–	–	–	–	L	L
409 Himera II	–	–	–	–	–	W	–	–	–	L	–	W	–	–	L
409 Oeta/Heraclea	–	W	–	–	–	–	–	W	–	W	–	–	–	–	W
409 Ta Kerata	–	–	L	–	–	W	–	–	L	–	–	–	–	–	L
409 Pygela	–	–	W	–	–	W	–	–	W	–	–	–	–	–	L
409 Ephesos II-Shore	–	–	W	–	–	–	–	–	W	–	W	–	–	L	W
409 Ephesos II-Swamp	–	–	W	–	–	L	–	–	W	–	–	–	–	–	W
409 Abydos	–	–	W	–	–	L	–	–	L	W	–	–	–	–	L
409 Punic Motya	–	W	–	–	–	W	–	–	–	–	–	–	–	–	L
409 Sicilian Panormus	–	–	W	–	–	W	–	–	W	–	–	–	–	–	L
408 Syracuse Mkt.	–	–	W	–	–	L	–	–	W	–	–	–	–	L	–
408 Chalcedon	W	–	–	–	–	W	–	–	–	W	–	–	–	–	L
408 Byzantium	–	W	–	–	–	–	W	–	W	W	–	–	–	L	–
407 Thasos	–	W	–	–	–	–	W	–	–	W	–	–	–	–	L
407 Gaurium	–	–	W	–	W	–	W	–	–	–	–	–	–	–	L
406 Acragas II	–	W	–	–	W	–	–	–	–	–	–	–	–	–	W
405 Gela-Beach	–	W	–	–	–	–	–	–	L	–	W	–	W	L
405 Gela-Plain	–	–	W	–	–	–	–	–	–	–	W	–	–	L
404 Neapolis	W	–	–	–	–	W	–	–	–	–	W	–	–	L	L
404 Pharsalos	–	–	–	–	W	–	–	W	–	–	–	–	–	–	L
403 Porus	–	W	–	–	–	–	–	W	–	–	–	–	–	L	W
403 Acharnae	–	–	–	–	–	L	–	–	–	W	–	–	–	–	W
403 Munychia	–	–	L	–	–	L	–	L	–	–	–	–	–	W	–
403 Halae Marsh	–	–	W	–	–	W	–	–	W	–	–	–	–	L	L
402 Elis	–	–	L	–	–	–	–	W	W	–	–	–	–	–	W
401 Cunaxa	–	–	W	–	–	L	–	–	L	–	–	–	–	–	L
401 Calah	–	–	W	–	–	L	–	–	L	W	–	–	–	W	L

KEY

Symbol   Explanation

W   Factor was an advantage to *winner* of the battle
L   Factor was an advantage to *loser* of the battle
HI Superior performance by heavy infantry with small or no numerical advantage*
HS Significant advantage (a third up to two times greater) in heavy infantry manpower*
HO Overwhelming advantage (two times or more) in heavy infantry manpower*
CV Superior performance by cavalry with small or no numerical advantage
CS Significant advantage (a third up to two times greater) in cavalry manpower
CO Overwhelming advantage (two times or more) in cavalry manpower
LI Superior performance by light infantry with small or no numerical advantage
LS Significant advantage (a third up to two times greater) in light infantry manpower
LO Overwhelming advantage (two times or more) in light infantry manpower
SA Surprise attack (assault/ambush not anticipated by its target)
SM Surprise mobilization (force's arrival in area not anticipated by its opposition)
MV Maneuver on the battlefield (tactical movement of troops in the midst of combat)
FM Exceptional formation design (nontraditional ordering of troops prior to combat)
TR Use of terrain elements (natural or manmade) to advantage on the battlefield
HM Fighting on or near "home ground" (action in direct defense of one's homeland)

* *Heavy infantry includes only sparabara with shields (usually 20 percent prior to 466 B.C.)*

Table 2: Decisive Factors in Greek Pitched Battles (500–401 B.C.)

See Keys on pages 296–297

BATTLE	SZ	WINNER(S)	LOSER(S)	DECISIVE FACTOR(S)
500 Argos/Corinth	GD	ARG	COR	Heavy infantry
500 Cleonai/Orneai	MN	CLE	ORN	Heavy infantry
500 Cleitor/Heraia	SK	CLT	HER	Heavy infantry
500 Lemnos	MN	ATH	LEM	Heavy infantry
500 Region/Gela	MN	RHG	GEL	Heavy infantry/Terrain
498 Ephesos I	GD	IRN/LYD/MYS	MIL/EPH/ATH	Cavalry/Light infantry
498 Cyp. Salamis I	GD	IRN/CYP/CAB	CYG	Cavalry/Surprise attack
497 Marsyas	GD	IRN/LYD/MYS	CRN	Heavy/Light infantry
496 Labraunda	GD	IRN/LYD/MYS	CRN/MIL	Cavalry
496 Pedasos	MJ	CRN	IRN/LYD/MYS	Hvy.Inf./Lt.Inf./Surp.attack
494 Hollows Chios	SK	LES/ION	CHI	Heavy Inf./Surprise attack
494 Malene	MN	IRN/MYS	LES/ION	Cavalry/Surprise attack
494 Sepeia	GD	SPR	ARG	Heavy Inf./Surprise attack
492 Helorus River	MJ	GEL	SYR	Cavalry
491 Heraian Hybla	MJ	GEL	SCL	Heavy infantry
490 Taras I	MJ	TAR	MSP	Heavy infantry/Terrain
490 Marathon	MJ	ATH/PLA	IRN/IONI/SYH	Heavy inf./Form./Terrain
487 Mylae I	MN	RHG/MSA	MYL/ZAN/LEP	Heavy infantry
485 Sicyon/Phlius I	MN	PHL	SCY	Heavy infantry
480 Thermopylae 1	MN	SPR/PEL/BOE	IRN	Heavy infantry/Terrain
480 Thermopylae 2	MN	SPR/PEL/BOE	IRA/SYH	Heavy infantry/Terrain
480 Thermopylae 3	MN	SPR/PEL/BOE	IRN	Heavy infantry/Terrain
480 Thermopylae 4	MN	SPR/PEL/BOE	IRN	Heavy infantry/Terrain
480 Thermopylae 5	MN	IRN	SPR/THB/THS	Heavy/Light infantry
480 Psyttaleia	SK	ATH	IRN	Heavy infantry
480 Himera I-Beach	GD	CAR/MRI/MRC	ACR/HIM	Heavy infantry/Terrain
480 Himera I-Hill	GD	SYR/MRG/SCG	CAR/MRI/MRC	Heavy inf./Surprise attack
479 Plataea-Cithaer.	MJ	ATH/MGR	IRN	Heavy/Light infantry
479 Plataea-Moloeis	GD	SPR/TEG	IRN/LYD	Heavy infantry/Terrain
479 Plataea-Oeroe	GD	ATH/PLA/THS	THB/BOE/THY	Heavy infantry/Terrain
479 Plataea-Asopos	MJ	BOI/THY	MGR/PHL/ISG	Cavalry
479 Plataea-Center	GD	COR/SCY/PEL	IRN/SAC	Heavy infantry/Terrain
479 Mycale	MN	ATH/COR/SCY	IRN	Heavy infantry
476 Eion	GD	ATH/DEL	IRN/PER	Heavy infantry/Terrain
475 Sicyon/Phlius II	MN	SCY	PHL	Heavy infantry
473 Taras II	GD	IAP	TAR/RHG	Heavy infantry
472 Acragas I	GD	SYR/MRG	ACR/MRG/HIM	Cavalry/Surp. mobiliz.
470 Tegea	GD	SPR	TEG/ARG.	Heavy infantry
466 Eurymedon	GD	ATH/DEL	IRN/PER	Heavy infantry/Terrain

293

Table 2

BATTLE	SZ	WINNER(S)	LOSER(S)	DECISIVE FACTOR(S)
466 Achradine I	GD	SYR/SCG	MRG	Heavy infantry
465 Drabescus	MN	THR	ATH/DEC/AIG/ARG	Cav./Lt. Inf./Surp. attack
465 Stenyklaras	SK	MES	SPR	Light infantry
464 Dipaea	MN	SPR	TEG/ARC	Heavy inf./Surp. mobiliz.
464 Mycenae	MN	ARG	MYC/TIR	Heavy infantry
463 Battle Isthmus	GD	SPT/ATH/PLA/PEL	MES	Heavy infantry
461 Oenoe	MJ	ARG/ATH	SPR	Cav./Lt. Inf./Terrain
461 Achradine II	GD	SYR/SCG	MRG	Heavy infantry
460 Owl's Plain	MJ	SYR	MRG	Heavy infantry
460 Crastos	MJ	ACR	MRG/HIM/GEL	Heavy infantry
460 Taras III	MJ	TAR	IAP	Heavy infantry
460 Papremis	GD	ATH/EGY	IRN/PER	Heavy infantry/Terrain
459 Halieis	MJ	COR/EPI/SCY	ATH	Heavy infantry
458 Cimolia I	GD	*ATN/MGR	*COR	Drawn engagement
458 Cimolia II	GD	ATH/MGR	COR	Heavy inf./Surp. mobiliz.
457 Tanagra I	GD	SPR/THB/BOE/THY	ATH/ARG/DEL	Cavalry/Surprise attack
457 Oenophyta	GD	ATH/DEL	THB/BOE	Heavy inf./Surp. mobiliz.
457 Sicyon I	MJ	ATH	SCY	Heavy inf./Surp. mobiliz.
454 Sicyon II	MN	ATH	SCY	Heavy inf./Surp. mobiliz.
454 Mazaros I	MJ	*SEL/ACR	*EGS/MOT	Drawn engagement
451 Greek Motya	MJ	SIC	SYR/ACR/SCG	Hvy.inf./Lt.inf.Surp. attack
450 Nomae	MJ	SYR	SIC	Heavy infantry
449 Cyp. Salamis II	GD	ATH/DEL/CYG	CYP	Heavy infantry
448 Megara	MJ	ATH	MGR	Heavy infantry
447 Coronea I	MJ	BOE/LOP/EUB	ATH/DEL	Heavy inf./Surp. mobiliz.
446 Himera River	GD	SYR/SCG	ACR/SCG	Cavalry
440 Taras/Thurii	MJ	TAR	THU/MSP	Heavy infantry/Terrain
433 Thurii/Lucania I	MJ	THU/MSP	LUC	Heavy infantry/Maneuver
433 Thurii/Lucania II	MJ	THU/MSP	LUC	Heavy infantry/Terrain
432 Potidaea	MJ	ATH/EUB	COR/MRG/POT	Heavy infantry
431 Phyrgia	MN	BOE	ATH/THY	Heavy infantry
431 Pheia	MN	ATH	ELI	Heavy infantry
431 Alope	MN	ATH	LOP	Heavy infantry
430 Cranae	MN	CEP	COR	Heavy/Light infantry
430 Lycia	SK	LYC	ATH/LYC	Light infantry
429 Spartolos	MN	SPA/MRG	ATH	Cavalry/Light infantry
429 Stratus	GD	ACA	PEL/ISG/AMB/BRH	Light infantry
428 Malea	MN	LES	ATH/DEL	Heavy infantry
428 Antissa	SK	ANT/MRC	MET	Heavy/Light infantry
428 Nericus	MN	LEU	ATH	Heavy inf./Surp. mobiliz.
428 Sandius	MN	CRN/SAM	ATH	Heavy/Light infantry
427 Corcyra	MN	COC	COC/BRH	Heavy infantry
426 Mylae II	MN	ATH	MSA	Heavy infantry
426 Locri	MN	ATH	LEP	Heavy infantry
426 Inessa	SK	SYR	SCL	Heavy infantry
426 Caicinus River	MN	ATH	LEP	Heavy infantry
426 Tanagra II	GD	ATH	THB/TAN	Heavy infantry
426 Ellomenus	MN	ATH/MES	LEU	Heavy inf./Surp. attack
426 Aegitium	MN	AIT	ATH/MES/ISG	Light infantry
426 Olpae	GD	ATH/ACA/AMP	PEL/MAN/AMB	Heavy inf./Surp. attack
426 Idomene	MJ	ATH/ACA/AMP	AMB	Hvy./Lt. inf./Surp. atk.
425 Halex River	MJ	LEP	ATH/DEL	Heavy/Light infantry
425 Naxos	MN	NAX	MSA	Heavy inf./Surp. attack

Decisive Factors in Greek Pitched Battles (500–401 B.C.)

BATTLE	SZ	WINNER(S)	LOSER(S)	DECISIVE FACTOR(S)
425 Messana	MJ	ATH/LEO	MSA/LEP	Heavy inf./Maneuver
425 Spaectaria	MN	ATH/DEL	SPR	Light infantry
425 Solygeia	MJ	ATH/DEL	COR	Cavalry
424 Cythera	MN	ATH/DEL	SPR	Heavy infantry
424 Cotyrta-Aphrod.	SK	ATH	SPR	Heavy infantry
424 Antandrus	MN	ATH/DEL	ANR/LES	Heavy infantry
424 Delium	GD	THB/THS/BOE	ATH	Cavalry
424 Sicyon III	MN	SYC	ATH	Heavy inf./Surp. mobiliz.
423 Lyncestis	MN	SPR/MRG/MCL	MCU	Heavy infantry
423 Mende	MN	MRG/SCI/MEN	ATH/DEL	Heavy/Light infantry
423 Scione	MN	ATH	MRG/SCI	Heavy infantry
423 Laodocium	MJ	*TEG/ARC	*MAN/ARC	Drawn engagement
422 Amphipolis	MJ	SPR/MRG/AMP	ATH/DEL	Heavy inf./Surp. atk.
421 Phocis/Locris	MN	PHO	LOZ	Heavy infantry
420 Heraclea	MN	MAL/AEN/DOL	HRC	Cavalry/Light infantry
419 Cumae	GD	SAN	CUM	Heavy infantry
418 Mantinea I	GD	SPR/ARC/TEG	ARG/ATH/MAN	Heavy inf./Maneuver
417 Argos/Phlius	MN	PHL	ARG	Hvy/Lt. inf./Surp. atk.
416 Mazaros II	MN	SEL	EGS	Heavy infantry
415 Anapus River	MJ	ATH/MRG/DEL	SYR/SCG	Heavy infantry
414 Terias River	MN	ATH	SYR	Heavy infantry
414 Euryelus	MJ	ATH/MRG/DEL	SYR/SCG	Heavy inf./Terrain
414 Syca	SK	ATH/EGS/SCL	SYR	Heavy infantry
414 Lysimel. C.W.	MJ	ATH/MRG/DEL	SYR/SCG	Heavy infantry
414 Epipolae C.W.I	MJ	ATH/MRG/DEL	SYR/SCG/PEL	Heavy infantry
414 Epipolae C.W.II	MJ	SYR/SCG/PEL	ATH/MRG/DEL	Cavalry/Light infantry
413 Mycalessus	MN	THB	THR	Heavy infantry
413 Enna Road	MN	SCL	SCG/SCL	Light infantry
413 Epipolae	MJ	THS/PEL/SCG	ATH/MRG/DEL	Heavy infantry
413 Helorus Gate	SK	SYR	ATH	Cavalry
413 Lysimeleia M.	MN	ETR/ATH	SYR/SCG	Heavy infantry/Terrain
413 Anapus Cross.	MN	ATH/MRG/DEL	SYR/SCG	Heavy infantry
413 Anapus Plain	MN	SYR/SCG/SCL	ATH/MRG/DEL	Cavalry/Light infantry
413 Acraean Bald R.	MN	SYR/PEL/SCG	ATH/MRG/DEL	Heavy inf./Terrain
413 Cacyparis River	MN	ATH/MRG/DEL	SYR/SCG	Heavy infantry
413 Est. Polyzelus	MN	SYR/SCG/SCL	ATH/DEL	Cavalry/Light infantry
413 Erineus River	MN	ATH/MRG/DEL	SYR/SCG/SCL	Heavy infantry
413 Assinarus Cr.	MJ	SYR/PEL/SCG	ATH/MRG/DEL	Heavy infantry
412 Spiraeum	MN	ATH	COR/PEL	Heavy infantry
412 Mytilene	MN	ATH	MYT	Heavy inf./Surp. mobiliz.
412 No. Chios	MN	ATH	CHI	Heavy inf./Surp. mobiliz.
412 Cape Phanae	MN	ATH	CHI	Heavy inf./Surp. mobiliz.
412 Leuconium	MN	ATH	CHI	Heavy inf./Surp. mobiliz.
412 Panormus	MN	ATH	SPR/ION/IRN	Heavy infantry
412 Miletus	MJ	ATH/ARG/DEL	MIL/CHI/PEL/CAR	Heavy infantry
412 Rhodes	MJ	ATH/DEL	RHO	Heavy inf./Surp. mobiliz.
412 Delphinium	MN	ATH	CHI/MRG	Heavy infantry
411 Lampsacus	MN	ATH	LAM/PEL	Heavy infantry
411 Athens I	SK	ATH	SPR	Cavalry/Light infantry
411 Cyzicus I	MN	ATH	BYZ	Heavy infantry
411 Cyzicus II	MJ	ATH/DEL	SPR/PEL/MRG/SYR	Heavy inf./Maneuver
411 Athens II	SK	ATH	SPR	Cavalry/Light infantry
410 Mazaros III	MJ	EGS/CMP/LYB	SEL	Heavy inf./Surp. mobiliz.

Table 2

BATTLE	SZ	WINNER(S)	LOSER(S)	DECISIVE FACTOR(S)
409 Selinous I	MJ	SEL	CMP/EGS/SCL	Heavy inf./Terrain
409 Selinous II	GD	IBR/CAR	SEL	Heavy infantry
409 Himera II	GD	CAR/IBR/EGS/SCL	SYR/HIM/ACR/SEL	Heavy inf./Maneuver
409 Oeta/Heraclea	MN	OET/PHT	HRC	Heavy inf./Surp. attack
409 Ta Kerata	MN	ATH	MEG/SPR	Cavalry
409 Pygela	MN	ATH	MIL	Heavy infantry
409 Ephs. II-Shore	MN	EPH/ION/SYR/LYD	ATH/DEL	Heavy infantry
409 Ephs. II-Swamp	MN	EPH/ION/SYR/LYD	ATH/DEL	Heavy infantry
409 Abydos	MN	ATH	IRN/PER	Cavalry/Surp. attack
409 Punic Motya	MJ	MRG/HIM/SCG	MOT/CRM	Heavy infantry
409 Sicil. Panormus	MJ	MRG/HIM/SCG	PAN	Heavy infantry
408 Syracuse Mkt.	MN	SYR	SYR	Heavy infantry
408 Chalcedon	MN	ATH	PEL/CHA	Cavalry/Surp. attack
408 Byzantium	MJ	ATH/DEL/BYZ	BOE/MRG/MEG	Heavy inf./Surp. attack
407 Thasos	MN	ATH	THA	Heavy infantry
407 Gaurium	MN	ATH	SPR/AND	Heavy inf./Cavalry
406 Acragas II	MJ	SYR/SCG/MSA/ITG	IBR/LYB/CMP	Heavy infantry
405 Gela-Beach	GD	SCP/IBR/CMP	SYR/MSA/ITG	Heavy inf./Man./Terrain
405 Gela-Plain	GD	LYB/CAR/IBR/CMP	SYR/SCG	Heavy inf./Maneuver
404 Neapolis	MJ	MRG/CMP	SYR/MRG	Heavy inf./Surp. mobiliz.
404 Pharsalos	MN	PHR/MRG	LAR/PHA/MRG	Cavalry/Light infantry
403 Porus	MN	SPR/BYZ	MRG	Heavy infantry
403 Acharnae	MN	ATH	SPR/ATH	Heavy inf./Surp. attack
403 Munychia	MJ	ATH	ATH/SPR/MRG	Light infantry/Terrain
403 Halae Marsh	GD	SPR/PEL/MRG	ATH/MRG	Heavy infantry
402 Elis	MN	AIT/ELS	SPR	Light inf./Surp. attack
401 Cunaxa	GD	MRG/THR	EGY/IRN	Heavy infantry
401 Calah	MN	MRG/THR	IRN/PER	Hvy. inf./Surp. atk./Terrain

NOTE: A Decisive Factor is a Combat Factor judged critical in the winner's avoiding a defeat or draw. Decisive Factor(s) for each battle must include at least one Manpower Factor and may include one or more Other Factors (those vitally complementary to the decisive manpower group[s] success).

KEY

Symbols	Explanation
SZ	Size/scale of battle based on the number of heavy infantrymen involved
SK	Skirmish (involving less than 1,000 heavy infantrymen)
MN	Minor battle (involving at least 1,000 but less than 5,000 heavy infantrymen)
MJ	Major battle (involving at least 5,000 but less than 10,000 heavy infantrymen)
GD	Grand battle (involving 10,000 or more heavy infantrymen)
*	Indicates a drawn battle with no clear-cut winner
Heavy infantry	Armored foot soldiers (hoplites or barbarian equivalents)
Light infantry	Light or unarmored foot soldiers (primarily missile troops)
Cavalry	Mounted troops (armored and unarmored)
Surprise mobilization	Arrival of an army that is unanticipated by its enemy
Surprise attack	An assault that is unanticipated by its target
Maneuver	A tactical movement of troops in the midst of a battle
Formation	Use of an exceptional design for troop arrangement
Terrain	Use of topography (natural or manmade) to advantage on the battlefield

Combatant Key

A: ACA=Acarnaria, ACR=Acragas, AEN=Aenis, AIG=Aigina, AIT=Aitolia, AMB=Ambracia, AMP=Amphilochia, AND=Andros, ANR=Antardrus, ANT=Antissa, APH=Amphipolis, ARG=Argos, ATH=Athens

B: BOE=Boeotia (undifferentiated), BYZ=Byzantium

(Combatant Key, *continued*)

- C: CAB=Cabalese, CAR=Carthage, CEP=Cephallenia, CHA=Chalcidia (undifferentiated), CHI=Chios, CLE=Cleonai, CLT=Cleitor, CMP=Campania, COR=Corinth, CRM=Carthaginian mercenaries, CRN=Carian, CUM=Cumae, CYG=Greek Cypriot (undifferentiated), CYP=Punic Cypriot (undifferentiated), CYR=Cyrene
- D: DEC=Decelea, DEL=Delian League (undifferentiated), DOL=Dolopia
- E: EGS=Egesta, EGY=Egypt (undifferentiated), ELI=Elis, EPI=Epidaurus, ETR=Etruscan (undifferentiated), EUB=Euboa (undifferentiated)
- G: GEL=Gela
- H: HER=Heraia, HIM=Himera, HRC=Heraclea
- I: IAP=Iapyians (undifferentiated), ION=Ionian (undifferentiated), IRN=Iranian (undifferentiated), ISG=Greek islanders (undifferentiated), ITG=Italian Greeks (undifferentiated)
- L: LEM=Lemnos, LEO=Leontini, LEP=Epizephyrian Locris, LES=Lesbos, LEU=Leucas, LOP=Opuntian Locris, LOZ=Ozolian Locris, LUC=Lucania, LYC=Lycia, LYD=Lydia
- M: MAL=Malis, MAN= Mantinea, MCL=Lower Macedonia, MCU=Upper Macedonia, MEN=Mende, MET=Methymna, MGR=Megara, MIL=Miletus, MOT=Motya, MRC=mercenaries (undifferentiated), MRG=mercenary Greeks (undifferentiated), MRI=mercenary Italians (undifferentiated), MSA=Messana, MSP=Messapia, MYC=Mycenae, MYL=Mylae, MYS=Mysia
- N: NAX=Naxos
- O: ORN=Orneai
- P: PEL=Peloponnesian (undifferentiated), PER=Persian (undifferentiated), PHL=Phlius, PHO=Phocis, PLA=Plataea, POT=Potidaea
- R: RHG=Rhegion
- S: SAC=Sacae, SAM=Samos, SAN=Samnites (undifferentiated), SCG=Sicilian Greeks (undifferentiated), SCI=Scione, SCL=Siculi (undifferentiated), SCP=Punic Sicilians (undifferentiated), SCY=Sicyon, SEL=Selinous, SPR=Sparta, SYH=Sythia, SYR=Syracuse
- T: TAN=Tanagra, TAR=Taras, TEG=Tegea, THB=Thebes, THR=Thrace (undifferentiated), THS=Thespiae, THY=Thessaly (undifferentiated), TIR=Tiryns,
- Z: ZAN=Zancle

Table 3: Pitched Battle Record of Major Combatants (500–401 B.C.)

Polis/Group	All Battles	Grand/Major	Minor/Skirmish	Hvy Manpower**	
Athens	95: 64–28–1*	39: 26–11–1*	56: 38–17–0*	+38–7–1	=16–7
	69% Success	68% Success	69% Success	–10–14	
Syracuse	38: 20–17–0*	23: 12–11–0	15: 8–6–0*	+10–5	=7–5
	54% Success	52% Success	57% Success	–3–7	
Mercenary Greek Hoplites	34: 15–15–0*	22: 8–11–0*	12: 7–4–0*	+8–2	=5–6
	50% Success	42% Success	64% Success	–2–7	
Sparta	29: 15–14–0	10: 8–2–0	19: 7–12–0	+7–4	=6–1
	52% Success	80% Success	37% Success	–2–9	
Iranians	23: 6–17–0 26% Success	12: 4–8–0	11: 2–9–0	+1–0	=2–3
		33% Success	18% Success	–3–14	
Corinth***	13:7–5–1	11: 6–4–1	2: 1–1–0	+6–1	=1–1
	54% Success	55% Success	50% Success	–0–3–1	
Gela***	13: 6–7–0	10: 4–6–0	3: 2–1–0	+2–0	=2–5
	46% Success	40% Success	67% Success	–2–2	
Thebes	11: 7–4–0	9: 6–3–0	2: 1–1–0	+4–0	=3–2
	64% Success	67% Success	50% Success	–0–2	
Argos	9: 3–6–0	7: 3–4–0	2: 0–2–0	+1–1	= 2–5
	33% Success	43% Success	0% Success	–0–0	
Sicyon***	9: 6–3–0	5: 4–1–0	4: 2–2–0	+5–2	=1–1
	67% Success	80% Success	50% Success	–0–0	
Selinous***	8: 4–3–1	7: 3–3–1	1: 1–0–0	+4–0–1	=0–1
	50% Success	43% Success	100% Success	–0–2	
Thespiae	8: 7–1–0	4: 4–0–0	4: 3–1–0	+4–0	=3–0
	88% Success	100% Success	75% Success	–0–1	

* *Discrepancy between the total number of battles and recorded results (victories/defeats/draws) is due to totals including actions in which a poleis/group was present on both sides. In such cases no unique result can be assigned.*

** *Heavy Manpower. Key: The symbol "+" means that the subject poleis/group had significantly superior heavy infantry manpower (+33% or more); the symbol "=" means that the subject poleis/group had near-even heavy-infantry manpower with its opponent, the symbol "-" means that the subject poleis/group had significantly less heavy infantry manpower (- 25% or less) than its opponent.*

*** *The battle record that follows includes actions in which this polis is not listed separately as a combatant in Table 2, but rather as part of an undifferentiated group.*

Note: A skirmish involves less than 1,000 heavy infantrymen, a minor battle has at least 1,000 but less than 5,000 heavy infantrymen, a major battle involves at least 5,000 but less than 10,000 heavy infantrymen, and a grand battle is one that has 10,000 or more heavy infantrymen.

Argos
Victories: 500 Argos/Corinth, 461 Oenoe, and 412 Miletus. *Defeats*: 494 Sepeia, 470 Tegea, 465 Drabescus, 457 Tanagra I, 418 Mantinea I, and 417 Argos/Phlius.

Athens
Victories: 500 Lemnos, 490 Marathon, 480 Psyttaleia, 479 Plataea-Cithaeron, 479 Plataea-Oeroe, 479 Mycale, 476 Eion, 466 Eurymedon, 461 Oenoe, 460 Papremis, 458 Cimolia II, 457 Oenophyta, 457 Sicyon I, 454 Sicyon II, 449 Cyprian Salamis II, 448 Megara, 432 Potidaea, 431 Pheia, 431 Alope, 426 Mylae II, 426 Locri, 426 Caicinus River, 426 Tanagra II, 426 Ellomenus, 426 Olpae, 426 Idomene, 425 Messana, 425 Spaectaria, 425 Solygeia, 424 Cythera, 424 Cotyrta-Aphrodisia, 424 Antandrus, 423 Scione, 415 Anapus River, 414 Terias River, 414 Euryelus, 414 Syca, 414 Lysimeleia Counter Wall, 414 Epipolae Counter Wall I, 413 Lysimeleia Marsh, 413 Anapus Crossing, 413 Cacyparis River, 413 Erineus River, 412 Spiraeum, 412 Mytilene, 412 Northern Chios, 412 Cape Phanae, 412 Leuconium, 412 Panormus, 412 Miletus, 412 Rhodes, 412 Delphinium, 411 Lampsacus, 411 Athens I, 411 Cyzicus I, 411 Cyzicus II, 411 Athens II, 409 Ta Kerata, 409 Pygela, 409 Abydos, 408 Chalcedon, 408 Byzantium, 407 Thasos, and 407 Gaurium. *Defeats*: 498 Ephesos I, 465 Drabescus, 459 Halieis, 457 Tanagra I, 447 Coronea I, 431 Phyrgia, 430 Lycia, 429 Spartolos, 428 Malea, 428 Nericus, 428 Sandius, 426 Aegitium, 425 Halex River, 424 Delium, 424 Sicyon III, 423 Mende, 422 Amphipolis, 418 Mantinea I, 414 Epipolae Counter Wall II, 413 Epipolae, 413 Helorus Gate, 413 Anapus Plain, 413 Acraean Bald Rock, 413 Estate of Polyzelus, 413 Assinarus River, 409 Ephesos II-Shore, 409 Ephesos II-Swamp, and 403 Halae Marsh. *Draw*: 458 Cimolia I. *Both sides*: 403 Acharnae and 403 Munychia.

Corinth
Victories: 480 Thermopylae 1–4, 479 Mycale, 463 Battle of the Isthmus, and 459 Halieis. *Defeats*: 500 Argos/Corinth, 458 Cimolia II, 432 Potidaea, 425 Solygeia, and 412 Spiraeum. *Draw*: 458 Cimolia I.

Gela
Victories: 492 Helorus River, 491 Heraian Hybla, 414 Epipolae Counter-wall II, 413 Anapus Plain, 413 Estate of Polyzelus, and 413 Assinarus Crossing. *Defeats*: 500 Rhegion/Gela, 460 Crastos, 415 Anapus River, 414 Euryelus, 414 Lysimeleia Counter Wall, 414 Epipolae Counter-wall I, and 406 Gela-Beach.

Greek Mercenary Hoplites
Victories: 480 Himera I-Hill, 429 Spartolos, 423 Lyncestis, 423 Mende, 415 Anapus River, 414 Euryelus, 414 Lysimeleia Counter-wall, 414 Epipolae Counter-wall I, 413 Anapus Crossing, 413 Cacyparis River, 413 Erineus River, 409 Motya II, 409 Sicilian Panormus, 401 Cunaxa, and 401 Calah. *Defeats*: 466 Achradine I, 461 Achradine II, 460 Owl's Plain, 460 Crastos, 432 Potidaea, 423 Scione, 414 Epipolae Counter Wall II, 413 Epipolae, 413 Acraean Bald Rock, 413 Anapus Plain, 413 Assinarus River, 412 Delphinium, 411 Cyzicus II, 408 Byzantium, and 403 Munychia. *Both sides*: 472 Acragas I, 404 Neapolis, 404 Pharsalus, and 403 Halae Marsh.

Iranians
Victories: 498 Ephesos I, 498 Cyprian Salamis I, 497 Marsyas, 496 Labraunda, 494 Malene, and 480 Thermopylae 5. *Defeats*: 496 Pedasos, 480 Thermopylae 1–4, 480 Psyttaleia, 479 Plataea-Cithaeron, 479 Plataea-Moloeis, 479-Plataea-Center, 479 Mycale, 476 Eion, 466 Eurymedon, 460 Papremis, 412 Panormus, 409 Abydos, 401 Cunaxa, and 401 Calah.

Selinous
Victories: 416 Mazaros II, 409 Punic Motya, 409 Selinous I, and 409 Panormus. *Defeats*: 410 Mazaros III, 409 Selinous II, and 409 Himera II. *Draw*: 454 Mazaros I.

Sicyon
Victories: 479 Plataea-Center, 475 Sicyon/Phlius II, 459 Halieis, 424 Sicyon III, and 403 Halae Marsh. *Defeats*: 485 Sicyon/Phlius I, 457 Sicyon I, and 454 Sicyon II.

Sparta
Victories: 494 Sepeia, 480 Thermopylae 1–4, 479 Plataea-Moloeis, 470, Tegea, 464 Dipaea, 457 Tanagra I, 423 Lyncestis, 422 Amphipolis, 418 Mantinea I, 403 Porus, and 403 Halae Marsh. *Defeats*: 480 Thermopylae 5, 465 Stenyklaras, 461 Oenoe, 425 Spaectaria, 424 Cythera, 424 Cotyrta-Aphrodisia., 412 Panormus, 411 Athens I, 411 Cyzicus II, 411 Athens II, 409 Ta Kerata, 407 Gaurium, 403 Acharnae, and 402 Elis.

Syracuse
Victories: 480 Himera I-Hill, 472 Acragas I, 466 Achradine I, 461 Achradine II, 460 Owl's Plain, 450 Nomae, 446 Himera River, 426 Inessa, 414 Epipolae Counter Wall II, 413 Epipolae, 413 Helorus Gate, 413 Acraean Bald Rock, 413 Anapus Plain, 413 Estate of Polyzelus, 413 Assinarus Crossing, 409 Ephesos II-Shore, 409 Ephesos II-Swamp, 409 Punic Motya, 409 Sicilian Panormus, and 406 Acragas II. *Defeats:* 492 Helorus River, 451 Greek Motya, 415 Anapus River, 414 Terias River, 414 Euryelus, 414 Syca, 414 Lysimeleia Counter Wall, 414 Epipolae Counter Wall I, 413 Lysimeleia Marsh, 413 Anapus Crossing, 413 Cacyparis River, 413 Erineus River, 411 Cyzicus II, 409 Himera III, 405 Gela-Beach, 405 Gela-Plain, and 404 Neapolis. *Both sides*: 408 Syracuse Market.

Thebes
Victories: 480 Thermopylae 1–4, 457 Tanagra I, 424 Delium, and 413 Mycalessus. *Defeats*: 480 Thermopylae 5, 479 Plataea-Oeroe, 457 Oenophyta, and 426 Tanagra II.

Thespiae
Victories: 480 Thermopylae 1–4, 479 Plataea-Oeroe, 424 Delium, and 413 Epipolae. *Defeat*: 480 Thermopylae 5.

Table 4: Hoplite Losses and Point/Cause of Formation Failure for Greek Pitched Battles (500–401 B.C.)

See Key on pages 304–305

BATTLE	PF	HL/HT WINNER	HL/HT LOSER	CAUSE OF FAILURE
500 Argos/Corinth	RR	250/6500	800/4800	Othismos
500 Cleonai/Orneai	FR	25/500	75/500	Front fighting
500 Cleitor/Heraia	FR	10/200	30/200	Front fighting
500 Lemnos	RR	45/1750	125/1000	Othismos
500 Region/Gela	FR	150/3000	450/3000	Front fighting
498 Ephesos I	RW	BB: 700/10000	1800/6000	Flank envelopment-M
498 Cyp. Salamis I	RW	BB: 800/10800	2900/9600	Flank envelopment-M
497 Marsyas	FR	BB: 1500*/10000	3000/8000	Front fighting-M
496 Labraunda	LW	BB: 450/8500	3200*/8000	Flank envelopment-M
496 Pedasos	FR	50/4500	BB: 4000/8000	Front fighting /SA
494 Hollows Chios	BW	10/320	300/500	Full envelopment /SA
494 Malene	SW	BB: 200/2500	900/3000	Flank envelopment-M
494 Sepeia	FR	25/5000	4000/6000	Front fighting/SA
492 Helorus River	SW	150/3000	500/2400	Flank envelopment
491 Heraian Hybla	FR	100/3000	BB: 500/2500	Othismos
490 Taras I	FR	100/4000	BB: 250/4000	Othismos
490 Marathon	BW	300*/5600	BG: 2500/5400	Double envelopment
487 Mylae I	FR	100/3000	250/1600	Othismos
485 Sicyon/Phlius I	FR	60/1250	300/3200	Front fighting
480 Thermopylae 1	MR	100/2700	BB: 1300/8000	Othismos
480 Thermopylae 2	MR	100/2800	BB: 1250/8000	Othismos
480 Thermopylae 3	MR	150/2650	BB: 550/7000	Othismos
480 Thermopylae 4	FR	50/2600	BB: 300/8000	Front fighting
480 Thermopylae 5	LW	BB: 1000/7000	950/1200	Flank envelopment-M
480 Psyttaleia	FR	10/625	360*/400	Front fighting
480 Himera I-Beach	FR	BB: 150/9000	300/4000	Front fighting
480 Himera I-Hill	LW	800/18000	BB: 7000/18000	Flank envelopment/SA
479 Plataea-Cithaer.	FR	30/3300	BB: Cavalry	Front fighting-M
479 Plataea-Moloeis	MR	250*/6500	BB: 2500/22000	Othismos
479 Plataea-Oeroe	FR	500*/6000	415/6000	Front fighting
479 Plataea-Asopos	FR	Cavalry	600*/4000	Front fighting-M
479 Plataea-Center	FR	125*/11500	BB: 150/13500	Front fighting
479 Mycale	MR	125*/2000	BB: 2500/5000	Othismos
476 Eion	MR	100/5500	BB: 450/4500	Othismos
475 Sicyon/Phlius II	LW	80/3200	150/1250	Flank envelopment
473 Taras II	CT	BB: 450/9000	1900/7000	Front fighting-M

301

Table 4

BATTLE	PF	HL/HT WINNER	HL/HT LOSER	CAUSE OF FAILURE
472 Acragas I	SW	400*/10000	800*/10000	Flank envelopment
470 Tegea	LW	100/5000	400/5000	Flank envelopment
466 Eurymedon	MR	150/8000	BB: 600/6000	Othismos
466 Achradine I	FR	500/11000	1250/10000	Front fighting
465 Drabescus	FR	BB: cavalry/peltasts	1500/2500	Front fighting-M
465 Stenyklaras	BW	30/600	300*/300	Double envelopment-M
464 Dipaea	LW	40/2000	300/4000	Flank envelopment
464 Mycenae	LW	50/4000	200/800	Flank envelopment
463 Battle Isthmus	RR	100/5500	400/5000	Othismos
461 Oenoe	LW	100/4000	150/2000	Flank envelopment
461 Achradine II	LW	300/7500	800/7000	Flank envelopment
460 Owl's Plain	RR	100/4000	300/3000	Othismos
460 Crastos	FR	150/3000	300/3000	Front fighting
460 Taras III	MR	200/4000	BB: 600/4000	Othismos
460 Papremis	LW	BG: 800/16000	BB: 4000/18000	Othismos
459 Halieis	RR	100/3500	200/2200	Othismos
458 Cimolia I	DR	(ATH)350/7000	(COR) 300/5100	Offsetting envelopments
458 Cimolia II	RR	200/6000	800/4000	Othismos
457 Tanagra I	LW	1000/11500	2500*/14000	Flank envelop./SA-M**
457 Oenophyta	RW	300/6500	1200/7800	Flank envelopment
457 Sicyon I	SW	50/2000	250/3000	Flank envelopment
454 Sicyon II	FR	30/1500	200/1600	Front fighting
454 Mazaros I	MR	200/3500	BB: 250/2500	Othismos
451 Greek Motya	FR	B: 50/3000	600/6000	Front fighting/SA-M
450 Nomae	MR	200/4500	BB: 750/3000	Othismos
449 Cyp. Salamis II	MR	200/7000	BB: 500/5000	Othismos
448 Megara	FR	100/3000	300/3000	Front fighting
447 Coronea I	RR	100/3000	300/1900	Othismos
446 Himera River	LW	350/7500	1000*/6500	Flank envelopment
440 Taras/Thurii	LW	100/4000	BG: 300/3000	Othismos
433 Thurii/Lucania I	RW	BG: 150/3000	BB: 400/2000	Flank envelopment-M
433 Thurii/Lucania II	FR	BG: 150/3000	BB: 1000/4500	Othismos
432 Potidaea	LW	180/3200	300/2400	Flank envelopment**
431 Phyrgia	FR	0/5000	Cavalry	Front fighting
431 Pheia	RR	10/500	20/300	Othismos
431 Alope	FR	20/1200	80/1000	Front fighting
430 Cranae	FR	15/700	90/1500	Front fighting/SA
430 Lycia	FR	BG: 10/800	50/240	Front fighting-M
429 Spartolos	BW	100/1800	430*/2000	Double envelopment-M
429 Stratus	CT	40/2000	BG: 500/11000	Front fighting-SA-M
428 Malea	FR	100/2350	100/2250	Front fighting
428 Antissa	FR	10/400	50/400	Front fighting-M
428 Nericus	RR	30/600	80/400	Othismos
428 Sandius	LW	30/1000	100/480	Flank envelopment
427 Corcyra	FR	100/2100	BG: 100/1400	Front fighting-M
426 Mylae II	BW	50/1600	400*/1000	Double envelopment
426 Locri	LW	30/1600	100/1500	Flank envelopment
426 Inessa	MR	10/500	BB: 100/800	Othismos
426 Caicinus River	FR	30/1600	150/2000	Front fighting
426 Tanagra II	RR	200/7000	500/4500	Othismos
426 Ellomenus	BW	20/1200	200/600	Double envelopment/SA
426 Aegitium	FR	Peltasts	600*/1600	Front fighting-M
426 Olpae	LW	300/4000	1000*/6000	Flank envelopment/SA**

BATTLE	PF	HL/HT WINNER	HL/HT LOSER	CAUSE OF FAILURE
426 Idomene	FR	30/3000	1200*/2000	Front fighting/SA
425 Halex River	RR	100/3000	200/2000	Othismos
425 Naxos	FR	30/1000	1000*/2500	Front fighting/SA
425 Messana	RW	500/3500	300/1650	Flank envelopment/SA
425 Spaectaria	RR	0/1000	128*/420	Front fighting/SA-M
425 Solygeia	RW	80*/3200	212*/1800	Flank envelopment-M**
424 Cythera	RR	60/2000	100/1000	Othismos
424 Cotyrta-Aphrod.	RR	10/1000	20/300	Othismos
424 Antandrus	LW	20/875	50/350	Flank envelopment
424 Delium	RW	500*/7000	1000*/7000	Flank envelopment/SA
424 Sicyon III	LW	30/3000	100/800	Flank envelopment
423 Lyncestis	RR	20/3000	400/1750	Othismos
423 Mende	FR	30/750	50/1000	Front fighting-M
423 Scione	RR	30/900	100/600	Othismos
423 Laodocium	DR	(TEG) 300/3500	(MAN) 300/3250	Offsetting envelopments
422 Amphipolis	CT	7*/2000	600*/3200	Front fighting-SA
421 Phocis/Locris	RR	75/1500	250/1100	Othismos
420 Heraclea	RW	75/1500	500/1250	Flank envelopment-M
419 Cumae	FR	BB: 500/24000	1000/4500	Front fighting
418 Mantinea I	CT	400*/9100	1100*/8000	Front fighting**
417 Argos/Phlius	FR	20/1000	80*/550	Front fighting/SA
416 Mazaros II	MR	100/2500	BB: 400/1500	Othismos
415 Anapus River	LW	50*/2550	400*/5000	Front fighting
414 Terias River	FR	25/500	50/500	Front fighting
414 Euryelus	RR	50/5000	300*/5000	Othismos
414 Syca	FR	0/500	Cavalry	Front fighting
414 Lysimel. C.W.	CT	200/4800	350/4500	Front fighting
414 Epipolae C.W.I	CT	100/4000	250/5200	Front fighting
414 Epipolae C.W.II	LW	100/4800	400/4000	Flank envelopment-M
413 Mycalessus	FR	10/1000	Peltasts	Front fighting
413 Enna Road	BW	BB: 40/2000	BG: 800*/3000	Double envelop./SA-M
413 Epipolae	RW	350/6000	2500*/9000	Front fighting
413 Helorus Gate	FR	Cavalry	35/350	Front fighting
413 Lysimeleia M.	FR	50/1000	50/1000	Front fighting
413 Anapus Cross.	RR	30/2500	60/900	Othismos
413 Anapus Plain	FR	Cavalry/light foot	100/5000	Front fighting-M
413 Acraean Bald R.	FR	40/2000	50/2500	Front fighting
413 Cacyparis River	FR	40/2000	50/900	Front fighting
413 Est. Polyzelus	FR	Cavalry/light foot	300/1500	Front fighting-M
413 Erineus River	FR	200/1500	Cavalry/light foot	Front fighting-M
413 Assinarus Cr.	FR	20/3000	400/1000	Front fighting
412 Spiraeum	FR	40/1000	120/800	Front fighting
412 Mytilene	FR	20/1000	100/800	Front fighting
412 No. Chios	FR	30/1000	100/1000	Front fighting
412 Cape Phanae	RR	30/950	60/500	Othismos
412 Leuconium	RR	30/900	60/500	Othismos
412 Panormus	RR	20/800	80/500	Othismos
412 Miletus	LW	350/3500	225/2800	Front fighting**
412 Rhodes	FR	100/2800	200/3000	Front fighting
412 Delphinium	FR	30/900	300/1450	Front fighting
411 Lampsacus	RR	50/1500	150/900	Othismos
411 Athens I	FR	0/300	30/600	Front fighting-M
411 Cyzicus I	LW	15/750	50/300	Flank envelopment

Table 4

BATTLE	PF	HL/HT WINNER	HL/HT LOSER	CAUSE OF FAILURE
411 Cyzicus II	BW	100/3440	200/2000	Othismos/front fighting
411 Athens II	FR	Cavalry/light foot	30/600	Front fighting
410 Mazaros III	BW	BB: 100/5300	800/2500	Double envelopment
409 Selinous I	MR	50/1000	BB: 100/800	Othismos
409 Selinous II	FR	BB: 300/6000	1500/2500	Front fighting
409 Himera II	FR	BB: 2500/9000	3500/7000	Front fighting
409 Oeta/Heraclea	LW	75/1500	700/1000	Flank envelopment/SA
409 Ta Kerata	RW	50/1000	470/2200	Flank envelopment-M
409 Pygela	FR	10/1000	160/200	Front fighting
409 Ephs. II-Shore	RW	50/3000	100*/1000	Othismos
409 Ephs. II-Swamp	BW	20/2900	200*/500	Double envelopment
409 Abydos	FR	50/1200	Cavalry/peltasts	Front fighting/SA
409 Punic Motya	MR	50/4000	BB: 300/2500	Othismos
409 Sicil. Panormus	MR	50/3900	BB: 380*/1900	Othismos
408 Syracuse Mkt.	FR	100/2000	200/1000	Front fighting
408 Chalcedon	RW	50/1600	200/1650	Flank envelopment/SA
408 Byzantium	FR	200/4500	1500/2400	Front fighting/SA
407 Thasos	RR	20/1200	200/750	Othismos
407 Gaurium	LW	50/2500	250/1250	Flank envelopment
406 Acragas II	MR	300/9500	BB: 500/7000	Othismos
405 Gela-Beach	FR	BB: 400/8500	1200/6000	Front fighting
405 Gela-Plain	FR	BB: 200/9000	600/3500	Front fighting
404 Neapolis	FR	50/3000	150/2500	Front fighting
404 Pharsalos	BW	75/1500	750/1250	Double envelopment-M
403 Porus	FR	50/1500	100/1000	Front fighting
403 Acharnae	FR	20/700	120*/600	Front fighting/SA
403 Munychia	FR	20/1200	70*/6000	Front fighting-M
403 Halae Marsh	RW	100/7500	180/3000	Othismos
402 Elis	FR	Peltasts	30*/500	Front fighting-M
401 Cunaxa	FR	0*/10400	BB: 500/6000	Front fighting
401 Calah	FR	10/2000	BB: Cavalry/lt. foot	Front fighting

NOTE: PF (point of failure) is that area of a battle formation that first decisively gives way to the enemy. Cause of Failure is the primary method used by the victors in overcoming their enemy at the point of failure. Figures for HL/HT (hoplite losses/hoplite total) are either derived from historical reports or represent the author's estimates (with mean averages for ranges). HL/HT are usually stated in round numbers and include no auxiliaries (those not ranked in the main formation), whether mounted or on foot. Front fighting is shock (hand-to-hand)/missile combat along the leading edge of the battlefront. Othismos is pushing by a formation file to apply forward pressure at the leading edge of the battlefront. Flank envelopment is the act of fully or partially surrounding the end (or both ends, in the case of a double envelopment) of an opposing linear battle array. Offsetting envelopments occur when opposing armies each envelop a single opposing flank and the battle is not subsequently resolved decisively.

KEY
Symbols Explanation

PF	Point of failure within the losing formation
RW	Failure on the right wing
LW	Failure on the left wing
SW	Failure on a single, undesignated wing
BW	Failure on both wings
CT	Failure in formation center
FR	Failure among the front ranks
RR	Failure among the rear ranks
MR	Failure among the middle ranks
DR	Drawn result

Symbols Explanation

HL/HT	Hoplite / line losses (deaths)/total hoplite / line manpower
BB	Barbarian line troops
BG	Mix of barbarian and Greek line troops
(ATH)	Athenian numbers for draw at Cimolia I
(COR)	Corinthian numbers for draw at Cimolia I
(TEG)	Tegean numbers for draw at Laodocium
(MAN)	Mantinean numbers for draw at Laodocium
*	Number includes at least some input from historical source(s)
-%	Percentage hoplite / line losses of total hoplite / line manpower
/SA	Surprise attack played a significant role in creating failure
-M	Missiles played significant role in creating failure
**	Losing side also carried out an envelopment

Bibliography

Ancient Sources

Aelian (c.165–235 A.D.): Eclectic Roman writer whose works include historical anecdotes relevant to 5th-century Greek warfare. (*Historical Miscellany [Varia Historia]*, Loeb Classical Library, Cambridge, Mass.: Harvard University Press, 1997)

Aeschylus (c.525–455 B.C.): Greek playwright who fought at Marathon and Salamis, describing the latter in one of his works. ("The Persians" in *Aeschylus, Prometheus Bound and Other Plays*, New York: Penguin Classics, 1961)

Aristophanes (late 5th-century B.C.): Greek playwright whose work provides insights on aspects of the Peloponnesian Wars. ("Lysistrata" in *Aristophanes, Lysistrata/Archarnians/The Clouds*, London: Penguin Books, London, 1973)

Aristotle (384–322 B.C.): Greek philosopher whose works provide details relevant to warfare in 5th-century Greece. ("The Athenian Constitution" in *Aristotle: Athenian Constitution, Eudemian Ethics, Virtues and Vices*, Loeb Classical Library, Cambridge, Mass.: Harvard University Press, 1952, and *Politics*, New York: Oxford University Press, 1995)

Callisthenes, (died c.327 B.C.): Greek historian whose works are now lost, but provided some information on 5th-century events to surviving histories, including that of Diodorus.

Cornelius Nepos (c.110–24 B.C.): Roman writer whose works included biographies of a number of 5th-century Greek generals. (*Cornelius Nepos*, Loeb Classical Library, Cambridge, Mass.: Harvard University Press, 1984) B.C.

Ctesias (late 5th-century B.C.): Greek doctor and historian at the Persian court of Artaxerxes II whose work on the history of Persia is mostly lost, but provides details on the 5th century in fragments and citations by other ancient writers.

Demosthenes (c.384–322 B.C.): Greek orator whose speeches yield details on 5th-century events. (*Demosthenes*, 3 volumes, Loeb Classical Library, Cambridge, Mass.: Harvard University Press, 1926–1930)

Diodorus Siculus (c.90–20 B.C.): Sicilian historian whose surviving works include coverage of events in the 5th-century Greek world. (*Library of World History*, 12 volumes, Loeb Classical Library, Cambridge, Mass.: Harvard University Press, 1933–1967)

Dionysius of Halicarnassus (late 1st-century B.C.): Greek historian whose surviving works detail early Roman history and shed light on events in Grecian Italy. (*Roman Antiquities,* 7 volumes, Loeb Classical Library, Cambridge, Mass.: Harvard University Press, 1937–1950)

Ephorus of Cyme (c.405–330 B.C.): Greek historian whose work is now lost, but was used extensively as a source on 5th-century events in the surviving works of others, including Diodorus and Plutarch.

epigrams (500–401 B.C.): Inscriptions preserved in stone from the historical period of interest. (see Meiggs and Lewis below)

Frontinus (c.35–103 A.D.): Roman writer whose collection of military stratagems includes many from 5th-century Greek warfare. (*Strategems*, Loeb Classical Library, Cambridge, Mass.: Harvard University Press, 1925) B.C.

Herodotus (c.490–430 B.C.): Greek historian whose work covers the conflict between Persia and the Greeks down to 479 B.C. (*Herodotus: The Histories*, New York: Penguin Classics, 1972)

Homer (late 8th century B.C.): Greek epic poet whose work reveals much about hoplite warrior culture that is of relevance to the 5th century B.C. (*The Iliad*, New York: Penguin Books USA, 1990)

Isocrates (436–338 B.C.): Greek orator whose speeches provide detail on 5th-century events. (*Isocrates*, 3 volumes, Loeb Classical Library, Cambridge, Mass.: Harvard University Press, 1928–1945)

Livy (59 B.C.–17 A.D.): Roman historian whose works include useful detail on the warfare among the Italians relevant to the 5th century. (*Livy, Rome and Italy, Books VI–X of The History of Rome from its Foundation*, New York: Penguin Books, 1982)

Onasander (1st century A.D.): Greek philosopher who wrote a treatise on generalship that includes information relevant to 5th-century warfare. (*Ateneas Tacitus, Asclepiodotus, Onasander*, Loeb Classical Library, Cambridge, Mass.: Harvard University Press, 1928)

"Oxyrhynchus Historian" (late 5th-early 4th century B.C.): Greek historian known from fragments found in Oxyrynchus (in Egypt) whose work includes coverage of the late stages of the Great Peloponnesian War that was a source for Ephoros and, hence, Diodorus.

Pausanias (2nd century A.D.): Greek travel writer whose works include numerous historical details relevant to the 5th century. (*Description of Greece*, 5 volumes,

Loeb Classical Library, Cambridge, Mass.: Harvard University Press, 1918–1955)

Philistus (c.430–356 B.C.): Sicilian historian whose work is now lost, but provided source material to Timaeus and, hence, to Diodorus on events in Sicily during the 5th century.

Plato (c.429–347 B.C.): Greek philosopher and student of Socrates (5th-century philosopher and participant in the Great Peloponnesian War) whose work contains details of his teacher's military exploits. (*Laches and Charmides*, Cambridge, Mass.: Hackett, 1973 and "The Symposium" in *Great Dialogues of Plato*, New York: New American Library, 1999)

Plutarch (c.45–120 A.D.): Greek philosopher and writer whose works include biographies of several Greeks of the 5th century and quotations from Sparta that are relevant to 5th-century warfare. (*The Rise and Fall of Athens: Nine Greek Lives*, New York: Penguin Books, and *Plutarch on Sparta*, New York: Penguin Books, 1988)

Polyaenus (2nd century A.D.): Macedonian rhetorician whose collection of stratagems include many from the 5th-century Greeks. (*Polyaenus, Stratagems of War, Vol. I and II*, ed. and trans. P. Krentz and E. L. Wheeler, eds., Chicago: Ares, 1994)

Polybius (c.208–124 B.C.): Greek historian whose works on the third and second centuries B.C. also shed some light on 5th-century military practices. (*The Histories*, 6 volumes, Loeb Classical Library, Cambridge, Mass.: Harvard University Press, 1922–1927)

Sun-Tsu (possibly late sixth to early 5th centuries B.C., though later dates have been proposed): Chinese general and philosopher whose work reflects martial concerns contemporary and compatible with those of classical Greece. ("Sun-tsu's Art of War" in *The Seven Military Classics of Ancient China*, trans. R. D. Sawyer, Boulder, Colo.: Westview Press, 1993)

Thucydides (c.460–400 B.C.): Greek general and historian of the Great Peloponnesian War. (*The Landmark Thucydides*, 1996, New York: Free Press, 1996)

Timaeus (c.350–260 B.C.): Greek historian whose works are now lost, but were an important source for the surviving works of others, including Diodorus and Plutarch.

Xenophon (c.430–350 B.C.): Greek general and historian whose works include coverage of the late stages of the Peloponnesian War and extend to the mid 4th century. (*Hellenica*, 2 volumes, Loeb Classical Library, Cambridge, Mass.: Harvard University Press, 1918–1921; *Anabasis*, Loeb Classical Library, Cambridge, Mass.: Harvard University Press, 1922; and *Scripta Minora*, Loeb Classical Library, Cambridge, Mass.: Harvard University Press, 1925)

Modern References

Adcock, F. E. 1957. *The Greek and Macedonian Art of War*. Los Angeles: University of California Press.

Akurgal, E. 1985. *Ancient Civilizations and Ruins of Turkey*. Ankara, Turkey: Haset Kitabevi.

Anderson, J. K. 1970. *Military Theory and Practice in the Age of Xenophon*. Los Angeles: University of California Press.

Ashley, J. R. 1998. *Xenophon*. New York: Charles Scribner's Sons.

Badian, E. 1993. *From Plataea to Potidaea: Studies in the History and Historiography of the Pentecontaetia*. Baltimore: Johns Hopkins University Press.

Barber, R. 1990. *Blue Guide Greece*. New York: W. W. Norton.

Bennet, M., ed. 1998. *Dictionary of Ancient and Medieval Warfare*. Mechanicsburg, Penn.: Stackpole Books.

Bradford, E. 1980. *The Year of Thermopylae*. London: Macmillan.

Buckley, T. 1996. *Aspects of Greek History, 750–323 B.C.: A Source Book Approach*, 126–435. London: Routledge.

Burn, A. R. 1968. *The Warring States of Greece*, 39–115. New York: McGraw-Hill.

_____. 1984. *Persia and the Greeks*. Guildford, U.K.: Biddles Ltd.

Bury, J. B. 1900. *A History of Greece to the Death of Alexander*, 242–530. London: MacMillan.

Cartledge, P. 2002. *Sparta and Lakonia, A Regional History 1300 to 362 B.C.*, 2nd ed. New York: Routledge.

_____. 2003. *The Spartans: The World of the Warrior-Heroes of Ancient Greece*. New York: Overlook Press.

_____. 2006. *Thermopylae: The Battle That Changed the World*. New York: Overlook Press.

Cassin-Scott, J. 1991. *The Greek and Persian Wars*. Oxford, U.K.: Osprey.

Casson, L. 1991. *The Ancient Mariners*, 81–115. Princeton, NJ: Princeton University Press.

Caven, B. 1990. *Dionysius I, War-Lord of Sicily*, 7–97. New Haven, Conn.: Yale University Press.

Cawkwell, G. L. 2002. "The Decline of Sparta" in *Sparta*, ed. M. Whitby, 236–257. New York: Routledge.

_____. 2005. *The Greek Wars: The Failure of Persia*. New York: Oxford University Press.

Cernenko, E. V., A. McBride, and M. V. Gorelik. 1983. *The Scythians 700–300 B.C.* Oxford, U.K.: Osprey.

Chrimes, K. M. T. 1949. *Ancient Sparta: A Re-examination of the Evidence*. Manchester: Manchester University Press.

Connolly, P. 1981. *Greece and Rome at War*, 10–63. London: Macdonald Phoebus Ltd.

Cornell, T. J. 1995. *The Beginnings of Rome: Italy and Rome from the Bronze Age to the Punic Wars (c. 1000–264 B.C.)*. New York: Routledge.

Creasy, E. S. 1987. *Fifteen Decisive Battles of the World, From Marathon to Waterloo*, 1–56. New York: Dorset Press.

Custance, R. 1970. *War at Sea: Modern Theory and Ancient Practice*. Conway Maritime Press.

Dawson, D. 1996. *The Origins of Western Warfare*, 47–110. Boulder, CO.: Westview Press.

_____. 2001. *The First Armies*, 75–211. London: Cassel.

Delbruck, H. 1990. *Warfare in Antiquity: History of the Art of War, Volume I*, 33–143. Lincoln: University Nebraska Press.

Bibliography

De Souza, P., W. Heckel and L. Llewellyn-Jones. 2004. *The Greeks at War, From Athens to Alexander*. Oxford, U.K.: Osprey.

Dodge, T. H. 1890. *Alexander: A History of the Origin and Growth of War from the Earliest Times to the Battle of Ipsus, Vol. I*, 27–170. London: Greenhill Books.

Ducrey, P. 1986. *Warfare in Ancient Greece*. New York: Schocken Books.

Ferrill, A. 1986. *The Origins of War From the Stone Age to Alexander*, 91–148. New York: Thames and Hudson.

Fine, J. V. A. 1983. *The Ancient Greeks: A Critical History*. Cambridge, Mass.: Harvard University Press.

Fitzhardinge, L. F. 1985. *The Spartans*. London: Thames and Hudson.

Forrest, W. G. 1969. *A History of Sparta 950–192* B.C. New York: W. W. Norton.

France, J. 1999. *Western Warfare in the Age of the Crusades 1000–1300*, 150–165. Ithaca, NY: Cornell University Press.

Freeman, E. A., 1891–1892. *The History of Sicily from the Earliest Times, Volumes I, II, and III*. Oxford, U.K.: Clarendon Press.

Fuller, J. F. C. 1987. *A Military History of the Western World: Volume I, From the Earliest Times to the Battle of Lepanto*, 15–82. New York: Da Capo Press.

Gabriel, R. A., and Boose, D. W. 1994. *The Great Battles of Antiquity: A Strategic and Tactical Guide to Great Battles that Shaped the Development of War*. Westport, Conn.: Greenwood Press.

Gabriel, R. A., and K.S. Metz. 1991. *From Sumer to Rome: The Military Capabilities of Ancient Armies*. New York: Greenwood Press.

Gaebel, R. E. 2002. *Cavalry Operations in the Ancient Greek World*. Norman: University of Oklahoma Press.

Garlan, Y. 1995. "War and Peace" in *The Greeks*, ed. J. Vernant, 53–85. Chicago: University of Chicago Press.

Garnsey, P. 1988. *Famine and Food Supply in the Graeco–Roman World: Responses to Risk and Crisis*, 89–166. Cambridge University Press.

Golding, W. 1961. *The Hot Gates and Other Occasional Pieces*, 13–20. New York: Harcourt, Brace, and World.

Goldsworthy, A. K. 1996. *The Roman Army at War, 100* B.C.–A.D. *200*, 171–247. Oxford, U.K.: Clarendon Press.

Grant, M. 1987. *The Rise of the Greeks*. New York: Collier Books.

Green, P. 1970a. *Armada from Athens: The Failure of the Sicilian Expedition, 415–414* B.C. Garden City, NY: Doubleday.

———. 1970b. *Xerxes at Salamis*. New York: Praeger.

Griffith, G. T. 1984. *The Mercenaries of the Hellenistic World*. Chicago: Ares.

Grossman, D. 1995. *On Killing: The Psychological Cost of Learning to Kill in War and Society*. New York: Little, Brown.

Grundy, G. B., 1901. *The Great Persian War and its Preliminaries: A Study of the Evidence, Literary and Topographical*. New York: Charles Scribner's Sons.

Hanson, V. D., 1989a. *The Western Way of War: Infantry Battle in Ancient Greece*. New York: Alfred A. Knopf.

———. 1989b. "Not Strategy, Not Tactics" in *Journal of Military History* 1, no. 3, 16–19.

———. ed., 1993. *Hoplites: The Classical Greek Battle Experience*. London: Routledge.

———. 1995a. *The Other Greeks: The Family Farm and the Agrarian Roots of Western Civilization*. New York: Free Press.

———. 1995b. "Genesis of the Infantry" in *Cambridge Illustrated History of Warfare*, ed. G. Parker, 12–31. Cambridge University Press.

———. 1998. *Warfare and Agriculture in Classical Greece*. Berkeley: University of California Press.

———. 2005. *A War Like No Other: How the Athenians and Spartans Fought the Peloponnesian War*. New York: Random House.

Head, D. 1992. *The Achaemenid Persian Army*. Stockport, U.K.: Montvert.

Higgins, M. D., and R. Higgins. 1996. *A Geological Companion to Greece and the Aegean*, 28–208. London: Gerald Duckworth.

Hillman, J. 2004. *A Terrible Love of War*. New York: Penguin Press.

Hodkinson, S. 1993. "Warfare, Wealth, and the Crisis of Spartiate Society" in *War and Society in the Greek World*, ed. J. Rich and G. Shipley, 146–176. New York: Routledge.

Holland, T., 2005. *Persian Fire, The First World Empire and the Battle for the West*. New York: Doubleday.

Holmes, R. 1985. *Acts of War: The Behavior of Men in Battle*. New York: Free Press.

Hopper, R. J. 1977. *The Early Greeks*, 109–222. New York: Harper and Row.

Hornblower, S. 1991a. *The Greek World, 479–323* B.C., revised edition, 1–180. New York: Routledge.

———. 1991b. *A Commentary on Thucydides, Volume I: Books I–III*. New York: Clarendon Press.

———. 1996. *A Commentary on Thucydides, Volume II: Books IV–V*. New York: Clarendon Press.

Hornblower, S., and A. Spawforth, eds. 1996. *The Oxford Classical Dictionary*. New York: Oxford University Press.

How, W. W., and J. Wells. 1912–1928. *A Commentary on Herodotus, Volumes I–II*. New York: Oxford University Press.

Howatson, M. C., ed. 1991. *The Oxford Companion to Classical Literature*. New York: Oxford University Press.

Hutchinson, G. 2000. *Xenophon and the Art of Command*. London: Greenhill Books.

Jones, A .H. M. 1967. *Sparta*. Oxford, U.K.: Blackwell.

Kagan, D. 1991a. *Pericles of Athens and the Birth of Democracy*, 65–90. New York: Simon and Schuster.

———. 1991b. *The Outbreak of the Peloponnesian War*. London: Cornell University Press.

———. 1992a. *The Archidamian War*. London: Cornell University Press.

———. 1992b. *The Peace of Nicias and the Sicilian Expedition*. London: Cornell University Press.

_____. 1992c. *The Fall of the Athenian Empire*. London: Cornell University Press.

Karl, D. 1990. *Glorious Defiance: Last Stands Throughout History*, 1–40. New York: Paragon House.

Keegan, J. 1993. *A History of Warfare*, 237–257. New York: Alfred A. Knopf.

Lazenby, J. 1990. "Hoplite Warfare" in *Warfare in the Ancient World*, ed. J. W. Hackett, 54–81. New York: Facts on File.

_____. 1993. *The Defence of Greece 490–479 B.C.* Warminster, U.K.: Aris and Phillips Ltd.

_____. 2004. *The Peloponnesian War: A Military Study*. New York: Routledge.

Lewis, D. M. 1984. "Postscript" in *Persia and the Greeks* by A.R. Burn, 587–612. Guildford, U.K.: Biddles Ltd.

Liddell, H. G., and R. Scott. 1996. *Greek-English Lexicon, With a Revised Supplement*. New York: Oxford University Press.

Lynn, J. A. 2003. *Battle: A History of Combat and Culture*, 1–28. Boulder, CO: Westview Press.

Macadam, A. 1993. *Blue Guide Sicily*. New York: W. W. Norton.

Marsden, E. W. 1969. *Greek and Roman Artillery: Historical Development*, 48–62. New York: Oxford University Press.

May, E. C., G. P. Stadler, and J. F. Votaw. 1984. *Ancient and Medieval Warfare*. Wayne, NJ: Avery Publishing Group.

Mayor, A. 2003. *Greek Fire, Poison Arrows and Scorpion Bombs: Biological and Chemical Warfare in the Ancient World*. New York: Overlook Duckworth.

McCartney, E. S. 1923. *(Greek and Roman) Warfare by Land and Sea*, 3–92. Boston: Marshall Jones.

McGregor, M. F. 1987. *The Athenians and Their Empire*. Vancouver, B.C.: University of British Columbia Press.

McInerney, J. 1999. *The Folds of Parnassos: Land and Ethnicity in Ancient Phokis*. Austin: University of Texas Press.

Meiggs, R. 1992. *The Athenian Empire*. Oxford, U.K.: Clarendon Press.

Meiggs, R., and D. Lewis. 1988. *A Selection of Greek Historical Inscriptions, To the End of the Fifth Century B.C.*, revised ed. Oxford: Oxford University Press.

Mitchell, S. 1996. "Hoplite Warfare in Ancient Greece" in *Battle in Antiquity*, ed. A.B. Lloyd ed., 87–106. London: Gerald Duckworth.

Montagu, J. D. 2000. *Battles of the Greek and Roman Worlds: A Chronological Compendium of 667 Battles to 31 B.C., from the Historians of the Ancient World*, 27–28, 51–83. London: Greenhill Books.

Morrison, J. S., and J. F Coates. 1986. *The Athenian Trireme, The History and Reconstruction of an Ancient Greek WarShip*. New York: Cambridge University Press.

Munn, M. H. 1993. *The Defence of Attica: The Dema Wall and the Boiotian War of 378–375 B.C.*, 1–128. Los Angeles: University of California Press.

Nelson, R. 1975a. *Armies of the Greek and Persian Wars*. Goring-by-Sea, Sussex: Wargames Research Group.

_____. 1975b. *The Battle of Salamis*, 1–95. London: William Luscombe.

Ober, J. 1991. "Fortress Attica" in *Journal Military History* 3, no. 2, 26–35.

O'Connell, R. L. 1989. *Of Arms and Men: A History of War, Weapons, and Aggression*, 30–68. New York: Oxford University Press.

Olmstead, A. T. 1948. *History of the Persian Empire*. Chicago: University of Chicago Press.

Parke, H. W. 1933. *Greek Mercenary Soldiers From the Earliest Times to the Battle of Ipsus*, 9–43. Chicago: Ares.

Pearson, L. 1987. *The Greek Historians of the West: Timaeus and His Predecessors*, 1–190. Atlanta: Scholars Press.

Phillips, T. R. 1985. *Roots of Strategy, Book I*, 301–441. Harrisburg, Penn.: Stackpole Books.

Polignac, F. 1995. *Cults, Territory, and the Origins of the Greek City-State*, 32–88. Chicago: University of Chicago Press.

Powell, A. 1991. *Athens and Sparta: Constructing Greek Political and Social History from 478 B.C.* London: Routledge.

Prevas, J. 2002. *Xenophon's March: Into the Lair of the Persian Lion*. Cambridge, Mass.: Da Capo Press.

Pritchett, W. K. 1960. "Marathon" in *University of California Publications in Classical Archeology* 4, no. 2, 137–190.

_____. 1965. *Studies in Ancient Greek Topography, Part I*. Los Angeles: University of California Press.

_____. 1969. *Studies in Ancient Greek Topography, Part II (Battlefields)*. Los Angeles: University of California Press.

_____. 1971–1991. *The Greek State at War*, 5 volumes. Los Angeles: University of California Press.

_____. 1980. "Amphipolis Restudied" in *Studies in Ancient Greek Topography, Part III (Roads)*, 298–346. Classical Studies Volume 22. Los Angeles: University of California Publications.

_____. 1985. "The Strategy of the Plataiai Campaign" in *Studies in Ancient Greek Topography, Part V*, 92–137. Classical Studies Volume 31. Los Angeles: University of California Publications.

_____. 1991: "Demosthenes' Campaign in Southern Aetoilia in 426 B.C." in *Studies in Ancient Greek Topography, Part VII*, 47–82. Amsterdam: J. C. Gieben.

_____. 1992. "Demosthenes' Amphilochian Campaign in 426 B.C." in *Studies in Ancient Greek Topography, Part VIII*, 1–78. Amsterdam: J. C. Gieben.

_____. 1994. *Essays in Greek History*. Amsterdam: J. C. Gieben.

_____. 1995. *Thucydides' Pentekontaetia and Other Essays*. Amsterdam: J. C. Gieben.

Rodgers, W. L. 1937. *Greek and Roman Naval Warfare: A Study of Strategy, Tactics, and Ship Design from Salamis (480 B.C.) to Actium (31 B.C.)*, 11–195. Annapolis, MD: Naval Institute Press.

_____. 1983. "Marathon, 490 B.C." in *Assault from the Sea, Essays on the History of Amphibious Warfare*, ed. M. L. Bartlett, 3–11. Annapolis, MD: U.S. Naval Institute.

Sage, M. M., 1996. *Warfare in Ancient Greece: A Sourcebook*, 1–134. London: Routledge.

Ste. Croix, G. E. M. de. 1972. *The Origins of the Peloponnesian War*. Ithaca, NY: Cornell University Press.

Santosuosso, A. 1997. *Soldiers Citizens and the Symbols of War—From Classical Greece to Republican Rome 500–167 B.C.*, 1–109. Boulder, CO: Westview Press.

Sekunda, N. 1987. *The Ancient Greeks: Armies of Classical Greece, 5th and 4th Centuries B.C.* Oxford, U.K.: Osprey.

———. 1989. "The Persians" in *Warfare in the Ancient World*, ed. J.W. Hackett, 82–103. New York: Facts On File.

———. 1998. *The Spartans*. Oxford, U.K.: Osprey.

Sekunda, N., and S. Chew. 1992. *The Persian Army 560–330 B.C.* Oxford, U.K.: Osprey.

Sekunda, N., and R. Hook. 2000. *Greek Hoplite 480–323 B.C.* Oxford, U.K.: Osprey.

Sekunda, N., S. Northwood and R. Hook. 1995. *Early Roman Armies*. Oxford, U.K.: Osprey.

Shay, J. 1994. *Achilles in Vietnam: Combat Trauma and the Undoing of Character*. New York: Simon and Schuster.

———. 2002. *Odysseus in America: Combat Trauma and the Trials of Coming Home*. New York: Scribner.

Snodgrass, A. M. 1967. *Arms and Armour of the Greeks*, 48–113. Ithaca, NY: Cornell University Press.

Spaulding, O. L., and H. Nickerson. 1993. *Ancient and Medieval Warfare*, 35–74. Abridged edition of *Warfare*. New York: Barnes and Noble.

Spence, I. G. 1993. *The Cavalry of Classical Greece: A Social and Military History*. Oxford, U.K.: Clarendon Press.

Strauss, B. S., and J. Ober. 1990. *The Anatomy of Error: Ancient Military Disasters and Their Lessons for Modern Strategists*. New York: St. Martins Press.

Stylianou, P. J. 1998. *A Historical Commentary on Diodorus Siculus, Book 15*. New York: Oxford University Press.

Szemier, G. J., W. J. Cherf, and J. C. Kraft. 1996. *Thermopylai: Myth and Reality in 480 B.C.* Chicago: Ares.

Talbert, J. A., ed. 1991. *Atlas of Classical History*, 18–49, 180–182. London: Routledge.

Tarn, W. W. 1984. *Hellenistic Military and Naval Developments*. Chicago: Ares.

Tomlinson, R. A. 1972. *Argos and the Argolid: From the End of the Bronze Age to the Roman Occupation*, 87–129, 175–186. Ithaca, NY: Cornell University Press.

Tritle, L. A. 2000. *From Melos to My Lai: War and Survival*. London: Routledge.

Vernant, J. 1991. "Between Shame and Glory: The Identity of the Young Spartan Warrior" in *Mortals and Immortals*, ed. F.I. Zeitlin, 220–243. Princeton, NJ: Princeton University Press.

Warmington, B. H. 1960. *Carthage*, 33–89. London: Robert Hale.

Warry, J. 1980. *Warfare in the Classical World*. London: Salamander Books.

Waterfield, R. 2006. *Xenophon's Retreat: Greece, Persia, and the End of the Golden Age*. Cambridge, Mass.: Belknap Press of Harvard University Press.

Wees, H., 1995: "Politics and the Battlefield" in *The Greek World*, ed. A. Powell, 153–178. London: Routledge.

———. 2000. "The Development of the Hoplite Phalanx: Iconography and Reality in the Seventh Century" in *War and Violence in Ancient Greece*, 125–166. London: Duckworth.

———. 2004. *Greek Warfare, Myths and Realities*. London: Duckworth.

Woodhead, A. G. 1962. *The Greeks in the West*. London: Thames and Hudson.

Worley, L.J., 1994. *Hippeis: The Cavalry of Ancient Greece*. Boulder, CO: Westview Press.

Yalichev, S. 1997. *Mercenaries of the Ancient World*, 80–149. London: Constable and Company.

Index

abatis 62, 63, 106, 235
Abrocomas 279, 280
Acarnania 154, 157, 166, 168, 223
Achaemenes 129
Achaemenid Empire 21
Achaemenides 129
Acharnae 152, 274, 275
Achradine 113, 114, 264, 271
acropolis 22, 67, 180
Aegean Sea 8, 28, 36, 40, 70, 124, 125, 128, 131, 190, 193, 222, 229, 236, 239, 246, 255–257
Aegialeis 138
Aegospotami 257
Aeolian Islands 164
Aeschylus 8, 65, 85
Agesilaus 237
agoge 118, 175
agora 162, 163
akinakes 31
akontistai 15
Alcamenes 28
Alcibiades 146, 185, 203, 210, 211, 222, 237, 238, 241–248, 252–257
Alexander 284
alloglossoi 40
Ambracia 91, 157, 168, 171, 172, 177, 213
amentum 14
Amompharetus 95
Amorges (Caria) 242, 243
Amorges (Persia) 45
Amphilochia 168, 169
Anaphes 75, 76
Anaxilas 52, 109
Anopaia 72, 78–80, 84, 201
antilabe 9
Antintanians 157
Antiochus 144
Archidamus 120–122, 151–155, 174, 197
Arginusae 256, 257
Argive plain 23
Argos, Gulf of 48, 206
Ariaeus 280–282
Arimandes 127
Arimnestos 61
Aristeus 144–146
Aristides 63, 65, 84–85, 95, 98, 99, 124
Aristippus 278, 279
Aristogoras 30, 33, 44
Aristokypros 39
Arrhabaeus 188–190

arstibara 69
Artabazus 95, 102, 103
Artanes 81
Artaphernes (father) 30, 33, 34, 40, 45
Artaphernes (son) 60, 65
Artaxerxes I 129, 130
Artaxerxes II 81, 278–280, 282
Artayntes 103, 105
Artemisium 43, 71, 72, 83
Artybius 37–39
Asopodoros 98, 101
aspis 8, 9
astu 61

baivaraba/myriads 32
barbarians (*barbaroi*) 7
battering rams 224, 259, 265
Bolcon 116, 117
Bosporus 252–255
Brasidas 153, 181, 182, 188–190, 193–195, 197, 205, 285
Brasidians 205, 207
Breltioi 51
Butes 125

Calasirian 90
Calimachus 63
Callibius 274
Callicrates 96
Callistratos 213, 234
camels 69, 70
Campania(ns) 202, 258, 259, 264–266, 269–271, 297
Carcinus 152
Caria(ns) 8, 33, 40–44, 86, 126, 161, 240–242, 278
Carnelian Feast 61
Cephallenia 153, 154, 166, 223
Chaereas 246
Chalcideus 238–240
Chalcidian League 155, 156, 189
Chalcidians 18, 146, 155, 156, 189, 190, 193, 199
Chaonians 157, 158
chariot(s) 18–20, 36–39, 68, 140, 183, 278–281
Charitimides 129, 130
Charoeades 164
Charopinos 33
Cheirisophus 279, 283
Chromon 167
Cimon 124–128, 131, 136, 139, 197
Cleander 52
Cleandridas 142, 143, 213

Clearchus 246–248, 254, 273, 274, 278–280, 282, 283
Clearidas 194, 195
Cleippides 159
Cleomenes 48–50, 62, 71
Cleon 174–177, 179, 193–195
Cleopompus 153
Cnemus 154, 157–159
Coeratadas 254
combined arms 20, 31
Comon 176
Conon 256
Corcyra 144, 146, 150, 152, 157, 162, 166, 199, 223
Coressos 33, 251
Corinthian Gulf 24, 124, 135, 138, 139, 157, 168, 169, 200, 223, 238
Critias 274, 275
Cuirass (*thorax*) 8–9, 31, 38, 54
Cyclades Islands 60, 66, 103, 124, 165, 210, 255
Cynegirus 65
Cynosura 84
Cyrus (the Great) 28, 81
Cyrus (the Younger) 81, 257, 273, 278–283

Daphnaeus 265, 266, 268
Darius I 29, 30, 33, 45, 46, 57, 59, 68
Darius II 278
Darius III 81
dathaba 32
Daunians 55, 110
Delian League 124, 125, 135–137, 140, 155, 159, 161, 162, 237, 239, 241–244
Demaratus 48, 84
demes 61
Demophilus 71
Demosthenes 165–172, 174–176, 181, 182, 185–187, 221–226, 229–235
Demoteles 173
Dercyllidas 244
Dexippus 265, 267
Diitrephes 222
Diomedon 239, 242
Diomilus 214
Dionysius 257, 266–272
doratismos 10
Dorians 22–24, 46, 140, 241
Dorieus 242
doru/enchos (spear) 10
doruphoroi 9

dromo 63
Ducetius 116, 117

Edonians 128
Egyptian(s) 84, 90, 93, 103, 129, 130, 279
Eleusis 142, 143, 151, 181, 275, 276
Elymians 51, 85, 110, 115, 116, 257
emporion 50
en chersi 26
enomotia 47, 183
Ephialties 79
epibatai 24
epilektoi 14, 148, 153, 210, 241, 246, 251, 260
Epitadas 174–176
epiteichismos 177, 179, 180, 222
epomides 9
eschatia 22, 28, 70, 115, 142, 143, 199, 200, 209
ethnos 188
Etruscans 87, 202, 218, 227
Eualcidas 33, 34, 36
Euboa 8, 50, 60, 61, 66, 71, 72, 91, 103, 104, 125, 136, 141, 142, 144, 153, 177, 237, 238, 243, 245
Eucles 65
Euripus Channel 83
Eurylochos 168–170, 197, 201
Eurymedon River 125, 163, 221, 223, 226
Euxine (Black) Sea 6, 30, 33, 156, 159–160, 188, 190, 196, 238, 244, 252, 283

falcata 258
field works 230–233, 235

gamoroi 53
Gorgus 36, 39
Gylippus 213, 218–223, 225–234, 250, 262
gymnesioi 25, 27

Habrocomes 81
Halipedon 276
Hamilcar 86–89, 257–259, 261, 262
hamippoi 19
Hannibal 257–266, 285
harmost 201
Harpagos 49
hazaraba 32
Helixus 254
Hellespont 30, 40, 44, 70, 85, 238, 244–246, 250, 252–255, 257
helmet types 8, 9
helots (*helotoi*) 46
heniochoi 183
Heracleidas 43
Heraion 122
Hermocrates 214, 228, 262–266
Hermophantos 33
Hermotybian 90
Herodotus 59, 142
hetairoi 188
Hieron 109–112, 116
Himilco 264–271, 285
hippagogos 210
hippeis 18

Hippeis 47
Hippias 30, 60, 62, 63, 65
hippobotai 188
Hippocrates (Athens) 181–183, 185
Hippocrates (Gela) 52–54, 57
Hippocrates (Sparta) 253, 254
hippotoxotai 19
Histiaeus 30, 44, 45
hopla 9
hoplitai (hoplites) 8
Hydarnes 76, 79, 80, 82
Hymaees 33, 40, 45
hyparchoi 28
Hyperanthes 81
hyperesia 60

Iapyians 55, 110, 111
Illyria 55, 157, 188
Imbros 159, 193–195
Immortals 69, 76–82, 84, 90, 96
Inaros 129, 130
Ionia 28
Ionian Sea 139, 144, 153
Iranian 31
Isthmus of Corinth 83, 91
Ithamitres 104, 105
Ithome 120, 123

kara (host) 32
knemides (greaves) 9
koinon 98
Kolonos 82
krypteia 118

Labotas 249
Laches 164, 165, 172, 173, 185, 197, 207
Lamachus 210–218, 227
lambda 9
Leagrus 128
Lemnos 22, 28, 159, 193–195
Leon 239, 242
Leonidas 50, 70–77, 79–83, 91, 99, 119, 187, 200, 235
Leontiades 71
Leotychides 91, 103–105
Lesbos 44, 45, 150, 154, 159–162, 182, 192, 237–239, 256
Leucas 91, 157, 158, 161, 166, 177, 213
Liby-Phoenicians 86, 87
lochoi 24
Lucanians 143, 146
Lyceum 249
Lycophron (Corinth) 177–179, 190, 197
Lycophron (Pherae) 272, 273
Lysander 256, 257, 276–277
Lysicles 161, 162

Macarius 168, 170
machairal kopis 10, 54, 55
makhimoi 15
Malian Gulf 22, 71, 72, 201, 249
Marathonomachai 63
Mardonios 59, 60, 70, 85, 90–96, 103, 120, 200
Mardontes 103, 105
Masistes 105
Masistios 93

Mediterranean loose 15
Medius 272, 273
Megabyzus 68, 69
Melanthios 33
Melesander 155
Menedaius 168
Menon 279, 280
mesogeia 61
Messapians 55, 56, 110, 142, 223
metoikoi 133
Micythus 109, 111
Miltiades 28, 30, 61–63, 65, 106, 123
Mindarus 245–248
Mithradates 283, 284
Molossians 157
mora 47
Myronides 133–135, 137, 138

nautae 60
Nemean Games 122
neodamodeis 123, 207, 226, 255, 279
Nicias 165, 166, 177–180, 185, 190, 191, 195, 197–201, 210–224, 226–234, 277
Nicomedes 135, 136
Nicostratus 163, 190, 191
Nine Ways 128, 129

obai 46
okhlos (attendants) 15
Olympiodoros 92, 93
Onesilus 36, 37, 39
Opis 111
Orestians 157
Orneates 49
Ortygia 113, 114, 271
Otanes 33, 40, 80
othismos 11
Oxyrhynchus 114

Paches 160, 162
Pagondas 148, 183, 186, 187, 197
Pallene 144, 145, 190
paltal akontia (javelin) 14
pandemei 24
panoplia 10
Panthoedas 273
pararrexis 27
parataxis 12
Parauaeans 157
parlia 61
Pasion 279
Pausanius (king) 276–278
Pausanius (regent) 91–96, 99, 119, 124
Peace of Nicias 195
pectorale 53, 110
Pedaritus 243
Peloponnese 8
Peloponnesian League 46, 118
pelta 15
peltastai 15
Pentacontaetia 109
pentekostyes 24, 44, 98
peraia 161
Perdiccas 188–191
Pericles 129, 138, 139, 141, 142, 146, 150–155, 159, 163, 181, 185

Perilaus 105
perioeci (*perioikoi*) 46
peripoli 181
Peucetians 55, 110, 111
pharmakon 17
Pharnabazus 246, 248, 252–254
Philippides 61
Phoenician fleet 37, 60
Phoenicians 18, 37, 39, 51, 60, 85–87, 115, 140
Phrynichus 242
phylai 19
Phyle 274, 275
Piraeus 151, 255, 275–277
Pisistratus 60, 61
Pixodarus 40
Pleistarchus 91
Pleistoanax 142
Plemmyrium 220–223, 227, 236
polemarchos 61
polis 7
Polydamidas 190, 191
Polyzelus 232
porpax 9
post-traumatic stress (PST) 13
Procles 165–167
promachoi 11
Propontis 245, 246, 253
Prosopitis 130
Proteas 152
Proxenus (Locri) 165
Proxenus (Thebes) 179, 280, 283
psiloi 14
pteruges 9
Pythen 219
Pythodorus 172–174

religious sanctuaries 22
reserves/age 24, 43, 47
reserves/tactical 178, 183, 187, 197, 246, 262, 266, 285
rhipsaspia 27
Rhodes 18, 52, 235, 242, 243

Sacred Band (Carthage) 86–90
Sacred Band (Thebes) 99, 148, 183
Sakae 31, 60, 61, 63–65, 70, 75, 76, 90, 95, 96, 102, 103
Salaethus 162
Sallentine Peninsula 55, 110
salpinx 13

Samos 103, 129, 142, 150, 239, 240, 242, 244, 245, 251
Saronic Gulf 23, 30, 132, 133, 139, 177
Saronic War 132, 135
sataba 32
satrap 28
sauroter/styrax 10
scutum/thureos 53–55
shield/Carian 40
shield/Carthaginian 86, 87
shield/Egyptian 90
shield/Illyrian 157
shock combat 11
sibyna 157, 189
Sicans 51, 53, 261
Sicilian Strait 50, 52, 109
Siculi 51, 85, 113, 225, 146, 165, 172, 173, 211, 213–215, 219, 223, 228, 229, 231, 232, 260, 265, 271
siege towers/engines 224, 259, 260, 262, 265, 267, 268 search
sigma 9
Sisimaces 44
Skala Ridge 123
skeuophoroi 15
Socrates (general) 152
Socrates (philosopher) 21, 57, 146, 185
Solon 62
Sophanes 128
soros 65, 67, 68
sparal gerrhon 30
sparabara 30, 31
spartiates (*spartiatoi*) 46
spear/Persian 31
Stasenor 39
Stesilaos 65
stratiotai 12
Strombichides 240, 244
Strymon River 125
Styphon 176

taka 126
taxis 61
Telesilla 49
Tempe 71
Terillus 86
Themistocles 63, 70, 84, 125, 126
Theramenes 245–248, 253–255
Thermopylae pass 71, 201

Theron 86, 88, 89, 109
Thersippos 65
Thesprotians 157
Thessalian(s) 18, 19, 83, 98, 101, 136, 138, 146, 152, 201, 272, 273
thetes 244
Thorax 98
The Thousand 136, 148, 206
Thrasybulus (Athens) 232, 245–247, 255, 256, 274–277
Thrasybulus (Syracuse) 112, 113, 116
Thrasycles 204, 205
Thrasydaeus 110–112, 121
Thucydides 188
Thyreatis 24, 48
Tigranes 72, 73, 75, 76, 104, 105
Tissaphernes 239, 240, 242, 251, 278–284
Tithraustes 125, 126
Tmolos 23
Tolmides 138, 139, 141, 185
toxon (bow) 15
toxotai (archers) 15
tresantes 12
triremes (*trierai*) 30
trope 27
trophy (*tropaion*) 27
Tyche 113
tyrants (*tyrannoi*) 29
Tyrrhastiadas 80

upaspistae 15

Vrana Valley 61–63, 65, 66, 68

White Wall/Fortress 130
wing (of formation) 11

Xanthippos 104, 138
Xenares 201, 202
Xenias 278–280
Xenophon (general) 156, 157
Xenophon (historian/general) 283, 285
Xerxes 59, 68–72, 76–86, 90, 103–105, 128, 129, 243
xiphos 10

Zacynthus 154, 166, 174, 223
zeugitai 245, 274
Zopyrus 69